Facilitating Judicial Cooperation in the EU

# Facilitating Judicial Cooperation in the EU

## *A Computable Approach to Mutual Recognition in Criminal Matters*

*Edited by*

Giulia Lasagni
Giuseppe Contissa
Michele Caianiello

BRILL | NIJHOFF

LEIDEN | BOSTON

This volume is the result of a research funded by the European Union. The research was conducted within the framework of the Justice Programme (2022) and is subject to the conditions of Grant Agreement No. 101089634. The views expressed herein are solely those of the authors and do not necessarily reflect those of the European Union.

Funded by
the European Union

The Library of Congress Cataloging-in-Publication Data is available online at https://catalog.loc.gov
LC record available at https://lccn.loc.gov/2025022890

Typeface for the Latin, Greek, and Cyrillic scripts: "Brill". See and download: brill.com/brill-typeface.

ISBN 978-90-04-70578-4 (hardback)
ISBN 978-90-04-70579-1 (e-book)
DOI 10.1163/9789004705791



This book is printed on acid-free paper and produced in a sustainable manner.

# Contents

# Figures and Tables

## Figures



## Tables

# Notes on Contributors

*Anna H. Albrecht*
Full Professor of Criminal Law and Criminal Procedure, University of Potsdam, Germany.

*Davide Audrito*
PhD Candidate in Legal Informatics, Alma Mater Research Institute for Human-Centered Artificial Intelligence, University of Bologna, Italy.

*Marco Billi*
PhD Candidate in Law, Science and Technology (LAST-JD), Alma AI Research Institute, University of Bologna, Italy – University of Luxembourg, Luxembourg.

*Marin Bonačić*
Associate Professor in Criminal Procedure, University of Zagreb Faculty of Law, Croatia.

*Zoran Burić*
Associate Professor in Criminal Procedure, University of Zagreb Faculty of Law, Croatia.

*Pedro Caeiro*
Associate professor and integrated researcher, Faculty of Law, UCILeR, University of Coimbra, Portugal.

*Michele Caianiello*
Full Professor in Criminal Procedure, University of Bologna, Italy.

*Raquel Cardoso*
Assistant professor, Faculty of Law, Univ Lusíada – Porto, CEJEIA, Portugal.

*Mariavittoria Catanzariti*
Assistant Professor in Legal Philosophy, University of Padua, Italy and Research Fellow, European University Institute.

*Eleonora Cervellera*
PhD Candidate in Criminal Law, University of Paris Nanterre, France.

*Giuseppe Contissa*
Associate professor in Legal Informatics, University of Bologna, Italy.

*Miguel João Costa*
Assistant professor and integrated researcher, Faculty of Law, UCILeR, University of Coimbra, Portugal.

*Luigi Di Caro*
Associate Professor in Computer Science, University of Turin, Italy.

*Menno Dolman*
Assistant Professor, Department of Criminal Law and Criminology, Maastricht University, the Netherlands.

*Zlata Đurđević*
Tenured Professor in Criminal Procedure, University of Zagreb Faculty of Law, Croatia.

*Agnieszka Frąckowiak-Adamska*
Professor at the Department of International and European Law, Faculty of Law, Administration and Economics, University of Wroclaw.

*Nicolò Gibelli*
PhD Candidate in Criminal Procedure, University of Pisa, Italy.

*Elizabeta Ivičević Karas*
Tenured Professor in Criminal Procedure, University of Zagreb Faculty of Law, Croatia.

*Wojciech Jasiński*
Professor at the Digital Justice Center, Faculty of Law, Administration and Economics, University of Wrocław.

*Eduard-Raul Kontos*
Junior Researcher, Maastricht Law and Tech Lab, Maastricht University, the Netherlands.

*Karolina Kremens*
Director and Professor at the Digital Justice Center, Faculty of Law, Administration and Economics, University of Wrocław.

*Giulia Lasagni*
Senior Assistant Professor in Criminal Procedure, University of Bologna, Italy.

*Miroslava Manolova*
Associate Professor in Criminal Law, Faculty of Law, Department of Criminal Law Studies, Sofia University "St. Kliment Ohridski", Bulgaria.

*Rachele Mignone*
Research Fellow in Computer Science, University of Torino, Italy.

*Rohan Nanda*
Assistant Professor, Maastricht Law and Tech Lab and Institute of Data Science, Maastricht University, the Netherlands.

*Ana-María Neira-Pena*
Associate Professor in Procedural Law, University of A Coruña, Spain.

*Isadora Neroni Rezende*
Research Fellow in Criminal Procedure, University of Bologna, Italy.

*Alessandro Parenti*
PhD Candidate in Law, Science and Technology (LAST-JD), Alma AI Research Institute, University of Bologna, Italy – University of Luxembourg, Luxembourg.

*Anna Piovan*
PhD Candidate in Criminal Procedure, University of Bologna, Italy.

*Antonio Pugliese*
Research Fellow in Criminal Procedure, University of Bologna, Italy.

*Ekaterina Salkova*
Associate Professor in Criminal Procedure, Institute for the State and the Law to the Bulgarian Academy of Sciences, Bulgaria.

*Alessandra Santangelo*
Senior Assistant Professor in Criminal Law, University of Bologna, Italy.

*Galileo Sartor*
Researcher in Legal Informatics, University of Swansea, Wales, UK.

*Anne Schneider*
Full Professor of German, European and International Criminal Law, Heinrich-Heine University Düsseldorf, Germany.

*Ivan Spada*
Research Fellow in Computer Science, University of Torino, Italy.

*Emilio Sulis*
Research Fellow in Computer Science, University of Torino, Italy.

*Camila Ugaz Heudebert*
Junior Researcher, Maastricht University, the Netherlands.

*António Vaz de Castro*
Guest Assistant professor and integrated researcher, Faculty of Law, UCILeR, University of Coimbra, Portugal.

*Gijs van Dijck*
Professor of Private Law, Maastricht Law and Tech Lab, Maastricht University, the Netherlands.

*Teddy Zwackhalen*
Junior Researcher, Maastricht University, the Netherlands.

# Introduction

Criminal law in the EU represents today a good example of how the interaction between law and legal informatics can bring important synergy that enhance the efficiency of the overall system and the protection of citizens' fundamental rights.

Enhancing smooth cooperation mechanisms is one of the main aims of the EU policy in the area of criminal justice. However, their effective implementation is heavily impacted by the highly varying legal frameworks which characterize Member States' regulation on procedural rights and investigative measures in criminal proceedings.

While we face such challenges in Europe, on a global level the domain of law is also on the brink of a period of fundamental and irreversible change and transformation. Information technologies and computer systems are the main drivers of this change. Increasingly capable machines, operating in support of experts are transforming the way that legal activities and procedures are undertaken. New legal applications and platforms appear, changing the practice of law, specifically by enriching legal texts with computational models of legal reasoning, providing users with automated assessments and explanations of their outcomes with reasons and arguments. New AI-enhanced tools, such as large language models (like GPT), are being introduced to analyse and reason also upon case law and legislation, although several significant challenges are still to be addressed here to make these tools really of support for the legal professions.

Against this background, we introduce the results of the FACILEX research project, that tried to address these problems from a multi-disciplinary perspective.[1]

Started in December 2022, the FACILEX project ("Facilitating mutual recognition: Analytics and Capacity building Information LEgal eXplainable tool to strengthen cooperation in the criminal matter") aimed to strengthen the implementation and application of the *acquis* on judicial cooperation in criminal matters through the help of digital tools, and not being limited to fact-finding research.

In light of the new Strategic Agenda 2019–2024, the project focused on three cooperation tools, that is: the European Arrest Warrant (FD 2002/584/JHA), the European Investigation Order (Directive 2014/41/EU) and Regulation 1805/2018

1 Grant Agreement no. 101089634; the project was funded by the European Union's Justice Programme (2022).

on freezing and confiscation orders, as implemented or anyway operational in nine Member States: Bulgaria, Croatia, France, Germany, Italy, Poland, Portugal, Spain, and the Netherlands.

The research study counted seven international partners including eminent scholars and researchers in the field of European law and Criminal Procedure, Legal Informatics and Computer Science, as well as private-sector experts working in the field of IT platform development.

FACILEX not only investigated the theoretical aspects, but also delivered concrete tools to support the legal professionals and citizens in retrieving the necessary knowledge to face criminal proceedings at the EU level.

## 1 From the CrossJustice Project …

The FACILEX research stands on the results gathered by a previous research programme, also coordinated by the University of Bologna, called CrossJustice ("Knowledge, Advisory and Capacity Building Information Tool for Criminal Procedural Rights in Judicial Cooperation").[2]

The CrossJustice study tackled the domain of criminal procedure law, by critically examining the procedural safeguards of the suspect and the accused as recognised by the six EU Procedural Rights Directives: Directive 2010/64/EU of 20 October 2010 on the right to interpretation and translation; Directive 2012/13/EU of 22 May 2012 on the right to information; Directive 2013/48/EU of 22 October 2013 on the right of access to a lawyer and to have a third party informed; Directive (EU) 2016/343 of 9 March 2016 on the presumption of innocence and the right to be present at trial; Directive (EU) 2016/800 of 11 May 2016 on procedural safeguards for juvenile defendants; Directive (EU) 2016/1919 of 26 October 2016 on legal aid.

All these Directives were analysed both with regard to the statutory legal framework and in their practical implementation in the case law of eleven EU jurisdictions (Bulgaria, Croatia, France, Germany, Italy, Portugal, Poland, Romania, Spain, Sweden, the Netherlands).

The research proposed an innovative perspective. First, the analysis of the shortcomings and obstacles that procedural rights of the Directives meet in

2 Crossjustice (University of Bologna) <https://site.unibo.it/cross-justice/en>. Grant Agreement no. 847346; the project was funded by the European Union's Justice Programme (2014–2020). The results of the project have been published in the volume Giuseppe Contissa, Giulia Lasagni, Michele Caianiello, Giovanni Sartor (eds.) *Effective Protection of the Rights of the Accused in the EU Directives. A Computable Approach to Criminal Procedure Law* (Brill, Leiden, 2022).

their national implementation was carried out through the lenses of legal reasoning. Second, the research integrated a legal informatics approach, consisting in the translation of the EU Procedural Directives, as well as samples of national legislation, into a computable language, that became the core of the *CrossJustice online platform*.

In particular, the project resulted in the development of a Legal Database and an Advisory Module, both freely accessible online.

The Legal Database aims at providing access to legislative, judicial and expert documents falling within the material scope of criminal procedure law, including international treaties and standards, relevant EU legislation and case law, as well as national legislation and case law, all provided in an English translation.

The Advisory Module, in turn, is an interactive expert module that helps legal professionals in identifying and applying relevant rules of EU and national legislations concerning procedural rights of persons suspected or accused of crimes, both at domestic and cross-border level. Within this Module, three computer tools were developed.

The first tool, called "Mass Testing", produces a comparative report showing the legal framework (legislation and case law) of the relevant national systems on a hypothetical legal case concerning a particular procedural right. This use modality is aimed at supporting policy makers in evaluating the level of harmonisation of national legal frameworks with the EU *acquis*.

The second tool, named "Single Assessment", requires the user to provide a series of concrete information concerning a specific legal situation, and, on that basis, produces a legal assessment concerning the significant potential critical legal issues. This use modality aims at supporting legal professional in a first legal assessment of practical cases.

The third and last tool, the "Automated Reasoner Assessment", aims at assisting users in developing and analysing the legal reasoning process of a given case. This tool represents a technological innovation in the application of computational models of legal reasoning to the domain of criminal law. The system is structured as a knowledge base containing the legal norms and a reasoning module that applies the rules to specific cases. The outcome provided by the tool includes all steps of the legal reasoning, leading to a specific conclusion, as well as an automated assessment of the level of harmonisation of the national legislation with the relevant Directive. Taking the lead from this research, the University of Bologna took the initiative to expand the investigation, adopting a similar approach also the matter of transnational cooperation among Member States in the criminal matter.

## 2 … To the FACILEX Project

The FACILEX project goes well beyond CrossJustice, in a twofold way.

On the one hand, it changed the subject matter of the analysis, bringing the focus of the research to the much more complex dimension of horizontal cooperation and taking into account mutual recognition instruments not previously examined.

On the other, the project also greatly improved the scientific methodology and approach, focusing on the innovative design and modelling of complex, multilayer legal norms in the field of criminal law cooperation and adopting novel legal informatics approaches for the development of online tools functionalities provided by the platform. Unlike other currently available legal information tools that only enable access to case law and legislation, the online platform developed within the FACILEX research thus includes an enhanced, AI-enabled advisory function providing accurate comparative analysis on the state-of-play of criminal cooperation across Member States.

FACILEX expanded the CrossJustice platform first by integrating the Legal Database Module, including the legal framework concerning the three chosen mutual recognition instruments, both at the EU and at the national level. Similarly to CrossJustice, all data are available in English and encompass also the relevant EU and national case law.

Secondly, the project developed a dedicated "Customized Single Test Advisory Module" focused on judicial cooperation, based on an explicit and computable representation of legal knowledge and reasoning, based on symbolic logic rules.

The tool has been designed to be user-friendly and accessible to legal experts. It is structured in a way to provide a deeper level of explainability, thanks to the adoption of novel technological approaches in logic programming, such as the use of Logical English, a logic programming language based on natural language. The explanations, as well as the rules themselves, are detailed and expressive, and enable a high degree of isomorphism in relation to the source legal material.

The module provides legal advice in a straightforward way, i.e. by answering to step-by-step questionnaire designed to take into even account users' inertia and general lack of tech abilities.

The system thus a) assesses the level of compliance of national legal systems with the relevant EU *acquis*; b) offers customized support to legal professional in the first legal assessment of practical cross-border cases; c) enables the generation of mock cases, for academic purposes, showing all possible different solutions for research purposes.

Finally, the FACILEX integrated platform includes a dedicated Harmonization Mass Test Advisory Module, that provides a harmonization index for each Member State, based on Natural Language Processing, that is an AI technique of textual and semantic analysis. The harmonization index is a measure of proximity between the terminologies of European and national legislation. This may enable legal professionals to assess the national law level of compliance with the EU *acquis* in matters of judicial cooperation, as well as to access an automated evaluation of the harmonization level of terminology.

The system also contains relevant case law from the Member States, used to assess the conformity between each State and the European Union. Case-based reasoning techniques are employed to evaluate the interpretation given by each State of relevant legal principles, in compliance with EU law. Such explanation is enhanced with the application of Large Language Models, which is applied for translating the explanations produced by the rule-based system, from high-level programming language to natural language, allowing all stakeholders a fast, clear, and accessible interaction with the technology.

Accessing the FACILEX platform, legal professionals receive a tailored legal assessment of potential cooperation flaws and available remedies, drawing all possible solutions relative to the given parameters. The FACILEX project thus represents a valuable tool to streamline EU judicial cooperation in criminal matters. By leveraging all the potential of digital technologies, the project fostered mutual knowledge, communication and ultimately trust among the relevant actors in the Area of Freedom, Security and Justice.

## 3 Exploring This Volume

The volume describes the results of the FACILEX twenty-four months international research project. However, the book goes also beyond such specific results, providing a generally applicable and integrated analysis, that results understandable also for readers who were not directly involved in the study.

The multi-disciplinary perspective of the research is mirrored in the approach adopted in this volume, that integrates criminal law and legal informatics analysis.

First, the analysis of the shortcomings and obstacles of the cooperation mechanisms at stake is carried out through the lenses of both legal reasoning and legal informatics. Secondly, the book proposes a multi-level perspective, since the legal analysis, carried out by highly specialised scholars, tackles both EU law and national legislation, as well as case law. Therefore, the practical implementation of the cooperation systems is also dealt with in the volume.

The book is composed of four parts.

Part 1, comprising three Chapters, serves as a general introduction to the increasing connection between cooperation in criminal matters and technological development. Chapter 1 opens the volume with an analysis of the impact of digital and AI technology on cooperation mechanism, with a specific focus on the role played, in this context, by the principle of mutual recognition. Chapter 2 looks at the global perspective, by focusing on investigations conducted by the International Criminal Court in cooperation with some EU institutions (as well as several EU Member States) in connection with international crimes committed during the war between Russia and Ukraine. It investigates the idea that mutual recognition cooperation instruments can serve as an inspiring model for cooperation also beyond the EU, between ICC States Parties and the ICC itself. Finally, Chapter 3 expounds on the application of Large Language Models in the justice domain in the context of the studies of legal text analytics, by exploring the developments from Natural Language Processing to generative pre-training models.

Part 2 presents nine, concise-yet-comprehensive Chapters on the state of implementation and application of the EAW Framework Decision, the EIO Directive and Regulation 1805/2018 at the national level. It includes legal analyses from Bulgaria, Croatia, France, Germany, Italy, Poland, Portugal, Spain and the Netherlands. The country selection ranges from North to South, from Western to Eastern European States and puts together inquisitorial and accusatorial traditions, allowing a broad representation of EU legal traditions and models.

The examination is innovative and integrated, as it illustrates the state of play of the most significantly critical or successful aspects in the cooperation among EU Member States, while taking into account both legislation and national case law. Each analysis, prepared by national experts, highlights the most problematic or significant issues emerging from the specific country context and provides a critical analysis that encompasses both the legislative transposition and case law implementation of the three cooperation mechanisms. The national analysis, however, does not cover an article-by-article analysis of the legal texts. Such analysis was nonetheless carried out in the course of the FACILEX research, and brought to the drafting of detailed national reports, that are currently available from the webpage of the Project.[3]

3 Facilex (University of Bologna) <https://site.unibo.it/facilex/en>.

Part 3, comprising three Chapters, provides a comparative and transnational analysis. The comparison of Chapter 13 builds upon the national law chapters of the previous section, as well as findings emerged by the semantic Natural Language Processing analysis, developed thanks to the computational approach previously illustrated. This perspective provides an innovative overview on the functioning of cooperation mechanisms grounded on mutual recognition in criminal matters and over the different (and sometimes contradictory) causes that reduce a smooth collaboration among Member States. Chapter 14 investigates the role played by fundamental rights' protection in the architecture of three judicial cooperation mechanisms. Chapter 15, lastly, entangles the double criminality test, facing the main inconsistencies of judicial application at both national and supranational levels.

Finally, Part 4 of our book covers the computable representation of EU law, showcasing a hybrid approach that combines Large Language Models and logic rules to offer users an overview of the applicable grounds for refusal. It also utilizes natural language processing to analyse the main legal concepts and their national implementation, achieved across the EU, and assists users in identifying relevant case law.

Last but not least, acknowledgements are in order.

This study was made possible only by a transnational teamwork, the enthusiasm of whose components deserves our most sincere thanks.

First and foremost, we wish to express our greatest appreciation and gratitude to the many researchers who chose to dedicate their precious time to our project and brought their boundless enthusiasm and expertise. Since the research, and also this volume, would never have seen the light of day without their hard work and patience in drafting with the project's demanding deadlines, we wish to thank each and every one of our national legal rapporteurs (in alphabetical order by Member State): Miroslava Manolova and Ekaterina Salkova (Bulgaria); Zlata Đurđević, Zoran Burić, Elizabeta Ivičević Karas and Marin Bonačić (Croatia); Eleonora Cervellera (France); Anna H. Albrecht and Anne Schneider (Germany); Isadora Neroni Rezende, Antonio Pugliese, Nicolò Gibelli, Anna Piovan, Alessandra Santangelo and Maria Corvaglia (Italy), Wojciech Jasiński, Karolina Kremens, Agnieszka Frąckowiak-Adamska (Poland); Miguel João Costa, Raquel Cardoso, António Vaz de Castro and Pedro Caeiro (Portugal); Ana-María Neira-Pena (Spain); Camila Ugaz Heudebert, Teddy Zwackhalen, Gijs van Dijck and Menno Dolman (the Netherlands).

An equally heartful thanks go to the researchers in the field of legal informatics and computer science, that accepted with patience to share and explain their expertise to criminal lawyers: Luigi Di Caro, Rohan Nanda, Galileo Sartor,

Marco Billi, Alessandro Parenti, Rachele Mignone, Davide Audrito, Ivan Spada and Eduard-Raul Kontos.

Research on these topics however is nothing without the capacity to transmit this knowledge and involve high-level academics and practitioners in a transnational debate: for all this, and much more, not less for her constant professional and personal support, a special thanks go to Mariavittoria Catanzariti and to the whole European University Institute in the person of Deirdre Curtin.

Naturally, very little of our research would have been really visible from the outside without the outstanding support of Hristo Konstantinov and his amazing APIS team, who concretely created the FACILEX Platform, and translated our theoretical debate into a (virtually) tangible tool.

In this regard, we would further like to extend our gratitude to the several stakeholders that, across five Member States, participated in the seminars organized on the topics covered by the Project, testing the FACILEX platform and providing precious feedback for its finalization and development.

Lastly, we must also extend a wholehearted and special thank you to Isadora Neroni Rezende, Antonio Pugliese and Marco Billi, who have been the very heart and soul of the research team since the very beginning, and remained with us until the end, surviving among tight deadlines, obscure administrative requirements and an immense amount of work.

Our most sincere gratitude also goes to Nicolò Gibelli, Anna Piovan, Alessandro Parenti, Gaetano Ancona, Lorenzo Farneti, Federico Messuti, Federica Gitto, Elena Nasi and Somaya Belcaid, without whose tireless efforts (in the middle of the Summer and Easter break) this book would have never come to being.

*Giulia Lasagni*
*Giuseppe Contissa*
*Michele Caianiello*

# PART 1

CHAPTER 1

# Effective Rights and Remedies in the Computable Era: Facing Informative Asymmetry When AI Adds to Transnational Cooperation

*Giulia Lasagni and Giuseppe Contissa*

## 1 Judicial Cooperation and AI Technology: a Complexity Challenge

Numerous contributions in the last years have dealt with identifying the advantages brought by the AI potential to the criminal justice systems, and perhaps even more authors have raised their voices about the risks posed by such technology for the integrity of fundamental rights in this domain.[1] These authors have also entered the debate by stressing the complexity of ensuring the effectiveness of remedies where algorithmic and AI decisions are in place. On that occasion, we had discussed how, to be able to challenge an individual decision effectively, the data subject must have access to all the information relevant to the decision, and in particular to the datasets, the data processing methods, and the source code expressing the algorithms underlying the functioning of the system.[2]

However, AI systems often present significant challenges for transparency: information on the dataset is usually not available to the parties or the judge using the system, and a similar consideration may be made with regard to the information on the data processing methods and algorithms. In fact, in many cases, they depend on the accessibility of the source code, the disclosure of

* The chapter is a joint reflection of the authors, but its drafting is broken down as follows: Contissa §§ 2, 4 (technological part), 5; Lasagni §§ 1, 3, 4 (legal part).

1 See, *ex m*ultis, Aleš Završnik 'Criminal justice, artificial intelligence systems, and human rights' (2020) 20 ERA Forum 567–583, https://doi.org/10.1007/s12027-020-00602-0; Serena Quattrocolo, *Artificial Intelligence, Computational Modelling and Criminal Proceedings. A Framework for A European Legal* (Springer, 2020); Brandon L. Garrett, Cynthia Rudin, 'The Right To A Glass Box: Rethinking The Use Of Artificial Intelligence In Criminal Justice' (2024) 103 (3) Cornell Law Review.

2 Giuseppe Contissa, Giulia Lasagni, 'When it is (also) algorithms and AI that decide on criminal matters: In search for an effective remedy' (2020) 28 3 European Journal of Crime, Criminal Law and Criminal Justice, 290.

DOI:10.1163/9789004705791_003

which may be limited by intellectual property rights. Moreover, as displayed by the *black box* image, in several AI systems based on machine learning, there are structural limits to the ability to provide information for reconstructing the system's functioning and the reasons for its decision.

This Chapter builds on those studies by focusing on the notion of effectiveness in the multi-layer context of judicial cooperation.

Such dimension, as known, presents its own specific challenges, especially in the European Union, where the procedural divergences among Member States may come to represent an obstacle to smooth cooperation. Indeed, the minimum harmonization realized with the Stockholm Programme, though extremely significant in approximating domestic systems,[3] only concerned a few aspects of procedural rules. In particular, the lack of common regulation persists regarding the performance of investigative measures, for instance, in relation to the need for judicial authorization or to the standard of proof that needs to be met to activate the measure itself. This lacuna grants the principle of mutual recognition not only a theoretical role as the "cornerstone" of judicial cooperation[4] but also a practical pivotal position in determining the effective functioning (or malfunctioning) of the cooperation game. While the limits and potential of this principle have been widely studied in the last decades[5] and are the subject of an increasing number of judicial decisions of the Court of Justice,[6] the growing technological dimension of the investigation calls for a specific reflection on the impact of this element not only for the efficiency of the cooperation mechanisms but also for the fairness of the whole procedure.

This calls for an integrated approach toward the deployment of AI technology in the criminal justice field that puts together, since the design of the

---

3 Giuseppe Contissa, Giulia Lasagni, Michele Caianiello, Giovanni Sartor (eds.), *Effective Protection of the Rights of the Accused in the EU Directives. A Computable Approach to Criminal Procedure Law* (Brill, 2022).

4 Tampere European Council, 15 and 16 October 1999, Presidency Conclusions, § 33.

5 With regard to different application fields, within the criminal matter see, *ex multis*, Hannah Brodersen, Vincent Glerum, André Klip, 'Improving Mutual Recognition of European Arrest Warrants for the Purpose of Executing in absentia Judgments' Funded by the European Union's Justice Programme (2014-2020); John A. E. Vervaele, 'The ne bis in idem principle as a domestic general principle of law' (2005) 1 (2) Utrecht Law Review 100-118; Helmut Satzger, 'Is mutual recognition a viable general path for cooperation? (201) 10 (I) New Journal of European Criminal Law 44-56; and, with a broader perspective Gisèle Vernimmen-Van Tiggelen et al., *The future of mutual recognition in criminal matters in the European Union / L'avenir de la reconnaissance mutuelle en matière pénale dans l'Union européenne* (Bruxelles 2009).

6 See CJEU Stefano Melloni v Ministerio Fiscal, 26 February 2013, Case C-399/11; Pál Aranyosi and Robert Căldăraru v Generalstaatsanwaltschaft Bremen, April 2016, Joined Cases C-404/15 and C-659/15 PPU; E.D.L., 18 April 2023, Case C-699/21.

tools, lawyers, computer scientists, and legal informatics. These are also the objectives of the FACILEX project, where a platform has been built and some AI applications have been developed by considering the requirements for transparency and explainability.[7]

With this perspective, the Chapter proceeds as follows: in section 2, an overview will be provided on the uses of AI systems in criminal justice, including investigations and judicial decision-making. In Section 3, a specific application of AI technology will be put in the context of the European Investigation Order cooperation mechanism. Looking at the EncroChat/Sky ECC transnational investigation that involved most EU Member States in recent years, the practical and systemic difficulties in ensuring fair trial rights will be highlighted when cooperation issues add up to technological challenges. Against such analysis, Section 4 stresses some proposals on how to approach the informative asymmetry typical of transnational technological investigations.

Last, Section 5 concludes by focusing on the policymaker perspective, examining the recently adopted AI act in light of the highlighted problematics, and proposing some corrective recommendations on better addressing such a complex state of affairs.

## 2 Potential Uses of AI in Criminal Justice

In recent years, a paradigm shift has occurred in AI: transitioning from human-made representation of knowledge to machine learning. Machine learning refers to a system that "improves its performance on future tasks after making observations".[8]

In machine learning-based systems, knowledge about the domain and the activities to be carried out is no longer provided by humans. Still, it is instead built by the system itself, applying a learning algorithm to vast datasets. Using this model, the system generates classifications, evaluations, and predictions for new cases submitted. Updating and expanding the dataset automatically improves the model and the system's predictive capabilities.

This direction has led to a large number of successful applications in many fields, including the judicial, enforcement, and investigations, enhancing the capabilities of law enforcement agencies, judges, and legal professionals.

---

7 For a detailed explanation of the technologies deployed in the FACILEX project, see *infra*, Chapter 15 and 16.

8 Stuart J. Russell and Peter Norvig, *Artificial Intelligence. A Modern Approach* (Prentice Hall, Englewood Cliffs, N.J., 3 edition, 2010).

AI applications in the judiciary can be classified into two main areas:[9] document-oriented and case-oriented approaches.

Document-oriented approaches are focused on the analysis of individual documents. The main goal of such systems is to extract information, that is, to identify named entities such as places, persons, organisations, dates, and claims, as well as to extract more complex information, such as events and narratives. Automated summarisation aims at creating summaries of case facts, decisions, and other legal documents by selecting phrases appropriate to a summary, combining and possibly rephrasing them into a coherent text. The automated parsing of statutory texts aims at the automated conversion of the original, natural language legislative documents into machine-interpretable rules.

Predictive retrieval aims at the automated selection of legal texts relevant to a specific legal task, such as drafting a new law or deciding a case. The entire corpora of documents can be analysed to discover correlations, extract implicit information, and organise cross-references between documents and parts of them.

Such systems may support identifying and selecting the most significant bits of previous cases and thus facilitate the reuse of portions of previous documents in new ones.

Document-oriented systems may benefit legal practice, enabling judges and other legal experts to be more efficient and accurate in doing legal analyses and generating legal documents. They can, therefore, also improve the quality of legal sources, such as judicial decisions and statutory texts.

Case-oriented approaches to legal machine learning typically rely on models extracted from vast sets of cases. They provide aggregate statistical information about such cases. Still, they may also be used to predict specific aspects of new instances, such as their duration, costs, and potential awards or punishments, as well as to calculate the probability that claims, motions, or other pleadings succeed.

The models constructed by such systems embed correlations between (sets of) features of cases on one side and decisions and/or factual forecasts on the other. One of the areas of primary interest is litigation assistance (i.e., systems providing information to increase the likelihood of success at trial). Based on an analysis dealing with factors related to the merit of the case (such as lexical features, events, narratives, and procedural history), but often also on the basis of factors not related to merit (such as the nature of the suit, the attorneys, the venue, the judge, and the parties), such systems can make predictions about the behaviour of the parties to a proceeding (e.g., under what conditions a

9 L. Karl Branting, 'Data-centric and logic-based models for automated legal problem solving' (2017) 25(1):5–27 Artificial Intelligence and Law.

settlement may be accepted) or the behaviour of judges (the decisions they may take).

Besides directly supporting the decision-making activities, Case-oriented AI systems can have a range of additional uses. Firstly, in the preparation of litigation: being prepared for litigation or an investigation involves having access to high-quality information about the potential outcome of the case, including the conditions or arguments that could enhance the chances of a positive result, the anticipated penalties or damages that might be assigned, and the expected time and expenses involved in resolving the matter. This type of information is crucial for a party's strategic planning in approaching the case.

Secondly, in analysing past decisions, AI systems can be used to analyse past decisions to uncover patterns in how judicial decisions have been made over time. These patterns might involve the method of judgement (the approach judges take to make their rulings), the nature of the decisions made (how these rulings differ based on variables like time and location), and through the use of network analysis, the connections between decisions (identifying which court opinions have the most impact on others and the reasons for this influence).

Thirdly, in enhancing the quality of the judiciary: like any professional, judges are fallible, and the quality of their work would benefit from using AI tools that can assist in analysing how judges arrive at decisions or in identifying any inherent biases in those decisions. Moreover, judges can make use of the insights gained from these technologies to assess and possibly enhance their decision-making skills.[10]

Systems that correlate the features of new cases with their possible future decisions may enable lawyers to get a sense of their chances of success (possibly reducing litigation), select or search for aspects of the case that increase their chances of success, and better develop their arguments. Such systems may also be helpful for judges, enabling them to gain a better sense of case law trends and see how a possible decision would stand in the context of case law.

A recent innovation is the development of legal applications for cognitive computing.[11] These applications aim at bridging the analysis of legal texts through machine learning with the relevant legal sources and rationales: the portions of texts that contain applicable provisions, judicial holdings, and

---

10 Examples of predictive systems for legal advice are Lexmachina, which aims at predicting the behaviour of courts, judges, lawyers, and parties in IP Law; Premonition, which focuses on analysing judicial tendencies and attorneys' performance and outcomes before judges; and Luminance, a platform that applies supervised and unsupervised machine learning to the process of document review and enables the automated annotation of legal documents and the detection of possible anomalies.

11 Kevin D. Ashley, *Artificial Intelligence and Legal Analytics: New Tools for Law Practice in the Digital Age* (Cambridge University Press, 2017).

findings of facts; the arguments that justify the proposed conclusions; and the legal and factual reasons in favour or against the proposed outcome. A cognitive computing approach may support judges and other legal experts in investigating and answering legal questions, providing explanations for their legal decisions or assessments, making arguments for and against legal conclusions, and improving predictions about case outcomes.

Cognitive computing in the legal domain can profit from argument mining, which includes a set of techniques and technologies focused on identifying and analysing argument-related information in text corpora, such as premises and conclusions, relationships between arguments and counterarguments, the substantive strengths or weaknesses of claims, and the rationale for legal decisions. An example of machine learning that includes elements of cognitive computing is Claudette (CLAUse DETecTEr),[12] a platform enabling machine learning analysis of consumer contracts and privacy policies. The system combines ML approaches and knowledge-based approaches to deliver explanation functionalities.

What is concerned with law enforcement activities, AI's most notable change is the ongoing shift from being reactionary to being proactive in their efforts to prevent crime.

In this context, an important and widespread application is that of predicting policing. The term refers to using data analytics, algorithms, and AI technologies to analyse historical crime data to anticipate future criminal activities. This approach enables law enforcement agencies to allocate their resources more effectively by predicting where and when crimes are more likely to occur. It involves analysing patterns in past crime data, including time, location, and other relevant factors, to identify potential risks and trends. The goal is to prevent crime proactively rather than responding reactively, allowing agencies to allocate their scarce resources to high-risk areas better before crimes happen, thus enhancing public safety and efficiency.[13] Similar AI systems aim to predict potential victims or categories of victims rather than crimes.[14]

---

12 Marco Lippi et al., 'CLAUDETTE: an automated detector of potentially unfair clauses in online terms of service' (2019) XXVII Artificial Intelligence and Law 117–139.

13 The perhaps most known being PredPol, now Geolitica (www.geolitica.com – accessed: 18/04/2025) but similar tools are today developed and deployed by most law enforcement agencies worldwide. For a comprehensive overview of predictive policing tools, see Albert Meijer, MartijnWessels 'Predictive Policing: Review of Benefits and Drawbacks' (2019) 42(12) International Journal of Public Administration, 1031–1039. https://doi.org/10.1080/01900692.2019.1575664.

14 For example, this research presents the use of AI to predict feminicide victims: Esperanza Garcia-Vergara, Nerea Almeda, Francisco Fernández-Navarro *et al.*, 'Artificial intelligence

A third category of AI applications that has raised many ethical and legal concerns is that of the systems making individual assessments, usually on the likelihood of risk of recidivism. Utilizing vast datasets – some of which may not be immediately accessible to law enforcement – these tools employ mathematical algorithms and machine learning capabilities to link statistical risk indicators with specific individuals. One of the most prominent examples of such predictive analytics tools is COMPAS, created by Northpoint Inc. (now known as Equivant), a private entity headquartered in California. This system is widely employed across various US states for estimating recidivism rates to inform alternative sentencing or probation decisions and has been widely analysed (and criticized) by legal scholars worldwide.[15]

Other systems that use AI predictive capabilities (that is, to predict and recognise anomalous patterns and to learn to recognise new patterns) are those aimed at detecting fraud risks in various fields and cybersecurity threats. Perhaps less known than those aiming at predicting recidivism, these systems find however a broad application in several countries.

Financial fraud detection applications are based on AI systems that can analyse and filter vast amounts of financial transactions to identify patterns indicative of fraudulent activities, such as money laundering or identity theft, much quicker and more accurately than human investigators.[16]

Healthcare fraud detection applications can analyse billing and clinical data across healthcare systems to detect unusual patterns and discrepancies that may indicate fraudulent claims or unnecessary medical procedures.[17]

---

extracts key insights from legal documents to predict intimate partner femicide' (2023) 13 18212 *Sci Rep*, , https://doi.org/10.1038/s41598-023-45157-5.

15 See, *ex multis*, 'Eric L. Loomis, Petitioner v. State of Wisconsin, on Petition for a Writ of Certiorari to the Supreme Court of Wisconsin: Brief for the United States as Amicus Curiae' <https://www.scotusblog.com/wp-content/uploads/2017/05/16-6387-CVSG-Loomis-AC-Pet.pdf> (accessed: 18/04/2025); Iñigo De Miguel Beriain, 'Does the Use of Risk Assessments in Sentences Respect the Right to Due Process? A Critical Analysis of the Wisconsin v. Loomis ruling' (2018) 17 Law, Probability and Risk 45–53; critics have been raised also from civil society, see for all Julia Angwin, Jeff Larson, Surya Mattu, Lauren Kirchner, 'Machine Bias: There's Software Used across the Country to Predict Future Criminals. And It's Biased against Blacks' (ProPublica, 23.05.2016) <https://www.propublica.org/article/machine-bias-risk-assessments-in-criminal-sentencing> (accessed: 18/04/2025).

16 Johan Perols 'Financial statement fraud detection: An analysis of statistical and machine learning algorithms.' (2011) 30.2 Auditing: A Journal of Practice & Theory 19–50; John O. Awoyemi, Adebayo O. Adetunmbi, Samuel A. Oluwadare, 'Credit card fraud detection using machine learning techniques: A comparative analysis' (International Conference on Computing Networking and Informatics (ICCNI), Lagos, Nigeria, 2017) 1–9, doi: 10.1109/ICCNI.2017.8123782.

17 Jing Li, et al. 'A survey on statistical methods for health care fraud detection.' (2008) 11 Health care management science 275–287.

Regarding cybersecurity threats, AI systems are employed to monitor network traffic in real time, identifying anomalies that could indicate a cyber-attack, phishing attempts, or malware infiltration. Moreover, AI systems are also used for cybersecurity incident response to help determine the scope and scale of a breach and recommend containment strategies.[18]

Coming closer to the investigation, AI systems are deployed in a vast set of tasks, ranging from eDiscovery to digital analysis of evidence to recognition of crime scenes, gunshots, and bombs. In eDiscovery, AI tools help investigators to analyse thousands of documents to find relevant case material, significantly reducing the time and cost associated with manual reviews.

In forensics, the main field of application is the digital analysis of videos and images. The typical case is facial recognition, which identifies suspects or finds missing persons by comparing faces against a database of known individuals. Recent developments have enhanced the accuracy of identifying individuals from images of low quality, taken from suboptimal angles, or where the face is partially concealed.[19] Another case in this area is the interpretation of radiological images to assist medical examiners with establishing causes and manner of death.

However, current AI technology provides law enforcement with capabilities that extend far beyond mere recognition of individuals and objects. For instance, it enables the analysis of accident and crime scenes, both as they occur and post-event: combining the information captured in crime scene photos with the analysis of gunshot pattern signatures, AI algorithms are used to differentiate each explosive shockwave and assign shots to a specific firearm and within a particular moment. Increasingly, AI technology is also used to decipher encrypted content, as illustrated below.

---

18 Javier Martínez Torres, Comesaña Carla Iglesias, Paulino J. García-Nieto, 'Machine learning techniques applied to cybersecurity' (2019) 10 (10) International Journal of Machine Learning and Cybernetics 2823–2836; Anand Handa, Sharma Ashu, K. ShuklaSandeep, 'Machine learning in cybersecurity: A review' (2019): 9.4 e1306 Wiley Interdisciplinary Reviews: Data Mining and Knowledge Discovery .

19 Justin Norman, Hany Farid, 'An Investigation into the Impact of AI-Powered Image Enhancement on Forensic Facial Recognition (Proceedings of the IEEE/CVF Conference on Computer Vision and Pattern Recognition (CVPR) Workshops', 2024) 4306–4314.

## 3 An Automated Approach to Mutual Recognition? The Cooperation Case of EncroChat and Sky ECC

A recent case, or better, a series of recent cases, present well the complexity of matching the use of AI techniques during criminal investigations with the application of cooperation mechanisms based on mutual recognition.

The reference goes to the EncroChat and Sky ECC affair, which involved a significant number of EU Member States and whose facts are so well-known that it is enough here to recall some of the main traits.

It was 2020 when the French and Dutch authorities, together with Eurojust and Europol, announced the official dismantling of the EncroChat server. Based (also) in France, EncroChat was one of the world's most extensive encrypted communication services, a parallel operating system to traditional ones (such as Android), with thousands of users in Europe alone. The service provided a 'secure' communication network, thanks to the deactivation of microphones, cameras, and GPS in the devices, the possibility of remotely wiping the contents of the hardware, and finally, encrypted software specifically for forwarding messages anonymously.

Having discovered the exploitation of such a network by several organised crime groups active in drug trafficking, in 2018, France and the Netherlands, with the support of the European agencies, set up a Joint Investigation Team (JIT). With the authorisation of the French judiciary, the investigators, thanks to an unspecified 'technical device', captured messaging for about two months until the platform, realising the hacking, alerted its users, informing them that a public authority had obtained access to the system and suggesting they dispose of their phones.[20] From a legal perspective, the operation was carried out in France using a specific investigative technique, which requires, in a similar way to the regime of wiretapping in most systems, an authorisation by a judge for its performance.[21]

The data collected, amounting to hundreds of thousands of messages, were first shared within the investigation team, giving rise to numerous criminal proceedings in the two countries. Subsequently, with the support of Eurojust

20 Eurojust/Europol, 'Dismantling of an encrypted network sends shockwaves through organised crime groups across Europe', joint press release, 2 july 2020, <https://www.europol.europa.eu/media-press/newsroom/news/dismantling-of-encrypted-network-sends-shockwaves-through-organised-crime-groups-across-europe> (accessed: 18/04/2025).

21 Specifically, the *captation des données informatiques* (Article 706-102-1 of the French Criminal Code, on which more *infra*, Chapter 6 – France).

and Europol, they were made available to other states through requests for judicial cooperation, precisely via the European Investigation Orders (EIO s).

After dismantling the EncroChat network, the French and Dutch investigators, joined by the Belgian ones, noted a shift of communications relating to international drug trafficking to the Sky ECC platforms. This was an encrypted messaging network boasting hundreds of thousands of users worldwide, based on the sale of smartphones that had been modified (deactivation of the video camera, microphone and GPS; impossibility of making calls outside the Sky ECC circuit) and equipped with unique security settings, such as the automatic deletion of messages received after a period of time predetermined by the users (even a very short one, such as 30 seconds) and the possibility of remotely deleting the contents of the device with a special password (so-called distress password/kill switch) in case of need. Sky ECC's complex hacking operation, once more carried out via the establishment of a JIT between France, the Netherlands, and Belgium, again with the support of Europol and Eurojust, resulted in the capture of at least one billion encrypted messages and the seizure of 70,000 cryptophones.

As in the EncroChat case, from a legal point of view, the inoculation into the encrypted platform was carried out in France (where the Sky ECC servers were also located) through the same investigative measure, with authorisation by the competent court. Technically, according to what has been disclosed, the operation was developed in three phases (not necessarily all clearly distinct, from a temporal point of view): a) use of a software to break into the server of reference; b) application of an AI tool to decrypt the content acquired, and attribute the content of the selected messages to specific defendants; and finally c) storage and analysis of the data collected through digital forensics platforms. All these technologies were developed within the JIT, with the fundamental contribution of the Dutch National Forensic Institute and Europol. Again, once collected, the data were also made available to third countries through international cooperation requests, which, within the EU, took the form of EIO s.[22]

The sharing of information in the EncroChat and Sky ECC cases gave rise to hundreds of criminal proceedings in Europe alone, in which several

---

22 For a more comprehensive analysis of the cases, see *ex multis*, Jan-Jaap Oerlemans, Sofie Royer, 'The future of data-driven investigations in light of the Sky ECC operation' (2023) 14 (issue 4) *New Journal of European Criminal Law* 434–458; Georgios Sagittae, 'On the lawfulness of the EncroChat and Sky ECC-operations', (2023) 14 (issue 3) New Journal of European Criminal Law 273–293; specific national aspects are also highlighted in Part 2 of this volume.

critical aspects related to the use of the collected data at trial were immediately apparent.

Of all the problems related to these affairs,[23] one is crucial for the focus of this paper: the AI-based tools used to (probably) hack the server and analyse the collected communications were not disclosed to the parties. This occurred not due to typical 'black box' technical issues but because the investigative authorities involved in the JIT made clear their interest in reusing the software for future repressive actions.[24]

Similarly, the data collected by the investigators was made available to the parties only to a limited extent. Expressly, parties within a given criminal proceedings were granted access to the so-called 'tertiary dataset', that is, the bulk of information relevant to that specific case, per the national law regulating access to file. However, no access was generally allowed to the raw dataset of all seized information ('primary dataset'), nor the data considered relevant for criminal investigations ('secondary dataset').[25]

Requests to access the AI tool and the dataset were also raised – and denied – in other Member States, where the information seized had arrived via EIO, reaching up to the highest instances in the respective court systems. The problems were also brought before the Court of Justice, which famously ruled on the application of the Landesgericht Berlin with judgment *M.N.* of 30 April 2024.[26]

In all such contexts, the question thus arose of whether these impediments could be regarded as an infringement of the rights of the defence and, if so, of what remedy could be effectively invoked against it. In particular, the problem posed by the defence concerned the alleged impossibility of trusting the reliability of the data contained in the tertiary dataset without the possibility of checking the latter with the bulk of data that have been seized and without knowing how the AI tool was set to operate on such data.

In the countries not included in the JIT, the issue was further complicated by the layer given by the transnational dimension of the investigation in light of the limited rules posed by the EIO Directive in this regard.

23 Among which whether the acquisition of the data, carried out in France according to forms of collection that do not necessarily find a correspondence in the domestic system, can be an obstacle to the use (or admissibility, in European States where the two profiles are not autonomous) of the data in domestic proceedings; and whether it is necessary to add, in the system that receives the data, a further measure of the judicial authority, certifying the usability of the data for domestic purposes, or whether it is sufficient to check that the French court has already carried out the acquisition at the time of the data.

24 Jan-Jaap Oerlemans and Sofie Royer (n 22) for the reference to the relevant domestic case-law.

25 Idem, ft 105.

26 CJEU, C-670/22.

Article 1(1) of the Directive provides that an EIO may be issued "for obtaining evidence that is already in possession of the competent authorities of the executing State". While this hypothesis was likely conceived as relatively unproblematic in origin, its recent application in the context of interceptions shows all the limits of the legal basis, especially in light of the principle of mutual recognition. In particular, the regulation of this type of EIO does not seem to consider the fact that when the bulk of evidence is remotely gathered in real-time investigating measures, the phase of data selection becomes crucial. Accordingly, the possibility for the defence to participate in such a selection is also essential, for instance, by contributing to defining the parameters (e.g., keywords) adopted to do so. This operation, however, occurs in the Member State where the investigative measure has been carried out (or, where relevant, in the countries involved by the JIT).

Defendants of further Member States that received the data via EIO, on the other side, did not have a chance to participate in the selection procedure and had to deal with packages of relevant data ('tertiary dataset') passively received in their case file. In such circumstances, the EIO Directive does not provide any specific safeguard to reinstate the right to be heard in the issuing Member State. This gap is then often examined at the national level in light of the principle of mutual recognition. The problem then emerges of whether or to what extent the principle of mutual recognition can compensate for the lack of access to information on both the selection process and the deployment of AI systems during the investigation.

## 4 Effective Rights and Remedies in a Transnational Computable Era

The question raised in the EncroChat and Sky ECC cases is exemplificative of a more general issue concerning the informative asymmetry that belongs both to the deployment of AI technology and to the transnational dimension of criminal investigations. In other words, in transnational technological investigations, there is a proliferation of information asymmetries that heavily impact the effectiveness of fundamental rights.

This makes the identification of effective remedies a highly complex task. On the one hand, total and detailed transparency in how the technology deployed or the foreign legal system works seems difficult to achieve for several reasons. Conferring to the defendant the right to know in detail how the AI technology works would likely impair the possibility of efficiently reusing that technology in the future, as it would enable strategic behaviours and ways to circumvent the use of the systems. In any case, detailed knowledge about an AI system would need to encompass not only the source code, not only the data set used by the investigators, as argued above, but also likely the user manual, i.e., the instructions on how the system works – an element that is also often covered by copyright or secrecy law.[27] Even where copyright or secrecy law would not apply, this amount of information is of such technical complexity that it would seem unlikely for an average defendant to be able to sort it in a meaningful way in the time constraints of a criminal proceeding. Similarly, a detailed knowledge of the functioning of another legal system can only be reached by a certain degree of approximation, given the legal and linguistic discrepancies. Studies that make foreign legislation and case law freely accessible, such as Crossjustice and FACILEX, try to reduce such gap. Still, of course, the specific knowledge required in one particular case is hardly reduced by a schematic approach and needs to be further integrated by direct contact between the two systems.

On the other hand, excluding these complexity factors appears unrealistic and unfeasible. Deployment of AI technology is increasingly necessary to address the challenges posed by encryption and anonymity, and transnational cooperation, especially in the common legal area of the EU, is, at this point, a matter of fact in a significant number of criminal investigations.

How to ensure, then, the effectiveness to both fair trial rights and, at least, the available remedies?

First, the assumption that the AI system, to be effective, must be utterly secret in its operation can be disputed.

True, it is often helpful to keep some elements of the functioning of an AI system secret, such as the model parameters, the key inputs, or the outcome. Specifically, maintaining aspects of an internal functioning logic secret can help prevent strategic "gaming" of a system.

However, presenting that as a necessity is reminiscent of the idea of "security through obscurity", namely the practice of concealing the details or mechanisms of a system to enhance its security. Experts have strongly criticised this approach and stand in contrast with more modern ones, such as "security by design".[28]

Instead, computer science nowadays offers several advanced techniques to enable the governance of secret decision systems, namely a set of computational methods that can provide accountability and a certain degree of understanding of the functioning of the system, even when some information is

27 Maja Brkan, 'Do Algorithms Rule the World? Algorithmic Decision-Making in the Framework of the GDPR and Beyond' (August 1, 2017). A revised version of this paper has been published in International Journal of Law and Information Technology, 11 January 2019, DOI; 10.1093/ijlit/eay017, Available at SSRN: https://ssrn.com/abstract=3124901 or http://dx.doi.org/10.2139/ssrn.3124901.

28 Peter P. Swire, 'A Theory of Disclosure for Security and Competitive Reasons: Open Source, Proprietary Software, and Government Agencies', (2006) 42 Houston Law Review SSRN 842228.

kept secret. Kroll et al.[29] give an overview of some of these methods: software verification, cryptographic commitments, zero-knowledge proofs, and fair random choices.

These methods ensure that the software and inputs meet the requirements for procedural regularity. Specifically, they can verify that the same decision policy was used for each decision, that the policy was established and implemented into the system before the inputs were known, and that the outcomes are reproducible. They can also be coupled with auditing, namely a set of techniques for the analysis of digital records documenting the responses of a computer system to the inputs it receives. The objective of auditing is to verify that proper procedures were adhered to (that is, compliant with the law) and to identify any unauthorized alterations in the system's functionality.

Second, access to the datasets must be addressed systematically, possibly by creating special rules at a centralised level. While access to the primary dataset seems difficult to achieve, for security and privacy issues,[30] structured access to the secondary dataset seems both feasible for the investigators and valuable for the defence.

In this regard, inspiring is the example of the Netherlands, where the defence, in Sky ECC cases, could file a motivated request to access parts of the secondary dataset. Once granted access, the examination of the information was realized via the same platform used by law enforcement authorities on the premises of the national forensic institute (but now also remotely).[31] This model could well be generalized and institutionalized in the various domestic systems. Last but not least, the claim for effective rights and remedies in such transnational and technological investigations can only call for a more conscious approach on the part of the defence. Investigators successfully carried out such a complex operation by creating Joint Investigation Teams and taking full advantage of the EIO cooperation mechanism.

To think, in the shoes of the defence, of countering such an organisation with a single set-up, in which each law firm is confronted with the difficulties of a transnational and technically complex investigation together, appears today to be guiltily naive. In this sense, at least for the more complicated general issues (e.g., how and where to get access to the secondary dataset, how to

---

29 Joshua A. Kroll, Joanna Huey, Solon Barocas, Edward W. Felten, Joel R. Reidenberg, David G. Robinson & Harlan Yu, 'Accountable Algorithms' (2017) 165 U. Pa. L. Rev. 633.

30 As the collected data in its most raw form is both likely used for intelligence purposes and certainly referring to a plethora of subjects, whose confidentiality shall be preserved.

31 As reported by Harm M. van Beek, Erwin J. van Eijk, RuudB. van Baar, Mattijs Ugen, J.N.C. Bodde & A.J. Siemelink 'Digital forensics as a service: Game on' (2015)15 Digital Investigation 27–28; see also Oerlemans, Royer (n 22) 456.

obtain information on the technical operations carried out, how to possibly challenge the use of EIO by the investigating authorities), the European bar has to take a step forward towards a common and more federated approach.

For example, it would seem essential to secure valuable information for an effective defence to present oneself in a unified manner before European agencies such as Europol (where the primary dataset of the EncroChat/Sky ECC data is stored).

## 5 The Lesson for Policymakers

All the challenges or difficulties outlined in the previous sections seem to be only partially addressed in the most recent legislation, i.e., the novel EU Regulation on Artificial Intelligence – or AI Act. The European Parliament adopted the AI Act on 14 March 2024 and published it on 12 July 2024 in the Official Journal of the EU as Regulation (EU) 2024/1689.[32]

The AI Act adopts a 'risk-based approach' to prevent and mitigate the risks of using AI. A risk-based regulation considers both the level and the characteristics of the risk associated with a practice to determine the applicable rules. At least in principle, legal restrictions should apply only to the extent necessary to prevent or mitigate risks.

Article 5 establishes some prohibited practices that constitute the highest risk associated with AI systems. The Regulation imposes a general prohibition on these practices, with some specific exceptions. Among them, and directly relevant to the uses of AI in investigation and judiciary activities, are the prohibitions of placing AI on the market, putting it into service, or using AI systems in two cases.

The first case is that of AI systems for criminal risk assessment of individuals (art 5(1)(d)): the AIA prohibits systems making risk assessments to predict criminal behaviour based solely on profiling or personality traits, supporting human assessment based on objective facts related to criminal activity. However, "this prohibition shall not apply to AI systems used to support the human assessment of a person's involvement in a criminal activity, which is already based on objective and verifiable facts directly linked to a criminal activity".

32 Regulation (EU) 2024/1689 of the European Parliament and of the Council of 13 June 2024 laying down harmonised rules on artificial intelligence and amending Regulations (EC) 300/2008, (EU) 167/2013, (EU) 168/2013, (EU) 2018/858, (EU) 2018/1139 and (EU) 2019/2144 and Directives 2014/90/EU, 2016/797/EU and 2020/1828/EU.

The second case is that of AI systems for real-time biometric identification in public spaces (art 5(1)(h)): the AIA prohibits systems using real-time remote biometric identification in publicly accessible spaces for law enforcement purposes. The Regulation provides a set of exceptions, namely when the use of these systems is strictly necessary for one of the following objectives: 1) for identifying victims of serious crimes such as abduction, trafficking, or sexual exploitation, and for locating missing persons; 2) for Preventing substantial and imminent threats to individuals' safety or preventing terrorist attacks; and 3) for Locating or identifying individuals suspected of major criminal offenses referred to in Annex II of the AIA, if also punishable for a maximum period of at least four years, to facilitate criminal investigations, prosecutions, or the execution of criminal penalties.

However, in the cases mentioned above, the adoption of real-time remote biometric identification systems requires the adoption of certain procedural guarantees. These safeguards consist, on the one hand, in assessing the preconditions authorising the use of such technologies and the potential consequences for rights and freedoms; on the other hand, in time, geographical and personal limitations are to be respected in using such systems. In all cases, prior authorisation is required by the judicial authority or an independent administrative authority of the Member State and granted upon reasoned application. Such authorisation, however, in a "duly justified situation of urgency" (Art 5(3)) may also be requested during or after use. The competent authority may only grant authorisation if, based on objective evidence or clear indications presented to it, the use of the system in question is necessary and proportionate to achieve one of the three objectives specified in (art 5(1)(h)). Due to the high risk that real-time biometric identification systems entail for individuals and groups, the prohibition outlined in the AIA is a welcomed choice; however, the exceptions' extension seems too large.

Pursuant to a risk-based approach, the Regulation also identifies high-risk AI systems (Art 6), referring to two lists in Annex I and III. These systems are subject to a series of provisions on their development, sale, and deployment in the EU market. The objective is to ensure the risk to safety, health, and protection of fundamental rights associated with such systems are mitigated without unnecessarily hindering their adoption.

Among the AI systems listed in ANNEX III are AI systems for law enforcement (annex III 7(a, b, c, d)). The reason for their inclusion is explained in recital 59 of the AI Act: "Given their role and responsibility, actions by law enforcement authorities involving certain uses of AI systems are characterised by a significant degree of power imbalance and may lead to surveillance, arrest or deprivation of a natural person's liberty as well as other adverse impacts on fundamental rights guaranteed in the Charter." Among the rights that could be hampered is the exercise of important procedural fundamental rights, such as the right to an effective remedy and a fair trial, as well as the right of defence and the presumption of innocence.

Other systems listed in Annex III that are relevant for our purposes are the AI systems used in migration, asylum, and border control management (annex III 8) since they affect persons who are often in particularly vulnerable positions and who are dependent on the outcome of the actions of the competent public authorities; and the AI systems used in the administration of justice (annex III 9), considering their potentially significant impact on democracy, the rule of law, individual freedoms as well as the right to an effective remedy and to a fair trial.

A core assumption of the AI Act is that risk can be calculated and classified in an objective and predetermined manner. While this may apply to a certain extent when we consider the safety and health of citizens, concerns arise as to whether the risk can be determined concerning fundamental rights: the AI Act is based on the idea that the impact on fundamental rights can be assessed according to a scale of values and that, to a certain extent, it can be deemed acceptable. However, the Act does not indicate how the acceptability judgment shall be made. The danger is that the risk assessment on fundamental rights will essentially be based on a subjective evaluation by the AI system provider and its greater or lesser risk aversion.

Concerning fundamental rights, what raises concerns is the decision by the EU legislator not to rely on a rights-based approach along the same lines as the Data Protection Regulation (GDPR).

Although it pursues the objective of protecting fundamental rights, the AI Act does not introduce any new rights that can be actionable and enforceable by individuals who may be adversely affected by the use of the AI system, other than the right to lodge a complaint with a market surveillance authority (Art 85) and the right – introduced only following an amendment proposed by the EU Parliament – to obtain an explanation "of the role of the AI system in the decision-making procedure and the main elements of the decision taken" (Art 86).

However, it should be noted that the right to obtain an explanation of the role of the AI system in decision-making does not involve a full right to the disclosure of detailed information on the functioning of the system, including all the elements, data and parameters that would be necessary to replicate and possibly challenge the fairness and procedural regularity of the system. Moreover, the right is subject to a significant limitation in the AI Act: Art 86(1), establishing this right, shall not apply to the use of AI systems "for which exceptions from, or restrictions to, the obligation under that paragraph follow from Union or national law in compliance with Union law." (Art 86(2)). This would leave open the problem of cases such as the EncroChat/Sky ECC mentioned above.

The problematic choice of the EU legislator of not providing actionable and enforceable by individuals who may be affected by AI systems is linked to a bold (but possibly wrong) assumption within the regulatory regime designed by the AI Act: that the use of AI systems may be fully regulated, just like any other product, by designing a set of obligations targeting specifically those persons creating the product (system developers) and using it (deployers). However, such strong assumptions may be rendered inaccurate by the technological peculiarities of an AI system, which, differently from other products, may evolve and learn by itself, sometimes in ways that escape the complete control of their developers and users. Maybe the idea that problems will and shall always be identified and solved *ex-ante* (during the development or deployment) could have been coupled with a regulatory empowerment *ex-post* of the individuals affected by AI, providing them actionable rights.[33]

Moreover, such focus on developers and deployers overshadows the transnational dimension of AI systems application, in particular in the context of criminal justice: no rules or directions are provided by the EU legislator, as highlighted above, to find a viable solution for situations like the Encrochat/Sky ECC cases, which clearly show a problem of compression or limitation of fundamental rights, in a transnational dimension.

In the face of these issues, the multidisciplinary and integrated approach proposed by this research project, in which, albeit with difficulty, law and technology have dialogued together since the design of the reference rules, can perhaps be an inspiring example.

33 On the problem of assumptions in technology regulation, see BJ Ard, Rebecca Crootof. 'Legal responses to techlaw uncertainties' in Bartosz Brożek, Olia Kanevskaia, Przemysław Pałka (eds.), *Research Handbook on Law and Technology* (2023) 28–44.

CHAPTER 2

# International Judicial Cooperation and the EU Principle of Mutual Recognition – towards a Convergence of Systems?

*Michele Caianiello*

## 1 Introduction

This chapter focuses on the investigations carried out by the ICC in cooperation with several EU institutions (as well as several EU Member States) in connection with international crimes committed during the war between Russia and Ukraine.

The idea is proposed that, on the one hand, EU cooperation instruments can serve as an inspiring model for cooperation between ICC States Parties and the ICC itself. On the other, that, in this investigation, what several scholars proposed in the first years after the Court's entry into force comes true: the ICC should play a predominantly 'Circuit Rider' role by facilitating State-level investigations and prosecutions of international crimes,[1] and by exploiting transnational networks.[2] These networks, thanks to their soft power, may be able, in comparison to top-down enforcement, to achieve effective results in the implementation of international criminal justice, which is still so strongly linked to the national interests of each State.[3]

The topic examined appears interesting because the actions taken by the EU, through its competent institutions and its Member States, to combat, investigate and help prosecute the commission of international crimes in the war conflict between Russia and Ukraine, cover, albeit with different modalities and measures, all the areas to which this research has been extended (arrest and surrender, collection and exchange of evidence, asset freezing and confiscation).

1 For an extensive and articulate reconstruction, see Jenia Iontcheva Turner, 'Nationalizing International Criminal Law' (2004) 41 Stanford Journal of International Law 1.

2 See Jenia Iontcheva Turner, 'Transnational Networks and International Criminal Justice' (2007) 105 Michigan Law Review 985.

3 See Turner (n 1) 994.

DOI:10.1163/9789004705791_004

A few considerations suffice to justify what has just been said. On the one side, the EU has consistently adopted economic sanctions, including asset freezing and confiscation measures, since 2014[4] and increasingly since Russia invaded Ukrainian territory in 2022, against individuals, organizations, and the Russian government.[5]

Furthermore, as of 2022, the EU is contributing significantly to the collection of evidence to help its Member States and the Office of the Prosecutor of the International Criminal Court (ICC's OTP) bring to justice persons responsible for international crimes. Finally, in a statement by the High Representative for External Action, the EU supported the decision of the Pre-Trial Chamber II of the International Criminal Court to issue an international arrest warrant against the President of the Russian Federation Vladimir Putin, and the Commissioner for Children's Rights in the Office of the President Maria Lvova-Belova, concerning the alleged crimes of illegal deportation and illegal transfer of children in the context of the situation in Ukraine.[6]

The analysis conducted in this chapter focuses mainly on the collection of evidence, a topic on which the doctrine is more abundant and allows for more in-depth considerations. However, from a methodological standpoint, the idea is that the principle of mutual recognition, through which the EU cooperates in criminal judicial matters with the ICC's OTP, can be an effective solution to improve the ICC's overall action and to realise in a more integrated way the principle of complementarity to which the ICC must be guided.

The chapter is divided into four parts. The first part (*infra,* §2 and 3) examines the operations the EU has put in place to cooperate with the ICC, mainly in evidence collection and exchange.[7] The second part (*infra,* §4) examines

4 See Council Decision 2014/145/CFSP of 17 March 2014 concerning restrictive measures in respect of actions undermining or threatening the territorial integrity, sovereignty and independence of Ukraine; and the Council Regulation (EU) No 269/2014 of 17 March 2014 concerning restrictive measures in respect of actions undermining or threatening the territorial integrity, sovereignty and independence of Ukraine.

5 See the complete framework at European Commission, 'Sanctions adopted following Russia's military aggression against Ukraine' (finance.ec.europa.eu) <https://finance.ec.europa.eu/eu-and-world/sanctions-restrictive-measures/sanctions-adopted-following-russias-military-aggression-against-ukraine_en?prefLang=it> accessed 24 July 2024.

6 See The Diplomatic Service of the European Union, 'Russia/Ukraine: Statement by the High Representative following the ICC decision concerning the arrest warrant against President Putin' (eeas.europa.eu, 19 March 2023) <https://www.eeas.europa.eu/eeas/russia ukraine-statement-high-representative-following-icc-decision-concerning-arrest-warrant-against_en> accessed 30 July 2024.

7 In this part, I take up several considerations developed in my editorial published in 2022: Michele Caianiello, 'The Role of the EU in the Investigation of Serious International Crimes

the important legal implications for the EU of this cooperation and the role it can play in countering the commission of serious international crimes. The third part (*infra*, §5) reflects on the prospects for the ICC considering its experience in countering international crimes by cooperating with the EU and using its legal system of judicial cooperation. Finally, the fourth part (*infra*, §6) addresses the topic from the perspective of the rule of law and due process, seeking to draw some general considerations on the three legal levels of judicial cooperation: international, transnational, and national. A specific reflection is devoted, in the fourth part, to the topic of digital evidence and AI. Digital evidence constitutes, in numerical terms, the main type of evidence collected in the context of the war between Russia and Ukraine (but a similar figure had already emerged during previous investigations of situations other than the one examined here). The use of AI, given the large amount of digital evidence, seems crucial to order to such a large amount of information and to move across it. The final idea is that, in this specific field, which constitutes one of the effects of the digital transition in the judiciary, there is room to develop, at the supranational level, a more uniform set of principles and rules than has been possible for more traditional form of evidence (such as testimony, or searches and seizures). This is because, in the field of digital evidence and AI, different national legal traditions have less influence.

## 2 EU Actions to Fight against the Commission of Core International Crimes (CIC)

It is well known that for at least two decades, the EU has been showing clear signs in favour of effective counteraction, both by its Member States and by its bodies, against serious forms of transnational crime, including Core International Crimes (CIC). Among these, it is worth mentioning the action adopted on a normative level by the EU in the late 1990s to contrast CIC commission: the establishment of a conditionality principle for countries interested in joining the EU from the break-up of the former Yugoslavia, as part of a new Stabilisation and Association Process kept by the Union in Western Balkans.[8] Furthermore, the EU has fully committed to the establishment of the International Criminal Court, to the Rome Statute, to which all EU Member

Committed in Ukraine. Towards a New Model of Cooperation?' (2022) 30 European Journal of Crime, Criminal Law and Criminal Justice 219.

8 Kei Hannah Brodersen, 'The ICTY's Conditionality Dilemma' (2014) 22 European Journal of Crime, Criminal Law and Criminal Justice 219.

States are parties, and to the financial support given to the ICC.[9] Political and economic sustain has also been accompanied by legal support. It is in this key that one can read those normative provisions which, since the EAW FD, have included the crimes over which the ICC has jurisdiction among those exempted from double criminality control. In this regard, it is useful to recall that the three legal sources examined in this research, the just mentioned EAW FD, the 2014 EIO D and the Regulation 1805/2018, all confirm that for offences falling within the jurisdiction of the ICC, a double criminality check is not required.

This means, as is well known, that when a national judicial institution of any EU Member State is proceeding against perpetrators of crimes covered by the Rome Statute, the principle of mutual recognition operates to its fullest extent, and a double criminality check is never required. In addition, using a Council Decision, the EU established, in 2002[10] (and reinforced one year later, in 2003),[11] the European Network for investigation and prosecution of genocide, crimes against humanity and war crimes ('Genocide Network').[12]

The framework depicted provides a better appreciation of recent developments following the outbreak of war between Russia and Ukraine.[13] There seem to be two specific elements worthy of mention. On the one hand, the creation of a joint investigation team (JIT) involving both EU and non-EU countries and an international institution. On the other, the attribution to Eurojust (and, to a lesser degree, to Europol) of a pivotal role in the collection and exchange of information, regarding investigations concerning serious international crimes (primarily those occurring in the Russia-Ukraine conflict).

---

9 The European Union has been one of the biggest financiers of the International Criminal Court from the beginning. Even after Brexit, the EU Member States finance approximatively the 40% of the ICC budget. See Assembly of the State Parties, 'Financial statements of the International Criminal Court for the year ended 31 December 2020' (July 2021) <https://asp.icc-cpi.int/sites/default/files/iccdocs/asp_docs/ASP20/ICC-ASP-20-12-ENG.pdf> accessed 30 July 2024.

10 Council Decision 2002/494/JHA of 13 June 2002 on setting up a European network of contact points in respect of persons responsible for genocide, crimes against humanity and war crimes [2002] OJ L 167/1.

11 Council Decision 2003/335/JHA of 8 May 2003 on the investigation and prosecution of genocide, crimes against humanity and war crimes [2003] OJ L 167/12.

12 The EU's firm commitment against the perpetration of CIC was confirmed, once more, in the support given to establishing the Specialist Chambers and Specialists Prosecutor's Office in Kosovo. In this regard Caianiello (n 7) 226.

13 See for a general analysis antecedent to the actual developments related to the war Natalia Bodnar, 'The EU-Ukraine Cooperation in Criminal Matters: "Justice" Dimension' (2018) 5 *European Political and Law Discourse* 13; Giulia Lanza, 'The Fundamental Role of International (Criminal) Law in the War in Ukraine' (2022) 66 *Foreign Policy Research Institute* 424.

## 3 The Establishment of a Joint Investigation Team. The Role Played by Eurojust (and Europol)

On 25 March 2022 two EU Member States, Lithuania and Poland, set up a JIT, together with Ukraine, a non-EU country. The initial composition of the group was later enriched by the involvement of three more EU States, Estonia, Lithuania, and Slovakia, and the participation of the Office of the Prosecutor of the International Criminal Court.[14]

This development should not appear surprising. First, the EU's willingness to actively cooperate with the ICC bodies is evident, as reflected in all the cooperation agreements mentioned above. Furthermore, with specific regard to Ukraine, it should be noted that it is one of the ten non-EU States that have a Liaison Prosecutor at Eurojust.[15]

The action taken establishing a JIT thus adapts a legal tool, the JIT FD, conceived in the framework of the mutual legal assistance Convention and translated in the mutual recognition regime, to the current scenario and the specific context of the international crimes committed in the conflict between Russia and Ukraine.[16]

The benefit of this choice is, in a nutshell, the extension of the mutual recognition principle, as far as the collection of information and evidence is concerned, to States and institutions outside the EU legal order, such as Ukraine and the OTP ICC.[17]

This outcome is made possible thanks to two factors. Firstly, by the application – as well as note – of the principle of mutual recognition, that rules

14 See the Eurojust, 'Estonia, Latvia and Slovakia become members of joint investigation team on alleged core international crimes in Ukraine' (31 May 2022) <https://www.eurojust.europa.eu/news/estonia-latvia-and-slovakia-become-members-joint-investigation-team-alleged-core-international> accessed 30 July 2024. See the further press release Eurojust, 'ICC participates in joint investigation team supported by Eurojust on alleged core international crimes in Ukraine' (25 April 2022) <https://www.eurojust.europa.eu/news/icc-participates-joint-investigation-team-supported-eurojust-alleged-core-international-crimes> accessed 30 July 2024.

15 See the recording Press conference held at the premises of Eurojust on May 31st, 2022, on the JIT on alleged core intl. crimes in Ukraine. Eurojust, 'Press conference – Joint investigation team on alleged core intl. crimes in Ukraine | Eurojust' (31 May 2022) <https://www.youtube.com/watch?v=_HW9AcF-AxI> accessed 30 July 2024.

16 It should be noted that the FD JIT allows the participation of non-EU entities in this body.

17 See on this topic Michele Caianiello, 'Models of Judicial Cooperation with *Ad Hoc* Tribunals and with the Permanent International Criminal Court in Europe' in Giulio Illuminati and Stefano Ruggeri (eds), *Transnational Inquiries and the Protection of Fundamental Rights in Criminal Proceedings. A Study in Memory of Vittorio Grevi and Giovanni Tranchina* (Springer 2013) 111–123.

in the cooperation between Member States in investigating the commission of CIC. Secondly, by the establishment of the JIT. This permits to expansion of some relevant advantages of the mutual recognition method to non-EU entities (Ukraine and the OTP ICC), as it allows several police officers or judicial authorities from different countries to work together, in conducting investigations and gathering evidence.[18] Such a hybrid JIT composition, with both EU and non-EU States, allows the former to work through the mutual recognition principles, and then to share, in real-time, the results achieved with the other partners in the team. A specific added value of the JIT is indeed fostering the spontaneous exchange of information,[19] thanks to the practice of parallel investigations into the same or related criminal facts. The JIT can serve as a forum where, more easily, the results of investigations conducted in parallel can be made available and exchanged. This way, the action of national law enforcement agencies should be more effective, as well as more comprehensive than if the efforts of the national States and the JIT remained separate and unconnected.

In the perspective under scrutiny, one must also appreciate the new role attributed to Eurojust, which, through the normative changes introduced, seems to become a privileged interlocutor in the fight against CIC not only at the EU level, but also on a wider geopolitical area (wherever directly or indirectly some legal interest of the Union is at stake).

Before examining the recent reform, however, one must remember that Eurojust has already competence to deal with investigations of serious international crimes. Indeed, this is provided for in Art 3(1) of Regulation (EU) No 1727/2018, which, in turn, refers to Annex 1. The Annex includes war crimes, crimes against humanity, and genocide among the crimes in respect of which Eurojust may act. In addition, Art 3(4) extends Eurojust's competence to instrumental crimes, that is those necessary to procure the means of committing the serious crimes enlisted in Annex 1, those made to facilitate or commit the formers, and those accomplished to ensure their impunity.

It may be useful to note that, within the framework of CIC, Eurojust enjoys a competence without constraints, compared to the one attributed to it in the field of offences affecting the financial interests of the EU. In fact, regarding

18 This operational mode helps to speed up the collection of information, which takes place, in a contextual manner, for the benefit of several judicial and law enforcement agencies. Above all, it considerably reduces the risks linked to the inadmissibility of evidence, since joint participation permits to respect each of the legal system involved in the JIT.

19 See Michele Simonato, 'The "Spontaneous Exchange of Information" between European Judicial Authorities from the Italian Perspective' (2011) 2 New Journal of European Criminal Law 220.

the latter, Eurojust must refrain from acting if EPPO has decided to intervene by initiating an investigation or prosecution.[20] On the contrary, about serious international crimes, Eurojust is the only major player at the EU judicial level and, as such, should not be subject to limitations or obstacles.

The recent developments that occurred last Spring give Eurojust an advanced role in the collection and exchange of information for countering the commission of CIC, this way improving the relevant role that this body already had, for the considerations just expressed. Indeed, to provide an adequate law enforcement response to the commission of international crimes in the conflict in Ukraine, on 30 May 2022, the European Parliament and the Council adopted a new Regulation (EU) No 838/2022, amending Regulation (EU) No 1727/2018 as regards the preservation, analysis, and storage at Eurojust of evidence relating to genocide, crimes against humanity, war crimes, and related criminal offences.[21] Thanks to this amendment, Article 4(1) of Regulation (EU) No 1727/2018 has been added a letter 'j', as a result of which Eurojust is entitled to

> support Member States' action in combating genocide, crimes against humanity, war crimes, and related criminal offences, including by preserving, analysing, and storing evidence related to those crimes and related criminal offences and enabling the exchange of such evidence with, or otherwise making it directly available to, competent national authorities and international judicial authorities, in particular the International Criminal Court.

To this end, the new Regulation mandates Eurojust to establish a new automated data management and storage facility that must collect, store, and order DNA profiles established from the non-coding part of DNA, photographs, and fingerprints and, about the CIC, videos, and audio recordings. For each item of evidence, the facility shall indicate the description and nature of the offences involving the person concerned, the date on which and the location at which the offences were committed, the criminal category of the offences, the

20 This holds except regarding offences committed in countries that do not participate in enhanced cooperation for EPPOs, or unless EPPO or a State participating in EPPO has asked Eurojust to participate.

21 See the press release of the European Council, 'Eurojust: Council adopts new rules allowing the agency to preserve evidence of war crimes' (25 May 2022) <https://www.consilium.europa.eu/en/press/press-releases/2022/05/25/eurojust-le-conseil-adopte-de-nouvelles-regles-permettant-a-l-agence-de-conserver-des-preuves-de-crimes-de-guerre/> accessed 30 July 2024.

progress of the investigations, and, about CIC, information relating to criminal conduct, including audio recordings, videos, satellite images, and photographs.

The purpose of these amendments is to give Eurojust a key role in judicial cooperation in the field of CIC. Indeed, as stated in Recital 11 at the new Regulation

> By preserving, analysing, and storing evidence related to genocide, crimes against humanity, war crimes, and related criminal offences and, when necessary and appropriate, by enabling its exchange following the applicable Union data protection rules, Eurojust can support case building in national and international investigations and provide additional support to the competent national authorities and international judicial authorities. Such analysis might be especially valuable for ascertaining the reliability of witness testimonies or establishing any relevant links. However, this Regulation does not introduce any obligation on national authorities to share evidence with Eurojust.

Since April 2022, when the EU legislator took action to introduce these legal changes, Eurojust has started to set up a new facility and preserve and catalogue evidence related to crimes committed during the war in Ukraine. Although the legal changes indicated are very recent, it is easy to foresee that their effects will soon be seen. On the one hand, this is due to Eurojust's great experience as a privileged mediator of judicial cooperation. On the other, this appears to be caused by the large amount of evidence that seems to be collected on the ground. Indeed, as has been observed, the conflict between Russia and Ukraine could be one of the most documented through digital evidence as well as one of the most "actively watched" by the community on social media.[22] In such a scenario, the enhanced capacity to collect, preserve, and sort digital evidence and make it directly accessible to the authorities conducting investigations – this is the role entrusted to Eurojust – may prove to be a choice that can make a difference in effectively prosecuting the commission of serious international crimes and bringing those responsible for them to justice.

Finally, European Commission President Ursula von der Leyen announced the creation of the International Centre for the Prosecution of the Crime of Aggression against Ukraine at the 24th EU-Ukraine Summit on 2 February 2023

---

22 See Sofia Aalto-Setälä and Maria F. Jaramillo Gomez, 'ICC investigations in Ukraine: How Digitally Derived Evidence can make a difference' (Leidenlawblog, 18 May 2022) <https://www.leidenlawblog.nl/articles/icc-investigations-in-ukraine-how-digitally-derived-evidence-can-make-a-difference> accessed 30 July 2024.

(ICPA).[23] According to the description on the Centre's website, the ICPA is a unique judicial pole, incorporated into Eurojust to support national investigations into the crime of aggression related to the war in Ukraine. At the ICPA, independent prosecutors from various countries can work together on a daily basis in the same location, exchanging evidence and agreeing on an integrated investigation and prosecution strategy. ICPA efforts should prepare and support any future prosecution of the crime of aggression, regardless of the jurisdiction in which these cases will be tried. ICPA participants benefit from Eurojust's specialised operational, technical, logistical and financial support. The Core International Crimes Evidence Database (CICED), managed by Eurojust, is central to the operations of the ICPA. Evidence already submitted to CICED for other international crimes, such as genocide, crimes against humanity and war crimes, may also be relevant to the investigation of the crime of aggression. In addition, ICPA participants can submit national evidence to CICED for analysis.

Eurojust is not the only EU network involved at the forefront of the investigation of crimes committed during the war in Ukraine. A significant role is also played by Europol. As of 2022, Europol has been involved in several support activities, including communication and intelligence gathering, support for war crimes investigations, and support for the EU Commission's initiatives to seize and confiscate assets, knowledge sharing and liaison investigation officers.[24]

## 4 The Prospects for the European Union

The picture outlined so far can be interpreted in several ways, all of which can be useful in trying to work out different perspectives for the future. Although the initiatives adopted in the past two years, taking advantage of the opportunity offered by the war between Russia and Ukraine, are undoubtedly significant, the two main players involved, the EU and the ICC, still have significant

23 See the website Eurojust, 'International Centre for the Prosecution of the Crime of Aggression against Ukraine' (eurojust.europa.eu) <https://www.eurojust.europa.eu/international-centre-for-the-prosecution-of-the-crime-of-aggression-against-ukraine> accessed 30 July 2024. See also Julia Geneuss and Florian Jeßberger, 'Russian Aggression and the War in Ukraine. An Introduction' (2022) 20 Journal of International Criminal Justice 783.

24 See the information shared at the Europol website: Europol, 'Europol's solidarity with Ukraine' (europol.europa.eu) <https://www.europol.europa.eu/europol's-solidarity-ukraine> accessed 30 July 2024.

weaknesses. Both institutions, albeit in different ways and different contexts, are working to find a more stable balance than the one achieved so far and to acquire fuller legitimacy in the international scenario.

They have metaphorically travelled a road that has led them to a crossroads through what they have achieved by cooperating up to now: faced with this, they can choose whether to put what they have managed to achieve so far to more stable use or rather to be satisfied with the experience they have had, without expecting to turn it into a new chapter in their history.

If we look at the overall picture from the EU perspective, it is evident the significant role that its police and judicial institutions are potentially able to play in the fight against the commission of CIC. Paradoxically, it is precisely the fact that they can mainly rely on soft power rather than vertical power in the strict sense, that seems to make these transnational bodies more efficient in the international arena.[25] Moreover, this should come as no surprise, given that in the supranational context, in which respect for the sovereignty of States is still so important, soft power, due to its elasticity and flexibility, can be more effective than vertical hierarchical power, which is often perceived as an undue intrusion into what are traditionally considered to be matters that are strictly or predominantly the responsibility of national governments.

As is well known, both Europol and Eurojust are, in essence, facilitators of the work carried out by their national police and judicial counterparts.[26] Both European bodies have no direct capacity to carry out investigations or prosecutions. Their added value, however, lies in their ability to process a wide range of data, obtained through their position as privileged mediators, and their power to conclude agreements and work with institutions outside the EU Member States. This puts both agencies in a position to receive information, reports, and evidence on a wider scale and of higher quality than individual States could if they acted in isolation.

On the other hand, both Eurojust and Europol are endowed with the power to direct the work of the respective investigation and prosecution agencies of the EU Member States. This is particularly evident in Eurojust, which can give written directions to national judicial authorities, requesting them to prosecute, set up joint investigation teams, or order special investigative measures (such as controlled deliveries). Even Europol, in recent times, thanks to the

---

25 Jenia Iontcheva Turner, 'Transnational Networks and International Criminal Justice?' (2007) 105 Mich. L. Rev. 994, 999.

26 Gaetano de Amicis, 'Centralised Bodies of Administrative and Police Cooperation' in Roberto E. Kostoris (ed), *Handbook of European Criminal Procedure* (Springer 2018) 202, 223.

amendment to the Regulation governing its work adopted in 2022 (Art 6(1)(a)), can require the authorities of a Member State to initiate investigations, communicating this request immediately to Eurojust and EPPO.

These possibilities of making formal requests to national authorities – which are made known among all EU institutions with competence in criminal matters – have an effect not too far from that of an order in the proper sense. The authority of the Member State that neglects the invitation to act would be subjected to unpleasant scrutiny, while the government of the Member State in which the authority operates would face delicate diplomatic issues. Moreover, the closely intertwined interests, economic and otherwise, of the various EU countries produce a not inconsiderable indirect push, capable, especially if the stakes are high, of considerably reducing the margin of choice for the individual national authority. For instance, a financial aid package can also be linked to the compliance a State can show in the field of law enforcement. From this specific point of view, compliance with international criminal law, one must consider that the fight against CIC, and the activation to bring the persons responsible for crimes to justice is conceived by the EU as strategic for strengthening the rule of law, which, in turn, constitutes one of the common foundations of the entire Union and its Member States.[27]

At the same time, the soft nature of the power exercised by these supranational bodies is such that it leaves in the hands of the national authorities a margin of appreciation, regarding, if nothing else, how to act and how to achieve the objectives set by Europol and Eurojust.

The experience during the Russia-Ukraine conflict makes it clear that the EU's transnational bodies are also able to develop their potential in the field of international criminal justice. Eurojust has been able, by exploiting the legal framework that was already in place (and by benefiting from the amendment to the Regulation made in 2022 precisely to address the emergency of the war in Ukraine) to play a pivotal role, at the crossroads of investigations conducted by several EU countries, by third countries, and by the ICC OTP. The ability to collect information, to store it, and to allow access to all 'members of the club', meaning by this definition both the judicial authorities of EU States and those outside the EU who are partners in the investigation of crimes committed in Ukraine, gives Eurojust the role of director of a broader strategy. A strategy in which, realistically, the most numerous prosecutions will take place before national jurisdictions,[28] both within and outside the EU countries; at the same

27 See Caianiello (n 7) 221–223.

28 To a certain extent, this strongly pro-national jurisdiction's approach is inspired by what is observed in Turner (n 1) 31. But while Turner maintains a radical approach to his theory

time, a symbolically pivotal role, for the most sensitive cases involving Heads of State or members of Government, will be played by the ICC OTP (and ultimately by the ICC itself).[29]

Moreover, it should not be overlooked that the EU's potential to promote countering the commission of CIC seems broader than hitherto. If, exploiting the potential of the Treaty, the EU legislator was to choose to extend the competence of EPPO to the CIC commission, the EU could play a more direct and active role in the actual prosecution of crimes, conducting investigations, and directly prosecuting through its own body.[30]

Another very important aspect, from a European perspective, is the application of the principle of mutual recognition (and the Framework decision on Joint Investigation Teams) to cooperation with the ICC. This choice, on a technical level, seems to fit well with the needs of the ICC. The principle in question, which operates – as far as it is relevant in the context of this research – in matters of arrest and surrender, collection and exchange of evidence, and confiscation, ensures swift action by the jurisdictions involved. It also allows for respect, at least in essential aspects, for national legal traditions, while taking care not to depart from the tracks set by the EU Charter of Fundamental Rights and ECtHR human rights jurisprudence. The model, although certainly not free of flaws, seems easily compatible with the requirements, from the outset marked by a certain flexibility, applied by the ICC, which refers in the Statute to a set of principles very similar to the European one.[31] Similarly, the reluctance to provide for overly specific and strict exclusion rules, particularly in

(whereby the ICC in practice should never hold trials), I believe that, as the reality of recent years has shown, a conception of the ICC as a mere 'circuit rider' is not optimal. Indeed, the ICC may have the capacity to go beyond the limits of national jurisdictions. One case, for example, concerns trials against Heads of State or members of government, who before national jurisdictions would always enjoy immunity. See Christoph Safferling, *International Criminal Procedure* (Oxford Un. Press 2012) 105. Of course, the issue of Heads of State and Head of governments is quite controversial. See Leila Nadya Sadat, 'Heads of State and other government officials before the International Criminal Court: the Uneasy revolution continues' in Margaret M. de Guzman, James E. Beasley and Valerie Oosterveld (eds), *The Elgar Companion to the International Criminal Court* (Edward Elgar 2020) 96–127; Gerhard Kemp, 'Immunity of High-Ranking Officials Before the International Criminal Court – Between International Law and Political reality' in Gerhard Werle and Andreas Zimmermann (eds), *The International Criminal Court in Turbulent Times* (Springer 2019) 61–82.

29 This should be the ideal set-up for the ICC, based on the principle of complementarity. See Safferling (n 28) 94.

30 See Caianiello (n 7) 227.

31 See Safferling (n 28) 378.

the field of evidence, which is typical of the ICC system,[32] bears a resemblance to the *modus operandi* of the EU directives on the admissibility of evidence: EU legislation, in fact, except in sporadic cases, tends to leave this aspect to national jurisdictions, tending not to impose standards or exclusion rules at the supranational level.

On reflection, the European model of exchange of information and evidence should apply not only in one direction (from the EU or its Member States to the ICC) but also in the opposite direction (from the ICC to the EU and its Member States). On the one hand, the operability of the JIT allows information, also collected by authorities operating within the EU, to be easily circulated through legal sources based on mutual recognition, within the Member States jurisdictions. On the other hand, a possible handing over by the ICC OTP to let us suppose Eurojust of evidentiary relevant information could then benefit from direct access for national authorities investigating a case (and wishing to make use of that information). Finally, the surrender by the ICC OTP to a national judicial authority within the EU, if considered admissible by the latter, could then be transmitted to other judicial authorities within the Union, under the aegis of the principle of mutual recognition, as also in the recent *Encrochat* case the Court of Justice established.[33]

Ultimately, the model at work seems to favour, if nothing else, celerity in cooperation, ensuring, on paper, respect for a set of common values, between the ICC and the EU.

---

32 See in this regard Michele Caianiello, 'First Decisions on the Admission of Evidence at ICC Trials – A Blending of Accusatorial and Inquisitorial Models?' (2011) 9 Journal of International Criminal Justice 385; John D. Jackson and Sarah J. Summers, 'Evidence in the international criminal tribunals' in *The Internationalisation of Criminal Evidence: Beyond the Common Law and Civil Law Traditions* (Cambridge University Press 2012) 108–148.

33 See Case C-670/22 *M.N.* (*EncroChat*) EU:C:2024:372. See Thomas Whal, 'AG: EncroChat Data Can, in Principle, Be Used in Criminal Proceedings' (Eucrim, 8 February 2024) <https://eucrim.eu/news/ag-encrochat-data-can-in-principle-be-used-in-criminal-proceedings/> accessed 30 July 2024; Bill Goodwin, 'Germany: European Court of Justice ruling on EncroChat could lead to new legal challenges. A ruling by the European Court of Justice could prompt legal challenges in EncroChat prosecutions in Germany and other EU States' (Computerweekly.com, 08 May 2024) <https://www.computerweekly.com/news/366583692/Germany-European-Court-of-Justice-ruling-on-EncroChat-could-lead-to-new-legal-challenges> accessed 30 July 2024; Lorenzo Bernardini, 'On Encrypted Messages and Clear Verdicts – the EncroChat Case before the Court of Justice (Case C-670/22, MN)' (EuLawLive, 21 May 2024) <https://eulawlive.com/op-ed-on-encrypted-messages-and-clear-verdicts-the-encrochat-case-before-the-court-of-justice-case-c-670-22-mn-by-lorenzo-bernardini/> accessed 30 July 2024.

## 5 The Prospects for the ICC

The collaboration between the International Criminal Court (ICC) and the European Union (EU) in the investigation and prosecution of war crimes in Ukraine is a significant example of how international and national institutions can work together to ensure justice.

The complementarity between the ICC and domestic prosecutions is a key element in enhancing the effectiveness of the ICC. The ICC can act as a catalyst for investigations by States, intervening only when national authorities are unable or unwilling to prosecute certain crimes. This provides an incentive for countries, such as EU Member States, to strengthen their investigative and judicial capacities in international crimes. Furthermore, the collaboration between the ICC and the European institutions allows for the construction of a transnational network of judicial cooperation, strengthening the impetus to investigate and prosecute such crimes.

Complementarity between the ICC's jurisdiction and actions at the national level, strengthened by collaboration with the EU, is key to overcoming some of the challenges the Court has faced in the past. Complementarity, first, is a method of work-sharing between the ICC and its Member States. It presupposes, but in practice mandates, that the ICC does not conduct most trials on serious international crimes. This is for two reasons. The first is that, although heavily funded by States, the Court does not have the necessary resources to cope with all the demands for justice that may arise across the globe to cases over which it would have jurisdiction under the Statute. Secondly, it should be noted that even if these resources would allow the ICC to administer every case that deserves to be tried, this would not be an optimal solution.[34] The Court's function is to encourage more widespread protection of rights that are compromised by the commission of serious international crimes.[35] To this end, the hope is that States Parties will develop their domestic systems to be able to do justice when an international crime is committed over which they could claim jurisdiction. Put another way, the political idea behind complementarity is not, as is obvious from the term itself, that of an isolated international court in an indifferent or inactive international context in the face

34 See what had already caught 20 years ago Turner (n 1) 18.

35 Nevertheless, it is true that the ICC has been less effective than hoped in encouraging national prosecutions. See Paul Seils, 'Putting Complementarity in Its Place' in Carsten Stahn (ed), *The Law and Practice of the International Criminal Court* (Oxford Un. Press 2015) 305–327.

of the commission of international crimes.[36] On the contrary, the Court can fully unleash its potential if it is placed in a position to act as the engine of an integrated system. To use the definition of the first Roman emperor, Octavian Augustus, the idea is that of an ICC '*primum inter pares*', not of a powerful but remote institution.

It is not only a question of resources or power, of course; it is first and foremost a question of culture, and of the dissemination of a set of shared principles in the international community. In this perspective, the active involvement of domestic judicial authorities, demanded by the principle of complementarity, allows for the best use of their contextual knowledge, investigative resources, and relations with local communities. This makes it possible to build stronger cases and ensure greater acceptance and legitimacy of proceedings at the national level.[37] Furthermore, the central role of States is crucial to overcome traditional cooperation and coordination challenges that have often limited the impact of international criminal justice.

In this way, the culture of international criminal justice should spread more pervasively among those countries that have ratified the Rome Statute of the ICC. When States actively prosecute the most serious crimes according to the standards of international justice, the legitimacy and acceptance of prosecutions at the local level are strengthened, the harmonisation of domestic criminal law with international law is promoted, specialised expertise is created at the national level, and cooperation between national authorities and the ICC is fostered.

Finally, trials held at the national level have a more direct and visible impact on communities and the population.[38] They become more proximate and tangible for the citizens concerned, fostering greater public discussion and awareness of international crimes, enhancing victims' and their families' sense of justice and reparation, fostering acceptance and legitimacy of verdicts, and stimulating the growth of a legal culture regarding international crimes.

In sum, promoting expertise at the national level, strengthening investigation and prosecution capacities on international crimes within Member States contributes to consolidating a substratum of shared knowledge and professionalism. It also enhances cooperation and dialogue between national authorities and the ICC, because the frequent exchange of information, best

---

36 Turner (n 1) 18.

37 Turner (n 1) 23. See also Irene Milazzo, 'Commentary' in Andre Klip and Stephen Freeland (eds), *Annotated Leading Cases of International Criminal Tribunals. The International Criminal Court: 2012–2014*, vol. 61 (Intesentia 2020) 296–306.

38 Milazzo (n 37) 296.

practices, and working methods creates a collaborative culture that transcends individual prosecutions.

In this way, the central role attributed to States in the administration of international criminal justice fosters the widespread dissemination of a common mentality and standards among the countries that are parties to the Rome Statute. This contributes to the consolidation of the ICC's legal and institutional framework over time, making it increasingly entrenched and accepted globally.

Transnational networks, such as Eurojust and Europol, or collaborative legal networks, such as the EU JITs, in this regard, are crucial in enhancing the effectiveness of cooperation between the ICC and EU institutions.[39] These networks make it possible to share information and evidence in a timely and effective manner, harmonise investigative and prosecutorial standards and best practices, enhance national investigative and judicial capacities, and promote political and diplomatic coordination. In the context of the conflict in Ukraine, these networks seem to play a high value role to overcome the traditional challenges of coordination and cooperation, ensuring that perpetrators of the most serious crimes do not go unpunished.

On the one hand, the ICC can act as a catalyst for State investigations, exploiting the principle of complementarity that allows it to intervene only when national authorities are unable or unwilling to prosecute certain crimes. This provides an incentive for countries, such as EU Member States, to strengthen their investigative and judicial capacities in international crimes. On the other hand, the collaboration between the ICC and the European institutions allows for the construction of a transnational network of judicial cooperation that strengthens the impetus to investigate and prosecute such crimes.

## 6 Perspectives on the Rule of Law. The Potential of EU and ICC Collaboration in the Field of Digital Evidence and AI in Criminal Justice

Many considerations in terms of the rule of law have already been expressed in the previous paragraphs and can therefore be summarised here.

39 A more skeptical approach worth to be read is taken by Sergey Vasiliev, 'Watershed Moment or Same Old? Ukraine and the Future of International Criminal Justice' (2022) 20 Journal of International Criminal Justice 893.

Effective cooperation between the different actors in the international criminal justice system is crucial to countering the commission of international crimes and bringing alleged perpetrators to justice. From this perspective, cooperation between the EU and the ICC seems to be facilitated by the fact that its supranational institutions are inspired by a fairly similar operational model: complementarity for the ICC and subsidiarity, as per Art 4 TEU, for the EU. Trying to simplify the two concepts, which in detail are not as close as the words used might suggest, it can be said that both pursue the goal of giving precedence to State sovereignty. This requires, of course, that States equip themselves to cope with the responsibilities that rest on their shoulders, also considering their membership in these supranational institutions. In the background, of course, remains the role played by these latter institutions, which can intervene when a State is unable to act.[40]

The ultimate goal is the harmonisation of national systems, whose traditions we try as much as possible to respect, supplemented by joining supranational institutions that softly bind them together, the International Criminal Court in one case and, much more strongly, the EU in the other.

In this general framework, a few more words should be said about the type of evidence that, in the Russia-Ukraine conflict, but also previous cases, is becoming predominant. This is digital evidence.

As well known, the term 'digital evidence' refers to any information or data stored, transmitted, or processed in digital form that can be used in a court of law to prove or disprove a fact in question. This evidence is crucial in modern investigations and trials due to the pervasive use of digital devices and the Internet. Digital evidence includes a wide range of data types and sources,

40 Of course, the two guiding principles, complementarity and subsidiarity, are very different, on closer inspection. Complementarity operates primarily as a criterion for dividing jurisdiction over criminal cases between the ICC and the States Parties. In contrast, subsidiarity is a guiding criterion for all EU action, which only sporadically deals with or intervenes in criminal cases (especially in criminal matters, an area that has developed in recent times compared to the more traditional areas of the common market and energy). Furthermore, complementarity allows the ICC to evoke the case when a national State that would have jurisdiction over it is unwilling or unable to act. These are two specific criteria, though also open to interpretation, denoting a situation of impossibility, whether objective or not. Conversely, subsidiarity allows the EU to prevail over the Member States even when the latter would be able and willing to act (or perhaps, with national solutions, have indeed already acted) and yet the EU is best placed to address the supranational nature of the problems involved in the case. A case that, it is worth repeating, may well be of a non-criminal nature (and, moreover, concern problems that are not of a judicial nature).

such as electronic documents,[41] multimedia files,[42] internet activity, computer logs, data from mobile devices, network traffic data, metadata and databases, and cloud storage.

### 6.1 *Use of Digital Evidence and AI in the ICC*

The ICC increasingly relies on freely available digital evidence from the web, often referred to as open-source evidence.[43] This trend has been driven by various technological advances and social changes. In the new millennium, there has been a significant increase in the volume of open-source evidence. This growth has been further amplified by the advent of Web 2.0, which facilitates interaction and user-generated content. The ability of individuals to upload and share information online has opened new avenues for collecting evidence of international crimes.

The market introduction and widespread use of smartphones and other digital devices have led to a substantial increase in available digital evidence. These devices have become ubiquitous, allowing people around the world to capture events as they happen. New applications have been developed specifically to document international crimes, allowing individuals to capture and share crucial evidence. Notable examples are EyeWitness[44] to Atrocities and CameraV.[45] These applications are designed to ensure that the evidence collected is secure, verifiable, and admissible in court. They provide tools to document atrocities in a way that preserves the integrity of the data, making it useful for future court proceedings.

Since around 2010, there has been a marked increase in open-source digital evidence, coinciding with the mass adoption of smartphones and related technologies. This trend reflects the growing recognition of the importance of

---

41 Electronic documents are a primary form of digital evidence. They include e-mails, text messages, word processing documents, spreadsheets, PDFs and other files created or stored on computers and digital devices. Such documents can provide a detailed record of communications and transactions relevant to a case.

42 Multimedia files also play an important role among digital evidence. Photos, videos and audio recordings captured with digital cameras, smartphones or other recording devices can document events, capture interactions and provide an often compelling visual and auditory context in court.

43 Alexa Koenig, 'From 'Capture to Courtroom': Collaboration and the Digital Documentation of International Crimes in Ukraine' (2022) 20 Journal of International Criminal Justice 829.

44 See <https://www.eyewitness.global/>. See ibid 833.

45 See <https://camerav.en.uptodown.com/android>. See Raquel Vazquez Llorente, 'Deepfakes in the Dock: Preparing International Criminal Justice for Deepfakes and Generative AI' (2024) 20 The SciTech Lawyer 29.

digital evidence in documenting and prosecuting international crimes.[46] The ability to capture high-quality video and photographic evidence has transformed the international criminal justice landscape, offering new opportunities for accountability.

The ICC OTP has adopted a new strategy to make effective use of digital evidence. This strategy is part of broader initiatives such as Project Harmony, which aims to harmonise the collection and use of digital evidence across jurisdictions.[47] The new ICC OTP strategy recognises the central role of open evidence in building cases against perpetrators of international crimes and seeks to integrate this type of evidence into the judicial process in a more systematic way.[48]

A recent collaboration between Eurojust and the ICC resulted in the publication of guidelines to assist civil society organisations in documenting international crimes. This joint effort is described in the document 'Documenting International Crimes and Human Rights Violations for Criminal Accountability Purposes'.[49] These guidelines provide a comprehensive framework for civil society organisations to collect and store information on international crimes and human rights violations. They include a set of 'do's and don'ts' to ensure that evidence collected is admissible in court and does not inadvertently damage criminal accountability efforts. The guidelines respond to the request of

46 A significant example of the impact of digital evidence is the Al-Mahdi case. In 2016, Ahmad Al-Faqi Al-Mahdi pleaded guilty at the International Criminal Court to the war crime of attacking historic and religious buildings in Timbuktu, Mali. Video evidence played a crucial role in illustrating the extent of the destruction and linking Al-Mahdi directly to the acts. Similarly, the arrest warrants issued for Mahmoud Mustafa Busayf Al-Werfalli in 2017 and 2018 relied heavily on video footage. Al-Werfalli, a commander in the Libyan National Army, has been involved in multiple extrajudicial killings. Videos circulated on social media showed him personally participating in or ordering executions, providing crucial evidence to support the charges against him. See Maria de Arcos Tejerizo, 'Digital evidence and fair trial rights at the International Criminal Court' (2023) 36 Leiden Journal of International Law 749.

47 See Hayley Evans and Mahir Hazim, 'Digital Evidence Collection at the Int'l Criminal Court: Promises and Pitfalls' (justsecrurity, 5 July 2023) <https://www.justsecurity.org/87149/digital-evidence-collection-at-the-intl-criminal-court-promises-and-pitfalls/> accessed 30 July 2024.

48 See also The OTP Strategic Plan 2023–2025, where the Prosecutor in Strategic Goal No. 3 aims to make of the OTP a "global technology leader". See the document at <https://www.icc-cpi.int/sites/default/files/2023-08/2023-strategic-plan-otp-v.3.pdf>.

49 Eurojust, 'Documenting International Crimes and Human Rights Violations for Criminal Accountability Purposes' (Eurojust.europa.eu, 21 September 2022) <https://www.eurojust.europa.eu/publication/documenting-international-crimes-and-human-rights-violations> accessed 30 July 2024.

several civil society organisations and stakeholders in the field of accountability, who have indicated the need for guidance to ensure that the information collected can be used as evidence in future national or international court proceedings. This publication was jointly developed by Eurojust, the EU Network for the Investigation and Prosecution of Genocide, Crimes against Humanity and War Crimes ('Genocide Network'), and the Office of the Prosecutor of the International Criminal Court.

These developments highlight the changing landscape of evidence collection and the critical role of digital technologies in promoting accountability for international crimes.[50] The ICC and its partners are harnessing the power of digital evidence to build stronger cases and ensure that perpetrators of international crimes are brought to justice. Through strategic initiatives and collaborations, they are improving the capacity of civil society organisations and individuals to effectively document atrocities, thereby contributing to the broader goals of international criminal justice.[51]

However, the use of digital evidence is not without its challenges. There are inherent risks of possible bias in the collection and presentation of this evidence. On the one side, in fact, it is good that people living in remote and conflict-ridden regions can use their phones to proactively submit evidence to the ICC, potentially creating a bottom-up narrative of international justice. This bottom-up approach allows ordinary people to directly contribute to the documentation of crimes, fostering a sense of participation and ownership in the justice process. However, on the other, those documenting events may

50 The use of footage and videos as evidence is not a new phenomenon. Films were also shown at the Nuremberg Trials to account for the atrocities encountered by the Allies upon their arrival in European territories after the defeat of the Axis regimes. These films provided stark and irrefutable images of the horrors of the Holocaust and other war crimes, helping to convey the extent and brutality of the crimes to the court and the world. The use of visual evidence at Nuremberg set a precedent for the inclusion of multimedia evidence in international criminal proceedings.

51 This is understandable and, in many respects, also useful. The possibility of filming events that ordinary people witness on the street is now unlimited. Thanks to the wide accessibility of smartphones and digital cameras, almost everyone can become a documentarist of events in real time. This democratisation of the media has profound implications for the documentation of international crimes and human rights violations. Audio and video footage is a highly evidentiary asset, very useful for providing an account of the context in which crimes were committed and sometimes to constitute evidence of the crimes themselves. The visual and auditory details captured in these recordings can provide a vivid and undeniable record that complements traditional forms of evidence such as witness testimony and forensic analysis.

have a personal interest in what they are recording, which may influence the perspective and content of the evidence collected. This selective nature means that user-generated evidence is more likely to be collected, at least in the international context, by users seeking to document incriminating evidence, rather than exculpatory evidence. This bias can affect the objectivity of the evidence, and the overall narrative derived from it.

Furthermore, a specific problem is the huge volume of digital evidence that is often collected. The quantity of digital information can be enormous, creating a substantial challenge in terms of data processing and analysis. Investigators and prosecutors must sift through huge amounts of footage, images, and audio recordings to separate what is relevant from what is useless. This task can be excessive and time-consuming, potentially delaying the judicial process. Another critical challenge is verifying the authenticity of digital information. Digital evidence can be manipulated and ensuring its integrity is crucial to maintaining the credibility of the judicial process.

To address these challenges, the ICC is leveraging artificial intelligence (AI) systems. Using AI, investigators can handle large volumes of data more effectively, quickly identifying the most relevant evidence. AI systems can be trained to recognise patterns, detect anomalies, and flag potentially significant information, thus streamlining the evidence-collection process.

There are two types of problems. The first is related to authenticity and the risk of credible fakes, constructed by exploiting the 'new' world of digital evidence. The second, on the other hand, is related to respect for the rights of the defence and more generally of due process.[52]

In relation to the first, essentially the risk is that spontaneous documentation of criminal actions or scenarios in a war context may result in misleading or incomplete evidence. Although images and videos easily arouse a feeling of trust in the viewer, due to the high demonstrative capacity we usually attribute to this kind of representative evidence, errors and limitations are always around the corner. Thus, for example, a partial shot, which does not allow one to see what has happened outside the range of the camera, can compromise the reliability of the evidence (but many and various examples could be given

52 See De Arcos Tejerizo (n 46) 750–751; Lindsay Freeman, 'Prosecuting Atrocity Crimes with Open Source Evidence' in Sam *Dubberley, Alexa Koenig and Daragh Murray (eds), Digital Witness: Using Open Source Information for Human Rights Investigation, Documentation, and Accountability (Oxford Un. Press 2019) 48–67*; Evans and Hazim (n 47).

on this point).[53] Added to this is the problem of fakes,[54] which are increasingly easy to make thanks to the development of technology. When faced with deep fakes, how can they be detected? Can technology develop not only to allow those who want to create forgeries to do so, but also to allow those seeking credible evidence to isolate forged documents?

In relation to the second, the need to ensure a fair trial in this new digital scenario, inevitably, serious concerns arise from such massive use of digital evidence. It is in fact crucial to ensure effective disclosure to the parties, particularly the defence. This is progressively challenging in the case of large volumes of digital data, which can be cumbersome to manage and examine thoroughly.

Under this perspective, the fundamental right of due process to allow the defence full access to the data available to the prosecution runs the risk of finding a practical limit and some theoretical or principled limits. As to the first, the problem concerns, as already mentioned, the large amount of data. Sometimes there can be so much of it that it is difficult for the prosecutor to fully access it, which in turn makes it difficult to catalogue and store it in an orderly fashion.[55]

But the biggest problem, inevitably, is one of principle. The data available to the prosecution may concern third persons: in these circumstances, the right to full access that the defence may claim, in the name of due process, risks being limited in the name of the right to privacy of third parties, whose data have been mistakenly or otherwise casually collected in the network of the data-driven investigation. Moreover, if by full access is meant, as it should be, the possibility for the defence to know also the artificial intelligence programmes used by the prosecutor to navigate through all the data, a further limitation could be intellectual property rights. This issue could be raised by

53 See Gabrielle McIntyre and Nicholas Vialle, *The Use of AI at the ICC: Should we Have Concerns? Part I* (OpinioJuris, 11 October 2023) <http://opiniojuris.org/2023/10/11/the-use-of-ai-at-the-icc-should-we-have-concerns-part-i/> accessed 30 July 2024. See also De Arcos Tejerizo (n 45) 753–754.

54 McIntyre and Vialle (n 53). See Vazquez Llorente (n 45) 30–31.

55 This, too, is not a new problem. The difficulty for the defence in navigating the information held by the prosecutor in a digital archive had already arisen with respect to the ICTY. In fact, to meet the defence's need to navigate the *mare magnum* of evidence collected by the Prosecutor, Rule 68(B) was amended, requiring the Prosecutor to "make available to the defence, in electronic form, collections of relevant material held by the Prosecutor, together with appropriate computer software with which the defence can search such collections electronically". See Salvatore Zappalà, 'The Prosecutor's Duty to Disclose Exculpatory Materials and the Recent Amendment to Rule 68 ICTY RPE' (2004) 2 *Journal of International Criminal Justice* 620–630.

the company that supplied or created the AI system used by the prosecutor.[56] The latter, in turn, would be faced with an unsolvable dilemma: Either allow access to the data to the defence, thus violating intellectual property rights (and risking future problems with the companies designing the AI for justice, which might decide to stop cooperating with the ICC OTP); or do not allow access to the defence, thus violating due process (with risks for the fairness of the trial, as the issue would seem to have some similarities with the Lubanga case and the non-disclosure agreement signed at the time by the prosecutor on the basis of Art 54 St.).[57]

The provisions of the Rome Statute and the ICC Rules of Procedure and Evidence are designed to ensure fair and transparent proceedings. However, the question remains whether they are adequate to tackle the specific challenges posed by digital evidence. To address these problems, the ICC may need to develop more detailed guidelines for the disclosure and verification of digital evidence. Such guidelines should include specified procedures for handling large datasets, deadlines for disclosure, and standards for independent verification. In addition, the court could consider implementing training programmes for defence lawyers on digital evidence management and access to digital forensics experts.

In conclusion, while the current provisions of the Rome Statute and the ICC Rules of Procedure and Evidence provide a flexible framework for the

---

56 See Lorena Bachmaier Winter, 'The Quest for Evidentiary Rules in EU in Cross-Border Criminal Proceedings: Electronic Evidence, Efficiency and Fair Trial Rights', in Lorena Bachmaier Winter and Farsam Salimi (eds), *Admissibility of Evidence in EU in Cross-Border Criminal Proceedings: Electronic Evidence, Efficiency and Fair Trial Rights* (Hart 2024) 1–27; Giulia Lasagni, 'Admissibility of Evidence in Criminal Proceedings: Lessons (and Problems) from the 'Data Retention Saga'' in Lorena Bachmaier Winter and Farsam Salimi (eds), *Admissibility of Evidence in EU in Cross-Border Criminal Proceedings: Electronic Evidence, Efficiency and Fair Trial Rights*, 29–48. Although not related to the experience of international criminal justice, the problems examined in this volume on cross-border judicial cooperation in the EU formally recall those outlined in this chapter with reference to the ICC.

57 As is known, in the above-mentioned case the need for complete access to exculpatory materials was revealed to be fundamental for the accused to prepare his trial (and pre-trial) strategy. That is why the judges ordered the stay of the proceeding and the interim release of the accused: ICC Trial Chamber I, *Decision on the Consequences of Non-Disclosure of Exculpatory Materials Covered by Article 54(3)(e) Agreements and the application to stay the prosecution of the accused, together with certain other issues raised at the Status Conference on 10 June 2008*, ICC-01/04-01/06-1401-13-06-2008; ICC Trial Chamber I, *Decision on the Release of Mr. Thomas Lubanga Dyilo*, ICC-01/04-01/06-1418-02-07-2008. See Michele Caianiello, 'Disclosure Before the ICC. The Emergence of a New Form of Policies Implementation System in International Criminal Justice?' (2010) 10 International Criminal Law Review 23.

admissibility of evidence, more specific guidelines and procedures seem to be needed to address the challenges of digital evidence. Ensuring effective disclosure to all parties, in particular the defence, and safeguarding the right to verify the authenticity and reliability of evidence are key to maintaining the fairness and integrity of the judicial process in the new digitalised environment.

### 6.2 *Interaction with the EU in the Development of Shared Principles and Rules in the Field of Digital Evidence and AI*

In the field we have briefly described the interaction between the ICC and the EU institutions can be particularly fruitful. The EU has long had a set of rules to progressively address the issue of digital evidence and the use of AI in justice, including criminal justice. For instance, both Directive No 680/2016 and Regulation (EU) No 679/2016 (the General Data Protection Regulation), provide that a decision based solely on automated processing shall be prohibited.[58]

The jurisprudence of the Court of Justice, developed in numerous decisions on digital data and metadata, has also introduced significant safeguards on how data are collected, processed, and stored. Thus, starting with the pivotal judgment in *Digital Rights and Ireland*, the Court has prescribed that intrusion into an individual's virtual privacy may only take place in the presence of serious criminal offences, predetermined by law, and only following an authorisation order by a judicial (or other independent) authority. After that, it was clarified that this concept must be understood as meaning a body guaranteeing the levels of independence of a judge in the strict sense of the term, the order of a public prosecutor not being sufficient for this purpose.

Finally, in recent years the EU has adopted several regulatory measures, for instance on the acquisition of data directly from service providers, with the European Regulation on production orders,[59] and on artificial intelligence (the recent AI Act), which innovatively regulate areas that were hitherto not regulated by law.

For instance, the use of AI for facial recognition is defined as high-risk and the system implementing it must meet certain safety and quality standards,

58 See Giuseppe Contissa and Giulia Lasagni, 'When it is (also) Algorithms and AI that decide on Criminal Matters: In Search of an Effective Remedy' (2020) 28 European Journal of Crime, Criminal Law and Criminal Justice 280.

59 Stanislaw Tosza, 'All evidence is equal, but electronic evidence is more equal than any other: The relationship between the European Investigation Order and the European Production Order' (2020) 11 New Journal of European Criminal Law 161. Stanislaw Tosza, 'The E-Evidence Package is Adopted: End of a Saga or Beginning of a New One?' (2023) 9 European Data Protection Law Review 163.

without which the admission of this type of algorithmic testing should not be permitted.

The interaction between EU legal norms and the ICC can be fruitful, as it helps the Court to give substance to the criteria of fairness and reliability that characterise the law of evidence and are enshrined in Art 69 St. But there is perhaps a further point worth making. The terrains of digital and AI evidence are much less subject to the influence of national traditions, of which each State is usually very jealous than those of more traditional evidence, such as the testimony or interrogation of the accused. This interaction between two supranational institutions such as the International Criminal Court and the European Union can help to develop common standards that, gradually, lend themselves to serve as a point of reference for States, which are also grappling with the problems related to digitisation of evidence, without having, almost always, mature experience in the field.

## 7 Concluding Remarks

The cooperation between the International Criminal Court (ICC) and the European Union (EU) during the war between Russia and Ukraine has led to several important outcomes. This collaboration has allowed the ICC to enhance its operational capabilities and investigative reach by leveraging EU networks in criminal justice. As a result, the ICC has been able to gather and process digital evidence more comprehensively and effectively, which is crucial in investigating the crimes committed in the current conflict. Furthermore, working closely with the EU may ensure, and probably is allowing, a more faithful implementation of the principle of complementarity, which means that national jurisdictions are supported and strengthened to prosecute international crimes more effectively and adhere to international standards. Additionally, the collaboration has extended the principle of mutual recognition of judicial decisions to the relationship with the ICC, streamlining the process of international cooperation in criminal justice, particularly regarding digital evidence.

However, there are common problems that need to be addressed for the continued success of this cooperation. One of the primary issues is the need for adequate standards of fairness for digital evidence, as well as to defect flaws that may affect such kind of evidence (and discover fakes, of course). Establishing rigorous standards is crucial to ensuring the reliability and admissibility of digital evidence in court and upholding the rights of the accused.

The EU can help address these challenges by sharing its experience and legal precedent, as well as making its own set of legal forecasts available, in handling digital evidence over the past decade. By providing guidance and support, the EU can assist the ICC and national jurisdictions enhance their capabilities in handling digital evidence, thereby promoting justice and accountability.

In conclusion, the cooperation between the ICC and the EU, originated in the context of the war between Russia and Ukraine, shows interesting potentialities. This, however, does not obviate the need to address common challenges, such as ensuring the fairness and reliability of digital evidence, to fully realize the potential of this cooperation. It is to be hoped that these two supranational institutions, which came into play with reference to a specific and unforeseen event such as the war in Ukraine, will maintain their willingness to cooperate on the issues touched upon in this chapter in a more stable manner. With reference to the field of digital evidence, new to the entire international community as well as to national jurisdictions, a fruitful collaboration can help to formulate effective standards, with the ability to influence the development of this new area of law in a global manner.

CHAPTER 3

# Large Language Models in the Justice Domain

*Giuseppe Contissa and Galileo Sartor*

## 1 Introduction

In the last few years, an important category of AI systems has appeared, and is spreading in use in different domains: generative AI. Generative AI is a category that includes very different and heterogeneous AI systems, broadly referring to any artificial intelligence capable of creating (more or less) original content, such as text, images, music, and even code, which in the most powerful systems is hardly distinguishable from analogous content created by humans.

Unlike traditional AI systems that are limited to analysing and interpreting data, generative AI tools leverage advanced algorithms and vast datasets to produce new and original outputs. This innovative capacity stems from complex machine learning models, particularly those based on deep learning architectures (like Generative Adversarial Networks (GAN s)).

Among generative AI systems, Large Language Models are text-based models trained on a very large dataset of textual content that can draft coherent and contextually relevant written content and are currently deployed for writing assistance, content creation, and language translation. Models like GPT (Generative Pre-trained Transformer) by OpenAI, or Gemini by Google, can write from scratch or manipulate pre-existing documents, code, and even legal texts, learning from vast datasets to mimic human writing styles, and on the basis of a set of instructions (prompts) given by the user.

In this chapter, we shall describe the functioning of LLM s, their abilities and issues (both technical and legal). Then, we will describe some possible uses in the legal domain, focusing in particular on applications in the area of justice.

## 2 AI and Law

Much of the research in the field of AI and Law in the last decades was aimed at creating computational models capable of legal reasoning, specifically by developing systems able to perform such reasoning and forecast the results of legal conflicts. Despite significant progress by researchers in AI and Law over recent years, their advancement towards significant contributions in legal practice has been hindered by the so-called knowledge representation bottleneck, namely, the essential legal knowledge required by these computational models had to be manually identified, interpreted and represented from legal documents, including cases, statutes, regulations, contracts, and other materials utilized by legal practitioners.

In recent years, advancements in AI, particularly in the realm of Natural Language Processing, and the introduction of Large Language Models (LLM s) promise to revolutionize the landscape. A broader categorization for these methodologies is "text analytics" or "text mining", which is defined as the process of extracting meaningful knowledge from text archives. This involves employing a combination of linguistic, statistical, and machine learning techniques to organize and interpret the information content of textual sources. This approach is utilized for purposes ranging from business intelligence to research and investigation.

When the texts to be analyzed are legal, we may refer to "legal text analytics" or more simply "legal analytics,",[1] namely the "deriving of substantively meaningful insight from some sort of legal data," including legal textual data.[2]

However, systems based on LLM s will not perform legal reasoning. They may be able to answer legal questions in a superficial sense, but they cannot explain their answers or make legal arguments. To understand why, we need to look at the technical aspects of NLP s and LLM s.

## 3 From NLP to LLMs

### 3.1 *NLP in the Legal Domain*

NLP, or Natural Language Processing is the field of research focused on understanding and manipulating text in order to extract information, or automate processes that are normally reserved to human understanding.

The ability to understand natural language texts is very important in building complex systems that interact with human generated data, and in the legal domain this is even more the case, as we have different types of legal resources (national and international provisions, legal cases of different courts, …) that differ in their structure and natural language presentation.

1 Kevin D. Ashley, *Artificial Intelligence and Legal Analytics: New Tools for Law Practice in the Digital Age* (Cambridge University Press 2017).

2 Daniel Martin Katz, Michael J Bommarito II, and Josh Blackman, 'Predicting the Behavior of the Supreme Court of the United States: A General Approach' (2014) arXiv preprint arXiv:1407.6333.

Traditional NLP systems relied on syntactic patterns present in the source text in order to classify it, rather than the more complex semantic meaning the texts convey. For this reason functions that appear simple and intuitive to human readers were complex for computers to understand or repeat. This has changed with the introduction of Language Models (of which Large Language Models are a subcategory).

While language models existed before the recent explosion in public availability, they were mostly used in specific contexts, such as summarization and machine translation.[3] In 2017 the landmark paper *Attention is all you need*[4] was published, where researchers at Google expanded the attention mechanism proposed by Bahdanau et al.[5] into the Transformer architecture, and posited its potential use for generating text.

Progress has continued rapidly in this novel direction, with many different models appearing since, that can be divided in two main categories: encoders and decoders, where the first generate vectors from the input, to classify and extract semantic meaning, and the second generate new text starting from a given input.

Encoder-only models (like BERT, *Bidirectional Encoder Representations from Transformers*) were quickly adopted in the NLP domain, presenting state of the art results in many benchmarks, on applications ranging from sentiment analysis, machine translation, and feature extraction. These systems replaced the previously used models for language translation, and language understanding more in general, due to their deeper understanding of the semantic meaning of text, compared to a system based solely on syntax or statistics of single word meaning.

In 2019 OpenAI released the first paper on a Generative Pre-Training (GPT) model[6] where they showed that "a general task-agnostic model, built on generative pre-training of a language model on a diverse corpus of unlabeled text" is more efficient than an ad-hoc trained system. The basic idea is to build a model that is able to create new information from a given input, not only classify the

3 Google translate was started as a "simple" statistical machine translation, pivoting then to a Neural Machine translation (via deep learning), and finally, since 2020, making use of transformers, the building blocks of Language Models.

4 Ashish Vaswani and others, 'Attention Is All You Need' (arXiv 2017) arXiv:1706.03762 <http://arxiv.org/abs/1706.03762> accessed 6 April 2023.

5 Dzmitry Bahdanau, Kyunghyun Cho and Yoshua Bengio, 'Neural Machine Translation by Jointly Learning to Align and Translate' (arXiv 2016) arXiv:1409.0473 <http://arxiv.org/abs/1409.0473> accessed 23 June 2024.

6 Alec Radford and Karthik Narasimhan, 'Improving Language Understanding by Generative Pre-Training' (2018) <https://api.semanticscholar.org/CorpusID:49313245> accessed 23 June 2024.

input data. These are generally decoder-only models. After the commercial success of OpenAI, different companies, such as Google Deepmind, Anthropic, Microsoft, etc started to train and integrate similar systems on their existing services.

GPT-style models have taken over the LLM discussion, and have since captured the attention of the public as well as research community, in a way that is much more pervasive than the approaches in the past. This is due not only to the capability of the systems, but their ease of use, being mostly presented to users as chatbots, usable with no previous programming knowledge.

These chatbots enable a simplified access to users, who do not need to be trained in formal programming languages, rather can express their goal in natural language, leaving the interpretation and execution to the system.

Large Language Models are trained generally through masking, removing a word (token) from a sentence, and asking the system what is the most likely token to fill that spot. By repeating this process numerous times, on a large dataset of sentences, the system learns to correlate tokens that appear in sequence. This process is also behind what we sometimes think as reasoning, and knowledge. For instance in the text that has been fed to the system it might have appeared in multiple occasions that a certain person is the President of a country, or that two countries share a border. The LLM will thus repeat the most probable sequence when asked.

The training of these systems is guided through a type of reinforcement learning. Since we are dealing with text, and there is no simple way to tell the system which solution is the better one (it has to do with human preference). Human feedback is collected by prompting humans to rank instances of the agent's behavior, either at runtime, as when the system asks if the answer was satisfactory, or choosing between different answers to a question.

The goal is to get a model that takes in a sequence of text, and returns a value which represents the human preference. This model can then be used in a Reinforcement Learning scenario to optimise the Large Language Model.[7]

In a second moment the system can be further "trained" either via few-shot learning (i.e., giving the system a limited number of examples, even directly in the prompt), or by uploading and fine-tuning on custom data, to improve the effectiveness of the model in specific applications.[8]

7 Lambert and others, 'Illustrating Reinforcement Learning from Human Feedback (RLHF)' (Hugging Face Blog, 2022) <https://huggingface.co/blog/rlhf> accessed 11 August 2024.

8 Davide Liga and Livio Robaldo, 'Fine-tuning GPT-3 for Legal Rule Classification' (2023) 51 Computer Law & Security Review 105864.

### 3.2 *How LLMs Work*

At a high level, Large Language Models (LLMs) like ChatGPT are advanced AI word-prediction systems that are designed to produce human-like text based on the input they receive. When generating a response, the model starts by analyzing the prompt, such as "Write a poem about dogs." This prompt is inserted into the model's "context window." The context window acts like the model's short-term memory, comprising context words that inform the model about the conversation's topic. The LLM uses this information to guess the word that statistically is the most likely to follow, drawing on patterns of grammar, writing, and the previous portions (the context) of the user's prompt.

The process begins with the model breaking down the prompt into individual tokens, which can be words or parts of words. These tokens are then processed through multiple layers of artificial neurons, with each layer extracting increasingly complex features of the text.

As the model generates each word, it updates the context window to include the words it has produced so far, and continuously recalculates the next probable word based on the expanded context.

Lately, Large Language Models (LLMs) have been trained on a growing amount of data, which helps them understand the statistical relationships between words. The attention mechanism and the arrangement of tokens in a multi-dimensional space enable the system to comprehend not just the likelihood of individual words, but also the context of the entire sentence.

Combining this vast amount of data with the computational power to train and run inference on these systems, with the addition of user friendly chatbot interfaces, LLMs are used in an increasing number of contexts, by people who previously would not have had access to similar systems.

### 3.3 *Emergent Abilities*

The relevant literature[9] often discusses emergent abilities in large language models (LLMs). They refer to capabilities that arise unexpectedly when a model reaches a certain scale or level of complexity, without being explicitly programmed into the model. The amount of data that is built into the model enables it to make apparently complex inferences, such as those required by logic reasoning and problem-solving tasks.

9 Jason Wei and others, 'Emergent Abilities of Large Language Models' (2022) <https://arxiv.org/abs/2206.07682> accessed 11 August 2024.

Whether this is reflects abilities or is the result of the specific metrics used is still debated,[10] and it appears that these abilities may be over amplified by the benchmarks used, and skewed by the information contained in the training data.

### 3.4 *Hallucinations*

With the term “Hallucinations” we refer to occasions where the LLM gives an untrue (but well written and plausible) answer to a query. Hallucinations are fairly frequent, especially in domains that are less known to the LLM (less present in the training dataset). Users should in fact be careful about using LLMs in low-probability situations,[11] and in general revise the output with a critical mind.

It is therefore important to understand why they occur, if and how they can be mitigated.

A good description of this problem comes from a tweet by Andewj Karpathy (previously co-founder of OpenAI), where he states[12] that

> I always struggle a bit with I'm asked about the “hallucination problem” in LLMs. Because, in some sense, hallucination is all LLMs do. They are dream machines.
>
> We direct their dreams with prompts. The prompts start the dream, and based on the LLM's hazy recollection of its training documents, most of the time the result goes someplace useful.

LLMs are next token predictors, and are inventing the sequence of tokens based on statistical analysis of the training corpus. They need to invent, especially to provide results that are novel, not strictly acting as a search engine, even though sometimes they seem to be a search engine. The strength of the system is that these statistical correlations and sequences of words, given the vast amount of data that has been ingested in the system, may vary wildly, and thus the system could offer a novel text. The system however has no way of determining if the sequence spells contains correct information or not.

---

10 Rylan Schaeffer, Brando Miranda and Sanmi Koyejo, ‘Are Emergent Abilities of Large Language Models a Mirage?’ in A. Oh and others (eds), *Advances in neural information processing systems* (Curran Associates, Inc 2023) <https://proceedings.neurips.cc/paper_files/paper/2023/file/adc98a266f45005c403b8311ca7e8bd7-Paper-Conference.pdf>.

11 R. Thomas McCoy and others, ‘Embers of Autoregression: Understanding Large Language Models Through the Problem They Are Trained to Solve’ (2023) <https://arxiv.org/abs/2309.13638> accessed 11 August 2024.

12 See <https://x.com/karpathy/status/1733299213503787018> accessed 11 August 2024.

An issue that is tied to this is the shrinking availability of new data. LLMs need an ever-increasing amount of information as training data to increase their accuracy and usefulness. However, the systems we have today have already been trained on (almost) all the high quality texts available, from books to newspapers, blogs to forums. It is unclear what the addition of data of an ever-decreasing quality, or even synthetic data (data generated from a LLM) would do on the quality of the output.

It is worth reminding that the vast amount of information contained in the system, and the apparent randomness of the output is in some sense their strength, i.e., why they can summarize text, generate new texts from a prompt, etc.

If we expect to use these systems to determine true or false statements, to act as search engines,[13] especially when used by non-technical users, who may not understand or be able to deal with this fact, it is necessary to adequately inform users of the reliability (or lack thereof) of the output. LLMs are very powerful systems that however need human supervision to ultimately determine their effectiveness at addressing a specific problem.

### 3.5 *Benchmarks*

Often, when discussing Large Language Models, we rank them according to how they deal with tests that are complex for humans (such as the bar exam, or medical diagnoses), and a set of artificial benchmarks that are published every time a new LLM is released.

It is worth considering however that these systems have no concept of right or wrong with regards to the answer they provide. They are statistical token (word) predictors, and they will always provide a possible answer. They are also for the most part non-deterministic, so it is worth keeping in mind that the output will not necessarily be repeatable.

While it is true that LLMs perform well in many of these sample use cases, it is also clear that this does not necessarily mean that the system has abstracted a world model, rather that it is statistically determining the correct token.[14]

Having said this, LLMs are still very powerful tools for the legal domain, and they can assist in numerous activities that are currently very time consuming, and that require some level of experience. The human factor is not removed from the equation, rather it is focused on explaining the issue that

13 See on this the recent launch of AI generated content in Google Search, or the new GPT Search launched by OpenAI.

14 Hanzi Xu and others, 'LLMs' Classification Performance Is Overclaimed' (2024) <https://arxiv.org/abs/2406.16203> accessed 11 August 2024.

needs solving, and a methodology that the AI system can use to provide an adequate answer.

## 4 Legal Issues of LLMs

LLMs (like most of Generative AI systems), while having many innovative applications, also raises a series of legal issues. These include intellectual property rights, data privacy, and liability, among others.

Copyright: the use of LLMs presents two orthogonal challenges. Firstly, the question of authorship: can authorship be attributed solely to human beings, or is it conceivable for an AI to be considered an author? Secondly, the question of whether authors' rights extend to the derivative work (output) generated by a LLM based on pre-existing works, and how they should be regulated and balanced with the rights attached to such pre-existing works. These issues challenge the traditional approach to intellectual property and copyright protection, which has historically been centred around human authorship. The second challenge is linked, in particular, to the legal evaluation of data mining activities carried out on copyrighted content. In this regard, in the EU, Directive (EU) 790/2019 on copyright in the Digital Single Market (often known as the DSM Directive) introduced a legal definition of data mining and a set of exceptions and limitations allowing reproductions and extractions of works or other subject matter, for the purpose of text and data mining, under certain conditions. Under these rules, rightsholders may choose to reserve their rights, expressing the choice (opt-out) that their work shall not be subject to data mining activities.

Data Protection: the majority of the training data for LLMs originates from texts taken from freely accessible internet sources, such as the Common Crawl dataset, which includes information from over 3 billion web pages. These datasets, obtained through web scraping, also include data about private individuals. This raises concerns under data protection laws, in particular, the GDPR in the EU. This personal data could be either correct or incorrect, and the datasets might also include false information. Implementing measures to mitigate the data protection risks inherent in utilising these datasets presents a significant challenge. Additionally, should the security measures not be robust, the outputs from LLMs could inadvertently expose sensitive or private data contained in the training datasets, raising the risk of actual data breaches. Moreover, unlike traditional databases, LLMs incorporate the learned data into their internal structure, encoding it within billions of parameter values. Consequently, amending, erasing, or even accessing the personal data absorbed by LLMs can be challenging or unfeasible.

Liability in relation to the output: determining liability when content generated by LLMs causes harm or financial loss is another legal challenge. For instance, if a LLM creates defamatory content, misleading information, or infringes on IP rights, it is unclear who – the developer, the user, or even the platform hosting the content – should be held responsible.

Deepfakes and Misinformation: LLMs' ability to create realistic-looking content has led to the proliferation of fake news. This raises concerns about misinformation, requiring legal frameworks to balance the freedom of expression with protections against defamation, fraud, and the manipulation of public opinion. The marketing of LLMs as search engines makes this even more of a problem, aggravating the issues seen in social networks in the last years. The incredible availability of these systems, as well as the lack of knowledge and training on their use, makes for the easy distribution of fake news, whether on purpose or not. In January 2024 the WHO released guidelines on the uses and risks of LLMs in the health domain,[15] where they list among the risks the possibility of "producing false, inaccurate, biased, or incomplete statements, which could harm people using such information in making health decisions".

## 5 LLMs in the Legal Domain

When using an LLM, as previously mentioned, it is important to understand not only it's strengths, but also limitations. In the legal domain it would be easy to imagine using an LLM as a smart search engine, to provide for example legal precedents for a case. This has happened in the past, and while the system did generate an accurate sounding list of precedents, complete with links to the online resources, they were completely invented, and the urls did not point to anything.

These systems cannot be considered reliable to generate something new from scratch, especially if there is a presumption of correctness and validation.

15 Chief Scientist and Science Division (SCI), Health Ethics & Governance (HEG), 'Ethics and governance of artificial intelligence for health: Guidance on large multi-modal models' (January 2024) <https://www.who.int/publications/i/item/9789240084759> accessed 11 August 2024.

It is possible however to use these systems as draft tools, to augment a text that has already been drafted, to analyze an existing text extracting legally relevant information, produce summaries,[16] and many other.

In the PRODIGIT project, where the goal was the automated summarizing of cases in the tax law domain. This is an activity that is generally carried out manually by legal experts, and made available by the courts or the legal service companies that maintain databases of case law.

The main issue with the generation, be it automated or manual, of legal summaries is that they differ from normal summaries, in that should provide the relevant information to the legal professional, highlighting the principles of law more than the specific details of the case.

In the project a comparison was carried out between specific NLP technologies (NLTK, TextRank, etc.), and LLM s (GPT 4 in particular). The latter offered a more satisfactory solution, especially when tasked with generating an "abstractive" summary, i.e., paraphrasing the output, rather than extracting the relevant sentences.

This work was carried out in different phases, with legal experts contributing to the description of the task in the prompt, composed of examples, a definition of the principles of law, and indications on where they could be found in the full text. Different LLM s then were used to generate a set of summaries, to be evaluated by the experts. This process was repeated until an adequate prompt was found, and applied to a larger dataset of cases.

Another project in which LLMs are a central focus is POLINE,[17] a project aimed at creating an AI-powered tool to retrieve and analyze judicial principles of law within the context of Value Added Tax (VAT) case-law from the Court of Justice of the European Union (CJEU) and the supreme courts of Italy, Sweden, and Bulgaria.

The main goal of the use of LLMs in POLINE is to identify and extract the principles of law, a task that could previously be carried out by specific language analysis NLP methods. There are two main obstacles in this task: the lack of definition of a judicial principle of law, and the lack of a uniform structure between judgements from different Member States.

Prompt engineering for this task requires a careful dialogue between legal and IT experts, to identify a general definition of judicial principles, and combine that in a prompt with additional information on the text structure

16 Giuseppe Pisano and others, 'La Sommarizzazione Delle Sentenze Tributarie Di Merito Nel Progetto PRODIGIT' (2024) 17 i-lex 1 <https://i-lex.unibo.it/article/view/19618> accessed 11 August 2024.

17 For more information on the project: <https://site.unibo.it/poline/en> accessed 11 August 2024.

(paragraphs, sentences). With this information the LLM can be used to identify the judicial principles, and extract the portions of text in which they appeared in the source document.

The project is currently ongoing, but the results are promising, with the tested systems able to identify different linguistic patterns.

Many private companies have started to integrate LLM models in their websites, for easier access to information, with varying levels of success. Examples of these are:

- LexisNexis+ where a legal search can be described in natural language, and documents can easily be analyzed[18]
- Robin AI leverages LLM s to provide advanced contract editing[19]

Legal consultation services can be provided to users, as a first level of interaction (backed by human experts), generating content such as summaries or drafts.[20]

Another potential use that is being explored is the use of LLM s to assist in creating legal knowledge bases, addressing the issue of formal logic models of the law, namely the data acquisition (rule modelling), and using LLM s as a tool to speed up the process.

Attempts are in progress to use LLM s to enrich existing knowledge bases with additional logic rules, constraining the system so that it is consistent with the previously given rules. This is a complex task, given the limited information that can be used as input (the "memory" in this case), and the tendency of these AI models to be non deterministic and non-reproducible. Given the right prompt this issue seems to be mostly mitigated.

In chapter 16 the use of LLM s in the FACILEX project will be described in more detail, and will showcase a different use of these tools, namely the translation of logic code (Prolog) in a more user accessible text. This methodology would enable the combination of a stricter rule-based system, enabling reasoning and determinism (the ability to consistently obtain the same output with the same input), while also providing the user of the system with an easy interface in natural language.

The last two approaches described are still guided by human experts, and would reduce the reliance on the LLM for legal reasoning and inference, relying on the LLM for its strength in code generation and natural language translation, and on the formal model for the consistent logic reasoning, and to

18 <https://www.lexisnexis.com/en-us/products/lexis-plus.page> accessed 18 July 2024.

19 <https://www.robinai.com/post/large-language-models-legal-industry> accessed 18 July 2024.

20 Jinqi Lai and others, 'Large Language Models in Law: A Survey' (2023) <https://arxiv.org/abs/2312.03718> accessed 11 August 2024.

ensure explainability. With these models able to translate natural language, it may become easier also to generate translations of the output as required by the users, although when dealing with legal texts this is a more complex task.

In the future we may see many more use cases of LLMs in the legal domain, and by understanding it's strengths and weaknesses it may become a useful tool to increase accessibility to legal content and solutions.

# PART 2

CHAPTER 4

# Bulgaria: the EAW, EIO and Regulation 1805/2018 in the Bulgarian Legislation and Case Law

*Miroslava Manolova and Ekaterina Salkova*

## 1 Introduction

All three European criminal mutual recognition instruments under examination – the European Arrest Warrant (EAW), the European Investigation Order (EIO), the Regulation 1805/2018 – have been introduced into Bulgarian legislation.

The regulation on the detention and surrender of persons for the purposes of conducting a criminal prosecution or executing a custodial sentence or detention order based on a EAW was already adopted in 2005 – by the *Extradition and European Arrest Warrant Act* (in the text, hereinafter "EEAWA").[1] Its introduction was related to Bulgaria's commitments regarding the country's accession to the European Union (EU). It began to be practically implemented on January 1, 2007, when Bulgaria became a full member of the Union. Its application does not raise any particular difficulties in the case law of the Bulgarian courts, as it will be outlined below. Nonetheless, the regulatory framework has been amended several times to bring the national law into full compliance with the European regulatory framework in this area, as well as to meet the standards for effective judicial protection in EAW proceedings established in the case law of the CJEU,[2] including through the recent amendments in this connection – from December 2023.[3]

As regards the EIO, the transposition of the Directive 2014/41/EUO[4] (EIO D) entailed the adoption in 2018 of a comprehensive law, namely the *European Investigation Order Act*.[5] The first amendment to the law so far was made in 2022 and was related to the closure in the same year of the specialized criminal

1 SG No. 46/3.06.2005.

2 Case C-648/20, *Svishtov Regional Prosecutor's Office* [2021] ECLI:EU:C:2021:187.

3 SG No. 100/1.12.2023.

4 Directive 2014/41/EU of the European Parliament and of the Council of 3 April 2014 regarding the European Investigation Order in criminal matters [2014] OJ L130/1.

5 SG No. 16/20.02.2018.

 | DOI:10.1163/9789004705791_006

courts and specialized prosecution offices as part of the Bulgarian judicial system.[6] However, the new amendments were adopted in April 2024,[7] motivated by the need to bring the national legislation in line with the requirements of the EIO D, as well as with two judgments of the CJEU delivered in 2021 (references for a preliminary ruling from Bulgarian courts).[8]

As regards the mutual recognition and execution of freezing or confiscation orders, in general the Bulgarian law is in compliance with the requirements as set out by the European legislation. Specifically, in July 2022 measures for implementing Regulation 1805/2018 were introduced in the domestic system,[9] by amending the two laws governing the matters of the mutual recognition of the freezing orders and confiscation orders, namely the *Recognition, Execution, Issuance and Transmission of Property Freezing Orders Act*[10] and the *Recognition, Execution and Transmission of Confiscation or Seizure Orders and Decisions Imposing Financial Penalties Act*.[11] Both laws were adopted more than 10 years ago, in 2006 and 2010 respectively, to bring national legislation into line with the European standards of the time, namely Framework Decision 2003/577/JHA and Framework Decision 2006/783/JHA respectively, now replaced by the Regulation 1805/2018.

Against this background, in this chapter we will discuss some of the requirements provided in the three European criminal mutual recognition instruments under examination and to what extent national legislation and case law are consistent with them.

## 2 European Arrest Warrant: Critical Profiles in Legislation and Case Law

### 2.1 *Scope*

The requirements of Art 2 of the Framework decision 2002/584 regarding the scope and double criminality of the acts are fully and explicitly transposed into

6 SG, No. 32/26.04.2022, in force from 27.07.2022.

7 SG No. 36/23.04.2024.

8 Case C-852/19, *Gavanozov II* [2021] ECLI:EU:C:2021:902 and Case C-724/19, *Spetsializirana prokuratura* [2021] ECLI:EU:C:2021:1020.

9 SG No. 56/19.07.2022.

10 SG No. 59/21.07.2006.

11 SG No. 15/23.02.2010.

the national legislation.[12] In the case law, there are also no problems related to the application of this provision.[13]

### 2.2 *Grounds for Non-recognition and Non-execution*

In general, the requirements of the Framework decision for grounds for non-recognition and non-execution of the European arrest warrant have been correctly introduced in the Bulgarian legislation – both with regard to the mandatory (Art 3 EAW FD) and optional grounds (Art 4 EAW FD).[14]

The mandatory grounds are established in Art 39 EEAWA and are fully in line with Art 3 EAW FD. The optional grounds for non-execution are provided for in Art 36(2) and Art 40 EEAWA, transposing the requirements of Art 4 EAW FD. Part of the recent changes in the national legislation in this area, made in December 2023, related precisely to one of these grounds, namely that under Art 4(1) EAW FD, according to which "the executing judicial authority may refuse to execute the European arrest warrant if, in one of the cases referred to in Art 2(4), the act on which the European arrest warrant is based does not constitute an offence under the law of the executing Member State". According to the doctrine,[15] the national regulation (Art 36(2) EEAWA) until then, had correctly introduced the ground in question as not mandatory, meeting the standards of the EAW FD.[16] Nonetheless, the Bulgarian legislator adopted amendments in the provision of Art 36(2) and Art 40 EEAWA in order to bring it into full compliance with the European act.[17]

---

12 Art 36 EEAWA.

13 See Judgment № 92/2019 of District Court – Haskovo. The court concluded that the execution of the EAW should be refused due to the lack of the double criminality of the act. The crime for which the surrender of the person is requested for the purpose of conducting a criminal prosecution (breaking a level crossing barrier and thus creating a danger for the life and the bodily integrity of the railway passengers), corresponds to some extent to a crime under the Bulgarian Criminal Code. However, the factual description of that crime shows that it is committed through negligence. It is, therefore, intentional as a form of guilt under Bulgarian Criminal Code (Art 340 CC).

14 See, in that regard, Pavlina Panova, *The European Arrest Warrant* (Ciela 2009) 129–140.

15 ibid 143.

16 Art 36(2), first sentence EEAWA in the version in force until 5 December 2023 states that "a surrender on the basis of a European arrest warrant shall be carried out if the act in respect of which the said warrant is issued, also constitutes a criminal offence under the laws of the Republic of Bulgaria".

17 Under Art 36(2), first instance EEAWA in its current wording, the court may refuse to allow the surrender of the person if the act for which a EAW has been issued is not included in the list under Paragraph (3) and it does not constitute a crime under the legislation of the Republic of Bulgaria. Moreover, Art 40(1) EEAWA on the grounds for optional non-execution of EAW was supplemented by a new point 6, according to which

### 2.3 *Fundamental Rights and Proportionality Issues*

As correctly stated in the doctrine, fundamental rights violations are not among the grounds for non-execution under Art 3 and 4 EAW FD.[18] At the same time, however, Art 1(3) EAW FD, in conjunction with recitals 12 and 13 of the Framework decision, are considered by some scholar as "independent grounds for refusal".[19] It is also accepted that, based on these provisions of the FD, both the issuing and executing States are obliged to respect human rights under the international treaties to which they are parties, as well as under their constitutional norms.[20]

Bulgarian legislation has not been explicitly transposed Art 1(3) EAW FD, which states that "this Framework Decision shall not have the effect of modifying the obligation to respect fundamental rights and fundamental legal principles as enshrined in Art 6 of the Treaty on European Union". However, the lack of explicitly transposition does not mean that, both as an issuing and executing country, Bulgaria can be exempt from the obligation to respect human rights. On the contrary,[21] this obligation arises from the commitments Bulgaria has undertaken as a party to the European Convention on Human Rights (ECHR), as well as from the Bulgarian Constitution. According to Art 4(1) thereof Bulgaria is a State governed by the rule of law. In addition, Art 5(4) of the Constitution provides for that any international treaty, ratified,

---

the District Court may refuse to execute a EAW in the absence of double criminality, save for cases under Arts 36(2) and (3).

18 ibid 169 and the literature quoted in the article; Gergana Marinova, *The Extradition and European Arrest Warrant* (Sibi 2009) 119.

19 Panova (n 14) 169.

20 Marinova (n 18) 120–121 and the literature quoted in the book. According to human rights activists, although "all Member States are bound by Article 6 TEU to protect the principles therein and that all Member States are signatories to the European Convention on Human Rights (ECHR) and are equally bound by its provisions", their views "as to whether or not Article 1(3) FD requires specific implementation in national laws" have differed. See for more details, S. Alegre and M. Leaf, 'Mutual Recognition in European Judicial Cooperation: A Step Too Far Too Soon? Case Study – the European Arrest Warrant' (2004) 10 European Law Journal 200–217, 203.

21 See in this regard Panova (n 14) 169–171. According to the author, although these texts have not been transposed into Bulgarian law, the judicial authorities should observe them pursuant to the interpretation made by the CJEU in Pupino judgment (Case C-105/03 *Pupino* [2005] ECR I-05285). In this judgment the CJEU concludes "that the principle of conforming interpretation is binding in relation to framework decisions adopted in the context of Title VI of the Treaty on European Union. When applying national law, the national court that is called upon to interpret it must do so as far as possible in the light of the wording and purpose of the framework decision in order to attain the result which it pursues and thus comply with Article 34(2) (b) EU" (para 43 thereof).

promulgated and entered into force for Bulgaria, shall be part of the domestic law. Such a treaty shall take precedence over any conflicting standards of the domestic legislation.[22]

In fact, there is national case law in regard to the possibility of refusing surrender in case of potential fundamental rights violation. For instance, the Appellate Court – Sofia annulled the ruling of the first instance court (Sofia City Court) and refused to execute EAW, issued by the Greek authorities for the purposes of conducting a criminal prosecution. The requested person is Bulgarian citizen, pregnant at the time of the proceedings and mother of a 3-year-old child with chronic nephritis. According to the Court, despite the presence of the formal prerequisites for the execution of the EAW, not all material legal grounds are present. Analysing the provision of Art 1(3) FD in conjunction with recitals 12 thereof, the court concluded that the specifics of the case define the surrender of the requested person as a disproportionate measure, because it would affect the fundamental rights of private and family life guaranteed by EU law of the mother, who would also be placed at risk for

---

22 The Bulgarian Constitutional Court has issued several decisions in this regard. For instance, in Decision № 3/2004, it noted that "The acts of primary law of the European Union constitute international treaties within the meaning of Article 5 (4) of the Constitution and subject to the stipulated conditions, their provisions become part of the domestic law of Bulgaria. Moreover, they take precedence over the norms of the domestic law that contradict them [...] The European Union also adopts so-called secondary law. Its main characteristic is that its acts are not international treaties within the meaning of Article 5 (4) of the Constitution and are not subject to ratification by national parliaments after their adoption [...] This is because the institutions of the European Communities act within their competences with a directly binding legal effect on the institutions and citizens of the Member States. At the same time, however, it should be borne in mind that the methods and mechanisms of the adoption of acts of secondary law, as well as its scope, are determined by the primary law, which, constituting international treaties, is necessarily subject to ratification". This understanding is confirmed in its basic sense in the Decision № 3/2012 of the Bulgarian Constitutional Court, in which the primacy of primary law is linked to the provision of Art 5 (4) of the Constitution, and the automatic effect of priority refers to the secondary law of the Union: "As soon as the international treaty has been ratified in accordance with the constitutional order, promulgated and entered into force, it has priority. The priority is unconditional. According to Article 5 (4), second sentence of the Constitution, the international treaties, promulgated and entered into force for the Republic of Bulgaria, are part of the domestic law and have priority over those norms of the national legislation that contradict them. This also applies to all acts of Community law, not only to regulations (Article 249 (2) of EC Treaty and Article 288 (2) of the Treaty on the Functioning of the European Union). The primacy operates automatically and does not require any special mechanism to establish or declare". See in this context also Decision № 7/2018 of the Bulgarian Constitutional Court.

her health and that for the foetus as well as the right of care and protection enjoyed by her 3-year-old son.[23]

### 2.4 *Issues for the Rights of the Suspect, Accused and Other Parties*

In general, the standards regarding the rights of persons suspected and accused in the criminal proceedings and provided for in the six procedural directives of the European Union are also applicable in the EAW proceeding.[24]

Specifically, under the EEAWA, the right of access to a lawyer in European arrest warrant proceedings is guaranteed in the proceedings for the imposition of remand in custody of the requested person by the court, as well as in the judicial proceedings for the examination of the European arrest warrant.[25] In both cases, the court shall appoint a defence counsel and an interpreter for the requested person, if the latter has no command of the Bulgarian language.[26] The participation of a lawyer is mandatory and does not depend on the will of the requested person. In this respect, therefore, according to some scholars, Bulgarian law provides a higher standard of protection than that granted in Directive 2013/48/EU.[27]

The legal aid is also guaranteed in cases of detention of requested persons under the EEAWA.[28] Moreover, in such cases, legal assistance is mandatory,

23 Judgment 48/2021 of Appellate Court-Sofia.

24 Directive 2010/64/EU; Directive 2012/13/EU; Directive 2013/48/EU; Directive (EU) 2016/800; Directive (EU) 2016/1919 and Directive (EU) 2016/343. For more details on the standards of the rights of the requested persons in EAW proceedings under the six directives and their transposition into Bulgarian law see the National Report of Bulgaria, CrossJustice, <https://site.unibo.it/cross-justice/en/project-results/publications>.

25 Arts 43(4) and 44(5) EEAWA.

26 According to Art 43(4) EEAWA, applicable in the proceedings for the imposition of remand in custody of the requested person, the court shall explain the grounds for his/her detention, the content of the European arrest warrant and his/her right to give consent to surrender to the competent authorities of the issuing Member States and the implications thereof. As regards the judicial proceedings for the examination of the European arrest warrant, the court shall explain to the request person the right to give consent to surrender to the issuing Member State, as well as to renounce entitlement to the speciality rule under Art 61 and the consequences of these steps (Art 44(3) EEAWA). At the court session the court shall hear the prosecutor, the person claimed and his/her defence counsel (Art 44(5) EEAWA). The rule ensures the participation of the lawyer in the judicial proceedings.

27 See Margarita Chinova, Pavlina Panova 'The new Directive on the right of access to a lawyer in criminal proceedings' in: Norma, 3/2014.

28 According to Art 43(4) EEAWA, applicable in the proceedings for the imposition of remand in custody of the requested person, the court shall appoint a defence counsel and an interpreter for the person if the latter has no command of the Bulgarian language and shall explain the grounds for his/her detention, the content of the European arrest

and the court is obliged to appoint a lawyer if the requested person has not retained one of his or her own.

As regards the right to information, under the EEAWA, in the proceedings for the imposition of remand in custody of the requested person, the court shall explain the grounds for his/her detention, the content of the European arrest warrant and his/her right to give consent to surrender to the competent authorities of the issuing Member States and the implications thereof.[29] The court is obliged to do the same in the judicial proceedings for the examination of the European arrest warrant where Bulgaria is an executing State.

In addition, in December 2023, the *Extradition and European Arrest Warrant Act* was amended to fully comply with the requirements of Art 5 of Directive 2012/13/EU. According to Art 42(6) EEAWA in its current wording, immediately after detention of the requested person by the police authorities, an official or contractual defender is provided, as well as an interpreter, in whose presence a declaration of the rights is served on the person detained and signed, in a language understandable to him/her.[30]

### 2.5 *Cooperation Issues between Executing and Issuing Authorities*

As regards cooperation issues between executing and issuing authorities, the national law is in full compliance with the requirements of EAW FD as laid down in Art 9 and 10 thereof.[31]

---

warrant and his/her right to give consent to surrender to the competent authorities of the issuing Member States and the implications thereof.

29 Art 43(4) EEAWA.

30 For more details on the standards of the rights of the requested persons in EAW proceedings under the Directive 2012/13/EU and its transposition into Bulgarian law see the National Report of Bulgaria, CrossJustice, <https://site.unibo.it/cross-justice/en/project-results/publications-> 24–34.

31 According to Art 9 EAW FD, when the location of the requested person is known, the issuing judicial authority may transmit the European arrest warrant directly to the executing judicial authority. The issuing judicial authority may, in any event, decide to issue an alert for the requested person in the Schengen Information System (SIS). Such an alert shall be effected in accordance with the provisions of Article 95 of the Convention of 19 June 1990 implementing the Schengen Agreement of 14 June 1985 on the gradual abolition of controls at common borders. An alert in the SIS shall be equivalent to a European arrest warrant accompanied by the information set out in Art 8(1) EAW FD. For a transitional period, until the SIS is capable of transmitting all the information described in Art 8, the alert shall be equivalent to a European arrest warrant pending the receipt of the original in due and proper form by the executing judicial authority. In addition, Art 10 EAW FD provides for detailed procedures for transmitting a European arrest warrant in various situations, such as where the issuing judicial authority does not know the competent

Practically, the same means are provided for, both for reception and transmission of a European arrest warrant, namely: the Schengen Information System; the telecommunications system of the European Judicial Network; the Interpol; electronic mail or fax or any secure means allowing establishment of the authenticity of the European arrest warrant.[32]

Moreover, according to Art 57(1) EEAWA, where the location of the requested person in the territory of a Member State is known, the issuing authority may transmit the European arrest warrant directly to the executing authority of said Member State. Where the issuing authority has no information about the executing authority of the said Member State, it shall consult the European Judicial Network. This rule applies in cases where Bulgaria is an issuing State but, as noted in the scientific literature, that provision is fully applicable also where Bulgaria is an executing State.[33]

### 2.6 *Remedies*

The possibility of appeals against the imposition of remand in custody, the decision to surrender the requested person or to refuse the execution of an EAW, as provided for in the *Extradition and European Arrest Warrant Act*,[34] can be considered to be an effective remedy under the EAW FD.

As argued in the case law and scientific literature, according to the practice of the CJEU, in EAW proceedings a dual level of protection must be provided.[35] In the *Parchetul de pe lângă Curtea de Apel Cluj/Bob-Dogi* case, the Court concluded that "the European arrest warrant system [...] entails, in view of the requirement laid down in Art 8(1)(c) of the Framework Decision, a dual level of protection for procedural rights and fundamental rights which must be enjoyed by the requested person, since, in addition to the judicial protection provided at the first level, at which a national judicial decision, such as a national arrest warrant, is adopted, is the protection that must be afforded at the second level, at which a European arrest warrant is issued, which may occur, depending on the circumstances, shortly after the adoption of the national judicial decision".[36]

executing judicial authority or if it is not possible to call on the services of the SIS or if the authority which receives a European arrest warrant is not competent to act upon it.

32 Arts 38a and 57(5) EEAWA.

33 See Panova (n 14) 81–82.

34 Arts 43, 44 and 48 thereof.

35 See André Klip, 'A Next Level Model for the European Arrest Warrant' (2022) 30 European Journal of Crime, Criminal Law and Criminal Justice 107.

36 Case C-241/15, *Parchetul de pe lângă Curtea de Apel Cluj/Bob-Dogi* [2016] ECLI:EU:C:2016:385, para 56.

In this regard, in Bulgaria, until recently, there was a problem in ensuring that both levels of protection were present when issuing an EAW in pre-trial proceedings.[37]

In these cases, the competent issuing authority is the public prosecutor.[38] Pursuant to Art 56(1) EEAWA, at the pre-trial stage of criminal proceedings an EAW may be issued by the competent prosecutor against an accused person or a person convicted by an enforceable sentence. The EAW is issued on the basis of the detention decree for up to 72 hours from the moment the person is detained (Art 64(2) of the *Bulgarian Criminal Procedure Code "CPC"*). In this scenario, neither the arrest decree, nor the EAW both issued by the prosecutor were subject to judicial review before the surrender of the requested person by the executing Member State.

The matter was examined by the CJEU, on a preliminary ruling raised by an English court and regarding the execution of an EAW issued by the Bulgarian Prosecutor's Office. In the *Svishtov Regional Prosecutor's Office* case, the Court noted (para 39 of the judgment) that "the prosecutor's decision ordering the detention of the requested person for a maximum of 72 hours, on which the European arrest warrant is based, must be classified as an 'enforceable judicial decision having the same effect' as a national arrest warrant, within the meaning of Art 8(1)(c) of Framework Decision 2002/584". In addition, the Court concluded that the requirements inherent to the effective judicial protection that must be afforded to a person who is the subject of a European arrest warrant for the purpose of criminal prosecution, are not satisfied where both the EAW and the judicial decision on which that warrant is based are issued by a public prosecutor. This was held true, even if the latter may be classified as an 'issuing judicial authority' within the meaning of Art 6(1) EAW FD, in case the decision cannot be reviewed by a court in the issuing Member State prior to the surrender of the requested person by the executing Member State.[39]

---

37 See in this context Ivo Hinov, Elena Popova 'The European arrest warrant in Bulgaria in the light of the latest case law of the CJEU' (9 April 2017) <https://evropeiskipravenpregled.eu/t174/> accessed July 2024; Andrey Jankulov, 'The European arrest warrants, issued by a prosecutor in our country, and the new case law of the CJEU' (3 January 2020) <https://defakto.bg/2020/01/03/%D0%B5%D0%B2%D1%80%D0%BE%D0%BF%D0%B5%D0%B9%D1%81%D0%BA%D0%B8%D1%82%D0%B5-%D0%B7%D0%B0%D0%BF%D0%BE%D0%B2%D0%B5%D0%B4%D0%B8-%D0%B7%D0%B0-%D0%B0%D1%80%D0%B5%D1%81%D1%82-%D0%B8%D0%B7%D0%B4%D0%B0%D0%B2/> accessed July 2024.

38 Art 56(1)(1) EEAWA.

39 Case C-648/20, *Svishtov Regional Prosecutor's Office* [2021] ECLI:EU:C:2021:187, para 60.

In practice, this CJEU's judgment caused an impossibility of executing Bulgarian European arrest warrants, issued by a prosecutor for the purposes of pre-trial proceedings on the basis of a detention decree under Art 64(2) CPC.

In order to overcome this problem, as well as to bring the national legislation into full compliance with the requirements of the EAW FD, amendments to the EEAWA were adopted in December 2023. Two levels of judicial control were introduced when a prosecutor issues an EAW. In pre-trial proceedings, if there are grounds for the detention of the requested person, the prosecutor issues a National detention warrant of the accused person and submits a request to the relevant court of first instance for permission to issue a European Arrest Warrant. The request is accompanied by the issued National detention warrant and by a draft of the European Arrest Warrant. The court issues a ruling, assessing the existence of the conditions justifying detention in relation to the presented National detention warrant, and the legality and proportionality of the issuance of the EAW. The ruling is subject to appeal before the relevant appellate court. When the ruling is final, the public prosecutor can actually issue the European Arrest Warrant. The issued EAW can be challenged before the relevant court of appeal by the accused, within 7 days from the date on which s/he learned that the EAW has been issued against her/him.[40]

In this way, the national legislation meets the first level of protection required by the case law of the CJEU.

Along with this, the second level of protection was also introduced, by providing a judicial review after the admittance of the requested person on Bulgarian territory. According to Art 59a EEAWA, in this case, the prosecutor immediately submits a request to the relevant court of first instance for taking the permanent measure of remand in custody of the requested person. In this proceeding, the accused and his defense counsel may contest the legality and proportionality of the European Arrest Warrant issued by the prosecutor pursuant to Art 56a EEAWA.

## 3 European Investigation Order: Critical Profiles in Legislation and Case Law

### 3.1 *Scope*

In accordance with Art 2 of Directive 2014/41/EU, Art 4(1) of the *European Investigation Order Act*[41] provides that this Act applies to all investigative

40 Art 56a EEAWA.

41 Art 4(1) of the *European Investigation Order Act:* "This Act shall apply to all investigative measures and other procedural measures for the carrying out of which a European

actions and other procedural actions for the performance of which a European Investigation Order has been issued, except for cases where a Joint Investigation Team has been established. Where a competent authority participating in a Joint Investigation Team requests the assistance of a Member State other than those participating in the said team, a European Investigation Order may be issued (Art 4(2) of the *European Investigation Order Act*). The *European Investigation Order Act*, however, shall not apply to freezing property with a view to confiscation and to confiscation of property,[42] and where cross-border surveillance has been requested.[43]

Specifically, the transposition law provides that an EIO may be issued with respect to: (1) criminal proceedings that are brought by, or that may be brought before, a judicial authority in respect of a criminal offence committed in the issuing State; (2) proceedings brought by administrative authorities in respect of acts which are punishable under the law of the issuing State, by virtue of being infringements of the rules of law, and where the decision may give rise to proceedings before a court having jurisdiction in criminal matters; (3) proceedings brought by judicial authorities in respect of acts which are punishable under the law of the issuing State by virtue of being infringements of the rules of law, and where the decision may give rise to proceedings before a court having jurisdiction in criminal matters; (4) acts in connection with these proceedings, which relate to criminal offences or infringements for which a legal person may be held liable or punished in the issuing State.[44]

With regard to the goals pursued by the EIO, the latter may be issued: (1) with a view to provisionally preventing acts of destruction, transformation, removal, transfer or disposal of items that may be used as evidence in the territory of the executing State; (2) for the temporary transfer to the issuing State of a person held in custody in the executing State for the purpose of carrying

Investigation Order has been issued with the exception of the cases where a joint investigation team under Art 476 (3) of the Criminal Procedure Code has been set up".

42 In these cases, it concerns actions that are not related to an investigation. They are regulated in two other acts – *Recognition, Execution, Issuance and Transmission of Property Freezing Orders Act (Title amended, SG No. 16/2018, SG No. 56/2022)* and *Recognition, Execution and Transmission of Confiscation or Seizure Orders and Decisions Imposing Financial Penalties Act (Heading amended, SG No. 56/2022)*.

43 In accordance with Art 40 of the Convention implementing the Schengen Agreement of 14 June 1985 between the Governments of the States of the Benelux Economic Union, the Federal Republic of Germany and the French Republic on the gradual abolition of checks at their common borders, OJ L 239/19 of 22 September 2000. A detailed analysis aimed at the training of magistrates is presented in 'Prosecutor's Guide. Book two, Project "Modern learning environment for judges, prosecutors, investigators and other representatives of the professional community"' (2024) National Institute of Justice.

44 Art 2(2) of the *European Investigation Order Act*.

out procedural measures requiring the presence of that person, or for the temporary transfer to the executing State of a person held in custody in the issuing State for the purpose of participating in the investigation as requested.[45]

### 3.2 *Grounds for Non-recognition and Non-execution*

The provisions of Art 11 of the EIO D have been fully implemented in Bulgarian legislation.

In Art 16 of the *European Investigation Order Act*, the same grounds for non-recognition and non-execution specified in the Directive are provided for. In the case law, no problems are identified in connection with their concrete application.[46] Nevertheless, Art 16 was recently amended[47] in order to clarify the approach in which the grounds for non-recognition and non-execution are formulated.[48]

---

45 Art 2(3) of the *European Investigation Order Act*.

46 This conclusion follows from a comprehensive review of the relevant case law, in which no such problem has been raised. It should be noted that, in principle, judges comply with the provisions of European acts, applying national legislation. Indicative of the desire to comply with the rules of European acts is the high number of preliminary ruling. In the last three years, Bulgaria is in second or third place in terms of preliminary ruling, right after Germany (for 2021 and 2023) and after Germany and Italy (for 2022), See 'Annual Report 2023. Statistics concerning the judicial activity of the Court of Justice' (CJEU, 2024) <https://curia.europa.eu/jcms/upload/docs/application/pdf/2024-04/en_ra_2023_cour_stats_web_bat_22042024.pdf> accessed July 2024.

47 The purpose of the language revision is to remove doubts about the use of some terms.

48 Art 16, Grounds for Refusal of Recognition or Execution, which states: "(1) The competent authority referred to in Article 9 (1) herein may refuse to recognise or to execute a European Investigation Order where:
1. there is an immunity or a privilege under Bulgarian legislation which make it impossible to execute the said order;
2. the execution of the European Investigation Order would harm essential national security interests or would jeopardise a source of information, or would involve the use of classified information relating to specific intelligence activities;
3. the execution of the European Investigation Order would be contrary to the principle of ne bis in idem, except in the cases where the said order is aimed to establish whether a possible conflict with the ne bis in idem principle exists, or where the issuing authority has provided assurances that the evidence transferred as a result of the execution of the said order would not be used to prosecute or impose a sanction on a person whose case has been finally disposed of in another Member State for the same facts;
4. (Amended, SG No. 36/2024) The European Investigation Order has been issued in connection with the proceedings referred to in Items 2 and 3 of Art 2 (2) herein and the measure requested is not authorised according to Bulgarian legislation in a similar case;
5. (Amended, SG No. 36/2024) the European Investigation Order relates to a criminal offence which has been committed outside the territory of the issuing State but wholly or

### 3.3 *Fundamental Rights and Proportionality Issues*

According to Art 16(1)(6) of the *European Investigation Order Act*, one of the grounds for refusing to recognize and execute an EIO is if there are substantial grounds to believe that the execution of the investigative action and other procedural actions would be incompatible with the observance of the rights and freedoms guaranteed by the Convention for the Protection of Human Rights and Fundamental Freedoms (ECHR) of the Council of Europe and the Charter of Fundamental Rights of the European Union (CFR).

Moreover, as a condition for issuing an EIO, according to Art 6 (1)(1) of the *European Investigation Order Act*, the competent authority must establish that the issuance of such Order is necessary and proportionate to the purpose of the criminal proceedings, taking into account the rights of the accused or the defendant. Also, Art 5(1)(1)(b) of the *European Investigation Order Act* expressly stipulates an obligation for the judge to make an assessment of the necessity and proportionality of the investigative action when giving prior permission for its performing in the pre-trial proceedings.

In judicial practice, no problems related to the application of these provisions have been identified, and the observance of fundamental rights and proportionality in the application of coercive measures are largely related to the aspiration of judges to comply with the decisions of the European Court of Human Rights.[49] As stated in the Decision No 24 of 10.03.2023 of the Supreme

partially on the territory of the Republic of Bulgaria, and which is not an offence according to Bulgarian legislation;

6. (Amended, SG No. 36/2024) there are substantial grounds to believe that the execution of the investigative measure and the other judicial investigation measures would be incompatible with the respect for the rights and freedoms guaranteed by the Convention for the Protection of Human Rights and Fundamental Freedoms of the Council of Europe and the Charter of Fundamental Rights of the European Union;

7. (Amended, SG No. 36/2024) a decision has been rendered under Art 18 (2) herein and the European Investigation Order has been revoked;

8. the conduct for which the European Investigation Order has been issued does not constitute a criminal offence under Bulgarian legislation, unless the European Investigation Order relates to a criminal offence on the list referred to in Art 10 (2) herein;

9. (Amended, SG No. 36/2024) the measure requested is inapplicable, according to Bulgarian legislation, to the criminal offence for which the European Investigation Order has been issued."

49 In Judgment No 10 of 11.06.2020 in appeal case No. 418/2020, the Sofia Court of Appeal emphasizes the requirements of necessity and proportionality: "At the same time, the conditions of Article 6, Paragraph 1, Item 1 and 2 of the European Investigation Order Act, namely that the issuance of the order was necessary for the full and comprehensive conduct of the judicial investigation in the case and was proportional to the purpose of the criminal proceedings, taking into account the rights of the defendant and giving him

Court of Cassation in Criminal Case No 1121/2021, III Criminal Division, "The standards adopted in the practice of the ECHR indicate that the execution of a search with a preliminary or subsequent a judicial sanction does not necessarily constitute a reliable guarantee against an arbitrary violation of the right to privacy of the home, from which it follows the need to assess the proportionality of the restriction of rights in accordance with the specific circumstances. This assessment takes into account the severity of the offense that led to the search; the circumstances that gave rise to the action; the order in which it was carried out; the precautions to limit coercive actions within reasonable limits; whether the premises subject to search are used by the offender or by a third party; the extent to which the search affected the good name of the person using the premises, etc. The assessment of the described criteria in relation to the searches carried out in the residences inhabited by the defendants indicates that these actions were proportional to the severity of the crime under investigation, that the legal order was observed when they were carried out, the coercion used was not related to the execution of the actions, but was aimed at the detention of the persons".

### 3.4 *Issues for the Rights of the Suspect or Accused Person*

As a condition for issuing a European Investigation Order, Art 6(1) of the *European Investigation Order Act* provides for a requirement to take into account the rights of the accused or the defendant, in addition to the requirement that there be necessity and proportionality to the purpose of the criminal proceedings. According to Art 15(1)(3) of the law, the competent authority shall have recourse to an investigative measure and other judicial investigation measures other than those indicated in the European Investigation Order where the measure selected would achieve the same result by means that intrude less into the privacy and the legitimate interests and rights of the person than the measure indicated in the European Investigation Order. Where there are substantial grounds to believe that the execution of the investigative measure and the other judicial investigation measures would be incompatible with the respect for the rights and freedoms guaranteed by the Convention for the Protection of Human Rights and Fundamental Freedoms of the Council

---

the opportunity to formulate and set the requested by him questions to the witness …". It is noteworthy that in many other matters, when judges find inconsistency of national law with the European Convention on Human Rights and with the interpretation made by the European Court of Human Rights, they directly apply the law of the ECHR, not the national law. This approach of the judges is correct and should be encouraged, because when it is necessary to protect the rights of individuals, the judicial practice precedes the national legislation.

of Europe and the Charter of Fundamental Rights of the European Union the competent authority may refuse to recognise or to execute a European Investigation Order (Art 16(1)(6) of the *European Investigation Order Act*). When conducting a hearing by videoconference or other audiovisual transmission, the competent authority shall be obliged to inform the accused person about the rights thereof in such a time as to ensure a possibility for the effective exercise of the right of defence (Art 28(2) of the law). In addition to the express provisions of the special law, in relation to the right of defense of the accused, respectively the defendant, the rules of the *Criminal Procedure Code* are also applicable.[50]

### 3.5 *Cooperation Issues between Executing and Issuing Authorities*

In the practice of the application of the Directive and the law, no particular difficulties related to cooperation have been noticed. It is noteworthy that in most cases the communication among Member States' authorities is sufficiently intense to ensure the normal conduct of the hearing, including the technical support and the provision of translators/interpreters.

In some cases, Bulgarian authorities reportedly conduct consultations with the assistance of the European Judicial Network.[51] Important for the qualification of Bulgarian magistrates and investigative bodies is moreover the

50 According to §3 of the Additional provisions of the European Investigation Order Act, "Except where this Act contains specific rules, the provisions of the Criminal Procedure Code shall apply".

51 See, for example, Ruling No 2829 of 13.12.2022 of the Sofia City Court in criminal case No 2870/2022. In both phases of the criminal process, the competent authority can use the Atlas, Contact Points and Library sections of the European Judicial Network (EJN) (europa.eu) website, can contact a contact point in the National Judicial Network for International Cooperation in Criminal Cases in the Republic of Bulgaria or with a contact point of the EJN. In more complex cases, where European Investigation Orders are drawn up to more than two countries or when operational coordination is required, the competent authority could also seek assistance from the National Bureau of Bulgaria at Eurojust, which also offers a legitimate channel for sending European Investigation Orders. When searching for initial information, it can also be specified whether the crime (criminal offense) is also punishable in the executing country; in what way the procedural actions for collecting the relevant evidence would be carried out; whether there are other "interested persons" under the law of the executing State who would have legal remedies against EIO enforcement actions, etc. See Sava Petrov, 'European Investigation Order' in 'Prosecutor's Guide. Book two, Project "Modern learning environment for judges, prosecutors, investigators and other representatives of the professional community"' (2024) National Institute of Justice.

compulsory training conducted by the National Institute of Justice,[52] which comprises separate training manuals for judges, prosecutors and investigators and dedicates a module to the European Investigation Order.[53]

### 3.6 *Remedies*

Art 18 of the *European Investigation Order Act* provides for a general regulation of legal remedies.

According to it, remedies and time limits available in similar cases under Bulgarian legislation shall apply to the defence of the persons concerned when carrying out an investigative measure and other procedural measures indicated in the European Investigation Order. This provision states that the substantive reasons for issuing an EIO may be appealed only in the issuing State, without prejudice to the guarantees of fundamental rights provided for in Bulgarian legislation. The law moreover provides that, where it would not undermine the need to ensure confidentiality of an investigation, the issuing authority and the authority competent to recognize the order shall take measures to ensure that information is provided about the possibilities for seeking the legal remedies when these become applicable and shall ensure in due time the effective exercise of the said remedies. These authorities must inform each other about the legal remedies sought against the issuing, the recognition or the execution of a European Investigation Order.

In addition to this general provision, the law also contains special rules regarding the performance of certain procedural actions. For example, in the procedure for the temporary transfer of persons held in custody for the purpose of carrying out investigative measure and other procedural measures, in addition to the cases referred to in Art 16, the execution of a European Investigation Order issued for temporary transfer may be refused on the grounds that the person in custody does not consent to it, or that the transfer is liable to prolong

52 According to Art 249 of the Judiciary System Act, the National Institute of Justice shall implement: (1) mandatory initial training of candidates for junior judge, junior prosecutor, and junior investigating magistrate; (2) mandatory induction training of judges, prosecutors and investigating magistrates when they are appointed for the first time in judicial authorities and when court assessors are elected for their first term of office; (3) maintaining and upgrading the qualification of judges, prosecutors and investigating magistrates, of members of the Supreme Judicial Council, of the Inspector General and inspectors of the Inspectorate with the Supreme Judicial Council, of public enforcement agents, recording magistrates, judicial assistants, prosecutorial assistants, judicial officers, court assessors, of the inspectors at the Inspectorate with the Minister of Justice and of other employees of the Ministry of Justice; (4) e-learning, and shall organise empirical legal research and analysis.

53 See <https://nij.bg/> accessed July 2024.

the detention of the person in custody (Art 26(3) of the Act). Such a rule is contained in Art 28 (3) of the *European Investigation Order Act*, according to which execution of an EIO by videoconference or other audiovisual transmission may be refused where the accused does not consent, or the execution of such an investigative measure and other procedural measures in the particular case is contrary to Bulgarian legislation. These rules are in accordance with the provisions of Art 22(2) and, accordingly, Art 24(2) of the EIO D.

So far, problems have been identified in the application of the Directive in Bulgaria, specifically in relation to the means of protection. They are related to the lack of a guaranteed possibility of defense in the proceedings for the issuance of the European Investigation Order and the lack of judicial sanction for certain actions, for which in similar cases a judicial authorization is required according to the *Criminal Procedure Code*.[54] Thus, the previous provisions in the law created a risk that the European Investigation Orders issued by the Bulgarian authorities would not be recognized by the authorities of other Member States.

In applying the law, in case No 1055/2022[55] the Bulgarian Specialized Criminal Court concluded that Bulgarian law does not provide for any legal remedies against decisions to search and seize or to hearing of a witness, nor against the issuance of a European Investigation Order, and made a preliminary reference to the Court of the European Union (CJEU) to seek the interpretation of certain provisions of the Directive.[56]

---

54 According to the Criminal Procedure Code, the permission of a judge is required to carry out a physical examination in the absence of the person's consent (Art 158(3) of the CPC), searches (including search of a person) and seizures (Art 161(1) of the CPC), submission of data by enterprises, providing public electronic communication networks and/or services (Art 159a(1) of the CPC), compulsory taking samples for comparative study (Art 146(3) of the CPC), interception and seizure of correspondence (Art 165(2) of the CPC), when these actions are carried out in the pre-trial proceedings. In cases of urgency, where this is the only possible way to collect and keep evidence, the pre-trial authorities may perform physical examination, searches (including search of a person) and seizures without authorisation from the judge, but the record of the investigative action being submitted for approval by the supervising prosecutor to the judge forthwith, but not later than 24 hours thereafter (Art 158(4), Art 161(2) and Art 164 of the CPC).

55 After the closure of the Specialized Criminal Court, a problem was noticed with access to the acts issued by this court. According to the information in the press release about the request for a preliminary ruling, the judicial act has been published (<https://spns.justice.bg/> accessed July 2024), but it is missing on the website of the Supreme Judicial Council (<https://legalacts.justice.bg/Search/Details?actId=txT87UWr1alD2rOE9HLtgg%3D%3D> accessed July 2024).

56 Art 6(1) of the European Investigation Order Act (SG No 16 of 20. 2. 2018) lays down "conditions for issuing a European Investigation Order":

In relation to this, in its decision in Case C-852/19 *Gavanozov*,[57] the CJEU held that the rules of Directive 2014/41/EU and of the Charter of Fundamental Rights of the European Union require Member States' legislation to provide for legal remedy against the issuing of a European Investigation Order, the purpose of which is the carrying out of searches and seizures as well as the hearing of a witness by videoconference. Also, the rules of EIO D, CFR and the Treaty on European Union do not allow the issuance of EIO, the purpose

---

*"The competent authority in accordance with Article 5(1) shall issue a European Investigation Order following an individual assessment, on condition that:*
*1. A European Investigation Order is necessary and appropriate in light of the purpose of the criminal proceedings, taking account of the rights of the accused or the defendant.*
*2. The investigative and other procedural measures for which the European Investigation Order is issued could be carried out in a similar case under the same conditions under Bulgarian law."*
No provision of the European Investigation Order Act provides for a possibility of challenging the issuance of a European Investigation Order. Art 161(3) of the Criminal Procedure Code (SG No 86/05, in the version applicable at the time of the order for reference SG No 83/19) states that "search and seizure measures in court proceedings shall be carried out on the orders of the court in which the proceedings are pending". Art 341(3) of the Criminal Procedure Code excludes the possibility of appealing against acts other than those expressly listed. The Criminal Procedure Code does not allow for orders for the hearing of witnesses or for a search and seizure of residential and business premises to be challenged. The person concerned by the search and seizure or the hearing of the witness cannot challenge the decision because he is not party to the proceedings.

57 See Case C-852/19 *Gavanozov II* [2021] ECLI:EU:C:2021:902 <https://curia.europa.eu/juris/liste.jsf?language=en&td=ALL&num=C-852/19> accessed July 2024. Mr Gavanozov is being prosecuted in Bulgaria for involvement in an organised criminal group formed for the purpose of committing tax offences. He is suspected of having imported sugar, via shell companies, into Bulgaria from other Member States, obtaining supplies from, inter alia, a company established in the Czech Republic and represented by Mr Y, and of subsequently having sold that sugar on the Bulgarian market without assessing or paying value added tax (VAT), by submitting incorrect documents according to which that sugar had been exported to Romania. The Specialised Criminal Court (Bulgaria) decided, on 11 May 2017, to issue an EIO requesting the Czech authorities to carry out searches and seizures at both the premises of the company established in the Czech Republic and the home of Mr Y, and to hear Mr Y as a witness by videoconference. In its order for reference, the Specialised Criminal Court states that Bulgarian law does not provide for any legal remedy against decisions ordering the carrying out of searches and seizures or the hearing of witnesses, or against the issuing of an EIO. In that context, that court asks whether Bulgarian law is contrary to EU law and, in such a case, whether it may issue an EIO seeking such investigative measures. In his Opinion, the Advocate General notes that "it is the duty of the issuing authorities to make sure that their own acts are not tainted by unlawfulness due to non-compliance with the minimum standards laid down in the ECHR when these acts enter the system of Directive 2014/41." Opinion of Advocate General Bobek (29 April 2021) <https://eur-lex.europa.eu/legal-content/EN/TXT/HTML/?uri=CELEX:62019CC0852> accessed July 2024.

of which is the carrying out of searches and seizures as well as the hearing of a witness by videoconference, where the legislation of the respective Member State does not provide any legal remedy against the issuing of such a European Investigation Order.[58]

In another case related to the implementation of the Directive, the Specialized Criminal Court found that there was no requirement in the special law (the *European Investigation Order Act*) for a judicial sanction, as required for similar actions under the *Criminal Procedure Code*.[59]

Specifically, following the commencement of criminal proceedings in Bulgaria for the financing of terrorist activities, the prosecutor issued four EIOs, with identical content, for the collection of traffic and location data relating to electronic communications. The four EIOs were issued by the Bulgarian prosecutor without a validation by a judge or a court,[60] and were transmitted to the relevant authorities in Belgium, Germany, Austria and Sweden.

---

58 See the Judgment of the Court (First Chamber, 11 November 2021) <https://eur-lex.europa.eu/legal-content/EN/TXT/HTML/?uri=CELEX:62019CJ0852> accessed July 2024: "1. Article *14 of Directive 2014/41/EU of the European Parliament and of the Council of 3 April 2014 regarding the European Investigation Order in criminal matters, read in conjunction with Article 24(7) of that directive and Article 47 of the Charter of Fundamental Rights of the European Union, must be interpreted as precluding legislation of a Member State which has issued a European investigation order that does not provide for any legal remedy against the issuing of a European investigation order, the purpose of which is the carrying out of searches and seizures as well as the hearing of a witness by videoconference. 2. Article 6 of Directive 2014/41, read in conjunction with Article 47 of the Charter of Fundamental Rights of the European Union and Article 4(3) of the Treaty on European Union, must be interpreted as precluding the issuing, by the competent authority of a Member State, of a European investigation order, the purpose of which is the carrying out of searches and seizures as well as the hearing of a witness by videoconference, where the legislation of that Member State does not provide any legal remedy against the issuing of such a European investigation order.*"

59 See Art 146, Art 158, Art 159a, Art 161, Art 164, Art 165 of the Criminal Procedure Code, as outlined *supra*, n 54.

60 According to Art 159a(1) of Criminal Procedure Code, "Upon request by a court as part of court proceedings or based on *motivated order by a judge of the respective court of first instance, issued by request of the supervising prosecutor of pre-trial proceedings* the enterprises, providing public electronic communication networks and/or services shall make available the data, generated in the course of performance of their activities, which may be required for:
1. tracing and identification of the source of the communication link;
2. identification of the direction of the communication link;
3. identification of the date, hour and duration of the communication link;
4. identification of the type of the communication link;
5. (amended, SG No. 20/2021) to identify the terminal equipment of the user or what purports to be a terminal equipment of the user;
6. establishment of an identification code of the cells used."

The public prosecutor's offices of such Member States executed the EIOs without authorisation or validation by a judge or a court either, except in the case of the Belgian public prosecutor's office. Based on the evidence gathered (including the information supplied in response to the EIOs), the defendant, *HP*, and five other persons were charged with financing terrorist acts and being part of a criminal group for the purpose of financing such acts. The Specialised Criminal Court in Bulgaria, which had to examine the evidence gathered in accordance with the EIOs, questioned whether that evidence was lawful since, under national law, that evidence could only have been obtained in Bulgaria following judicial authorisation, including from the public prosecutor. Against that background, that court has made a preliminary ruling to the Court of the European Union whether the public prosecutor's office of a Member State is competent to issue a European Investigation Order in a criminal matter ('EIO'), requesting traffic and location data relating to electronic communications, when, in accordance with the national law of the issuing State, only a judge or a court is entitled to authorise the gathering of such evidence.[61]

In its preliminary ruling, the Bulgarian Specialized Criminal Court stated that Art 2(c) of Directive 2014/41 refers to national law to designate the competent issuing authority. The Specialized Criminal Court notes that under Bulgarian law, pursuant to Art 5(1)(1) of the *European Investigation Order Act*, the competent issuing authority is the public prosecutor. However, that Court notes that, in a similar domestic case, the authority with competence to order the transfer of traffic and location data associated with telecommunications is a judge of the first instance court having jurisdiction and that the public prosecutor has, in such a situation, only the power to make a reasoned request to that judge. Thus, the Specialized Criminal Court asked the CJEU whether, having regard in particular to the principle of equivalence, the competence to issue an EIO may be governed by the national law transposing Directive 2014/41, or

61 See Request for a preliminary ruling from the Specialised Criminal Court (Bulgaria) lodged on 1 October 2019 – Criminal proceedings against HP (Case C-724/19), <https://curia.europa.eu/juris/document/document.jsf?text=&docid=221379&pageIndex=0&doclang=EN&mode=req&dir=&occ=first&part=1&cid=7001808> accessed July 2024: "Is a national law (Article 5(1)(1) of the Law on the European investigation order; 'the ZEZR'), according to which, during the pre-trial stage of the criminal proceedings, the authority competent to issue a European investigation order for the provision of traffic and location data related to telecommunications is a public prosecutor, consistent with Article 2(c)(i) of Directive 2014/41 and the principle of equivalence, provided that in an identical domestic case the competent authority is a judge?

Does recognition of that European investigation order by the competent authority of the executing State (public prosecutor or an investigating judge) replace the court order required under the law of the issuing State?".

whether Art 2(c) of that Directive confers competence on the authority which is competent in a similar domestic case.

In relation to this reference for a preliminary ruling, in its decision in Case C-724/19, the Court of the European Union held that the rules of Directive 2014/41/EU do not allow a prosecutor to have the power to issue, during the pre-trial phase of criminal proceedings, a European Investigation Order an investigation aimed at obtaining traffic and location data related to telecommunications, when in a similar national case only the judge has the exclusive competence to grant permission for this.[62]

In order to address these problems, Bulgarian law was recently amended.[63] In 2024, an amendment to the *European Investigation Order Act* was adopted and in Art 6, two new paragraphs are included. The new rules introduce the possibility for persons affected by the execution of the European Investigation Order to appeal the grounds for its issuance and regulate the procedure for appeal.[64] In addition, explicitly in Art 5 of the *European Investigation Order*

---

62 See the Judgment of the Court (Fourth Chamber) of 16 December 2021 (Case C-724/19) <https://eur-lex.europa.eu/legal-content/en/TXT/?uri=CELEX:62019CJ0724> accessed July 2024: "*1. Article 2(c)(i) of Directive 2014/41/EU of the European Parliament and of the Council of 3 April 2014 regarding the European Investigation Order in criminal matters must be interpreted as precluding a public prosecutor from having competence to issue, during the pre-trial stage of criminal proceedings, an European Investigation Order, within the meaning of that directive, seeking to obtain traffic and location data associated with telecommunications, where, in a similar domestic case, the judge has exclusive competence to adopt an investigative measure seeking access to such data.*

*2. Article 6 and Article 9(1) and (3) of Directive 2014/41 must be interpreted as meaning that recognition, on the part of the executing authority, of an European Investigation Order issued with a view to obtaining traffic and location data associated with telecommunications may not replace the requirements applicable in the issuing State, where that European Investigation Order was improperly issued by a public prosecutor, whereas, in a similar domestic case, the judge has exclusive competence to adopt an investigative measure seeking to obtain such data*".

63 SG No. 36/23.04.2024.

64 "*Conditions for Issuing European Investigative Order*

*Article 6. (1) [...]*

*(4) (New, SG No. 36/2024) Persons whose individual rights or property rights are directly and immediately affected by the execution of the European Investigative Order may appeal the substantive reasons for issuing the said order within 14 days after becoming aware of the carrying out of the investigative measure or the judicial investigation measure before:*

*1. the relevant court of first instance, where the order has been issued in the pre-trial proceeding;*

*2. the court which issued the said order in the trial proceeding;*

*3. the relevant regional court, where the order has been issued by an administrative authority in the cases referred to in Article 44 (2) and Article 52 (4) of the Administrative Violations and Sanctions Act.*

*Act* provides that in the pre-trial phase of the criminal proceedings, the prosecutor issues a European Investigation Order based on prior permission from a judge, when such is required under Bulgarian legislation and the EIO shall be issued by the relevant court on a motion by the prosecutor, where the court is the sole authority to order the carrying out of an investigative measure in a domestic case.[65]

## 4 Regulation 1805/2018: Critical Profiles in Legislation and Case Law

### 4.1 *Legal Basis in the National System and Scope*

As already mentioned above, before the adoption of the Regulation 1805/2018, the European requirements regarding the mutual recognition and enforcement of freezing or confiscation orders as laid down in FD 2003/577 and FD 2006/783 were implemented in national legislation, by the adoption of two laws regulating this matter, namely the *Recognition, Execution, Issuance and Transmission of Property Freezing Orders Act* of 2006, and the *Recognition, Execution and Transmission of Confiscation or Seizure Orders and Decisions Imposing Financial Penalties Act* of 2010.

In 2022, both laws were amended to introduce implementing measures for the Regulation 1805/2018 into national legislation.[66] In view of the direct

---

*(5) (New, SG No. 36/2024) The interlocutory appeal shall be lodged care of the authority referred to in Article 5 (1) herein which has issued the European Investigative Order. The court, sitting in camera, shall examine the appeal within 7 days from the lodgement thereof and shall adjudicate on the lawfulness, necessity and proportionality of the European Investigative Order as issued by a ruling which shall be final. Where the court revokes the European Investigative Order, the competent authority referred to in Article 5 (1) herein shall so notify the executing State.".*

65 *"Authority Competent to Issue European Investigative Order*
*Article 5. (1) (Amended, SG No. 36/2024) A European Investigative Order in the Republic of Bulgaria shall be issued:*
*1. in a pre-trial proceeding:*
*(a) by the relevant prosecutor:*
*(b) by the relevant prosecutor: on the basis of a prior authorisation granted by a judge, where such authorisation is required by Bulgarian legislation in order to carry out the investigative measure; the judge shall assess the necessity and proportionality of issuing the European Investigative Order and shall adjudicate according to the procedure and within the time limits established in a similar domestic case;*
*(c) by the relevant court on a motion by the prosecutor, where the court is the sole authority to order the carrying out of an investigative measure in a domestic case;*
*[...]".*

66 SG No. 56/19.07.2022.

applicability of the Regulation, the grounds established in it for non-recognition and non-execution of the freezing or confiscation orders do not need to be repeated in the domestic law. Therefore, the changes made in both laws in 2022 refer to the designation of the competent authority in Bulgaria as an executing or issuing State, the jurisdiction, the procedure for recognition of the freezing or confiscation orders.

The Bulgarian legal system provides several legal regimes for freezing and confiscation of property. In addition to confiscation as a punishment in the meaning of Art 44 of the *Criminal Code* (CC),[67] the *Criminal Code* under its Art 53 also provides for the confiscation in favour of the state of: a) objects belonging to the culprit that were intended or served for the perpetration of an intentional crime; b) objects belonging to the culprit, which were subject of intentional crime – in the cases expressly provided in the Special Part of the Code. According to the Code, the direct and indirect benefits acquired through the crime are also subject to confiscation, if they are not subject to return or recovery.[68] The confiscation within the meaning of Art 53 CC is not a punishment. It is defined in the doctrine as a measure that is applicable regardless of the criminal liability.[69]

Besides these, Bulgarian legislation also provides for the so-called civil forfeiture, i.e. forfeiture of unlawfully acquired assets (any assets for the acquisition of which a legitimate source has not been identified). The unlawfully acquired assets forfeiture proceeding is conducted without prejudice to the criminal proceeding against the person under examination and the parties related thereto. The matter is governed by the Unlawfully Acquired Assets Forfeiture Act.[70] As per its Art 5(3) the procedures and sanctions regarding identification of such assets are applied without prejudice to the taking of steps and measures under other laws, including the initiation of criminal proceedings.

In the literature, this civil forfeiture is distinguished from the crime-related confiscation in so far it concerns the forfeiture of unlawfully acquired assets, i.e. any assets for the acquisition of which a legitimate source has not been identified and not necessarily proceeds of crime.[71] It is also noted that EU legal framework, which includes FD 2006/783, Directive 2014/42/EU and currently

67 Art 44 CC states that confiscation shall be compulsory appropriation without compensation of property in favour of the state, of assets belonging to the convict or of part thereof, of specified pieces of property of the culprit, or of parts of such pieces of property.

68 Art 53 CC.

69 Alexander Stoynov, *Criminal Law* (Ciela 2019); Lazar Gruev, *Punishment of Crime* (Prof Marin Drinov Publishing House of BAS 2020).

70 SG No. 7/19.01.2018 (Heading amended, SG No. 84/2023, effective 6.10.2023).

71 Gruev (n 69) 119.

Regulation 1805/2018, applies precisely to the crime-related confiscation and not to the so-called civil forfeiture.[72]

### 4.2 *Grounds for Non-recognition and Non-execution*

There are differences between the grounds for non-recognition and non-execution of the freezing or confiscation orders, provided for in the two Framework Decisions, and implemented into Bulgarian law, and those established in the Regulation.

For instance, according to Art 14(1) of the *Recognition, Execution and Transmission of Confiscation or Seizure Orders and Decisions Imposing Financial Penalties Act*, confiscation orders issued in another Member State shall be recognised and executed in Bulgaria if they relate to acts which constitute offences and for which confiscation is also envisaged under the Bulgarian legislation, regardless of the components comprising the *corpus delicti* under the legislation of the issuing State. Accordingly, in such way one of the grounds for non-recognition or non-execution of a confiscation order under Art 19(1), p. 8 thereof is formulated.[73] Thus, the requirements established in Art 6(3) and 8(2) (b) of FD 2006/783 have been introduced into national law.[74]

72 ibid 120–123. The differences in these two types of confiscations provided for into national legislation have also been discussed by the CJEU. For instance, in its judgment in Case C-319/19, the Court concluded that the Directive 2014/42 [...] is an act aimed at obliging Member States to establish common minimum rules for confiscation of crime-related instrumentalities and proceeds, in order to facilitate the mutual recognition of judicial confiscation decisions adopted in criminal proceedings. Therefore, according to the Court the directive does not govern the confiscation of instrumentalities and proceeds resulting from illegal activities that is ordered by a court in a Member State in the context of or following proceedings that do not concern the finding of one or more criminal offences. Such confiscation falls outside the scope, in fact, of the minimum rules laid down by that directive, in accordance with Article 1(1) thereof, and the rules governing it fall within the scope of the power of the Member States, referred to in recital 22 of that directive, to provide more extensive powers in their national law (Case C-319/19, *Komisia za protivodeystvie na koruptsiyata i za otnemane na nezakonno pridobitoto imushtestvo* [2021] ECLI:EU:C:2021:883, paras 36–37).

73 Art 19(1), p. 8 states that the court may refuse to recognise or to allow the execution of a confiscation order if it establishes that according to the terms of Article 14(1) the confiscation order relates to acts which do not constitute an offence, which permits confiscation pursuant to the Bulgarian legislation.

74 According to Art 6(3) of FD 2006/783, for offences other than those covered by paragraph 1 [namely those without need of the verification of the double criminality], the executing State may make the recognition and execution of a confiscation order subject to the condition that the acts giving rise to the confiscation order constitute an offence which permits confiscation under the law of the executing State, whatever its constituent elements or however it is described under the law of the issuing State.

However, the Regulation does not provide for a similar condition for recognition and execution of confiscation orders for crimes, other than those for which double criminality is not necessary.[75]

These differences are reflected in the case law. In particular, some courts continue to apply the national law introducing the requirements of the FD, although, in relation to confiscation certificates transmitted on or after 19 December 2020, Regulation 1805/2018 should now apply.[76]

---

In addition, Art 8(2)(b) of FD 2006/783 provides for that the competent judicial authority of the executing State, as defined in the law of that State, may also refuse to recognise and execute the confiscation order if it is established that in one of the cases referred to in Art 6(3), the confiscation order relates to acts which do not constitute an offence which permits confiscation under the law of the executing State; however, in relation to taxes, duties, customs duties and exchange activities, execution of a confiscation order may not be refused on the ground that the law of the executing State does not impose the same kind of tax or duty or does not contain the same types of rules concerning taxes, duties, customs duties and exchange activities as the law of the issuing State.

75 As laid down in Art 3(2) thereof, for criminal offences other than those referred to in paragraph 1, [namely those without need of the verification of the double criminality], the executing State may make the recognition and execution of a freezing order or confiscation order subject to the condition that the acts giving rise to the freezing order or confiscation order constitute a criminal offence under the law of the executing State, whatever its constituent elements or however it is described under the law of the issuing State.

In addition, Art 19(1)(f) of Regulation 1805/2018 states that the executing authority may decide not to recognise or execute a confiscation order only where in a case falling under Art 3(2), the conduct in connection with which the confiscation order was issued does not constitute a criminal offence under the law of the executing State; however, in cases that involve taxes or duties or customs and exchange regulations, the recognition or execution of the confiscation order shall not be refused on the grounds that the law of the executing State does not impose the same kind of taxes or duties or does not provide for the same type of rules as regards taxes and duties or the same type of customs and exchange regulations as the law of the issuing State.

76 See in this context Judgment № 114/17.06.2021 of the District Court-Blagoevgrad. The proceedings is initiated on the basis of a confiscation certificate under Art 4 of FD 2006/783 for the recognition and execution of a confiscation order, issued by a competent authority of the Lithuania against a Bulgarian citizen, that concerns an amount of money – 3200 euros, representing the value of the instrumentality of crime, namely the vehicle used to transport the goods.

According to the court, the most similar crime under the Bulgarian Criminal Code to the described act is that under Art 234 of the Criminal Code (the distribution or storage of excise goods without an excise tax banderol sticker where such banderol is required by the law shall, in non-negligible cases), but it does not provide for "confiscation" of the instrumentality of crime. Additionally, the offence committed on the territory of the Republic of Lithuania does not fall under the exceptions of crimes for which double criminality is not required. Against all these factors, the court concluded that the recognition and execution of the confiscation order should be refused.

The situation is similar with regard to another ground for non-recognition and non-execution of confiscation orders, specified in the FD 2006/783 (Art 8(2)(h) thereof)[77] and provided for in Bulgarian legislation,[78] but which, again, is missing among the grounds set out in Regulation, namely – where the execution of the confiscation order is with expired prescription barred under the Bulgarian legislation. Until the entry into force of the Regulation, such requirements have been commonly applied by the case law.[79] However, some

---

77 According to Art 8(2)(h) of FD 2006/783, the competent judicial authority of the executing State, as defined in the law of that State, may also refuse to recognise and execute the confiscation order if it is established that the execution of a confiscation order is barred by statutory time limitations in the executing State, provided that the acts fall within the jurisdiction of that State under its own criminal law.

78 An identical norm is introduced in national legislation. Art 19(1), p. 3 of the *Recognition, Execution and Transmission of Confiscation or Seizure Orders and Decisions Imposing Financial Penalties Act* states that the court may refuse to recognise or to allow the execution of a confiscation or seizure order if it establishes that the execution of the order is with expired prescription barred under the Bulgarian legislation and the order is related to an act which falls within the jurisdiction of a Bulgarian court.

79 See in this context Judgment № 2/4.07.2017 of the District Court-Sliven. The proceedings is initiated on the basis of a confiscation certificate received in the District Court – Sliven under Art 4 of FW Decision 2006/783 for the recognition and execution of a confiscation order, issued by a Netherlands court (entered into force on 15 March 2005), by which a confiscation was imposed on the defendant, Bulgarian citizen, that concerns an amount of money – 22 218 euros, representing proceeds derived from the crime of trafficking in human beings.

According to national law (Art 10(1) of the *Recognition, Execution and Transmission of Confiscation or Seizure Orders and Decisions Imposing Financial Penalties Act*), the execution of confiscation orders in the Republic of Bulgaria shall be governed by the Bulgarian legislation. For the confiscation Bulgarian Criminal Code provides for that the punishment imposed shall not be served where the term of two years have elapsed following the entry into force of the sentence (Art 82(1), p. 5 thereof). In addition, the Code states that irrespective of the interruption and termination of prescription, the punishment shall not be enforced where a term has elapsed which exceeds the previously mentioned term by one half (Art 82(4) thereof). Therefore, in the present case, the enforcement of the punishment was time-barred.

Moreover, under national law confiscation orders, issued in another Member State are recognised and executed in Bulgaria if they relate to acts which constitute offences and for which confiscation is also envisaged under the Bulgarian legislation. Thus, the requirements of the FW Decision 2006/783 are transposed. However, the provisions of the Bulgarian Criminal Code on human trafficking do not provide for confiscation as a punishment.

Against all these factors, the District Court – Sliven refuses to recognise and execute the confiscation order.

courts continue to refer to this ground for non-recognition and non-execution of confiscation orders in the proceedings even after 19 December 2020.[80]

### 4.3 *Fundamental Rights and Proportionality Issues*

It is the existence and enforcement of the so-called civil forfeiture, as explained above, that raises a lot of issues, mostly relating to protection and guarantee of the rights of the affected persons. Specifically for Bulgaria, the problem is deepening due to the numerous judgments of the ECtHR against the country, concerning the civil confiscation under the two repealed laws governing this matter, namely the *Criminal Assets Forfeiture Act* adopted in 2005, repealed in 2012[81] and the *Act on Forfeiture to the Exchequer of Unlawfully Acquired Assets,* enacted in 2012 and repealed in 2018.[82]

The European Court found that national courts did not look for a causal link between the crime committed and the acquisition of the assets for which the confiscation was requested.[83] According to Court, it is not enough to simply prove a discrepancy between the established "legitimate" income and the expenses incurred by the applicants. Due to this too formalistic approach, the Court concluded that there had been a violation of Art 1 of the Additional Protocol of ECHR, namely the right to property. In addition, in the *Yordanov and others v. Bulgaria* case, the European Court pointed out that the *Unlawfully Acquired Assets Forfeiture Act,* adopted in 2018[84] and currently in force provides essentially for the same mechanism for the forfeiture of "unlawfully

80 See in this context Judgment № 36/3.05.2022 of the District Court-Vidin. The proceedings is initiated on the basis of a confiscation certificate received in the District Court – Vidin under Art. 17 of Regulation 2018/1805 for the recognition and execution of a confiscation order, issued by a Slovenian court against a Bulgarian citizen, that concerns an amount of money – 1100 euros, representing proceeds derived from the crime of trafficking in human beings. According to the court, there are no reasons for non-recognition and non-execution of confiscation order, including that relating to the expired statute of limitations. Against all these factors, the court recognises the confiscation order.

81 SG N 19/1.03.2005. It provides for confiscation of the benefits of crimes after a final criminal conviction, as well as, in accordance with the national case law, a causal link between the crime committed and the property subject to confiscation.

82 SG N 38/18.05.2012. The main novelty is that it provides for the forfeiture of "unlawful" assets and not necessarily proceeds of crime. The law remained in force until 2018 when it was repealed with the adoption of the Unlawfully Acquired Assets Forfeiture Act currently in force.

83 *Todorov and Others v Bulgaria* App nos 50705/11 and 6 others (ECtHR, 13 July 2021); *Sabouni and Others v. Bulgaria* App nos 25795/15 and 59286/16 (ECtHR, 2 March 2023); *Lyapchev and Others v Bulgaria* App nos 75478/13 and 30713/15 (ECtHR, 2 March 2023); *Yordanov and others v Bulgaria* App nos 265/17 and 26473/18 (ECtHR, 26 September 2023).

84 SG No. 7/19.01.2018 (Heading amended, SG No. 84/2023, effective 6.10.2023).

acquired assets" as the one under the repealed 2012 Act, namely assets "for the acquisition of which a legitimate source has not been identified" (Art 5(1) thereof), and does not require a criminal conviction.[85] Therefore, according to the opinion of some Bulgarian human rights defenders, these decisions of the Court require a change both in the current law (also providing for confiscation of illegally acquired property, not based on a verdict and independently from the criminal proceedings), and in case law regarding their compliance with the ECHR principles and standards.[86] In addition, according to some scholars, the civil forfeiture regime, as explained above, provided for in the Bulgarian legislation, which extends the confiscation outside the field of criminal law, is potentially problematic and significantly influences the rights of the affected persons,[87] while at the same time excludes the same rights from the "(protective) assessment of the CJEU".[88]

The matter related to the expansion of the scope of confiscation not only at the national but also at the European level is a subject of scientific interest.[89] According to some scholars, "*the expectation that, e.g., the instruments from the wider spectrum of non-conviction-based confiscation (usually associated with lower standards), in order to meet the requirements of the Regulation (EU)*

---

85 *Yordanov and Others v Bulgaria* App nos 265/17 and 26473/18 (ECtHR, 26 September 2023), para 36.

86 See Mirela Veselinova 'ECtHR: Only property related to criminal activity is confiscated, Capital' (13 July 2021) <https://www.capital.bg/politika_i_ikonomika/pravo/2021/07/13/4232261_espch_konfiskuva_se_samo_imushtestvo_koeto_ima_vruzka/> accessed July 2024; Mirela Veselinova, Jonko Grozev, 'Civil forfeiture is not a universal instrument, Capital' (6 October 2023) <https://www.capital.bg/politika_i_ikonomika/pravo/2023/10/06/4535371_ionko_grozev_grajdanskata_konfiskaciia_ne_e/> accessed July 2024.

87 See in this context Elżbieta Hryniewicz-Lach, 'Expanding Confiscation and its Dimensions in EU Criminal Law' (2023) European Journal of Crime, Criminal Law and Criminal Justice (online publication, 27 December 2023) 253–254 <https://brill.com/view/journals/eccl/31/3-4/article-p243_003.xml?language=en> accessed July 2024. The article presents the partial results of a research project called 'Extended confiscation and its justification in light of fundamental rights and general principles of EU law', financed by the National Science Centre, Poland, in years 2021–2024. The article refers to the Bulgarian report on the subject drawn up within the project.

88 ibid 254. The "protective assessment of the CJEU" mentioned above means the Judgment of the CJEU of 28 October 2021 (Case C-319/19) on a preliminary inquiry of a Bulgarian court, according to which "Directive 2014/42/EU ... must be interpreted as not applying to legislation of a Member State which provides that confiscation of illegally obtained assets is to be ordered by a national court in the context of or following proceedings which do not relate to a finding of one or more criminal offences".

89 See Elżbieta Hryniewicz-Lach (n 87) and the literature quoted in the article.

*2018/1805, will either be reinforced with enhanced protection of the rights of affected persons or will not be recognized or executed, might be too optimistic".*[90]

### 4.4 *Issues for the Rights of the Suspect, Accused and Other Parties*

With the recent legislative changes made in July 2022 concerning the recognition and execution of freezing or confiscation orders, the relevant competent authorities in Bulgaria as an executing State under Regulation 1805/2018 were explicitly indicated, namely the district courts.[91]

When it comes to proceedings for recognition of a freezing order, such court shall hear the case in a single-judge panel and in a closed session.[92] As regards the proceedings for recognition of a confiscation order, the court shall hear the case in a panel of three judges in an open session with the participation of a prosecutor and the affected person.[93]

As regards the rights of the affected persons, and in particular the rights of the persons that own the property covered by the freezing order, there is national case law where the courts refuse to recognize and execute such freezing orders. The courts conclude that where at the time of imposing the foreclosure on the property, the latter is not the property of the affected person, but is acquired by a *bona fide* third party, the freezing order could not fulfill its purpose and could not oppose to the right of ownership of that third party.[94]

90 ibid 256 and the literature quoted in the article.

91 Art 24 (1) of the *Recognition, Execution, Issuance and Transmission of Property Freezing Orders Act* and Art 44 of the *Recognition, Execution and Transmission of Confiscation or Seizure Orders and Decisions Imposing Financial Penalties Act*, respectively.

92 Art 24(2) of *Recognition, Execution, Issuance and Transmission of Property Freezing Orders Act.*

93 Art 45(1) of *Recognition, Execution and Transmission of Confiscation or Seizure Orders and Decisions Imposing Financial Penalties Act.*

94 See in this context Ruling No 272/21.05.2018 of the Appellate Court – Sofia. The proceedings is initiated by appeal against a decision of the Sofia City Court, which recognises a freezing order, issued by a Spanish court for seizure of property of four Bulgarian citizens for purposes of execution of subsequent confiscation order issued by Spain authority. Criminal proceedings are being conducted against them in Spain on charges of participation in an organized criminal group for human trafficking, fraud and money laundering. By the decision under appeal, a foreclosure was imposed on real estate property located in the territory of Bulgaria, including an immovable property, for which the attached freezing certificate states that it is owned by one of the affected persons. However, it is clear from the documents submitted as evidence, that at the time of imposing the foreclosure on that immovable property, the latter was not the property of the one of the affected persons, but was acquired by the appellant through a purchase contract between them a few years ago. Therefore, the freezing order based on the recognized and executed judgment of the Spanish judicial authorities could not fulfill its purpose and could not

In general, this approach appears to be consistent with European law insofar as in the relevant European acts the freezing order is defined as a preventive measure concerning property with a view to possible subsequent confiscation thereof. Therefore, if in the proceedings for recognition of a freezing order it is established that the property is acquired by a *bona fide* third party, this calls into question the subsequent confiscation of such property. However, it should be noted that such national case law is settled prior to the entry into force of Regulation 1805/2018.

### 4.5 *Cooperation Issues between Executing and Issuing Authorities*

As regards cooperation issues between executing and issuing authorities, the Bulgarian legislator held that it was not necessary to introduce in national law specific provisions other than those set out in Regulation 1805/2018.

### 4.6 *Remedies*

Both laws on recognition and execution of freezing or confiscation orders provide for legal remedies for persons involved in these proceedings.

Specific provisions in this regard were introduced by the 2022 amendments. According to Art 26 of the *Recognition, Execution, Issuance and Transmission of Property Freezing Orders Act*, each interested party, including a *bona fide* third party, may appeal the ruling on the recognition of the freezing order before the Court of Appeal in accordance with the Code of Civil Procedure within 14 days

---

oppose to the right of ownership of the applicant. Against all these factors, the Appellate Court – Sofia annuls the decision of the Sofia City Court.

A similar approach has been followed in Ruling № 526/1.11.2017 г. of the same court. The proceedings is initiated by an appeal against a ruling of the Sofia City Court, which recognises a freezing order, issued by a Romanian court for seizure of property of Bulgarian citizens for purposes of execution of subsequent confiscation order issued by said Romanian authority. Criminal proceedings are being conducted against them in Romania for participation in an organized criminal group and money laundering.

By the decision under appeal, a foreclosure was imposed on real estate property located in the territory of Bulgaria, including an immovable property, for which the attached freezing certificate states that it is owned by one of the affected persons. The complainant claims that she is the owner of the foreclosed property in question and should be considered as a third interested party.

However, it is clear from the documents submitted as evidence, that with regard to the same property, its confiscation was ordered in favor of the Bulgarian State. Subsequently, this property was sold by the National Revenue Agency at an auction to the applicant. Therefore, the freezing order based on the recognized and executed judgment of the Romanian judicial authorities could not fulfill its purpose and could not oppose to the right of ownership of the applicant. Against all these factors, the Appellate Court – Sofia annuls the ruling of the Sofia City Court. See in this context Ruling No 330/11.10.2016 and Ruling No 84/17.03.2014 of the Appellate Court – Sofia.

from coming into knowledge of the issuance of such ruling. Such an appeal does not stay the execution. The parties may also appeal, in accordance with the Code of Civil Procedure, actions for the execution of the freezing order within 14 days of knowledge thereof.

The *Recognition, Execution and Transmission of Confiscation or Seizure Orders and Decisions Imposing Financial Penalties Act* provides for similar rule. Pursuant to Art 46, any person concerned, including a *bona fide* third party, may appeal the decision of the district court on recognition of the confiscation order before the Court of Appeal within 7 days of becoming aware of the ruling of the court. The appeal shall not stop the process of execution of the order. The case is decided in an open court session, in the presence of a prosecutor, the person concerned and his/her counsellor, and the *bona fide* third party admitted to participate. The ruling of the Court of Appeal is final.

These remedies as laid down in domestic law seem to be satisfactory and in compliance with Regulation 1805/2018, and more particularly with Art 33 thereof. Nevertheless, it should be noted that as laid down in Art 33 of the Regulation, this national legislative framework refers to the remedies in Bulgaria as the executing State. As regards the legal remedies in the issuing State, the situation is problematic, in so far as the Regulation itself does not contain sufficient provisions in this regard. Such a lack raises questions about the way in which the affected persons can protect their rights, especially since *per argumentum a contrario* the substantive reasons for issuing the freezing order or confiscation order could be challenged before a court in the issuing State.[95]

## 5 Concluding Remarks

With regard to the EAW FD, it seems that, by the latest changes in the regulatory framework made in December 2023, national legislation in the field of recognition and execution of European arrest warrants has been brought into line with the European standards established both in the Framework decision 2002/584 and in the case law of the CJEU. In the national case law, no special issues emerge. This is largely due to the fact that the European requirements in this area were introduced a long time ago and have been consistently applied

95 For critical appraisal whether the rights of defence of affected persons under Regulation 1805/2018 are sufficient to effectively safeguard the interests of such persons see Nuno Brandão, 'The right of defence under Regulation (EU) 2018/1805 on the mutual recognition of freezing orders and confiscation orders' (2022) 13(1) New Journal of European Criminal Law 28–41 and the literature quoted in the article.

by the national competent judicial authorities for more than 15 years. A challenge for the practice will rather be the recent legislative amendments, which implemented the two levels of protection in the cases of European arrest warrant, issued by a prosecutor in the pre-trial proceedings.

A positive assessment can be drawn also with regard to EIO D. In particular, it is clear from the preliminary ruling of the Bulgarian judges that they apply national law taking into account the ideas and meaning of the Directive. Their continuous training and their good cooperation with the judges of other Member States in the implementation of the Directive ensure a timely reaction in identifying and solving the problems related to the application of the rules of the Directive.

The greatest challenge in Bulgaria stems instead from the application of Regulation 1805/2018. The issues arise, on the one hand, from the fact that, at the European level, the matter related to the mutual recognition and the execution of freezing or confiscation orders was initially regulated by two Framework Decisions, duly implemented into Bulgarian law since 2006 and 2010, respectively. The settlement of this matter, however, by an European legislative act with direct applicability, such as Regulation 1805/2018, which replaces the Framework Decisions and introduces different requirements both in terms of the grounds for refusal and the rights of the affected persons, causes difficulties especially in the implementation by the national competent authorities.

In addition, it should be taken into account the too broad scope of freezing and confiscation of property provided for in Bulgarian legislation in the cases of the so-called civil forfeiture (forfeiture of unlawfully acquired assets, i.e. any assets for the acquisition of which a legitimate source has not been identified) and the problems resulting from the application of this regime, related to the violation of the rights of the affected persons, established in the practice of the ECtHR in cases against Bulgaria.

The relatively recent introduction into the national legislation of measures for the implementation of the Regulation 1805/2018 and the insufficient case law of the national courts in this regard, make the application of the European standards on recognition and execution of freezing or confiscation orders a challenge. It remains to be seen how and to what extent the application of these standards will be ensured in Bulgaria.

To sum up, the implementation of the rules of the EU cooperation mechanisms in the criminal law matter represents a serious test for the Bulgarian legislator.

This is because, regardless of the participation of the Member States in the legislative procedure for the adoption of the acts of the European Union, the national legislation has its specificities, and sometimes they can hardly be overcome.

Traditionally, Bulgarian legislation is characterized by a high level of abstraction of legal norms, and this makes it possible to take into account the specifics of each case when applying the law. Conversely, the acts of the European Union are characterized by the detailed settlement of all issues that are subject to discussion in the legislative procedure. This makes it difficult to implement provisions in the domestic legislation, because, on the one hand, the excessive detailing of the legal framework risks always leaving specific cases without a clear answer, and on the other hand, this approach of excessive detailing creates a visible discrepancy between the style of national and European legislation.

This is also the reason for the adoption of more and more normative acts, that follow the style of European acts, different from the style of national laws. On the one hand, this approach ensures an almost identical content of national normative acts to that of European acts, but on the other, it displaces the codification of law. The desire of the Bulgarian legislator to fully implement the rules of the European acts created a new trend, as some issues related to criminal proceedings are regulated in special laws, which are applied together with the *Code of Criminal Procedure* (*Extradition and European Arrest Warrant Act; European Investigation Order Act; Act on the Recognition, Enforcement and Forwarding of Judicial Instruments Imposing Custodial Sentences or Measures Involving Deprivation of Liberty; Recognition, Execution and Transmission of Decisions on Supervision Measures Other Than Measures Which Require Detention Act; Act on Recognition, Execution and Forwarding of Judgments and Probation Decisions with a View to Exercising Supervision of Probation Measures and Alternative Sanctions; Recognition, Execution, Issuance and Transmission of Property Freezing Orders Act; Recognition, Execution and Transmission of Confiscation or Seizure Orders and Decisions Imposing Financial Penalties Act; European Protection Order Act*). This creates a danger of internal contradiction in the legislation and ambiguity for citizens.

In particular, it makes it difficult for citizens to know the rules and their easier understanding and interpretation, given not only their increasing quantity, but also their quality. And as Voltaire says, "The multitude of laws is, in a state, what the great number of doctors is: a sign of illness and weakness".[96]

96 Voltaire Lettre à l'abbé Moussinot, le 14 septembre 1736: "La multitude des lois est, dans un état, ce qu'est le grand nombre de médecins: signe de maladie et de faiblesse." <https://citations.ouest-france.fr/citation-voltaire/multitude-lois-etat-grand-nombre-117047.html> accessed July 2024.

CHAPTER 5

# Croatia: Effective Enforcement of Mutual Recognition Instruments and Cases Exposing Political Influences on EU Judicial Cooperation

*Zlata Đurđević, Elizabeta Ivičević Karas, Marin Bonačić and Zoran Burić*

## 1 The Implementation of the EU Mutual Recognition Instruments[1]

In addition to international agreements, international cooperation in criminal matters in Croatia is regulated by two distinct Acts, one for classical mutual legal assistance outside the European Union (EU) and the other for supranational cooperation with EU Member States. The 2004 *Act on mutual legal assistance in criminal matters*[2] regulates cooperation with States outside the EU or with States that opted out from the Area of freedom, security and justice. The EU mutual recognition instruments are implemented in a separate *Act on Judicial Cooperation in Criminal Matters with the Member States of the European Union* (AJCCMEU).[3] Besides the AJCCMEU, implementation of some instruments required legislative amendments of other criminal justice laws, including the Criminal Procedure Act, which covers aspects such as arrest procedures, detention, the rights of individuals, evidence collection and pre-trial supervision, and the Criminal Code, which defines the criminal offenses for which EU mutual recognition decisions can be issued.

The AJCCMEU is a comprehensive law that serves as the foundation for implementing various EU mutual recognition instruments. It was adopted before Croatia's accession to the EU in 2013, when Croatia, as a candidate country, was obliged to establish the necessary legal framework for the

1 Đurđević wrote sections 1, 2.1, 2.2.1 and 2.2.3; Ivičević Karas wrote section 4; Bonačić wrote section 3.1, 3.3–3.5; Burić wrote sections 2.2.2, 2.3 and 2.4; and Ivičević Karas and Bonačić wrote section 3.2.

2 Act on International Legal Assistance in Criminal Matters (*Zakon o međunarodnoj pravnoj pomoći u kaznenim stvarima*) The Official Gazette No. 178/04.

3 Act on Judicial Cooperation in Criminal Matters with the Member States of the European Union (*Zakon o pravosudnoj suradnji u kaznenim stvarima s državama članicama Europske unije*) Official Gazette No. 91/10, 81/13, 124/13, 26/15, 102/17, 68/18, 70 /19, 141/20, 18/24.

© ZLATA ĐURĐEVIĆ ET AL., 2025 | DOI:10.1163/9789004705791_007 implementation of EU framework decisions and directives on judicial cooperation in criminal matters. The AJCCMEU has been amended eight times so far and has implemented 20 framework decisions and directives, including the EAW FD, the EIO D, and the Regulation 1805/2018.

The AJCCMEU consists of general provisions that refer to all implemented EU instruments of mutual recognition, after which, as a rule, each individual instrument is implemented in a separate chapter. The general part contains the basic terms and principles, the central authorities responsible for coordinating the implementation and execution of mutual recognition instruments, the competent national judicial authorities, the procedure for communication between Croatian authorities and their counterparts in other EU Member States, the list of criminal offenses for which verification of the double criminality is excluded, as well as provisions on Eurojust and joint investigation teams. Since all EU mutual recognition instruments in Croatia have been implemented by the AJCCMEU, the overview of the implementation roadmap follows the amendments of this Act.

The EAW FD has been enforced in Croatia for more than two decades, resulting in a well-established, effective, and comprehensive use of the EAW, as well as enduring political and legal implications that shake Croatian society and the legal system. In contrast, the implementation of the EIO and the Regulation 1805/2018 has a significantly lower critical profile in both legislation and case law. Therefore, we will focus more extensively on the EAW than on the other two instruments.

## 2 European Arrest Warrant: Critical Profiles in Legislation and Case Law

The legislative and judicial implementation of the EAW in Croatia has been and remains one of the most controversial legal issues that has been agonising the national political and legal scene for decades. It spans from the pre-accession period in the early 2000s[4] through legislative implementation in 2010, which served only to meet the formal requirements during the accession

4 Croatia acceded to the European Union on 1 July 2013, after a lengthy and difficult process of accession that started with signing the Stabilisation and Association Agreement in October 2001. It applied for EU membership on 21 February 2003, acquired candidate status in June 2004, accession negotiations were launched on 3 October 2005 and closed on 30 June 2011.

negotiations, to the true enactment in 2013, immediately preceding accession on 1 July 2013. This enactment, however, led to long-standing political and legal challenges, including an infringement procedure initiated by the Commission in 2021, which resulted in the latest AJCCMEU amendments in 2024.

From a practical perspective, the enforcement of the EAW in Croatia has been undeniably successful. Since its introduction in 2013, Croatian prosecutors and courts have readily accepted the use of the EAW. In 2014, 21 EAWs were issued, 73 were received.[5] Over the subsequent decade, the number of issued EAWs increased multiple times, while the number of received EAWs doubled. In 2016, 51 EAWs were issued and 154 were received, whereas in 2023, 102 EAWs were issued and 167 were received.[6]

This chapter, after a detailed review and analysis of these legislative reforms, examines the two most significant Croatian EAW criminal cases, one related to the statute of limitation and the surrender of nationals (Perković and Mustač) and the other to the *ne bis in idem* principle (*Hernardi* case), addresses human rights violations as grounds for refusal of an EAW in legislation and case law, and provides an overview of procedural issues including the rights of the accused and other parties, remedies, and execution procedures.

### 2.1 *Implementation of the Framework Decision on European Arrest Warrant*

#### 2.1.1 Pre-accession Nominal Implementation in 2010

The implementation of the EAW FD, which was one of the benchmarks of Croatia's accession negotiations, initially required amending the Constitution. After heated political debates, largely influenced by the uneasy experience of surrendering its own citizens to the International Criminal Court, the necessary constitutional amendments were adopted in June 2010.[7] These amendments abandoned the previous constitutional guarantee of a complete ban on the extradition of Croatian nationals to other States, thereby paving the way for Croatian accession to the EU.[8]

---

5 State Attorney's Office, 'Report of the State Attorney's Office of the Republic of Croatia for 2014 (Izvješće Državnog odvjetništva Republike Hrvatske za 2014. godinu)' (Zagreb, April 2015) 155.

6 Chief State Attorney of the Republic of Croatia, 'Report of the Chief State Attorney of the Republic of Croatia on the work of State attorneys' offices in 2023 (Izvješće Glavnoga državnog odvjetnika Republike Hrvatske o radu državnih odvjetništava u 2023. godini)' (Zagreb, April 2024) 260.

7 Official Gazette No. 76/10 of 18 June 2010.

8 'A citizen of the Republic of Croatia cannot be expelled from the Republic of Croatia, nor can his citizenship be revoked, nor can he be extradited to another country, except when a decision on extradition or surrender made in accordance with an international treaty or the

In July 2010, the AJCCMEU[9] was adopted to implement the EAW FD into Croatian legislation, and it was supposed to enter into force on 1 July 2013, the date of Croatia's accession to the EU. Croatia generally had very limited discretion in implementing EU measures and as concerns EAW FD was under special scrutiny from the European Commission, not only as a candidate country but also due to negative assessments of the existing EAW implementing legislation in other Member States.[10] Special attention was paid to the reasons for the non-execution of the EAW, spotted as one of the weakest points of its implementation in Member States, and described by the European Commission as "a patchwork which is contrary to the Framework Decision."[11] Accordingly, the mandatory and optional grounds for refusal to execute an EAW, as outlined in Arts 3 and 4 of the EAW FD, have been incorporated almost *verbatim* into Arts 20 and 21 of the AJCCMEU. No additional grounds for refusal were introduced, and executing judicial authorities have been given discretionary power to apply the optional grounds for refusal, guided by the principles of effective cooperation, opportunity, and the right to a fair trial (Art 21(1) AJCCMEU).[12] Although the Act was adopted correctly from the perspective of EU law, the Croatian legislator's primary objective was to fulfill a benchmark for closing Chapter 23, 'Justice, Freedom and Security,' of the *acquis communautaire*, rather than genuinely implementing the EAW in the Croatian criminal justice system.

### 2.1.2 Politically and Legally Contentious Implementation in 2013

From July 2010 until Croatia's accession in July 2013, the legislator had sufficient time to ensure practical implementation of the AJCCMEU. However, no efforts were made to provide the necessary technical, personnel, and educational prerequisites. Consequently, three months before accession to the EU, the Act was found to be inapplicable and had to be quickly amended. As a

acquis of the European Union must be carried out'. Art 9 of the Constitution of the Republic of Croatia.

9 Official Gazette No. 91-2569/10 of 23 July 2010.

10 See Report from the Commission on the implementation since 2005 of the EAW FD [COM(2007) 407 final]. E.g., point 3.6: '... the transposition of the grounds for non-execution in particular indicates that the principle of mutual recognition is not fully observed in a significant number of Member States'.

11 Annex to the Report from the Commission on the implementation since 2005 of the EAW FD [COM (2007) 407 final], 11.

12 See Zlata Đurđević, Iris Goldner Lang and Maja Munivrana Vajda, 'Croatia – National Report', in Julia Laffranque (ed), *The Area of Freedom, Security and Justice, including Information Society Issues – FIDE XXV National Reports* (University of Tartu Press 2012) 235–259.

result, on 28 June 2013, three days before accession, the Croatian Parliament adopted comprehensive amendments to the AJCCMEU,[13] revising almost all Arts and adding 30 new ones.[14]

However, while these amendments led to the genuine and practical implementation of the EAW in the Croatian institutional setting, there were two amended provisions that attracted huge domestic and European political and public attention as they allegedly violated EU law. One was the introduction of a temporal limitation on the EAW, which prevented authorities from surrendering anyone suspected of a crime committed before the 7 August 2002. Such a clause, which represented one of the key elements of harmonization of national law in this area, could have been inserted during the negotiations when the European Commission could decide whether it accepts such an important limitation of the most important instrument of criminal justice cooperation in the EU or not. Subsequent important legislative amendments, after the European Commission had verified Croatia's compliance, compromised accession negotiations by enabling the institutional and procedural framework for cooperation with EU Member States in criminal matters to escape the Commission's scrutiny. Under severe criticism and the threat of financial sanctions from the European Commission, the temporal limitation was removed on 1 January 2015.[15]

The second critical change was related to transforming the five grounds for optional non-execution of the EAW (Art 4 (1–5) EAW FD) into grounds for mandatory non-execution. The shift of codifying the statute of limitations on prosecution as a mandatory ground for refusal unleashed the political and legal controversy that has marked Croatian political and judicial life to date, with its extensive consequences discussed in detail below.[16]

#### 2.1.3 The 2024 Amendment Prompted by the EU Infringement Proceedings: Broadening the EAW Scope of Application

Due to the deficiencies in the transposition, as for the other countries, the European Commission decided on 23 September 2021 to initiate infringement

13 Act amending the Act on Judicial Cooperation in Criminal Matters with the Member States of the European Union of 28.06.2013, (*Zakon o izmjenama i dopunama Zakona o pravosudnoj suradnji u kaznenim stvarima s državama članicama Europske unije*), Official Gazette No. 81-1708/13.

14 See Zlata Đurđević, 'Lex Perković ima čak i gramatičke pogreške' (Tportal, 28 June 2013) <www.tportal.hr/vijesti/clanak/lex-perkovic-ima-cak-i-gramaticke-pogreske-20130628> accessed 15 July 2024.

15 E.g., Euroactive Reuters, 'Croatia surrenders on EU arrest warrant' (Euractiv, 29 August 2013) <www.euractiv.com/section/justice-home-affairs/news/croatia-surrenders-on-eu-arrest-warrant/> accessed 5 June 2024.

16 See *infra*, § 2.2.1. Statute of limitation and surrender of nationals.

proceedings against Croatia by issuing official warnings for failing to properly transmit the EAW FD.[17] Although the Commission gave Croatia only two months to take the necessary measures to ensure the correct transposition, the infringement case is still active, as Croatia only adopted the required amendment of the AJCCMEU on 8 February 2024, almost three years later.

In particular, shortcomings were identified in relation to the transposition of optional grounds for non-execution.[18] Hence, the 2024 Amendment of the AJCCMEU provided the legislative epilogue to the 2013 Amendment by restoring the provisions on the grounds for mandatory and optional non-execution of the EAW from the original 2010 text of the AJCCMEU, literally rewriting the provisions on three grounds for mandatory non-execution (Art 3 EAW FD) and seven grounds for optional non-execution of the EAW (Art 4 EAW FD).

The 2024 Amendment also broadened the scope of the EAW regarding the double criminality requirement in two other ways. Firstly, the verification of double criminality is excluded in the case of recognition of a financial penalty, regardless of the prescribed prison sentence for the committed criminal offense (Art 3(3) AJCCMEU). Secondly, in line with the CJEU interpretation of the double criminality requirement in *KL* judgment C-168/21,[19] in case when EAW refers to several criminal offences some of which do not meet the conditions for issuing the EAW in relation to the length of the sentence or measure (punishable by at least 12 months or conviction of at least four months), an EAW can also be issued for these criminal offences (Art 17(3) AJCCMEU).[20] The High Criminal Court, in accordance with the KL judgment, has already interpreted this provision as stating that there is no obstacle to surrendering the requested person for executing a prison sentence for a single criminal offense composed of multiple acts, even if one of these acts, for which the requested person was sentenced to a custodial sentence, constitutes a misdemeanour.[21]

---

17 INFR(2021)2111, 23/09/2021, Incomplete and incorrect transposition of the EAW FD by Croatia, https://ec.europa.eu/atwork/applying-eu-law/infringements-proceedings/infringement_decisions.

18 See Letter of formal notice 'European Arrest Warrant: Commission calls on CROATIA and FINLAND to address shortcomings in transposition of EU rules', https://ec.europa.eu/commission/presscorner/detail/EN/INF_21_4681.

19 The KL judgment, Case C-168/21 *Procureur général près la cour d'appel d'Angers* [2022] ECLI:EU:C:2022:558

20 See Pavelin, Kapikul, *Izmjene Zakona o pravosudnoj suradnji u kaznenim stvarima s državama članicama*, Ius-Info, 13.02.2024.

21 '7.4. In this case, the requested person has been sentenced to two years and four months (of which the person still has to serve 1 year, 10 months, and 10 days) for the criminal offense of aggravated theft and a misdemeanour. There is no doubt that the offense of aggravated theft meets the requirement of dual criminality. Therefore, in accordance with (...) the CJEU's interpretation in the KL judgment, it can be concluded that there is no obstacle to surrendering the requested person on the grounds that one of the acts for

Although such a solution has already been applied in practice,[22] The 2024 Amendment expressly provided that the domestic court will proceed with the recognition and execution of the EAW when the issuing State fails to provide the necessary documentation for the execution of the foreign sanction within the deadline set by the court (Art 22(4) AJCCMEU). The 2024 Amendment of the AJCCMEU also corrected other shortcomings that the European Commission warned about in the letter of official notice related to time limits for deciding if the person does not consent (Art 32(2) AJCCMEU), temporary transfer (Art 33 and 34 AJCCMEU), and privileges and immunities (Art 25 AJCCMEU).[23]

## 2.2 *Grounds for Non-recognition and Non-execution*

### 2.2.1 Statute of Limitation and Surrender of Nationals: Perković and Mustač Cases

Croatia is likely one of the few EU Member States whose courts have given clear precedence to the concept of mutual trust over the protection of its citizens and the prohibition of their surrender in case of time-barred offences according to national law. This judicial interpretation was provoked by the transformation of the statute of limitations from an optional to a mandatory ground for non-execution, introduced by the 2013 Amendment to the AJCCMEU, commonly known as "Lex Perković". Namely, it was generally alleged in the Croatian media[24] that its concealed political aim was to prevent the surrender of Josip Perković and Zdravko Mustač, former members of the Yugoslav and Croatian intelligence agencies suspected of participating in the organisation of the murder of Stjepan Đureković, a Croatian emigrant in Germany, in Műnich in 1983, for whom Germany had issued EAWs.[25] To enable the surrender of Perković

---

which the person was sentenced to deprivation of liberty is a misdemeanour'. VKSRH, I Kž-eun-13/2024-5, 19 March 2024.

22 Pavelin Kapikul (n 20).

23 Final Draft of the Law on Amendments to the Law on Judicial Cooperation in Criminal Matters with the Member States of the European Union, Government of the Republic of Croatia of 25. 5. 2023 (Konačni prijedlog zakona o izmjenama i dopunama Zakona o pravosudnoj suradnji u kaznenim stvarima s državama članicama Europske unije, Vlada Republike Hrvatske) 12, PZE_502.pdf (accessed 5 July 2024).

24 See e.g. www.vecernji.hr/vijesti/hrvatska-zbog-perkovica-mijenja-zakon-o-ekstradiciji-570793; www.vecernji.hr/vijesti/nalog-za-uhicenje-perkovica-stize-prvog-dana-ulaska-u-eu-570258; https://hr.wikipedia.org/wiki/Europski_uhidbeni_nalog (accessed 5 July 2024).

25 For the chronicle of the Perković Mustač cases, see Hina, 'Od tjeralice do izručenja i presude: Kronologija slučaja Perković-Mustač' (Indexhr, 03 August 2013) <www.index.hr/vijesti/clanak/od-tjeralice-do-izrucenja-i-presude-kronologija-slucaja-perkovicmustac/910395.aspx> accessed 5 July 2024.

and Mustač to Germany for crimes committed 30 years earlier, which were time-barred for prosecution in Croatia, and to bypass the newly introduced implementing law, Croatian courts devised an infamous interpretation. This interpretation exempted the verification of the statute of limitations for prosecution for offences where the principle of double criminality does not apply.

It is generally accepted in international and European law, as well as in the theory of mutual legal assistance, that a double criminality requirement is considered to be a substantive requirement referring to the identity of norms in criminal codes, necessitating the criminalization of the act in both the issuing and executing states. The double criminality concept, which questions whether the behaviour constitutes an offence in both states, does not include the statute of limitations for the prosecution.[26] The application of the statute of limitations on prosecution presupposes an act that constitutes a criminal offense for which prosecution could be conducted within a time limit prescribed by law. Therefore, these are distinct legal requirements with no overlapping content and are not mutually exclusive, and both requirements must be checked separately. This distinction is also recognised by the EAW FD, which regulates these two concepts as separate legal issues, and two different optional grounds for refusal.[27]

This interpretation was also adopted by Croatian courts in extradition and surrender procedures[28] prior to the *Perković* and *Mustač* cases, where they assessed double criminality and the statute of limitations separately, ensuring that both legal requirements were independently verified. Since these cases, the Croatian Supreme Court introduced the rule that where the verification of double criminality is excluded (Art 2(2) EAW FD), the verification of the

26 On the content and the function of the double criminality principle see Petter Asp, Andrew von Hirsch, Dan Frände, *Double Criminality and Transnational Investigative Measures in EU Criminal Proceedings: Some Issues of Principle* (2006) 11 ZIS 512, 512–13; Neil Boister, *A History of Double Criminality in Extradition* (2023) *Journal of the History of International Law*, 25(2) 218; On the diverse concept of the double criminality, none of which includes the statute of limitations, see G. Vermeulen, W.D. Bondt, Charlotte Ryckman, *Rethinking international cooperation in criminal matters in the EU: moving beyond actors, bringing logic back, footed in reality* (Maklu, 2012) 107.

27 E.g., Poland executes an EAW even for an offence that is statute-barred under its own law, but because it is the optional ground for refusal. See Gudrun Hochmayr, 'A Comparative Analysis of Statutes of Limitation', in Walter Gropp and Gudrun Hochmayr (eds), *Die Verjährung als Herausforderung für die grenzüberschreitende Zusammenarbeit in Strafsachen* (Nomos 2021) 708, 781.

28 See the decisions of the Supreme Court cited in Josip Čule, Danka Hržina, *Primjena europskog uhidbenog naloga u Republici Hrvatskoj – očekivanja i stvarnost* (2013) 20 Hrvatski ljetopis za kazneno pravo i praksu (Zagreb), 715, 746.

statute of limitations is also excluded.[29] This interpretation, which was contrary to European law, to the principle of reciprocity in interstate relations, to the previous jurisprudence of the Supreme Court, to the concept of double criminality in the theory of criminal law and international legal assistance,[30] was challenged before the Constitutional Court of the Republic of Croatia, which held that it was not competent to decide on the judicial interpretation of legal provisions in the surrender procedure under the EAW.[31]

The judicial interpretation of the Supreme Court, according to which Croatian courts are obliged to surrender Croatian citizens to EU States for criminal offenses whose prosecution or execution of the sentence has expired in Croatia, has been widely criticised by the Croatian academic community members[32] as well as a number of other experts.[33] However, after the surrender of Perković and Mustač in 2014,[34] it has become established case law[35] and, for example, resulted in the surrender of a person in 2014 for acts of theft that were committed from 1985 to 1987, i.e., almost 30 years before.[36] The Croatian courts, to justify their interpretation, have expressly assumed the role

29 'When executing an EAW, the court shall not apply domestic legal provisions regarding the statute of limitations for a criminal prosecution, because the court does not verify double criminality', VSRH, Kž-eun 11/13, 20 September 2013. 'The statute of limitation is organically linked to the prescribed punishment for a criminal offence' and therefore, 'the statute of limitations is an integral part of the concept of double criminality'. VSRH, Kž-eun 2/14-5; VSRH, Kž-eun 8/14-4.

30 See Davor Derenčinović, 'Doseg isključenja provjere dvostruke kažnjivosti iz Zakona o pravosudnoj suradnji u kaznenim stvarima s državama članicama Europske unije' (2014) 21 Hrvatski ljetopis za kazneno pravo i praksu 249.

31 The Constitutional Court held that the surrender procedure is not a criminal procedure but rather a *sui generis* judicial proceeding, the aim of which is to enable criminal prosecution and not to decide on the guilt of the suspect. Therefore, the scope of potential constitutional complaints is very narrow, and the Constitutional Court 'is not allowed to question the interpretations of domestic courts regarding domestic law and its application in concrete cases of surrender on the basis of an EAW, unless reasons are presented indicating that the assessment of the courts in a concrete case was 'flagrantly and obviously arbitrary'. U-III-351/2014, 24 January 2014.

32 E.g., following professors of Croatian law faculties Petar Novoselec, Igor Martinović, Ivo Josipović, Davor Derenčinović, Elizabeta Ivičević Karas, Zoran Burić, Zlata Đurđević.

33 E.g., Josip Čule, Danka Hržina, Miljenko Giunio, Tomislav Sokol i dr.

34 In August 2016, Perković and Mustač were in Germany both sentenced to life in prison for abetting the murder of Đureković.

35 E.g. ruling from 2021, VSRH Kž-eun 1/2021-4.

36 VSRH, Kž-eun 20/14-6, 15 April, 2014.

of staunch proponents of loyal cooperation, efficiency and trust in the EU in their decisions.[37]

Unlike the Croatian Supreme Court and the Constitutional Court, the courts of Germany, France, Austria, Italy, Sweden, the Netherlands, Slovenia, and numerous other EU countries refuse to hand over requested persons if prosecution is statute-barred, regardless of the type of criminal offense.[38] Thus, Croatian citizens are better protected in Germany than in Croatia, because German courts regularly refuse to execute EAW issued by Croatian courts due to the statute of limitations when it comes not only to German citizens, but also other EU citizens, including Croatians.[39]

However, the European Commission did not abandon its initial interpretation of the implementation of the grounds for refusal of the EAW, according to which the intention of the EAW FD was that the grounds for optional non-execution should be determined by judges and not by the national legislator. It was a violation of EU law to make an optional ground for refusal

37 VSRH, Kž-eun 5/14-4 and Kž-eun 14/14-4: 'To achieve the goals and to respect the principles expressed in EU law, national courts are bound to apply national law in the light of the letter and spirit of EU law. This means that national law must be interpreted in the application as much as possible in the light of the wording and the purpose of relevant framework decisions and directives in order to achieve the result pursued by such framework decisions and directives'.

County court in Varaždin, Kv-eun 2/14: 'Criminal proceedings in another State have priority over criminal proceedings conducted before a Croatian court'.

VSRH, Kž-eun 17/14-4 [2014]: 'The EAW is an instrument of mutual judicial cooperation between the Member States of the EU that is based on the principles of mutual recognition between the Member States and effective cooperation, and contains a legal obligation and moral responsibility of the national courts of the Member States of execution to grant the surrender of the person requested, unless there are the few and expressly prescribed grounds for refusal to surrender'.

38 Certainly, the most famous decision of the German courts not to extradite a person because of the statute of limitations is the refusal to extradite Sören Kama, a member of the Danish SS unit and a Dane who acquired German citizenship in 1956. Denmark had asked for his surrender on the basis of an EAW for the murder of a number of journalists in Copenhagen in 1943. In 2007, the appeals court in Műnich decided that the surrender did not relate to a case of qualified murder (Mord), which is not subject to a statute of limitations, but rather to a case of ordinary manslaughter (Totschlag) and that therefore, the prosecution was time-barred. See Đurđević, Zlata in: Iris Goldner Lang, Zlata Đurđević and Mislav Mataija, *The Constitution of Croatia in the Perspective of European and Global Governance*, in Anneli Albi and Samo Bardutzky (eds), *The Role of National Constitutions in European and Global Governance: Democracy, Rights, the Rule of Law. National Reports* (T.M.C. Asser Press 2019) 1139, 1160–62.

39 Thus, Germany rejected the EAW issued by the Croatian court for Croatian citizens from the Rilović family for economic crimes because the statute of limitations had expired. See Derenčinović (n 30) 264.

mandatory,[40] despite the fact that the majority of EU Member States prescribed time-limitations for criminal prosecution as a mandatory reason for refusing surrender based on a EAW (Austria, Belgium, Czech Republic, Finland, France, Greece, Italy, Lithuania, Hungary, Malta, Netherlands, Germany, Slovenia, Slovakia, Sweden).[41] Therefore, as mentioned, the Commission initiated infringement proceedings against all these States in order to force them to give discretion to the courts to decide on a case by case basis whether to surrender a person whose prosecution is time-barred. Such a judicial discretion in executing the EAW raises the rule of law issues with regard to principles of legality (equality before the law) and legal certainty.

### 2.2.2 *Ne bis in idem*: the Hernadi Case

#### 2.2.2.1 *Circumstances of the Case*[42]

Another EAW case that attracted a lot of public and media attention in Croatia is the surrender of Zolt Hernadi, a famous Hungarian businessman best known for his role as the Chairman and CEO of MOL Group, a major Hungarian multinational oil and gas company. In 2003, MOL Group acquired a 25% plus one share stake in INA, the Croatian oil and gas company, from the Croatian government. In the period between 2008 and 2009, MOL increased its stake in INA to 47.16% by purchasing additional shares on the market and through a direct agreement with the Croatian government, thereby succeeding in gaining management control over INA.[43]

On 10 June 2011, the Croatian Office for the Suppression of Corruption and Organized Crime (USKOK) opened an investigation against former Croatian

40 See Report from the Commission on the implementation since 2005 of the EAW FD [COM(2007) 407 final]. E.g., point '3.8.2. Grounds for optional non-execution (Articles 4 and 4a): Articles 4 and 4a of the Framework Decision provide for eight optional grounds for non-execution .... a number of Member States have made all of the transposed grounds mandatory, giving no discretion to their executing authorities. Only a small number of Member States have made all of the transposed grounds optional'.

41 Đurđević, Zlata, *The Constitution of Croatia* (n 38) 1159.

42 Presentation of the facts of the case is based on the author's inspection of the case files of the proceedings conducted against Hernadi before the County Court in Zagreb: 5-K-US-29/15 and Kv-eun-25/2016. Compare Florentino-Gregorio Ruiz Yamuza, *The AY Case – Construing EAW ne bis in idem within the Boundaries of the Preliminary Ruling Reference*, eucrim, 4/2020, 336–343.

43 For the chronicle of the relationship between INA and MOL, see Slavica Cvitanić, 'Velika kronologija INA-MOL Sve je počelo još 2003, dionice MOL-u prodao je i Fond hrvatskih branitelja' (Indexhr, 29 november 2017) <www.index.hr/vijesti/clanak/sve-je-pocelo-2003-donosimo-veliku-kronologiju-inamol/1004098.aspx> accessed 15 July 2024.

prime minister Ivo Sanader and Zolt Hernadi.[44] Sanader, the Croatian prime minister in the incriminated period, was suspected of receiving bribes from Hernadi to help MOL gain management control over INA. USKOK tried to have Hernadi interrogated as a suspect by the Hungarian competent authorities and therefore sent two letters rogatory to Hungary in June and December 2011, but these requests for international legal assistance were refused, with the explanation that undertaking this action would run contrary to Hungarian national interests. In March 2012, a third letter of rogatory was sent; this time, it concerned the delivery of the summons for Hernadi's first interrogation as a suspect by USKOK, but this request was also refused with the same explanation. At the same time, the Croatian authorities were informed that Hungarian authorities, based on information accompanying the letters rogatory sent by the Croatian authorities, had opened an investigation against an unknown person. The investigation was opened on suspicion that a criminal offence of bribery in international relations had been committed; it concluded that there was insufficient evidence of the commission of the alleged offence; it was therefore terminated on 20 January 2012. Hernadi was interrogated as a witness during this investigation.

This cooperation between Croatian and Hungarian national authorities took place in the framework of traditional international legal assistance in criminal matters. Croatia was not a Member State of the EU at the time, so EU instruments of judicial cooperation in criminal matters, including the EAW, could not be used. Letters rogatory were sent and answered on the basis of the European Convention on Mutual Assistance in Criminal Matters from 1959.[45] Pursuant to the provisions of this Convention, Hungary was entitled to refuse to cooperate with Croatia if it considered 'that execution of the request [was] likely to prejudice the sovereignty, security, *ordre public* or other essential interests of its country'.[46]

After Croatia became a member of the EU, on 1 July 2013, EU instruments on judicial cooperation in criminal matters, including the EAW, became available to Croatian judicial authorities. On 1 October 2013, USKOK issued an EAW

44 The third defendant was Damir Polančec, then Vice President of the Government of the Republic of Croatia, Minister of the Economy and Chairman of the Government Commission for Negotiations with MOL. For the course of the criminal proceedings in the INA MOL case up to the decision of the Constitutional Court in 2015, see Zlata Đurđević, *Nedostatni i irelevantni ustavni razlozi za ukidanje kaznenih presuda po ustavnoj tužbi bivšeg predsjednika Vlade RH u predmetu "INA MOL" (Odluka Ustavnog suda RH U-III-4149/2014)* (2018) 25 Hrvatski ljetopis za kaznene znanosti i praksu 261, 262.

45 European Treaty Series – No. 30.

46 Art 2(b) of the Convention.

against Hernadi. Already on 7 October 2013, recognition and execution of this EAW were refused by the competent Hungarian court. The basis for the refusal was the decision of the Hungarian authorities rendered on 20 January 2012, by which the investigation against an unknown person for bribery in international relations – in the framework of which Hernadi had been interrogated as a witness – was terminated. It seems that the Hungarian court considered that recognition and execution of the Croatian EAW and the surrender of Hernadi to Croatia, which would be followed by an investigation into his alleged criminal activities, would represent a violation of the *ne bis in idem* principle.

After the recognition and execution of the Croatian EAW was refused by the Hungarian competent court, also Austria and Germany, to whose territories Hernadi travelled and was occasionally present there, refused to act on the basis of the Croatian EAW, fearing a possible violation of the *ne bis in idem* principle.[47] For the same reason, INTERPOL decided to suspend its red notice for Hernadi in December 2015. Finally, in November 2016, INTERPOL decided to erase the red notice for Hernadi from its system.[48] Croatia did not have access to the Schengen Information System (SIS) at the time, and the fact that the red notice for Hernadi was suspended and then finally erased from the INTERPOL system significantly reduced the possibility that Hernadi would be arrested and surrendered on the basis of the Croatian EAW.

However, the investigation against Hernadi in Croatia continued, and in March 2014, USKOK filed an indictment against Hernadi before the Zagreb County Court and asked the court to try Hernadi *in absentia*. This proposal was accepted, and the trial against Hernadi started in his absence. In December 2015, the Zagreb County Court issued a new EAW against Hernadi, but the Hungarian competent authorities refused to act upon it. They did not refuse to surrender Hernadi but remained silent on the matter, not undertaking any action on the basis of the Croatian EAW. In January 2017, an EAW was again issued by the Zagreb County Court and sent to Hungarian competent authorities, but they again refused to act upon it.

Faced with the silence of the Hungarian competent authorities, the Zagreb County Court addressed the Court of Justice of the EU in May 2017 and asked it to give its opinion on several issues in relation to the interpretation of the

---

47 See 'Austrija i Njemačka suspendirale hrvatsku tjeralicu za Hernadijem' (Ius-Info, 13 November 2015) <https://www.iusinfo.hr/aktualno/dnevne-novosti/austrija-i-njemacka-suspendirale-hrvatsku-tjeralicu-za-hernadijem-24065> accessed 15 July 2024.

48 See 'Interpol izbrisao međunarodnu tjeralicu za Hernadijem' (Lider, 19 November 2016) <https://lidermedia.hr/aktualno/biznis-i-politika/hrvatska/interpol-izbrisao-medunarodnu-tjeralicu-za-hernadijem-121930> accessed 15 July 2024.

EAW FD. Particularly, Zagreb County Court wanted to know how provisions of Arts 1(2), 3(2) and 4(3) should be interpreted in light of the circumstances of this specific case.

#### 2.2.2.2 *Judgment of the CJEU*

##### 2.2.2.2.1 Obligation of the Executing Authority to Decide on Every EAW Forwarded to It

Art 1(2) of the EAW FD stipulates that 'Member States shall execute any European arrest warrant on the basis of the principle of mutual recognition and in accordance with the provisions of this Framework Decision' The Zagreb County Court asked if the silence of the Hungarian authorities and their refusal to act on two EAWs that were issued by that court against Hernadi was in compliance with Art 1(2) of the EAW FD. The Zagreb County Court argued that the facts underlying the EAW issued by USKOK were not the same as the facts underlying the EAWs issued by the Zagreb County Court. The EAW issued by USKOK, whose recognition and execution were refused by the competent Hungarian court in October 2013, was issued during the investigation. In the meantime, new evidence had been gathered against Hernadi, and suspicion that he had committed a criminal offence had solidified. So, the case had been transferred from USKOK to the Zagreb County Court. The Hungarian Government maintained that there was no need to decide on the EAWs issued by the County Court in Zagreb since they were issued against the same person within the same criminal proceedings as the EAW which has been issued by USKOK and which has already been decided on.

The CJEU ruled that, by not replying to the EAWs issued by the Zagreb County Court, the Hungarian competent authorities acted in breach not only of Art 1(2) of the EAW FD but also of the provisions of Arts 15(1), 17(1) and (6), and 22.[49] The Court reminded that recognition and execution of EAWs is a rule in the framework of judicial cooperation in criminal matters in the EU, which may be refused only when a limited list of grounds for refusal of cooperation are invoked. Furthermore, cooperation, which is based on the EAW, is regulated by strict time limits, demand or urgency, the obligation to state reasons for any refusal to recognize and execute an EAW, and the duty of swift and direct communication between the issuing and the executing authority. There is, therefore, a duty of the executing judicial authority to adopt a decision on any EAW forwarded to it, even when, in that Member State, a ruling has already been made on a previous EAW concerning the same person and the same acts,

49 Case C-268/17 AY [2018] ECLI:EU:C:2018:602, para. 32–36.

but the second EAW has been issued only on account of the indictment, in the issuing Member State, of the requested person.[50]

#### 2.2.2.2.2 Scope and Limits of the *Ne bis in idem* Principle in EAW Framework Decision

The Zagreb County Court also wanted to know whether a decision terminating the investigation against an unknown person, which was conducted for the offence of bribery in international relations and in the framework of which Hernadi was only interrogated as a witness, is enough to qualify as one of the grounds for refusal of cooperation recognized by the EAW FD which are based on the *ne bis in idem* principle. When it comes to the application of the *ne bis idem* principle between the Member States of the EU, two grounds for refusal in the EAW FD are inspired by it. The first one is the mandatory ground for refusal of cooperation of Art 3(2).[51] The second one is the optional ground for refusal cited in Art 4(3).[52]

In relation to Art 3(2) of the EAW FD, the Court emphasised that the 'delivery of a 'final judgment' (...) implies that criminal proceedings had previously been instituted against the requested person' and that the principle *ne bis in idem* applies 'only to persons who have been finally judged in a Member State" and 'it does not extend to persons who were merely interviewed in the course of a criminal investigation, such as witnesses'. Since no criminal proceedings were brought against Hernadi in Hungary, he cannot be considered to have been finally judged within the meaning of Art 3(2) of the EAW Framework Decision.[53]

In relation to Art 4(3) of the EAW FD, the Court clarified that it regulates three distinct optional grounds for refusal of cooperation: when judicial authorities of the executing State have decided not to prosecute the offence on which the EAW is based; when judicial authorities of the executing State have decided to halt proceedings in respect of the offence on which the EAW

50 Compare Ruiz Yamuza (n 42).

51 The judicial authority of the Member State of execution (hereinafter 'executing judicial authority') shall refuse to execute the EAW in the following cases: '(...) 2. if the executing judicial authority is informed that the requested person has been finally judged by a Member State in respect of the same acts provided that, where there has been sentence, the sentence has been served or is currently being served or may no longer be executed under the law of the sentencing Member State (...)".

52 The executing judicial authority may refuse to execute the European arrest warrant: (...) '3. where the judicial authorities of the executing Member State have decided either not to prosecute for the offence on which the European arrest warrant is based or to halt proceedings, or where a final judgment has been passed upon the requested person in a Member State, in respect of the same acts, which prevents further proceedings; (...)'.

53 Case C-268/17 (n 49), para. 38–46.

is based; when a final judgment has been passed upon the requested person in a Member State in respect of the same acts, which prevents further proceedings. The Court immediately concluded that the first and the third grounds for refusal were not relevant in this case and went on to consider whether the decision of the Hungarian authorities to terminate the investigation against an unknown person could fall within the second optional ground for refusal regulated by Art 4(3) EAW FD. The Hungarian Government and the Commission maintained that the identity of the person against whom criminal proceedings are brought is irrelevant in the context of this ground for refusal of cooperation and invoked the text of the provision, which refers only to the offence on which the EAW is based, and not to the person requested. The Court considered this interpretation manifestly too broad, entailing a risk that the obligation to execute an EAW could be circumvented. The Court reminded that the second ground for refusal of cooperation from Art 4(3) must be interpreted in light of the need 'to promote the prevention and combating of crime'. It also looked at the provisions of the European Convention on Extradition and its Explanatory Report, which served as the model for Art 4(3) of FD. Finally, the Court concluded that the second optional ground for refusal of cooperation regulated in Art 4(3) – judicial authorities of the executing State have decided to halt proceedings in respect of the offence on which the EAW is based – could not be called upon in a situation where the criminal proceedings in the executing State were not conducted against the requested person.[54] Since investigation in Hungary was conducted against an unknown person and Hernadi was only interrogated as a witness, there was no room for application of this ground for refusal of cooperation in the instant case.[55]

#### 2.2.2.3 *Post CJEU Judgment Development*

Following the decision of the CJEU, the Hungarian competent authorities decided on the EAW issued by the Zagreb County Court and found that it cannot be recognized and executed. The Hungarian court considered that there was a risk that Hernadi would not be guaranteed a fair trial in Croatia. The Court referred to the decisions of the Croatian Constitutional Court and the UNCITRAL Tribunal.[56] In its decision from 24 July 2015, the Croatian Constitutional Court annulled the decisions of the County Court in Zagreb

54 Case C-268/17 (n 49), para. 47–63.

55 Compare Ruiz Yamuza (n 42).

56 Ana Raić Knežević, 'Doznali smo zašto Mađarska neće izručiti Hernadija; pozivaju se na onu zgodnu presudu našeg Ustavnog suda' (Telegram, 23 August 2018) <https://www.telegram.hr/politika-kriminal/doznali-smo-zasto-madarska-nece-izruciti-hernadija-pozivaju-se-na-onu-zgodnu-presudu-naseg-ustavnog-suda> accessed 15 July 2024.

and the Supreme Court of the Republic of Croatia by which Ivo Sanader was found guilty of receiving bribes from Hernadi and sentenced to 7 years and 6 months in prison.[57] On 23 December 2016 the UNCITRAL Tribunal decided in favour of MOL and refused to set aside the contract which was signed between the Croatian government and the company and by which MOL gained management rights in INA. The UNCITRAL tribunal did not find it convincing that the bribe was at the heart of the contract.[58]

In December 2019, Sanader and Hernadi, who was tried in absence, were convicted for corruption in the case INA-MOL. Sanader was sentenced to six and Hernadi to two years in prison. The judgment was confirmed by the Croatian Supreme Court and it became final in October 2021.[59]

Proceedings before the CJEU were not the only proceedings before a European court originating from this case. In 2015, Hernadi filed an application before the ECtHR.[60] He complained that the Republic of Croatia violated his right to freedom of movement guaranteed under Art 2 of Protocol No. 4, arguing that he was effectively prohibited from leaving Hungarian territory as a result of the detention order and the EAW issued by the Croatian authorities. Hernadi claimed that the interference with his freedom of movement caused by the EAWs had been unlawful and unjustified. The ECtHR did not address all the parties' arguments since it found that the applicant did not properly exhaust all available domestic legal remedies and thus did not provide the national authorities with the opportunity to address the particular alleged Convention violation. His application was, therefore, declared inadmissible by the Court.[61]

#### 2.2.2.4 *Preliminary Conclusion*

The Hernadi case shows how challenging EU judicial cooperation in criminal matters can be in cases that are politically sensitive. One of the main goals of developing an EU-specific system of judicial cooperation in criminal matters

57 For an analysis of this highly disputed decision of the Constitutional Court, see Đurđević (n 44).

58 Trishna S. Menon, 'UNCITRAL tribunal dismisses allegations of Hungarian investor's bribery and refuses to set aside contract with Croatia' (IISD, 21 December 2017) <www.iisd.org/itn/en/2017/12/21/uncitral-tribunal-dismisses-allegations-hungarian-investors-bribery-refuses-set-aside-contract-with-croatia-republic-croatia-mol-hungarian-oil-gas-plc-pca-case-2014-15-trishna-menon/> accessed 15 July 2024.

59 Ivana Jakelić, 'Vrhovni sud potvrdio presudu: Kako je osuđen Sanader – 10 milijuna eura mita' (Vecerni list, 25 October 2010) <www.vecernji.hr/vijesti/vrhovni-sud-potvrdio-presudu-kako-je-osuden-sanader-10-milijuna-eura-mita-1533962> accessed 15 July 2024.

60 Hernardi v. Croatia (ECtHR (First Section) 3 September 2019).

61 ibid 95.

was to create a system immune to political considerations based on cooperation between judicial (rather than political) authorities regulated by clear legal norms (rather than extra-legal interests and considerations). However, social, economic, and political realities can be quite convincing and present a serious obstacle to the proper functioning of an effective system of judicial cooperation in criminal matters in the EU.

### 2.2.3 Protection of Fundamental Rights and Principle of Proportionality

#### 2.2.3.1 *Legislative Amendment in 2017*

As in most Member States, in Croatia the initial implementation of the EAW FD did not include human rights violations as grounds for refusal of an EAW. Following the CJEU judgment in the *Aranyosi* and *Caldararu* case of 2016, Croatia amended the AJCCMEU accordingly. The amendment of 2017[62] introduced the new Art 3.a of the AJCCMEU entitled 'The principle of respecting fundamental rights'. It binds the competent authorities to issue orders and decisions that are proportional to the specific needs of each individual case (Art 3.a (1)). This entails that courts must apply the principle of proportionality and balance the right to respect private and family life with the surrender procedure and the interests of prosecution. Additionally, it clarifies that procedures under this Act are not exempt from the obligation to respect the fundamental rights and freedoms defined by the Charter of Fundamental Rights of the European Union (henceforth: Charter) (Art 3.a (2)). Therefore, as in EAW proceedings, if there is a real risk of violating Art 4 of the Charter, i.e., Art 3 of the ECHR, prohibiting torture and inhuman or degrading treatment, the surrender must be refused.

#### 2.2.3.2 *The Principle of Proportionality and Respect for Private and Family Life*

Although these international human rights obligations have bound Croatia long before their inclusion in the AJCCMEU and represent constitutional guarantees, Croatian courts in the last decade generally did not consider human rights violations as a ground for refusal of the EAW, showing a very high level of trust in criminal justice systems of other Member States. Regarding the principle of proportionality, the Supreme Court has consistently held that 'personal,

62 Act amending the Act on Judicial Cooperation in Criminal Matters with the Member States of the European Union of 18.10.2017. (*Zakon o izmjenama i dopunama Zakona o pravosudnoj suradnji u kaznenim stvarima s državama članicama Europske unije*), Official Gazette No. 102/ 2017.

family, or health reasons'[63] do not influence the decision to approve a surrender request but may serve as grounds for a temporary postponement (Art 23(4) EAW FD) of the surrender in cases of serious humanitarian reasons, such as a clear threat to the life or health according to Art 35 (3) of the AJCCMEU.[64] It was claimed that these reasons can be taken into consideration only after the decision on the surrender becomes final and therefore, e.g. 'the health issues of the requested person do not constitute an obstacle for a substantive decision on the EAW but can be the subject of determination and assessment only in the process of its execution, i.e., the surrender of the requested person after the decision approving the surrender becomes final'.[65]

However, an exception to this approach is found in the High Criminal Court ruling of 26 May 2022 concerning the surrender to Poland of a mother of two children, one aged 15 years and one 9 months, for conducting criminal proceedings for fraud. In this decision, the Croatian court has, for the first time (and only), invoked Art 3.a of the AJCCMEU as concerns the principle of proportionality and the right for respect to the family and private life of Art 8 of the ECHR.[66] It said that before executing the EAW it is necessary to obtain data on the private and family circumstances of the requested person, on the capabilities of other individuals (grandmother) to care for the children, especially the child under one year of age, considered to be an infant.[67] It should be assessed whether the surrender is proportional to the specific needs of this case, taking into account where and how long the requested person has resided in Croatia, the time of commission, severity and circumstances of the criminal offense, the best interests of the requested person's children according to Art 3 of the Convention on the Rights of the Child, which includes the child's right to protection and care, as well as the maintenance of personal and direct contact with parents.[68]

---

63 VSRH, Kž-eun 44/2019-4, 28 November 2019. See also VSRH, Kž-eun 8/13-4, 22 August 2013; VSRH, 19 Kv-eun-2/14-7z, 9 January, 2014; VSRH Kž-eun 25/2019-4, 9 July, 2019.

64 VSRH, Kž-eun 39/2018-4, 8 January 2019, VSRH, Kž-eun 44/2019-4, 28 November 2019.

65 VSRH, Kž-eun 6/2020-4, 19 February 2020.

66 VKSRH, I Kž-eun-10/2022-6, of 26 May 2022, § 7–10.

67 The High Criminal Court, upheld the appeal stating that there would be no one to care for the children in the event of extradition, as their grandmother is of advanced age and in poor health. The court of first instance did not previously verify the claims of the requested person and obtain data from the competent Social Welfare Center about the private and family circumstances of the requested person." ibid § 5.1.

68 'The court will apply the criteria for assessing proportionality and obstacles arising from the right to family and private life outlined in several decisions of the ECHR (*Üner v. Netherlands* of 18 October 2006; *Boultif v. Switzerland* of 2 August 2001) and CJEU (Land

This High Criminal Court's ruling from 2022 anticipated the GN judgment in case C-261/22 of 21 December 2023, which set a more stringent threshold by developing a two-step approach as in the *Aranyosi* and *Caldararu* case. In the GN judgment, the CJEU decided that the executing judicial authority can refuse the surrender of mother of young children living with her if, on account of systemic or generalised deficiencies in the condition of detention of mothers of young children and of the care of those children in the issuing Member State, there are substantial grounds for believing that, in the light of their personal situation, the persons concerned will run a real risk of a breach of the right to respect for her private and family life and a disregard for the best interest of her children.[69]

#### 2.2.3.3 *Prohibition of Torture and Inhuman or Degrading Treatment or Punishment*

The standards set by the CJEU in the *Aranyosi* and *Caldararu* cases[70] have been applied in Croatia for the first time in 2023 in the well-covered case in national and European media of the surrender proceedings of Croatian football fans (Bad Blue Boys), who were charged with numerous crimes related to sports events by the Prosecutor's Office in Athens, Greece.[71] The Croatian first-instance courts refused the execution of the EAW because the Greek judicial authorities had not provided sufficient guarantees that the requested persons would not be subjected to inhuman and degrading treatment in a Greek prison, but only general and vague information about the observance

Baden-Württemberg v. Panagiotis Tsakouridis, No. C-145/09, of 23 November 2010)', ibid 10.

69 CJEU, C-261/22, GN, Judgment (Grand Chamber) of 21 December 2023, § 59.

70 CJEU, C-404/15 and C-659/15 PPU – *Aranyosi und Căldăraru*, Judgment of 5 April 2016.

71 In the summer of 2023, more than a hundred members of the Bad Blue Boys (BBB), the ultras group of the Croatian football club Dinamo Zagreb, were arrested in Greece. The arrests followed violent clashes between rival football supporters in Athens, resulting in the tragic death of a young Greek fan, Michalis Katsouris. Greek authorities also issued 11 EAW for the BBB members who fled to Croatia after the incident. The detained BBB faced serious charges, including involvement in the riots and the death of the Greek supporter. After more than four months in detention, they were released when suspicion of the murder shifted toward a Greek fan, as his DNA was found on the knife used to kill Katsouris. The arrests and subsequent developments were widely covered in the media, leading to diplomatic communications between Croatia and Greece and involving the highest-level politicians. See, e.g. total-croatia-news.com/news/whats-happening-with-the-bad-blue-boys-in-greece/; en.wikipedia.org/wiki/Murder_of_Michalis_Katsouris; www.index.hr/tag/1135297/bbb-grcka.aspx; www.euronews.com/2023/08/25/greece-treats-jailed-croatian-football-fans-like-prisoners-of-war-says-president; n1info.hr/english/news/greek-media-dna-on-knife-belongs-to-greek-man-but-is-not-enough-to-charge-him/.

of minimal necessary standards in Greek prisons. The High Criminal Court vacated all first-instance decisions upon the appeals by the public prosecutor and stressed that the refusal of the execution of an EAW is an exception that must be interpreted narrowly.[72] The proof of shortcomings regarding the conditions in Greek prisons stems from the Report of the CPT[73] of 31 August 2023, which was compiled following a visit to *Korydallos* prison, where the requested persons were to be detained. The High Criminal Court specified that it is necessary to specifically and precisely examine whether, under the circumstances of the case, there are serious and established reasons to believe that the requested person, after the surrender, will be exposed to a real risk of being subjected to inhuman and degrading treatment.[74] Therefore, before refusing surrender, specific data must be requested on the institution in which the requested persons will be kept and the conditions of accommodation, such as the personal space available to each detainee in a cell in that prison (especially for a person suffering from asthma), sanitary conditions, and the extent of the detainee's freedom of movement within the prison in accordance with EU standards (CJEU, *Dorobantu*)[75] and the ECHR (*Muršić v. Croatia*).[76]

#### 2.2.3.4 *The Fair Trial Rights*

Additionally, in the same case, the High Criminal Court clarified that the executing authority must verify whether the requested persons in Greece have the possibility to challenge the decision to issue the EAW, particularly its proportionality, by means of a legal remedy that fully meets the requirements of effective judicial protection.[77] This obligation pertains to the fair trial guarantee, which, if at risk of violation, can also prevent the surrender under the EAW. Unfairness at trial in the issuing State is one of the most common grounds for appeal against a surrender decision in Croatia, which the Supreme Court has regularly been dismissing.[78] The Supreme Court, as a rule, refers to

72 VKSRH, I Kž-eun-2/2024-4 of 13 February 2024; VKSRH, I Kž-eun-7/2024-4 of 14 March 2024; VKSRH, I Kž-eun-10/2024-4 of 14 March 2024.

73 European Committee for the Prevention of Torture and Inhuman or Degrading Treatment or Punishment.

74 VKSRH, I Kž-eun-2/2024-4 of 13 February 2024, § 8; VKSRH, I Kž-eun-7/2024-4 of 14 March 2024; VKSRH, § 8; I Kž-eun-10/2024-4 of 14 March 2024, § 8.

75 CJEU, C-128/18 Dumitru-Tudor Dorobantu, Judgment (Grand Chamber) of 15 October 2019.

76 ECtHR, *Muršić v. Croatia* [GC], no. 7334/13, Judgment of 20 October 2016, § 171.

77 VKSRH, I Kž-eun-2/2024-4 of 13 February 2024; VKSRH, I Kž-eun-7/2024-4 of 14 March 2024; VKSRH, I Kž-eun-10/2024-4 of 14 March 2024.

78 See the same Matko Pajčić, *Europski uhidbeni nalog u praksi Vrhovnog suda Republike Hrvatske* (2017) 24 Hrvatski ljetopis za kaznene znanosti i praksu, 553–581, 574.

the *Ahorugeze v. Sweden* judgment, where the ECtHR stated that extradition may be refused if the individual would risk suffering a flagrant denial of a fair trial in the issuing State,[79] but that this is a stringent test, it goes beyond mere irregularities and has to constitute a fundamental violation, amounting to destruction of the very essence, of the right guaranteed by that Art 6.[80] Following the same judgment, the Supreme Court also required that the appellant must adduce evidence capable of proving that there are substantial grounds for believing that s/he would be exposed to a real risk of being subjected to a flagrant denial of justice.[81]

However, Croatian appellate courts have, in several cases, vacated rulings on surrender due to violations of the requested person's defense rights with respect to the right to translation (Art 24(3)(6) of the AJCCMEU). The Supreme Court found a violation of the right to a fair trial because the court did not provide the requested person with a translation of the ruling approving the surrender into Dutch, a language the requested person understands.[82] The High Criminal Court found a violation of defense rights because the court rejected the requested person's proposal to translate the issued EAW into Croatian, instead providing the EAW in Hungarian and English. According to Art 8 of the CPA, the Croatian language and Latin script are used in criminal proceedings in Croatia, and the requested person has the right to translate documentation not in a language they understand.[83] Therefore, besides the translation of the EAW into Croatian being a formal requirement in the procedure of deciding on surrender,[84] it is also a defense right of the requested person, the violation of which leads to a breach of the right to a fair trial.

#### 2.2.3.5 *Preliminary Conclusion*

At the legislative level, the 2017 amendment to the AJCCMEU introduced Art 3.a, which explicitly mandates respect for fundamental rights and requires that orders and decisions be proportional to the needs of individual cases. Despite these long-standing international obligations, Croatian courts, since joining the EU in 2013, have shown high trust in the criminal justice systems of other Member States and have rarely considered human rights violations as grounds for refusal. However, this judicial practice, which was previously

79 ECtHR, *Ahorugeze v. Sweden*, Judgment 27 October 2011, § 113.
80 ibid § 115. See Pajčić (n 78) 575.
81 ibid § 116. See Pajčić, (n 78) 575; VSRH, Kž-eun 46/15-4 of 30 December 2015.
82 VSRH, Kž-eun 39/15-5 prema Pajčić (n 78) 574.
83 VKSRH, I Kž-eun-11/2023-4, § 6.1. to 6.3.
84 VKSRH, I Kž-eun-6/2023-4 of 3 February 2023, § 6.

upheld by the Supreme Court, has been altered by the newly established High Criminal Court (in 2021) acting as the appellate court. In a few key decisions, as previously mentioned, the High Criminal Court has made significant breakthroughs regarding the principle of proportionality and inhuman treatment in prisons. In a 2022 ruling, the court invoked the principle of proportionality for the first time, considering the family circumstances of a requested person before approving a surrender. This trend continued with the well-publicised case of Croatian football fans in 2023, where Croatian courts refused to execute EAWs due to concerns over inhuman and degrading treatment in Greek prisons. The High Criminal Court emphasised the need for a specific and precise examination of the conditions in the issuing State's prisons and the availability of effective judicial protection for the requested persons. Moreover, Croatian appellate courts have annulled rulings approving surrenders due to violations of the right to translation, reinforcing that the right to a fair trial includes the right to understand legal proceedings in one's language. These developments mark the end of an era of automatic recognition of foreign judicial decisions without verifying compliance with fundamental rights in Croatia.

## 2.3 *Rights of the Suspect, Accused, and Other Parties*

### 2.3.1 Rights of the Requested Person

Immediately after the arrest of a person requested for the purpose of executing an EAW, the police will instruct that person in writing about his/her rights, which s/he exercises in accordance with the provisions of domestic criminal procedural law (Art 24(1) AJCCMEU). This means that the person arrested on the basis of an EAW in Croatia enjoys all the rights guaranteed to arrested persons under Croatian CPA. This includes the right to legal aid; upon arrest, the police will instruct the requested person of his/her right to a defense attorney in Croatia, even when the defense is not mandatory, with a warning that the decision to cover the costs of such an appointed defense attorney will depend on the later determined financial status of that person. Additionally, if the EAW has been issued for the purpose of criminal prosecution, the police will inform the requested person upon arrest that s/he has the right to request a defense attorney in the issuing State. The police, without delay, inform the competent county court, which will appoint a defense attorney for that person, and the State attorney's office, which will notify the competent authority of the issuing State about the request for a defense attorney in that State (Art 24(2) AJCCMEU).

Before the interrogation, the State attorney will instruct the requested person about his/her rights, which s/he exercises in accordance with the provisions of domestic criminal procedural law (Art 24(3) AJCCMEU).[85] If the person has not been instructed about his/her rights in accordance with the law, this will generally result in the inadmissibility of the statement given by the requested person. In this regard, general rules of criminal procedure apply, which provide that the statement of the arrested person who has not been adequately informed about his/her rights prior to the interrogation may not be used as evidence before the court (Art 108c in connection with Art 208.a(8) CPA).

If the competent authority of the issuing State has requested a limitation of the right to notify a third person or the right to communicate with a defense attorney, the State attorney will act in accordance with that request if it does not contradict the legal order of the Republic of Croatia (Art 24(6) AJCCMEU).

If the requested person wants to exercise the right to a defense attorney in the issuing State, the State attorney shall notify the competent authority of the issuing State thereof without delay. Exercising the right to a defense attorney in the issuing State does not affect the deadlines in the procedure for the execution of the EAW (Art 24(7) AJCCMEU).

If the EAW refers to the execution of a judgment rendered *in absentia*, which imposes a prison sentence or a measure that includes deprivation of liberty, the requested person may, before surrendering to the issuing State, request the delivery of the said judgment if it was not personally served on him/her before, nor did s/he receive an official notification that criminal proceedings are being conducted against him/her. In that case, the State attorney will ask the authority that issued the warrant to deliver the judgment without delay so that it can be delivered to the requested person. The delivery of the judgment will not be considered an official delivery for calculating the deadlines for submitting a request for renewal of the procedure or an appeal. This does not delay the

85 These rights are: – the right to a defense attorney of his/her own choice, i.e. a defense attorney appointed by the court, – the right to demand the appointment of a defense attorney even when defense is not mandatory, – the right to have the defense attorney present at the interrogation of the requested person and the right to free, undisturbed and confidential communication with him/her, – the right to appoint a defense attorney in the issuing State, – the right to request that a defense attorney be appointed in the issuing State in the proceedings regarding the EAW at the expense of the issuing State when the EAW was issued for the purpose of criminal prosecution, – the right to interpretation and translation, – the right to remain silent, – the right to inspect the case file before the interrogation by the State attorney, – the right to emergency medical assistance, – the right to have a person nominated by the requested person and the consular authority notified of the deprivation of liberty by the, with whom s/he also has the right to communicate.

process of surrender of the requested person or the deadline for rendering a decision on surrender (Art 24(8) AJCCMEU).

#### 2.3.2 Consent to Surrender

The requested person can consent to surrender to the issuing State and waive the application of the principle of specialty. The consent and waiver shall be entered in the minutes drawn up in a manner from which it undoubtedly follows that the requested person acted voluntarily and was fully aware of the consequences. The consent and waiver are irrevocable. The court shall notify without delay the issuing authority of the consent of the requested person (Art 27 AJCCMEU).

#### 2.3.3 Measures to Secure the Surrender of the Requested Person

In order to execute the EAW, measures must be applied in accordance with domestic law, which will ensure the surrender of the requested person. Upon the proposal of the State attorney, the judge will order pre-trial detention for the purpose of surrender, which may last until the execution of the decision on the surrender of the requested person. Instead of pre-trial detention for the purpose of surrender, the court may order one of the milder measures, provided that the application of such a measure can achieve the same purpose as pre-trial detention (Art 26 AJCCMEU).

#### 2.3.4 Remedies

Decision on recognition and execution of an EAW can be rendered either by the judge of the investigation or the judicial panel (composed of three professional judges). The judge of the investigation can render a decision only on the basis of the consent of the requested person. If the requested person does not consent to the surrender, the decision can only be rendered by the panel. Both decisions granting and refusing the surrender of the requested person can be appealed by the requested person, his/her defense attorney, and the State attorney. If the appealed decision has been rendered by the judge of the investigation, the appeal is decided by the panel of the same court (Art 28(3) AJCCMEU). If the appealed decision has been rendered by the panel, the appeal is decided by the panel of a higher court (Art 29(6) AJCCMEU). With these provisions, an effective remedy has been guaranteed to the requested person in compliance with EU law.

#### 2.3.5 Preliminary Conclusion

With regard to the rights of the suspect, accused, and other parties, four issues have been analysed: the rights of the requested person, consent to surrender, measures to secure the surrender, and remedies. With regard to the rights of the requested person, Croatian law is fully in line with the provisions of the EAW FD. A person who is arrested on the basis of an EAW enjoys all the rights that are regularly guaranteed by the CPA to persons arrested within the criminal procedure framework in Croatia. The requested person's right to consent to surrender is also guaranteed in compliance with the EAW FD. The personal liberty of the requested person may be limited or deprived in order to ensure execution of the EAW, and for this purpose, measures normally available within the criminal procedure in Croatia are also available in the EAW execution procedure. Finally, the requested person's right to appeal the decision granting surrender is also guaranteed by Croatian legislation in compliance with the EAW FD.

## 2.4 *Execution Procedure*

### 2.4.1 Starting the Proceedings for the Execution of the EAW: Arrest, Custody, and Interrogation of the Requested Person

The execution procedure regularly starts with the arrest of the requested person. Pursuant to Art 23(1) AJCCMEU, the police may arrest a person against whom an EAW has been issued or an alert in the Schengen Information System (SIS) at the request of the Member State has been entered. When justified reasons exist (Art 32(2) AJCCMEU), the requested person does not have to be arrested. In the latter case, the execution procedure will start with his/her first interrogation.

The arrested person must be handed over to the custody supervisor within 24 hours of the arrest, and the competent State attorney will be informed thereof and will deliver an EAW or/and an alert from the SIS that led to the arrest. If the EAW or the alert is not translated into Croatian, the police shall request a translation from the issuing State within 48 hours of the arrest. Alternatively, the competent State attorney may request the translation directly from the competent authority of the issuing State. If the alert lacks all the information that the EAW needs to contain, the police shall ask the issuing State's authority to supplement the alert without delay (Art 23(1) AJCCMEU).

After the arrested person has been handed over to the custody supervisor, the competent State attorney will interrogate the person about the circumstances from the documentation provided by the police within 16 hours of the handover (Art 23 (2) AJCCMEU). The State attorney shall inform the requested person about his/her rights according to domestic criminal procedural law (Art 24(3) AJCCMEU). The State attorney will also inform the requested person of the content and grounds for issuing an EAW, the possibility of consenting to surrender to the issuing State, and the option of waiving the application of the principle of specialty, along with the consequences of such a waiver. The State attorney will interrogate the requested person about his/her personal circumstances, citizenship, and relations with the issuing State, and whether and for what reasons s/he objects to the surrender (Art 24(4) AJCCMEU).

If the State attorney, on the basis of the EAW or the SIS alert, concludes that the offence in question is not a criminal offence under national law, s/he may issue a decision refusing to execute the EAW (Art 23(4) AJCCMEU). This decision needs to be delivered without delay to the judge of the investigation of the competent county court, who will confirm or revoke the State attorney's decision within 48 hours of the arrest (Art 23(5) AJCCMEU). If the judge of the investigation confirms the State attorney's decision, s/he shall immediately order the release of the arrested person (Art 23(6) AJCCMEU). If the judge of the investigation revokes the State attorney's decision, the latter may order the release of the arrested person and apply precautionary measures or bring the arrested person before the judge of the investigation, who will decide on detention (Art 23(9) AJCCMEU).

If the State attorney concludes that the offence for which the EAW or the SIS alert has been issued is a criminal offence under national law, s/he needs to decide concerning the liberty of the requested person who has been arrested. The State attorney may release the arrested person and order the application of precautionary measures (Art 23(4) AJCCMEU), However, if the State attorney considers that further deprivation of liberty is necessary, s/he needs to address the competent court and request a decision on detention against the requested person. The arrested person needs to be brought before the judge of the investigation at the latest within 48 hours from the moment of the arrest.

If the State attorney has not received the EAW or the SIS alert and their translation into Croatian, s/he may order the custody of the arrested person for up to 48 hours from the moment of the arrest (Art 23(7) AJCCMEU). If the State attorney has still not received the EAW or the SIS alert and their translation in Croatian within 48 hours of the arrest, s/he may request the judge of the investigation to prolong the custody of the arrested person for a further 36 hours (Art 23(8) AJCCMEU). Once the State attorney receives the EAW or the SIS alert and their translation into Croatian, s/he may order the release of the arrested person and apply precautionary measures or bring the arrested person before the judge of the investigation, who will decide on detention (Art 23(9) AJCCMEU).

If the necessary documentation and their translations have not been delivered to the State attorney within the statutory deadlines, the arrested person needs to be released (Art 23(10) AJCCMEU). Once the documentation is delivered, the released person may be arrested again and, in that case, must be brought before the judge of the investigation within 24 hours from the moment of the arrest (Art 23(11) AJCCMEU).

### 2.4.2 Proceedings before the Judge of the Investigation

If, after interrogating the requested person, the State attorney considers that detention is necessary, s/he shall submit a proposal to the judge of the investigation. The proposal needs to be accompanied by the EAW or the SIS alert and their translation in Croatian. The judge of the investigation shall schedule a detention hearing and notify the State attorney, the requested person, and his/her attorney and, if necessary, the interpreter of its time (Art 24.a(1) AJCCMEU). The detention hearing can only take place if the arrested person's attorney is present. If the arrested person does not have an attorney, the court will appoint one (Art 24.a(2) AJCCMEU). The judge of the investigation may also decide on the surrender of the requested person, but only if the requested person consents to surrender. In such cases, the judge of the investigation shall issue a decision approving the surrender without delay and within three days of the consent if there are no reasons for refusing the execution of the EAW (Art 24.a(4) AJCCMEU).

### 2.4.3 Proceedings before the Judicial Panel

If the detention hearing did not take place, or if the detention hearing did take place but the requested person did not consent to his/her surrender, the panel of the competent county court decides on the surrender (Art 24.b(1) AJCCMEU). After receiving the EAW or the SIS alert and their translation, the president of the panel must schedule the hearing within three days (Art 24.b(2) AJCCMEU). The State attorney, the requested person, his/her defense attorney, if any, and an interpreter, if necessary, will be summoned to the hearing (Art 24.b(3) AJCCMEU). The State attorney will state the basis for issuing the EAW, the criminal offense on which the warrant is based, as well as the reasons for its issuance, and propose the recognition and execution of that warrant. The State attorney will also address the further validity of detention or precautionary measures if they have been ordered (Art 24.b(5) AJCCMEU). The requested person and his/her attorney will have the opportunity to respond to the allegations from the warrant, state their reasons for opposing the surrender, and present evidence to support their allegations. The requested person may, at the session of the panel, consent to surrender to the issuing State. In that case, the panel will issue a decision on surrender (Art 24.b(6) AJCCMEU).

If the requested person objects to surrender, the court will question him/her about the reasons for the opposition. The competent State attorney can and the defense attorney must always be present during this questioning (Art 29(1)

AJCCMEU). The court may request additional information or documentation from the authority that issued the warrant, setting a deadline for their submission, but not longer than seven working days (Art 29(2) AJCCMEU). If necessary, the court carries out evidentiary actions in order to determine whether conditions for surrender are fulfilled (Art 29(3) AJCCMEU). After completing all the procedural actions, the panel shall render a decision either granting or refusing the surrender of the requested person (Art 29(4) AJCCMEU).

#### 2.4.4 Preliminary Conclusion

The procedure for the execution of the EAW in Croatia is fully regulated in compliance with the provisions of the EAW FD. The procedure typically starts with the arrest of the requested person by the police, who hands over the requested person to the State attorney, who finally brings the requested person before the competent court to decide on his/her surrender. There are two peculiar characteristics of the Croatian procedure for the execution of an EAW. First, the procedure does not have to start with the arrest of the requested person. The police may decide that the arrest is not necessary. In that case, the procedure for the execution of an EAW shall start with the State attorney interrogating the arrested person. Second, in cases in which it is obvious that the criminal offence underlying the surrender is not a criminal offence under Croatian law, the State attorney (and not the court) may decide to refuse to surrender the requested person. However, in this case, the court also makes the final decision on the surrender because the decision rendered by the State attorney needs to be validated by the court.

## 3 European Investigation Order: Critical Profiles in Legislation and Case Law

### 3.1 *Overview of the Transposition of the EIO Directive and Its Use in Practice*

The EIO D was transposed with the amendments of the AJCCMEU, which entered into force on 26 October 2017.[86] The Amendments introduced the EIO as a new form of judicial cooperation in a new Chapter 2.A, titled 'The European Investigation Order', with two sections: 'General Provisions' and 'Special Provisions for Individual Evidence Proceedings'. In addition to this, the introduction of EIO led to the amendment of some general provisions of

86 Act amending the Act on Judicial Cooperation of 2017 (n 62).

the AJCCMEU, the deletion of Chapter 4 on European Evidence Warrant, and of Chapter 3 in regard to freezing orders for securing evidence. To date, the Chapter on EIO has had three amendments: in 2018, 2019, and 2024.[87] With regard to the implementation of the EIO in Croatia, the conducted study established that 'Croatia did not face any substantial problems in the practical implementation of the EIO'.[88]

According to the Art 42.a AJCCMEU, transposing Art 3 of the EIO D, an EIO may be issued when it is necessary to conduct evidentiary actions in criminal or misdemeanour proceedings, in the territory of another Member State, with exception of Denmark and Ireland. It is explicitly prescribed that the EIO cannot be issued for the purpose of establishing a joint investigative team and collecting evidence in such a team.

In practice, there has been a steady increase in the use of EIOs in the last five years. According to the report of the Attorney General of the Republic of Croatia for 2023. in 2019, there were 583 EIO s with Croatia as issuing or executing State; in 2020, there were 648 EIOs; in 2021. 681 EIOs; in 2022, 758 EIOs and in 2023 909 EIOs.[89] The increase in the number of issued EIOs is related to the 'increase in the number of computer criminality, offenses committed within the framework of a criminal association, especially offenses of drug abuse and illegal investment of movement and residence in Croatia, another Member of the EU or a signatory to the Schengen Agreement'.[90] The first study of the use of EIO in 2018 found no issues in practice but did indicate some possible difficulties.[91]

### 3.2 *Grounds for Non-recognition and Non-execution*

Contrary to Art 11 of the EIO D, the AJCCMEU in Art 42.j distinguishes between optional and mandatory grounds for non-recognition and non-enforcement

87 Act amending the Act on Judicial Cooperation in Criminal Matters with the Member States of the European Union (*Zakon o izmjenama i dopunama Zakona o pravosudnoj suradnji u kaznenim stvarima s državama članicama Europske Unije*), Official Gazette No. 68/2018, No. 70/2019 and No. 18/2024.

88 Elizabeta Ivičević Karas and others, 'European Investigation Order in Croatia – Normative Framework and Practical Challenges' in Kai Ambos and others (eds), *The European Investigation Order: Legal Analysis and Practical Dilemmas of International Cooperation* (Duncker und Humblot, 2023) 48.

89 *Report of the Chief State Attorney in 2024* (n 6).

90 ibid 261.

91 Željko Karas and Silvija Pejaković Đipić, 'Evaluation of the Results of the European Investigation Order' (2019) 3 EU and comparative law issues and challenges series, 503–504.

of the EIO. Croatian legislation prescribes two optional and six mandatory non-recognition and non-execution grounds.

As regards optional grounds, the competent judicial authority is authorised to decide whether to execute or refuse the recognition and execution of the EIO, being guided by the principles of effective cooperation, expediency, and the right to a fair trial (Art 42.j(1)(a) AJCCMEU). Firstly, the competent judicial authority can refuse the EIO in case of immunity or privilege existing in domestic law that prevents the execution of the EIO or if rules on the limitation of criminal liability relating to freedom of the press and freedom of expression prevent the execution of the EIO (Art 42.j(1)(a) AJCCMEU, transposing Art 11(1)(a) of the EIO D). If the domestic authority is responsible for lifting the privilege or immunity, the competent judicial authority shall request it to exercise that power forthwith. On the other side, if the authority of another State or an international organization is competent for lifting the privilege or immunity, the issuing authority will request the authority competent for lifting the privilege or immunity to exercise that power (Art 42.j(5) AJCCMEU, transposing Art 11(5) of the EIO D). Secondly, the competent judicial authority can also refuse the EIO if it was issued in proceedings initiated by administrative or by judicial authorities for acts that violate the domestic law of the issuing State and if such a decision may lead to proceedings before a court competent in criminal matters, provided that the evidentiary action would not be authorised under the law of the executing State in a similar domestic case (Art 42.j(1)(b) AJCCMEU, transposing Art 11(1)(c) of the EIO D).

As regards mandatory grounds, the competent judicial authority will refuse the EIO if executing the EIO would harm essential national security interests, jeopardise the source of information, or involve the use of classified information related to specific intelligence activities (Art 42.j(2)(a) AJCCMEU, transposing Art 11(1)(b) of the EIO D). Second, executing the EIO would be contrary to the principle of *ne bis in idem*. Yet, there is an exception to this rule if the issuing authority guarantees that the evidence obtained by the EIO will not be used for the purpose of criminal prosecution or punishment of a person for an offense for which s/he has already been finally sentenced in the Member State (Art 42j(2)(b) AJCCMEU, transposing Art 11(1)(d) and Rec 17). Third, if the EIO relates to a criminal offense alleged to have been committed outside the territory of the issuing State and was partially or wholly committed on the Croatian territory, and the conduct for which the EIO is issued is not a criminal offense in Croatia (Art 42.j(2)(c) AJCCMEU, transposing Art 11(1)(e) of the EIO D). Fourth, if there are substantial grounds indicating that executing the evidentiary action specified in the EIO would be incompatible with the obligations from Art 6 of the Treaty on EU and the Charter (Art 42(j)(2)(d)

AJCCMEU, transposing Art 11(1)(f) of the EIO D). In these four cases (and the first optional ground described above), before deciding, the competent judicial authority must inform the issuing authority of the reasons for the refusal of the EIO and, if necessary, request the necessary information from the issuing authority without delay (Art 42.j(4) AJCCMEU, transposing Art 11(4) of the EIO D).

Fifth, the competent judicial authority will not recognize and execute the EIO if the conduct for which the EIO was issued is not a punishable act under domestic law unless it refers to a criminal offense included in the categories listed in Art 10(2) of the AJCCMEU. For fiscal offences, the execution of the EIO cannot be refused just because domestic law does not prescribe the same type of taxes or fees or lacks the same provisions on taxes, fees, customs duties, or currency exchange as the law of the issuing State (Art 42.j(2)(e) AJCCMEU, transposing Art 11(1)(g) of the EIO D). Sixth, the EIO will be refused if it is issued in relation to an evidentiary action whose application under domestic law is limited to a catalog of criminal offenses or to offenses with a determinate minimum sanction and a criminal offense for which proceedings are being conducted in the issuing country are not included in the catalog (Art 42.j(2)(f) AJCCMEU, transposing Art 11(1)(h) of the EIO D). The fifth and the sixth grounds do not apply to the following evidentiary actions listed in Art 42(2) of the AJCCMEU: obtaining information or evidence that is already in the possession of the competent authorities of the Republic of Croatia, and that information or evidence could be obtained, in accordance with domestic law within the framework of criminal proceedings or for the purposes of a EIO; obtaining information contained in databases maintained by the police or judicial authorities and directly accessible to the judicial enforcement authority within the framework of criminal proceedings; examination of witnesses, expert witnesses, injured parties and victims, suspects or defendants or third persons on the territory of the executing State; any evidentiary action which, according to domestic law, is carried out without a court order; and identity data of persons who have a subscription to a specific telephone number or IP address (Art 42.j(3) AJCCMEU, transposing Art 11(2) of the EIO D).

The explanation of the proposed amendments of the AJCCMEU did not give reasons for distinguishing between optional and mandatory grounds for non-recognition and non-enforcement of the EIOs.[92] Commentators stated

92 The Government of the Republic of Croatia, 'Proposal of the Law on Amendments to the Law on Judicial Cooperation in Criminal Matters with the Member States of the European Union' (*Prijedlog Zakona o izmjenama i dopunama Zakona o pravosudnoj suradnji u kaznenim stvarima s državama članicama Europske unije*) (Zagreb, May 2017) 52.

that this distinction was made according to established practice[93] and was not problematised.[94] Although the introduction of mandatory grounds has not been recognized as problematic so far, taking into account CJEU judgment C-396/22 *Generalstaatsanwaltschaft Berlin* (conviction *in absentia*),[95] it can be considered contrary to Art 11 of the EIO D. The recent experience with the European Commission requesting the harmonization of mandatory and optional refusal grounds for the EAW[96] suggests that a similar could happen with the EIO refusal grounds.

### 3.3 *Execution Procedure and Cooperation Issues*

Arts 5(1)(2) and 42.h(1) of the AJCCMEU define the County State Attorney's Office in the location where the evidentiary action is to be conducted or where the evidence is located as a competent authority for receiving EIO s. The County State Attorney's Office must undertake all the necessary actions for the execution of EIO as prescribed by domestic law. In this way, the reception of the EIO is separated from its execution, and the executing authority is, in accordance with domestic law, the State Attorney's Office or criminal or misdemeanour courts upon its proposal.[97] During the execution of the EIO, authorities of the issuing State can be present if this is not contrary to fundamental principles of domestic law or harms essential national security interests (Art 42.h(4) AJCCMEU). However, their representative is bound by domestic law and does not have the authority to take evidentiary actions independently unless it is in accordance with domestic law and to the extent agreed (Art 42.h(5) AJCCMEU).

Recourse to a different type of investigative measure, as foreseen in Art 10 of the EIO D, is also provided. The competent judicial authority will carry out

---

93 Ivan Crnčec and Tamara Mišerda, 'Novela Zakona o pravosudnoj suradnji u kaznenim stvarima s državama članicama Europske unije' (2017) 24 Hrvatski ljetopis za kaznene znanosti i praksu, 543.

94 See e.g. Danka Hržina, 'Novela Zakona o pravosudnoj suradnji u kaznenim stvarima s državama članicama Europske unije' (Pravosudna akademija, 2018) 23–25; Damir Primorac, Maja Buhovac and Marko Pilić, 'Europski istražni nalog kao novi instrument pravosudne suradnje država članica u kaznenim predmetima s posebnim osvrtom na hrvatsko pravo' (2019) 10 Godišnjak Akademije pravnih znanosti Hrvatske, 361; Ivičević Karas and others (n 88) 38–40.

95 Case C-396/22 Generalstaatsanwaltschaft Berlin (Conviction in absentia) [2023] ECLI:EU:C:2023:1029, in which the Court in the context of EAW established that the national legislation which does not leave that executing judicial authority any discretion in case of optional grounds is contrary to the provision of EU law.

96 See supra, § 2.1.3.

97 Crnčec and Mišerda (n 93) 542–543.

an evidentiary action different from the one provided for in the EIO if this evidentiary action does not exist according to the domestic law or it could not be ordered in a comparable domestic case (Arts 42.i(1)(a) and (b) AJCCMEU). However, in accordance with Art 10(2) of the EIO D, Art 42i(2), the evidentiary actions must be carried out if they refer to: a) obtaining information or evidence already in possession of the competent Croatian authorities, and such information or evidence could be obtained, under domestic law, in criminal proceedings or for the purposes of an EIO; b) obtaining information already contained in databases maintained by the police or judicial authorities and directly accessible to the judicial authority in the course of criminal proceedings; c) examination of witnesses, experts, injured persons, and victims, suspects or defendants or third parties in the territory of the State of execution; d) any evidentiary action which, according to domestic law, is carried out without a court order;[98] or e) identity information of persons who have a telephone number subscription or IP address.

In addition to cases of non-existent or inapplicable evidentiary actions, the competent judicial authority can also carry out an evidentiary action that is by its nature less intrusive than the action provided for in the EIO if the same result would be achieved (Art 42.i(3) AJCCMEU).

In regard to cooperation, partial implementation of several provisions of the EIO D has been established. Art 42.h(6) of the AJCCMEU does not have an explicit provision on consulting the issuing authority specifically 'on the importance of executing the EIO' and that 'after that consultation, the issuing authority may decide to withdraw the EIO', as provided in Art 6(3) of the EIO D. In regard to Art 26 of the EIO D, Art 42.af(1) of the AJCCMEU provides that the competent County Attorney's Office may, after obtaining the decision of the investigating judge, issue an EIO for the purpose of obtaining data on banking operations to conduct domestic criminal proceedings, but it does not transpose the request that in such cases, the execution of the EIO may also be refused (in addition to the grounds referred to in Art 11 of the EIO D) if the execution of the investigative measure would not be authorised in a similar domestic case.[99]

98 In this regard, Croatia adopted a formal criterion and all measures which require court authorization are considered coercive measures. Although, as a rule, the court authorisation is required for the measures limiting human rights and freedoms, there are exceptions. Ivičević Karas and others (n 88) 37–38.

99 For a more detailed presentation of the execution procedure and cooperation issues, see Ivičević Karas and others (n 88) 35–38 and 41–44.

As a problem in practice, it is pointed out that some EIOs require multiple, often conditional, evidentiary actions, which sometimes amount to conducting an entire investigation on behalf of the judicial authority of the issuing State.[100] In addition to that, it has been noted that EIOs are not always clearly drawn up, particularly when they are 'issued in the pre-investigation phase of the procedure, so the actions required by them are not clearly specified'.[101]

### 3.4 *Remedies*

The AJCCMEU provides legal remedies against the decision to refuse an EIO when Croatia is the executing State. According to Art 14(1) of the AJCCMEU, parties and third persons who, in good faith, have acquired certain rights to property subject to these decisions have the right to appeal, in accordance with domestic law, against decisions on the recognition and execution of property insurance orders, EIO s or decisions on the confiscation of property or objects, in order to protect their legitimate interests. In addition to that, the State attorney has the right to appeal against the decision by which the court refuses to recognize and execute the EIO within three days (Art 42.m(1) AJCCMEU).

An appeal against a decision on the recognition of an EIO postpones its execution until the end of the appeal procedure (Art 14(2) AJCCMEU). The request to review the validity and existence of the conditions for issuing an EIO can only be submitted to the competent authority in the issuing country in accordance with the national law of that country (Art 14(3) AJCCMEU). In addition to that, Art 42.m(2) of the AJCCMEU prescribes that the substantive reasons for issuing the EIO may only be challenged in proceedings initiated in the issuing State. This provision only partially transposes Art 14(2) of the EIO D, as it lacks the second part of this provision, which states that it is 'without prejudice to the guarantees of fundamental rights in the executing State'. The position of the defence or third persons is also undermined by the failure to transpose Art 14(3) of the EIO D, which requires both the issuing and the executing authorities to take the appropriate measures to ensure that information is provided about the possibilities under national law for seeking legal remedies when applicable and in due time, and to ensure that they can be effectively exercised without undermining the need to ensure confidentiality of an investigation. Also, Art 14(6) of the EIO D, providing that a legal challenge shall not suspend the execution of the investigative measure unless it is provided for in similar domestic cases, is also partially implemented since Art 42.m(4) AJCCMEU does not refer to any legal challenge, but only to legal remedy filed

100 *Report of the Chief State Attorney* (n 6) 262.

101 ibid.

in the issuing State (of which the competent State attorney notified the issuing State).

On the other hand, it has been observed that in Croatia, there is no legal remedy provided against the decision to issue EIO since it is not foreseen by the AJCCMEU nor by the CPA for evidence-gathering actions in general.[102] In this situation, the defence can only challenge the admissibility of the evidence gathered abroad.[103] In these cases, it is stated that the courts have almost without exception accepted the principle of *locus regit actum*, i.e. the evidence is considered valid if it was obtained in accordance with the law of the State where the evidence was gathered.[104] The issue of the admissibility of evidence arose in one case where the defendant's interrogation in Romania was not recorded, as required by Art 275(2) of the CPA.[105] Although it was requested, the interrogation was not recorded with an audio-video recording device due to the lack of the necessary technical equipment. Due to this, the defendant appealed to have these minutes excluded from the file. The Supreme Court rejected the appeal with the argument that the State executing the EIO conducted the investigation in accordance with the request of the competent judicial body, and the defendant's right to legal assistance was fully respected. Since the absence of a recording did not constitute a violation of the right of defense guaranteed by international law or the AJCCMEU, the way in which the evidence was obtained does not contradict the basic principles of domestic criminal law, and the evidence was deemed admissible. The evidence was presented in accordance with the prosecutor's request, and its legality and reliability were not questioned according to the law of the executing State. Therefore, the evidence was not considered illegal within the meaning of Art 10 of the CPA.[106]

The CJEU, in C-852/19 *Gavanozov II* judgment, established that the legislation of the issuing Member State that does not provide for any legal remedy

102 Ivičević Karas and others (n 88) 47. Although there are no provisions on legal remedy, Hržina states that the appeal can be submitted to the State attorney's office, which issued the EIO. Hržina (n. 94) 20. For a question whether Member States should provide legal remedies against the decision to undertake investigative measures see Igor Materljan and Gordana Materljan, 'Europski istražni nalog i nacionalni sustavi pravnih lijekova: pitanje primjerene razine zaštite temeljnih prava u državi izdavanja naloga' (2020) 27 Hrvatski ljetopis za kaznene znanosti i praksu, 757–758.

103 Ivičević Karas and others (n 88) 47.

104 Šime Matak, 'Dokazi iz inozemstva iz pozicije obrane – mogućnost pribavljanja, kontrola zakonitosti i pouzdanosti' (2020) 27 Hrvatski ljetopis za kaznene znanosti i praksu, 537.

105 VSRH, I Kž-Us 120/2020-4 of 17 December 2020.

106 ibid.

against the issuing of an EIO for searches, seizures, or witness hearing by videoconference is not in accordance with Arts 6 and 14 of the EIO D.[107] This issue was raised by the defence in an appeal against a decision on pre-trial detention in a case before High Criminal Court. The High Criminal Court did not decide on whether the evidence is admissible in a situation where the Croatian legislation does not provide for a legal remedy against the issuing of the EIO. Instead, the Court confirmed the first-instance decision on pre-trial detention and instructed the appellant that the admissibility of this evidence should be assessed in a separate procedure, as provided in Arts 350 and 351 of the CPA.[108]

### 3.5 *Preliminary Conclusion*

The EIO D was implemented in the AJCCMEU in 2017, and since then, the provisions of EIO have undergone only minor changes. Analysis reveals that while the EIO D has been largely transposed into Croatian law, significant issues remain. Specifically, switching some optional into mandatory grounds for non-recognition and non-enforcement of the EIO in Art 42.j AJCCMEU, taking into account the recent CJEU case law, cannot be considered to comply with Art 11 of the EIO D. In addition, it was established that Art 14(3) of the EIO D was not transposed and that there are some cases of partial transposition. After the CJEU *Gavanazov II* verdict, a potential problem was also observed with legal remedies since the Croatian legal system does not provide for a legal remedy to challenge the issuance of an EIO for certain evidentiary actions. It remains to be seen whether and in what way this will affect the execution of the EIOs issued in Croatia in the executing States and the admissibility of this evidence in proceedings before Croatian courts.

## 4 Regulation 1805/2018: Critical Profiles in Legislation and Case Law

### 4.1 *Overview of the Direct Application of the Regulation*

In Croatia, there is no special legislation transposing the Regulation 1805/2018 (hereinafter: Regulation). Therefore, the Regulation is applied directly as a standard. However, it is explicitly proclaimed that the implementation of the Regulation 'is ensured' (and not 'incorporated' into Croatian legislation) by the AJCCMEU (Art 1(3) AJCCMEU). This legal provision was introduced in the

107 Case C-852/19 Gavanozov II [2021] ECLI:EU:C:2021:902. For the analysis of the judgment see Zoran Burić, 'Postojanje pravnog sredstva protiv europskog istražnog naloga kao pretpostavka za njegovo izdavanje' (2021) 10 Zagrebačka pravna revija, 186–192.

108 VKSRH, II Kž-Us 2/2023-5 of 1 February 2023.

legislative amendments of 2020.[109] In the explanatory notes, the Government of the Republic of Croatia stated that the Regulation replaces the Framework Decision 2003/577/JHA and the Framework Decision 2006/783/JHA and that on the day the Regulation enters into force, the existing provisions of the AJCCMEU on the freezing of property and the confiscation of property and objects [which are in line with the aforementioned framework decisions, authors' note], cease to be valid, except in relation to Ireland and Denmark.[110] Yet, with the legislative amendment, it was necessary to determine the authorities responsible for receiving and recognition, as well as for issuing freezing orders and confiscation orders, and it was done in the AJCCMEU.[111] According to the current legislation, county State attorneys are responsible for receiving freezing orders and confiscation orders according to the place where the property or objects are located, or where a natural person has a place of domicile or residence, and a legal person has a registered seat (Art 5(1)(3) AJCCMEU). The order to secure confiscation and the freezing order is issued by the State attorney and the court conducting the proceedings (Art 6(2) AJCCMEU), while the decision on confiscation of property or objects, or the confiscation order according to the Regulation, is made by the competent court (Art 6(4) AJCCMEU). Finally, county courts have jurisdiction for filling out and verifying the content of certificates that are submitted with decisions on confiscation of property and objects, and now they have the same jurisdiction for confiscation orders in accordance with the Regulation (Art 7 AJCCMEU).

The High Criminal Court, in its recent decision, confirmed that, since the AJCCMEU now ensures the implementation of the Regulation, it actually derogates from the application of the aforementioned instruments of judicial cooperation – freezing and confiscation orders regulated in the AJCCMEU.[112] The direct application of the Regulation and its primacy over the AJCCMEU was also explicitly confirmed in another decision of the High Criminal Court.[113]

On the other side, the Directive 2014/42/EU, which establishes minimum rules on the freezing and the confiscation of property, was transposed to the

---

109 Act amending the Act on Judicial Cooperation in Criminal Matters with the Member States of the European Union (*Zakon o izmjenama i dopunama Zakona o pravosudnoj suradnji u kaznenim stvarima s državama članicama Europske unije*), Official Gazette No. 141/20.

110 Vlada Republike Hrvatske, *Prijedlog Zakona o dopunama Zakona o pravosudnoj suradnji u kaznenim stvarima s državama članicama Europske unije* (2020) 2 <https://www.sabor.hr/sites/default/files/uploads/sabor/2020-10-01/104409/PZE_36.pdf> accessed 16 July 2024.

111 ibid.

112 I Kž-eu-26/2022-4[2023] VKSRH, point 7.

113 I Kž-eu-10/2023-4[2023] VKSRH, point 10.

CPA with the legislative amendment in 2017.[114] Since then, besides traditional confiscation of instrumentalities and proceeds of crime, the CPA regulates the confiscation procedure in the cases of illness or absconding of the suspect or accused person – the so called non-conviction-based confiscation (Arts 560.a–560.f CPA), in cases where criminal proceedings have already been initiated regarding a criminal offence. The CPA also regulates the procedure of confiscation from a person to whom the property gain was transferred. This person has important procedural rights, including the right to a proxy (who may be a lawyer), the right to be summoned to the main hearing, the right to propose evidence, and to pose questions to the defendant, witnesses, and expert witnesses (Art 558 CPA). The same rights are guaranteed to the 'third person' who claims to have certain rights in relation to the property gain, which is the object of the procedure (Art 558 CPA).

In Croatian law, the confiscation of property gain acquired through a criminal offence is traditionally regulated in a Criminal Code,[115] as a measure *sui generis*,[116] or *in rem* measure,[117] which primarily serves to achieve a restorative and not a punitive purpose (Art 77 CC). Thus, the application of the confiscation measure does not imply the determination of guilt nor the determination that a criminal offence has been committed – it is sufficient to determine that an 'illegal act' was committed. Yet, this does not refer to the extended confiscation (Art 78 CC), which is possible in cases of criminal offences under the jurisdiction of the Office for Suppression of Corruption and Organized Crime, criminal offences of sexual abuse and exploitation of children, criminal offences against computer systems, programs, and data, as well as in cases of unauthorised production and trafficking of drugs, and enabling the consumption of drugs (Art 78(1) CC). If the perpetrator of any of these criminal offences has or had assets that are disproportionate to his or her legal income, it is assumed that these assets are the proceeds of the crime, and they will be the object of extended confiscation unless the perpetrator makes it probable that its origin is legal (Art 78(2) CC). On one side, the court does not have to be completely convinced that the entire property included in the extended confiscation derived from a criminal offence, and on the other side, the extent

114 Act amending the Criminal Procedure Act (*Zakon o izmjenama i dopunama Zakona o kaznenom postupku*), Official Gazette No. 70/17.

115 Criminal Code (*Kazneni zakon*), Official Gazette No. 125/11, 144/12, 56/15, 61/15, 101/17, 118/18, 126/19, 84/21, 114/22, 114/23, 36/24.

116 Marin Mrčela and Igor Vuletić, *Komentar Kaznenog zakona* (Libertin naklada 2021) 467; Ksenija Turković, et al., *Komentar Kaznenog zakona* (Narodne novine 2013) 113.

117 Elizabeta Ivičević Karas, *Kaznenopravno oduzimanje nezakonito stečene imovinske koristi* (2007) 14 Hrvatski ljetopis za kazneno pravo i praksu 674.

of the extended confiscation of the perpetrator's property can be quite significant. Therefore, the measure of extended confiscation does reveal some punitive features,[118] and that is why its application implies the determination of the perpetrator's guilt, as well as the determination of the commission of a criminal offence in a judgment of conviction. All these types of confiscation in Croatian law are in line with the Directive 2014/42/EU and are therefore included in the scope of the Regulation.[119]

### 4.2 *Critical Profiles of the Regulation 1805/2018 in Practice*

As concerns the direct application of the Regulation, so far, there are only four published decisions of the High Criminal Court of the Republic of Croatia, which decided as a court of the second instance.[120] In one of these decisions[121] the High Criminal Court decided to refer for a preliminary ruling to the CJEU, in accordance with Art 267(3) TFEU.

In this case, the first-instance judgment of the County Court in Zagreb, based on the provision of Art 18(1) of the Regulation and in connection with Art 1(3) AJCCMEU, recognized the order for confiscation of illegal property gain from the judgment of the District Court in Maribor, Republic of Slovenia. In the judgment of the District Court in Maribor, four defendants were acquitted of the criminal offence of abuse of position and authority due to the lack of evidence.[122] Yet, the court decided that the shares of another trading company were to be confiscated from trading company D. d.o.o. in favor of the Republic of Slovenia.[123] Finally, the court decided that the method of execution of confiscation would be determined in the executing State, in accordance with the provisions of the AJCCMEU, which refer to the recognition and execution of decisions regarding the confiscation of objects and property gains pronounced in another State.[124]

Both the State attorney and the company D. d.o.o., to which the confiscation order applied, appealed against that decision. The State attorney pointed to significant procedural and factual errors with the proposal that the contested

118 Elizabeta Ivičević Karas, *Komentar Zakona o postupku oduzimanja imovinske koristi ostvarene kaznenim djelom* (Narodne novine 2011) 13.

119 See the Regulation, Recitals 7, 8, 13 and 14.

120 The search of the case law was conducted with the search tools of the official website of the Supreme Court of the Republic of Croatia, using the keyword '2018/1805' <https://sudskapraksa.vsrh.hr/search> accessed 12 June 2024.

121 I Kž-eu-8/2023-4[2023] VKSRH.

122 Under Art 244(2), in relation to Art 244(1) and to Art 25 of the Slovenian Criminal Code.

123 According to Art 498.a(1) point 1 of the Slovenian Criminal Procedure Act.

124 I Kž-eu-8/2023-4[2023] VKSRH, point 1.

judgment be vacated and the case returned to the first instance court for a new decision.[125] The company D. d.o.o. filed an appeal due to violation of the CPA and the CC and due to factual errors, with a proposal to reverse the judgment so as to refuse to recognize and execute the order for confiscation of property gain from the judgment of the District Court in Maribor, which was passed in a procedure that represents a serious violation of fundamental rights and freedoms, or alternatively to vacate the judgment and return the case to a new trial.[126]

The High Criminal Court, determined that the interpretation of the CJEU was necessary for the correct application of the Regulation and, therefore, referred to the CJEU a request for a preliminary ruling, in accordance with Art 267(3) of the Treaty on the Functioning of the European Union.[127] Consequently, the procedure before the High Criminal Court was suspended until the decision of the CJEU.

The following questions were referred to the CJEU, as quoted:

> 1) Does the term 'proceedings in relation to a criminal offence that may result in confiscation of property, including confiscation without a conviction' within the meaning of Art 2(3) of Regulation 2018/1805 also include criminal proceedings concluded with an acquittal?
>
> 2) Does the term 'proceedings in relation to a criminal offence that may result in confiscation of property, including confiscation without a conviction' within the meaning of Art 2(3) of Regulation 2018/1805 also include criminal proceedings concluded with a judgment of acquittal that includes an order to confiscate property as undue proceeds derived from another criminal offence, which is not the criminal offence of which the defendants were acquitted, and in whose commission the defendants were not involved, but rather persons against whom no indictment was brought?
>
> 3) Is it contrary to Regulation 2018/1805, Art 1(2) thereof, and Art 47 of the Charter of Fundamental Rights to recognise a confiscation order issued in criminal proceedings in which an affected person, within the meaning of Art 2(10) of the Regulation:
>
> was not summoned to participate in all stages of the criminal proceedings;
>
> was not advised of his or her right to a lawyer throughout the proceedings;

125 ibid point 2.1.

126 ibid point 2.2.

127 ibid point 5.

> did not receive the full text of the judgment containing the confiscation order in a language s/he understood, but only excerpts from that judgment, and did not appeal against the judgment thus served.[128]

The first question referred to the CJEU on the possibility of confiscation of property in case of an acquittal asks for the correct interpretation of the relevant provisions of the Regulation. Namely, on one side, Art 18(1) of the Regulation prescribes that '[T]he executing authority shall recognise a confiscation order transmitted in accordance with Art 14 and shall take the measures necessary for its execution in the same way as for a domestic confiscation order issued by an authority of the executing State unless the executing authority invokes one of the grounds for non-recognition and non-execution provided for in Art 19 or one of the grounds for postponement provided for in Art 21.' On the other side, in Croatian law, the property gain may only be confiscated by a court decision that establishes *that an illegal act has been committed*, even in case of non-conviction-based confiscation (Art 77(1) CC, also Art 560(1) CPA and Art 560.d(1) CPA). This should lead to the conclusion that it is not possible to confiscate property gain on the basis of an acquittal, even in cases when acquittal is due to the exclusion of guilt,[129] although there are some different opinions in domestic literature. Namely, some authors actually hold that confiscation should also be possible in case of exclusion of guilt, for example, due to an unavoidable mistake as to the elements constituting a crime, or due to an unavoidable mistake as to illegality, or exceeding the limits of self defence or necessity.[130] So this question is obviously still open and it was, among others, referred to the CJEU, since in the concrete case the Slovenian court acquitted the accused persons and ordered the confiscation of property gain from a third person (or 'affected person').

Regarding the second question, in Croatian law, there is no possibility to confiscate in criminal proceedings the property gained through another criminal offence and not the one that was specified in the indictment, with the exception of extended confiscation when it is assumed that assets which are disproportionate to perpetrator's legal income are the proceeds of (any) crime (and not necessarily of the crime for which the perpetrator was pronounced

128 Case C-8/24, D.d.o.o., Request for a preliminary ruling from the Visoki kazneni sud Republike Hrvatske (Croatia) lodged on 9 January 2024 – Criminal proceedings involving D. d.o.o. and Županijsko državno odvjetništvo u Zagrebu [2024] .

129 Mrčela and Vuletić (n 116) 468.

130 Mrčela and Vuletić point to the attitudes of these authors, with whom they actually disagree. See ibid.

guilty), as already explained. The confiscation of property gain may only be pronounced by the court in a conviction or in a decision that establishes that the defendant has committed an illegal act that is the object of the accusation, and the property was gained through that illegal act (Art 560(1) CPA). The same principle applies to the non-conviction-based confiscation (Art 560.d(1) CPA).

Finally, regarding the third question, as was already mentioned, the Croatian law provides for the interested 'third person', or 'affected person' from Art 2(10) of the Regulation, important procedural rights allowing him or her to actively participate in the confiscation procedure and represent his or her interests (Art 558 CPA). It is alleged that the aforementioned rights were not guaranteed in the proceedings before the Slovenian courts, so the High Criminal Court is asking the CJEU for an interpretation as to whether this is an obstacle to the recognition of the confiscation order.

It should be mentioned that, in the same case, the High Criminal Court previously rejected the appeal filed by the company D. d.o.o. against the prolongation of provisional measures ordered by Zagreb County Court. It explained that the District Court in Maribor prolonged the provisional measure of securing the confiscation of property gain and added that '[A]t the same time, the first-instance court cannot get involved in the examination and determination of facts related to the validity of the decision on confiscation of property gain'.[131] Although the High Criminal Court pointed out that the Regulation is directly applicable in this case, it actually explicitly referred to the principle of mutual recognition and the principle of effective cooperation from Arts 3 and 4 of the AJCCMEU.[132]

This concrete case is still pending, since the proceedings before the High Criminal Court are suspended while awaiting the preliminary ruling of the CJEU.

### 4.3 *Preliminary Conclusion*

In Croatia, the Regulation is applied directly, and its implementation is ensured in the AJCCMEU, which determines the authorities responsible for receiving and recognition, as well as for issuing freezing orders and confiscation orders. Currently, only a few court decisions concerning the direct application of the Regulation have been published, and only one pointed out several open questions. In this case, the High Criminal Court, as the court of the second instance, concluded that the interpretation of the CJEU was necessary for the correct

---

131 I Kž-eu-10/2023-4[2023] VKSRH, point 13.

132 ibid point 13.1.

application of the Regulation and therefore referred to the CJEU a request for a preliminary ruling, which is still expected.

## 5 Concluding Remarks

Croatia has normatively separated Mutual Legal Assistance and EU cooperation in criminal matters, establishing the AJCCMEU as the *sedes materiae* for implementing all EU mutual recognition instruments. In order to achieve complete and correct implementation of the EAW FD, the AJCCMEU has undergone several amendments, with the latest in 2024 prompted by the EU infringement procedure. The most contentious amendment was from 2013, adopted three days before Croatia's EU accession, known as 'Lex Perković'. It introduced the statute of limitations on prosecution as a mandatory ground for refusing an EAW, aligning with the solution adopted in most EU Member States. However, the political and judicial interpretation of this amendment focused on its potential to block the surrender of Perković and Mustač to Germany. This issue became a highly charged topic in Croatian political discourse and had profound legal repercussions in Croatia. To bypass this legislative obstacle, Croatian courts, led by the Supreme Court, developed an innovative interpretation that excluded the verification of the statute of limitations for offenses not subject to the principle of double criminality. Consequently, Croatia became one of the few EU Member States prioritizing mutual trust over reciprocity and protection of its citizens from surrender in cases of time-barred offenses. It led to the automatic surrender of Croatian citizens for economic crimes committed decades earlier without considering the principle of proportionality. The *Hernardi* case, the second politically sensitive Croatian EAW criminal case, also underscores the challenges of EU judicial cooperation in politically charged matters. It highlights that discretionary refusal of extradition in the MLA system is possibly not always improved under the EU mutual recognition system, even in the case of clear instructions given in the judgment of the CJEU. In this case, the interpretation of the *ne bis in idem* principle proved to be fertile ground for misuse to prevent the surrender of the politically shielded individuals. Both cases illustrate that while the EU's judicial cooperation system was designed to be free from political interference and based on clear legal norms rather than political interests, real-world political dynamics can still pose significant challenges. These political realities often undermine the effectiveness of the EU's judicial cooperation framework, showing that even European judicial systems can be disrupted by prevailing political conditions.

Concerning using the protection of human rights as grounds for refusal, Croatian courts heavily relied on other Member States' criminal justice systems for a long time, often neglecting human rights concerns. In 2017, Croatian legislation was aligned with the *Calderaru* and *Aranyosi* judgments, and since 2022, notable advancements were made in judicial decisions by invoking the principle of proportionality, considering family life, the right to translation as well as requiring thorough examination of prison conditions and the effective judicial protection in the issuing State. These developments represent a shift from automatic recognition of foreign judicial decisions, leading to enhanced protection of fundamental rights in Croatia.

The normative analysis has shown that Croatian law ensures the rights of accused individuals in line with the EAW FD and that persons arrested under an EAW have the same rights as those in domestic criminal procedures. Two unique aspects of the EAW execution procedure are that it may begin with an interrogation by the State Attorney instead of an arrest if deemed unnecessary by the police and that while the State Attorney can refuse to surrender if the offense is not recognized under Croatian law, this decision must still be validated by the court.

Over the past decade, Croatian judicial authorities have shown exceptional diligence in executing decisions based on mutual recognition, effectively integrating Croatia into the European system of criminal cooperation. They have taken a proactive approach in harmonizing its national legislation with EU standards, enhancing cross-border judicial cooperation in criminal matters. The practical implementation of EAWs and EIOs has generally been extensive, with a steady increase in Croatia's active participation in both issuing and executing warrants.

However, significant shortcomings remain in the implementation of the EIO D through the 2017 AJCCMEU, with only minor amendments since. The major problem is that while the 2024 amendment to the AJCCMEU converted the EAW mandatory grounds to optional, the same adjustment for the EIO did not occur, which is contrary to the EIO D. Additionally, partial implementation of several other EIO FD provisions was identified. The CJEU's *Gavanazov II* ruling exposed a critical gap: Croatia lacks legal remedies for challenging the issuance of an EIO for certain evidentiary actions, potentially affecting the execution of EIOs and the admissibility of evidence in Croatian courts. These discrepancies with recent CJEU judgments and conflicts with EU law highlight the need for further adjustments to align with evolving EU standards.

In Croatia, Regulation 1805/2018 is applied directly without additional transposing legislation, as confirmed by the AJCCMEU amendments in 2020, which designates the State attorneys and courts as competent authorities. Croatian law regards property confiscation as a restorative measure, not implying guilt, but requires a conviction for extended confiscation related to serious crimes. Few court decisions exist regarding the Regulation's application, but notably, the High Criminal Court referred a case to the CJEU for a preliminary ruling. This case concerns the recognition of a Slovenian confiscation order despite an acquittal and raises questions about procedural rights and the scope of 'proceedings in relation to a criminal offence' under the Regulation. The High Criminal Court is awaiting the CJEU's interpretation to resolve these issues.

In conclusion, Croatia has effectively integrated EU mutual recognition instruments into its legal system, demonstrating commitment to EU standards and principles. While challenges remain, recent legislative and particularly judicial developments indicate a stronger focus on protecting fundamental rights and ensuring proportionality in judicial cooperation.

CHAPTER 6

# France: Cooperation in Criminal Matters between Mutual Recognition and Protection of Fundamental Rights – the Contribution of France

*Eleonora Cervellera*

## 1 Introduction

The process of adapting French law to the instruments of judicial cooperation in criminal matters and mutual recognition began exactly twenty years ago. The Law of 9 March 2004[1] introduced a new chapter in the Code of criminal procedure relating to the European Arrest Warrant (EAW),[2] in application of the Framework Decision no. 2002/584/JHA of 13 June 2002 (EAW FD). France was a bit late on the roadmap laid down by the Council of the European Union – the new European arrest warrant system should have been operational by 1 January 2004 – but tried to make up for it by adopting the Law of 9 March 2004, which was immediately applicable. In the same terms as the Framework Decision, Art 695-11 of the Code of criminal procedure (CPP) defines the arrest warrant as "a judicial decision issued by a Member State of the European Union, called the issuing Member State, with a view to the arrest and surrender by another Member State, called the executing Member State, of a person sought for the purposes of a criminal prosecution or the execution of a custodial sentence or detention order". In accordance with the Framework Decision, the French Code of criminal procedure provides for a fully jurisdictional procedure for the execution of the EAW, excluding any intervention by political authorities. The European arrest warrant is directly transmitted by the issuing judicial authority to the public prosecutor (Art 695-26 Code of criminal procedure). Once the person who is the subject of the arrest warrant is arrested in France, he or she is first presented to the public prosecutor (Art 695-27 Code of criminal procedure). He or she then appears before the investigating chamber, which has jurisdiction to rule on the execution of the EAW (Art 695-29 Code of criminal procedure). Finally, if the investigating chamber has granted

1 Law no. 2004-204 of 9 March 2004 adapting the judicial system to evolutions in criminal matters, JORF no. 59, 10 March 2004.

2 Chapter IV of Title X, Book IV (Arts 695-11 to 695-58).

DOI:10.1163/9789004705791_008

authorization, the public prosecutor arranges for the person to be surrendered to the issuing State (Art 695-37 Code of criminal procedure).

More than a decade after the transposition of the Framework Decision on the European Arrest Warrant, the second cooperation instrument, Directive no. 2014/41/EU of 3 April 2014 regarding the European Investigation Order in criminal matters (EIO D), was transposed into national law by the *Ordonnance* of 1 December 2016.[3] France is thus one of the first countries to transpose the Directive, meeting the deadline set by the Parliament and the Council.[4] The *Ordonnance* inserts a new section 1 (Arts 694-15 to 694-50) into the chapter of the Code of criminal procedure relating to mutual assistance in criminal matters between the States of the European Union.[5] As with Framework Decision 2002/584, the provisions transposing Directive 2014/41 are codified 'in one block', in a specific section of the Code of criminal procedure, following a progression faithful to the European text.[6] The section of the French Code of criminal procedure concerning the European Investigation Order (EIO) opens with Art 694-15, which states that, except where the Code provides otherwise, requests for mutual legal assistance between France and other EU Member States are made via EIOs. As with the EAW, the EIO requires direct communication between the issuing judicial authority and the executing judicial authority. The authority competent under French law to execute the EIO depends on the act to be carried out. It is sent to and recognized by the investigating judge when it relates to acts that cannot be ordered or carried out other than in the course of a judicial investigation, or which can only be carried out in the course of an inquiry with the authorization of the liberty and custody judge. In all other cases, the decision is addressed to and recognized by the public prosecutor (Art 694-30 Code of criminal procedure).[7]

3 The *ordonnance* has been adopted in accordance with the authorization given to the government by Art 118 of Law no. 2016-731 of 3 June 2016 strengthening the fight against organized crime, terrorism and their financing and improving the effectiveness and guarantees of criminal procedure, JORF no. 0129, 4 June 2016. Under Art 38 of the French Constitution, an *Ordonnance* is an act taken by the government in matters that normally fall within the scope of the law. The government receives legislative authorization from Parliament to adopt regulations in this field.

4 22 May 2017.

5 Chapter 2, Title x, Book IV.

6 Eliette Rubi-Cavagna, 'La transposition des directives de l'Union européenne en droit pénal français' (2019), 1, Archives de politique criminelle, 147.

7 In French criminal procedure, there are two possible investigation frameworks. On the one hand, the inquiry (*enquête*) is the investigation carried out by judicial police officers under the supervision of the district prosecutor (*procureur de la République*), who is not an independent magistrate: he operates under the supervision of the public prosecutor (*procureur*

In 2018, when the Freezing and Confiscation Regulation 2018/1805 (Regulation 1805/2018) came into force, the national legal system for the mutual recognition of freezing and confiscation orders was already largely compliant with the EU framework, the French legislator having previously transposed into national law the existing European cooperation instruments relating to freezing orders and confiscation of assets. Council Framework Decision 2003/577/JHA of 22 July 2003 on the execution in the European Union of orders freezing property or evidence was transposed into French law in Arts 695-9-1 to 695-9-30 of the Code of criminal procedure by Law 2005-750 of 4 July 2005.[8] Council Framework Decision 2006/783/JHA of 6 October 2006 on the application of the principle of mutual recognition to confiscation orders was transposed into French law by Law 2010-768 of 9 July 2010.[9] This law enshrines in domestic law the principle of mutual recognition of confiscation orders in the EU judicial area, by introducing into the Code of criminal procedure a new chapter entitled "On the transmission and enforcement of confiscation orders pursuant to the Framework Decision of the Council of the European Union

*général*), who is himself under the supervision of the Minister of Justice. The enquiry is the common framework for investigation in France. On the other hand, the judicial investigation (*instruction*) is conducted by an investigating judge, who is an independent magistrate (*juge d'instruction*). Judicial investigation is mandatory for the most serious offences (criminal offences) and possible for other offences, particularly complex cases. To strengthen the judicial control during this pre-trial stage, the Law no. 2000-516 of 15 June 2000 reinforcing the protection of the presumption of innocence and the rights of victims, created a new judicial institution: the liberties and custody judge (*juge des libertés et de la detention, JLD*), considered as "*the Judicial Authority,* [*which acts as a*] *guardian of the freedom of the individual*". This Judge takes all deprivation of liberty decisions relating to the judicial investigation: the JLD has responsibility for ordering and extending pre-trial detention (*détention provisoire*) (art 137-1 CPP).

8 Law no. 2005-750 of 4 July 2005, containing various provisions adapting French law to European Union legislation in the justice field, JORF no. 156, 6 July 2005. With the transposition of the directive creating the European Investigation Order in 2016, Arts 695-9-1 to 695-9-30 of the CPP now only concern the freezing of assets liable to confiscation, since the European Investigation Order has become the only framework for requests for cooperation for probatory purposes. The 2016 Ordonnance transposing Directive 2014/41 therefore amended the version of most of Arts 695-9-1 et seq. of the CPP to take account of this change.

9 Law no. 2010-768 of 9 July 2010 aimed at facilitating seizure and confiscation in criminal matters, Chantal Cujatar, 'Commentaire des dispositions de droit interne de la loi du 9 juillet 2010 visant à faciliter la saisie et la confiscation en matière pénale', (2010) 35 Dalloz, 2305; Eric Camous 'Les saisies en procédure pénale: un régime juridique modernisé, commentaire des dispositions pénales de droit interne de la loi no. 2010-768 du 9 juillet 2010 visant à faciliter la saisie et la confiscation en matière pénale', (2011) 1 Droit pénal, étude 1.

of 6 October 2006" (Arts 713 to 713-35).[10] Even if the Regulation 1805/2018 is directly applicable in national law without any need for transposition, Law no. 202-1729 of 22 December 2021 introduces two new sections into the Code of criminal procedure specifying the competent transmission authorities and the remedies available for freezing[11] and confiscation orders.[12]

The French legislator, thus, appears to be concerned about transposing European provisions as faithfully as possible. However, an in-depth analysis of national law and case law reveals a number of critical points, showing the difficulty of balancing the requirements of effective cooperation under European law with the national sovereignty in criminal matters.

## 2 European Arrest Warrant: Critical Profiles in Legislation and Case Law

The procedure for execution of the EAW by the French authorities is structured in three phases: presentation to the public prosecutor after arrest, presentation before the investigating chamber,[13] and surrender of the person to the issuing authority. It is therefore the investigating chamber that is competent to rule on the execution of the EAW. The respect for the principle of mutual recognition between the judicial authorities of EU Member States, which is the essence of the EAW, means that the judicial authority's control over execution is limited to the existence of a ground for non-execution, as set out from Arts 695-22 to 694-24 of the French Code of criminal procedure. It is therefore not for the investigating chamber "to assess the merits of the prosecution carried out by the judicial authorities of the issuing Member State".[14] Thus, the investigating chamber is not required to verify the existence of serious or concordant

10 Chapter 3 Title I Book V of the CPP.

11 Section 5*bis* Chapter 2 of Title X Book IV, entitled "On the transmission and execution of freezing orders pursuant to Regulation 2018/1805 of the European Parliament and of the Council of 14 November 2018, on the mutual recognition of freezing orders and confiscation orders".

12 Section 1*bis* in Chapter 3 of Title I of Book V of the CPP, entitled "On the transmission and enforcement of confiscation orders pursuant to Regulation 2018/1805 of the European Parliament and of the Council of 14 November 2018, on the mutual recognition of freezing orders and confiscation orders".

13 The investigating chamber oversees all questions concerning the legality or proportionality of the acts of the pre-trial stage in case of a judicial investigation (judicial investigation without preliminary inquiry or judicial investigation after a preliminary inquiry).

14 Cass. Crim., 19 April 2005, no. 05-81.677; Cass. Crim., 5 April 2006, no. 06-81.835.

evidence against the person sought for prosecution.[15] As the deprivation of liberty is itself a particularly important issue, it becomes even more so when France must surrender a person within its territory based on a judicial decision taken by a foreign jurisdiction, without being able to verify the merits of the decision. The legal conditions for refusing to execute an arrest warrant (1), and the control over respect for fundamental rights during the execution of this measure (2), are thus fundamental issues of cooperation.

### 2.1 *The Gradual Extension of Optional Grounds for Refusal*

Art 3 of EAW FD lists the mandatory grounds for non-execution of the European arrest warrant. The three mandatory grounds for refusal set out in the EAW FD have been faithfully transposed into French law. The French authorities shall refuse to execute the arrest warrant: (1) If the offences on which the warrant was issued could have been prosecuted and judged by the French courts and the public prosecution is extinguished by amnesty; (2) If the requested person has been the subject, by the French judicial authorities or by those of a Member State other than the issuing State, of a final decision for the same offences as those which are the subject of the European arrest warrant provided, in the case of a judgment, that the sentence has been served or is currently being served or may no longer be executed under the law of the sentencing State; (3) If the requested person was aged under thirteen at the time of the offences covered by the European arrest warrant). In addition to these three grounds for refusal,[16] Art 695-22 adds another mandatory ground for non-execution of the European arrest warrant that is not provided for as either a mandatory or an optional ground for non-execution in the EAW FD, relating to the risk of discrimination of the person sought: Art 695-22 (5) provides that the European arrest warrant must be refused if it is established that the arrest warrant was issued for the purpose of prosecuting or convicting a person on account of that person's sex, race, religion, ethnic origin, nationality, language, political opinions, sexual orientation or gender identity, or that that person's position may

15 Cass. Crim., 30 March 2021, no. 21-81.554.

16 There were five mandatory grounds for refusal before 2021. The 4th paragraph of the article included, among the mandatory grounds for refusal, the case where the acts for which it was issued could be prosecuted and judged by the French courts and the statute of limitations had expired on the prosecution or the sentence. The Law no. 2021-1729 of 22 December 2021, for trust in the judicial system, JORF, no. 0298 of 23 December 2021, abolished this provision and transferred it to the optional grounds for refusal (Art 695-24 6° CPP).

be prejudiced for any of these reasons. This provision, which is based on the preamble to the EAW FD,[17] has been applied extensively in case law.[18] While the Court of cassation generally prohibits refusal of the European arrest warrant on the grounds of political opinion,[19] it nevertheless requires the trial courts to ensure, under Art 695-33 of the Code of criminal procedure, that the person is not at risk of serious violations of his or her fundamental rights, in particular for being detained for purely political reasons, following surrender.[20] It is interesting to note that in a recent judgment subsequent to the *Aranyosi and Căldăraru*[21] decision handed down by the Court of Justice, the French Court of cassation nonetheless relied on Art 695-22(5) of the Code of criminal procedure to overturn a decision by the Investigating Chamber, which had not sufficiently verified whether this ground for refusal had been met.[22] When the European arrest warrant is based on political prosecution, the refusal to surrender is therefore not based on the general clause of respect for fundamental rights, but on the specific ground for refusal set out in Art 695-22 (5)of the CPP.

The optional grounds for refusal are set out in Arts 695-24, 695-23(1) and 695-22-1 of the French Code of criminal procedure. In the original version of Art 695-24 resulting from the 2004 transposition law, there were only four grounds for optional refusal (existence of a French decision on the prosecution

17 To find a reference to the issue of discrimination, it is necessary to refer to point 12 of the preamble of the EAW FD, where it is stated that "Nothing in this Framework Decision may be interpreted as prohibiting the refusal to surrender a person" where the arrest warrant has been issued for the purpose of prosecuting or punishing that person "on account of his or her sex, race, religion, ethnic origin, nationality, language, political opinions or sexual orientation [...]". The list of grounds for discrimination in Art 695-22(5) CPP is almost identical to that in point 12 of the preamble to the Framework Decision, except that the Code of Criminal Procedure adds discrimination on grounds of gender identity.

18 In particular, it has been used by political refugees in France, members of the Marxist-Leninist Communist Party of Turkey (TKPML) and the Kurdistan Workers' Party (PKK), as well as by people belonging to organization campaigning for Basque independence. Cass. crim., 21 November 2007, no. 07-87.499; Crim., 9 June 2015, no. 15-82.750; Crim., 4 Octobre 2022, no. 22-85.259.

19 Cass. Crim., 30 March 2005, n° 05-81.221.

20 Cass. Crim., 26 September 2007, n° 07-86.099; Cass. Crim., 21 November 2007, n° 07-87.499; Cass. Crim., 9 June 2015, n° 15-82.750. Juliette Lelieur, "Réfugiés politiques: la protection des droits fondamentaux s'articule sur la confiance mutuelle", (2016) AJ pénal, 92.

21 Case C-404/15 and C-659/15 *Aranyosi and Căldăraru* [2016] ECLI:EU:C:2016:198.

22 Cass. Crim., 4 Octobre 2022, no. 22-85.259.

of the facts,[23] execution of the sentence on French territory,[24] commission of all or part of the offences on French territory,[25] incompetence of the issuing judicial authority under French law),[26] which became six from 2021. Indeed, two grounds for refusal that were originally included among the mandatory ones (existence of a final decision by a third State[27] and existence of a statute

23 Art 4 (2) and (3) Framework Decision. Under Art 695-24(1) CPP, execution of the EAW may be refused by the investigating chamber if "the requested person is being prosecuted [for the same acts] before the French courts or if the French courts have decided not to prosecute or to end the prosecution". It is understandable that the French courts would prefer to allow French proceedings to be concluded or to avoid a French decision not to prosecute being challenged in another EU Member State, rather than handing over to that State a person who is on French territory.

24 Art 695-24 2° CPP authorizes the investigating chambers to refuse to execute a European arrest warrant If the person sought for the execution of a custodial sentence or detention order is a French national, has established his or her residence on French territory or lives on French territory, and if the sentencing decision is enforceable on French territory pursuant to Art 728-31. The application of Art 695-24(2) CPP is subject to the condition that the requested person asserts the application of this provision before the investigating chamber. According to the Court of cassation, this court is not required to determine whether the sentence can be enforced on national territory (Cass. crim.,5 August 2004, n° 04-84.511; Cass. crim.,23 November 2004, n° 04-86.131, Bull. crim. n° 293). In its initial version, Art 695-24(2) CPP did not apply to foreign nationals who had been resident in France for at least five years. Following a warning from the Court of Justice (Case C-42/11 *Lopez Da Silva Jorge* [2012] ECLI:EU:C:2012:517), Law no. 2013-711 of 5 August 2013, containing provisions for adapting the justice system to European Union law and France's international commitments, JORF no. 0181 of 6 August, amended Art 695-24(2) CPP. It now covers all foreign nationals (and not just European Union nationals) provided that they have been "lawfully and continuously resident in France for at least five years" (Cass. crim.,5 November 2014, no. 14-86.553, Bull. crim. n° 229. The condition relating to length of time of residence was removed by Law no. 2021-1729 of December 22.

25 Art 695-24(3) CPP thus allows the investigating chamber to refuse to surrender a person if all or part of the offences with which the person is charged have been committed on French territory, even if no investigation or prosecution has been initiated in France (Cass. crim.,8 July 2004, n° 04-83.662, Bull. crim. n° 181).

26 Art 695-24(4) CPP authorizes refusal of enforcement where the issuing authority bases its international jurisdiction broader than a French judicial authority could do. Thus, if the offence was committed outside the territory of the issuing Member State and French law does not authorize prosecution of the offence on the basis of an extraterritorial ground of jurisdiction, the investigating chamber is justified in refusing enforcement.

27 Art 695-22(5) CPP authorizes refusal of enforcement where the requested person has been finally judged by a third State for the same acts as those which are the subject of the European arrest warrant, provided, in the case of a sentence, that the sentence has been enforced or is in the process of being enforced or can no longer be enforced under the laws of the sentencing State.

bar)[28] have been moved by the Law no. 2021-1729 of December 22, among the optional grounds for refusal.[29] Finally, another optional ground for refusal is set out in Art 695-22-1 of the Code of criminal procedure. This article transposes, two years late,[30] the new Art 4a of the EAW FD introduced by Framework Decision 2009/299/JHA (Decisions rendered following a trial at which the person did not appear in person). The first version introduced by the French legislator did not faithfully transpose the Framework Decision. Whereas Art 4a of the Framework Decision provides for an optional ground for refusal where the person who is the subject of the EAW issued for the purpose of enforcing a custodial sentence or detention order did not appear in person at the trial, Art 695-22-1 of the Code of criminal procedure considered this to be a mandatory ground for refusal.[31] Law no. 2021/1729 of 22 December 2021 amended Art 695-22-1 and made it compliant with EU law, transforming the mandatory ground for refusal into an optional ground. The decision to refuse delivery is therefore no longer automatic but depends on the sovereign appreciation of the trial judges.[32]

As regards the nature of the offence for which the European arrest warrant may be executed, Art 2(4) of the EAW FD states that surrender may be subject to the condition that the offence for which the warrant is issued constitutes an offence under the law of the executing Member State. In 2004, the French legislator, manifesting a rather nationalist attitude,[33] made double criminality a necessary condition for the execution of the measure (695-23 (1) CPP). So, France was not going to cooperate with another Member State for an act that it could not prosecute under French law.[34] Thus, in the original version of the article, the first paragraph provided for the obligation to refuse to execute a European arrest warrant if the offence for which the warrant was issued did not constitute an offence under French law. Nevertheless, it should be stressed that the concept of dual criminality has always been interpreted flexibly.

28 Art 695-22(5) CPP authorizes refusal of enforcement where the acts for which the European arrest warrant was issued could be prosecuted and judged by the French courts, and whether the statute barred prosecution or sentence has expired.

29 Law no. 2021-1729 of December 22.

30 Law no. 2013-711 du 5 August 2013.

31 Cass. Crim., 19 January 2021, no. 20-87.149.

32 "Whether or not to refuse to surrender […] falls within the sovereign assessment of the trial judges", Cass. Crim., 8 November 2022, no. 22-85.929; Cass. Crim., 10 May 2022, no. 22-82.379.

33 Jean Pradel, 'Le mandat d'arrêt européen. Un premier pas vers une révolution copernicienne dans le droit français de l'extradition' (2004) Recueil Dalloz, 1392.

34 Cass. Crim., 5 August 2004, n° 04-84.511.

According to the Court of cassation, for this condition to be met, it suffices that the offences can be classified as criminal offences under French law, even if the legal definition is not identical in the two countries. Therefore, although the national transposition was not formally compatible with the European text, the national court's flexible interpretation of the concept of double criminality made it possible to attenuate the non-compliance of domestic legislation.[35] Later on, Law no. 2021-1729 of 22 December 2021[36] replaced the word "must" with "may", thereby removing the mandatory nature of the principle of double criminality.[37] The provision can therefore now be deemed fully compliant with the Directive.

### 2.2 *The Extensive Protection of Fundamental Rights*

Respect for fundamental rights during the execution of a European arrest warrant is a major issue in French case law. Over the years, national courts have paid increasing attention to respecting the fundamental rights of the person subject to a European arrest warrant. Respect for fundamental rights is essential both when the domestic courts are deciding whether to execute the measure and surrender the person to the issuing State (a), and during the procedure for execution of the measure by the French authorities (b).

#### 2.2.1 Respect of Fundamental Rights in the Issuing State and Proportionality of the Surrender

National legislation does not indicate, nor does the European text, how the French jurisdictions should behave in the event of a violation of fundamental rights resulting from the execution of the arrest warrant.[38] The Court of cassation strives to implement the principle of mutual recognition as far as possible, as shown by the many decisions stating that, in the absence of grounds for refusing to execute the European arrest warrant, the investigating chambers are not justified in rejecting requests for the surrender of persons from other EU Member States. In the early years of the European Arrest Warrant, the Court of cassation applied this principle even when the argument raised concerned the violation of fundamental rights.[39] Subsequently, the Court has progressively extended its control in two situations: on the one hand, when

35 Cass. Crim., 5 April 2018, nº 18-81.528.

36 Law no. 2021-1729 of 22 December 2021.

37 This optional nature has been confirmed by the Court of cassation, Cass. Crim., 12 July 2022, no. 22-83.646.

38 Juliette Lelieur, Chloé Fauchon, 'Mandat d'arrêt européen' (2023) Répertoire de droit pénal et de procédure pénale.

39 Cass. Crim., 5 April 2006, nº 06-81.835; Cass. Crim., 8 August 2007, nº 07-84.621.

there is a risk that the fundamental rights of the person surrendered under the arrest warrant will be infringed in the issuing State; on the other hand, when the execution of the arrest warrant, and therefore the surrender of the person to another State, constitutes a disproportionate measure in relation to a fundamental right.

As for the risk of violation of the fundamental rights of the person surrendered in the issuing State, in a 2010 decision the Court of cassation annulled the decision of the investigating chamber, which had decided to execute a European arrest warrant without verifying whether the surrendered person had been subjected to torture in the issuing State, as she had claimed.[40] Furthermore, since 2012, the Court of cassation has accepted that a violation of fundamental rights constitutes a general ground for refusing enforcement that may prevent France from surrendering a person covered by an EAW, even when there are no legal grounds for refusing enforcement.[41] The Court of cassation bases this general exception on Art 1(3) of the EAW FD of 13 June 2002, which requires respect for "the fundamental rights of the person sought, and the fundamental legal principles enshrined in Art 6 of the Treaty on European Union". The European Court of Justice, in the *Aranyosi and Căldăraru* case,[42] has also tempered the principle of mutual recognition in the context of the execution of a European arrest warrant, by allowing the executing authorities to refuse to execute the arrest warrant where this is justified by the protection of the fundamental rights of the person subject to the measure. However, the Court of Justice has set strict conditions for this exception to the principle of automatic surrender: the executing judicial authority must establish that the person has failed to comply with the warrant on the basis of objective, reliable, precise and up-to-date information; and it must check, on the basis of serious and proven grounds, whether there is a concrete and precise risk to the individual covered by the arrest warrant. These checks therefore require a dialogue between the executing and the issuing authority. The clause introduced by the French Court of cassation in the event of a risk of violation of fundamental rights is similar, in principle, to the judgment of the Court of Justice. But whereas the latter set out particularly strict conditions for this exception, the French Court of cassation simply created a new ground for refusal justified by the risk of violation of the fundamental rights of the person surrendered,

40 Claim based on the violation of Art 15 of the Convention against Torture and Other Cruel, Inhuman or Degrading Treatment or Punishment signed in New York on 10 December 1984.

41 Cass. Crim., 28 February 2012, no. 12-80.744.

42 CJEU, *Aranyosi and Căldăraru* (n 21).

without imposing any further conditions.[43] Furthermore, the Court of cassation, when there is a suspicion that the person may suffer serious violations of fundamental rights, requires the investigating chambers to check with the issuing judicial authority, under Art 695-33, that the wanted person will not subsequently be extradited or handed over to a State where he or she could risk his or her life or liberty.[44] This provision, interpreted by the Court of cassation as a means of obtaining additional guarantees to those which already naturally found mutual recognition, may therefore constitute an obstacle to cooperation. The implementation of this Art also has an impact on the speed of execution of the European arrest warrant. The time limits of seven days (if there is agreement to surrender) or twenty days (if there is agreement to surrender) within which the investigating chamber must rule on the surrender, may be extended when the chamber applies Art 695-33. The investigating chamber shall ask the issuing judicial authority to provide the requested information within ten days. Although the French legislator has set a time limit of ten days for the provision of additional information, the request made under Art 695-33 justifies the decision of the investigating chamber not to rule within the time limits set out in Art 695-31 (3) and (4).

As regards the risk of violation of the fundamental rights of the person subject to the EAW, the execution of the measure is subject, as is the case for extradition, to a proportionality check in relation to the right to respect for private and family life, in accordance with the conditions set out in Art 8(2) of the European Convention on Human Rights (ECHR).[45] Art 695-24 (2) of the Code of criminal procedure, as does the Art 4 (6) of the EAW FD, provides that execution of the arrest warrant may be refused "if the person sought for the enforcement of a custodial sentence or detention order is of French nationality, has established his or her residence on French territory or remains on French territory and if the conviction is enforceable on French territory pursuant to Art 728-31". This article is certainly intended to protect respect for family life in the context of the European arrest warrant, by providing an optional ground

---

43 Cass. Crim., 28 February 2012, no. 12-80.744: "Considering that, subject to respect, as guaranteed by Art 1 (3) of the Framework Decision of 13 June 2002, of the fundamental rights of the person sought and of the fundamental legal principles enshrined in Art 6 of the Treaty on European Union, the execution of a European arrest warrant may not be refused on grounds other than those provided for in the Framework Decision and the texts adopted for its application".

44 Cass. Crim., 7 February 2007, no. 07-80.762, *AJ penal*, 2007, p. 188; Cass. Crim., 21 Nov. 2007, no. 07-87.499; Cass. Crim., 9 June 2015, no. 15-82.750.

45 Vissarion Giannoulis, 'Le principe de reconnaissance mutuelle des décisions judiciaires pénales et les droits fondamentaux' (2021) Phd Thesis Paris Nanterre.

for refusal when the person sought has close connections with France, and this effect is amplified by the reforms that have broadened the categories of the persons concerned by this ground for refusal. Indeed, in its original version, this article provided that enforcement could be refused only where the person sought for the purposes of enforcing the sentence was of French nationality; in 2013, the case was also added where the foreign national had established his or her residence on French territory for an uninterrupted period;[46] in 2021, the temporal condition (5 years) of residence was removed, and the case where the person sought simply lives in France was also added.[47] This article therefore now complies with the provisions of Art 4(6) of the Framework Decision, which allows the execution of the European arrest warrant to be refused not only when the wanted person is a national or resident of the Member State but also when he or she is simply living in France.

An overview of the national case law on the European arrest warrant shows that the Court of cassation requires an effective prior check on the proportionality between the surrender to the issuing State and the respect for the sought person's right to private and family life. The Court requires trial judges to ensure that the surrender of the wanted person does not disproportionately affect respect for his or her private and family life within the meaning of Art 8 ECHR. In a 2010 ruling, the Court of cassation overturned a decision by the investigating chamber that had agreed to the surrender.[48] The case concerned the surrender of a person who had been living in France for several years, with her five school-going children, for the theft of a wallet worth €40. The Court of cassation pointed out that any interference by the public authorities in a person's private life must be proportionate to the legitimate aim pursued, and criticized the judges for approving the execution of the arrest warrant without checking whether the surrender did not entail a disproportionate breach of respect for the private and family life of the person sought. If so, it is up to the French authorities to undertake to enforce the sentence. The Court of cassation's decision, based on Art 4 of the Framework Decision and on Art 8(2) of the ECHR, requires an *in concreto* control, in that it demands the trial judges to consider all the circumstances making it possible to assess the proportionality of the interference with the right to respect for private and family life. For example, the Court of cassation agreed with an investigating chamber's refusal to surrender a wanted person to the German courts for driving without a license, on the grounds that surrender would cause a disproportionate breach

46 Law no. 2013-711 of 5 August 2013.

47 Law no. 2021-1729 of 22 December 2021.

48 Cass. crim.,12 May 2010, no. 10-82.746.

of the right to respect for private and family life under Art 8 of the European Convention. The person concerned had worked regularly on French territory for several years, shared his life with a French woman and was the father of two children.[49] Similarly, the Court also approved of an investigating chamber that authorized the surrender to the Portuguese authorities, having fully justified the reasons for ruling out a disproportionate infringement of private and family life.[50] In a 2016 ruling, the investigating chamber authorized the execution of the arrest warrant on the grounds that the conditions set out in Art 695-24(2) (the person requested to serve a custodial sentence or a custodial security measure is a French national, has established his or her residence on French territory or lives on French territory, and if the sentence is enforceable on French territory) had not been met. If these conditions are not met, the connection with France cannot be considered sufficiently strong to affect, in the event of surrender, the family ties that the person maintains there. However, the Court of cassation overturned the ruling, on the grounds that the judges had not sufficiently verified whether the surrender would have a disproportionate impact on the right to respect for private and family life. This decision clarifies that the absence of the conditions set out in Art 695-24(2) does not absolve the investigating chamber from checking the proportionality of the offence.[51] It is therefore possible that the harm caused by the surrender may appear disproportionate even beyond the cases for which the optional ground for refusal of Art 4(6) is explicitly provided, thus confirming the existence of an autonomous ground for refusal such as to justify the refusal to execute the European arrest warrant that would create a disproportionate breach of the right to private and family life.[52]

#### 2.2.2 Respect for the Fundamental Rights before the French Courts Responsible for Executing the EAW

The French legislator applied to the execution of the European arrest warrant the same rules applicable at the domestic level concerning the deprivation

49 Cass. crim.,5 May 2015, no. 15-82.108. François Cordier, 'Le refus de remise suite à l'émission d'un mandat d'arrêt européen pour atteinte disproportionnée au droit au respect de la vie privée et familiale' (2015) Revue de Science Criminelle 906 Guillaume Taupiac-Nouvel, 'La protection du droit au respect de la vie privée et familiale dans la procédure du mandat d'arrêt européen: la chambre criminelle aurait-elle délié l'outre des vents contraires (2016) Les Petites Affiches no. 213, 6.

50 Cass. crim.,8 June 2011, no. 11-83.622.

51 Cass. crim.,12 April 2016, no. 16-82.175.

52 Dorothée Goetz, 'Mandat d'arrêt européen et droit au respect de la vie privée et familiale' (2016) Dalloz actualité.

of personal liberty and the rights of persons deprived of their liberty. Other rights, specific to the European arrest warrant, are also recognized.

The regime applicable to persons deprived of their liberty under a European arrest warrant is that of police custody (*garde à vue*) to which Art 695-27 Code of criminal procedure refers.[53] Police custody is a measure involving deprivation of liberty taken during a judicial investigation against a person suspected of having committed an offence. It is important to point out that the French police custody system was challenged by the European Court of Human Rights in 2008–2009 for its incompatibility with the rights of liberty and defense guaranteed by Arts 5 and 6 ECHR, notably due to the absence of a lawyer from the outset of the measure and during interrogations.[54] By reviewing compliance with the Convention, the Court of cassation directly verified the respect for the rights of the defense during police custody, where necessary disapplying domestic law and directly applying the requirements of the ECHR.[55] This control, therefore, also concerned the procedure carried out in France with a view to executing the European arrest warrant. In a 2010 decision of the Court of cassation, the requested person challenged the violation of his rights of defense during the surrender procedure by the French authorities to the Polish authorities. The person covered by the arrest warrant challenged the breach of his rights of defense, as she had not been given the opportunity to speak to an interpreter before appearing before the investigating chamber. In fact, the only article that refers to the assistance of an interpreter during EAW proceedings is Art 695-30 (3), which provides for it exclusively during the hearing before the investigating chamber, and not before the hearing. The Court of cassation, applying Arts 5 and 6 ECHR, affirmed that any person sought for the purposes of executing a European arrest warrant and benefiting from legal aid, has the right to be assisted free of charge by an interpreter in order to speak, in a language he or she understands, with the lawyer appointed to prepare his or her defense, even before being presented to the investigating chamber. The guarantees provided by the Convention, even in the absence of any legislative recognition, are granted by the Court of cassation to persons arrested under

53 Art 62-2 CPP procedure provides that "The custody is a coercive measure decided by a judicial police officer, under the supervision of the judicial authority, with which a person against whom there exist one or more plausible reasons to suspect that they have committed or attempted to commit a crime, or an offence punished with an imprisonment remains at the disposal of the investigators".

54 *Salduz v Turkey* App no 36391/02 (ECHR, 27 November 2008); *Dayanan* v Turkey App no 7377/03 (ECHR 13 October 2009); *Brusco v France*, App no 1466/07 (ECHR 14 October 2010).

55 Crim. 7 mars 2012, no. 11-88.118, D. 2012. 818; AJ pénal 2012. 346, obs. L. Ascensi; *Procédures* 2012, no. 157, obs. A.-S. Chavent-Leclère.

a European arrest warrant.[56] The fundamental rights of suspects deprived of their liberty during police custody have been considerably strengthened[57] by three successive laws, in 2011,[58] 2014[59] and 2016.[60] However, the Code of criminal procedure does not provide for any notification of the right of the person subject to the European arrest warrant to benefit from legal aid, neither does explicitly require the appointment of an interpreter to help the lawyer of the person subject to the arrest warrant to prepare his defense before appearing before the investigating chamber.[61] It can therefore be seen that, despite the rulings of the Court of cassation and the legislative reforms aimed at bringing domestic law into line with European standards, the provisions concerning the rights of persons deprived of their liberty under the European arrest warrant are still deficient on certain points. Although they are laid down in principle, the lack of information provided to the person concerned about his or her right to exercise them raises compatibility issues with the procedural directives of the Stockholm Programme.

A particularly problematic point raised before the French courts concerns the right of the person sought under a European arrest warrant to appeal against the decision authorizing his surrender. The EAW FD is not explicit on the question of appeals against decisions taken by the executing authorities. Under French law, when the person has consented to surrender, the decision of the investigating chamber is not subject to remedy, either before the court of appeal or before the Court of cassation (art 695-31 (3) of the Code of criminal procedure). On the other hand, where the person sought has not consented to surrender, the decision of the investigating chamber may be appealed by the

56 Cass. crim.,8 December 2010, no. 10-87.818.

57 Sébastien Pelle, 'Garde à vue et audition libre: acte final? Bilan d'un cycle de réformes (lois du 14 avril 2011, 27 mai 2014 et 3 juin 2016)' (2017) *Recueil Dalloz* 359 et s.

58 Law no. 2011-392 of 14 April 2011 on police custody, JORF no. 0089 of 15 April 2011. Anne-Sophie Chavent-Leclère, "La garde à vue est morte, vive la garde à vue! À propos de la loi no. 2011-392 du 14 avril 2011", (2011) Procédures, 7.

59 Law no. 2014-535, of 27 mai 2014 transposing Directive 2012/13/EU of the European Parliament and of the Council of 22 May 2012 on the right to information in criminal proceedings, JORF, no. 0123 of 28 May 2014.

60 Law no. 2016-731 of 3 June 2016.

61 When the requested person is presented to the public prosecutor, according to Art 695-27 CPP, he or she shall inform him or her of the existence and content of the European arrest warrant; of the possibility of consenting to his or her surrender and of the legal consequences thereof; and of the right to be assisted by a lawyer. The right to be assisted by an interpreter is not expressly mentioned in Art 695-27 CPP. However, the prosecutor's obligation to inform the arrested person of his or her rights "in a language he or she understands" implicitly implies the support of an interpreter if required.

person sought or by the public prosecutor, within three days of the decision. The Court of cassation must rule within forty days of the date of submission of the appeal (art 568-1 and 574-2). This distinction made by the French legislator is certainly explained by the fact that the consent to surrender and the guarantees attached to it – the person who is the subject of the European arrest warrant is informed of the legal consequences of this consent, as well as of its irrevocable nature (Arts 695-37 and 695-31) – justify the absence of an appeal against the decision of the investigating chamber. Inversely, the aim is therefore clearly to offer more guarantees, by providing additional control by the Court of cassation, when the person subject to the European arrest warrant has explicitly opposed his/her surrender. Although this difference in treatment in the event of consent or non-consent does not formally raise any problems with the Framework Decision – the FD does not require an appeal against the decision of the executing authority, but neither does it prohibit it – the absence of an appeal in the event of consent to surrender does raise questions, particularly in view of the consequences this decision entails for the person concerned. For the moment, however, this issue has not raised any doubts of compatibility with the right to an effective remedy, either before the domestic courts or the European courts.

On the other hand, one issue that has been the subject of much discussion concerns the situation envisaged by Arts 27 and 28 of the EAW FD and transposed into French law in Art 695-46 of the Code of criminal procedure. This is the case where a person who has been surrendered is subsequently sought by the same State that issued the EAW, or by another State for an offence other than that justifying surrender by the executing French authority. The investigating chamber is the competent authority to rule on the extension of the initial EAW. However, French law does not provide for the possibility of appealing against a decision by the investigating chamber to extend the surrender to offences other than those covered by the initial warrant. Initially, Art 695-46 of the French Code of criminal procedure provided that the investigating chamber's decision was "without appeal". The Court of cassation then referred a QPC (*question prioritaire de constitutionnalité*) to the Constitutional Council,[62] considering the risk of violation of the right to an effective remedy. The Court of cassation noted that "while a decision to hand over to foreign judicial authorities a person who has not consented to the execution of a European arrest warrant may be appealed to the Court of cassation, this is not the case for a decision

62 A *question prioritaire de constitutionnalité* (QPC) consists, in the course of a trial before an administrative or judicial court, in questioning the Constitutional Council as to the compatibility with the Constitution of the law that should apply during the trial.

of the investigating chamber, which rules without appeal on the request of the issuing Member State to consent to prosecution or to the enforcement of a sentence or security measure imposed for offences other than those for which the person was surrendered", and asks the Constitutional Council whether the absence of such an appeal is contrary to the Constitution, in particular to the principle of equality before the law and to the principle of the right to an effective judicial remedy.[63] Requested by the Constitutional Council to give a preliminary ruling, the CJEU considered that the EAW FD, while not explicitly providing for a remedy, did not preclude Member States from providing for one, as long as the time limit laid down in Art 17 was respected.[64] The Constitutional Council then carried out a constitutionality review and concluded that the domestic law not providing for a remedy constitutes an "unjustified restriction on the right to an effective remedy". It therefore declared the words "without appeal" in Art 695-46 to be unconstitutional.[65] The article was then amended by the law of August 5, 2013, giving access to an appeal to the Court of cassation against the decision of the investigating chamber authorizing the extension of the arrest warrant to other offenses.

## 3 European Investigation Order: Critical Profiles in Legislation and Case Law

The French government has proposed a very faithful transposition of the EIO D. Indeed, the transposition into national law is extremely faithful to the European text.[66] The article specifying the scope of the European Investigation Order is also to be commended for its clarity, grouping together in its various paragraphs all the measures that can be the subject of a European investigation order, which are scattered throughout the Directive (Arts 1 (1), 32 (1), 22 and 23). Thus, the first three paragraphs of Art 694-16 Code of criminal procedure set out the three purposes of a European investigation order: carry out investigations aimed at obtaining evidence relating to a criminal offence or at communicating evidence already in the possession of the authorities; provisionally prevent, on the territory of the executing State, any destruction, transformation, displacement, transfer, or alienation of items likely to be used as

63 Cass. crim.,19 February 2013, no. 13-80.491.

64 Case C-168/13 *Jeremy F* [2013] ECLI:EU:C:2013:358.

65 Cons. const., no. 2013-314 QPC, 14 June 2013.

66 François-Xavier Roux-Demare, "La décision d'enquête européenne ou l'adoption d'un instrument inédit de l'Europe penale", (2017) AJ pénal, 115.

evidence; temporarily transfer to the issuing State a person detained in the executing State, in order to enable procedural acts requiring that person's presence to be carried out in the issuing State, or temporary transfer to the executing State of a person detained in the issuing State for the purpose of participating on that territory in investigations requested. Although less problematic than the European arrest warrant, in that it does not involve deprivation of personal liberty, the European investigation order does affect evidence in criminal matters, which remains a highly sensitive aspect of criminal proceedings. Three critical points emerge from an analysis of French national law. Firstly, the non-compliant transposition of the grounds for refusal (1); secondly, the problematic status of the French Public prosecutor's office (2); and finally, the absence of a remedy for acts carried out during the inquiry (3).

### 3.1 *Non-compliant Transposition of Grounds for Refusal*

Art 694-17 of the French Code of criminal procedure extends the principle of mutual recognition to the EIO, providing that "Member States shall recognize a European Investigation Order without any formality, and shall execute it in the same way and under the same conditions as if the request had come from a national judicial authority, unless a valid reason provided for in this section for non-recognition, non-execution or postponement of the decision applies, and subject to the application of formalities expressly requested by the issuing authority which are not contrary to the fundamental principles of the law of the executing State", echoing the provisions of Art 9 (1) of the Directive.

In accordance with Art 11 of the Directive, grounds for non-recognition and non-execution of the decision are set out in Art 694-31(1–9) of the Code of criminal procedure. While the grounds for refusal set out in the Code of criminal procedure are similar in content to those set out in the Directive,[67] there is one major difference. Whereas the Directive provides for refusal to be optional (the executing State "may refuse", Art 694-31 provides for refusal to be mandatory (the magistrate to whom the case is referred "refuses" to recognize or execute the decision). This obviously raises a major issue in terms of compliance with the Directive. The French legislator thus refuses to accept the major advance in terms of cooperation offered by the EIO D, which provides only optional grounds for refusal and excludes all mandatory grounds.

67 Cf. Art 694-31 no. 1–9 CPP.

The French legislator has faithfully transposed, in Arts 694-36[68] and 694-39[69] of the Code of criminal procedure, the provisions of the Directive which introduce a clause relating to the failure to respect fundamental rights. But while in the case of the European arrest warrant, as mentioned above, there are many rulings by the Court of cassation limiting cooperation in the event of a violation of the fundamental rights of the person sought, this does not seem to be the case in the case of the European investigation. Although a basis for refusal of the investigation decision is explicitly provided for both in the European instrument and at domestic level, there seem to be no rulings whatsoever on this ground.

Among the grounds for non-recognition and non-execution by the executing judicial authority, Art 11(1)(b) of the Directive lists cases in which execution of the European Investigation Order risks harming essential national security interests, jeopardizing the source of information or involving the use of classified information relating to specific intelligence activities. Art 694-34(3) of the French Code of criminal procedure transposes this article and provides that "if the execution of the European investigation order risks harming essential national security interests, jeopardize the source of the information or involve the use of information that has been classified in accordance with the provisions of Art 413-9 of the Criminal Code and relates to intelligence activities, Arts 694-4 and 694-4-1 of the same code shall apply, and recognition or execution of the European investigation order may be refused by the Minister of Justice". So, where the request for a European investigation could be damaging to these interests, Arts 694-4 and 694-4-1 which require the intervention of the Minister of Justice, apply, in derogation of the principle of mutual recognition.[70] Art 694-34 clearly represents an obstacle to mutual recognition:

68 Art 694-36 CPP provides that «The investigation decision shall be executed in accordance with the formalities and procedures expressly indicated by the issuing authority, unless the law provides otherwise and provided, on pain of nullity, that these rules do not reduce the rights of the parties and the procedural guarantees applying the fundamental principles laid down in the preliminary article of this Code» (Art 9(2) of the Directive).

69 Art 694-39 CPP provides that "The judge hearing the case may refuse to allow the authorities of the issuing State to assist in the execution of the investigation decision on national territory only if it appears likely to reduce the rights of the parties and the procedural safeguards applying the fundamental principles laid down in the Preliminary Article or likely to harm the fundamental interests of the Nation" (Art 9(4) of the Directive).

70 Art 694-4 CPP provides that, when the execution of a request for judicial cooperation is likely to harm public order or the essential interests of the country, the Public Prosecutor will forward the request to the General Prosecutor, who may, if necessary, refer the matter to the Minister of Justice. In turn, the Minister of Justice will inform the

jurisdiction for enforcement is transferred from the judicial authority to the Minister of Justice, and recognition or enforcement of the investigative decision may be refused by the by the executive.

### 3.2 *Problematic Status of the French Public Prosecutor*

One of the main difficulties that may arise when executing the European Investigation Order concerns the status of the French public prosecutor's office. Under the terms of Arts 694-20 and 694-30 of the Code of criminal procedure, the EIO is issued, when France is the issuing State, or received, when France is the executing State, by the authority competent at national level to order or carry out the measure which is the subject of the EIO.

When the investigation order relates to acts which, in national proceedings, can only be ordered or carried out in the course of a judicial investigation, or which can only be ordered or carried out in the course of an investigation with the authorization of the liberty and custody judge, the EIO is issued by the investigating judge when France is the issuing State. It is recognized by the investigating judge and is carried out by the latter or by officers or agents of the judicial police acting on a rogatory commission from this judge, when France is the executing State. Where the investigative act covered by the European Investigation Order falls within the competence, under national law, of the public prosecutor, it is the latter who can issue or execute a European Investigation Order.[71] Under French law, during the inquiry phase, several acts may be carried out by the police under the supervision of the public prosecutor: house searches, deprivation of personal liberty (police custody), requisitioning of any private or public establishment or public authority likely to hold information relevant to the inquiry. As regards measures carried out by the public prosecutor, a potential issue of compliance with the ECHR could arise. Indeed, the French public prosecutor is placed under the authority of the

requesting authority, if necessary, of the total or partial impossibility of acting on the request. Art 694-4-1 provides that when the execution of a request for mutual assistance interferes with the mission of the special intelligence service to defend and promote the fundamental interests of the Nation, the Public Prosecutor forwards it to the General Prosecutor, who must refer the matter to the Minister of Justice. The Minister of Justice then informs the Minister responsible for the special intelligence service concerned, who must give an opinion within one month as to whether the request can be executed. In the event of a negative response, the Minister of Justice will inform the requesting authority, if necessary, of the total or partial impossibility of carrying out the request.

71 Cf. Introduction of the French national report.

Minister of Justice,[72] and thus operates under the influence of the executive. As the European Court of Human Rights has ruled on several occasions, the French public prosecutor's office is not a judicial authority as required by the Convention, since it lacks the necessary guarantees of independence.[73] As a result, he cannot ensure that the guarantees set out in the ECHR are respected during the execution of an inquiry (guarantees relating to the deprivation of personal liberty, guarantees relating to respect for the right to privacy, etc.). This can clearly also raise issues within the European Union as regards the guarantees that underpin mutual trust between Member States.

The question of the public prosecutor's jurisdiction to issue a EIO has arisen on several occasions before the Court of Justice. The Court has generally accepted that the public prosecutor is competent to issue an investigation order, ruling that Art 1(1) and Art 2(c) of the Directive must be interpreted as meaning that the public prosecutor's office of a Member State falls within the concepts of "judicial authority" and "issuing authority", regardless of the subordinate relationship that may exist between members of the public prosecutor's office and the executive.[74] The French Public Prosecutor's Office can therefore issue a EIO without being independent of the executive. The Court of Justice of the European Union has provided further clarification on the competence of the public prosecutor to issue a EIO in the *Encrochat* case.[75] This case, which has transnational dimensions, sees France in the front line:

---

72 Art 5 Ordonnance of the 22th December 1958: "*Les magistrats du parquet sont placés sous la direction et le contrôle de leurs chefs hiérarchiques et sous l'autorité du garde des sceaux, ministre de la justice. A l'audience, leur parole est libre*".

73 The European Court of Human Rights has taken the view that owing to their status, public prosecutors in France did not satisfy the requirement of independence from the executive which, according to its well-established case law, was, like impartiality, one of the guarantees inherent in the autonomous notion of "officer" within the meaning of Art 5 (3) (*Moulin v France*, App no 37104/06 (ECHR, 23 November 2010) § 57; *Medvedyev v France*, App no 3394/03 (ECHR, GC, 29 March 2010)). But the Constitutional Council has expressed disagreement with Strasbourg in a line of cases. In an important judgment published on the 8th of December 2017 (Cons. const., no. 2017-680 QPC, 8 December 2017), the Council held that, regarding the public prosecutor, the principle of independence of the judicial authority (no individual instruction, the principle of the opportunity of the prosecution …) was compatible with the powers given to the Government by the Art 20 of the Constitution ("*the Government shall determine and conduct the policy of the Nation*", which includes the power to determine the prosecution policy). This is also the position of the CJEU in the context of the European arrest warrant, see joint cases C-566/19 PPU and C-626/19 PPU *JR and YC* [2019] ECLI:EU:C:2019:1077.

74 Case C-584/19 [2020] ECLI:EU:C:2020:1002; *Dr. pénal*, 2021, comm. 35, A. Gogorza; *AJ pénal* 2021. 95, obs. M. Lassalle.

75 Case C-670/22 *Encrochat* [2024] ECLI:EU:C:2024:372.

during an investigation, the French authorities discovered an encrypted communication system used from various countries to commit drug trafficking offences. The data collected was transmitted by the French authorities to the Member States concerned via European investigation orders. Beyond the question raised at both national and supranational level as to the legality of the procedure followed in France to collect this connection data,[76] a major issue concerns the authority responsible for issuing a EIO to obtain the data collected from the French authorities. Indeed, the German judge asked the Court of Justice whether the German public prosecutor was competent to request the transmission of interceptions carried out by the French authorities, or whether respect for fundamental rights required the authorization of a court judge for such intrusive measures. The question of the breach of the right to a fair trial arises all the more since the technical system set up by the French authorities to collect the data is covered by national defense secret, making it impossible to verify the data transmitted.[77] According to the Court of Justice, Art 6(1) of the Directive does not preclude a public prosecutor from adopting an EIO for the transmission of evidence already in the possession of the competent authorities of the executing State, where such evidence has been acquired as a result of interception by those authorities on the territory of the issuing State, provided that the decision complies with all the conditions laid out by the law of that State for the transmission of such evidence in a domestic case. The Court of Justice has thus reduced mistrust of the Public Prosecutor, allowing him to control the issuing of a EIO with a view to the transmission of evidence already collected by the executing State, if the law of the executing State so provides.

As regards French law, Art 694-20 of the Code of criminal procedure states that where the measure requires the authorization of a judge, the EIO may only be issued by the public prosecutor with the prior authorization of that judge. It should be noted that, under the influence of the ECHR, the French legislator has progressively restricted the powers of the public prosecutor, by requiring that a magistrate with guarantees of impartiality and independence authorizes acts carried out during an enquiry. For example, until 2014, the public prosecutor could authorize the implementation of geolocation

76 Maxime Lassalle, "L'affaire Encrochat", Recueil Dalloz 2023, 1833.

77 This procedure allows the public prosecutor to use means covered by national defense secrecy at his or her own discretion, thereby excluding the procedures used to capture computer data from the adversarial debate (Art 706-102-1 CPP). The French Constitutional Council has validated the possibility of using these means of national defense secrecy (Cons. const. no. 2022-987 QPC, 8 April 2022).

measures (geographical location of mobile phones), on the basis of his general power to establish offences and gather evidence before opening a judicial investigation.[78] The power of the public prosecutor to authorize such measures was challenged before the Court of cassation as being contrary to Art 8 ECHR.[79] According to the Court, geolocation constitutes an interference with private life, whose seriousness requires that it be carried out under the supervision of a judge. In line with the case law of the Court of cassation, in 2014 the French legislator subjected geolocation to a new legal framework which requires the authorization of the liberty and custody judge.[80]

### 3.3 *The Lack of Appeals against Investigative Acts*

As regards the appeals that may be lodged against measures carried out under an EIO, Art 694-41 of the Code of criminal procedure provides, in accordance with the Directive, that measures carried out on national territory may be challenged in the same way and under the same conditions as if they had been carried out under a national procedure. The persons concerned are informed of their right to lodge an appeal where this is provided for in the Code of criminal procedure. Art D. 47-1-4 of the Code of criminal procedure specifies that when an appeal is lodged against the investigation decision, the magistrate must inform the issuing authority of the existence of the appeal as well as its outcome, but the absence of this information does not constitute a ground for nullity of the European investigation order.

Although the provisions of the Directive relating to remedies have been faithfully transposed into domestic law, it should be noted that under French procedural law, the right to appeal against investigative acts is limited. Under French law, no appeal is possible against investigative measures carried out during the police inquiry phase. The person suspected during the inquiry is not considered to be a party to the proceedings. An appeal against these measures can only be lodged when the person becomes a party to the proceedings, that is during the judicial investigation following the inquiry (in this case, an appeal against the investigative measures can be lodged with the investigating chamber) or during the trial (in this case, the appeal against the investigative measures can be lodged directly with the trial court). The absence of any means of appeal during the inquiry phase poses even more difficulties since most acts

---

78 Arts 12,13, 14 CPP.

79 Cass. crim.,22 Oct. 2013, no. 13-81.949.

80 The public prosecutor may only use geolocation for a limited period, after which authorization from a trial judge (liberty and custody judge or investigating judge) is required. Art 230-32 et seq. CPP.

are carried out by the judicial police under the supervision of the public prosecutor, who is not considered to be an independent judicial authority within the meaning of the ECHR.

## 4 Regulation 1805/2018: Critical Profiles in Legislation and Case Law

In French law, the rules governing the procedures for recognizing and enforcing freezing and confiscation orders between Member States are respectively contained in Arts 695-9-1 et seq. and 713 et seq. of the Code of criminal procedure.

As mentioned above, these rules result from the transposition of the two framework decisions on freezing and confiscation. With regard to freezing orders, Art 695-9-1 of the Code of criminal procedure states that a freezing order is an order issued by a judicial authority of a Member State of the European Union, known as the issuing State, to prevent the destruction, transformation, movement, transfer or disposal of property that may be subject to confiscation and that is on the territory of another Member State, known as the executing State. Property that may be subject to a freezing order, as provided for in Art 695-9-2, is any movable or immovable, tangible or intangible property, as well as any legal instrument or document evidencing title to or interest in such property, which the judicial authority of the issuing State considers to be the proceeds of an offence or to be wholly or partly equivalent to the value of such proceeds, or to be the instrument or object of an offence.

The French legislator faithfully reproduces the expression used in the Framework Decision 2003/577/JHA of 22 July 2003 on the execution in the European Union of orders freezing property or evidence, using the term *gel* (freeze) instead of *saisie* (seizure). In domestic law, the term *saisie* is used indistinctly for the temporary unavailability of property for both probatory and confiscation purposes. In EU law, on the other hand, the term "freezing" is used only for a measure of temporary unavailability for confiscation purposes, and not for probatory purposes. The Court of cassation recently stated that it follows from Art 2 of Regulation 2018/1805 that the freezing order constitutes an autonomous concept of European Union law. In domestic law, a freezing order corresponds to a decision to seize assets for which confiscation is provided for in Art 131-21 of the Criminal Code.[81] In the context of EU cooperation, the concept of freezing therefore now refers only to seizure for the purpose of confiscation.

81 Cass. crim.,13 December 2023, no. 22-87.237.

With regard to confiscation orders, Art 713 of the Code of criminal procedure states that a confiscation order is a penalty, or a definitive measure ordered by a court in a Member State of the European Union, known as the issuing State, following proceedings relating to one or more criminal offences, resulting in the permanent deprivation of one or more items of property. Property that may be subject to a confiscation order is, in accordance with Art 713-1, movable or immovable, tangible or intangible, as well as any legal act or document attesting to a title to or right over this property, on the grounds that: (1) they constitute the instrument or object of an offence; (2) they constitute the proceeds of an offence or correspond wholly or in part to the value of such proceeds; (3) they are liable to confiscation under any other provision of the law of the issuing State even though they are not the instrument, object or proceeds of the offence. The scope of property that may be subject to a confiscation order is therefore broader than that provided for in Art 695-9-1 in respect of freezing, in accordance with the Framework Decision of 6 October 2006 on confiscation, which Arts 713 et seq. transpose.

The development of cooperation between States on the seizure and confiscation of criminal assets depends not only on the correct and faithful transposition of EU provisions, but also on the substantial extension of the scope of seizure and confiscation procedures within national law. This is certainly the case in French law, which in the last decade has seen a significant increase in the number of cases where temporary or permanent deprivation of criminal assets is possible.[82] The extension of the scope of freezing and confiscations has a considerable impact on the effectiveness of cooperation in the recovery of criminal assets, as it increases the number of cases in which France can request the execution of a freezing or confiscation order on assets located in another Member State.

In the past, the additional penalty of confiscation only concerned dangerous or harmful objects, as well as objects that had been used to commit the offence or that were the proceeds of the offence. It was thus necessary to bring the seizure provisions in line with the broader scope of confiscation, in order to guarantee the enforcement of confiscation sentences. A major innovation was introduced by Law 2007-297 of 5 March 2007,[83] which transposed Council Framework Decision 2005/212/JHA of 24 April 2005 on the confiscation of crime-related proceeds, instrumentalities, and property and amended Art 131-21 of the Criminal Code. The law considerably extends the powers of

82 Lionel Ascensi, 'Droit et pratique des saisies et confiscations pénales' (2023) Dalloz, 728.

83 Law no. 2007-297 of 5 March 2007 on the prevention of delinquency, JORF no. 0056 of 7 March 2007.

the judge in confiscation matters. It is now possible for the judge to confiscate: a) all or part of the property belonging to the convicted person without any link to the offences prosecuted;[84] b) property whose illegal origin is only presumed, since neither the convicted person nor the owner of the property of which the convicted person is the holder is able to justify its origin;[85] c) the instrument, object or proceeds of an offence may also be confiscated in value, i.e. by equivalent, from any property in the convicted person's assets.[86]

The scope of seizure has therefore been extended. The provisions of the Code of criminal procedure only provided for the seizure for probatory purposes, without providing that seizure could be a preventive measure aimed at facilitating confiscation. Law no. 2010-768 of 9 July 2010[87] authorizes the seizure of assets subject to confiscation under Art 131-21 of the Criminal Code. Seizures made during searches, carried out by the public prosecutor[88] or by the investigating judge[89] in the course of an inquiry or a judicial investigation, can be now carried out not only on property for which evidence must be preserved, but also on property for which confiscation is provided for under Art 131-21 of the Criminal Code.[90]

In order to ensure better management of confiscated and seized assets, and to support the courts responsible for ordering these measures, the Law of 9 July 2010 also created the Agency for the Management and Recovery of Seized and Confiscated Assets (AGRASC),[91] whose operation and missions are specified by decree.[92] Its missions are to improve the seizure, management, confiscation and sale of criminal assets. But AGRASC plays also a fundamental role in international cooperation. It advises national courts, helping them to draw up freezing and confiscation certificates, and manages the sums seized

84 Art 131-21 (6) Criminal Code.

85 Paragraph 5 of Arts 131-21 Criminal Code is the most innovative provision. It now makes it possible, when a person is convicted of an offence punishable by five years' imprisonment or more and has directly or indirectly enriched himself, to confiscate assets for which he has not been able to justify their origin. This provision therefore reverses the burden of proof, since it requires proof that the assets are legal.

86 Art 131-21 (9) Criminal Code.

87 Law no. 2010-768 of 9 July 2010.

88 Art 56 and 76 CPP.

89 Art 97 CPP.

90 Art 56, 76 et 97 CPP.

91 Fournier Alain, 'La nouvelle Agence de gestion et de recouvrement des avoirs saisis et confisqués (AGRASC). À propos du décret du 1er février 2011' (2011) JCP, 334.

92 Decree no. 2011-134 of 1 February 2011 relating to the Agency for the management and recovery of seized and confiscated assets, JORF, no. 0028, 3 February 2011.

in France on foreign request, which are centralized in the AGRASC account (Art 706-159 et seq. Code of criminal procedure).

While national law strives to ensure that EU provisions are faithfully transposed and that the scope of application of measures enabling the temporary seizure or permanent confiscation of criminal assets is ever wider, some points remain critical and may weaken the effectiveness of cooperation. On the one hand, national law differs from the Regulation 1805/2018 in that it provides for grounds for refusal that are not entirely in line with the provisions of the Regulation (1), and in that it does not set time limits for the recognition and execution of freezing and confiscation orders (2). On the other hand, the increasing attention paid to the rights of third parties by national courts may restrict the effectiveness of the confiscation order (3).

### 4.1 *Grounds for Refusal That Not Entirely in Line with the Regulation*

As regards the grounds for refusal, both when the order concerns freezing and when it concerns confiscation, national law differs in several aspects from the Regulation 1805/2018.

First of all, whereas the Regulation provides that the enforcement authority "may" not recognize or execute an order on the grounds indicated, French law provides, for the grounds referred to in Art 695-9-17 (refusal of freezing order) and in Art 713-20 (refusal of confiscation order) that the order "is refused". The national legislation does not comply with the Regulation, in that it provides for mandatory grounds for refusal, whereas the Regulation only provides for optional grounds. Moreover, domestic law does not include a general clause addressing the risk of a manifest breach of fundamental rights provided for in the Regulation – such as the right to an effective remedy, the right to a fair trial, or the rights of the defense – that could result from executing a freezing or confiscation order. As there is no national case law on these points following the entry into force of the Regulation 1805/2018, it is difficult to assess whether the national legislation that existed before the Regulation has been implicitly repealed by the entry into force of the Regulation.

Secondly, a ground for refusal not provided for in the Regulation is set out in Arts 695-9-17, no. 3 and 713-20, no. 4, where the freezing or confiscation order has been issued with a discriminatory purpose. However, no ruling has been handed down by the national courts on this basis, and it is therefore difficult to carry out a relevant conformity assessment.

Thirdly, Arts 695-9-17 and 713-20 open with a clause providing that the freezing and confiscation order must be refused in the cases indicated, "without prejudice to the application of Art 694-4". Pursuant to Art 694-4 of the Code of criminal procedure, where the freezing or the confiscation order is likely to harm public order or the essential interests of the Nation, the Public Prosecutor will forward the request to the General Prosecutor, who will decide if there are grounds to refer the matter to the Minister of Justice, who will then decide whether or not to execute the request. It is therefore clear that Art 694-4 is an obstacle to mutual recognition: in this case, jurisdiction for enforcement is transferred from the judicial authority to the government, and recognition or enforcement of the order may be refused by the Minister of Justice.

### 4.2 *Lack of Time Limits for Recognizing and Enforcing Freezing and Confiscation Order*

One aspect on which domestic law differs from the regulations concerns the deadlines for recognizing and enforcing a freezing and a confiscation order.

As regards the freezing order, Art 695-9-13 provides that the investigating judge, after verifying the legality of the request, "shall decide on the execution of the freezing order as soon as possible and, if possible, within twenty-four hours of receipt of the order. S/he immediately executes or orders the execution of the freezing order. S/he shall inform without delay the judicial authority of the issuing State of the execution of the freezing order by any means which leaves a written record". Domestic law establishes no provision for cases where the issuing authority has indicated in the freezing certificate that execution must take place on a specific date (Art 9(2) of the Regulation 1805/2018), nor for cases where the issuing authority has indicated in the certificate that immediate freezing is necessary, due to the risk of destruction of the property or the needs of the investigation (Art 9(3) of the Regulation 1805/2018). In the latter case, the Regulation stipulates that the executing authority must decide whether to recognize the freezing order no later than 48 hours after receiving it and must execute it within 48 hours of the decision. Domestic law provides, as a general rule, that the decision must be taken as soon as possible and, if possible, within 24 hours of receipt of the order, but it does not lay down any mandatory time limit for urgent cases.

No time limits are set for execution of the confiscation order either. The Regulation 1805/2018 provides that the enforcement authority must adopt its decision on the recognition and enforcement of the confiscation order without delay and no later than 45 days after receipt of the certificate of confiscation (art 20 (1)). Under national law, on the other hand, Art 713-15 provides only that the correctional court shall rule "without delay" on the enforcement of the confiscation order, without setting any mandatory time limit.

As regards the time limits for enforcing the decision that has already been recognized by the court, while the Regulation 1805/2018 provides that the executing authority shall take the necessary measures to enforce the confiscation order without delay and, at the very least, with the same speed and the same degree of priority as for a similar domestic case, nothing is provided for in national law. Art 713-30 only states that the Public Prosecutor's Office of the court that has issued the ruling "shall continue the execution of the authorization decision", without further specifying the timeframe for execution. While the provision laid down in national law was applied by the national courts before the Regulation came into force,[93] no ruling has yet applied the provision of the Regulation which requires time limits for recognizing and enforcing freezing and confiscation order.

### 4.3 *Increasing Attention to the Rights of Third Parties*

A tricky point in freezing and confiscation matters concerns the rights of third parties, other than the person concerned by the freezing or confiscation measure, who are affected by it. Indeed, the measure may affect not only the person prosecuted or convicted, but also the person who has rights over the property subject to freezing or confiscation. Under the Regulation 1805/2018, these persons fall into the very broad category of "person concerned", which includes not only the natural or legal person against whom a freezing order or confiscation order is issued, but also the natural or legal person who owns the property that is the subject of the order, as well as any third party whose rights in respect of that property are directly affected by the order in accordance with the law of the executing State.

In French law, the concept of third parties acting in good faith in relation to freezing or confiscation refers to the person who is subject to these coercive measures due to the fact that he is the owner of the property, for offences that he did not commit. Under certain conditions, French law limits the possibility of implementing a freezing or confiscation measure to protect his or her interests. Art 713-20(6) of the Code of criminal procedure provides, in accordance with Art 19 of the Regulation 1805/2018, that the impossibility under French law of enforcing a confiscation order issued by another Member State because of the rights of third parties acting in good faith constitutes a ground for refusing a confiscation order.[94] In accordance with Recital 15 of the Regulation, determining whether a confiscation order affects the interests of third parties and can therefore be refused on this ground depends on the definition of the rights of third parties recognized by French law, the law of the executing State. French law does not define the concept of good faith in the context of seizures

93 Crim.,10 October 2017, no. 17-80.118.

94 Refusal is mandatory under French law, whereas it is optional under the Regulation 1805/2018.

and confiscations.[95] The courts, although they make their own assessment of the good faith of the third party in order to preserve their rights,[96] do not provide a definition either. However, an analysis of the rulings handed down in this field reveals criteria for assessing good faith. In the case of a natural person, the family ties between the third party and the person being prosecuted may prevent it from being held that the third party was unaware of the criminal activity.[97] In the case of a legal person, the links that exist between it and the offender may also constitute a criterion excluding good faith.[98]

Determining the rights of third parties in freezing and confiscation proceedings is far from straightforward in French law.[99] Both the legislator and the judges try to find a balance between the aim of hitting criminal assets as hard as possible and protecting the fundamental rights of those who own the property. Thus, while the property liable to be freezing or confiscated is constantly expanding,[100] the protection afforded to owners acting in good faith is also being extended. In fact, where the confiscated object is dangerous or harmful or its possession is unlawful, there is no exception to confiscation: there are no provisions protecting the rights of the third-party owner.[101] When it comes to the object or direct or indirect proceeds of the offence, Art 131-21(3) of the Criminal Code mentions as the only exception to confiscation only property liable to restitution to the victim, without making any mention of the rights of the third party in good faith. However, the Court of cassation has extended the protection of the owner in good faith by recognizing that, in accordance with the provisions of Art 6(2) of Directive 2014/42/EU of the European Parliament and of the Council of 3 April 2014, the rights of the owner in good faith must be preserved even where the property constitutes the direct or indirect proceeds of the offence.[102] Applying European Union law, the Court of cassation

---

95 Haritini Matsopoulou et Hervé Robert, 'Confiscation des biens des tiers: les conditions de la libre disposition et de la bonne foi' (2020) JCP G 209.

96 Cass. crim.,15 January 2014, no. 13-81.874.

97 E.g. the partner of an accused person, who had lived with her partner since 1997 and was aware of his criminal record, could not "seriously claim to have been unaware of the fraudulent origin of the funds that enabled the couple to repay the loans granted for the acquisition of this property, given her partner's financial situation", Cass. crim.,9 December 2014, no. 13-85.150).

98 E.g. the good faith of the company was excluded when the accused was its sole manager, Cass. crim.,15 January 2014, no. 13-81.874).

99 Jean Pradel, 'Droit pénal général' (2019) 22 edition, 611.

100 Cf. French national report.

101 Art 131-21 paragraph 7 of the Criminal Code specifies that such property may be confiscated from whomever it belongs, even if the convicted person is not the owner.

102 Cass. crim.,7 November 2018, no. 17-87.424.

therefore extends the reservation of the rights of a third party in good faith to a situation not provided for in the text. In other forms of confiscation (when the confiscated property is the instrument of the offence,[103] when it is a confiscation of property for which the convicted person cannot justify the origin,[104] when it is a confiscation of property from the convicted person's assets that has no connection with the offence,[105] or when it is a value confiscation),[106] the property that may be confiscated must belong to the convicted person or be at his or her free disposal, subject to the "rights of the owner in good faith". In order to prevent offenders from hiding their assets and to ensure that the confiscation penalty is effective, the law authorizes the confiscation of property owned by the convicted offender, as well as that which is freely at the convicted offender's disposal. The only limit set is respect for the rights of third-party owners acting in good faith. This means that confiscation cannot be ordered against property of which the convicted person has free disposal when the property belongs to a third party who has no knowledge of its unlawful use. The concept of good faith is assessed on a case-by-case basis by the trial judges.[107] There is therefore an undeniable increase in the attention paid to the rights of third parties, which may constitute grounds for refusing a confiscation order, thus limiting cooperation on this point.

One of the key points handled by the Regulation is that of the restitution to the victim (Art 29 of the Regulation), which allows the issuing authority to inform the executing authority when it has taken a decision to return frozen property to the victim, so that the latter can take the necessary measures to implement the decision as quickly as possible. The decision to return the seized property to the victim is taken by the public prosecutor, pursuant to Art 41-4 of the Code of criminal procedure (during the inquiry) or by an order of the investigating judge, pursuant to Art 99 (during the judicial investigation). The decision to make restitution to the victim taken on these grounds and sent to the foreign courts must state that the funds shall be transferred to the agency's account at the *Caisse des Dépôts et Consignations*. The funds must pass through the agency and not be returned directly by the foreign authorities to the victim. The AGRASC report of 2022 clearly shows that the French courts have taken up this possibility offered by the Regulation since it came

103 Art 131-21 paragraph 2 Criminal code.
104 Art 131-21 paragraph 5 Criminal code.
105 Art 131-21 paragraph 6 Criminal code.
106 Art 131-21 paragraph 9 Criminal code.
107 Cass. crim.,15 January 2014, no. 13-81.874.

into force. In 2020, only 6 restitutions were executed by foreign authorities at the request of the French authorities; in 2021, they doubled to 12; in 2022, they doubled again to 23 (for a total of 7,498,008.24 euros returned to victims only in 2022).[108]

## 5 Concluding Remarks

An overall analysis and confrontation of French national law with European cooperation instruments reveals that, on the whole, national law is in line with European expectations. France is formally a good performer in the development and implementation of its legislation on European cooperation in criminal matters. The EAW FD and the EIO D have been explicitly transposed into national law. As for the provisions of the Regulation 1805/2018, they are well coordinated with the national rules already existing before their entry into force, since the French legislator had carefully transposed instruments relating to the freezing and confiscation of criminal assets existing before the Regulation 1805/2018.

The transposition of the cooperation instrument on the European arrest warrant into national law can be considered satisfactory overall and in line with the expectations of the Framework Decision. The analysis of national law reveals two interesting aspects, which point in the opposite direction.

On the one hand, as regards the grounds for refusal, the legislator who transposed the EAW FD in 2004 extended the list of mandatory grounds for refusal compared with European provisions. But in 2021, certain grounds for mandatory refusal were transferred to the list of grounds for optional refusal. For example, the absence of the condition of double criminality, formerly a mandatory ground for refusal under French law, has become an optional ground for refusal, in accordance with the Framework Decision. This trend towards transforming mandatory grounds for refusal into optional grounds contributes to bringing national law more into line with the Framework Decision and promotes cooperation in that execution of the EAW is not automatically refused but is assessed on a case-by-case basis by the judicial authority.

On the other hand, the French courts that have to execute the EAW are increasingly careful about the risks of violating the fundamental rights of the person surrendered. The risk that the surrendered person may suffer a violation

108 Rapport activité AGRASC 2022, p 192, <https://crimhalt.org/2023/07/21/rapport-dactivite-de-lagrasc-2022-un-an-dusage-social-des-biens-confisques/> accesed 30 july 2024.

of their fundamental rights in the issuing State, as well as the finding that the surrender leads to a violation of the right to private and family life, constitute frequent grounds for refusal of surrender by national courts. Contrary to the Court of Justice, the French Court of cassation does not subject the control of the breach of fundamental rights to the strict conditions of the *Aranyosi and Căldăraru* ruling. If the protection of fundamental rights inevitably benefits from this lax control, mutual recognition necessarily loses in effectiveness.

The transposition of the Directive on the European Investigation Order is particularly faithful to the text of the Directive; the domestic provisions are almost a copy-paste of the European text. However, a number of critical points have been raised.

The first point of criticism concerns the grounds for refusal of a EIO submitted to the French authorities. While the Directive only provides for optional grounds for refusal, the French legislator has a long list of mandatory grounds for refusal, which severely restricts cooperation between States in matters of evidence. In addition, where the execution of the investigative decision is likely to harm national interests, recognition or execution of the investigative decision may be refused by the Minister of Justice. We are therefore seeing the return of the government's power, which the 2014 Directive was intended to remove.

A second critical point arises from the status of the French public prosecutor. The effectiveness of cooperation between Member States has been seriously undermined by the doubts relating to the competence of the public prosecutor to issue an EIO when the intrusive nature of the investigation measure is particularly harmful to fundamental rights. Although the Court of Justice has tried to mitigate this danger in the context of the transmission of connection data previously collected within a Member State, the competence of the public prosecutor to authorize the acquisition of an investigation document remains a sensitive issue. This is even more the case when, as in France, the status of the public prosecutor's office is problematic because of its lack of independence from the executive.

A third and final point of criticism concerns the surprising absence of rulings by national courts on European investigation decisions. This lack raises doubts about the reasons behind it. Does this mean that the instrument of cooperation is rarely used, evidence still being a field in which national control is sought? Or does it mean that, while it is used, it generates few contentious cases?

The French legal framework governing the recognition and enforcement of freezing and confiscation orders within the European Union shows solid alignment with European action in this field, underlining France's commitment to fighting transnational crime by striking at criminal assets.[109] This is due both to the direct transposition into French law of the cooperation instruments that precede the Regulation 1805/2018, and to the progressive broadening in national law of the scope of seizure and confiscation measures. However, certain national provisions, such as the broadening of grounds for refusal and the absence of strict deadlines for the enforcement of orders, represent potential obstacles to seamless cooperation.

Indeed, although the Regulation 1805/2018 is directly applicable in national law – i.e. the grounds for refusal and time limits provided therein apply without the need for transposition – it might be appropriate to clarify these points at legislative level, in order to facilitate the action of national courts in an already highly complicated matter. In addition, the increasing focus on the rights of third parties, while crucial to the protection of fundamental rights, may further complicate the enforcement of confiscation orders. The analysis of French law on this point has also revealed a more general difficulty that could hinder effective cooperation between States in this area. While the extension of the scope of freezing and confiscation measures at the national level constitutes a major advancement in the fight against cross-border crime, it also evidently leads to a complication of the rules related to seizure and confiscation. The issuance and execution of freezing and confiscation orders requested by or from another Member State follow the rules established in the sections of the Code of criminal procedure relating to cooperation between France and other Member States regarding freezing and confiscation. These provisions refer to the conditions under which freezing and confiscation orders are adopted or executed under national law. Internal rules, which are very complex in this matter (different forms of seizure and confiscation depending on the nature, the object, and the modalities of execution), must therefore be coordinated with the specific provisions that must be applied when the freezing or confiscation order concerns assets located in another Member State or assets located in France for which foreign authorities request freezing or confiscation. Despite the formal alignment of domestic legislation with the Regulation 1805/2018, the effectiveness of cooperation in French law is hampered by a fragmented and interwoven discipline, which is constantly evolving and whose complexity still eludes the understanding of the courts.[110]

---

109 Lionel Ascensi, Pascal Beauvais, Raphaële Parizot 'La confiscation des avoirs criminels' (2021) *LGDJ*.

110 Ibid.

CHAPTER 7

# Germany: a Clash of Systems between EU Mutual Legal Assistance Instruments and National Law

*Anna H. Albrecht and Anne Schneider*

## 1 Introduction

Germany has always been a staunch supporter of the EU. This is not surprising when considering that Germany is one of the EU Member States with the most bordering States and thus profits more from free cross-border transfers than many other countries, but is also more threatened by cross-border crime. The German positive outlook on the EU has led to a general willingness to implement EU law.

True to form, the German legislator implemented all mutual legal assistance instruments into German law. In doing so, the legislator opted for the integration of the EU-based rules into the existing law on mutual legal assistance and amended the Act on International Legal Assistance (*Internationale Rechtshilfegesetz – IRG*)[1] accordingly. However, this chapter will show, by using the examples of the European Arrest Warrant (EAW), European Investigation Order (EIO) and Regulation 1805/2018, that this integrative approach has not always been successful. In order to do so, the implementation of the three instruments into German law will first be discussed with a focus on controversial issues and case law. This contribution then argues that many controversies come from differences in the EU and German legal systems, in particular a diverging understanding of the way power is distributed between legislative and executive powers, as well as between the issuing and the executing State in mutual legal assistance.

1 Bundesgesetzblatt (Federal Law Gazette) 1994 I, 1537.

## 2 European Arrest Warrant: Critical Profiles in Legislation and Case Law

### 2.1 *Scope and Double Criminality*

The rules on the scope of the EAW are straightforward and are oriented on Art 2 EAW FD. In Germany, the main rules are set out in Art 81 IRG, which refers to Art 3 IRG. The latter generally requires double criminality in cases of extradition or surrender, but the law makes exceptions for offences that are punishable by a sanction involving deprivation of liberty of a maximum of at least three years and belong to one of the categories listed in Art 2(2) EAW FD (see Art 81 No. 4 IRG).

A prominent example of the double criminality requirement was the *Puigdemont* case. Carles Puigdemont, the leader of the Catalan separatist movement, was arrested in Germany on the basis of an EAW by the Spanish authorities for "rebellion" and "corruption". The Higher Regional Court Schleswig found that there was no German equivalent for "rebellion" because the relevant provisions in German law required violence.[2] Double criminality was required because "rebellion" was not listed in Art 2(2) EAW FD. In contrast, "corruption" was one of the categories in which double criminality should not be assessed, and the reasoning that the act in question (wasting public money) qualified as "corruption" was plausible for the court.[3]

### 2.2 *Grounds for Non-recognition and Non-execution*

The German legislator has implemented most of the grounds for non-recognition and non-execution of the EAW.[4] As will be seen below, this is due to the fact that the German Constitutional Court required further protection of German nationals than was initially foreseen in the first implementation law,[5] which did not make use of many of the exceptions provided in the EAW FD.

The German legislator first implemented the EAW FD with the "Act implementing the Framework Decision on the European arrest warrant and the surrender arrest warrant and the surrender procedures between the Member States of the European Union of 21.07.2004 (EAW I)".[6] However, the German

2 OLG Schleswig, decision of 12.07.2018, BeckRS 2018, 19152.

3 OLG Schleswig, decision of 12.07.2018, BeckRS 2018, 19152; OLG Schleswig, decision of 05.04.2018, BeckRS 2018, 4762.

4 The only grounds not implemented into German law are Art 4(5) (*ne bis in idem*) and Art 4a(3) (detention while waiting for a retrial).

5 See BVerfG, judgment of 18.07.2005, BVerfGE 113, 273.

6 Bundesgesetzblatt – BGBl. (Federal Law Gazette) 2004 I, 1748.

Constitutional Court held that this law violated the constitutional rights of the person concerned, in particular Art 16(2) and 19(4) Basic Law (*Grundgesetz* – GG, the German Constitution).[7] Art 16(2) GG forbids the extradition of German citizens to foreign countries, but not within the EU.[8] Although the amended version of Art 16 GG allowed the surrender of German citizens, the Constitutional Court held that the law was disproportionate in not making use of the exception provided in Art 4(7) EAW FD.[9] Moreover, the Court found a violation of the guarantee of judicial protection (Art 19(4) GG) because the decision authorizing the surrender was not subject to judicial review.[10] The German legislator then drafted a second law for implementing the EAW FD,[11] taking account of the judgment of the Constitutional Court. This version restricted the surrender of German citizens but kept the old rules for foreign citizens.

#### 2.2.1 Fundamental Rights and Proportionality Issues

One of the most controversially discussed topics in EU criminal law is whether EU instruments in general, and the EAW in particular, protect fundamental rights sufficiently. There was a particular focus on the question whether or not recognition and execution of the EAW can be refused by referring to fundamental rights. The IRG has a so-called "public order clause" in section 73 that applies to all types of mutual legal assistance.[12] The first sentence contains the rule on violations of the national public order. However, for cooperation within the EU, the second sentence applies (so-called "EU public order"). For a long time, it was unclear whether section 73 IRG was in breach of the EAW FD because the EAW FD does not explicitly allow refusing the execution of an EAW in case of fundamental rights violations. However, the CJEU has in the

7 BVerfG, judgment of 18.07.2005, BVerfGE 113, 273.

8 In order to facilitate mutual legal assistance within the EU, sentence 2 had been added in 2000, which reads: "*The law may provide otherwise for extraditions to a Member State of the European Union or to an international court, provided that the rule of law is observed*".

9 BVerfG, judgment of 18.07.2005, BVerfGE 113, 273, 304 ff.

10 BVerfG, judgment of 18.07.2005, BVerfGE 113, 273, 309 ff.

11 Act implementing the Framework Decision on the EAW and the surrender arrest warrant and the surrender procedures between the Member States of the European Union of 20.07.2006 (EAW II), Bundesgesetzblatt – BGBl. (Federal Law Gazette) 2006 I, 1721.

12 Section 73 IRG reads as follows: "The rendering of mutual assistance and the transmission of data without a request is not permissible if it would contradict core principles of the German legal system. In the case of requests pursuant to Part 8, 9, 10 and 13, the rendering of assistance is not permissible if executing the request would go against basic principles as set out in Article 6 of the Treaty on European Union".

meantime recognized that fundamental rights violations can provide a reasonable ground for refusal in *Aranyosi und Căldăraru*.[13]

Since then, section 73 sentence 2 IRG has often been invoked. Most of the judgments that refer to Art 73 sentence 2 IRG relate to the surrender to countries with bad imprisonment conditions. For example, surrender to Bulgaria has often been refused due to the bad conditions in Bulgarian prisons.[14] The same happens for Greece.[15] Similar arguments have been made consistently for Romania, Latvia, Hungary and Lithuania, but also for Poland, France, Belgium and Spain.[16] A trustworthy guarantee by the State in question can, however, help the courts to allow surrender.[17] Other arguments in the context of section 73 IRG were a disproportionate penalty in the issuing State, e.g., a penalty of lifelong imprisonment that did not take into account imprisonment that had already taken place in another State,[18] or excessive penalties.[19] Surrender has also been refused in case of a severe violation of defence rights, such as the right of access to a lawyer or of access to the file.[20]

It should also be noted that the German Constitutional Court has developed a right to refuse surrender if this would violate fundamental rights guaranteed in the German Constitution and thus threaten the identity of the Constitution (so-called "*Identitätskontrolle*" = identity control).[21] The identity control was a condition set by the Constitutional Court for Germany's agreement to the Lisbon Convention: if a measure taken by the EU or necessary under EU law violates the inviolable guarantees referred to in Art 79(3) GG and is thus irreconcilable with German Constitutional Law, the Constitutional Court reserves the right to defy the supremacy of EU law.[22] This exceptional measure was

13 Case C-404/15 *Aranyosi and Căldăraru* [2016] ECLI:EU:C:2016:198.

14 See, e.g., OLG München, decision of 12.12.2018, BeckRS 2018, 17663; KG Berlin, decision of 28.08.2015, BeckRS 2015, 12531 mn. 7 ff.; OLG Celle, decision of 17.12.2014, BeckRS 2015, 9794 mn. 10 ff.

15 See, e.g., OLG Brandenburg, decision of 22.03.2022, BeckRS 2022, 5759; OLG München, decision of 09.01.2018, BeckRS 2018, 263; OLG Hamm, decision of 30.11.2017, BeckRS 2017, 136404; OLG Stuttgart, decision of 08.06.2016, BeckRS 2016, 11835.

16 See the overview of German jurisprudence in Neil Goerge, 'Menschenrechtswidrige Haftbedingungen als Ablehnungsgrund in der Praxis des Europäischen Haftbefehls aus Perspektive der deutschen Gerichtsbarkeit unter besonderer Berücksichtigung des Grundsatzes gegenseitigen Vertrauens' (2024) ZfIStW 107, 111 ff.

17 See OLG Bremen, decision of 16.02.2023, BeckRS 2023, 5079 (for Cyprus).

18 OLG Hamm, decision of 09.09.2016, BeckRS 2016, 16677; KG Berlin, decision of 22.12.2009, BeckRS 2010, 453.

19 OLG Zweibrücken, decision of 22.04.2021, BeckRS 2021, 8805.

20 OLG Karlsruhe, decision of 26.02.2020, BeckRS 2020, 27088.

21 First applied to the EAW in BVerfG, decision of 15.12.2015, BVerfGE 140, 317.

22 BVerfG, judgment of 30.06.2009, BVerfGE 123, 267, 340 ff. – *Lisbon Treaty*.

designed in order to safeguard fundamental principles of German Constitutional Law and was, among other things, a reaction to the *Melloni* case of the CJEU.[23]

Its first application was in a case on the surrender of a person who had been convicted *in absentia*.[24] The Higher District Court Düsseldorf felt obliged under the EAW FD to surrender the person, even though there were some doubts about whether Italian courts would grant a sufficient retrial.[25] In this decision, the Constitutional Court recapitulates the reasoning of the identity control:

> Within the framework of the identity review, one has to review whether the principles laid down as inalienable by Art 79 sec. 3 GG are affected by an act of the European Union [...]. The result of such a review may be that in exceptional cases [...] Union law must be declared inapplicable in Germany.[26]

The Constitutional Court found that the decision to surrender the person in this case violated their human dignity (Art 1 GG), which is one of the unchangeable and inviolable guarantees referred to in the so-called "eternity clause" in Art 79(3) GG.[27] This result was in clear contrast to the CJEU jurisprudence in *Melloni*, which was recognized by the Constitutional Court. It recapitulated the CJEU's findings in *Melloni* and went on to explain that:

> [t]hese stipulations, however, do not relieve German authorities or courts of their obligation to ensure that the principles of Art. 1 sec. 1 GG

---

23 Case C-399/11 *Stefano Melloni v Ministerio Fiscal* [2013] ECLI:EU:C:2013:107.

24 BVerfG, decision of 15.12.2015, BVerfGE 140, 317.

25 See, in more detail, Frank Meyer, 'From Solange II to Forever I – the German Federal Constitutional Court and the EAW (and How the CJEU Responded)' (2016) NJECL 277, 278 ff.

26 BVerfG, decision of 15.12.2015, BVerfGE 140, 317 mn. 43 (official English translation).

27 "Art. 1 sec. 1 GG can be violated by executing the Framework Decision on the European arrest warrant, because, in extraditing a person with the purpose of executing a sentence rendered in the absence of the requested person, one enforces, through criminal law, a reaction to socio-ethical misconduct, a reaction that is incompatible with the guarantee of human dignity and the rule of law (Rechtsstaatsprinzip) unless the individual blameworthiness (individuelle Vorwerfbarkeit) of the person concerned has been determined by the competent court (a). Therefore, one must also ensure compliance with the minimum procedural rights of the accused guaranteed under the rule of law and aimed at establishing the true facts of the case, rights that are necessary to ensure the effectiveness of the substantive component of the principle of individual guilt, in the extradition procedure determined by Union law that is triggered by a European arrest warrant (b).", BVerfG, decision of 15.12.2015, BVerfGE 140, 317 mn. 52.

> are complied with in the context of extraditions executing a European arrest warrant [...]. Rather, they must ensure that [...] the minimum guarantees of the rights of the accused required by Art. 1 sec. 1 GG will also be observed in the requesting Member State, or – where this is impossible – refrain from extraditing the person concerned. To this extent, the principle of mutual trust that governs extraditions within Europe is limited by human dignity guaranteed under Art. 1 sec. 1 GG.[28]

Scholars have pointed out that EU law would have allowed to refuse surrender in the case in question and that the problem was, in fact, the misapplication of EU law by the German court and the lack of appeal in extradition and EAW cases.[29] Nonetheless, the case shows that the Constitutional Court is willing to subject surrender on the basis of an EAW to the scrutiny of the German Constitution. This reasoning also applies to other areas of mutual legal assistance (and other areas of EU supremacy).[30]

From the point of view of EU law, this practice clearly defies the goals of mutual recognition and goes against the *Melloni* jurisprudence. It is one thing to allow EU fundamental rights to prevent the surrender of a person, but another to grant this right to any constitutional provision in the Member States. Such an approach makes the applicable law effectively unforeseeable and defeats the purpose of the mutual legal assistance rules.[31] Nonetheless, the struggle in creating human rights-based arguments in EAW cases shows the consequences of the EU's failure to give room to fundamental rights considerations. Later EU directives and regulations are clearer on the role of fundamental rights and prevent some of the confusion attached to the EAW by explicitly allowing the refusal of mutual legal assistance in case of a violation of fundamental rights.[32]

---

28 BVerfG, decision of 15.12.2015, BVerfGE 140, 317 mn. 83.

29 See, e.g., Frank Meyer (n 25) 277, 279 ff.; Christoph Schönberger, 'Anmerkung zu BVerfG, Beschluss v. 15. 12. 2015-2 BvR 2735/14.' (2016) JZ 422 ff.; Helmut Satzger, 'Grund- und menschenrechtliche Grenzen für die Vollstreckung eines Europäischen Haftbefehls? – "Verfassungsgerichtliche Identitätskontrolle" durch das BVerfG vs. Vollstreckungsaufschub bei "außergewöhnlichen Umständen" nach dem EuGH' (2016) NStZ 514 516 ff.

30 As a general principle, this reasoning applies to any area of mutual legal assistance and any instance in which EU law is applied. So far, this has been the only case.

31 See, in more detail, Anne Schneider 'In absentia trials and transborder criminal procedures. The perspective of EU law' 605, 628 ff. in Serena Quattrocolo, Stefano Ruggeri (eds), *Personal Participation in Criminal Proceedings* (Springer 2019).

32 See, e.g., *infra*, §1.4.2.1.

#### 2.2.2 *In absentia* Trials

*In absentia* trials are covered by section 83(1) no. 3 IRG. Generally, surrender is forbidden if the person sentenced was absent from the trial which is the foundation for the sentence. This is in line with German procedural law, which has always put a huge emphasis on the presence of the defendant and does not allow for *in absentia* trials in principle. However, the law allows for exceptions from this rule in the following paragraphs of section 83(1) IRG. These exceptions are based on Art 4a EAW FD and are to be interpreted similarly. It should also be noted that the doctrine of the "identity control" was developed in a case of an *in absentia* trial (*supra*, §1.2.2.1).

Recently, the issue has been raised in German law whether the implementation of Art 4a EAW FD was successful. The problem relates to the fact that Art 4a(1) gives the judicial authority the *right* to refuse the execution of the EAW, so the option to do so, whereas section 83(1) IRG *forbids* the extradition under these circumstances. This means that the German judicial authorities do not have discretion to decide on surrender but must refuse it. This raises the question of whether German law, in not granting the discretion foreseen in the EAW FD, is too narrow and thus in breach of EU law. This question was recently transferred to the CJEU by German courts.[33] The CJEU decided that the mandatory refusal of surrender laid down in German law was indeed contrary to EU law.[34] The consequences of this decision are unclear: generally, the primacy of EU law would require national law to provide the discretion foreseen. As this is not the case and cannot be assumed to the detriment of the person concerned, a change of law will be necessary. An interpretation of section 83 IRG that allows for discretion goes against the wording of the provision and is thus not an adequate ground for such discretion under German law.[35]

---

33 KG Berlin, submission decision of 14.06.2022, BeckRS 2022, 13807; OLG Brandenburg BeckRS 2022, 39762. In the case in question, the Polish authorities had requested the surrender of a person for the execution of a sentence. The person concerned had attended the Polish trial, but had been absent from the final sentencing trial, in which several offences with individual sentences were combined to a common sentence. The German authorities were willing to surrender because the combination of sentences does not require the presence of the defendant in German law, but they felt bound by the law to refuse surrender.

34 Case C-396/22 *Generalstaatsanwaltschaft Berlin* [2023] ECLI:EU:C:2023:1029.

35 Dieter Inhofer, '§ 83 IRG mn. 3', in Graf (ed), Beck'scher Online-Kommentar zur StPO (50th edn, 2024).

### 2.2.3 *Ne bis in idem*

The grounds for refusal that are based on the *ne bis in idem* principle have been implemented in three provisions of the IRG, that is section 9, section 83(1) no. 1 and section 83b(1) no. 1, 2 IRG. Section 83b IRG contains obstacles to the authorization of the surrender by the competent executive authorities and is thus subject to discretion. It allows the authorities to refuse surrender when there are criminal proceedings for the same facts by German authorities or when these have refused to open or continue with criminal proceedings (Art 4 (2, 3) EAW FD). It does not apply to criminal proceedings ongoing in other EU countries.[36]

Section 83(1) IRG deals with final judgments in other Member States (including the issuing State)[37] on the same facts. If there was such a judgment, surrender must be refused, provided that the sanction was, in case of conviction, enforced, is currently being enforced or could not be enforced under the law of the sentencing State (cf. Art 54 CISA).[38] This provision differs in two respects from Art 4(3) EAW FD: first, Art 4 contains optional grounds for refusal, but section 83 IRG does not give discretion to the authorities. This has been regarded as a breach of EU law in the case of *in absentia* trials (see *supra,* §1.2.2.2). Secondly, Art 4 refers to "a final judgment [...] which prevents further proceedings" and does not contain the so-called "enforcement clause".

Nonetheless, despite these differences, the German law does not violate the EAW FD in this respect, for a twofold reason. On the one hand, since the CJEU has upheld the applicability of the enforcement clause of Art 54 CISA to Art 50 CFR,[39] a final judgment only prevents further proceedings within the EU if it has been enforced, is actually in the process of being enforced or can no longer be enforced under the laws of the sentencing Contracting Party. Accordingly, the different wording in the German law is arguably a valid interpretation of EU law. On the other hand, the second issue is the lack of discretion foreseen in the German law, which has proven to be a problem in the case of *in absentia* trials (*supra,* §1.2.2.2). However, under EU primary law, the executing State does not have discretion in allowing surrender or not. If there is a final decision with *ne bis in idem* effect, the Member States are forbidden to initiate criminal proceedings. The CJEU has recently included extradition and surrender

36 OLG Braunschweig, decision of 16.09.2022, BeckRS 2022, 25122.

37 OLG Celle, decision of 23.05.2018, BeckRS 2018, 10787.

38 Convention implementing the Schengen Agreement of 14 June 1985 between the Governments of the States of the Benelux Economic Union, the Federal Republic of Germany and the French Republic on the gradual abolition of checks at their common borders, OJ 2000 L 239.

39 Case C-129/14 *Spasic* [2014] ECLI:EU:C:2014:586.

proceedings into the scope of the *ne bis in idem* principle, which means that extradition or surrender are contrary to EU primary law when the case has already been finally judged.[40] The wording of the EAW FD is thus misleading. Because there is no discretion on EU primary law level, the German implementation law complies with EU law.

Section 9 IRG deals with criminal offences that are punishable under German law and have been the subject of certain judicial decisions with *res judicata*. Again, there is no discretion for the German authorities: surrender must be refused. In contrast to section 83 IRG, section 9 IRG does not contain an enforcement clause for final judgments, but obliges the authorities to refuse surrender even if a convicting judgment has not yet been enforced. From the perspective of EU law, this is not a problem because surrendering a person that has been finally convicted in the executing State is a situation in which not the transnational *ne bis in idem* principle (Art 54 CISA) applies, but the national one which is laid down only in Art 50 CFR. This provision forbids multiple proceedings within a State even if the first judgment was not (yet) enforced. Because Art 50 CFR is also primary law, the lack of discretion is in compliance with EU law.

#### 2.2.4 Surrender of Citizens and Residents

German law distinguishes between German citizens and citizens of EU Member States and third States. The surrender of German citizens is regulated by section 80 IRG that contains rules implementing Art 4(6, 7) EAW FD. Section 80 IRG forbids the surrender unless the criteria contained in there are met. Again, there is no discretion in the German transposition law. The reason for this is the influence of German Constitutional Law, in particular Art 16(2) GG. According to this provision, the extradition of German citizens is generally not allowed. An exception can be made for EU Member States, but this exception must be as narrow as possible. The lack of protection of German citizens was the reason why the first implementation law was considered to be in breach of the Constitution (*supra*, §1.2.2). Now, the law forbids the surrender of German citizens, unless the issuing State promises to transfer the person back for the enforcement of the sentence and there is a substantial link between the criminal offence and the issuing Member State. A substantial link exists when the crime was committed in the issuing State and when, in minor cases, the effects of the crime took place in this State (§ 80(1) sentence 2 IRG).

40 Case C-435/22 *Maersk* [2024] ECLI:EU:C:2024:349.

The nationality of the victim does not suffice.[41] Again, German law leaves no discretion to the judge: if the conditions of the provision are not met, the person must not be surrendered. However, section 80 IRG is very complex and requires, besides the substantial link, in certain cases as a condition a balancing of the interests of the German national not to be surrendered and the interests of the issuing State to prosecute.[42] From a theoretical point of view, the balancing of interests is a condition for a set consequence: if the judge finds that the interests of the German national do not prevail and the other criteria of the paragraph are met, the judge is obliged to allow the surrender, so has no discretion in this respect. However, from a practical point of view, the norm effectively gives the judge a huge leeway to decide in favour of or against the surrender. Accordingly, section 80 IRG conforms to the EAW FD.

In contrast, the surrender of foreign citizens is permitted in similar circumstances, i.e. without a substantial link to the issuing State, but can be refused if the foreign citizens are habitually resident in Germany and their interests to

---

41 OLG Dresden, decision of 13.12.2022, BeckRS 2022, 35753. In this case, Poland wanted to have a German citizen, a former Stasi officer, surrendered for a murder of a Polish national that had occurred at the border between Western and Eastern Berlin in 1974.

42 Section 80(2) IRG reads: "If the conditions of subsection (1) sentence 1 no. 2 are not met, extradition of a German national for the purpose of criminal prosecution is only permissible if
1. the conditions of subsection (1) sentence 1 no. 1 are met and
2. the offence has a substantial link to Germany and
3. the offence is also an unlawful act under German law which fulfils the elements of a criminal provision or would also be such an act under German law in the case of analogous conversion of the facts, and, after weighing up the various concrete, contradictory interests, the person pursued's legitimate expectation in not being extradited does not prevail.

An offence generally has a substantial link to Germany if the entire offence or essential parts of the offence were committed within the area of application of this Act and at least essential parts of the result occurred there. When considering the various interests, the criminal charge, the practical requirements and possibilities in respect of effective criminal prosecution, and the person pursued's constitutionally protected interests are specifically to be weighed up and set in proper relation to one another, giving due consideration to the goals associated with the creation of a European judicial area. Where a public prosecution office or a court has given a decision to terminate or not to institute criminal proceedings in Germany for the offence which is the subject matter of the request for extradition, this decision and its reasoning are to be included when considering the various interests; the same applies accordingly where a court has opened main proceedings or has issued a summary penalty order."

remain there prevail (section 83b IRG).[43] The rule is an obstacle to the authorization of surrender (*Bewilligungshindernis*) that is decided upon by the executive authorities, not the court, and gives discretion to these authorities. The reason for the distinction between German and foreign citizens is Art 16(2) GG, which limits the right to extradite German citizens, but does not apply to foreign citizens. Foreign citizens are thus worse protected than German nationals. This is also apparent by the larger amount of court decisions on the surrender of foreign citizens.[44] It appears to be unclear under which circumstances the interests of the habitually resident foreign citizen not to be surrendered prevail. The courts look at external factors such as language, work, family, in order to decide if someone is to be surrendered or if this person's interests of staying in Germany are dominant.

It has been argued that section 83b(2) no. 2 IRG constitutes discrimination against other EU nationals because they cannot prevent the surrender in these cases as easily as Germans, and are subject to a discretionary decision.[45] Although there might be reasons for distinguishing between German and foreign citizens, the threshold for justifying the difference is higher for EU citizens than for other foreign nationals. Accordingly, after a certain period of time spent in Germany (CJEU in *Wolzenburg*:[46] five years), EU citizens must be treated equally to Germans in order to prevent a violation of Art 18 TFEU.

---

43 § 83b(2) IRG:
(2) Authorisation of the extradition of a foreign national who is habitually resident in Germany may, further, be refused if,
1. in the case of extradition for the purpose of prosecution, the extradition of a German national would not be permissible pursuant to section 80 (1) and (2),
2. in the case of extradition for the purpose of enforcement of a penalty, the foreign national, following instruction, does not consent to extradition, such non-consent being declared before and placed on record by a judge, and that person's legitimate interests in enforcement in Germany prevail; section 41 (3) and (4) applies accordingly.

44 See in the past couple of years OLG Saarbrücken, decision of 11.05.2023, BeckRS 2023, 10817; OLG Brandenburg, decision of 20.09.2021, BeckRS 2021, 32351; however, OLG Karlsruhe, decision of 02.06.2014, BeckRS 2014, 15796; OLG Brandenburg, decision of 13.09.2021, BeckRS 2021, 29137; OLG Brandenburg, decision of 07.07.2021, BeckRS 2021, 19029; OLG Brandenburg, decision of 15.09.2022, BeckRS 2022, 29232; OLG Brandenburg, decision of 04.06.2020, BeckRS 2020, 12235; OLG Bremen, decision of 11.09.2013, BeckRS 2013, 17627; KG Berlin, decision of 28.08.2012, BeckRS 2013, 1207; OLG Frankfurt a.M., decision of 08.12.2016, BeckRS 2016, 13556; KG Berlin, decision of 15.03.2016, BeckRS 2016, 9285; OLG Karlsruhe, decision of 01.10.2019, BeckRS 2019, 12670.

45 See Martin Böse, '§ 83b IRG' in Heinrich Grützner, Paul-Günter Pötz, Claus Kreß, Nikolaos Gazeas, Dominik Brodowski (eds), *Internationaler Rechtshilfeverkehr in Strafsachen* (C. F. Müller, 107th installment July 2012) margin note 34 ff.

46 Case C-123/08 *Wolzenburg* [2009] ECLI:EU:C:2009:616; see also OLG Frankfurt a.M., decision of 08.12.2016, BeckRS 2016, 13556.

In these cases, the German authorities are obliged to refuse the authorization of the surrender.

## 2.3 *Execution Procedure*

German law on judicial cooperation traditionally differentiates between two phases: the admissibility phase and the authorization phase.[47] In matters of extradition, the courts have to decide whether extradition is admissible or not. The Higher Regional Court (*Oberlandesgericht*) has jurisdiction in first instance for decisions about extradition (section 13 IRG). If extradition is admissible, the executive authorities (*Generalstaatsanwaltschaft*, the Attorney General's office) can decide whether they wanted to extradite or not, often based on questions of policy.[48] This authorization decision (*Bewilligungsentscheidung*) was traditionally regarded to be a policy matter between the States and was thus not subject to judicial review.

### 2.3.1 Admissibility and Authorization Decision

The German legislator has kept the distinction between admissibility decision and authorization decision for EAW matters. While some of the grounds for refusal in the EAW FD have been implemented as grounds for the inadmissibility of surrender (e.g., section 80, 83 IRG), others are merely obstacles to authorization (e.g., section 83b IRG). It should be kept in mind that grounds for inadmissibility render surrender inadmissible while obstacles to authorization allow the authorities to refuse surrender, i.e. they give the authorities discretion. Moreover, the courts traditionally decided on the admissibility of surrender while the authorization decision was not subject to judicial review. However, the rules have been modified as a result of the aforementioned decision of the German Constitutional Court on the first implementation law.[49] In this judgment, the German Constitutional Court decided that some of the refusal grounds in the EAW FD concerned fundamental rights of the person concerned and thus required judicial review.[50]

As a result of this judgment, the German legislator needed to draft a second implementation law that provided for judicial review of the obstacles to

47 A more detailed description of the execution procedure can be found in Martin Böse and Maria Bröcker, 'Country Report "Germany"' in Martin Böse, Maria Bröcker and Anne Schneider (eds), *Judicial Protection in Transnational Criminal Proceedings* (Springer 2021) 93, 95 ff.

48 Suzan Denise Hüttemann, § 13 'Grundlagen der Zusammenarbeit' in Martin Böse (ed), *Europäisches Strafrecht*, (Nomos 2020), margin note 36.

49 BVerfG, judgment of 18.07.2005, BVerfGE 113, 273.

50 BVerfG, judgment of 18.07.2005, BVerfGE 113, 273.

authorization. In this law, the German legislator chose to keep the traditional procedure also in EAW cases, but to enable prior judicial review of not only the admissibility of surrender but also of the obstacles to authorization, in which some of the grounds for refusal had been implemented (see section 79 IRG). The procedure is now as follows:

Traditionally, the decision on the admissibility of surrender taken by the Higher Regional Court comes first, the authorization of surrender later. In order to enable judicial review, the executing authority that is competent to authorize the surrender has to decide whether they see obstacles to authorization prior to the court's assessment of admissibility (section 79(2) IRG). The executing authorities then need to give reasons if they do not see obstacles and thus plan on granting authorization. These reasons can be assessed by the court when deciding on the admissibility. The court then decides whether there are obstacles that will prevent the authorization of the surrender (which is decided upon later). If the court finds that surrender is admissible and that no obstacles to authorization are apparent, the executing authorities can then decide whether or not they want to authorize surrender, which is the actual authorization. It should also be noted that authorization can only be refused for one of the grounds laid down in section 80 ff. IRG, i.e., the provisions implementing the EAW FD. The actual authorization, which follows after the Higher Regional Court deems the surrender admissible, has consequently lost its importance.

This traditional system of judicial cooperation does not fit with the system of the EAW FD, in which the grounds for refusal are limited and the surrender of a person is not subject to political considerations. Therefore, the German legislator has been criticized for keeping this distinction and trying to apply it to EU governed legal assistance.[51] Moreover, the existing procedure is very complicated because the Higher Regional Court must decide on admissibility and take a preliminary assessment of the authorization decision, but cannot actually authorize the surrender.[52]

51 Suzan Denise Hüttemann (n 48); Frank Zimmermann, '§ 83b IRG' in Wolfgang Schomburg, Otto Lagodny, Sabine Gleß, Thomas Hackner and Sebastian Trautmann (eds), *Internationale Rechtshilfe in Strafsachen* (C.H. Beck 2020), mn. 2 ff.; Martin Böse, Maria Bröcker and Anne Schneider, 'Rechtsschutz in der internationalen Rechtshilfe in Strafsachen – Defizite und Reformbedarf' (2021) JZ 81, 84.

52 Martin Böse and Maria Bröcker (n 47) 93, 95 ff.

### 2.3.2 Judicial Authority

In the past couple of years, another problem with the German implementation law has become apparent: the existence of an ambiguity on the notion of "judicial authority". In 2019, with *OG and PI*, the CJEU decided that the German public prosecution office was not a judicial authority because it lacked independence from the executive authorities.[53] The reason for this was that the Ministry of Justice can give orders to the public prosecutors on how to use their discretion for dispensing with criminal proceedings in the cases foreseen by the law. It should be noted that German authorities are required under the principle of legality to initiate criminal proceedings, but can dispense with the proceedings under certain circumstances, e.g., in case of minor offences or compensation outside the framework of criminal law (sections 153 ff. StPO). The German legislator has not changed the law as a result of *OG and PI*, so that, on paper, the public prosecution office is still the competent judicial authority for issuing the EAW. Since then, however, all EAWs are issued by the judge, as are national arrest warrants under German law (section 112 StPO).[54] Even before *OG and PI*, an EAW could only be issued when a national arrest warrant, which is issued by a judge, was in existence, but the EAW itself, which is a different document, was only issued by the public prosecution office. Now, the judge needs to decide on both the national arrest warrant and the EAW.

The public prosecution office at the Higher Regional Court or District Court is also competent for the authorization of surrender to other Member States of the EU, or, more precisely, matters of international cooperation.[55] Therefore, the question arises whether the public prosecution office is competent, under the EAW FD, to decide on authorizing the surrender after the courts have admitted it, i.e. after the courts have found that there are no grounds for refusing the EAW. If the actual authorization is undertaken by an authority that is not a "judicial authority" in the sense of EU law, this might be contrary to EU law, even if it does not have discretion. The EAW FD does not distinguish

53 Case C-508/18 and C-82/19 *Minister for Justice and Equality v OG e PI* [2019] ECLI:EU:C:2019:456.

54 See Martin Böse, Maria Bröcker and Anne Schneider (n 51) 81, 83 ff.; Klaus Michael Böhm, 'Aktuelle Entwicklungen im Auslieferungsrecht' (2020) NStZ 204, 206.

55 See e.g. the circular on the competences in international cooperation in criminal matters in the State of Northrhine-Westphalia of 16.12.2016 (*Ausübung der Befugnisse im Rechtshilfeverkehr mit dem Ausland in strafrechtlichen Angelegenheiten, Berichtspflichten und die Zusammenarbeit im Europäischen Justiziellen Netz sowie mit transnationalen Verbindungsstellen – Gemeinsamer Runderlass des Justizministeriums – 9350 – III. 19 –, des Ministeriums für Inneres und Kommunales – 424 – 57.01.48 – und des Finanzministeriums – S 1320 – 5 – V B 5/ S 770 – 4 – V A 1 – vom 16. Dezember 2016*), JMBl. NRW 2017, 74.

between admissibility and authorization decisions and provides no help in dealing with the aftermath of *OG and PI*.

In 2021, the Higher Regional Court Frankfurt a.M. had to decide on a case in which Italy had issued an EAW for the surrender of a person in order to enforce a sentence.[56] The Attorney General (*Generalstaatsanwalt*) was of the opinion that the obstacle to authorization of section 83b(2) no. 2 IRG applied, according to which foreign citizens who refuse to be extradited for the enforcement of a sanction cannot be surrendered if their legitimate interests to pass their sentence in Germany prevail. The Attorney General therefore asked the Court to hold that the surrender was not allowed because there was an obstacle to authorization. The Court rejected the application of this rule by claiming that there was no legal foundation for deciding on the admissibility of surrender if the competent administrative authority, the Attorney General, had already decided not to authorize the surrender (cf. section 79(2) IRG, which applies to cases in which the AG sees no obstacles). The fact that the Attorney General was not a "judicial authority" in the sense of EU law did not suffice to make the Court competent to decide on authorization instead of the Attorney General because this was contrary to German law.

### 2.4 *Remedies*

Judicial protection in transnational criminal proceedings in general and EAW proceedings in particular is complicated. Studies have shown that most States have deficits in this respect, and Germany is no exception[57] With regard to legal remedies, it is again important to distinguish between the different types of decision that could be subject to judicial review: the admissibility decision and the authorization decision.

Extradition and surrender have to be admitted by the Higher Regional Court prior to the authorization decision (section 13 IRG). The Higher Regional Courts are the highest courts of the *Länder* and judges there are more experienced than at the lower courts. While ordinary arrest warrants are signed by the local courts and most criminal proceedings are decided in first instance by the local and district courts, the German legislator wanted the higher-ranking courts to decide on the complex matter of extradition and surrender.[58] At the same time, the legislator found that it was not necessary to provide for

56 OLG Frankfurt a.M., decision of 10.03.2021, BeckRS 2021, 8518, see also OLG Braunschweig, decision of 12.10.2021, BeckRS 2021, 31689.

57 Martin Böse, Maria Bröcker and Anne Schneider (eds), *Judicial Protection in Transnational Criminal Proceedings* (Springer 2021).

58 Legislative materials, BT-Drs. 9/1338, S. 47.

judicial review against this decision, because it had already been taken by a higher court.

This reasoning has been criticized in literature because surrender has a massive effect on the individual concerned and a wrong application of the law in question can lead to a severe violation of fundamental rights.[59] The effects of wrongful surrender are often irreversible because the EAW FD does not provide for an obligation to transfer the individual concerned back if the admissibility decision is shown to be wrong after the surrender. Moreover, the requirements of EU law, in particular the exclusive list of grounds for refusal, have made the decision on surrender much more complicated than the decision on extradition initially was. Indeed, there have been cases in which surrender could only be prevented by a constitutional complaint after the Higher Regional Court had wrongfully applied EU law.[60] It has therefore been suggested to change the law and allow judicial review of the admissibility decision.[61]

The authorization decision was traditionally not subject to judicial review because it was considered a purely international matter. However, the German Constitutional Court held that the first implementation law was in breach of Art 19(4) GG, which is the guarantee of judicial review, because there was no legal remedy against the authorization decision.[62] Taking into consideration that the obstacles to authorization based on the EAW FD had their foundation in individual rights of the person concerned, this person had to have the option to challenge the authorization decision before the courts. Now, the law clarifies that the obstacles to authorization need to be evaluated before the admissibility decision and are assessed by the courts (section 79(2) IRG). This makes the procedure more cumbersome. Indeed, the execution authorities, i.e. the public prosecution office, need to state whether they intend to authorize or they see an obstacle. Subsequently, the court decides whether the assessment on the obstacles was correctly made and the surrender is allowed. The procedure ends with the final decision of the public prosecutor to authorize or not the surrender, taking into account the decision of the court. This latter authorization decision is completely predetermined and does not allow for discretion

59 Martin Böse, Maria Bröcker and Anne Schneider (n 51) 81, 84; Klaus Leipold and Moritz Lochmann, 'Mehr Rechtsschutz im Auslieferungsverfahren' (2018) Zeitschrift für Rechtspolitik, 43, 45.

60 BVerfG, decision of 15.12.2015, BVerfGE 140, 317.

61 On different models, see Martin Böse, Maria Bröcker and Anne Schneider (n 51) 81, 84.

62 BVerfG, judgment of 18.07.2005, BVerfGE 113, 273, 309 ff.

any longer. This set-up has rightly been criticized for being overcomplicated and responsible for increasing the length of proceedings.[63]

## 3 European Investigation Order: Critical Profiles in Legislation and Case Law

### 3.1 *Scope*

The scope of application of the German regulations implementing the EIO D is defined in section 91a IRG for both incoming and outgoing requests for EIO s.

Overall, the material scope of application of the German transposition provisions, like that of the Directive, is very broad: in principle, all repressive investigative measures for conducting criminal and administrative offence proceedings in all their stages are covered, such as searches and seizures or methods of covert investigations. This does not, however, include measures of criminal procedure that do not serve to gather evidence, i.e., measures that are taken to determine the whereabouts or to apprehend the suspect, as well as the arrest and surrender of the suspect for prosecution, since the provisions on the EAW apply in this respect. Also, preventive police measures are not encompassed.[64] With regard to personal scope, national law does not contain any restrictions, for example, to accused persons. This appears in line with the Directive itself, where potential restrictions can only be inferred from Recital 27. It is therefore feared that measures will also be ordered or taken against third parties, insofar as national law provides for this possibility.[65]

### 3.2 *Grounds for Non-recognition and Non-execution*

#### 3.2.1 Discretion

Also with regard to the EIO D, the legislator has again retained the traditional terminology of German mutual legal assistance law[66] and the traditional

63 Martin Böse, Maria Bröcker and Anne Schneider (n 51) 81, 84.

64 Martin Böse, 'IRG § 91a' in Heinrich Grützner, Paul-Günter Pötz, Claus Kreß, Nikolaos Gazeas, Dominik Brodowski (eds), *Internationaler Rechtshilfeverkehr in Strafsachen* (C. F. Müller, 135th installment December 2023) margin notes 3 ff.; Liane Wörner, in Kai Ambos, Stefan König, Peter Rackow (eds), Rechtshilferecht in Strafsachen (2020) 2nd edn, Pt. 3 Div. 4 margin note 542.

65 Anna Oehmichen, in Thomas Knierim, Anna Oehmichen, Susanne Beck, Claudius Geisler (eds), *Gesamtes Strafrecht aktuell* (2018) chapter 23 margin note 10.

66 Sebastian Trautmann, 'IRG Vor § 91a' in Wolfgang Schomburg, Otto Lagodny (eds), *Internationale Rechtshilfe in Strafsachen* (6th edn 2020) margin note 2; Liane Wörner (n 64) margin note 541.

division of the procedure for recognition into admissibility and authorization (see *supra,* 2.3.). However, with regard to the EIO, the distinction between these two categories is essentially limited to the question of whether, despite the existence of a ground for refusal, the authority retains discretion over the execution of the EIO.[67]

The grounds for refusal of an EIO in Art 11(1) are classified into two different categories: the ones named in letters (a), (c), (f), (g) and (h) are set out in sections 91b (general conditions) and 91c(2)(1) IRG (additional conditions for special types of mutual assistance) as mandatory conditions for admissibility, while the ones in letters (b), (d) and (e) are set out in section 91e IRG as obstacles to authorisation that leave discretion to the competent German authorities. This differentiation corresponds to the legal situation of other so-called '*kleine Rechtspflege*' (ancillary mutual legal assistance), i.e., the service of documents, the examination of witnesses and the gathering of evidence: section 59 IRG grants the German authorities a wide margin of discretion as to whether they provide ancillary mutual legal assistance even if obstacles to authorisation exist. It could have seemed contradictory if legal assistance towards other States could be provided to a greater extent than in relation to EU Member States.[68]

However, as this subdivision finds no equivalent in the Directive, it could be cause to misunderstandings in practice.[69] Also, the alignment of the implementation of the Directive with the traditional wording and categories of mutual legal assistance in German law is perceived as an indication of the legislator's reluctance to comprehensively implement the concept of mutual recognition and to understand mutual legal assistance as an extension of the issuing State's decision-making power.[70]

Especially the discretionary power granted in section 91e IRG is criticized by the German Federal Bar Association and in academia, insofar as the procedural rights of the person concerned might be affected.[71] It is pointed out

67 Sebastian Trautmann (n 66) margin note 4.
68 Legislative materials, BT-Drs. 18/9757 p. 57; Liane Wörner (n 64) margin note 550.
69 Sebastian Trautmann (n 66) margin note 4.
70 Sebastian Trautmann (n 66) margin note 3.
71 BRAK Stellungnahme Nr. 11/2016, p. 7 <https://www.brak.de/fileadmin/05_zur_rechtspolitik/stellungnahmen-pdf/stellungnahmen-deutschland/2016/mai/stellungnahme-der-brak-2016-11.pdf> last accessed on 05/03/2024; Martin Böse, 'IRG § 91e' in Heinrich Grützner, Paul-Günter Pötz, Claus Kreß, Nikolaos Gazeas, Dominik Brodowski (eds), *Internationaler Rechtshilfeverkehr in Strafsachen* (C. F. Müller, 135th installment December 2023) margin notes 6 ff., 9 ff.; Liane Wörner (n 64), margin note 550.

that the Directive only partially guarantees the rights of the accused person as well as uninvolved third persons in the executing State, and that the German law made insufficient use of the existing leeway to ensure adequate protection through implementation. In particular, it is criticized that the grounds for refusal of *ne bis in idem* (section 91e (1) No. 2 IRG), the primacy of domestic law in domestic cases (section 91e (1) No. 3 IRG) and the lack of consent of the detained person to a temporary transfer (section 91e (1) No. 4 IRG) were formulated only as optional grounds for refusal, whereas the Directive generally permits a refusal of enforcement in these cases. The German legislator should at least have declared refusal as a general rule and only authorized enforcement in narrow exceptional cases instead of granting open discretion,[72] or even should have excluded any discretion at all.[73] The fact that this would result in a stricter standard for mutual legal assistance on the basis of an EIO compared to mutual legal assistance with non-European States is seen to be justified by the fact that the European Union is also committed to safeguarding the rights of the accused.[74]

It can also be argued that the granting of such a discretion is provided for in the Directive: in fact, Art 11(2) specifies the grounds as optional ('may be refused'). In this respect, the criticism in the literature also relates to the Directive itself.[75] Against the background of the decision of the CJEU on the interpretation of Art 4a(1) of the Directive EAW (see above 2.2.2.),[76] it can therefore be assumed that, at least in the view of the court in Luxembourg, the legislator was right to provide for a discretionary power where the Directive does so in order to avoid an insufficient transposition of the Directive.

72 Liane Wörner (n 64) margin note 583; Marc Wortmann, 'Die Europäische Ermittlungsanordnung in Strafsachen' (2020) 164 with regards to *ne bis in idem*.

73 BRAK Stellungnahme Nr. 11/2016, p. 7 <https://www.brak.de/fileadmin/05_zur_rechtspolitik/stellungnahmen-pdf/stellungnahmen-deutschland/2016/mai/stellungnahme-der-brak-2016-11.pdf> last accessed on 05 March 2024; Martin Böse (n 71) margin note 7.

74 Liane Wörner (n 64) margin note 550.

75 Martin Böse, 'Die Europäische Ermittlungsanordnung – Beweistransfer nach neuen Regeln?' (2014) ZIS 152, 154; European Criminal Policy Initiative, 'Manifest zum Europäischen Strafverfahrensrecht' (2013) ZIS 412, 418; Andrea Leonhardt, 'Die Europäische Ermittlungsanordnung in Strafsachen' (2017) 286 ff.

76 Case C-396/22 *Generalstaatsanwaltschaft Berlin* [2023] ECLI:EU:C:2023:1029.

### 3.2.2 Recourse to a Different Type of Investigative Measure

Related to the question of refusal is the possibility of a recourse to a different type of investigative measure according to Art 10 EIO D,[77] because the non-existence or non-availability of a measure in national law may result in a request being refused. The German legislator has transposed Art 10 EIO D in section 91f IRG: paragraph 1 prescribes recourse to less intrusive measures ('that less intrusive measure *is to be* taken') and is therefore stricter than Art 10(3) of the EIO D ('*may* also take recourse'). Paragraph 2 addresses the case referred to in Art 10(1) EIO D where the requested measure could not be carried out in the national procedure either because the investigative measure does not exist in German criminal proceedings in the first place (No 1), or because its requirements under national law are not met in the specific case (No 2). In such instances, paragraph 5 specifies, in implementation of Art 10(5) of the EIO D, that if no alternative investigative measure exists effective in achieving the same objective as outlined in the request, the relevant authority in the requesting Member State must promptly be informed of the inability to provide the requested assistance. The German legislator has considered it unnecessary to implement the exemption provision outlined in Art 10(2) of the EIO D. This decision stems from the view that the investigative measures listed are predominantly of low intrusiveness, for which no specific intervention thresholds were established in the overarching mutual legal assistance law.[78]

The provision in section 91f (5) IRG is understood in the literature as a further reason for rejecting an EIO. With Art 10(5) of the EIO D, the EU legislator had implicitly recognised that the non-availability of the investigative measure or a substitute would lead to the request being rejected. For example, Recital (10) suggests that existing requirements for the lawfulness of the investigative measure under the law of the executing State may result in its non-availability in the specific case; and the relevant examples are not limited to the grounds for refusal expressly specified in the Directive. This would lead to a broad obstacle to enforcement, and not only in cases where a measure is not provided for in national law at all, but also in cases where only its requirements are not met. Such an interpretation would therefore ensure that the interests of foreign criminal prosecution would not justify a more extensive infringement upon fundamental rights than the public interest in criminal prosecution in

77 Cf. Liane Wörner (n 64) 591 ff.

78 Legislative materials, ministerial draft for an Act amending the Act on International Mutual Legal Assistance in Criminal Matters, p. 26.

the context of national criminal proceedings. This also corresponded to constitutional requirements: the national provisions on the EIO in sections 91a *et seq.* did not extend the powers of the prosecution authorities and, in cases where the investigative measure is not available under national law, there would be no legal basis for carrying out the investigative measure.[79] Some even argue that since these prerequisites for an investigative measure encompass the suspicion of an offense, it would mean that the condition of double criminality is maintained, which runs counter to the limitations specified in Art 11(1)(e) and (g) of the EIO D.[80]

Others reject this interpretation of the Directive and of the corresponding provision in national law on the grounds that it would be incompatible with the drafting history and the inner coherence of the EIO D. They point out that the Directive contains an exhaustive catalogue of grounds for refusal, which does not list the general unavailability of the measure. Either a refusal was only permitted on certain grounds or the general ground for refusal of the unavailability of the measure was provided only for certain investigative measures. These provisions would be redundant if Art 10 (1), (5) and therefore also section 91f IRG contained a general ground for refusal for all investigative measures.[81] Especially the unrestricted retention of the double criminality requirement is countered by the argument that this would make the listing

79 Legislative materials, BT-Drs. 18/9757 p. 73; Heiko Ahlbrecht, 'Europäische Ermittlungsanordnung – Durchsuchung à la Europäischer Haftbefehl' [2018] StV 601, 604; Bachmaier in Brière, Weyembergh, *The Needed Balances in EU Criminal Law: Past, Present and Future* S. 313, 317; Martin Böse, 'IRG § 91f' in Heinrich Grützner, Paul-Günter Pötz, Claus Kreß, Nikolaos Gazeas, Dominik Brodowski (eds), *Internationaler Rechtshilfeverkehr in Strafsachen* (C. F. Müller, 135th installment December 2023) margin notes 5 ff.; Katrin Brahms, Till Gut, 'Umsetzung der Richtlinie Europäische Ermittlungsanordnung in das deutsche Recht – Ermittlungsmaßnahmen auf Bestellschein?' (2017) NStZ 388, 390; Ulrich Eisenberg, Beweisrecht der CCP (10th edn 2017), margin note 477; Dagna Knytel, Die Europäische Ermittlungsanordnung und ihre Umsetzung in die deutsche und französische Rechtsordnung (2020) p. 80; Andrea Leonhardt, *Die Europäische Ermittlungsanordnung in Strafsachen* (2017) 55 ff.; Peter Rackow, 'Überlegungen zu dem Gesetz zur Änderung des IRG vom 5.1.2017' [2017] KriPoZ 79, 80, 82; Marc Wortmann (n 72) 138.

80 Martin Böse (n 75) 152, 156.

81 Frank Zimmermann, 'Die Europäische Ermittlungsanordnung: Schreckgespenst oder Zukunftsmodell für grenzüberschreitende Strafverfahren?' (2015) ZStW 143, 164 ff.; Frank Zimmermann, 'IRG § 91f' in Wolfgang Schomburg, Otto Lagodny (eds), *Internationale Rechtshilfe in Strafsachen* (6th edn 2020) margin notes 16 ff.; see also Dominik Brodowski, Verdeckte technische Überwachungsmaßnahmen im Polizei- und Strafverfahrensrecht (2016) p. 447; Liane Wörner (n 64) margin note 590 fn 297.

of individual measures unnecessary and would contradict the principle of mutual recognition.[82]

Also, the non-implementation of Art 10(2) of the EIO D, referring to the investigative measures that must always be available under the law of the executing State, is subject to criticism. The German Federal Bar Association points out that German law did not contain a definition of "non-invasive" investigative measures. Therefore, it was not sufficiently clear which measures did not require an examination of mutual legality. The examples of taking photographs and fingerprints cited by the national legislator could certainly not be considered 'non-invasive'. The national legislator should therefore only have waived the double legality tests for the measures explicitly mentioned in Art 10(2)(a), (b), (c) and (e).[83] Conversely, it has been pointed out in the literature that a rejection of the measures listed in Art 10(2) of the EIO D for the reasons stated in section 91f (2) IRG – non-availability of the measure under national law in general or in the specific case – would be contrary to EU law. It is therefore suggested to interpret national law in accordance with European law, insofar as the wording permits, to the effect that the authorities can nevertheless resort to the measure in the specific case.[84]

### 3.3 *Execution Procedure*

With regard to incoming requests, section 91h(1) IRG ensures that a judicial authorisation must always be obtained if this is required by national law. However, it is not clear what precisely the judge is required to assess. In this respect, the legislator has 'left the clarification to legal practice'.[85] In the literature, it is assumed that the jurisdiction of the ordering judge to examine an incoming request is limited: If a measure is legally challenged, it is the courts of the issuing State that have jurisdiction to examine whether substantive grounds for an EIO including a suspicion of an offence are given (Art 14(2) of

82 Klaus Böhm, 'Die Umsetzung der Europäischen Ermittlungsanordnung' (2017) NJW 1512, 1513.

83 BRAK Stellungnahme Nr. 11/2016, p. 6 (https://www.brak.de/fileadmin/05_zur_rechtspolitik/stellungnahmen-pdf/stellungnahmen-deutschland/2016/mai/stellungnahme-der-brak-2016-11.pdf; last access on 05/03/2024).

84 Frank Zimmermann, 'IRG § 91f' in Wolfgang Schomburg, Otto Lagodny (eds), *Internationale Rechtshilfe in Strafsachen* (6th edn 2020) margin note 14; see also Liane Wörner (n 64) margin note 592.

85 Legislative materials, BT-Drs 18/9757, p. 31.

the EIO D). Therefore, the assessment of these requirements was also excluded from preventive scrutiny by a judge when ordering the measure in execution of an EIO.[86] For this reason, there are fears of a deficit in legal protection compared to a corresponding measure in national proceedings, if the measure is not subject to a judicial authorization in the issuing State. The validation of the EIO in the issuing State in accordance with Art 2 lit. c no. ii sentence 2 EIO D did not offer sufficient compensation: Although it also takes into account the fundamental and procedural rights of the accused person, it can be carried out by the public prosecutor's office, which would not offer the same level of preventive legal protection as a judicial review. It is therefore proposed that the German judge when ordering a measure should be given the power to conduct a summary review or plausibility check to determine whether the substantive requirements for the measure are met.[87]

This latter approach is now supported, at least to a limited extent, in the case law of the CJEU: in its decision on *Spetsializirana prokuratura*[88] from 2019, the CJEU still held without reservation that the review of the conditions for the issuing of an EIO in accordance with Art 6 EIO D was not subject to any review by the executing authority. Accordingly, in the decision on *G.K. et al.*[89] regarding the EPPO Regulation in late 2023, it confirmed that the review in

---

86 Martin Böse, 'IRG § 91h' in Heinrich Grützner, Paul-Günter Pötz, Claus Kreß, Nikolaos Gazeas, Dominik Brodowski (eds), *Internationaler Rechtshilfeverkehr in Strafsachen* (C. F. Müller, 135th installment December 2023) margin notes 4 ff.; Martin Böse (n 75) 152, 158 ff.; Frank Zimmermann, 'IRG § 91h' in Wolfgang Schomburg, Otto Lagodny (eds), *Internationale Rechtshilfe in Strafsachen* (6th edn 2020) margin note 7.

87 LG Köln, decision of 23.09.2020-111 Qs 32/20; AG Köln, decision of 04.06.2020-504 Gs 1117/20; Klaus Böhm (n 82) 1512, 1513; Martin Böse (n 86) margin note 5; Martin Böse (n 75) 152, 158, 159; Dagna Knytel, Die Europäische Ermittlungsanordnung und ihre Umsetzung in die deutsche und französische Rechtsordnung (2020), p. 77; Andrea Leonhardt, Die Europäische Ermittlungsanordnung in Strafsachen (2017), pp. 281 et seqq.; Peter Rackow, 'Überlegungen zu dem Gesetz zur Änderung des IRG vom 5.1.2017' [2017] KriPoZ 79, 85 et seq.; Frank Peter Schuster, 'Die Europäische Ermittlungsanordnung – Möglichkeiten einer gesetzlichen Realisierung' [2015] StV 393, 396; Frank Zimmermann (n 86) margin note 8; see also legislative materials, BT-Drs. 18/9757 p. 31.

88 Case C-724/19 *Spetsializirana prokuratura* [2021] ECLI:EU:C:2021:1020, margin notes 46 ff.

89 Case C-281/22 *G.K. et al.* [2023] ECLI:EU:C:2023:1018, margin notes 38 ff. Both the German and Austrian governments in their proposals had gone even further than the CJEU and the opinion expressed in the literature by arguing in favour of a full review by authorizing judge if the national law of the European Delegated Prosecutor required prior judicial authorization, as mentioned in the opinion of the AG of 21.6.2023.

the context of a judicial authorisation required under the law of the Member State of the assisting European Delegated Prosecutor was limited to matters concerning the enforcement of the measure; if, however, measures are concerned which seriously interfere with fundamental rights guaranteed in the EU Charter, namely Art. 7 and 17, the national law of Member State of the handling European Delegated Prosecutor had to provide adequate and sufficient safeguards to ensure the legality and necessity of such measures, e.g. by judicial review with regards to matters concerning the justification and adoption of that measure. As the court in its reasoning strongly endeavours to establish a uniform approach to the various instruments of judicial cooperation in criminal matters between the Member States, it can be assumed that these considerations can be transferred to the EIO.

In the case of an outgoing EIO, there may be no preventive judicial review at all, even if the findings originate from investigative measures that are subject to a judicial authorisation under the national law of the issuing State. For the transmission of evidence already obtained with such a measure, under the CJEU ruling on *M.N.*,[90] a public prosecutor's order would suffice, if also under national law the prosecution is competent to order a transmission. And even if, according to the CJEU decision *A et al.*,[91] the German public prosecutor's offices are a sufficiently independent authority to issue an EIO, a review by a judge can be expected to ensure greater independence and thus a better guarantee of the rights of the accused. This deficit in protection is, indeed, inherent in national law, to which the EIO D insofar refers.

### 3.4 *Remedies*

Art 14 of the Directive is understood by the German legislator and the literature to mean that the legal protection against the substantive grounds for issuing an EIO, such as suspicion of an offence, the legality of the measure in the issuing State and its proportionality, can only be obtained in the issuing State.[92] The only provision on the subject of legal protection enacted in implementation of the Directive is section 91i IRG.[93] It contains regulations on legal

90 Case C-670/22 *M.N.* [2024] ECLI:EU:C:2024:372.

91 Case C-584/19 *A et al.* [2020] ECLI:EU:C:2020:1002.

92 Legislative materials, BT-Drs. 18/9757 p. 29; Frank Zimmermann (n 86) margin note 2.

93 Section 91i IRG – Appeals; suspending transmission of evidence
(1) Where a submission is made as specified in section 61 (1) sentence 1 or an application is made as specified in section 61 (1) sentence 2, the higher regional court also reviews, upon application, the decisions referred to in section 91e (3) and in section 91f (1) and (2).

protection against the execution of an incoming EIO, which supplements the general provisions on legal protection against the rendering of mutual legal assistance and the execution of the necessary investigative acts. Paragraph 1 extends the jurisdiction of the Higher Regional Court to decide on the admissibility of legal assistance (section 61) to decisions pursuant to sections 91e and 91f. Paragraph 2 allows suspension of the transmission of the evidence obtained through execution of the EIO, if an appeal against the issuing of the investigation order has been lodged in the issuing State or an appeal against its execution has been lodged in Germany. With this sole exception, the legislator did not provide for any other specific provision as, according to Section 77 IRG,[94] the remedies envisaged in the Code of Criminal Procedure are applicable.[95]

This leads to the following system of legal remedies:[96]

- Section 61(1) sentence 2 IRG[97] contains a specific legal remedy for the review of mutual legal assistance aimed at surrender of property (section

Where the decisions referred to in section 91e (3) were based on an abuse of discretionary powers, the court makes such a determination, reverses the decisions to that extent and returns the files for a new decision, in which due consideration must be given to the court's legal opinion; otherwise, the court finds that discretionary powers were properly exercised.

(2) The transmission of evidence to the requesting Member State may be suspended until a decision is given on an appeal which was filed

1. in the requesting Member State against the issuing of a European Investigation Order or
2. within the area of application of this Act.

(3) It is for the competent agency in the requesting Member State to give notification about any appeals filed pursuant to subsection (2) no. 2; section 91d (3) sentence 2 applies accordingly.

94 Section 77 IRG – Application of other procedural rules
(1) In the absence of special procedural rules provided for under this Act, the provisions of the Courts Constitution Act and of the Introductory Act to the Courts Constitution Act (Einführungsgesetz zum Gerichtsverfassungsgesetz), of the Code of Criminal Procedure, of the Youth Courts Act, of the Fiscal Code (Abgabenordnung) and of the Act on Regulatory Offences (Gesetz über Ordnungswidrigkeiten) apply analogously.

95 Legislative materials, government draft for an Act amending the Act on International Mutual Legal Assistance in Criminal Matters, pp. 29 et seqq.

96 Martin Böse, 'IRG § 91i' in Heinrich Grützner, Paul-Günter Pötz, Claus Kreß, Nikolaos Gazeas, Dominik Brodowski (eds), *Internationaler Rechtshilfeverkehr in Strafsachen* (C. F. Müller, 135th installment December 2023) margin notes 3 ff.; Ludmila Hustus, § 34. In Ulrich Karpenstein, Markus Kotzur, Johann Vasel (eds), *Handbuch Rechtsschutz in der Europäischen Union* (4th edn 2024) margin notes 322 ff.; Liane Wörner (n 64) margin note 619.

97 Section 61 IRG – Court decision
(1) [...] The higher regional court likewise gives a decision in respect of whether the conditions for rendering assistance are met upon application by the public prosecution office

66 IRG). However, according to the prevailing view in practice, only third parties who are not directly affected by the mutual legal assistance are entitled to file such an application. Persons who are directly affected by legal assistance pursuant to section 66 IRG or who are affected by other forms of legal assistance can therefore raise objections to the admissibility of legal assistance as part of an appeal against the execution proceedings (so-called '*Integrationslösung*').[98]

- Section 98(2) sentence 2 CCP[99] opens an application for a court decision against a seizure. However, it is generally recognised that the provision is also applied by analogy to other coercive measures, as otherwise there would be a significant shortfall in legal protection.[100] Such an application is admissible if the coercive measure has been ordered by the public prosecutor's office or the police or if the person affected by the measure only objects to the manner in which the coercive measure is carried out.
- In the case of a judicial order, a complaint ('*Beschwerde*') must be lodged in accordance with section 304 CCP.
- Section 101(7) CCP[101] provides a specific legal remedy for undercover measures.[102]

at the higher regional court or, in the case under section 66, upon application by persons asserting that their rights would be infringed on account of the surrender.

98 BVerfG, decision of 24.06.1997, BVerfG BeckRS 1997, 126335; Klaus Böhm (n 82) 1512, 1514; Martin Böse (n 96) margin note 5.

99 Section 98 CCP – Procedure for seizure
(2) [...] The person concerned may at any time apply for a court decision. [...]

100 Instead of many legislative materials, government draft for an Act amending the Act on International Mutual Legal Assistance in Criminal Matters, pp. 29 ff.; Liane Wörner (n 64) margin note 619; Marc Wortmann (n 72) 211.

101 Section 101 CCP – Procedural rules for undercover measures
(7) [...] Even after completion of the measure and for up to two weeks following their notification, the persons referred to in subsection (4) sentence 1 may apply to the court competent pursuant to sentence 1 for a review of the lawfulness of the measure and of the manner and means of its implementation. An immediate complaint against the decision is admissible. If public charges have been preferred and the defendant has been notified, the court seized of the matter decides upon the application in its concluding decision.

102 Section 304 CCP Admissibility
(1) A complaint is admissible against all orders made by the courts of first instance or in proceedings on an appeal on points of fact and law and against directions given by the presiding judge, by the judge in the preliminary investigation, and by a commissioned or a requested judge, unless such orders are expressly exempted from appellate remedy by law. [...].

- An application for a court decision pursuant to sections 22 and 23 ff. of the *Einführungsgesetz zum Gerichtsverfassungsgesetz* (Introductory Act to the Courts Constitution Act)[103] is admissible if no preliminary measures are required for the provision of legal assistance, for example in the case of information from an official register.

Scholars and legal practitioners criticise the fact that no specific judicial reservation prior to the enforcement of an EIO has been created and that the diverse and confusing legal remedies under national law remain in place.[104] Judicial redress against the provision of legal assistance, i.e. an assessment of the admissibility of legal assistance, is to be obtained only by contesting the execution.[105] To make matters worse, the scope of review by national courts is limited (see *supra*, 3.3.).[106] Any discretion granted by law regarding the provision of legal assistance is also not subject to review.[107] Moreover, decisions rejecting a request can only be reviewed to a limited extent, which means that there are deficiencies in the legal protection in this respect as well.[108] Furthermore, there are concerns about a non-transparent fragmentation of jurisdiction because, beyond sections 61 and 91i (1) IRG, challenges to authorisation decisions would fall under the jurisdiction of the administrative courts;

103 Section 23 EGGVG
(1) Upon application, the ordinary courts shall decide on the legality of orders, decrees or other measures taken by the judicial authorities to regulate individual matters in the areas of civil law, including commercial law, civil procedure, voluntary jurisdiction and the administration of criminal justice. The same shall apply to orders, decrees or other measures of the enforcement authorities in the execution of pre-trial detention as well as those custodial sentences and measures of correction and security that are executed outside the prison system.

104 BRAK Stellungnahme Nr. 11/2016, p. 9 <https://www.brak.de/fileadmin/05_zur_rechtspolitik/stellungnahmen-pdf/stellungnahmen-deutschland/2016/mai/stellungnahme-der-brak-2016-11.pdf> last accessed on 05 March 2024; Kai Ambos, Peter Rackow, Stefanie Schork, 'Die Europäische Ermittlungsanordnung aus Verteidigersicht' [2021] StV 126, 128 et seq.; Klaus Böhm (n 82) 1512, 1513 et seq.; Anna Oehmichen, Björn Weißenberger, 'Die Europäische Ermittlungsanordnung – praxisrelevante Aspekte der deutschen Umsetzung im IRG' (2017) StraFo 316, 322 ff.; Liane Wörner (n 64) margin note 617.

105 Martin Böse (n 96) margin note 5.

106 Martin Böse (n 96) margin note 3.

107 Martin Böse (n 96) margin note 6.

108 Klaus Böhm (n 82) 1512, 1513 ff.; Martin Böse (n 96) margin note 7; Anna Oehmichen, Björn Weißenberger (n 104) 316, 322 ff.; Liane Wörner (n 64) margin note 620.

depending on the legal remedy, it would have to be submitted to the local court, the higher regional court or the administrative court.[109]

In order to at least reduce the challenges for the appellant resulting from the division of legal protection between the issuing State and the executing State, a procedure is therefore favoured which allows the appellant to comprehensively appeal in the executing State and to oblige the authorities of the requested State to forward objections to the grounds for issuing the EIO to the competent authorities of the requesting State, as provided for in Recital 22 sentence 3 of the Directive. This idea was actually put forward by Germany in the negotiations for the EIO D and the legislator had envisaged a corresponding amendment to the *Richtlinien für den Verkehr mit dem Ausland in strafrechtlichen Angelegenheiten* (RiVaSt; Directives on Cooperation with foreign States in criminal matters)[110] when implementing the directive, but this never materialised.[111]

The challenges regarding legal remedies may also be a reason why there is very little national case law on the EIO D and its transposition into national law,[112] as well as little discussion with regard to the scattered legal remedies and the question of an adequate protection of the rights of the accused person.[113]

## 4 Regulation 1805/2018: Critical Profiles in Legislation and Case Law

### 4.1 *Legal Basis in the National System and Scope*

The rules on issuing confiscation orders within the framework of criminal proceedings are laid down in sections 73 ff. German Criminal Code (*Strafgesetzbuch – StGB*). These rules include third-party confiscation and non-conviction based confiscation.[114] Before 2017, the law distinguished

109 Liane Wörner (n 64) margin note 620; Frank Zimmermann, 'IRG § 91j' in Wolfgang Schomburg, Otto Lagodny (eds.), Internationale Rechtshilfe in Strafsachen (6th edn 2020) para. 14.

110 The RiVaSt are administrative regulations which, however, have the function of supplementing the law.

111 Liane Wörner (n 64) margin note 617; Frank Zimmermann (n 109) para 15.

112 Cf Liane Wörner (n 64) margin note 508.

113 Liane Wörner (n 64) margin note 616.

114 See also Suzan Denise Hüttemann, 'Grundlagen und Bedeutung der grenzüberschreitenden Vermögensabschöpfung unter besonderer Berücksichtigung der Verordnung (EU) 2018/1805 – Teil 2' (2019) NZWiSt 248, 253.

between the confiscation of objects (*Einziehung*) and the confiscation of the value of such proceeds (*Verfall*). In implementing Directive 2014/42/EU, the legislator deleted the term "*Verfall*" and used the word "*Einziehung*" (confiscation) for both objects and value. Nonetheless, the former distinction is still obvious in the fact that both types of confiscation are contained in different provisions. Specifically, section 111b Code of Criminal Procedure (*Strafprozessordnung – StPO*) allows the seizure of objects that are likely to be confiscated, e.g. cash money or weapons, while section 111e allows a freezing order of assets such as bank accounts.

The legal framework for international cooperation can be found in the IRG. There are rules on executing confiscation and freezing orders that were issued by other Member States in sections 88 ff., and 94 IRG, but these only apply outside the scope of Regulation 1805/2018, e.g., for cooperation with Ireland and Denmark. Outgoing requests to other Member States are covered by section 90. Sections 96a ff. IRG include additional rules for cooperation that falls within the framework of the Regulation. These rules were implemented to supplement the Regulation, which applies directly and is the main source for international cooperation in the matter of confiscation.

### 4.2 *Grounds for Non-recognition and Non-execution*

#### 4.2.1 Fundamental Rights and Proportionality Issues

Germany fought hard to include Art 8(1)(f) and 19(1)(h) in the Regulation.[115] The initial idea was to model a ground for non-recognition and non-execution which was similar to Art 11(1)(f) of Directive 2014/41/EU, but this found no consent. Arts 8(1)(f), 19(1)(h), that contain a ground for non-recognition and non-execution in case of a breach of fundamental rights, are based on the CJEU jurisprudence on the EAW[116] and are a compromise between Germany's wish for the protection of fundamental rights and the other Member States' wish for expediency and effectiveness.[117] The provisions have been severely criticized in literature. The reasons were, first, that providing discretion for the authorities would be contrary to EU primary law; second, that the provision was too narrow in focusing on the execution of confiscation orders only; thirdly, that property rights could – contrary to Recital 34 – not be excluded; and, fourthly,

---

115 See Martin Böse, VO 2018/1805/EU in Heinrich Grützner, Paul-Günter Pötz, Claus Kreß, Nikolaos Gazeas, Dominik Brodowski (eds), *Internationaler Rechtshilfeverkehr in Strafsachen* (C.F. Müller, 135th installment December 2023) margin note 4.

116 Cases C-404/15 *Aranyosi and Căldăraru* [2016] ECLI:EU:C:2016:198 and C-659/15 *Căldăraru* [2016] ECLI:EU:2016:140.

117 See, in more detail, legislative materials, BT-Drs. 19/19852, p. 22 ff.

that the provision should not only apply in exceptional situations, but always when its requirements are met (which should be the exception, not the rule).[118] However, this criticism does not relate to the German laws implementing the Regulation, but to the EU text itself.

As for German law, Arts 8(1)(f), 19(1)(h) take precedence over section 73 sentence 2 IRG, which covers violations of EU public order in other areas of mutual legal assistance.[119] It should also be kept in mind that the German Constitutional Court does not allow the execution of a request for mutual assistance either if the execution would violate the core of German fundamental rights and thus threaten the identity of the German Constitution (see above 2.2.1).[120] This exception was developed in an EAW case, but applies to all types of mutual legal assistance. Admittedly, it is less likely that a confiscation order will go against the core of German fundamental rights than an EAW, and Art 8(1)(f), 19(1)(h) should suffice to prevent this type of conflict. It was the complete lack of provisions for fundamental rights issues in the FD EAW that led to this jurisprudence.

#### 4.2.2 Territoriality Issues

The provisions on territoriality, Art 8(1)d, 19(1)(d), were the subject of the so far only decision by the German Federal Court of Justice on Regulation 2018/1805/EU.[121] The low number of cases is surprising in the light of the binding nature of the Regulation. The reason might be a general unwillingness of the German judicial authorities to deal with matters of EU Criminal Law in general, and mutual legal assistance in particular. In this decision, the Federal Court of Justice (*Bundesgerichtshof*) had to decide on a case in which a Dutch citizen had been surrendered to Germany for drug offences. In a search of the defendant's apartment, the Dutch authorities found drugs and more than 100.000 Euros in cash. The German district court (*Landgericht*) ordered the confiscation of a large amount of this money on the basis of section 73a Criminal Code (extended confiscation), referring to unnamed other drug offences.

One argument raised by the defence during the German trial was that the confiscation was contrary to Art 8(1)(d) of the Regulation. However, the court rejected the relevance of this argument. Because the executing authority was

118 See Suzan Denise Hüttemann (n 114) 248, 255; Frank Meyer, 'Recognizing the Unknown – the New Confiscation Regulation' (2020) EuCLR 140, 167 ff.

119 Martin Böse (n 115) margin note 6; see also *supra*, §1.2.2.1.

120 BVerfG, decision of 15.12.2015, BVerfGE 140, 317.

121 BGH, judgment of 22.03.2023, NJW 2023, 2956.

not *obliged* to refuse the execution on the basis of Art 8, the court ordering confiscation did not need to refrain from issuing the initial confiscation order. It would be up to the Dutch authorities to decide on whether to refuse the execution of the confiscation order due to the territoriality clause.

With regard to this case, it should first be noted that the Federal Court of Justice referred to the wrong article. The subject matter was the "*Einziehung*", a final measure imposed by the district court following proceedings in relation to a criminal offence and thus a confiscation order under Art 2(2). Accordingly, it would have been correct to refer to Art 19(1)(b) of the Regulation (which, however, is identical to Art 8(1)(d)).

Aside from this, it had also been criticized in the literature that the executing State has discretion about whether or not to make use of Art 8(1)(d) or Art 19(1)(d).[122] This discretion can lead to gaps in the protection of the defendant's rights.[123] However, the Regulation is clear in giving discretion to the executing authorities. Bearing in mind that it was considered a violation of the EAW FD when the national legislator limited the discretion given to the judicial authorities in Art 4 EAW FD,[124] it seems to be an informed choice by the EU legislator and a general principle to give a lot of leeway to the executing authorities.

### 4.3 *Execution Procedure*

#### 4.3.1 Judicial Authority

In its legislative draft to the Sixth Act amending the Act on International Mutual Assistance in Criminal Matters,[125] the German legislator pointed out that the use of the term "issuing authority" was ambiguous. In the context of the EAW FD, the CJEU had decided that German public prosecutors were not "judicial authorities" because they lacked formal independence.[126] If this reasoning applied to freezing orders – which also have an impact on fundamental rights – it might not suffice that the public prosecutor issues the freezing order, although this authority was explicitly listed in Art 2(8)(i) of the Regulation.[127] Confiscation is ordered by the courts which are judicial authorities in the understanding of EU law. In the light of the (later) CJEU decision *A et al.* on

122 See Suzan Denise Hüttemann (n 114) 248, 254; Martin Böse (n 115) margin note 26.

123 Maximilian Lenk, 'Anmerkung zu BGH-Urteil vom 22.3.2023-1 StR 335/22' (2023) NJW 2959.

124 case C-396/22 *Generalstaatsanwaltschaft Berlin* [2023] ECLI:EU:C:2023:1029.

125 Bundesgesetzblatt – BGBl. (Federal Law Gazette) 2020 I, 2474.

126 Case C-508/18, C-82/19 Minister for Justice and Equality v *OG and PI* [2019] ECLI:EU:C:2019:456.

127 Legislative materials, BT-Drs. 19/19852, p. 50 fff.

the EIO,[128] in which the court held that the German public prosecutor was competent to issue an EIO, these scruples seem unfounded. Bearing in mind that a freezing order is a temporary measure directed against property and not personal freedom, it is likely that the CJEU would accept German public prosecutors as competent authorities in this context, too.

#### 4.3.2 Confiscation Certificate and Order

With regard to Art 14(2) of the Regulation, it was argued in the literature that German law should not only rely on the confiscation certificate, but ought to demand the original order because it is more difficult to assess potential grounds for refusal if the original confiscation order is not transmitted with the certificate.[129] For example, the grounds for refusal of the order cannot be evaluated properly if the order is not available. Nor can mistakes in the confiscation certificate be detected. The legislator refrained from including an obligation to ask for the original order because this document is without much value if it is not translated, and such a translation cannot be asked for under the Regulation. It is true that a translated confiscation order would have more value and allow for a better assessment of the certificate. However, even with a limited knowledge of the language of the original order, obvious mistakes such as the wrong addressee would probably be noticed. Moreover, nowadays, AI-based translation programs make it easy to understand what the order is about and would enable the executing authority to translate the order in case of doubts. In any case, the protection of fundamental rights, *ne bis in idem* etc., that is foreseen in the Regulation is severely hampered if the executing State does not have access to the original order.

Germany's unwillingness to ask for the original order is even more surprising when considering that Germany sends a copy – whether asked for or not – of the order when issuing a certificate.[130] Although this is not translated into the foreign language (other than the certificate, see No 190(2) lit. b RiVASt), it at least enables the executing authority to find out what the basis of the original order was.

128 Case C-584/19 *A et al.* [2020] ECLI:EU:C:2020:1002.

129 Suzan Denise Hüttemann (n 114) 248, 253.

130 See No 190(2) lit. c Directives on Cooperation with foreign States in criminal matters (*Richtlinien für den Verkehr mit dem Ausland in strafrechtlichen Angelegenheiten – RiVASt*). These are ministry-issued directives with lower legislative value than proper laws that contain (numbered) rules on formalities.

### 4.4 *Remedies*

According to the German legislator, it was obvious that implementation of a new remedy was required by the Regulation, which was done in section 96d IRG. Section 96d refers to the immediate complaint in Criminal Procedure Law (section 311 StPO). This is a remedy against decisions in criminal proceedings other than judgments that has to be filed quickly in the course of one week. Other complaints are not permitted.[131] The immediate complaint has no suspensive effect under German law, nor was one intended.

A slight difference to Criminal Procedure law is that only "affected persons" can file this complaint. "Affected persons" refers to the definition in Art 2(10) Regulation 2018/1805 and includes the persons against whom an order is issued, persons owning property that is covered by the order and "any third parties whose rights in relation to that property are directly prejudiced by that order under the law of the executing State".[132] Persons who participate as private accessory prosecutor (*Nebenkläger*) because they were victims of the crime do not have recourse to this legal remedy. Nor does the public prosecution office, which is not affected in its property rights.[133]

There are also the legal remedies against freezing and confiscation orders under national law, which apply against actual enforcement measures (sections 111j ff., 98(2) analogously for freezing orders, sections 304 StPO and the rules on appeal for confiscation orders that are mostly part of the criminal judgment). Complaints against the issuing of the order must be directed at the issuing State.[134] Damages for a violation of mutual legal assistance law can be claimed under Art 34 GG and section 839 of the German Civil Code (*Bürgerliches Gesetzbuch* – BGB). This is sometimes regarded as not helpful when it comes to an actual claim for damages because the burden of proof is rather high.[135]

---

131 OLG Saarbrücken, decision of 28.4.2023-1 Ws 73/23, BeckRS 2023, 10818.

132 Legislative materials, BT-Drs. 19/19852, S. 49.

133 Martin Böse, '§ 96d IRG' in Heinrich Grützner, Paul-Günter Pötz, Claus Kreß, Nikolaos Gazeas, Dominik Brodowski (eds), *Internationaler Rechtshilfeverkehr in Strafsachen* (C. F. Müller, 135th installment December 2023) margin note 2.

134 Ralf Riegel, VO 2018/1805/EU in Wolfgang Schomburg, Otto Lagodny, Sabine Gleß, Thomas Hackner and Sebastian Trautmann (eds), *Internationale Rechtshilfe in Strafsachen* (C.H. Beck 2020) margin note 16.

135 Sebastian Peters and Karl-Christoph Bode, 'Die grenzüberschreitende Abschöpfung von Vermögenswerten im Steuerstrafverfahren de lege lata und de lege ferenda (Teil 1)' (2020) ZWH 233, 243.

## 5 Concluding Remarks

This analysis has shown that the German legislator has implemented the Framework Decision on the EAW, the Directive on the EIO, and applies the Regulation on the mutual recognition of freezing orders and confiscation orders to a large extent. Deficits can be identified only in rather few instances. The general level of compliance with EU criminal law is thus good.

That said, it is worthwhile to look at the instances in which German law does not comply with the requirements of EU law. One of the key issues in the past couple of years has been the interpretation of the notion "judicial authority" in the EU instruments. Most of the legal instruments discussed here become relevant in phases of the criminal proceedings for which the public prosecution office is responsible, so the investigation and the execution phase. From the perspective of German law, it thus made sense to name the public prosecution office as the national competent authority.

The problem that the CJEU found with this approach in its decision *OG and PI* was that the German public prosecution office is part of the executive power and part of the hierarchical structure of the Ministry of Justice and thus lacks formal independence.[136] A lot of Germans were dissatisfied with this decision because it made it sound as if the German public prosecution office was politically swayable when, in fact, public prosecutors are bound by the law and orders by the Ministry are incredibly rare. However, the point of view of EU law becomes clearer when *OG and PI* is read together with *Generalstaatsanwaltschaft Berlin*,[137] in which the CJEU held that the German law implementing Art 4a EAW FD was too narrow in not allowing for discretion. The system envisaged by the EU legislator is, therefore, that of an independent judicial authority which decides on the basis of EU law taking into account the grounds for refusal in the EU instruments to the extent to which they are allowed. When EU law allows for discretion, the EU legislator trusts in the *judicial authority* to find the best solution for the case in question. This trust is earned by the judicial authority's independence.

The German legal system follows a different approach. The initiation of criminal investigations is not left to the discretion of the public prosecution office. Instead, the latter is obliged by law to start an investigation whenever a crime has allegedly been committed (section 152(2) StPO) and can only dispense with

136 Case C-508/18, C-82/19 *Minister for Justice and Equality v OG and PI* [2019] ECLI:EU:C:2019:456.

137 Case C-396/22 *Generalstaatsanwaltschaft Berlin* [2023] ECLI:EU:C:2023:1029.

proceedings in specifically named cases (section 153 ff. StPO). This example shows that the discretion of the public prosecution office is severely limited by law. One reason for this is that the Constitution requires major infringements of fundamental rights to be regulated by law. In order to assure equal treatment, individual preferences of the prosecutors should ideally not be allowed to play a role in criminal proceedings. Accordingly, the national legislator puts its trust in the *written law*. From the point of view of German law, limiting the discretion of the judicial authority in EAW cases would be the best way to protect fundamental rights and prevent arbitrariness. Because the decision of the judicial authority is to a large extent predetermined, the independence of this authority is of lower importance.

The importance of written law in the German legal system can also explain other critical issues that have been identified in this chapter. For example, several frictions arise from the fact that the legislator sought to accommodate the requirements of the EU instruments in the existing legal assistance law. As with the implementation of the six EU Directives on criminal procedural rights,[138] it seems that the fundamental openness towards Europe is countered by a certain reluctance to abandon traditional structures in national law. The effects are partly to the benefit of the rights of the persons concerned, such as the application of identity control or the exclusion of extradition in cases of *in absentia* trials; but some are to their detriment, for example with regard to the provisions on legal remedies against EIOs or the distinction between foreign and German citizens in EAW cases. These indiscriminating effects indicate that the instances of non-compliance are not the result of a specific political agenda, but rather of the wish not to destabilize the system of written law that is already in existence. This is probably also the reason why German courts have proven to be unwilling to deny the protection of fundamental rights in EAW cases.

The differences between the EU legal system and the German legal system are, arguably, the reason why the German legislator has been slow to address the shortcomings in implementation. The relevant actors in the national system seem baffled by the EU system expressed by the CJEU: public prosecutors are unsure what they are still competent to decide on, the legislator seems unable to grasp why limiting discretion by law does not qualify as exercising discretion under EU law, and judges apply EU law wrongly. Adapting

138 Anna Albrecht and Anne Schneider, 'Between Laissez-faire and Literal Regulation – the German approach to the Implementation of the Directive on Defence Rights,' 114 ff. in Giuseppe Contissa *et al.* (eds), *Effective Protection of the Rights of the Accused in the EU Directives* (Brill 2022).

to a different system will be a challenge, particularly when considering that German history has shown the risks of taking power away from Parliament. Nonetheless, the German legislator is required to make certain amendments in order to comply with EU law. Under the previous government, the Federal Ministry of Justice therefore presented a draft bill for a fundamental reform of the IRG. With the dissolution of this government, this initiative has also come to nothing for the time being. It remains to be seen whether the new government will take it up again.

CHAPTER 8

# Italy: the EU Criminal Cooperation Instruments at the Test in Italy – Procedures and Critical Profiles

*Isadora Neroni Rezende, Antonio Pugliese, Nicolò Gibelli and Anna Piovan*

## 1 Introduction*

The implementation into the Italian legal system of the EU instruments of judicial cooperation – namely, the European Arrest Warrant (EAW), the European Investigation Order (EIO), and the Regulation 1805/2018 on the Mutual Recognition on Freezing and Confiscation Orders – followed very different paths, depending on the margin of discretion allowed by each EU legislative instrument and the entity of discrepancies with the national procedural law.

The present Chapter aims to illustrate the process of implementation of these EU cooperation instruments in Italian procedural law, carefully analysing the most noteworthy issues that emerged over the years. To this end, relevant pieces of legislation, related amendments, and salient case law will be considered. Before delving into the critical issues affecting the implementation of each specific instrument, we provide an overview of their transposition in the Italian system.

### 1.1 *Overview of the Implementation Roadmap*

The European Arrest Warrant has been established by the "Council Framework Decision of 13 June 2002 on the European arrest warrant and the surrender procedures between Member States 2002/584/JHA" (EAW FD). In the Italian context, the instrument has been transposed – with a significant delay – in Law no. 69 of 22 April 2005 (Law no. 69/2005), establishing requirements, procedures, and safeguards for the issuance and execution of EAWs involving Italy.

* Although the Chapter is a joint reflection of all the authors, its drafting is broken down as follows: Isadora Neroni Rezende (§2), Antonio Pugliese (§4), Nicolò Gibelli (§3), Anna Piovan (§§1, 5).

The transposition process has been long and highly debated,[1] as several perplexities have emerged on the compatibility of the EAW FD with principles and guarantees provided in the Italian Constitution.[2] At the time of the adoption of the EAW FD, the Italian Government published a declaration suggesting a reversal of the adaptation process, *i.e.* the EAW to the national system, and not *viceversa*.[3] This emblematically represents the controversial approach adopted by Italy at the first stage of the transposition process and outlines the ideological mindset grounding the first version of the implementation law.[4]

From a formal perspective, the initial text of Law no. 69/2005 presented serious issues of consistency, due to, *inter alia*, exceeding the list of grounds for refusal that hampered the smooth operability of the instrument. Indeed, the Italian legislator took advantage of the room for manoeuvre typically left by framework decisions, and transposed the original text at times creatively, at times *verbatim*.

The lack of correspondence of certain provisions of Law no. 69/2005 in the EAW FD fostered the necessity for more conformity. Eventually, on the 2nd of February 2021, Legislative Decree no. 10 (Legislative Decree no. 10/2021)[5] brought substantial changes to Law no. 69/2005 through the amendment of

---

1 On the topic, see Lorenzo Salazar, 'La decisione quadro sul mandato d'arresto europeo: genesi, contenuto e finalità del nuovo sistema normativo' (Programma "Grotius penale" della Commissione europea. Incontro di studio sul tema "Cooperazione Giudiziaria Europea: dall'estradizione al mandato d'arresto europeo", Rome, 10–12 November 2003) 13–17; Vincenzo Caianiello and Giuliano Vassalli, 'Parere sulla proposta di decisione-quadro sul mandato di arresto europeo' (2002) Cassazione Penale 462.

2 For instance, considering the constitutional principle of legality of criminal offences, criticisms were moved against the exemption from the double criminality check of the categories of offences listed in Art 2(2) EAW FD, as their wording did not correspond to the formulation of their national equivalents; likewise, concern was manifested for the infringement of the constitutional principle of equality due to the potentially lower guarantees for the suspect or accused than those provided for in the Italian system.

3 In the press release issued by the Italian government on 11 December 2001, the text of the declaration was as follows: "In order to implement the Framework Decision on the European arrest warrant, the Italian Government will have to initiate the internal procedures to make the Framework Decision itself compatible with the supreme principles of the constitutional order about fundamental rights". The declaration was of non-binding nature.

4 Vincenzo Picciotti, 'La riforma del mandato d'arresto europeo. Note di sintesi a margine del D.Lgs. 2 febbraio 2021, n. 10' (2021) Cassazione Penale 2.

5 Legislative Decree no. 10 of 2 February 2021, "Provisions for the full alignment of national legislation with the provisions of Framework Decision 2002/584/JHA, on the European arrest warrant and surrender procedures between Member States, implementing the delegations provided for in Article 6 of Law no. 117 of 4 October 2019. (21G00013)" (*Disposizioni per il compiuto adeguamento della normativa nazionale alle disposizioni della decisione quadro 2002/584/GAI, relativa al mandato d'arresto europeo e alle procedure di consegna tra stati*

several Articles. The core purpose of the reform was to circumvent the criticalities that hindered the principle of mutual recognition underpinning the EAW and to enhance the consistency of the transposition with the EAW Framework Decision.

Among all modifications, Legislative Decree no. 10/2021 has intervened on Art 1 of Law no. 69/2005, deleting the clause that limited the execution in the event of incompatibility with the supreme principles of the Italian constitutional order in terms of fundamental rights, freedom, and due process. Thus, paragraph 1 of Art 2 has been reformulated so that the execution of the EAW may not, under any circumstances, entail the violation of the supreme principles of the constitutional order of the State, the inalienable rights recognised by the Constitution, and the fundamental rights and principles enshrined in Art 6 of the Treaty on European Union (TEU) and the European Convention of Human Rights (ECHR). This change aimed to narrow the grounds for non-execution of a EAW, limiting the circumstances for refusal to those enlisted in the EAW FD, in order to enhance the effectiveness of the instrument.

By the same token, paragraph 1-*bis* has been added to Art 6 of Law no. 69/2005, following the amendment of the EAW FD that introduced Art 4(a), in order to regulate the conditions for refusal in case of a trial held *in absentia*, as introduced by the Framework Decision 2009/299/GAI. Furthermore, the last paragraphs of Art 6 have been repealed, as they aimed at controlling the merits of the warrant, thus restricting, and even inhibiting, the execution in a way deemed incompatible with the principle of mutual trust.

The reform also touched on the double criminality clause, reviewing the list of cases for which surrender is mandatory, contained in Art 8 of Law no. 69/2005. That list has been extensively criticized for being more demanding than the EAW FD, thus mandating a double criminality check that was contrary to the rationale of mutual trust.[6] In its new shape, the list transposes Art 2(2) of the EAW FD more consistently.

Similarly, the list of grounds for non-execution contained in Arts 18 and 18-*bis* has been reduced, deleting those circumstances not directly provided for by Arts 3 and 4 of the EAW FD.[7] Furthermore, Art 18-*ter* has been added to implement the new Art 4-*bis* of the EAW FD on *in absentia* trials. In this new

*membri, in attuazione delle delega di cui all'articolo 6 della legge 4 ottobre 2019, n. 117*), GU no. 30 of 05/02/2021.

6 Picciotti (n 4) 17.

7 In Article 18 of Law no. 69/2005, those pertaining to the *ne bis in idem*, the minor age of the surrendee, and the amnesty remain. In Art 18-*bis* the optional ground for non-execution in case of a decision involving an Italian citizen or a person residing in Italy, applies when the period of residence or stay in Italy is at least of five years.

version of Art 18-*bis*, not all optional grounds for refusal provided in the EAW FD are recognized. It is curious that the Italian law first exceeded in formulating grounds for refusal while, later on, made the possibility of not executing a EAW even narrower than what was provided by the EU standards.

The European Investigation Order, introduced with the "Directive 2014/41/UE of 3 April 2014 regarding the European Investigation Order in criminal matters" (EIO D), has been transposed into the Italian legal framework by means of Legislative Decree n. 108 of 21 June 2017 (Legislative Decree no. 108/2017). The instrument has been enacted in Italy after two years of legislative interventions for the adaptation of the Italian procedural law to the existing EU legislation.[8] Thus, differently from what happened with the EAW FD, the EIO D has been implemented in the context of a general effort to align the Italian system with the EU procedures for judicial cooperation and create an organic and long-lasting framework.[9] So far, Legislative Decree no. 108/2017 has been affected by a sole reform, broadening the circumstances requiring the involvement and coordination with the Anti-terrorism and Anti-mafia Prosecutor in the execution of a EIO.[10]

As will be illustrated in this Chapter, the Italian Government has preserved a certain degree of autonomy in the implementation process. Some provisions of Legislative Decree no. 108/2017 mirror the EIO D thoroughly, sometimes even *verbatim*, while other provisions are overabundant. For instance, concerning the grounds for refusal, Arts 10(1)(a) and 10(3) of the Legislative Decree no. 108/2017 are not based on any provision of the EIO D. At the same time, certain paragraphs of the EIO D about the grounds for non-recognition or execution lack an explicit or even indirect transposition, such as Arts 11(1)(a), 11(1)(b), 11(1)(c), 11(1)(h), 11(1)(e), 11(5).

The great innovation brought by the EIO – as transposed in the Italian system – is the central role of the district prosecutor,[11] both in the passive and active procedure. This marks a turning point, since the protagonist of the

8 On this topic, see Gaetano De Amicis, 'Dalle rogatorie all'ordine europeo d'indagine: verso un nuovo diritto della cooperazione giudiziaria penale' (2019) 1 Cassazione Penale, 22 et seq.; Luigi Kalb, 'Cooperazione Giudiziaria: le novità del recepimento delle fonti sovranazionali' (2016) Diritto Penale e Processo, 989 et seq.; Michele Caianiello, 'L'OEI dalla Direttiva al Decreto N. 108 del 2017' in R. Kostoris and M. Daniele (eds), *L'Ordine Europeo D'Indagine Penale. Il nuovo volto della raccolta transnazionale delle prove nel d.lgs. n. 108 del 2017* (Giappichelli 2018) 18.

9 Caianiello (n 8) 19.

10 Art 2-bis(6) of Legislative Decree no. 105 of 10 August 2023 amended to a small extent Art 4(1) Legislative Decree no. 108/2017.

11 Art 51 of the Italian Code of Criminal Procedure (CCP).

judicial cooperation used to be the General prosecutor of the Court of Appeal. Furthermore, the EIO D fosters direct contact between judicial authorities: compared to Law no. 69/2005, in Legislative Decree no. 108/2017 the role of the Ministry of Justice throughout the process is reduced, as it is not involved in the transmission procedures – it must only be provided with a copy of the EIO.

From a formal point of view, the active and the passive procedures of recognition and execution have been almost correctly transposed in the Italian legislation – even though a few inconsistencies can still be detected.

"Regulation 2018/1805 of 14 November 2018 on the mutual recognition of freezing orders and confiscation orders" is self-executing by nature; therefore, it applies to the Italian system directly. Before delving into the detailed analysis of the implementation process, some considerations on the Italian procedural regime must be pointed out. According to the Italian Code of Criminal Procedure (CCP), the seizure of assets is twofold: it can be "conservative" or "preventive".[12] The "conservative" seizure may be activated, as provided by Art 316 CCP, when there can be a lack or dispersal of guarantees for the payment of the costs of the process or damages (the so-called "*periculum in mora*"). Differently, the "preventive" seizure was conceived in Art 321 CCP for protection purposes: it may be requested in case of risk that the free availability of an asset pertaining to the offence aggravates or prolongs its consequences or facilitates the commission of other offences or, lastly, it may be ordered in case of property for which confiscation is possible. As it will be further illustrated in the present Chapter, reading the Regulation in line with the Italian CCP suggests that the kind of seizure targeted by the EU legislator is likely to be the "preventive" one.

The Italian perspective on the matter of freezing and confiscation of assets had a significant impact on the negotiation process for the drafting of a unified EU instrument. With respect to the original version of the Regulation proposed by the European Commission, which established the mutual recognition of freezing and confiscation orders issued in the context of "criminal proceedings", the final text has been extended on the Italian initiative to include the mutual recognition of orders issued in the context of "proceedings in criminal matters". Accordingly, the scope of application has been broadened to orders adopted in the context of the Italian prevention proceedings (Legislative Decree no. 159/2011), which are non-conviction-based. Even though such adjustment allowed the Regulation to encompass also anti-mafia proceedings, it was not welcomed by States like Germany, which do not provide for similar

12 On this topic, see § 4.

measures in their systems and thus flagged a potential violation of fundamental rights.[13]

The entry of this instrument into the Italian legislative framework has been followed in 2021 by an internal informative act (so-called "Circular") of the Minister of Justice[14] and one of the Minister of the Interior,[15] indicating the measures of patrimonial prevention falling within the scope of the Regulation. However, at the initial stage, the Italian legislator has not intervened through a proper normative act to adapt the Italian system by smoothing potential contrasts and allowing a thorough implementation. Therefore, the enactment of EU freezing and confiscation orders has been initially conducted through the direct application of the Regulation and an analogical interpretation of existing instruments on the matter (namely, the Legislative Decree 137/2015 on the recognition of confiscation orders,[16] and the Legislative Decree 35/2016 on the recognition of seizure orders),[17] combined with the abovementioned Circulars. Eventually, in 2023, Legislative Decree no. 203 (Legislative Decree no. 203/2023)[18] has been approved to regulate comprehensively all procedural

---

13 For a more in-depth reading on the issue, see: Ciro Grandi, 'Il Mutuo Riconoscimento dei Provvedimenti di Confisca alla luce del Regolamento (UE) 2018/1805' (2021) La Legislazione Penale <A://www.lalegislazionepenale.eu/wp-content/uploads/2021/05/Grandi-App-edit.2021.5.25.pdf> accessed 14 August 2024.

14 Minister of Justice, Circular of 18 February 2021, "Implementation of Regulation (EU) 2018/1805 on the mutual recognition of freezing and confiscation orders" (*Attuazione del Regolamento (UE) 2018/1805 relativo al riconoscimento reciproco dei provvedimenti di congelamento e di confisca*).

15 Minister of Interior, Department of Public Security, Circular of 12 January 2021 on the "Regulation (EU) 2018/1805 on the mutual recognition of freezing and confiscation orders" (*Regolamento (UE) 2018/1805 del Parlamento Europeo e del Consiglio del 14 Novembre 2018, relativo al riconoscimento reciproco dei provvedimenti di congelamento e confisca*).

16 Legislative Decree no. 137 of 15 August 2015, "Implementation of Framework Decision 2006/783/JHA on the application of the principle of mutual recognition to confiscation orders (15G00152)", (*Attuazione della decisione quadro 2006/783/GAI relativa all'applicazione del principio del reciproco riconoscimento delle decisioni di confisca*), GU no. 203 of 02/09/2015.

17 Legislative Decree no. 35 of 15 February 2016, "Implementation of Council Framework Decision 2003/577/JHA of 22 July 2003 on the execution in the European Union of orders freezing property or evidence" (*Attuazione della decisione quadro 2003/577/GAI del Consiglio, del 22 luglio 2003, relativa all'esecuzione nell'Unione europea dei provvedimenti di blocco dei beni o di sequestro probatorio*), GU no. 59 of 11/03/2016.

18 Legislative Decree no. 203 of 7 December 2023, "Provisions for the full adaptation of national legislation to the provisions of Regulation (EU) 2018/1805 of the European Parliament and of the Council of 14 November 2018 on mutual recognition of freezing and confiscation orders. (23G00213)" (*Disposizioni per il compiuto adeguamento della normativa nazionale alle disposizioni del Regolamento (UE) 2018/1805 del Parlamento europeo*

issues for implementation, such as the grounds for refusal, and align the Italian procedural law with the EU provisions.

The present Chapter will deal with the most noteworthy issues that have arisen in the implementation of the EAW, the EIO, and Regulation 1805/2018 in the Italian system, dwelling on those interpretative and concrete aspects that have marked the way towards the compliant transposition of EU legislation and the effective application of the principle of mutual recognition enshrined therein.

## 2 European Arrest Warrant: Critical Profiles in Legislation and Case Law

As indicated in the introduction, the EAW FD was transposed in the Italian system with Law no. 69/2005, which was amended multiple times over the years to align the domestic provisions with the EU text. After providing a general overview of domestic provisions for executing and issuing EAWs, some of the inconsistencies still affecting the national transposition law, as well as the improvements made so far, will be highlighted. In particular, the analysis will focus on the transposition of the grounds for refusal – including that inspired by the risk of serious fundamental rights violations – and on the procedural safeguards afforded to the surrendee in the execution procedure.

### 2.1 *Overview of EAW Proceedings in the National System*

Law no. 69/2005, transposing the EAW FD, foresees an active and a passive procedure for executing a EAW.[19] The active procedure takes place when the Italian authorities issue a warrant to obtain the surrender of a person located in the territory of another EU Member State (Arts 28–33, Law no. 69/2005). Conversely, the passive procedure occurs when the Italian authorities are requested to surrender someone in the national territory (Arts 5–27, Law no. 69/2005).

The passive proceedings can be articulated in a twofold way, according to how the Italian authorities receive the EAW. On the one hand, the ordinary procedure begins when the EAW is directly transmitted to the competent judicial authority (Arts 9–10, Law no. 69/2005). On the other hand, the

---

*e del Consiglio, del 14 novembre 2018, relativo al riconoscimento reciproco dei provvedimenti di congelamento e di confisca*), GU no. 298 of 22/12/2023.

19 For a more detailed overview of EAW proceedings in Italy, see the Italian FACILEX report, available at <https://site.unibo.it/facilex/en> accessed 14 August 2024.

passive procedure can be initiated by the police if they receive an alert for the requested person through the Schengen Information System (SIS) (Arts 11–12, Law no. 69/2005), and proceed with the arrest. In both cases, the competent authority to execute the EAW is the Court of Appeal (Art 5, Law no. 69/2005), which falls within the concept of "judicial authority" of Art 6(2) EAW FD. Specific competence rules, however, apply when the EAW concerns a person who is underage at the time of the facts. In such cases, the jurisprudence has clarified that a twofold competence exists for issuing the precautionary measures – preventing absconding – and deciding on the final surrender of the person. First, the President of the Court of Appeal remains competent to validate the arrest made by the judicial police and, if requested, to issue the precautionary measure before the surrender. Then, the juvenile section of the Court of Appeal is responsible for ascertaining whether the conditions for surrender exist. For this purpose, once the precautionary measure is adopted, the case file must be forwarded by the President of the Court of Appeal to the juvenile section for the final decision on surrender.[20]

When the issuing authority intends to transmit a EAW directly to the Italian judicial authorities, it must do so with the intermediation of the designated central authority, the Minister of Justice (Art 4, Law no. 69/2005). Upon reception of the warrant, the President of the territorially competent Court of Appeal proceeds with the urgent acts and gathers the whole Court, composed of a panel of three judges. The Court hears the general public prosecutor on the matter and, if necessary, applies a precautionary measure by reasoned order, paying special attention to the need to prevent that requested person absconds (Art 9(4), Law no. 69/2005). If the Court orders a measure, the judicial police shall proceed with its execution, informing the person concerned that s/he may appoint a lawyer in the issuing State (Art 9(5-*bis*), Law no. 69/2005). Within five days of the execution of the precautionary measure, the President of the Court of Appeal (or a delegated magistrate) shall proceed to hear the person subject to the measure, informing in a language known to him or her, of the procedural right (Art 10(1), Law no. 69/2005)[21] to be heard "if present" (Art 17(1), Law no. 69/2005). While this wording may raise issues concerning the right to be present in the case of detained persons, whose participation at the hearing is subject to the availability of services for accompanying him or her to court, the case law seems to avert this risk. In fact, the Court of Cassation has established that the hearing for the decision on the execution of

20 Cass. pen., sez. VI, no. 23259 of 19/05/2016.

21 For a more detailed overview of this provision and related compliance issues, see *infra*, §2.3.

the EAW must be postponed when the surrendering person, having indicated the wish to be heard, is legitimately prevented from appearing (such as in the case of administrative detention).[22] On this occasion, the person concerned may give consent to the surrender (Art 14, Law no. 69/2005). The national provision does not include any specifics on the voluntary nature of the consent, as required by Art 13(2) EAW FD, but the necessary presence of the lawyer and an interpreter could be considered a sufficient guarantee for the voluntariness of the statements.

The final decision on the execution of the warrant is made at the outcome of another hearing that shall take place within fifteen days from the execution of the precautionary measure (Art 9(4), Law no. 69/2005) or from the decision of the Court not to apply one (Art 9(4-*bis*), Law no. 69/2005).

When the judicial police execute a EAW transmitted through the SIS, a validation hearing shall take place within forty-eight hours from the arrest of the person. In this hearing, the President of the territorially competent Court of Appeal (or a delegated magistrate) must hear the arrested person in the presence of a retained or court-appointed lawyer and, if necessary, of an interpreter (Art 13, Law no. 69/2005).[23] If the arrest is validated,[24] the Court proceeds with issuing a precautionary measure according to the rules established for the ordinary procedure (Arts 9 and 10(4), Law no. 69/2005), except when there are reasons to believe that grounds for refusal may apply. When the measure is applied, the hearing for the final decision shall take place within fifteen days from its execution (Arts 13(3) and 10(4), Law no. 69/2005).

Against the surrender decision, the surrendering person has the right to appeal to the Court of Cassation, only on the grounds of violation of the law (Art 606(1)(a)-(b)-(c) of the Italian Code of Criminal Procedure, CCP), within five days of having acquired knowledge of the ruling. The Court of Cassation must decide within ten days of receipt of the file, which shall occur the next day of the appeal's filing at the latest (Art 22, Law no. 69/2005). Pending the decision, the surrender is suspended. The same remedy is provided against an

---

22 Cass. pen., sez. F, no. 36397 of 29/08/2023.

23 The jurisprudence (see Cass. pen., sez. VI, no. 27357 of 19/06/2013) has cleared up that the time limit of forty-eight hours laid down for validating the arrest also extends to the adoption of the precautionary measure, meaning that the two decisions shall be made within the same timeframe.

24 The case law has clarified the scope of the control exercised by the judge when validating the arrest. Specifically, the Court of Cassation (see Cass. pen., sez. VI, no. 5547 of 19/01/2016) explained that the validation of an arrest of a person whose data has been entered in the SIS is limited to a paper verification that does not affect the outcome of the surrender proceedings.

order consenting to surrender upon the person's consent, within three days (Art 22(5-*bis*)). Despite having a suspensive effect, this remedy may not be considered "effective" by European standards. First, the Court of Cassation does not have the power to intervene on the merits of the case, as required by the case law of the ECtHR.[25] This shortcoming could be critical when the surrender poses a risk of inhuman and degrading treatment: in this regard, national case law has specified that such grievances can be raised before the Cassation, for the first time, only when the risk of violation of fundamental rights is notorious or recently established by other judgments of the Court.[26] In this sense, the Cassation appeal on the grounds of risk of inhuman and degrading treatment seems "mediated" *de facto*, that is, effective only in relation to the existence of other decisions on the merits of the possible fundamental rights violation. Second, the remedy cannot always be considered effective for the defendant who does not understand Italian. The Supreme Court has established that there is no right to the translation of the surrender judgment and that the person requested may be assisted by a trusted interpreter, possibly paid by legal aid; in this case, a postponement of the deadline for filing the appeal is also possible to allow for translation.[27] The possibility of access to legal aid is not, however, always assured in EAW proceedings. Indeed, while in the ordinary procedure the arrested person receives all the information on procedural rights provided for in domestic law, including information on the right to legal aid, this is not the case in the (more frequent) procedure at the initiative of the judicial police.[28] Without this support, the right to the translation of the judgement – and consequently, to challenge it – may be jeopardized.

In the active procedure, the competence to issue a EAW belongs to different authorities, depending on the phase which the domestic proceedings are at. Art 28, Law no. 69/2005 provides that the warrant is issued: (a) when the proceedings are ongoing, by the judge who adopted the precautionary measure

25 cf *Glas Nadezhda Eood and Elenkov v. Bulgaria* App no 14134/02 (ECHR, 11 October 2007), para. 69. For example, the Court of Cassation declared inadmissible an appeal in which the individualising information provided by the issuing State had already been assessed and found to be adequate by the Court of Appeal. See Cass. pen., sez. F, no. 32465 of 9/08/2024.

26 Cass. pen., sez. VI, no. 10119 of 7/03/2024.

27 Cass. pen., sez. VI, no. 17535 of 30/04/2024.

28 In fact, Art 9(5), concerning the ordinary procedure, includes a general reference to the rules relating to precautionary measures, among which there is Art 293 CCP, providing for all the information rights to be given to the person arrested at the moment of the execution of a precautionary measure. The same reference is not provided, however, in Art 12, concerning the arrest made at the initiative of the judicial police.

of pre-trial detention or house arrest; (b) when the judgement has become final, by the public prosecutor competent for its enforcement (Arts 656 and 665 CCP), if the custodial penalty is at least of one year of imprisonment and there is no suspension of the enforcement;[29] (c) when a security measure is applied, by the public prosecutor competent under Art 658 CCP.[30] The Minister of Justice is the central authority competent for assisting the national bodies in forwarding (and translating) EAWs (Art 28(2), Law no. 69/2005). When the whereabouts of the suspect or accused are not known, an alert shall be entered in the SIS (Art 29, Law no. 69/2005). Such an alert is equivalent to a EAW when it includes all the information provided by Art 30, Law no. 69/2005 (correctly implementing Art 8 EAW FD).

Having presented an overview of the passive and active EAW proceedings in Italy, some critical issues stemming from the national legislation are examined, focusing on the implementation of the grounds of refusal, including those based on fundamental rights risks, and the procedural rights of the people involved in such proceedings.

### 2.2 *Grounds for Refusal and Fundamental Rights Issues*

The regulation of grounds for refusal has been one of the most troubled areas in Italy's transposition of the EAW FD. While at first Art 18, Law no. 69/2005 listed twenty grounds for refusal, to which other hypotheses were added throughout the text, today the catalogue has been greatly reduced, especially regarding optional grounds for refusal. The evolution of the regime of grounds for refusal has also been affected by the gradual introduction of fundamental rights considerations into the EU system of mutual recognition in criminal matters.

29 Under Art 665(5) CCP, there is suspension of the enforcement of a custodial penalty when the "imprisonment does not exceed three or four years in the cases provided for in Article 47-*ter*, paragraph 1, of Law No 354 of 26 July 1975, or six years in the cases referred to in Articles 90 and 94 of the Consolidated Text approved by Decree No 309 of the President of the Republic of 9 October 1990, as amended".

30 In the Italian system, security measures (Art 199 of the Criminal Code) are aimed at keeping the person away from the opportunity of committing further crimes. They are applied to offenders, regardless of whether they can be punished, after ascertaining their social dangerousness, in order to prevent the risk of reoffending. They differ from punishment because they do not have a retributive function but only and exclusively a function of re-educating the offender. Therefore, they are also applied to non-chargeable offenders, and their application presupposes the concrete ascertainment of the social dangerousness of the subject. For a general overview of security measures in the Italian system, see Giorgio Marinucci, Emilio Dolcini and Gian Luigi Gatta, *Manuale di diritto penale* (12th edn., Giuffrè) 897 ff.

The mandatory grounds for refusal are implemented in Art 18, Law no. 69/2005, with minor issues. For instance, Art 18(1)(b) transposes the ground of refusal based on the *ne bis in idem* principle. The national provision clarifies the meaning of "finally judged", provided in Art 3(2) EAW FD, by listing the types of decisions satisfying this requirement in the domestic system: irrevocable judgements, criminal decrees of conviction,[31] judgements of no grounds to proceed[32] which are no longer subject to an appeal, and final judgments of other EU Member States. Among these, the reference to judgements of no grounds to proceed raises some issues. In fact, these decisions do not become "final" under national law even when they are no longer subject to appeal, meaning that the case can always be reopened if new evidence comes to light (Art 434 CCP). It should be borne in mind, however, that the CJEU has considered judgements of no ground to proceed as "final judgements" barring further prosecution in the EU under Art 54 of the Schengen Convention.[33] Considering this case law, which however creates ambiguity between national and EU law, judgements of no grounds to proceed appear more in line with the concept of a "final" judgement that has been passed upon the requested person in a Member State and that prevents further proceedings. Under Art 4(3) EAW FD, such decisions can only serve as a basis for a *non-mandatory* refusal. Therefore, the Italian law does not seem to correctly implement the EAW FD in this respect.

The interpretation of this ground of refusal is also contradictory in the case law. Specifically, it is not clear whether the final decision triggering the application of Art 18(1)(b) shall include an assessment of the merits of the case (as required by the CJEU)[34] or may dispose of it on procedural grounds only. Two judgements of the Court of Cassation have dealt with this issue in relation to judgements that had finally closed previous EAW proceedings, refusing surrender. Firstly, in a 2014 judgement, the Court of Cassation excluded the applicability of the *ne bis in idem* principle regarding a judgement based on procedural

31 The proceedings by decree (Arts 459 ff. of the Criminal Procedural Code, CCP) are a special form of proceedings where the prosecutor, if s/he considers that only a financial penalty shall be applied, submits a reasoned request for issuing a criminal decree of conviction to the judge for preliminary investigations. The judge, where s/he agrees with the prosecutor's request, issues the criminal decree of conviction (Art 460 CCP).

32 The judgements of no grounds to proceed is the decision of dismissal issued by the judge of the preliminary hearing at the end of such hearing (Art 425 CCP). Judgements of no grounds to proceed have been introduced in Art 18(1) of the transposition law only in the last 2021 reform.

33 Case C-398/12 *M* [2014] ECLI:EU:C:2014:1057.

34 Case C-469/03 *Miraglia* [2005] ECLI:EU:C:2005:156.

grounds only.[35] The case involved a EAW issued by the Romanian authorities to Italy. Previously, the French authorities had refused to surrender the person concerned to Romania for procedural issues. In line with the CJEU case law, the Italian Court of Cassation decided not to consider this circumstance for refusing the surrender, given that the European *ne bis in idem* principle applies only to substantive assessments of liability for criminal acts, and not also to purely procedural ones. A more recent judgement, however, apparently contradicts this approach. In particular, the Court of Cassation has established that an irrevocable judgement refusing the execution of a EAW for the lack of supplementary documentation could trigger the applicability of the *ne bis in idem* under Art 3(2) EAW FD.[36] In this case, Poland had transmitted a EAW to the Italian authorities, which had requested further documentation to decide on the request, with no answer from the issuing authorities. Consequently, the EAW proceedings had been closed with a decision refusing surrender, which became final. The Polish authorities later reiterated the request with all the necessary documentation. However, the Court of Cassation excluded that the competent Court of Appeal could rule again on the same request, modifying the previous decision of refusal. This last decision seems to embrace a more extensive interpretation of the *ne bis in idem* principle, acknowledging that also final decisions relying on procedural grounds (e.g., the lack of documentation) can serve as grounds for mandatory refusal. Arguably, this approach is not in line with the interpretation of the CJEU but the judgement seems to be an isolated case, so it might be too soon to state that the national provision's practical implementation raises compliance issues with EU law.

As mentioned above, the regime of the non-mandatory grounds for refusal has undergone significant changes in the transposition law.[37] This development shows a path of progressive adherence to the principle of mutual recognition, considering that at present not even all optional grounds for refusal are transposed into the Italian system.[38] Because of their non-mandatory nature,

35 Cass. pen., sez. VI, no. 1695 of 14/01/2014.

36 Cass. pen., sez. VI, no. 35290 of 19/07/2018.

37 For an overview of the evolution, see Guido Colaicovo, 'La nuova disciplina del mandato di arresto europeo tra esigenze di semplificazione della procedura e tutela del diritto di difesa' (2021) 7 Dir Pen Proc 872 ff.

38 The grounds of refusal provided at Art 4(3), (4), and (5) are not implemented in the national system. To be true, as explained above, Art 4(3) is a case of bad transposition because the judgements of no grounds to proceed have been included in the list of decisions grounding a mandatory refusal of the EAW, rather than an optional one.

the lack of transposition of some grounds does not raise criticism in relation to EU law.[39]

For instance, important changes have concerned Art 18-*bis*(2-2-*bis*), Law no. 69/2005, which transposes Art 4(6) EAW FD and allows to refuse the surrender of the Italian citizen or a person who lawfully and effectively resides or has resided continuously for at least five years on the Italian territory, provided that it orders that such penalty or security measure be executed in Italy by its domestic law. The Italian Constitutional Court has scrutinized this regime several times, also by dialoguing with the CJEU. In the first transposition of the EAW FD, this ground for refusal protected only Italian citizens and was later extended to EU citizens by a 2010 ruling of the Constitutional Court.[40] Because the regime still excluded third-country citizens legally residing in Italy, it was again subject to constitutional review. When asked about the issue, the Constitutional Court referred a question to the CJEU for a preliminary ruling. In *O.G.*, the Luxembourg Court indicated that the principle of non-discrimination in EU law precludes legislation such as Italy's, which excludes absolutely and automatically from the optional refusal provided for in Art 4(6) EAW FD, any third-country national who is staying or residing in the territory of the State of execution of the warrant, without the judicial authority being able to assess that national's links with that Member State.[41] Following this judgement, the Constitutional Court has settled the question in the national system,[42] extending the scope of Art 18-*bis*(2) also to third-country citizens, residing for at least five consecutive years in Italy. Following the indications of the Constitutional Court, a Law Decree[43] inserted a paragraph 2-*bis* in Art 18-*bis*, obliging the Court of Appeal to ascertain – for the purpose of verifying the lawful and effective residence or abode on the Italian territory of the person requested to be surrendered – whether the execution of the punishment

39 Case C-700/21 *O.G.* [2023] ECLI:EU:C:2023:444, para. 35.

40 Italian Constitutional Court, no. 227 of 21/06/2010.

41 *O.G.* (n 39).

42 Italian Constitutional court, no. 178 of 6-28/07/2023.

43 Law Decree No. 69 of 13 June 2023, Urgent provisions for the implementation of obligations arising from acts of the European Union and from pending infringement and pre-infringement proceedings against the Italian state (*Disposizioni urgenti per l'attuazione di obblighi derivanti da atti dell'Unione europea e da procedure di infrazione e pre-infrazione pendenti nei confronti dello Stato Italiano*), in Official Gazette No. 136 of June 13, 2023, provided (by Art 18-bis, paragraph 1, letter a)) for the amendment of Art 18-bis, paragraph 2 and the introduction of paragraph 2-bis to Art 18-bis. The Law Decree was converted with amendments by Law No. 103 of 10 August 2023, Urgent provisions related to severe acute respiratory syndrome (SARS) (*Disposizioni urgenti relative alla sindrome respiratoria acuta severa* (*SARS*)). (in Official Gazette No. 186 of August 10, 2023).

or security measure on the territory is in practice suitable to enhance the opportunities for social reintegration, considering: the duration, nature and manner of residence or abode, specifically, the time elapsed between the commission of the crime on the basis of which the EAW was issued and the beginning of the period of residence or abode; the commission of offenses and the regular fulfilment of social security and tax obligations during that period; compliance with national rules on the entry and residence of foreigners; family, linguistic, cultural, social, economic or other ties that the person has on Italian territory; and any other relevant factors. The judgment is null and void if it does not contain a specific indication of the elements referred to in the first sentence and the criteria for their evaluation. Despite this positive development, jurisprudence is divided on the assessment of the five-year residence requirement referred to in Article 18-bis(2) of Law no. 69/2005. While some judgments of the Court of Cassation consider that this period should be counted both before and after the commission of the offence for which surrender is sought,[44] others take a more restrictive view, requiring the person concerned to have resided legally in Italy for five consecutive years *after* the facts in question.[45] However, this latter interpretation does not seem to have any basis in the text of Article 4(6) EAW FD, in the case law of the CJEU,[46] or in the rationale of the provision, which aims to ensure the social reintegration of the person concerned. Additionally, part of the case law considers that the lack of knowledge of Italian on the part of the person concerned is in itself an obstacle to the recognition of the ground for refusal.[47] This approach may conflict with the wording of Art 18-*bis*(2-*bis*), which refers to linguistic competencies as only one of the factors (among others) that may be assessed to refuse surrender. Nonetheless, given the margin of discretion left to Member States in implementing this ground for refusal, it is doubtful that this line of interpretation would raise problems of compliance with EU law.

---

44 Cass. pen., sez. VI, no. 5013 of 25/06/2024. The same decision, however, states that the evidence to prove the period of legal residence cannot be presented for the first time before the Court of Cassation, which, as explained above, can only review the decision on grounds of violation of law (Art 606(1)(a)-(b)-(c) CCP) and cannot make any assessment on the merits of the case (a task that is delegated only to the Court of Appeal).

45 Cass. pen., sez. VI, no. 10929 of 13/03/2024.

46 In *Wolzenburg*, the CJEU examined the five-year residence requirement in 4(6) EAW FD but made no distinction according to whether the offence covered by the EAW was committed before or within that period. See Case C-123/08 *Dominic Wolzenburg* [2009] ECLI:EU:C:2009:616.

47 Cass. pen., sez. VI, no. 17317 of 24/04/2024.

Although not explicitly configured as a ground for refusal,[48] also the violation of fundamental rights can lead to the failure to surrender the requested person.

Art 2 Law no. 69/2005, as amended by the Legislative Decree no. 10/2021, provides indeed for a general clause that excludes the execution of a EAW when this may entail a violation either of the supreme principles of the Italian constitutional order or the inalienable rights of the person recognised by the Constitution, or of the fundamental rights and principles enshrined by Art 6 of the Treaty on European Union (TEU), as well as the fundamental rights guaranteed by the European Convention on Human Rights. Furthermore, the EAW execution is to be refused whether the issuing State has been suspended by the EU Council due to serious and persistent violation of Art 6(1) TEU.

The domestic case law arguably pays much attention to fundamental rights considerations in passive EAW proceedings. For instance, the Court of Cassation has underscored the need to apply the two-step approach developed by the CJEU in *Aranyosi and Căldăraru* and later developed in *LM* and *EDL*. The "real" risk of inhuman or degrading treatment shall be inferred by the supplementary information provided by the issuing State and refusals can only be decided on a case-by-case basis, thus avoiding mere general assessments on that Member State[49] or the conditions of the surrendee.[50] If the Court of Appeal complies with the obligation to request additional information, but the issuing State avoids providing detailed information that excludes the risk of inhuman and degrading treatment, case law has considered that the surrender may be refused.[51]

Lastly, the Constitutional Court has recently included the protection of health among the fundamental rights considerations that may lead to a

48 As clarified by the *Relazione illustrativa*, in *Senato della repubblica, XVIII legislatura, Atto del governo sottoposto a parere parlamentare N. 201, Schema di decreto legislativo recante disposizioni per il compiuto adeguamento della normativa nazionale alle disposizioni della decisione quadro 2002/584/GAI, relativa al mandato di arresto europeo e alle procedure di consegna tra Stati membri*, 8. In the first transposition of the EAW FD, this ground was explicitly provided for in Art 18(1)(h), Law no. 69/2005.

49 Cass. pen., sez. VI, no. 44015 of 16/11/2022; Cass. pen., sez. II, no. 6633 of 17/02/2021; Cass. pen., sez. VI, no. 18352 of 11/06/2020; Cass. pen., sez. VI, no. 44397 of 29/10/2019; Cass. pen., sez. VI, no. 52541 of 09/11/2018; Cass. pen., sez. VI, no. 47891 of 11/10/2017; Cass. pen., sez. VI, no. 22249 of 03/05/2017; Cass. pen., sez. II, no. 3679 of 24/02/2017; Cass. pen., sez. VI, no. 5472 of 01/02/2017; Cass. pen., sez. VI, no. 23277 of 01/06/2016.

50 Cass. pen., sez. VI, no. 51798 of 28/12/2023 (concerning a pregnant surrendee).

51 Court of Appeal of Milan, no. 155 of 28/03/2024 (rejecting the surrender of an Italian citizen following the refusal of the Hungarian authorities of providing individualized information on detention facilities).

refusal – *rectius*, a postponement for (indefinite) time – of a EAW. Following a preliminary ruling to the CJEU,[52] the Constitutional Court has established that, under Arts 4 CFREU and 2 and 32 of the Italian Constitution – the national executing authority may temporarily postpone the surrender of the requested person, provided that there are serious reasons for believing, on objective grounds such as medical certificates or expert reports, that the execution of the EAW manifestly risks endangering the health of that person. In these circumstances, a direct dialogue shall be established between the judicial authorities to find a solution that avoids serious risks to the person's health. When such a solution cannot be found, a final decision refusing surrender may be issued.[53]

### 2.3 *Issues for the Rights of the Suspect or Accused in EAW Proceedings*

Art 11 EAW FD, which provides for the rights of the requested person, is transposed by Arts 10(1), 9(5-*bis*), and 12(1), Law no. 69/2005. While the implementation of the rights to information and access to a lawyer can be considered satisfactory overall, the case law has interpreted these prerogatives in a rather flexible fashion, possibly raising issues in practice. The right to interpretation and translation, instead, has not been fully transposed by the national legislator, as outlined below.

Concerning the right to information, in the ordinary passive procedure it is provided that the person concerned is informed of the right to appoint a lawyer in the issuing state at the moment of execution of precautionary measure ordered by the Court of Appeal (Art 9(5-*bis*), Law 69/2005). In the subsequent hearing before the Court, the President informs the subject, in a language known to him or her, of the content of the EAW and the procedure for its execution, of the right to consent to the surrender and waive the application of the speciality rule (Art 10(1), Law 69/2005). When the procedure is initiated by the police, instead, the officer making the arrest shall provide the same warnings in a language the arrested person understands (Art 12(1), Law 69/2005). Under Art 12(1-*bis*), the police must also inform the person concerned of the right to appoint a lawyer in the issuing State. To ensure the effectiveness of these rights, Art 12(3) foresees that the arrest report shall, under penalty of nullity of the act, indicate that the information of Art 12(1) has been provided. The same is not required for the information on the right to appoint a lawyer in the issuing state: this gap may be explained by the fact that Art 12(1-*bis*) was introduced into the text of the transposition law only at a later stage and was

52 Case C-699/21 *E.D.L.* [2023] ECLI:EU:C:2023:295.

53 Italian Constitutional Court, no. 177 of 28/07/2023; cf, also, Cass. pen., sez. F., no. 34816 of 8/08/2023.

not coordinated with the reporting obligation of Art 12(3), although the Court of Cassation has argued otherwise.[54]

The case law, however, has interpreted these provisions in quite an anti-formalistic fashion. In relation to the duty to inform the subject of the right to appoint a defence counsel in the issuing State, the Court of Cassation has clarified that no nullity arises where this notice is given to the person concerned by the judge at the time of validation of the arrest, rather than by the judicial police immediately upon arrest.[55] Despite this approach not being entirely satisfactory, it does not raise any compliance issues. Art 11 EAW FD only foresees that the information is delivered to the person concerned "in accordance with its national law" but does not set any specific requirements or limits to the provision of such information. Given this, any implementation gap can only be discerned considering the effectiveness of such information rights: if, for example, the notice is given too late in the procedure, the requested person might be deprived of an effective right to legal assistance before the issuing and executing authorities. This risk does not, however, seem to rise in the national procedure. Art 13(1), Law no. 69/2005 provides indeed that the judge presiding the arrest validation hearing must give to the requested person all the information on procedural rights. Considering that such a hearing takes place within forty-eight hours of the arrest, this timeframe seems short enough to ensure the fairness of the procedure.

Jurisprudence shows similar flexibility in the interpretation of the right to access a lawyer. Concerning the right to be assisted by a retained lawyer, the Court of Cassation has established that there is no provision to observe a period of notice for notifying the defence counsel of the validation hearing.[56] The need to facilitate the participation of the defence counsel must be balanced

54 cf Cass. pen., sez. VI, no. 52013 of 16/10/2018, which has argued that the lack of any sanctions for the failure to inform the arrested person of the right to appoint a lawyer in the issuing State corresponds to an intentional choice of the legislator, considering that no sanctions are also provided for the same failure in the ordinary procedure (Art 9(5-*bis*), Law no. 69/2005).

55 Cass. pen., sez. VI, no. 52013 of 16/10/2018; Cass. pen., sez. VI, no. 51289 of 6/11/2017. In such cases, the Court considered the supplementary notices given by the judge at the validation hearing to be sufficient, according to the general rules of Arts 294(1-bis) and 391(2) CCP. Previously, however, the case law had established that the absence of the notice gave rise to an intermediate nullity, that had to be flagged by the defence at the latest at the hearing to validate the arrest, see Cass. pen., sez. VI, no. 51289 of 06/11/2017; Cass. pen., sez. VI, no. 24301 of 9/05/2017.

56 Cass. pen., sez. VI, no. 7025 of 08/01/2021; Cass. pen., sez. VI, no. 28/04/17918 of 2009. This applies also where the court-appointed lawyer was not notified of the validation hearing, cf Cass. pen., sez. F, no. 34958 of 04/09/2008.

against the urgency of the procedure, so that no nullity can be found where the defence counsel is not able to participate in the hearing or, at least, to appoint a substitute. This approach does not raise issues when the requested person was informed of the right to appoint a retained lawyer when arrested and exercised this right before the validation hearing. Nonetheless, problems may arise when the person concerned was not placed, from the moment of the arrest, in a position to exercise this prerogative. In fact, the Court of Cassation considers that the failure to record the delivery of information about procedural rights in the arrest report constitutes only a relative nullity, whose effects can be remedied according to the general rules of Art 183 CCP.[57] Besides, in this case, the nullity is merely linked to the arrest report, and not the defendant, meaning that no check is made on the fact that the arrestee has been effectively informed of his or her right.[58]

Moreover, the approach applied in EAW proceedings seems to contradict that adopted in domestic cases, where courts tend to interpret the right to be assisted by a lawyer to a high standard. Generally, suspects or accused persons have a right to be assisted not by any lawyer, but by the lawyer of their choice.[59] Specifically, in a decision not on the EAW, the Court of Cassation has acknowledged that the failure to give notice of the hearing to the retained lawyer promptly appointed by the person concerned constitutes an absolute nullity when his or her presence is mandatory, although the notification was made to another lawyer and that a substitute was present at the hearing.[60] Following this line of reasoning, one could wonder whether an absolute nullity occurs at the validation hearing, where the presence of the lawyer is mandatory, when

57 Cass. pen., sez. VI, no. 48127 of 29/11/2013. From the point of view of sanctions, there are three types of nullities in the Italian criminal procedural system: absolute nullities (*nullità assolute*), intermediate nullities (*nullità intermedie*), and relative nullities (*nullità relative*). Relative nullities have the least serious consequences on the procedure, as they can be raised only by the parties (and not *ex officio* by the judge), within the strict time limits of Art 181 CCP, and the with the general limitations of Arts 182–183 CCP.

58 Marianna Biral and others 'The Italian implementation of the EU Directives on Procedural Safeguards for Accused Persons in Criminal Proceedings' (*SP*, 22 November 2023), 51 <https://www.sistemapenale.it/pdf_contenuti/1669131660_report-italiano-cross justice.pdf> last accessed 14 August 2024.

59 ibid 57–58.

60 Cass. pen., sez. V, no. 181 of 26/11/2020. Art 13 EAW FD does not specify whether the presence of the lawyer at the validation hearing is necessary. However, the case law has already admitted to the possibility of extending the general rules of the Italian CCP on arrest validation hearings (Art 391) to the police-initiated procedure (Art 13). According to this line of reasoning, the presence of the lawyer at the validation hearing in the EAW should be considered mandatory.

the requested person was not informed of the right to be assisted by a retained lawyer. The Court of Cassation would likely exclude such a possibility, given the urgency underlying EAW proceedings. It is also unsure whether such an issue would raise actual compliance problems with the EAW FD. In this case as well, Art 11(2) establishes the right to be assisted by a legal counsel "in accordance with the national law of the executing Member State" and does not set any specific standards in terms of being assisted by a retained or court-appointed lawyer. Given this, the impossibility of being assisted by a retained lawyer at the validation hearing does not raise compliance issues. Nonetheless, from a purely domestic perspective, more coherence on the contents of the right to be assisted by a lawyer would be welcomed.

Lastly, there are reasons to argue that the right to translation of essential documents is not fully implemented in the national system. Art 11 EAW FD establishes that the person concerned has a right to be informed of the EAW and its contents and should be assisted by an interpreter.[61] While such prerogatives should be ensured "in accordance with the national law of the executing Member State", the standards of protection granted in the national system should also be aligned with those foreseen in Directive 2010/64/EU.[62] Art 3(6) of the Directive provides that "[i]n proceedings for the execution of a European arrest warrant, the executing Member State shall ensure that its competent authorities provide any person subject to such proceedings who does not understand the language in which the European arrest warrant is drawn up, or into which it has been translated by the issuing Member State, with a written translation of that document". Therefore, *as a rule*, the person arrested for the execution of a EAW should be handed a written translation of the warrant. Such a prerogative is aimed at ensuring the effectiveness of the participation in the proceedings of the defence: it is certainly better for the person requested to have a written document, which can be later analyzed

61 The right to be assisted by an interpreter is instead guaranteed to a high standard. The Court of Cassation has clarified that, if the person requested to be surrendered who does not know the Italian language, he or she has the right to be assisted by an interpreter for the purpose of signing the declaration of waiver of participation in the hearing, otherwise determining an absolute nullity pursuant to Art 178(1)(c) CCP, which is irremediable and extends to the sentence pronounced at said hearing. cf Cass. pen., sez. VI, no. 3726 of 25/01/2024.

62 Directive 2010/64/EU of the European Parliament and of the Council of 20 October 2010 on the right to interpretation and translation in criminal proceedings OJ L 280, 26.10.2010, p. 1–7.

with the interpreter and the defence counsel.[63] When the transposition law for the Directive was adopted,[64] the Italian legislator did not intervene on Art 12, Law no. 69/2005, which enshrines the rights of the person arrested for the execution of a EAW. The current version of the text only foresees an oral summary of the warrant's contents. This situation is seen as an exception according to the Directive, while the written translation of the document should be the rule. Given this, the implementation of the right to translation in the EAW procedure cannot be considered fully satisfactory.[65]

## 3 European Investigation Order: Critical Profiles in Legislation and Case Law

The EIO D has been implemented in Italy by Legislative Decree no. 108 of 21/06/2017.[66] The transposition law consists of three parts: the first contains some general provisions (Arts 1–3 and 47); the second regulates the passive procedure, with Italy acting as executing authority (Arts 4–26); the third regulates the active procedure, with Italy acting as issuing authority (Arts 27–46). It is remarkable that the very first provision of Legislative Decree no. 108/2017 establishes that the implementation respects the principles of the Italian constitutional order and the Charter of Fundamental Rights of the European Union regarding fundamental rights, freedoms, and fair trial. This general provision should serve as a guide in the interpretation of the entire text of the law of implementation.

63 Marta Bargis, 'Il mandato di arresto europeo dalla decisione quadro del 2002 alle odierne prospettive' (2015) 4 Dir Pen Cont 61, 65.

64 The Directive was transposed with the Legislative Decree 4 March 2014, no. 32, *Implementation of Directive 2010/64/EU on the right to interpretation and translation in criminal proceedings* (Attuazione della direttiva 2010/64/UE sul diritto all'interpretazione e alla traduzione nei procedimenti penali) in Official Gazette no. 64 of 18-03-2014.

65 Marta Bargis (n 63) 66. The case law has not provided a useful response to this gap. The Court of Cassation acknowledges that the EAW constitutes an essential act of the proceedings, which the accused has a right to have translated according to Art 143 CCP. However, it recognises this prerogative *only if* the requested person presents a reasoned request, while the Directive provides for this right to be implemented automatically. See Cass. pen., sez. VI, no. 50814 of 24/11/2016.

66 Legislative Decree no. 108/2017 has been recently amended by Law no. 137 of 9 October 2023. The amendment only concerns Art 4 Legislative Decree no. 108/2017, which deals with the powers of the public prosecutor in EIO matters. The amendment is relatively minor and will be reported when appropriate.

The following sections will first consider the procedures for executing and issuing a EIO in Italy in general. The focus will then turn to the specific provisions for certain types of investigations.

### 3.1 *Scope and Types of Proceedings for Which a EIO Can Be Issued*

The broad material scope of the EIO D is confirmed, at the national level, by Art 2 Legislative Decree no. 108/2017, according to which a EIO can be issued and executed in Italy for carrying out virtually every investigative act, with some minor exceptions.[67] At the outset, it is important to highlight two key aspects of the procedures in which an EIO can be issued in Italy.

First, Italian authorities can issue EIOs "in criminal proceedings or proceedings for the application of a measure of asset prevention" (Art 27 Legislative Decree no. 108/2017). This definition arguably transposes Arts 4(a) and (c) of EIO D, while the Italian legislator does not appear to have conferred the competence to issue a EIO on administrative authorities, as is the case under Art 4(b) EIO D. It is beyond question that this constitutes a significant distinction.[68]

Second, the national system also provides for the possibility to issue a EIO in criminal proceedings where a legal person is involved as a defendant. That is possible in criminal proceedings relating to offences committed by a natural person in the interest or advantage of a legal person (i.e., in most cases, a company).[69]

---

67 These exceptions depend on the overlap of Legislative Decree no. 108/2017 with other pieces of legislation, notably the European Convention on Mutual Assistance in Criminal Matters adopted by the Council of Europe on 20/04/1959; the Convention implementing the Schengen Agreement of 14/06/1985, ratified by Italy by Law no. 388 of 30/09/1993; the Brussels Convention of 29/05/2000 on Mutual Assistance in Criminal Matters between the Member States of the European Union, implemented in Italy through Legislative Decree no. 52 of 5 April 2017.

68 On the possibility of including administrative authorities such as OLAF within the category of Art 4(c) EIO D, cf Salvatore Tesoriero, 'La cooperazione transnazionale nelle indagini in materia di frodi IVA e doganali: strumenti tradizionali e nuove opportunità' in A. Di Pietro and M. Caianiello (eds), *Indagini penali e amministrative in materia di frodi IVA e doganali. L'impatto dell'European Investigation Order sulla Cooperazione Transnazionale* (2016) 68.

69 In such cases, the liability of the company, although formally administrative in nature, is ascertained through a criminal proceeding. Consequently, Art 27 Legislative Decree no. 108/2017 is applicable. The matter is regulated by the Legislative Decree no. 231 of 8 June 2001. For further details, please refer to the Italian FACILEX Report, available at <www.site.unibo.it/facilex/en>.

### 3.2 *Execution Procedure*

When Italy acts as the executing Member State, the EIO is transmitted – compulsorily in Italian – to the public prosecutor of the district where the investigative acts must be conducted (Art 4 Legislative Decree no. 108/2017), who must inform the issuing authority of the reception (Art 6 Legislative Decree no. 108/2017).[70] The prosecutor then assesses the occurrence of reasons preventing recognition, which include not only grounds for non-recognition but also serious proportionality issues.[71]

Once the evaluation is complete and no later than 30 days after receiving the EIO, the prosecutor decides whether to issue a EIO recognition decree or to refuse recognition (Art 4 Legislative Decree no. 108/2017). Before refusing recognition, however, s/he must inform the issuing authority of the reasons for denial, in order to initiate the appropriate discussions to remove them (Art 6(2) and (3) Legislative Decree no. 108/2017). If, on the other hand, there are no grounds for refusing recognition, the prosecutor issues a reasoned decree of recognition,[72] which is notified to the lawyer of the accused only if, under Italian law, the defence counsel would have the right to take part in the act of investigation.[73] Within 5 days of notification, the decree may be challenged by the defendant before the judge for preliminary investigations, who may set it aside (Art 13 Legislative Decree no. 108/2017).

After recognition, the EIO must be executed observing the specific requests indicated by the issuing authority, provided that such compliance does not contravene the supreme principles of Italian law (Art 4(2) Legislative Decree no. 108/2017). For the execution of the EIO either the general rules or those dictated for specific acts (Arts 16–25 Legislative Decree no. 108/2017) are followed.

70 The Ministry of Justice, on the one hand, and the National Anti-Mafia Prosecutor, on the other, must also be informed (Art 4 Legislative Decree no. 108/2017), but the latter only if the EIO is issued in the context of proceedings for offences covered by Arts 51 (3-bis), (3-quater) and 371-bis (4-bis) CCP. The list of offences has been extended by an amendment to Legislative Decree no. 108/2017.

71 Cass. pen., sez. VI, no. 14413 of 7/02/2019.

72 Under the sanction of nullity of the act, the decree must state why there is no obstacle to recognition and the proportionality principle is respected, cf Cass. pen., sez. VI, n. 14413 of 7/2/2019.

73 No communication is due if the recognized EIO relates to an investigative act for which Italian law does not provide for the right of the defendant to be present (e.g., the interception of communications), cf Ministry of Justice, Operational Manual of 26/10/2017 on the Implementation of Directive 2014/41/EU on the European Investigation Order in Criminal Matters ('*Attuazione della direttiva 2014/41/UE relativa all'ordine europeo di indagine penale – Manuale operativo*'), *sub* para 4.1.

After execution, the evidence collected is transmitted without delay to the issuing authority, together with the reports of the acts performed (Arts 12 and 14 Legislative Decree no. 108/2017). The time limits for the execution of the EIO prescribed throughout the whole procedure by the Directive (Art 12 EIO D) are, in general, correctly implemented.

### 3.2.1 Grounds for Non-recognition and Non-execution

Although overall accurate, the transposition of grounds for non-recognition and non-execution in Italian law (Art 10 Legislative Decree no. 108/2017), presents some gaps and inconsistencies with respect to the EIO D.

As to immunities (Art 11(1)(a) EIO D), Italian law does not explicitly prevent recognition in case of crimes relating to freedom of the press and expression. Nonetheless, the latter deficiency can be covered by Art 10(1)(e) Legislative Decree no. 108/2017, which allows to refuse execution when it would be incompatible with CFREU. National case law has specified the conditions for exclusion of criminal liability when an act is carried out in the exercise of freedom of speech.[74]

Similarly, with regard to the ground for refusal based on national security (Art 11(1)(b) EIO D), the Italian transposition is too synthetic, as it does not refer specifically to cases where execution would involve the use of classified information relating to specific intelligence activities (Art 10(1)(c) Legislative Decree no. 108/2017). Anyway, by only mentioning "national security reasons" as a possible reason for refusal, the wording of the law of implementation seems capable of including all the specific cases mentioned in the Directive.

Art 11(1)(c) EIO D – the investigative measure would not be authorized in a similar domestic case in proceedings referred to in Arts 4(b) and (c) – and (h) – restrictions to some offences – are not explicitly implemented in the list of Art 10 Legislative Decree no. 108/2017. Nonetheless, the implementing law explicitly states that if the Italian prosecutor cannot perform the requested investigative act because the Italian requirements are not met, they must carry out those acts available under Italian law that achieve the same objectives (Art 9(1) Legislative Decree no. 108/2017). If that is impossible, the prosecutor must refuse execution (Art 9(3) Legislative Decree no. 108/2017). The latter provisions, by directly implementing Arts 10(1) and 10(5) EIO D, would seem to provide an indirect implementation also of the grounds for refusal at hand. Their application, however, remains subject to the impossibility of

74 See, *ex multissimis*, Cass. pen., sez. un., no. 37140 of 30/05/2001 and Cass. pen., sez. II, no. 51439 of 19/12/2013. For further references, please refer to the Italian FACILEX Report, available at <www.site.unibo.it/facilex/en>.

having recourse to another type of investigative measure that would be available under Italian law.

The *ne bis in idem* principle as a ground for refusal, the respect of fundamental rights, and double criminality (Arts 11(1)(d), (f), (g) EIO D) are fully implemented and pose no issues (Arts 10(1)(d), (e)(f) Legislative Decree no. 108/2017).

Despite the generally appropriate implementation of the above-mentioned grounds for refusal, three significant inconsistencies between the Directive and Italian legislation have been identified. One is the direct omission of an essential ground for non-recognition, while the other two can be characterized as 'undue additions' to the national legislation.

First, Art 11(1)(e) EIO D, on the territoriality of the offence, is completely omitted and cannot find any equivalent in the transposition law. Anyway, considering that the EIO D explicitly states that execution 'may' be refused in those cases listed in its Art 11, the lack of the territoriality ground does not amount to a case of non-compliance with the EIO D. Indeed, the absence of a ground for refusal in national legislation appears to reinforce the principle of mutual trust. Second, Art 10(1)(a) Legislative Decree no. 108/2017 establishes that a EIO may be non-recognized or non-executed if it contains manifestly wrong or mismatched information. Although the case law has mitigated this ground for non-recognition,[75] this remains a major discrepancy with the EIO D, which reflects the intention of the legislator to strictly enforce Art 5 EIO D on the content and form of the EIO. Lastly, according to Art 10(3) Legislative Decree no. 108/2017, a EIO issued by an authority other than a judicial one, or not validated by it, must not be recognized and must be returned to the issuing authority. This enforces, by way of a specific ground for non-recognition, Art 2(c) EIO D, which notoriously defines 'issuing authorities' as either judges, courts, investigating magistrates, and public prosecutors (Art 2(c)(i) EIO D) or any other competent authority, subject to validation by one of the latter.

The latter two cases can be regarded as situations of formal non-compliance, as the content and origin of the EIO are not formally included by the European legislator among the possible grounds for non-recognition.

75 The Court of Cassation has specified that it is the responsibility of the prosecutor to assess the completeness and precision of the EIO. Furthermore, the court has stated that mere formal flaws cannot be grounds for the annulment of a decree that recognizes a EIO (respectively, decision no. 14412 of 2/2/2019 and no. 30885 of 15/9/2020).

### 3.2.2 Proportionality and Fundamental Rights

During recognition and execution, Italian authorities must verify the proportionality between the rights of the suspect (or any other person involved in the proceedings) and the needs of the investigation (Art 7 Legislative Decree no. 108/2017). The latter provision is far more precise than the corresponding Art 6(1)(a) EIO D, as it specifically states the parameters according to which proportionality must be assessed: the respect of rights and liberties of the suspect or third parties, the investigative or evidentiary needs, the seriousness of the offences for which proceedings are being conducted and the penalty established for these offences (Art 7 Legislative Decree no. 108/2017). However, Italian law does not prescribe how compliance with such standards should be assessed (as done in Art 6(1)(b) EIO D); it merely leaves the agreement on how to overcome any possible disproportionality to communications between authorities. This results in the principle of proportionality being well integrated within the national system as a whole.[76]

As for fundamental rights, on the other hand, the Italian implementation proves particularly effective (at least formally), considering that Art 10(1)(e) Legislative Decree no. 108/2017 reproduces *verbatim* the ground for refusal of Art 11(1)(f) EIO D for violation of Art 6 TEU and the CFREU. The national provision is interpreted as meaning that, when Italy is the executing Member State, the decree by which the prosecutor recognises the EIO can only be challenged when its defects significantly affect the fundamental rights of the person concerned.[77]

A crucial point for the rights of the defendant in the proceedings is that of the communication to the defence counsel of the execution of investigative acts relating to the EIO (see *supra*, §3.2). The Supreme Court has established that the failure to timely communicate the decree recognising the EIO to the defence counsel constitutes a violation of the suspect's right to a fair trial, as it prevents the suspect and the defence counsel from lodging a timely appeal. However, in such a case, the execution of the EIO is not halted (Art 13(4) and

76 See also Arts 6(3) and 9(2) Legislative Decree no. 108/2017. Indeed, when the investigative measure indicated in the EIO is deemed to be disproportionate, Italian authorities should contact the issuing authority in order to agree on how to proceed with a less intrusive act, cf Cass. pen., sez. VI, no. 8320 of 31/01/2019. Extensively on this topic, see Cosimo Emanuele Gatto, 'Il principio di proporzionalità nell'ordine europeo di indagine penale' (2019) 2 Dir pen cont 69 ff. <www.archiviodpc.dirittopenaleuomo.org/d/6482-il-principio-di-proprzionalita-nell-ordine-europeo-di-indagine-penale> last accessed 14 August 2024.

77 Cass. pen., sez. VI, no. 30885 of 15/09/2020. Therefore, the Italian judge is not obliged to ascertain the correctness of the acts of execution and is entitled to presume it.

(7) Legislative Decree no. 108/2017), but the transfer of the results of the activities conducted may be postponed if the prosecutor deems it necessary.[78]

#### 3.2.3 Issues for Cooperation between Executing and Issuing Authorities

When Italy is the executing Member State, potential issues of cooperation may emerge as a result of discrepancies between the EIO D and its transposition in Italian law. Three categories of potential problems were identified.

First, communications with the issuing Member State may be hampered by the fact that, according to the Italian law of implementation, not every delay in the execution procedure must be communicated to the issuing Member State. In particular, contrary to what is prescribed by Art 12(5) EIO D, a notice about delays in the procedure is only due if such delays concern the execution, and not also the recognition of the EIO (Art 6 Legislative Decree no. 108/2017).[79]

The second issue concerns costs. When Italy is the executing Member State and the execution of the order turns out to be particularly costly, the public prosecutor must indeed consult with the issuing authority on cost-sharing (Art 15 Legislative Decree no. 108/2017). But there is no reference in the Italian implementation to the fact that Italy should notify the issuing authority in advance of cost specifications (Art 21(2), second subparagraph EIO D).

The last issue relates to the possibility of recurring to an investigative measure other than the one requested as an alternative to refusing the execution of the EIO (Art 10 EIO D and Art 9 Legislative Decree no. 108/2017). Art 10(2) EIO D lists a number of investigative acts that must always be available in the executing Member State. In such exceptional cases, the EIO could not be refused and the investigative act should be executed. Although the list of Art 10(2) EIO D is generally correctly implemented, sub-paragraph (a)[80] is only partially: Art 9(5) Legislative Decree no. 108/2017 states that "the execution of the investigation order concerning the obtaining of evidence gathered in other proceedings shall be carried out in any event". It is clear that Art 9(5) Legislative Decree no. 108/2017 outlines a narrower exception compared to that of the EIO D, and this

78 In particular, the prosecutor suspends the execution if "serious and irreparable harm" may be caused to the suspect, the accused or other affected parties (cf. Cass. pen., sez. VI, no. 8320 of 31/01/2019).

79 Moreover, no consultation obligation is imposed on the Italian authorities when delays in enforcement occur. It can thus be concluded that Arts 12(5) and (6) EIO D have not been fully implemented in Italian law.

80 This refers to the investigative measure of "obtaining of information or evidence which is already in the possession of the executing authority and the information or evidence could have been obtained, in accordance with the law of the executing State in the framework of criminal proceedings or for the purposes of the EIO".

could hinder cooperation, allowing Italian authorities to avoid direct execution in a wider range of cases.

Anyway, in general, these imperfections in the implementation of the EIO D can be considered minor and not likely to prevent effective cooperation between Italy and the other Member States, as they can easily be solved through informal contacts.

### 3.3 *Active Procedure*

The EIO can be issued in Italy in the context of a criminal proceeding or in that of preventive measures, by the prosecutor or by the judge according to their respective competence (Art 27 Legislative Decree no. 108/2017).[81] The judge issues the investigation order after hearing the parties. The accused, through his defence counsel, may request a EIO to be issued by the prosecutor,[82] who may refuse by means of a reasoned act of refusal (Art 31 Legislative Decree no. 108/2017).

The order is then transmitted directly to the executing authority in the official language of the executing Member State, or in the other language indicated by the latter (Art 32 Legislative Decree no. 108/2017).[83] Upon receipt of the EIO, the Italian authorities will agree with the executing Member State on the modalities for carrying out the requested investigative acts, stating rights and faculties recognized by Italian law to the defendant and other parties (Art 33 Legislative Decree no. 108/2017). After execution, once they receive documentation of the investigative acts conducted in the executing MS, Italian authorities shall make it available to the parties of the Italian proceeding (Art 35 Legislative Decree no. 108/2017).

Due to the prevailingly adversarial nature of the Italian criminal procedural system, the documentation of investigative acts conducted abroad cannot be directly known by the trial judge, unless it is considered by Italian law to be a mere "document" or the counsel of the defendant has participated to the act (Art 36 Legislative Decree no. 108/2017).[84] With regard to possible

81 The competence to issue a EIO therefore lies with authorities that are certainly judicial in nature and independent of the executive. Issues such as the one in Case C-16/22 *Staatsanwaltschaft Graz* [2023] ECLI:EU:C:2023:148 do not therefore arise in relation to Italy.

82 The defendant must indicate, under penalty of inadmissibility of the request, the investigative act whose execution is requested and the reasons justifying the request (Art 31(2) Legislative Decree no. 108/2017).

83 In accordance with the provisions of the Directive, transmission may take place via the European Judicial Network (Art 7 EIO D and 32 Legislative Decree no. 108/2017).

84 Therefore, documentation from abroad should in principle be placed in a file that is not accessible to the trial judge. If during the trial it turns out that it is impossible to

consequences of the violation of fundamental rights by the executing Member State, the Court of Cassation has repeatedly stated that concrete evidence of non-conformity with fundamental rights enshrined in the CFREU or the principle of proportionality is needed to overcome the presumption of compliance by the executing authority.[85]

The active procedure does not pose significant issues for the implementation of the EIO D.

### 3.4 *Special Investigative Acts*

Let us now examine the status of implementation of the specific investigative acts mentioned in Chapter 4 of the EIO D.

#### 3.4.1 Temporary Transfer of Persons Held in Custody

Both the procedure for transferring persons held in custody to the issuing (Art 22 EIO D) and to the executing Member State (Art 23 EIO D) are, in general, correctly implemented in Italian law. In particular, as imposed by the EIO D, the temporary transfer of an inmate is only granted upon their free consent, provided that the person has had the opportunity to confer with their lawyer. According to Art 16(1) Legislative Decree no. 108/2017, the transfer is, in any case, subject to the clearance of the judge.

As for the passive procedure itself, there are some implementation flaws that can, however, be overcome through a broad reading of Legislative Decree no. 108/2017. Indeed, Art 16(2) Legislative Decree no. 108/2017 provides that, for executing the EIO, the authorizing judge shall take into account the age of the person and their physical or mental health condition but does not explicitly foresee that the legal representative of the person in custody may express his or her opinion on the temporary transfer (as requested by Art 22(3) EIO D). This seems to be a major defect that can only be remedied by taking into account the age, as well as the physical and mental health, of the person to be transferred.[86]

Art 22(5) EIO D, regarding the practical arrangements of the transfer, is not fully implemented. In fact, the corresponding Art 16(3) Legislative Decree

---

cross-examine the person whose testimony was obtained abroad (e.g., because s/he has died), the documents will then be transferred to a file that can be accessed by the judge (Art 36 Legislative Decree no. 108/2017, recalling Art 512-bis CCP).

85 cf e.g., Cass pen., sez. VI, no. 48330 of 25/10/2022. Therefore, the Italian judge is not obliged to ascertain the correctness of the acts of execution and is entitled to presume it.

86 See the Italian FACILEX Report, available at <www.site.unibo.it/facilex/en> for further details.

no. 108/2017 does not explicitly consider custody conditions, safeguards for the person's physical and mental conditions, and the level of security required in the issuing State as terms of the agreement. Therefore, national authorities are under no obligation to specifically agree on such conditions to ensure the well-being of the person concerned.

Instead, the active procedure is fully implemented by Art 37 Legislative Decree no. 108/2017.

### 3.4.2 Hearing by Videoconference and Phone Conference

Hearing by videoconference (Art 24 EIO D)[87] seems to run smoothly both when Italy is the executing and the issuing Member State.

In the passive procedure, Art 18(1) Legislative Decree no. 108/2017 allows for the execution of the request for the hearing by videoconference of the accused, the defendant, witnesses, and expert witnesses, after prior agreement with the issuing authority on the modalities of the hearing. Consent is mandatory in the case of suspects and accused persons (Art 18(2) Legislative Decree no. 108/2017). It must be noted that Legislative Decree no. 108/2017 does not prescribe that execution must be refused if contrary to the fundamental principles of Italian law (as does Art 24(2)(b) EIO D). Nonetheless, it is provided that during the execution of the act, the Italian prosecutor or the judge must ensure the respect of the fundamental principles of Italian law (Art 18(6) Legislative Decree no. 108/2017).[88] This can be classified as defective implementation. In contrast, the rules of Art 24(5) EIO D are correctly transposed.

In the active procedure, Art 39(3) Legislative Decree no. 108/2017 specifies the conditions that allow a EIO for the hearing by videoconference to be issued.[89] Consistently with the Directive (Art 24(3) EIO D), the modalities of execution shall be agreed upon by the Italian and the executing authorities (Art 39(4) Legislative Decree no. 108/2017).

---

87 The same rules apply also with regard to the hearing by means of a telephone conference (Art 25 EIO D, correctly transposed by Art 19 Legislative Decree no. 108/2017).

88 The hearing is conducted directly by the issuing authority or under its direction (Art 24(5)(c) EIO D and Art 18(6) Legislative Decree no. 108/2017). This is why the prosecutor or the judge have, in principle, only a supervisory role.

89 These are: (a) when for the listed persons there are justified reasons rendering their presence on the national territory inappropriate; (b) when the person to be questioned or examined is in any capacity detained in the Member State; (c) in cases of need to examine undercover operators, state witnesses and accused of crimes connected with the main proceedings.

### 3.4.3 Information on Bank and Financial Accounts

With regard to the execution of EIOs requesting information on bank and financial accounts, Art 20 Legislative Decree no. 108/2017, which describes the passive procedure, is largely based on the regime for the seizure of documents held by banks provided for in the CCP.[90]

This would seem to limit the execution of such EIOs to the cases and modalities in which the seizure of documents held by banks would be authorised under national law. However, the latter is so undemanding that this reference can hardly be seen as posing obstacles to cooperation.

The active procedure is briefly described and presents no issues of implementation.[91]

### 3.4.4 Real-Time Monitoring and Controlled Deliveries

The procedure established by Legislative Decree no. 108/2017 for real-time monitoring (Art 28(1)(a) EIO D) is particularly noteworthy, as this investigative act is formally unknown in Italian law.

Faced with this absence on the domestic scene, the choice of the Italian legislator was to remain silent on the possibility for the prosecutor to send a EIO addressed to another country to perform such an investigative act (i.e., in the active procedure). Nonetheless, it may be that real-time monitoring activities could be ordered by national prosecutors as 'atypical investigative acts', i.e., the category that includes all investigative acts not specifically regulated by law. Such acts are subject to very limited safeguards in the Italian system.[92]

On the contrary, the Italian legislator has chosen to regulate real-time monitoring when Italy is the executing State by referring to the rules on interceptions (for which see *infra*, §3.4.6), given the similarities between the two instruments. Accordingly, the prosecutor, after receiving the EIO shall proceed, if necessary, by means of a request to the judge for preliminary investigations (Art 20(2) Legislative Decree no. 108/2017).[93]

It is evident that there is a significant discrepancy between the guarantees provided in the active and passive procedures: in essence, the authorisation of the judge is solely necessary in the passive procedure. This difference does not

---

90 In particular, Art 20 Legislative Decree no. 108/2017 prescribes to execute the order according to the rules of Arts 255 and 266 CCP.

91 Art 40 Legislative Decree no. 108/2017 only prescribes to use the model of Annex A, subsection H4 for the request and its content.

92 On the qualification of real-time monitoring activities as 'atypical investigative acts', see Cass. pen., sez. V, no. 48370 of 20/05/2017. It is the jurisprudence that basically dictates the framework for the execution of these investigative acts.

93 See Arts 266 et seq. CCP.

represent an implementation defect but rather an evident disparity in treatment that necessitates intervention from the Italian legislature.

Controlled deliveries (Art 28(1)(b) EIO D) are also no longer directly envisaged by Italian law. In particular, the law explicitly provided for controlled deliveries with regard to drug-related offences, but the relevant rules were then replaced by a general regulation included in Art 9, Law no. 146 of 16 March 2006 on undercover operations. The latter establishes that, for a limited number of crimes, police officers may omit or delay acts within their jurisdiction, thus for instance allowing a controlled delivery.[94] Yet, Legislative Decree no. 108/2017 does not mention controlled deliveries, but cites Art 9 Law no. 146 of 16 March 2006 with respect to covert investigations and to a specific procedure called 'delay or omission of acts of arrest or seizure' (Art 22 and 42 Legislative Decree no. 108/2017).

It is therefore reasonable to assume that EIOs relating to controlled deliveries are issued in accordance with Art 9 Law no. 146 of 16 March 2006 and therefore follow national regulations. Since controlled deliveries are not mentioned in Legislative Decree no. 108/2017, neither are the conditions of Art 28 EIO D, so one cannot speak of explicit implementation into Italian law. However, the result obtainable through the possible application of Art 9 Law no. 146 of 16 March 2006 could lead to a satisfactory indirect implementation, considering that the Directive itself widely refers to the applicable national law.[95]

#### 3.4.5 Covert Investigations

With regard to covert investigations, Legislative Decree no. 108/2017 expressly refers, for both active and passive proceedings, to the Italian law regulating these activities in domestic proceedings, i.e., Art 9, Law no. 146 of 16 March 2006 (cited by Arts 21 and 41 Legislative Decree no. 108/2017). The latter law establishes the procedural framework for covert investigations and provides police officers with immunity from criminal prosecution for their actions undertaken in the course of such investigations, in relation to a wide range of criminal offences. Overall, the combination of the two laws the Italian implementation

94 The police shall however give immediate notice to the prosecutor and transmit a reasoned report within forty-eight hours. When it is necessary for the acquisition of relevant evidence, the public prosecutor may request that assets, money or other utility be used for the execution of controlled transactions (e.g., for the payment of the ransom), and the judge shall issue a reasoned decree. See Art 9 (6), (6-bis) (7), Law no. 146 of 16 March 2006.

95 E.g.: the execution may be refused if the investigative measure would not be authorised in a similar domestic case (Art 28(1) EIO D); the right to act, direct and control operations related to the execution shall lie with the competent authorities of the executing Member State (Art 28 (4) EIO D).

of EIO D satisfactory, as the latter largely relies on the legal framework of covert investigations (including the grounds for refusal) existing in the executing Member State.[96]

The only flaw in the Legislative Decree no. 108/2017 seems that it does not expressly state the ground for refusal arising from the lack of agreement between issuing and executing authorities on the modalities of execution of covert investigations. But the defect could be overcome via contacts between authorities.

### 3.4.6 Interception of Telecommunications

Overall, the rules established by the EIO D on interception of telecommunications are correctly implemented.

Some deviations from the general EIO execution procedure are highlighted here, which largely depend on the fact that, in the Italian system, only a judge can authorise wiretapping, except in cases of absolute urgency.

Thus, in the passive procedure, the public prosecutor must forward the received EIO to the judge for the preliminary investigation (Art 23(2) Legislative Decree no. 108/2017). If no technical assistance from Italy is required, the prosecutor will send the notification of the beginning of operations to the same judge (Art 24(1) Legislative Decree no. 108/2017).

The range of control of the judge seems to vary depending on whether the operations require technical assistance from the Italian authorities.[97] In case of interceptions that require technical assistance, the judge may deny execution according to Art 10 Legislative Decree no. 108/2017 (ordinary grounds for refusal) and "if the conditions of admissibility provided for by domestic law are not met". Italy has therefore used the possibility provided for in paragraph 5 of Art 30 EIO D.[98]

On the other hand, where the assistance of Italy is not required, the judge should verify solely whether the offence being prosecuted by the issuing authority is one for which Italian law permits interceptions. The latter check is undoubtedly milder than both that imposed by Art 31(3) EIO D ("where

96 See Art 29(3)(a) and (4) EIO D, which largely rely on the rules existing in the executing Member State.

97 This results from a comprehensive reading of Legislative Decree no. 108/2017 and of the Operational Manual issued by the Ministry of Justice on the execution of the EIOs. See Ministry of Justice, Operational Manual of 26/10/2017 on the Implementation of Directive 2014/41/EU on the European Investigation Order in Criminal Matters (*'Attuazione della direttiva 2014/41/UE relativa all'ordine europeo di indagine penale – Manuale operativo'*) *sub* para 17.3.

98 Paragraph 5 of Art 30 EIO D allows Member States to deny execution "where the investigative measure would not have been authorised in a similar domestic case".

the interception would not be authorized in a similar domestic case") and that requested in case of interceptions that require the technical assistance of Italy.[99]

As regards the active procedure (Arts 43 ff. Legislative Decree no. 108/2017), there are no implementation issues to be highlighted. However, similarly to other European countries, a heated debate has sparked concerning the legal classification of the encrypted messages from the SKY-ECC platform (or similar ones) obtained through EIOs issued by Italian authorities. The hubbub stemming from the issue[100] ended with the decision no. 23755 of the Supreme Court of Cassation of 29/02/2024. According to the Court, the transfer to the Italian judicial authority of the content of communications made through 'cryptophones' and already acquired and decrypted by a foreign judicial authority does not necessarily have to be subject to the authorisation of the judge in Italy to be used as evidence at trial. The transmission of such evidence is only subject to control concerning the respect of fundamental rights and the rights of defence.[101]

Also, with regard to traffic and location data associated with telecommunications, Legislative Decree no. 108/2017 correctly implements the EIO D, stipulating that the normal procedure of the European Investigation Order – together with Art 256 CCP on the duty of disclosure and confidentiality – be followed in the passive procedure.[102]

---

99 Also, in case the judge decides to interrupt the interception, Legislative Decree no. 108/2017 does not provide the possibility to subject the use of intercepted material to conditions, as does Art 31(3)(b) EIO D.

100 According to a dominant line of case law of the Supreme Court, such conversations, once transmitted to Italy, were admissible in the form of documents (See, e.g., Cass. pen., sez. I, no. 6364 of 13/10/2023 and previously Cass. pen., sez. IV, no. 16347 of 18/04/23). But tables have turned with decision no. 44154 of 02/11/2023, with which the sixth chamber of the Supreme Court outlined a distinction: if the activity of the executing authority consists in the covert apprehension or seizure of the content of a server, then the rules on seizures should apply; if, on the other hand, the executing authority carries out actual interceptions, then rules on interceptions are to be followed (including the authorisation of the judge). On 3/11/2023, the matter was referred to the *Grand Chambre* of the Supreme Court of Cassation, the body appointed to settle these contrasts.

101 This principle is actually expressed in two so-called 'twin' judgments of the Court of Cassation: no. 23755 and 23756 of 29/02/2024. For further details, see also Marcello Daniele 'Le sentenze "gemelle" delle Sezioni Unite sui criptofonini' (2024) SP <www.sistemapenale.it/it/scheda/daniele-le-sentenze-gemelle-delle-sezioni-unite-sui-criptofonini> last accessed 14 August 2024. The author relates the two judgments to that of the Court of Justice of the European Union in Case C-670/22 *M.N.* [2024] ECLI:EU:C:2024:372.

102 According to Recital 30 EIO D, "Possibilities to cooperate under this Directive on the interception of telecommunications should not be limited to the content of the telecommunications, but could also cover collection of traffic and location data associated with such

### 3.5 *Remedies*

Art 14 EIO D requires the Member States to ensure that legal remedies equivalent to those available in a similar domestic case are applicable to the investigative measures indicated in the EIO. Also, the substantive reasons for issuing the EIO may be challenged only in an action brought in the issuing State (Art 14(2) EIO D). At the national level, such provisions must be confronted with the almost total absence of direct legal remedies against the investigative acts carried out by the prosecution. Indeed, also in national proceedings, most investigative acts cannot be challenged directly, but only on a later stage, with regard to the admission or use of such evidence at trial, and subject to the specific rules applicable.

As a result, the remedies available against the issuance of EIOs in Italy in the active procedure are extremely limited and are essentially confined to seizure to secure a source of evidence. Against such measure Art 28 Legislative Decree no. 108/2017 entitles the person from whom the evidence or property has been seized (and the person who would be entitled to their return) to submit a request for review to the competent court.[103] As for the other investigative acts, the only way the defendant can challenge the evidence collected through a EIO in the active procedure is by contesting its admissibility in court *ex post facto*, i.e., after the collection of the evidence.[104] In general, considering the equivalence clause in Art 14 EIO D, the Italian implementation cannot be considered non-compliant. However, it must also be said that an increase in the guarantees provided for in the issuing Member State would be desirable, in line with what the CJEU has established in the *Gavanozov II* decision.[105] In Italy, the latter judgment has not yet had the hoped-for effect of raising the level of protection of the defendant's rights.

In the passive procedure, Art 13 Legislative Decree no. 108/2017 allows the defendant to appeal the decree by which the prosecutor has recognized the EIO within five days of its notification.[106] The problem is that communication of the decree of recognition to the defendant is not always mandatory for the prosecution, but only for those investigative acts in which the defence counsel of the defendant has the right to participate. It follows that only the execution

---

telecommunications, allowing competent authorities to issue a EIO for the purpose of obtaining less intrusive data on telecommunications".

103 The procedure mirrors that of Art 324 CCP.

104 Cass. pen., sez. VI, no. 44154 of 26/10/2023.

105 Case C-852/19 *Ivan Gavanozov* [2021] ECLI:EU:C:2021:346.

106 If the competent judge upholds the appeal of the defendant, the decree of recognition is annulled and the execution of the EIO is blocked (Art 13(3) Legislative Decree no. 108/2017).

of some investigative acts must be timely communicated to the lawyer of the defendant (see *supra*, §§3.2 and 3.2.2).

## 4 Regulation 1805/2018: Critical Profiles in Legislation and Case Law

### 4.1 *Legal Basis in the National System and Scope*

As illustrated in the introduction, Italy has recently adopted the Legislative Decree no. 203/2023,[107] in force since 6 January 2024, "for the complete adaptation of national legislation to the provisions of Regulation (EU) 2018/1805".[108] Nevertheless, the recent legislative decree has not fully resolved all coordination problems between the Regulation and national legislation, requiring the interpreter to make a coordinated approach between various sources: Regulation 1805/2018, the recent Legislative Decree 203/2023, but also the previous legislation, Legislative Decrees no. 137/2015,[109] 35/2016[110] and, no less important, the Ministry of Justice Circular of 18 February 2021 and that of the Ministry of the Interior, Department of Public Security, of 12 January 2021.

Italy, therefore, has not adapted to the Regulation for a long time, in the sense, it should be pointed out, that it did not make the small changes necessary to allow its broader application. Before Legislative Decree no. 203/2023, in fact, in Italy the application of the Regulation was made through: (i) direct application of the Regulation, as an immediately applicable legal act; (ii) analogical procedural interpretation, using as a term of comparison Legislative Decree no. 137/2015, on the recognition of confiscation orders and Legislative Decree no. 35/2016, on the recognition of seizure orders; (iii) reference to the Circulars of the Ministry of Justice and the Interior already mentioned and that, with a pragmatic approach, address quite a few application issues.

As is well known, the Regulation was immediately applicable in Italy even before the Legislative Decree no. 203/2023, which adapted the domestic

107 Legislative Decree No. 203 of 7 December 2023, in force since 6 January 2024, Official Gazette No. 298 of 22 December 2023.

108 For a more detailed overview of Regulation 1805 in Italy, see the Italian FACILEX report, available at <https://site.unibo.it/facilex/en>.

109 Legislative Decree No 137 of 7 August 2015 '*on the implementation of Framework Decision 2006/783/JHA on the application of the principle of mutual recognition to confiscation orders*', in force since 17/09/2015 (Official Journal No 203 of 2 September 2015).

110 Legislative Decree No. 35 of 15 February 2016, '*implementing Council Framework Decision 2003/577/JHA of 22 July 2003 on the execution in the European Union of freezing orders*', in force since March 26, 2016 (Official Journal No. 59 of March 11, 2016).

procedural system to the EU instrument.[111] And yet, it must be underlined that, especially at this initial phase, there are several interpretative issues unresolved by Legislative Decree no. 203/2023, and for which one must still refer to the other sources already mentioned above, or to the interpretative role of the case law.[112] Among these, the Circulars of the Ministry of Justice and of the Ministry of the Interior maintain centrality, as they have taken care, since the beginning, for example, of expressly indicating which measures of patrimonial prevention fall within the scope of the Regulation (thus, for example, the same Circulars, to be read together, already clarified that the Regulation must also be applied to the cases of the so-called seizure of prevention, i.e. issued in the ambit of the anti-mafia legislation, regulated by Legislative Decree no. 159/2011).[113]

With this brief overview of the recent legislative evolution, it should be immediately appreciated that with Regulation 1805/2018 the European Union intended to bring judicial cooperation between Member States to a new level for at least two reasons: 1) the legislative instrument used; 2) the breadth and specificity of the regulatory intervention.

Under the first profile, it must be considered that with the Regulation, the EU attempted to overcome the fragmentary nature of the instruments that existed until then, specifically, Directive 2014/42/EU. By comparing the two opening articles of the two legislative acts (Directive 2014/42 and Regulation 1805/2018), the direction that the Regulation intended to give to the cooperation between

---

111 Especially from the perspective of recognition and execution procedures, i.e. where Italy is the executing State. For active procedures, therefore, the Regulation operates directly, and it continues to be useful to refer, insofar as they are compatible, to other and pre-existing national legislation as well. E.g., Arts 11 and 12 of Legislative Decree 35/2016 provide some useful directive for requests to execute a freezing order in the territory of another Member State.

112 It's sufficient to read this judgment issued before the Legislative Decree 203/2023 to appreciate this issue. Court of Cassation, 06/10/2023, no. 47141 stated: "on the subject of recognition and execution of freezing orders of assets functional to confiscation issued by the authority of an EU member state, the "self-executing" provisions of the Regulation apply – pending the approval of the implementing legislation of the EU Regulation 2018/1805 – and, for matters not fully regulated therein, the provisions of Legislative Decree No. 35 of 15 February 2016, and Legislative Decree No. 137 of 7 August 2015".

113 The Ministry of the Interior Circular, specifically, states that "*the expression 'proceedings in criminal matters,' used by the European legislator, is also suitable to include the measures governed by the Code of Anti-Mafia Laws and Measures of Prevention (Legislative Decree 159/2011), since they presuppose an assessment of social dangerousness, based on the existence of indicia of the commission of crimes, and an ascertainment of the illicit origin of assets*".

States is clear. The Directive set out a series of "minimum rules"[114] on freezing property with a view to possible subsequent confiscation. The Regulation, for its part, aspires more simply and widely to regulate (all) the procedures for the recognition and execution of freezing and confiscation orders within the EU Member States.[115]

Regarding the object of the regulatory intervention, from an Italian perspective, it is necessary to define what can and should be understood by "freezing"[116] at the level of domestic procedural law. There is no processual instrument going by the same name in the Italian Code of Criminal Procedure (CCP). The most closely related instruments are seizures ("*sequestri*" in Italian).

In Italy, there are two types of seizures understood as real precautionary measures: preventive (*sequestro preventivo*) and conservative (*sequestro conservativo*). Without claiming to be exhaustive, consider that, in a nutshell, the preventive seizure is that measure requested by the prosecutor to prevent that property, in the availability of the defendant, may lead to more serious consequences of the crime. This seizure may also be ordered on things for which confiscation would be possible.[117] This instrument, therefore, has purely public purposes. On the other hand, the *conservative seizure* is that measure requested to protect credit,[118] that is, in order to prevent the defendant from dissipating

114 Art 1 Directive 2014/42/EU states "[t]his Directive establishes *minimum rules* on the freezing of property with a view to possible subsequent confiscation and on the confiscation of property in criminal matters". Differently, the Regulation states "This Regulation *lays down the rules* under which a Member State recognises and executes in its territory freezing orders and confiscation orders issued by another Member State within the framework of proceedings in criminal matters".

115 Art 1, § 1, states "This Regulation lays down the rules under which a Member State recognises and executes in its territory freezing orders and confiscation orders issued by another Member State within the framework of proceedings in criminal matters".

116 Confiscation, for its part, does not generate too many problems of interpretation, as it corresponds to the Italian institution of "*confisca*". Reference should be made to Article 240 and ff. of the Criminal Code. Simplifying, the measure's purpose is to deprive the subject of the assets seized within the confiscation order, which become part of the public assets.

117 Art 321 CCP, Preventive Seizure, states that "when there is a risk that the free availability of an asset relating to the offence may aggravate the consequences of the offence or facilitate the commission of other offences, at the request of the public prosecutor, the judge (...) shall order its [preventive] seizure (...). *The judge may also order the seizure of the objects whose confiscation is allowed*".

118 For our purposes, we consider in particular the claim arising from damages. For exhaustiveness, Art 316 CCP states that "If there are reasonable grounds to believe that the securities for the payment of a financial penalty, costs of proceedings and any other sum owed to the Treasury of the State are lacking or will be dispersed, the Public Prosecutor, at any stage and instance of the proceedings, after the initiation of criminal prosecution, shall request the conservative seizure of the accused person's movable or immovable property

the economic guarantees aimed to safeguard, for example, compensation for damages. Although the conservative seizure can also be requested by the prosecutor, it must be said that there is another procedural party particularly interested in this measure, and that is the *civil party*, i.e. who acts in the criminal trial for the sole purpose of claiming compensation for damages suffered and arising from the crime.[119] It is well understood, therefore, how this measure is mostly of a private nature, that is, to protect the private interests of the creditor.

Among these types of seizure, therefore, for the purposes of the Regulation, prevalence should be given to preventive one (*sequestro preventivo*), in the Italian CCP. Such preventive seizure can, presumably, be assimilated to the freezing order foreseen in the Regulation 1805/2018, as deduced from the finality of the freezing order indicated by Art 2 of the Regulation, which describes the "freezing order means a decision issued or validated by an issuing authority in order to prevent the destruction, transformation, removal, transfer or disposal of property with a view to the confiscation thereof". Considering that these are freezing orders aimed at confiscation, also Art 321 CCP comes to mind, which has a similar approach and states that a *preventive seizure* may be requested in cases where there is a risk of aggravating the consequences of the offence or facilitating the commission of other offences and, not least, the preventive seizure of assets for which confiscation would then be allowed.

If this is true in general, the absence of a clear statement by the European and national legislators, brings the interpreter face to face with a complex legal question, if seen from an Italian perspective: *can the freezing order under the Regulation be issued only in cases where a preventive seizure would be possible in Italy? And then, can the victim request it directly*?

This brings us to one of the *critical profiles* on the matter, which is the role of the victim according to the Regulation. After looking at this aspect in depth in the following paragraph, it will be necessary to focus on the meaning of the concept of "criminal matter", when viewed from the perspective of Italian law. Finally, the procedural aspects will be analysed in order to understand the concrete functioning of the instrument, including the reference to the "double criminality" requirement and whether it operates in the Regulation. Finally,

or the sums or objects owed to him, within the limits set by law for their distress. If there are reasonable grounds to believe that the securities for civil obligations deriving from the offence are lacking or will be dispersed, the civil party may request the conservative seizure of the property of the accused or of the person with civil liability for damages as provided for in paragraph 1. The seizure ordered upon the request of the Public Prosecutor shall also be in favour of the civil party".

119 See previous footnote on the reasons why the civil party may apply for a conservative seizure.

attention will be devoted to the freezing and confiscation certificates, through which the Regulation "comes to life".

### 4.2 *The Role of the Victim*

The role of the victim is one of the issues that raises most of the difficulties in the interpretation and application of the Regulation. To properly understand the problem, it is necessary to briefly frame the opportunities recognized to the victim in Italian criminal proceedings. The victim of a crime can choose whether to exercise his or her right to damages directly in a criminal trial (or not). If s/he makes this decision, then s/he will have to formalize it through the so-called act of "constitution as a civil party" (assuming this name as a party in the proceedings). This act must comply with strict formalities that make it clear that only civil interests are at stake. Indeed, it must be considered that under Art 78 CCP, "The declaration of constitution as civil party (...) *must contain, under penalty of inadmissibility*: (...) a statement of the reasons justifying the claim for *civil purposes*".[120] As is evident, the civil party acts in a criminal trial to have compensation for the damages suffered. If follows that the civil party may also have an interest in taking precautionary action in order to prevent, having reasonable grounds, the defendant from dissipating the guarantees protecting the civil claim (e.g., if the defendant disposed of his or her assets to avoid payment of damages). As mentioned in the previous paragraph, the procedural tool exists, and it is the *conservative seizure*. With this instrument, the civil party requests (and aspires to obtain) a restriction on the defendant's property, which becomes unavailable to him or her, as a guarantee for the civil party's claims. At this point, the Regulation comes into relevance for the civil party's interests. As it can easily be imagined, the possibility to apply for a freezing order under the Regulation, i.e., being able to rely on an EU-wide instrument, would be a huge procedural advantage for the

120 This is particularly true after the so-called "Cartabia" Reform, the wide-ranging reform introduced by Legislative Decree 150/2022 to reorganize criminal justice in Italy. The Cartabia Reform also intervened on Article 78 of the Italian Code of Criminal Procedure, making it even clearer that the civil party exercises purely civil claims in criminal proceedings. This was also expressed by the Cass. Pen., sez. un., no. 38481 of 25/05/2023, which states that "*a precise indication of the* causa petendi *will be necessary similarly to the forms prescribed for the claim brought in civil proceedings* (...) *for the purposes of the admissibility of the constitution, it will no longer be sufficient to refer to the commission of an offence but it will be necessary to refer to the reasons on the basis of which it is claimed that prejudicial consequences have arisen from the offence, as well as the title legitimating the claim*".

civil party.[121] Indeed, the civil party would be able to freeze assets held in other EU countries, and, for the practical application of the instrument, it could also count on the human and logistical resources of the States involved in the mutual recognition instrument (the issuing and executing Member States).

To answer the theoretical question,[122] it is necessary to see what the Regulation says on this subject. It must be observed that it is a bit cryptic and, likewise, the Italian legislation does not help to immediately understand the solution to the question. According to the Regulation (Art 1), it is called to operate "in criminal matters" and not "(...) in civil or administrative matters". In Italy, a civil action in a criminal trial, although formally instituted in criminal proceedings, must nevertheless be considered as a civil action. The formalities of a civil action make this assumption clear (Art 78 CCP). The doctrine on this point also specifies that "[the *civil action* can be] exercised in the criminal trial, attributing to the latter a further part (...) qualified as "possible/eventual" (...) because its presence in the trial depends on a free and unquestionable option – in this sense uncertain and, therefore, eventual: that of deciding whether to apply to the criminal judge and not to the civil one to find satisfaction of his

121 *Fair* or *unfair*? That's the question.

A few examples may help to understand the issue.

Imagine that the victim (and civil party in the proceeding) of one of the offences included in the list of those covered by the Regulation request a conservative seizure. The civil party, having seen the investigation documents, discovers, based on investigations by the judicial authority, that there have been numerous money transfers to another Member State in order to prevent the victim from recovering his or her loss in Italy. At that point, the victim would have to embark on a long road to recover the sums that he or she believes are owed to him or her. S/he would then have to obtain a condemnation to reimbursement of damage and then take the difficult road to recovery.

And instead, if s/he could take advantage of the Regulation s/he would have, in order:

1. information derived from the judicial police that it could immediately exploit for the purpose of applying for a seizure;
2. if requested and obtained, the public authorities, the State, within the framework of this judicial cooperation, would take charge of executing the freezing order; in doing so, the victim would not only be able to rely on the human resources of Italy (which is assumed here as the issuing State), which would actually prepare the file to be sent to the executing State, but also on the human resources of the executing country. There, in fact, public security officers would seize the assets to meet the request for cooperation.

Whether this was the intention of the European legislator, or, on the contrary, such an approach could be considered a stretch, however, remains uncertain. The considerations that follow are intended to outline a guideline of possible interpretation that is in agreement with both the literal datum emerging from the Regulation and the *ratio legis*.

122 It is useful to repeat the interpretative question that is being researched: *can the freezing order under the Regulation be issued only in cases where a preventive seizure would be possible in Italy? And then, can the victim request it directly?*

or her claim deriving from a crime (...). The relationship between [the two actions, civil and criminal] is governed (...) on the basis of the principle of the autonomy of the respective [ascertainment]: the tendency to separate the civil trial from the criminal trial, in fact, testifies to the pre-eminence of the requirements of celerity (...) of the criminal proceedings with respect to the interest of the victim in exercising his or her [civil] action before the same judge who also ascertains the conditions for punishment".[123] In addition to this, it is worth recalling Art 2 of the Regulation, which, on the subject of Definitions, states that "[f]or the purpose of this Regulation, the following definitions apply: (1) 'freezing order' means a decision issued or validated by an issuing authority in order to prevent the destruction, transformation, removal, transfer or disposal of property with a view to the confiscation thereof". As can easily be seen, there is no mention of the possibility of immediately satisfying civil interests through the Regulation, nor the possibility for the victim to apply for the freezing order to protect civil reasons directly.

Lastly, it is necessary to point out a clue that can be deduced from the Legislative Decree no. 203/2023 and that seems to point definitively towards the hermeneutic option proposed here, namely the lack of legitimacy of the civil party to be able to directly apply for a freezing order under the Regulation. Art 2 of Legislative Decree no. 203/2023, in fact, states that for the execution of freezing orders issued pursuant to the Regulation "the provisions of the Code of Criminal Procedure concerning the execution, revocation, and appeal of the *preventive seizure* decree shall be observed, insofar as they are compatible". Here, too, therefore, albeit seen from the Italian perspective, no mention of the conservative seizure is to be found, which further supports the validity of the interpretative choice advanced here.[124]

Finally, it must be admitted that the Regulation is concerned with the victim, recognising the latter as a sort of right of priority over the sums which the issuing State has obtained through the Regulation procedure. In these terms, however, it would seem that, in the vision of the European legislator, the victim would not be allowed to apply directly for a freezing order under the Regulation, but s/he would come back into play at the end of the procedure and, at that point, his or her right to restitution would be particularly valued, recognising him or her as the beneficiary of the assets which the executing State will have succeeded in recovering. This appears to be the solution most in

123 Maria Lucia Di Bitonto, 'I Soggetti', in Alberto Camon, Marcello Daniele, Daniele Negri and others (eds), Fondamenti di procedura penale (Cedam, 2023), p 200 ff.

124 Namely the lack of legitimacy of the civil party to be able to directly apply for a freezing order under the Regulation.

line with the *ratio* of the discipline. Therefore, granting the victim the possibility to apply directly for a freezing order for civil purposes (i.e. for cases where in Italy it would be possible to apply for a so-called *conservative seizure*) may lead to a distortion of the implementation, with significant practical repercussions. This obliges the interpreter to wonder, finally, about possible friction with the rights of the defendant if this were to become the prevailing interpretation. Allowing the civil party to directly leverage the tools of the Regulation may raise an issue of legal basis and a doubt as to whether the victim has direct legal capacity to apply directly for a freezing order under the Regulation. This may also pose a question as to whether the right to an effective remedy and the right of defence of the person affected by the freezing order has been violated.

On the first aspect, recalling the arguments presented above, it should be added that even a glance at the freezing certificate, in the section on 'restitutions', provides further arguments in favour of the interpretative approach proposed here (namely the lack of legitimacy of the civil party to be able to directly apply for a freezing order under the Regulation.). Section "K" of the freezing certificate is entitled "possible restitution to the victim" and asks whether there is, in accordance with domestic law, a decision (which, therefore, already appears to be a decision additional and different from the freezing order) that has recognized the victim's right to restitution. In addition, the last part of section "K" specifically asks the issuing State to indicate whether, on the contrary, a procedure is pending which will establish the right of the victim to the possible return of "frozen" goods (to be understood, therefore, as *already frozen* for reasons falling within the Regulation's reasons of public interest).[125]

No less important is Art 29 of the Regulation, which regulates precisely the 'restitution of frozen property to the victim' which again refers to the restitution of (already) frozen property and identifies the cases in which it is possible, i.e. "(a) the victim's title to the property is not disputed; (b) the property is not sought as evidence in criminal proceedings in the executing State; and (c) the rights of the persons concerned are not affected".[126] The verbal tense ("frozen") and the listing of cases in which assets are returned to the victim suggest that

---

125 Art 29 of Regulation also expresses in similar terms, stating that "Where the issuing authority or another competent authority of the issuing State has issued a decision, in accordance with its national law, to return frozen property to the victim, the issuing authority shall include information on that decision in the freezing certificate or communicate information on that decision to the executing authority at a later stage".

126 There are also other useful references in the Regulation to explore the issue in depth, but they cannot all be cited in the space of this paper. Consider, however, recitals NN. 45 and 46.

s/he cannot directly request a seizure under Regulation. "*Frozen*" seems to refer to assets already blocked and, therefore, for another reason[127] and the listing represents a *numerus clausus* in which the victim's direct action to request a seizure is *not* included.

Still on the role of the victim, it is also useful to look at the issue from the perspective of the provisions about remedies. Art 33 Regulation 1805/2018, titled "[l]egal remedies in the executing State against the recognition and execution of a freezing order or confiscation order", states that "[a]ffected persons shall have the right to effective legal remedies in the executing State against the decision on the recognition and execution of freezing orders (...). The right to a legal remedy shall be invoked before a court in the executing State in accordance with its law (...). 2. The substantive reasons for issuing the freezing order or confiscation order shall not be challenged before a court in the executing State". The rule provides that the person affected by the order should be able to appeal in the executing State the decision to recognize and execute the freezing order. Questions of merit, however, can only be appealed in the issuing State. However, *what remedies if the freezing order could also be issued for purely civil purposes? What remedies could the person affected by the freezing have and in which State? What grounds could he or she assert in the executing State? And what remedies could he or she exercise in the issuing State?* Here, theoretically, the defendant will have to assert issues on the merits, but these will concern the merits of the victim's claim for damages, not the merits of the criminal charge, and will likely be raised in the very early stages of criminal proceedings. In addition to the grounds on the merits, *can the lack of a legal basis for the civil party also be invoked in the issuing State?*

Questions such as these, which are not resolved *per tabulas* by the European legislator (nor by the Italian one) attract the interest of the interpreter, whose efforts must be aimed to prevent the Regulation from becoming responsible for a deprivation of the rights of defendants. The reading advanced here also shows that these hurdles can be solved by linking the application of the Regulation both to the strict literal interpretation of its provisions and to the overall *ratio* of this mutual recognition instrument.

### 4.3 *Like Wildfire: about the Alleged Elasticity of the Criminal Matter*

The scope of application of the Regulation is ambiguous if seen from the Italian perspective in relation to the definition of "criminal matters".

---

127 Those referred to in Arts 1 and 2 of Regulation and this because it is already clear from the title of Art 29 that these are operations of restitution to the victim of already frozen assets.

Art 1 Regulation 1805/2018, indeed, states that it applies in the field of proceedings "in criminal matters". Moreover, its Recital 13 states that "[p]roceedings in criminal matters is an autonomous concept of Union law interpreted by the Court of Justice of the European Union, notwithstanding the case law of the European Court of Human Rights. The term therefore covers all types of freezing orders and confiscation orders issued following proceedings in relation to a criminal offence (...) It also covers other types of orders issued without a final conviction. While such orders might not exist in the legal system of a Member State, the Member State concerned should be able to recognise and execute such an order issued by another Member State (...)".

The issue is relevant in Italy, especially concerning the anti-mafia prevention legislation and proceedings. In the national system, there exists a structured para-sanctioning system (or, at any rate, a preventive one, simplifying as much as possible) aimed at striking the assets of mafia-type criminal associations. Within this mechanism, the instruments of seizure and confiscation are of the utmost importance.

Therefore, *can the scope of the Regulation cover also anti-mafia prevention proceedings?* To reconstruct the answer to the question, two ministerial Circulars on the subject are worth mentioning: the Ministry of Justice Circular of 18 February 2021 and that of the Ministry of the Interior, Department of Public Security, of 12 January 2021. The latter considers that the Regulation can also be applied in so-called "anti-mafia prevention proceedings", i.e. proceedings based on the deemed "social dangerousness" inferred from "indications of commission of offences" (in Italy governed by Legislative Decree no. 159/2011). The Ministry's interpretation should be underlined because it extends to the possibility of applying the Regulation.

As it can be read in the Circular of the Ministry of Justice, this was one of the goals of the Italian authorities on the road that led to the Regulation. In fact, the legislator intended to facilitate the mutual recognition of freezing orders even if issued, in Italy, under anti-mafia legislation, i.e. as preventive measures. On this point, therefore, it is convenient to mention, in excerpts, the salient parts of the Circular that concern this theme. "On December 21, 2016, the European Commission therefore presented a proposal for a Regulation on the mutual recognition of freezing and confiscation orders issued in the context of 'criminal proceedings', a proposal (...) was then extended during the negotiations (...) to include the mutual recognition of orders issued in the context of 'proceedings in criminal matters', so as to broaden the scope of application also to orders adopted in the context of Italian prevention proceedings (...). It can be said that a correct interpretation of the Regulation can today extend its applicative perimeter to the Italian measures of patrimonial prevention (which must, therefore, be recognized and executed also in the Member States whose national legislation does not provide for such measures)".[128] This considered, however, it must be admitted that the resolution of the issue is not so straightforward and has long interested scholars. The concept of criminal matter to which the Italian Circular also refers concerns the jurisprudence of the European Court of Human Rights (ECHR)[129] for the benefit of defendants, namely to reiterate the principle that even where, formally, a sanction is not described as criminal in a legal system, it is necessary to observe whether, in substance, it should be considered so. If the answer to this question is positive, then the measure is in substance criminal and the person subjected must be accorded some rights, including respect for the principle of legality or due process. The application advocated by the Ministry intends to resume that long debate but leveraging it "against the accused", that is, favouring the enforcement extension of measures with a sure sanctioning character (in this case: freezing and confiscation orders).[130]

---

128 In the Report on Eurojust's Casework in Asset Recovery, published in February 2019, the following was noted: "difficulties caused due to different styles of preventive measures utilised in some national legislation in the pursuit of criminal assets, such as unexplained wealth, non-conviction-based orders or civil confiscation orders. The difficulty becomes acute if national legislation in the requesting/issuing State is not reflected in the requested/executing State" (footnote also mentioned in the Ministry of Justice Circular of 18 February 2021).

129 *De Tommaso v. Italy*, App no. 43395/09 (ECHR, 23 February 2017). In doctrine on this point, see, among others Francesco Menditto, 'La sentenza De Tommaso c. Italia: verso la piena modernizzazione e la compatibilità convenzionale del sistema della prevenzione' (2017), on Dir Pen Cont 4; Anna Maria Maugeri, 'Misure di prevenzione e fattispecie a pericolosità generica: la Corte europea condanna l'Italia per la mancanza di qualità della "legge", ma una rondine non fa primavera. Nota a Corte EDU, Grande Camera, sent. 23 febbraio 2017, de Tommaso c. Italia' (2017), on Dir Pen Cont3. The author, already in 2017, moreover, acutely noted that "If the approach of the European Court expressed in the De Tommaso judgment were to be consolidated in future rulings, it could represent a vital stimulus to rethink the personal and patrimonial prevention measures, perhaps together with the future Regulation on the mutual recognition of confiscation orders issued in criminal proceedings, – should the Commission's proposal of 21 December 2016 be approved –, a regulation that will require the consideration of the possibility of bringing the patrimonial prevention proceedings back to the criminal matter and the related guarantees". See also *Case of G.I.E.M. S.R.L. and others v. Italy*, App no. 1828/06 and 2 others (ECHR, 28 June 2018). See also Vittorio Manes and Michele Caianiello, 'Introduzione al diritto penale europeo' (Giappichelli 2020).

130 If on the efficacy and incidence of the interpretative option endorsed by the Ministry, one cannot doubt, on the procedural guarantees, some doubt can arise, due to the particularly expeditious procedure that is that of prevention, with fewer guarantees compared to the "purer" criminal trial.

The recently adopted Legislative Decree no. 203/2023 does not mention the type of proceedings to which the Regulation applies. So, pending to see how the case law will orient itself, the practice proposed in the Circulars must still be considered.

### 4.4 *Procedure*

A quick overview of the procedure may help to understand the functioning of the Regulation in the Italian system.

The instrument is obviously based on mutual recognition between Member States and this aspect characterises several provisions of the Regulation. Through this cooperation, a 'double criminality' check for the facts being prosecuted is also overcome (in some cases). Specifically, for the purpose of Art 3 Regulation 1805/2018, the double criminality check is not carried out if the facts are punishable in the issuing State with a penalty of not less than three years and constitute one or more of the offences listed in Art 3, according to the issuing State legal system. It is, therefore, a requirement to be fulfilled jointly and not separately. Outside such cases, double criminality may be verified by the executing State before adopting the requested measure, and Legislative Decree no. 203/2023 (Art 1) provides for such a control in the passive procedure (that is when Italy is the executing State).[131]

As for the dynamic part of the procedure, i.e. the request for cooperation, this takes place through the issuance and transmission of the freezing[132] and confiscation certificate and the related order. Regarding this, it should be noted that once the freezing or confiscation order is compiled in the issuing State, this will have to be transmitted to the authority of the executing State. At the same time, the issuing State must transmit the freezing or confiscation certificate, which is attached to the Regulation. When Italy is the executing State, the

131 This aspect may also come to the fore as a ground for refusal under Arts 8 (1(e)) and 19 (1(f)). In order to properly apply this ground for refusal, it is possible to interpret the double criminality principle in light of the case law of the Italian Supreme Court of Cassation. The Cass. Pen., sez. VI, judgment no. 35818 of 14/12/2020, when referring to the double criminality principle as a possible ground for refusal of the European Arrest Warrant, stated that it is not strictly necessary for the abstract scheme of the incriminating rule of the foreign legal system to have an exact correspondence in a rule of the Italian legal system. It is instead sufficient for the concrete case to be punishable as a crime in both legal systems, regardless of any differences in the penalty treatment or in title or other elements required.

132 Art 4 of Regulation states "A freezing order shall be transmitted by means of a freezing certificate". Similarly, Art 14 provides for confiscation: "A confiscation order shall be transmitted by means of a confiscation certificate".

order must be transmitted to the competent national authorities in a certified copy, as required, most recently, by Art 1(3), Legislative Decree no. 203/2023.

Scrolling quickly through the freezing certificate (or confiscation one, both of them annexed to the Regulation), a not-at-all marginal set of information is indicated, which may be useful for the executing State to carry out the issuing State's request for execution correctly. The general rule would be that the certificate, i.e. the request for execution of the order on the territory of another State, is addressed to only one State at a time.[133] Only exceptionally, when, for example, there are reasons for considering that the enforcement requires continuous actions in more than one member State, may it be transmitted to more than one State.[134]

The executing authority, upon receipt of the order, executes it in the manner it would have done in a domestic procedure. The passage is not irrelevant because it touches on the essence of the mutual recognition of measures between States. Recalling the modalities that would have been proper in the execution State also means referring to an ambitious "principle of equivalence" of the foreign measure with respect to the domestic one, perhaps the highest point of mutual recognition instruments.[135] For freezing orders, where Italy is executing State, "on the request for recognition and execution of the freezing order the judge for preliminary investigations decides by reasoned decree, having acquired the opinion of the public prosecutor and having taken (...) all necessary information. The prosecutor shall render the opinion within ten days (...). Once these time limits have expired, the judge (...) shall also take action in the absence of the prosecutor's opinion" (Art 2 Legislative Decree n. 2023/2023). For confiscation, when Italy is the executing State, the competent authority is the Court of Appeal where the assets to be confiscated are located, or, if credits are involved, the Court of Appeal where the debtor resides (Art 3 Legislative Decree no. 203/2023). The Court of Appeal must set a hearing within twenty days of receiving the certificate and confiscation order. The notice of the hearing is communicated to the Prosecutor General at the Court of Appeal, the authority that requested the confiscation order, the person against whom the order is issued, and those who have rights to the property for

133 See Arts 5 and 15 of the Regulation.

134 On this point, Legislative Decree no. 203/2023 does not add anything further, the aforementioned and related provisions of the Regulation therefore apply directly.

135 Some practical aspects of the execution of preventive seizure (i.e. those to be followed in the case of execution of a freezing order under the Regulation) can be found in Arts 104 ff of the implementing rules of the Code of Criminal Procedure.

which confiscation is claimed. The Court decides (by sentence) on the request for recognition and execution of the confiscation.

If that is true in general terms, it must also be acknowledged that there are some grounds for refusal which are briefly mentioned below. The cases are enumerated in Art 8 Regulation 1805/2018 for freezing orders (Art 19 for confiscation ones) and, while not mentioning all of them, they may refer to: cases of *ne bis in idem*; formal and/or procedural flaws, such as incompleteness of the certificate; or in the event that – when there are serious grounds and with specific and objective elements – fundamental rights may be affected. However, a special duty of cooperation is also prescribed in these circumstances. In fact, the executing State, before proceeding with non-execution, is called upon to enter an adversarial process with the issuing Member State. The aim is evidently to save the enforcement of the order, by means of any additional information that the issuing State may be able to send because of the executing State's rejection notice. It may be argued that this "cross-examination" is indeed somewhat informal. Indeed, consider also that beyond the formal procedure of the instrument under consideration, there are also eminently political logics that at least in part support this freer approach in form. Legislative Decree 203/2023 does not specifically deal with grounds for refusal, either with reference to freezing or confiscation. The Regulation, therefore, remains the standard of reference[136] and it becomes interesting to add a few quick considerations on how the practice has intended to relate to these grounds for refusal in Italy. Since it is not possible to mention all of it, it seems useful here, given the eminently practical slant to the paragraph, to focus just on the cases of the incompleteness of the certificate. In fact, the Regulation lays down a safeguard clause for cases where the certificate (of freezing or confiscation orders) is incomplete. Instead of immediately refusing execution, the executing State should initiate an exchange of information with the issuing State to allow the latter to remedy any errors detected. The Italian approach, when Italy is the executing State, can be considered in line, as it appears clear even in the Circular of the Ministry of Justice of 18 February 2021: the "recognition may be refused when the certificate of freezing or confiscation is incomplete or manifestly inaccurate, provided that the issuing authority has not completed or amended the same certificate following consultations that the executing authority is required to initiate".

136 Insofar as they are compatible, it may also be useful to refer to the relevant pre-existing national legislation (e.g. Art 6, Legislative Decree no. 35/2016 and Art 6, Legislative Decree no. 137/2015).

Art 9 Regulation 1805/2018 specifies that the executing State should enforce the order as quickly as possible, in the same way it would do, again, in a similar domestic case. This type of act is characterized by the need to be executed within a certain timeframe. This applies even more to freezing orders, which by their nature are characterized by a higher need for celerity. In this respect, however, it is necessary to point out a difference between the provisions of the Regulation and those of the Code of Criminal Procedure. The Italian legislation has a mechanism for the urgent execution of preventive seizure orders. In cases of urgency, in fact, either the public prosecutor or the police may provide for preventive seizure, subject to validation by the judge for preliminary investigations within 48 hours. Well, in the case of the Regulation, Art 9 (3) operates as a special norm (derogating the general one and provided for by Art 321 CCP), requiring Italy, when it is the executing State, to comply with it. Specifically, the issuing Member State also can request the urgent performance of the freezing order from the executing State, which, in these circumstances, must decide within 48 hours on recognition and then within the following 48 hours provide for the execution. The aforesaid time limits are not stated to be peremptory – not least because they would otherwise reverberate against the issuing State itself – and therefore, even if the executing State should fail to comply in time, the expiry of the time limits does not exempt it from compliance in any event. This procedure is regulated in Italy by Art 2(4) of Legislative Decree no. 203/2023, which reiterates the provision of the Regulation (Art 9). Specifically, it imposes the prosecutor to give an opinion on the request for cooperation within 24 hours of receipt of the request for execution, after which the judge may proceed even without the prosecutor's opinion, precisely in order to ensure compliance with the reasons for urgency.

## 5 Concluding Remarks

This Chapter has explored the implementation of the three instruments of judicial cooperation into the Italian framework, recalling the process of adaptation of national legislation to the EU laws and the reforms adopted over the years, while highlighting inconsistencies in the transposition of provisions and troubles in the compliant interpretation by the case law.

Concerning the EAW, the analysis has illustrated two aspects of the national implementation that have raised the most concerns in terms of compliance with the original text of the instrument, namely the grounds for refusal and the rights of the suspect or accused.

The Italian transposition of the mandatory grounds for refusal, and the related case law, cannot be considered fully compliant with EU law. Nonetheless, the inconsistencies are minor, such as the definition of judgements of no grounds to proceed as a "final judgment" for the purposes of *ne bis in idem* under Art 3(2) EAW FD, or the application of the *ne bis in idem* clause for procedural flaws. As for the non-mandatory grounds for refusal, the Italian transposition still does not encompass all the optional grounds provided in the EU law; however, their absence does not cause concrete concerns, as they are optional by nature.

Considering the rights of the suspect or accused, the Chapter has shown that the formal transposition of the rights to information and access to a lawyer conforms to EU law, even though the jurisprudential interpretation of the relevant safeguards appears less rigorous than in domestic circumstances. On the contrary, the right to translation cannot be considered fully implemented since the transposition does not mirror the original text of the instrument.

The analysis conducted has evinced that, after a quite tortuous process of implementation, the Italian text is now mostly compliant with the EAW FD. Nevertheless, certain aspects would still require further legislative or judicial intervention to allow for a smoother issuance and execution of EAWs. As emerged in this Chapter, it would be advisable to enhance conformity in the transposition of the grounds for refusal and the provisions on the right to translation, and to increase consistency in the interpretation of the right to be assisted by a lawyer compared to domestic standards.

Concerning the EIO, this Chapter has shown that the transposition into the Italian system is overall compliant with the EIO D, even though some inconsistencies have been detected. Regarding the grounds for non-recognition or execution, the EIO D can be considered correctly implemented, except for the deliberate elevation of two formal requirements as grounds for non-recognition or execution (Arts 2(c) and 5 EIO D). Some minor inconsistencies have also been flagged in the cooperation procedure and in the implementation of the principle of proportionality, but they may be easy to overcome in practice through communication between authorities.

With regard to the special investigatory acts, apart from slight discrepancies that can be solved through a broad interpretation of the legislation – as for the temporary transfer of persons held in custody – or through the contact between authorities – as for covert investigations, the spotlight has been on real-time monitoring and controlled deliveries, which are not formally provided by Italian law. The former has been regulated by the legislator for the sole execution phase, generating significant discrepancy between the guarantees provided in the active and passive procedures; the latter have been omitted from the transposition law. In light of this, a legislative intervention to bridge the gap left in the Italian transposition of these special investigatory acts is highly recommended.

The last noteworthy issue concerning the EIO is related to the transposed provisions on remedies. While no remedy is provided for the active procedure (except for seizures for evidentiary purposes), in the passive one remedy is linked to the notification of recognition by the prosecutor, which is not always mandatory. The Italian legislation is therefore not fully in line with the Directive as interpreted in the *Gavanozov II* case, and a legislative intervention to fix such deficiency is highly recommended.

Concerning Regulation 1805/2018, the implementation process has been less linear. The Italian legislator has adopted the necessary changes for the smooth application of the Regulation only in 2023, with the enactment of Legislative Decree no. 203. Nevertheless, as emerged in this Chapter, even after the recent legislative intervention, serious uncertainties remain at the interpretative level.

In the first place, the question of whether victims are entitled to request a freezing order under the Regulation has been left unsolved in both national and European legislations. The reasoning conducted in this Chapter combined both the literal interpretation of the Regulation and the Italian legislation – emblematically, Art 1 Regulation 1805/2018 and Art 78 CCP – and the *ratio* underpinning the instrument. Considering that such a prerogative in the hands of the victim might impair the balance towards the accused and contravene express legal provisions, the most suitable conclusion proposed at the end of the analysis is that the victim should not be considered attributed the right to request a freezing order under the Regulation.

Second, the ambiguity surrounding the definition of "criminal matter" casts doubts on the scope of application of the Regulation and questions the possibility of applying this instrument to anti-mafia prevention proceedings when such measure is not envisaged by the law of the executing Member State. Considering that ministerial Circulars have confirmed the application of the Regulation to anti-mafia prevention proceedings and that Recital 13 of the Regulation affirms that Member States should recognise and issue an order even though such an order does not exist in its legal system, it could be suggested that the Regulation does cover anti-mafia prevention proceedings. However, the recent Legislative Decree no. 203/2023 does not rule this aspect.

Therefore, since the Regulation has still not been so frequently deployed in Italy, upcoming case law must be awaited in order to infer the judicial orientation on the matter.

Third, the procedural aspects illustrated so far, as implemented in the Italian system, can be classified as compliant with EU law.

To conclude, notwithstanding the often-debated process of transposition, the implementation in the Italian system of the three instruments is overall consistent, in the sense that it does not present serious hampers for the smooth functioning of cooperation procedures between Member States. Still, some inconsistencies have emerged throughout the analysis conducted in the present Chapter and have been carefully examined to highlight concrete effects in the cooperation practice. Therefore, aiming for a more compliant implementation into the national system, the authors have flagged those provisions where a harmonizing intervention by the Italian legislation would be advisable.

CHAPTER 9

# Poland: EAW, EIO and Freezing and Confiscation Orders – Implementation and Transposition Process and Its Deficiencies

*Wojciech Jasiński, Karolina Kremens and*
*Agnieszka Frąckowiak-Adamska*

## 1 Introduction[1]

This chapter discusses the implementation and transposition of the European Arrest Warrant Framework Decision (EAW FD), European Investigation Order Directive (EIO D) and Regulation 2018/1805, into the Polish legal system. While European Arrest Warrant (EAW), European Investigation Order (EIO) and freezing and confiscation orders serve the same purpose – building the area of freedom, security, and justice – they differ in several important aspects. The EAW is regulated by a framework decision, the EIO through a directive, and freezing and confiscation orders find their legal basis in the EU regulation. The EAW has the longest history, dating back to 2002. The EIO is more recent, adopted in 2014, while the Regulation on freezing and confiscation orders only became functional in 2020. In this time, EU Member States have been able to gain experience of these tools and to adjust their approaches to mutual trust and recognition. This evolution can be noticed in particular when comparing the grounds for refusal of an EAW or an EIO, as regulated in the EAW FD and EIO D. Finally, the subject matter and scope of the analyzed instruments differ significantly.

Since Poland only joined the EU after the first instruments devoted to cooperation in criminal matters were adopted, the transposition of the EAW FD[2]

1 This work came about within the framework of the Academic Excellence Hub – Digital Justice Center carried out under the Initiative of Excellence – Research University at the University of Wrocław. The authors are grateful to Kalina Romanowska for her remarkable help in editing the chapter.

2 Law amending the Criminal Code, Code of Criminal Procedure and Petty Offences Code 2004 (*Ustawa z dnia 18 marca 2004 r. o zmianie ustawy – Kodeks karny, ustawy – Kodeks postępowania karnego oraz ustawy – Kodeks wykroczeń*) DzU 2004 Nr 69 poz 626.

took place when European Arrest Warrants were already functional. To fully implement the EAW FD, apart from the amendments made to the Polish Code of Criminal Procedure[3] (CCP), the Constitution of the Republic of Poland also had to be adjusted to the new EU scheme of cooperation in criminal matters.[4] Moreover, the initial shape of statutory provisions for issuing and executing EAWs was amended a few times.[5] This was not the case in the transposition process of EIO D[6] as the amendments of the CCP triggered by the Directive were introduced in 2018 and no further changes were made. The case of Regulation 1805/2018 is quite different. It does not require transposition into the domestic system and can – and should be – used directly. However, the new framework of mutual recognition of freezing and confiscation orders provided by Regulation 1805/2018 was preceded by older provisions introduced to the Polish domestic system based on FD 2003/577/JHA and FD 2006/783/JHA. The former frameworks impacted the practice of issuing and executing freezing and confiscation orders in transnational cooperation between Poland and other EU Member States which appears to be hard to replace by the direct use of Regulation 1805/2018 without additional efforts on the normative level.

Taking this into account, the challenges faced by the Polish lawmakers in the process of transposition and implementation of the discussed instruments are numerous and also very much dependable on the type of EU legislation that introduced them. Thus, no easy single scheme for the adoption of the EAW, EIO, and freezing and confiscation orders into Polish domestic law can be identified. Considering the differences that exist among discussed mutual recognition instruments, the way in which they were incorporated into the Polish legal system will be analyzed. Due to space constraints only the most

---

3 Code of Criminal Procedure 1997 (*Kodeks postępowania karnego*) with amendments.

4 Amendments concerned Art 55 of the Polish Constitution 1997 which prohibited the extradition of a Polish citizen.

5 See for example Law amending Criminal Code, Code of Criminal Procedure, Criminal Enforcement Code, Criminal Fiscal Code and other laws 2009 (*Ustawa z dnia 5 listopada 2009 r. o zmianie ustawy – Kodeks karny, ustawy – Kodeks postępowania karnego, ustawy – Kodeks karny wykonawczy, ustawy – Kodeks karny skarbowy oraz niektórych innych ustaw*) DzU 2009 Nr 206 poz 1589 which according to justification of the bill presented to the Parliament introduced amendments eliminating the errors and lacunas in CCP's provisions in force at that time identified in the judicial practice. 'Rządowy projekt ustawy o zmianie ustawy – Kodeks karny, ustawy – Kodeks postępowania karnego, ustawy – Kodeks karny wykonawczy, ustawy – Kodeks karny skarbowy oraz niektórych innych ustaw' available at <https://orka.sejm.gov.pl/Druki6ka.nsf/wgdruku/1394>, accessed 29 June 2024.

6 Amendment to the CCP introduced by: Law amending Code of Criminal Procedure and other laws (*Ustawa z dnia 10 stycznia 2018 r. o zmianie ustawy – Kodeks postępowania karnego oraz niektórych innych ustaw*) DzU 2018 poz 201.

important aspects of this process will be presented in the context of the normative framework and the judicial practice.[7]

## 2 European Arrest Warrant: Critical Profiles in Legislation and Case Law

### 2.1 *Constitutional Challenges Related to the Implementation of the EAW FD*

The EAW FD was implemented in Poland by the Law of 18 March 2004.[8] At the time of its implementation, Art 55(1) of the Polish Constitution prohibited the extradition of a Polish citizen. Soon after, the Polish Constitutional Tribunal ruled that the surrender procedure under the EAW is a form of extradition,[9] making the freshly introduced provisions of the CCP permitting the surrender of a Polish national to an EU Member State under the EAW[10] inconsistent with the Polish Constitution. This quickly led to the amendment of the Constitution by adding exceptions to the prohibition of extradition of Polish nationals which allowed for the application of the EAW.[11] However, the amendment introduced new barriers to the execution of EAWs, creating favorable treatment for Polish citizens. The surrender of Polish citizens is only made possible if the offense for which the individual was accused of was committed outside of the territory of Poland (Art 55(2)(1)), with the additional requirement of double criminality (Art 55(2)(2)).[12] The favorable treatment of Polish citizens stemming from Art 55 of the Constitution is repeated in Art 607p § 2 CCP.[13]

---

7 For more details on the implementation process see the national report at <https://site.unibo.it/facilex/en> accessed 29 June 2024.

8 Special chapters on the EAW were added to the CCP. Chapter 65a (Art 607a–607j) governs the procedure when Poland is an issuing State and Chapter 65b (Art 607k–607zc) governs the procedure when Poland is an executing state. Several additional acts of lower level supplemented the implementation.

9 Judgment of the Constitutional Tribunal of 27 April 2005 P 1/05 OTK ZU 4/A/2005 item 42 para 5.9 (text in English available at <http://trybunal.gov.pl/fileadmin/content/omowienia/P_1_05_full_GB.pdf> accessed 28 June 2024).

10 Art 607t § 1 CCP.

11 The amendment entered into force on 7 November 2006.

12 The amendment also added to the existing prohibition of the extradition of a person suspected of having committed a crime for political reasons but without the use of force, a prohibition of an extradition which would violate rights and freedoms of persons and citizens (§ 4).

13 A common view expressed in Polish academic literature is that Art 607p § 2 CCP is contrary to the EAW FD. See Małgorzata Wąsek-Wiaderek and Adrian Zbiciak, 'The practice of Poland on the European Arrest Warrant' in Renata Barbosa and others, *European Arrest*

### 2.2 *Issuing and Executing Authorities*

The issuing judicial authority is a regional court (*sąd okręgowy*) having territorial jurisdiction over the place where the relevant proceedings are conducted. In Poland, decisions on both detention on remand and on the EAW are issued by a court. The executing judicial authority is also a regional court.[14] In the case of Poland, therefore, there is no doubt that the relevant authorities are judicial authorities within the meaning of Art 6 EAW FD. However, the reforms limiting the independence of the judiciary introduced between 2016 and 2020 led to four preliminary references from other Member States – two from Ireland[15] and two from the Netherlands[16] – as to whether they should refuse to execute EAWs from Poland. The CJEU upheld the principle of mutual trust, and while it allowed a refusal to execute EAWs due to the risk of violation of Art 47 of the Charter, it set very strict criteria in the form of a two-step test.[17]

Both issuing and executing authorities in Poland communicate directly with the equivalent authorities in other Member States.[18] Neither the central authority, nor the Minister of Justice is involved in the communication.

### 2.3 *Procedure for Issuing and Executing EAW*

In principle, the requirements for issuing an EAW were transposed correctly. In practice, in the first years after the transposition of the EAW FD into Polish law,

---

*Warrant. Practice in Greece, the Netherlands and Poland* (Boom Juridisch 2022) 249 and the literature cited therein.

14 There are 47 regional courts in Poland. See: Regulation of the Minister of Justice of 28 December 2018 on determining the seats and areas of jurisdiction of courts of appeal, regional courts and district courts and the scope of cases heard by them (*Rozporządzenie Ministra Sprawiedliwości z dnia 28 grudnia 2018 r. w sprawie ustalenia siedzib i obszarów właściwości sądów apelacyjnych, sądów okręgowych i sądów rejonowych oraz zakresu rozpoznawanych przez nie spraw*) DzU 2018 poz 2548 with amendments.

15 CJEU Case C-216/18 *LM* [2018] ECLI:EU:C:2018:586; Case C-480/21 *W O, J L v. Minister for Justice and Equality* [2022] ECLI:EU:C:2022:592.

16 CJEU joined Cases C-354/20 and C-412/20 *Openbaar Ministerie vs. L and P* [2020] ECLI:EU:C:2020:1033; Joined Cases C-562/21 and C-563/21 *X and Y v Openbaar Ministerie* [2022] ECLI:EU:C:2022:100.

17 For a critical analysis of this case law, see Agnieszka Frąckowiak-Adamska, 'Trust until it is too late! Mutual recognition of judgments and limitations of judicial independence in a Member State: L and P' (2022) 59 Common Market Law Review 113–150.

18 According to Art 607d § 2 CCP if the location of the requested person is known the EAW is sent directly to the judicial authority of the executing state. Only a copy of the warrant will be sent to the Minister of Justice. According to Art 607z § 1 CCP if information transmitted by the EAW issuing state is not sufficient to take a decision on the surrender of the requested person, the court shall call on the judicial authority that has issued the EAW to supplement the information within a specified time limit.

the main problem was the abuse of the EAW by Polish authorities for trivial cases.[19] The Polish criminal justice system is based on the principle of mandatory prosecution. According to Art 10 CCP, with respect to an offense prosecuted *ex officio*, the authority responsible for the prosecution of offenses is obliged to initiate and conduct the investigation, and the public prosecutor is moreover obliged to file an indictment with a court and support it throughout the proceedings. This has resulted in a very high number of EAWs,[20] which in turn has led to criticism from other Member States. In response to the complaints about the absence of the principle of proportionality in Polish law, in 2013 a general clause of "the interest of justice" was added to Art 607b CCP.[21] Since then, an EAW must not be issued if it does not serve the interest of the administration of justice, which, even if not defined in the legal provision and decided case by case, covers the principles of necessity and proportionality. In particular, according to the Supreme Court, the need for engaging the authorities of foreign States should be considered when issuing the warrant.[22] Despite its general wording, which does not explicitly refer to the principle of proportionality, this clause is efficient in practice. The data indicate that EAWs are now used by Polish courts in a more appropriate manner.[23]

The execution procedure seems to be in conformity with the EAW FD with two notable exceptions of the lack of abolition of the double criminality requirement in the case of Polish citizens and the insertion of a few additional grounds for refusal.

---

19 See for example Witold Klaus, Justyna Włodarczyk-Madejska, Dominik Wzorek See for example Witold Klaus, Justyna Włodarczyk-Madejska and Dominik Wzorek 'In the Pursuit of Justice: (Ab)Use of the European Arrest Warrant in the Polish Criminal Justice System' [2021] 10 Central and Eastern European Migration Review 1, 95–117 <http://ceemr.uw.edu.pl/content/pursuit-justice-abuse-european-arrest-warrant-polish-criminal-justice-system> accessed 29 June 2024.

20 For example, in 2006, Poland issued 2,421 out of a total of 6,889 EAWs in the EU; in 2008, 4,829 out of 14,910 EAWs; and in 2009, 4,844 out of 15,827.

21 Law amending the Code of Criminal Procedure and other laws (*Ustawa z dnia 27 września 2013 r. o zmianie ustawy Kodeks postępowania karnego oraz niektórych innych ustaw*) DzU 2013 poz 1247 with amendments. The amendment entered into force on 1 July 2015.

22 Order of the Court of Appeal in Cracow of 28 April 2020, II AKa 207/20, LEX nr 3145371.

23 For example, in 2015, Poland issued only 2,390 out of a total of 16,144 EAWs in the EU, in 2021; 1,541 out of 14,789. See also Małgorzata Wąsek-Wiaderek and Adrian Zbiciak, 'The practice of Poland on the European Arrest Warrant' in Renata Barbosa and others, European Arrest Warrant. Practice in Greece, the Netherlands and Poland (Boom Juridisch 2022) 258–259 and examples cited therein. In 2020 Polish courts issued 1,795 EAW s and in the same year they refused to issue an EAW in 551 cases. Most of these refusals were justified by the proportionality principle, which means that this principle is expressly addressed in EAW practice.

As to the first exception, Poland partially transposed Art 2(2) EAW FD introducing an abolition of the double criminality requirement in the case of 32 offenses only in relation to persons other than Polish nationals.[24] In the case of Polish citizens, a verification of this requirement is still necessary according to Art 55(2)(2) of the Constitution and Art 607p § 2 CCP. Both provisions foresee a qualified test of double criminality, i.e. the act on which the EAW is based should constitute an offense under the law of the Republic of Poland both at the time of its commission and when the EAW was submitted. However, regarding the way in which it is verified in practice, the Polish Supreme Court does not require a detailed verification. It stated that in proceedings for the execution of an EAW concerning a Polish citizen, the court is not – as a rule – required to verify the factual circumstances of the offense the requested person allegedly committed, or to examine the issue of guilt, social harmfulness, or illegality of the alleged prohibited act. The competence of the court "is limited only to verifying whether the behavior alleged against a Polish citizen prosecuted in another country of the European Union finds – in an abstract sense – a counterpart in Polish criminal law".[25]

The list of offenses of Art 2(2) EAW FD has been correctly implemented.[26]

### 2.4 *Grounds for Refusal*

The EAW FD stipulates three mandatory grounds for refusing the execution of an EAW (Art 3), seven optional grounds for refusal (Art 4), and four situations where refusal of execution of the EAW in the case of trial *in absentia* is not possible (Art 4a). All of them were transposed into the Polish CCP. However, additional mandatory grounds for refusal were adopted, alongside the distinction of the differentiating situations of Polish nationals and nationals of other Member States in the case of surrender. Thus, the Polish CCP provides for a greater protection of Polish citizens not provided for in the EAW FD. Additionally, the nature of the reasons for refusal has also been changed in some cases (mandatory instead of optional).

To begin with, Poland in principle correctly transposed all three mandatory grounds for refusal of execution of the EAW. However, it widened the scope of the *ne bis in idem* exception, which covers rulings issued in any State[27] and not

24 Art 607w CCP.

25 Order of the Supreme Court of 12 May 2021, II KK 415/20, LEX nr 3289306.

26 Art 607w CCP. There are only minor stylistic differences. In the case of one offense (robbery with a firearm) in the Polish CCP it is split into two offences. That is why Art 607w CCP lists 33 such offences while Art 2(2) EAW FD only 32.

27 Art 607p § 1(2) CCP.

only EU Member States as is provided for in the EAW FD. The refusal of an EAW based on the *ne bis in idem* principle is mandatory both in the case of an EU Member State and a third State final ruling.[28]

Poland has also introduced five additional mandatory grounds for refusal to execute an EAW not provided for in the EAW FD (three formulated expressly as grounds for refusal and two of them formulated as conditions *sine qua non*).[29] Some of them stem from Art 55(2) and (4) of the Polish Constitution, as we will see below. This potentially has important constitutional consequences as, according to the Polish Constitutional Tribunal, in the case of a collision between EU law and the Polish Constitution, the latter always prevails.[30]

The first mandatory ground for refusal to execute an EAW is related to the protection of fundamental rights.[31] The remaining four additional grounds for refusing to execute an EAW not provided for in the EAW FD are as follows. The execution of an EAW will be refused in the case of Polish citizens, if the criminal act to which the EAW applies has been committed on the territory of the Republic of Poland or on board of a Polish vessel or aircraft. The same will be in a situation of a lack of double criminality. In both cases it is a consequence stemming from the requirements from the Constitution and Art 607p § 2 CCP. Moreover, the execution of an EAW issued for execution purposes will be refused in the case of Polish nationals and persons exercising their asylum right in the Republic of Poland if they do not agree to be surrendered.[32] Finally, according to Art 607p § 1 point 3 CCP, the execution of an EAW shall be refused if a final decision on

28 This is the result of linguistic interpretation, legislative work and the opinion of the majority of doctrine – see S. Steinborn, Komentarz do artykułu 607p kodeksu postępowania karnego in Lech Krzysztof Paprzycki (ed), *Komentarz aktualizowany do art. 425–673 Kodeksu postępowania karnego* (Lex/el. 2015) and the literature referred to therein.

29 Art 607p CCP and Art 607s § 1 CCP. Two situations defining the *sine qua non conditions* for the execution of an EAW are set out in Art 607p § 2 and 607s § 1 CCP. According to Art 607p § 2 CCP "If the European warrant has been issued in respect of a person prosecuted who is a Polish national, the warrant may be executed on condition that the act to which the European warrant relates was not committed on the territory of the Republic of Poland or on a Polish ship or aircraft and constituted an offence under the law of the Republic of Poland or would have constituted an offence under the law of the Republic of Poland had it been committed on the territory of the Republic of Poland, both at the time when it was committed and at the time when the European warrant was received." Art 607s § 1 CCP "A European warrant issued for the purpose of executing a custodial sentence or a measure involving deprivation of liberty against a prosecuted person who is a Polish citizen or who enjoys the right of asylum in the Republic of Poland shall not be executed if he or she does not consent to the surrender."

30 Judgment of the Constitutional Tribunal of 11 May 2005, K 18/04, OTK ZU 5A/2005, poz 49.

31 See *infra* § 2.5.

32 Art 607s § 1 CCP.

surrender to another Member State of the EU has been issued against a requested person. This is a procedural impediment introducing the principle of chronological priority in the case of several surrender decisions under the EAW.

As to the optional grounds for refusal, Poland has transposed most of them correctly. However, a few deficiencies can be identified. The optional refusal in the case of a lack of double criminality for offenses other than the thirty-two offenses listed in Art 2 of the EAW FD[33] has been transposed to Polish law in an excessively narrow manner – only in the case of non-Polish citizens.[34] The refusal of execution of an EAW based on the *ne bis in idem* principle in the case of a final ruling from third States is an optional ground for refusal in the EAW FD.[35] In the Polish CCP, conversely, the refusal of an EAW based on the *ne bis in idem* principle is mandatory both in the case of an EU Member State and that of a third State final ruling. Last, Art 4(6) EAW FD provides for the possibility of refusing the recognition of an EAW issued for the execution of a judgment if the person concerned is a national or resident of the executing state. This provision has been transposed into Polish law in Art 607s CCP. The latter provision differentiates the nature of this ground according to nationality (mandatory in the case of Polish nationals and persons exercising their asylum right in the Republic of Poland, and optional for persons who have the place of residence or permanently reside in the territory of the Republic of Poland). Therefore, the implementation is not fully compliant with the EAW FD, in which the refusal of execution in such a situation is always optional.[36] Additionally, Art 4(7)(b) EAW FD (regarding extra-territorial offenses) has not been transposed into Polish law.

Referring to trials *in absentia*, Art 4a(1) EAW FD has been transposed into Polish law in Art 607r § 3 CCP[37] as an optional ground for refusal. A detailed assessment of the transposition of this provision was done within the

33 Art 4(1) of EAW FD.

34 Art 607r § 1(1) and § 2 CCP. As stated above, in the case of Polish citizens it is a mandatory ground for refusal.

35 Art 4(5) EAW FD.

36 In the case of refusal of surrender, the foreign sentence will be executed in Poland (Art 607s § 3 CCP). Art 607s § 4 CCP specifies how the Polish court shall adjust the imposed penalty to the catalogue of penalties provided by Polish law.

37 Poland transposed the Framework Decision 2009/299/JHA by means of a legislative amendment to the CCP – Law Amending the Criminal Code, the Code of Criminal Procedure and Corporate Criminal Liability Act 2011 (*Ustawa z dnia 29 lipca 2011r. o zmianie ustawy – Kodeks karny, ustawy – Kodeks postępowania karnego oraz ustawy o odpowiedzialności podmiotów zbiorowych za czyny zabronione pod groźbą kary*) DzU 2011 poz 1135.

framework of the *InAbsentiEAW* project.[38] It is worth underlining here that Poland transposed some of the exceptions of Art 4a in such a way that the level of protection of fundamental rights as envisaged by this provision was lowered.[39] The *InAbsentiEAW* report points out that as to the first exception of Art 4a, it is not required that the requested person was summoned in person, nor that he or she be informed of the date of the hearing "in such a manner that it was unequivocally established that he or she was aware of the scheduled trial".[40] Moreover, as to the second exception – concerning defense by a mandated legal counsel – it is not required that the requested person was aware of the scheduled trial.

### 2.5 *Protection of Fundamental Rights in the Context of* EAW

Polish law provides for a general ground for refusal based on the protection of fundamental rights. Art 55(4) of the Polish Constitution states that "The extradition of a person suspected of the commission of a crime for political reasons but without the use of force shall be forbidden, so as an extradition which would violate rights and freedoms of persons and citizens." Art 607p § 1 CCP confirms that "The execution of the EAW shall be refused, if: [...] 5) it would infringe freedoms and rights of human and citizen [...], 6) the offence was committed without violence for political reasons." As to the notion of "freedoms and rights of human and citizen," it is broad and not limited to a specific right or freedom. The Polish Constitutional Tribunal interpreted it as covering both rights that are guaranteed by the provisions of binding international law, including the European Convention on Human Rights (ECHR), as well as constitutionally protected rights and freedoms.[41] However, in practice, courts are reluctant to apply this ground for refusal of the EAW.[42] They emphasize that the sole probability of a violation of freedoms and rights is not sufficient. What is required is a finding, or at least a probability approaching certainty,

---

38 The research project, financed by the European Union's Justice Programme, concerns European Arrest Warrants issued for the enforcement of sentences after in absentia trials. It studies the application of Art 4a of EAW FD by means of case studies from Belgium, Hungary, Ireland, the Netherlands, Poland and Romania. The research report: 'Improving Mutual Recognition of European Arrest Warrants for the Purpose of Executing Judgments Rendered Following a Trial at which the Person Concerned Did Not Appear in Person' <https://www.inabsentieaw.eu/publications/> accessed 29 June 2024.

39 Ibid.

40 Ibid.

41 Ibid.

42 Ibid.

that such a violation will occur.[43] Moreover, the general information about irregularities, concerning groups of people or specific correctional facilities, does not imply that in a particular case a person will experience inhuman or degrading treatment after transfer to the issuing state.[44] This aspect is in line with CJEU jurisprudence, which also, for the time being, requires an examination of whether there is a risk in an individual case.

Grounds for refusal based on human rights considerations (Art 607p § 1(5) and (6) CCP) at first glance seem to be contrary to the EAW FD, because of the *numerus clausus* of grounds of refusal in Art 3–4a EAW FD. Yet the picture is not entirely clear, considering the pending discussion on whether the protection of human rights could be a separate, overriding ground for refusal. Especially Art 1(3) and recitals 12 and 13 of the EAW FD emphasize the importance of the protection of fundamental rights, as does the recent case law of the CJEU which admitted that in some circumstances the infringement of some fundamental rights could lead to non-execution of an EAW.[45] The issue of the compatibility of Polish legislation with the EAW FD thus needs to be clarified by the Court of Justice.

Not all rights provided by six EU directives on procedural rights of the suspected and accused person were properly implemented in the Polish CCP.[46] However, recent amendments to the CCP enhancing the rights of children have partially improved the situation.[47] Important guarantees for surrendered persons also result from a Supreme Court judgment, which stated that in the case of detention on remand of an EAW surrendered person, all general rules concerning detention are applicable.[48] The person is thus entitled to appeal

43 Ibid.

44 Order of the Court of Appeal in Katowice of 4 April 2018, II AKz 167/18, LEX nr 2557275.

45 The prohibition of torture and inhuman and degrading treatment (CJEU C-404/15 and C-659/15 PPU *Pál Aranyosi and Robert Căldăraru* [2016] ECLI:EU:C:2016:198) or the right to a fair trial (C-216/18 PPU LM [2018] ECLI:EU:C:2018:586).

46 With reference to rights provided by six EU directives on procedural rights of the suspect and accused, see: Karolina Kremens and others, 'Poland. There and Back Again. A Struggle with Transposition of EU Directives' in Giuseppe Contissa and others (eds), *Effective Protection of the Rights of the Accused in the EU Directives. A Computable Approach to Criminal Procedure Law* (Brill 2022) 154–169 and the detailed report prepared within the framework of the CrossJustice project https://site.unibo.it/cross-justice/en/project-results/publications accessed 29 June 2024.

47 Law amending Code of Criminal Procedure and other laws 2023 (*Ustawa z dnia 14 kwietnia 2023 r. o zmianie ustawy – Kodeks postępowania karnego i niektórych innych ustaw*) DzU 2023 poz 818. The law entered into force on 15 February 2024.

48 Judgment of the Supreme Court of 12 October 2021, IV KK 249/19, LEX nr 3520443.

against a detention order[49] and submit a motion for quashing it at any time.[50] In addition, the Supreme Court decided also that the phrase "detention on remand or arrest" used in Art 552 § 4 of the CCP (provision allowing an arrested person to obtain compensation for wrongful detention in domestic cases) also encompasses the actual deprivation of liberty applied by a foreign State to a requested person as a result of an EAW issued by a Polish court.[51]

In the end, the European Commission opened in 2020 an infringement proceeding against Poland for an incorrect transposition of the EAW FD, on the basis of Art 258 TFEU. The procedure, still ongoing, relates to the preferential treatment of Polish citizens compared to EU citizens from other Member States, providing additional grounds for refusal of warrants not provided for in the EAW FD and a few, less significant, implementation shortcomings.[52]

## 3 European Investigation Order: Critical Profiles in Legislation and Case Law

### 3.1 *The Scope of Application of the EIO*

EIO D was transposed with over eight months' delay into the Polish CCP in 2018. Since then, no additional amendments to the created legal framework for EIOs have been made. Two chapters devoted to the EIO (Chapter 62c "Request to a European Union Member State to conduct investigative measures on the basis of a European Investigation Order" and 62d "Request from a European Union Member State to conduct investigative measures on the basis of a European Investigation Order") were added to the existing procedural provisions.

---

49 Art 252 CCP.

50 Art 254 CCP.

51 Judgment of the Supreme Court of 12 October 2021, IV KK 249/19, LEX nr 3520443.

52 The Commission sent to Poland (and some other Member States) a letter of formal notice on 3 December 2020 and an additional letter of formal notice on 14 July 2023 (INFR(2020)2308). The first formal notice concerned the preferential treatment of Polish citizens compared to EU citizens from other Member States and providing additional grounds for refusal not provided for in the EAW FD. The additional letter of formal notice concerned the failure to correctly transpose the provisions on: the temporary transfer of the requested person pending the decision on surrender; the conditions for the hearing of the requested person pending the decision on surrender; the judgments where the sentenced person was not personally present at the trial and competing international obligations. The proceeding is ongoing and it has not yet reached the stage of a reasoned opinion of the Commission which is the step required by Art 258 TFEU before a case can be brought before the Court of Justice of the European Union.

Under Polish law, the EIO can be primarily issued in criminal proceedings regulated by the CCP and providing procedure for criminal offenses (felonies and misdemeanors) as regulated in the Criminal Code (CC) and other statutes. Additionally, the CCP's provisions regarding the EIO are also applicable to petty offenses. Petty offenses are a separate category of minor offenses (subject to a fine, community service, and in exceptional cases subject to a penalty of maximum 30 days' detention) which are codified in the Petty Offenses Code of 1971[53] as well as in numerous other statutes. The procedure applied in petty offense cases is codified separately from the CCP in the Petty Offenses Procedure Code of 2001.[54] It is explicitly provided there that Chapters 62c and 62d CCP regarding the issuing and executing of EIOs shall apply, *mutatis mutandis*, to petty offense proceedings (Art 116c § 1 of the Petty Offenses Procedure Code). However, the scope of application of provisions regarding the issuing of the EIO is limited only to petty offenses provided in Chapters XI and XIV of the Petty Offenses Code, i.e., petty offenses against the safety of traffic and against property.

Additionally, Chapters 62c and 62d of the CCP are also applicable in criminal fiscal proceedings (Art 113 § 1 Criminal Fiscal Code).[55] In this type of proceeding, the liability of natural persons accused of committing a fiscal criminal offense or a fiscal petty offense codified in the Criminal Fiscal Code is addressed.

Polish criminal and petty offense law does not provide for a liability of legal persons. Nonetheless, a separate legal act – Law of 28 October 2002 on liability of collective entities for acts prohibited under the threat of penalty[56] – enables the court to hold legal persons liable for offenses committed by natural persons – broadly speaking, those who represent the legal entity. While this type of liability is not treated as criminal *sensu stricto*, it is obviously repressive in its nature, as the financial penalty that can be ordered can exceed 1 million euros and the legal persons may also be banned from applying for various public funding schemes or public procurement. Art 22 of the Law on liability of collective entities for acts prohibited under the threat of penalty provides

53 Petty Offences Code 1971 (*Ustawa z dnia 20 maja 1971 Kodeks wykroczeń*) DzU 1970 Nr 12 poz 114 with amendments.

54 Petty Offences Procedure Code 2001 (*Ustawa z dnia 25 sierpnia 2001 Kodeks postępowania w sprawach o wykroczenia*) DzU 2001 Nr 106 poz 1148 with amendments.

55 Criminal Fiscal Code 1999 (*Ustawa z dnia 10 września 1999 r. Kodeks karny skarbowy*) DzU 1999 Nr 83 poz 930 with amendments.

56 Law on liability of collective entities for acts prohibited under the threat of penalty 2002 (*Ustawa z dnia 28 października 2002 r. o odpowiedzialności podmiotów zbiorowych za czyny zabronione pod groźbą kary*) DzU 2002 Nr 197 poz 1661.

that the provisions of the CCP shall apply *mutatis mutandis* to proceedings regarding the liability of collective entities for acts prohibited under penalty. Since Chapters 62c and 62d are not explicitly excluded from the scope of the mentioned reference, there is, at least theoretically, a possibility of issuing an EIO in a discussed corporate liability proceeding.[57]

### 3.2 *Issuance of the EIO*

The broad range of Polish authorities that can issue EIOs consists of district courts, regional courts, courts of appeal,[58] the Supreme Court, prosecutors of any of the prosecutorial units in Poland,[59] the police, and numerous other specialized agencies responsible for the conduct of criminal investigations (e.g., Border Guard, Internal Security Agency, the Central Anticorruption Bureau).[60]

Art 589w § 1 CCP clarifies that it is the court before which the case is pending or the public prosecutor conducting criminal investigation, which is competent to issue the EIO. The EIO may be issued *ex officio* or at the request of a party, defense counsel, or attorney representing the victim. The EIO can also be issued by the police or the specialized agencies indicated above if they conduct the investigation. However, in such a case it has to be validated by the prosecutor supervising the investigation (Art 589w § 7 CCP). The validation by the prosecutor or by the court (if the relevant provisions regarding an investigative measure provide that the court is authorized to decide on

57 This view is however questioned by some scholars. See: Joanna Klimczak, Dominik Wzorek and Eleonora Zielińska, Europejski nakaz dochodzeniowy w praktyce sądowej i prokuratorskiej – ujawnione problemy i perspektywy rozwoju (Wydawnictwo Instytutu Wymiaru Sprawiedliwości 2022) 31.

58 The structure of common courts in Poland is three-fold – district courts (sądy rejonowe), regional courts (sądy okręgowe) and courts of appeal (sądy apelacyjne). Apart from common courts there are also military and administrative courts which are separate as well as, at the top of the judicial structure in Poland, the Supreme Court.

59 The structure of the Public Prosecution Office is similar to the structure of common courts – district prosecution offices (prokuratura rejonowa), provincial prosecution offices (prokuratura okręgowa) and regional prosecution offices (prokuratura regionalna). At the very top of the organizational structure of the Polish prosecution service is the National Prosecution Office (Prokuratura Krajowa). For more on the prosecution service in Poland see: Karolina Kremens and Wojciech Jasiński, 'The prosecution service in the Polish legal system' (2024) 62 DPCE Online 1 <https://www.dpceonline.it/index.php/dpceonline/article/view/2083> accessed 29 June 2024.

60 For the full list see: European Judicial Network, 'Notification on the implementation by Poland on the Directive on the European Investigation Order in criminal matters. Competent authorities' (EJN) <https://www.ejn-crimjust.europa.eu/ejn/libdocumentproperties.aspx?Id=2072> accessed 29 June 2024.

its application) is also needed if the police or other authorized agencies (e.g., Internal Security Agency, the Central Anticorruption Bureau) issued an EIO during covert investigative measures conducted outside of an ongoing investigation within the legal framework provided in the Police Act and other statutes (Art 589w § 7 CCP).

Art 6(1) of EIO D provides that two conditions have to be met in order to issue the EIO. First, the issuing of an EIO must be necessary and proportionate for the purpose of the proceedings and the rights of the suspected or accused person have to be taken into account. Second, the investigative measure(s) indicated in the EIO could be ordered under the same conditions in a similar domestic case. While this second condition has been transposed to Art 589x CCP explicitly, the same cannot be said about the first one. In this case, the Polish lawmaker decided to modify the wording of the condition enlisted in Art 6(1)(a) of EIO D and provided in Art 589x point 1 CCP that the issuance of an EIO is not permissible if the interest of the administration of justice does not require it. Although this interest undoubtedly covers the principles of necessity and proportionality, as well as the need to observe the rights of suspects and accused persons, the very broad and general character of the discussed condition may negatively influence the practical operation of the EIO, if the issuing authorities decide to interpret it without reference to Art 6(1)(a) of EIO D. Especially the lack of direct reference to proportionality in a country like Poland, where the criminal justice system is based on a principle of mandatory prosecution, may result in an excessive use of this mutual recognition tool. In this context, it is worth remembering that, as mentioned in *supra* § 2.3., Poland already faced charges of overuse of the EAW after this tool was introduced. From this perspective, it would have been better to refer in the Polish CCP explicitly to the proportionality principle. Nonetheless, in the case law of Polish courts it is underlined that "the interest of justice clause (...) should be interpreted in the same way as in the case of the EAW (European Arrest Warrant), that is, when issuing the warrant, the need for involving foreign authorities should be considered".[61]

Polish CCP does not limit the type of investigative measures that can be carried out on the basis of an EIO. Art 589w § 1 CCP is very general in its wording, as it provides that the EIO can be issued if it is necessary to take or obtain any piece of evidence that is located or may be taken on the territory of another EU Member State.

61 Order of the Court of Appeal in Cracow of 28 April 2020, II AKa 207/20, LEX nr 3145371; see also: Order of the Court of Appeal in Katowice of 14 August 2018, II AKz 403/18, LEX nr 2633164.

The provisions of the CCP provide for legal remedies against an investigative measure that are equivalent to those accessible in a national context (Art 589w § 5 and Art 589ze § 1 CCP). The only concern, in light of the *Gavanozov II* judgment,[62] that can be raised refers to calling a witness for a videoconference. There is no appeal available in Polish law in such a case, regardless of whether in the context of an EIO or a domestic one. However, if this investigative measure is believed to be disproportionate, the witness can always reach for *post hoc* remedy and claim damages in front of the civil court for loss suffered as a result of an unjustified summons. Of course, the effectiveness of such a remedy can be questioned, but it should be considered that the ECtHR in general does not exclude this type of remedy as potentially effective.[63]

Poland fully transposed the provisions regarding the transmission of the EIO and ensured that the communication as a rule will take place directly between the issuing authority and the executing authority. The same can be said about the provisions of EIO D on the form of EIO set out in Annex A. They have also been fully transposed into the Polish legal system.[64]

### 3.3 *Execution of the EIO*

The authorities executing EIOs in Poland are district and regional courts as well as prosecutors in the provincial public prosecution offices. The courts are competent if the case is at the judicial stage of criminal proceedings. The prosecutors are competent in cases at the investigative stage of proceedings. There are three exceptions to these rules. First, if according to Polish law the competence for obtaining, taking, or deciding on the admissibility of evidence is entrusted to a court (district or regional), this court is also competent to issue a decision on the execution of the EIO, regardless of the stage of proceedings (Art 589ze § 2 CCP). Second, the regional court is always competent in the execution of an EIO regarding the temporary surrender of a person deprived of liberty to the issuing State for the purpose of conducting an investigative measure in that State (Art 589ze § 3 CCP). Third, the regional court is also competent in the execution of an EIO regarding the temporary surrender of a person

62 CJEU C-852/19 Gavanozov II [2021] ECLI:EU:C:2021:902.

63 Depending of course on the individual circumstances of the case. See: 'Guide on Art 13 of the European Convention on Human Rights. Right to an effective remedy' (ECHR) <https://ks.echr.coe.int/>.

64 Regulation of the Minister of Justice of 8 February 2018 on the model form of the European Investigation Order (*Rozporządzenie Ministra Sprawiedliwości z dnia 8 lutego 2018 r. w sprawie określenia wzoru formularza europejskiego nakazu dochodzeniowego*) DzU 2018 poz 366.

deprived of liberty to the Republic of Poland for the purpose of conducting an investigative measure (Art 589ze § 4 CCP).

The general rule expressed in EIO D is that the positive grounds for issuing the EIO (i.e., necessity, proportionality, protection of the rights of the suspected or accused person) are assessed by the issuing authority. However, as provided in Art 6(3) of EIO D, where the executing authority has reason to believe that the conditions for issuing an EIO have not been met, it may consult the issuing authority on the importance of executing the EIO. The consultations may result in a withdrawal of the EIO. This provision has been fully implemented in Art 589zn § 1 CCP. The same refers to the provision allowing the executing authority to return the EIO to the issuing State, when it has not been issued by a competent issuing authority.

Another main rule regarding the execution of the EIO is that, in general, the executing authority shall recognize an EIO without any further formality being required, and ensure its execution in the same way and under the same modalities as if the investigative measure concerned had been ordered by an authority of the executing state, unless one of the grounds for non-recognition or non-execution materializes. All these rules are fully transposed into the CCP. Art 589zi § 1 CCP states that unless otherwise provided, the provisions of Polish law shall be applied in the execution of the EIO. However, the request of the authority issuing the EIO to apply a special procedure or formality in the execution of the procedural measure shall be complied with, if it is not contrary to the principles of the legal order of the Republic of Poland. The reference to the term "legal order of the Republic of Poland" does not mean that the executing authority should approach the request of the issuing state in a very formalistic manner, in particular by a detailed comparison of the content of the request and national legal provisions regulating the investigative measure in question. What matters are the general principles of the Polish legal system which have to be observed, such as the right to a fair trial.[65] As a consequence, cross-examining the witness (not applicable in Polish criminal cases in its original American form) or changing the wording of the witness' commitment, for example, are fully acceptable.[66]

From the perspective of the executing authority, the most important issue is how the grounds for refusal are transposed. The Polish lawmaker decided to divide the grounds for non-recognition or non-execution into two

---

65 Andrzej Sakowicz in Andrzej Sakowicz (ed) *Kodeks postępowania karnego. Komentarz* (C.H. Beck 2023) 1675 and case law cited therein.

66 Andrzej Sakowicz in Andrzej Sakowicz (ed) *Kodeks postępowania karnego. Komentarz* (C.H. Beck 2023) 1675.

categories – mandatory and optional. This seems to be acceptable since the wording of Art 11 of EIO D indicates that the existence of a relevant ground does not oblige the competent EU Member State's judicial authority to refuse to recognize or execute an EIO. It is only an option and the final assessment of whether it is necessary is left to the EU Member States' lawmakers or competent judicial authorities. The transposition of the grounds for non-recognition or non-execution of an EIO is thus full and correct.[67] The only minor flaws in the transposition process refer to the exceptions to applicability of these grounds provided in Art 11(2–3) of EIO D. So far, the grounds for refusal were not subject to extensive judicial interpretation and controversies. Therefore, not much can be said about potential doubts as to the understanding of their scope in judicial practice. However, case law regarding the equivalent grounds referring to EAW, including particularly the one based on human rights issues, might be helpful and should be applied *mutatis mutandis* also to the EIO.

The procedure of executing an EIO is in general in compliance with the provisions of EIO D. Only minor deficiencies can be identified in this regard. The possibility of recourse to a different type of investigative measure can serve as an example. This modality is not applicable, among others, to cases of any non-coercive investigative measures as defined under the law of the executing state. Art 589zi § 3(4) CCP states that substitute investigative measure shall not be carried out if the EIO concerns evidence the admission, obtaining, or taking of which does not require in a similar domestic case the issuance of a decision by a judge or prosecutor. The Polish lawmaker decided not to refer expressly to non-coercive investigative measures as provided in EIO D, but to use the expression "evidence the admission, obtaining, or taking of which does not require, in a similar domestic case the issuance of a decision by a judge or prosecutor". The rationale for this choice is unclear. Although in general

67 Similar views are expressed in the legal doctrine. See: Joanna Klimczak, Dominik Wzorek and Eleonora Zielińska, *Europejski nakaz dochodzeniowy w praktyce sądowej i prokuratorskiej – ujawnione problemy i perspektywy rozwoju* (Wydawnictwo Instytutu Wymiaru Sprawiedliwości 2022) 61, 62 and sources cited therein. The discussed case is different than the case of an EAW. EAW FD makes a clear distinction between mandatory and optional grounds for refusal, which leaves a lesser margin of discretion for the domestic lawmaker in the transposition process. Moreover, what is crucial, when transforming an optional ground from the directive into a mandatory one in the domestic legislation is whether it does not excessively limit the power of the court to assess the relevant factors in a specific case (see: Judgment of the Court (Grand Chamber) of 6 October 2009. C-123/08 *Dominic Wolzenburg* [2009] ECLI:EU:C:2009:616). Taking that into account in the case of Directive 2014/41/EU of the European Parliament and of the Council of 3 April 2014 regarding the European Investigation Order in criminal matters [2014] the assessment of the implementation should be positive.

the non-coercive investigative measures and measures that do not need to be authorized by a judge or a prosecutor seem to overlap, in practice the implementation might turn out to be deficient, as in practice a measure may turn out to be coercive and at the same time it will not have to be authorized by a judicial or prosecutorial decision.

Another shortcoming concerns the obligation to consult with the issuing authority on the appropriate timing to carry out the investigative measure, if the competent executing authority cannot meet the initial 90-day time limit. This obligation has not been transposed to Polish law. Although there is a general provision in the CCP encouraging consultations, they are not mandatory. However, this is just a minor deficiency in transposition, and nothing prohibits the executing authority from following the obligation stemming from EIO D.

### 3.4 *Specific Investigative Measures*

Apart from general provisions referring to all investigative measures, EIO D also contains a set of provisions concerning the specific investigative measures (Chapter 4). Important shortcomings in the national implementation concern videoconference or other audiovisual transmission, as well as hearing by telephone conference. The CCP provides for a hearing of a witness by videoconference in Polish domestic criminal proceedings (Art 177 § 1a–1d CCP). These regulations apply *mutatis mutandis* in the case of EIOs, as according to Art 589zi § 1 CCP the general rule is that unless otherwise provided, the provisions of Polish law shall be applied in the execution of the EIO. The problem is, however, that there are no provisions in the Polish CCP allowing *in general* to hear a suspect or accused person via videoconference. The hearing of an accused person by videoconference is allowed only during trial. It is thus doubtful whether these provisions (Art 374 § 4–8 CCP) can serve as a legal basis for carrying out a videoconference with the suspect or accused during an investigation or any out-of-trial procedure. Therefore, a separate legal basis for such a hearing should be introduced into the Polish CCP.

Moreover, the provisions regarding a hearing by videoconference or other audiovisual transmission are tailored in order to fit into domestic investigations and they do not take into account the specificity of the videoconference conducted on the basis of an EIO, where the issuing authority is in fact interrogating the person and the procedure is modified in comparison to a domestic case (Art 24(3–7) of EIO D). So even though the necessary arrangements can be made between issuing and executing authority, there are no firm legal grounds for carrying out the measure as designed in EIO D. Therefore, like in the case of hearing of a suspect or accused person, a more developed body of provisions should be adopted to guide domestic authorities in executing EIOs regarding videoconference.

Hearing by telephone conference is also problematic. In this case, the main issue is that Polish criminal procedure does not provide at all for the possibility of this kind of hearing. Therefore, there is no explicit legal ground to conduct it in the context of an EIO.

### 3.5 *Admissibility of Evidence Obtained by the EIO*

Admissibility of evidence gathered with the application of an EIO is a very important issue. Art 14(7) of EIO D deals with this problem, but only in a very general and vague way. Poland has not adopted any specific legal regulation transposing this provision. Moreover, the CCP does not contain any general or explicit regulation on the admissibility of evidence obtained abroad. The only provision addressing this issue directly is Art 587 CCP, stating that the reports of inspection, interrogation of defendants, witnesses, expert witnesses, or other evidentiary measures, prepared at the request of a Polish court or prosecutor, carried out by courts or prosecutors of foreign countries or authorities acting under their supervision, may be read during trial, under the rules set forth in Art 389, 391, and 393 CCP, if the manner in which the measures were carried out does not violate the principles of the legal order of the Republic of Poland. This provision allows for an admissibility test limited only to the verification of compliance with the principles of the Polish legal order. However, the scope of Art 587 CCP is reduced only to evidentiary measures enumerated therein and does not encompass all types of evidence that can be gathered abroad, including evidence obtained with the use of the EIO. While there is a visible tendency, in practice, to apply the discussed provision *per analogiam* to other types of evidence (enlisted reports which were not drafted on request of the Polish criminal justice authorities),[68] it is nonetheless doubtful whether Art 587 CCP can be treated as a general rule in the case of admissibility of evidence obtained abroad (including within the EU). In fact, the legal doctrine perceives the situation described as deficient.[69] This flaw is systemic as the evidence gathered abroad requires special rules of admissibility. Moreover, even if the test of admissibility of evidence is limited only to the verification of whether the fundamental rights (right to a fair trial, right to defense) were

68 See: Barbara Nita-Światłowska in Jerzy Skorupka (ed), *Kodeks postępowania karnego. Komentarz* (C.H. Beck 2023) 1626–1627.

69 Hanna Kuczyńska in Jerzy Skorupka (ed), *Kodeks postępowania karnego. Komentarz* (C.H. Beck 2023) 1698–1699.

observed, which may seem rational as the technicalities obviously differ in EU Member States, it does not offer much guidance in real-life situations, where determining whether the rights of defense were violated is problematic and often dependent on how the role of procedural technicalities (e.g. how a procedural measure has been conducted or documented) is treated. Therefore, at least for the sake of clarity, the lawmaker's intervention is desirable.

### 3.6 *Controversies over the EIO in the Case Law of Polish Courts*

The analysis of the case law of Polish courts reveals that there are few controversies over provisions transposing the EIO into the domestic legal system. The only remarkable difference in opinions regards the gathering of information covered by banking secrecy. The source of controversies was the interpretation of domestic provisions on the procedure of issuing EIOs covering banking information during criminal investigation. The relevant provisions (Art 589w § 1 and § 5 CCP) state that, in general, it is the prosecutor who is competent to issue the EIO. Moreover, if it is necessary to issue a warrant to obtain evidence (e.g., to conduct a search, to demand information from various institutions), the EIO replaces this warrant. Most importantly, however, domestic provisions on obtaining evidence shall apply accordingly in the procedure for issuing an EIO. The latter provision is very important in the discussed context because in domestic cases, if a piece of information covered by banking secrecy is needed and it does not concern a suspect, the prosecutor should, before addressing the bank, request the regional court to grant the authorization to use that information in criminal proceedings.

This led to significantly divergent practices confirmed in case law. According to the first interpretation, the EIO should be issued by the regional court as a competent authority to lift banking secrecy and it should be a separate decision than the one referring to the banking secrecy.[70] The second view implied that the warrant lifting the banking secrecy replaces the order on the issuance of the EIO.[71] The third approach was that the general rules on the authorities competent to issue EIO s are applicable, so the order is issued by the prosecutor, and it is not mandatory to obtain the regional court's permission for lifting the banking secrecy. The reasons for that are twofold. Domestic procedure is not applicable in EIO cases, as the verification of whether the information can be obtained for the purpose of criminal proceedings is conducted in the executing state. Moreover, the provisions regarding the lifting of banking secrecy

70 Judgment of the Court of Appeal in Gdańsk of 23 May 2018, II AKz 408/18, LEX nr 2553721.
71 Judgment of the Court of Appeal in Katowice of 29 January 2019, II AKz 53/19, LEX nr 2728416.

concern only banks that fall under Polish jurisdiction.[72] The fourth approach was that the authority authorized to issue the EIO is the prosecutor. However, before issuing such an order, the prosecutor must apply for and obtain the regional court's permission to use banking information, as in a similar domestic case.[73] The latter view was accepted by the Supreme Court in an order of 2 June 2022,[74] which should put an end to the dispute regarding this matter.[75]

What should be underlined is that these controversies cannot be reduced solely to the interpretation of national legal provisions. While *prima facie* it may seem so, in reality the view allowing the prosecutor to issue an EIO regarding banking secrecy without judicial authorization is not compliant with EIO D to the extent this legal act obliges the issuing authority to conduct a necessity and proportionality test on the same basis as in domestic cases. Polish law, considering the sensitive nature of information covered by banking secrecy, does not provide for the power of the prosecutor to obtain such information. An independent body, namely the court, should decide on the issue. Taking into account the wording of Art 6(1)(a) of the EIO D assessment of necessity and proportionality is precisely what has to be done by the issuing authority. At the same time, according to Art 6(1)(b) of EIO D, the issuing authority may only issue an EIO where the investigative measure indicated in the EIO could have been ordered under the same conditions in a similar domestic case. Consequently, the prosecutor willing to issue an EIO must obtain the authorization of the court first. This authorization is an integral part of the decision-making process encompassing the assessment of the necessity and proportionality of issuing an EIO. Moreover, if the issuing State is obliged to follow the same rules in the EIO procedure as in a domestic case, judicial

72 Judgment of the Court of Appeal in Cracow of 23 October 2018, II AKz 524/18, LEX nr 2645341; Judgment of the Court of Appeal in Łódź of 19 September 2018, II AKz 496/18, LEX nr 2601868.

73 Judgment of the Court of Appeal in Katowice of 4 September 2018, II Akz 645/18, LEX nr 2615563.

74 Order of the Supreme Court of 2 June 2022, I KZP 17/31, OSNK 2022, nr 7, poz 26.

75 Divergent views were also expressed in the legal doctrine, however the majority view is consistent with the Supreme Court's approach. See: Hanna Kuczyńska in Jerzy Skorupka (ed), *Kodeks postępowania karnego. Komentarz* (C.H. Beck 2023) 1694; Ariadna Ochnio, 'Glosa do postanowienia Sądu Apelacyjnego w Katowicach z dnia 4 września 2018 r., II AKz 645/18' [2021] Orzecznictwo Sądów Polskich 101–117; Anna Błachnio-Parzych, 'Organ uprawniony do wydania europejskiego nakazu dochodzeniowego w celu uzyskania informacji stanowiących tajemnicę bankową na podstawie art. 106b ust. 1 Prawa bankowego – glosa do postanowienia Sądu Apelacyjnego w Łodzi z 19.09.2018 r., II AKz 496/18' [2022] Glosa 33–41.

authorization cannot simply be dispensed with by arguing that the procedure is inapplicable as the bank is not subject to Polish jurisdiction.

## 4 Regulation 1805/2018: Critical Profiles in Legislation and Case Law

### 4.1 *Legal Basis in the National System and Scope*

The Polish legal framework concerning freezing and confiscation in the context of judicial cooperation in criminal matters between EU Member States was initiated by the introduction of four separate Chapters within Section XIII of the Polish Code of Criminal Procedure, namely "Transnational Criminal Proceedings" (*Postępowanie w sprawach karnych ze stosunków międzynarodowych*).[76]

The first two chapters (Chapters 62a and 62b) were introduced to the Polish CCP by the Law of 7 July 2005, which implemented Council Framework Decision 2003/577/JHA of 22 July 2003 on the execution in the European Union of orders freezing property or evidence. They are in force since 2 August 2005. Conversely, the latter chapters (Chapters 66c and 66d) were introduced to the Polish CCP by the Law of 19 December 2008, which implemented Council Framework Decision 2006/783/JHA of 6 October 2006 on the application of the principle of mutual recognition to confiscation orders. They have been binding continuously since 5 February 2009 with almost no changes.

Importantly, the adoption of Directive 2014/42/EU on the freezing and confiscation of instrumentalities and proceeds of crime in the European Union did not change anything within the Polish CCP and the procedure concerning freezing and confiscation orders. The implementation of this Directive focused solely on the substantive criminal law and concerned amendments to the definition and description of forfeiture of things, benefits, etc. (Art 44–45 CC).

The adoption of Regulation 1805/2018 also had no effect on the existing normative framework in CCP concerning freezing and confiscation orders. Although there was no official reaction from the Ministry of Justice to that matter, it should be assumed that rules concerning freezing and confiscation orders arising from the Polish CCP may still be used, but only in relation to those states that opted out of Regulation 1805/2018, i.e., Denmark and Ireland,

76 Chapter 62a – Request to a Member State of the European Union to execute orders freezing evidence or property (Art 589g–589k CPP); Chapter 62b – Request from a Member State of the European Union to execute orders freezing evidence or property (Art 589l–589u CPP); Chapter 66c – Request to a Member State of the European Union to execute a confiscation order (Art 611fn–611ft CPP); Chapter 66d – Request from a Member State of the European Union to execute a confiscation order (Art 611fu–611fze CPP).

and not toward any other EU Member State due to the direct applicability of Regulation 1805/2018 among them.

Certainly, for the clarity and predictability of law, it would have been better if the legislator had decided to add an explanation in Chapters 62a–62b and 66c–66d, stating that these rules are not binding by default among all Member States as their titles suggest. Regulating freezing of evidence is a good example of how it could have been done. Freezing of evidence among EU Member States originally was regulated by Chapters 62a and 62b. When the implementation of EIO Directive became necessary they were not removed and additional chapters (62c and 62d) were introduced. This allowed in relations with most of the EU Member States to use Chapters 62c and 62d in the context of EIO s. But issuing and executing freezing of evidence with Denmark and Ireland may be continuously conducted under old regime provided in Chapters 62a and 62b. However in case of freezing and confiscation orders became less clear as the use of Regulation 1805/2018 will be direct, leaving Chapters 62a and 62b only for cooperation in criminal matters with Ireland and Denmark. This is not reflected in the wording of the Polish CCP nor explained in any other way. In result the criminal justice authorities as well as practitioners and people concerned may falsely assume that the old CCP regime provided in Chapters 62a and 62b are still applicable to freezing and confiscation orders in all EU Member States without any adjustments.

This complex and ambiguous normative framework raises questions as to the effective use of instruments devoted to mutual recognition of freezing and confiscation orders among EU Member States. It may be suspected that, since Chapters 62a–b (freezing) and 66c–d (confiscation) coexist with Regulation 1805/2018, the proper use of the pertinent legal regime will demand specific and precise knowledge not only from prosecutors and judges, but also from the legal representatives of accused persons. As the low understanding of other EU instruments in the Polish criminal justice system has translated into their low level of practical use, with a notable exceptions of EAW and EIO, it can be assumed that freezing and confiscation orders based on Regulation 1805/2018 will continue to be used moderately.

Under the Polish legal framework, there is a strict division between the authorities competent to engage with freezing orders and confiscation orders, both within domestic criminal justice schemes and concerning the mutual recognition of those instruments. Thus, freezing orders, being treated as a tool to be used in a strong relation with a criminal investigation,[77] are vested almost

77 On the notion of criminal investigation (*postępowanie przygotowawcze*) in Poland and its forms see Karolina Kremens, *Powers of the Prosecutor in Criminal Investigation: A Comparative Perspective* (Routledge 2022) 81–83, 158–159.

entirely in the hands of the public prosecution (which does not exclude ordering this measure by a court in a national scheme), while confiscation orders (known in Poland under the name forfeiture)[78] are the sole responsibility of the court. The same scheme has been adopted by Poland for cross-border cases.[79]

Authorities competent to issue freezing orders under Regulation 1805/2018 are all units of the Polish public prosecution service, including provincial public prosecution offices, district public prosecution offices, and the Organized Crime and Corruption Department of the National Public Prosecution Office and its regional departments. At the same time, the only authorities competent to execute freezing orders issued by other Member States are provincial public prosecution offices. The situation is easier in the case of confiscation orders, as the authorities competent to issue and execute them are district and regional courts. In the event of any concerns the central authority responsible for freezing orders is the Internal Cooperation Bureau of the National Public Prosecution Office. In the absence of a designated central authority for confiscation orders, if it proves challenging to identify the competent court (including through the contact points within the European Judicial Network in criminal matters), the confiscation order may be forwarded through the Department of International Cooperation and Human Rights at the Ministry of Justice.

### 4.2 *The Normative Framework of Confiscation and Freezing Orders in Poland*

Even though Regulation 1805/2018 is directly applicable and there are no national procedural provisions explaining how issuing and executing freezing and confiscation orders among EU Member States should be carried out (since the chapters in Section XIII of the Polish CCP are no longer relevant in this context, as discussed earlier), it is important to note that the normative framework established by Regulation 1805/2018 does not operate in isolation. The basic rules on confiscation are provided in the Polish CC. The law provides for forfeiture of items (Art 44 CC), forfeiture of enterprise (Art 44a CC),[80] and forfeiture of benefit (Art 45 CC). Meanwhile, the national mechanism of freezing

78 See on the relation between "confiscation" and "forfeiture" in Polish criminal legal system below.

79 According to the declaration made by Poland on 18 December 2020 (<https://www.ejn-crimjust.europa.eu/ejn/libdocumentproperties/EN/3319> accessed 28 June 2024) in accordance with Art 2 (9) and Art 24 (2) of Regulation 1805/2018.

80 This provision was added in 2017 as a result of the implementation of Directive 2014/42/EU of the European Parliament and of the Council of 3 April 2014 on the freezing and confiscation of instrumentalities and proceeds of crime in the European Union [2014].

orders is adopted in the CCP in Chapter 32 entitled "Freezing of assets" (*zabezpieczenie majątkowe*) (Art 291–296 CCP). The way in which both mechanisms are regulated in domestic law raises several issues affecting in different ways the reception of Regulation 1805/2018 in the Polish system.

First, the Polish CC uses the term "forfeiture" (*przepadek*) instead of confiscation (*konfiskata*). Even after the coming into force of Council Framework Decision 2006/783/JHA and Regulation 1805/2018, the wording has not changed in the CC or in the CCP. Also CCP remained its traditional wording in the part of the code directly related to international cooperation in criminal matters between Member States (Chapters 66c and 66d). As a result, the term "confiscation" used in EU documents was translated against its most natural translation (*konfiskata*) into traditional Polish wording – forfeiture (*przepadek*). This may be explained by the historical context. Traditionally, "confiscation of property" (*konfiskata mienia*) available in Polish law under the communist CC of 1969, after 1989 was perceived as "contradictory to the principles of justice and individual criminal liability, and even to the concept of human rights".[81] This instrument was abolished in 1990 and for historical reasons, negative associations with the term "confiscation" remained. This led to the introducing and keeping of the notion of "forfeiture" in the Polish legal framework with the new code of 1997.[82] There are currently no known plans to amend this divergence between Regulation 1805/2018 also in the Polish language version and the wording of CC and CCP in that regard.

Second, the scope of forfeiture as provided in Polish criminal law provides for several different forms: 1) forfeiture of items derived from the crime directly (Art 44 § 1 CC); 2) forfeiture of items used to commit a crime (Art 44 § 2 CC); 3) forfeiture of items prohibited from manufacture, possession, circulation, transmission, transfer, or transportation (Art 44 § 6 CC); 4) forfeiture of the equivalent value of items directly derived from the crime or items that were used or intended to be used in the commission of the crime (Art 44 § 4 CC); 5) forfeiture of the share belonging to the perpetrator or forfeiture of the equivalent value of that share (Art 44 § 7 CC); 6) forfeiture of enterprise (Art 44a CC); and 7) forfeiture of benefit (Art 45 CC). Thus, the definition of forfeiture is broader although it seems to cover all possibilities and remain in compliance with the requirement of Art 2 of Regulation 1805/2018 to that matter.

---

81 See Elżbieta Hryniewicz-Lach, 'Poland. Report on extended confiscation in scope of the fundamental rights and general principles of EU' 1 <https://konfiskata.web.amu.edu.pl/wp-content/uploads/2022/02/Country-Report-Poland-1.pdf> accessed 28 June 2024 and literature quoted in footnotes 1–2.

82 Cf. German regulations to that matter.

Third, and most importantly, a 2015 amendment to the Polish CC[83] relocated forfeiture from its conventional position within the catalogue of penal measures (*środki karne*)[84] to a newly established Chapter Va, alongside what are termed "compensation measures" (*środki kompensacyjne*). This created a new legal category of *sui generis* measure that is neither a compensatory measure (as the title of Chapter Va reads "Forfeiture and compensation measures," suggesting these are two separate categories jointly defined in one chapter) nor a penal measure (as forfeiture was excluded from Chapter 5 of CC entitled "Penal measures").[85] The distinctiveness of forfeiture from compensation measures is also visible through functions that forfeiture played – and still plays – in Polish criminal law, which are primarily preventive and retributive.[86] The lack of connection between forfeiture and compensation may also be seen through the fact that forfeiture is aimed at transferring an item (or equivalent value or enterprise or benefit, etc.) to the State Treasury and not to the victim. It is clearly stated in Art 44 § 5 CC that it is impossible to order forfeiture of items derived from the crime directly (Art 44 § 1 CC), as well as items used to commit a crime (Art 44 § 2 CC), if they are to be returned to the victim or other eligible entity. The same rule applies to forfeiture of benefit or equivalent value (Art 45 § 1 CC *in fine*). This legal framework has been functioning without change in the Polish legal order to this day, having severe consequences for the role that confiscation orders play in compensation of victims under Regulation 1805/2018 (see further *infra* § 4.3).

Finally, the shape of the normative regulation of forfeiture in Polish national law has important implications for the way in which the freezing of assets in cross-border context is carried out. The basic provision concerning the latter is provided in Art 291 § 1 CCP. It states that if the accused is charged with a crime for which such measures as fine, pecuniary payment, forfeiture, compensation, or restitution to the victim may be pronounced, the execution of

83 Law amending Criminal Code and other laws (*Ustawa z dnia 1 lipca 2015 roku o zmianie ustawy – Kodeks karny i niektórych innych ustaw*) DzU 2015 poz 396.

84 Penal measures are measures of penal response the aim of which is to complement the effect of the penalty imposed on a convicted person. The catalogue of penal measures is available in Art 39 CC. See briefly on penal measures in Polish criminal law in Wojciech Jasiński and Karolina Kremens, *Criminal Law in Poland*, (Kluwer Law International 2019) 144–158.

85 See Ryszard A. Stefański in: Ryszard A. Stefański (ed), *Kodeks karny. Komentarz* (Wolters Kluwer 2015) 351.

86 Anna Płońska, 'Charakter prawny instytucji przepadku po zmianach nowelizacyjnych wprowadzonych do Kodeksu karnego ustawą z dnia 20 lutego 2015 r.' (2015) 37 Nowa Kodyfikacja Prawa Karnego 92.

the confiscation order of the property of the accused may be secured. This may only be done if there is a reasonable fear that without such freezing the execution of the confiscation order would be impossible or significantly hindered. Such regulation suggests that freezing orders concerning compensation and restitution measures shall be treated as distinctive instruments from freezing orders concerning forfeiture. This must affect the scope of freezing orders that can be issued or executed by Poland in the process of mutual recognition among EU Member States based on the Regulation 1805/2018.

### 4.3 *Compensation for Victims through Freezing and Confiscation Orders in Poland*

The most problematic issue from the Polish perspective is the general non-compliance of the Polish normative framework when it comes to the rights of victims and the compensatory nature of the instruments provided in Regulation 1805/2018. Strengthening the rights of victims to restitution and compensation remains one of the most obvious objectives of Regulation 1805/2018. It is provided that the rights of victims should take precedence over the rights of states in that regard, and confiscation should facilitate the exercise of these rights by victims.[87] Thus, it has been argued that "it should be possible to use the recovered assets for the purposes of restitution and compensation at the stage of execution of the confiscation both in domestic and cross-border enforcement proceedings".[88]

Considering the above, it has been made clear that freezing and confiscation orders under Regulation 2018/1805 emphasize their restorative function, rather than just the traditional retributive and preventive functions. This aim becomes, however, impossible to achieve if the national confiscation (forfeiture in the case of Poland) mechanisms exclude the possibility of serving compensatory purposes. Certainly, Regulation 1805/2018 directly highlights that its provisions "should apply to all freezing orders and to all confiscation orders issued within the framework of proceedings in criminal matters" and "[w]hile

87 See for example Recital 45 and Art 29–30 of Regulation (EU) 2018/1805 of the European Parliament and of the Council of 14 November 2018 on the mutual recognition of freezing orders and confiscation orders [2018]. This aim has also been highlighted in EU Commission report by Joëlle Milquet, Strengthening victims' rights: from compensation to reparation. EU Commission Report from the Commission on 'Strengthening victims' rights: from compensation to reparation' (Luxembourg 2019), 57 <https://db.eurocrim.org/db/en/doc/3204.pdf> accessed 29 June 2024.

88 Ariadna H. Ochnio, 'Addressing Barriers to Victim's Rights to Recovered Assets in the Mechanism for Mutual Recognition of Freezing and Confiscation Orders' in Ariadna H. Ochnio and Hanna Kuczyńska (eds), *Current Issues of EU Criminal Law* (ILS PAS 2022) 149.

such orders might not exist in the legal system of a Member State, the Member State concerned should be able to recognize and execute such an order issued by another Member State".[89] Nevertheless, freezing orders and confiscation orders that are aimed at compensation will be excluded from mechanisms provided by Regulation 1805/2018 "when the national legal order makes that State the beneficiary of the assets recovered through confiscation, not the crime victims".[90]

Taking into account the above, it should be argued that Polish law creates a contradiction in which Regulation 1805/2018 cannot exercise its task to provide restitution and compensation for victims. Under Polish law, ordering forfeiture is a concurrent mechanism to restitution and compensation, and not a way to enable them (see Art 44 § 5 CC). The disconnection between the functioning of those mechanisms is confirmed through the normative regulation of freezing orders under Polish law, that allows the issuing of such orders either with a purpose of forfeiture (Art 291 § 1 point 3 CCP) or with a purpose of compensation (Art 291 § 1 point 4 CCP) or with a purpose of restitution (Art 291 § 1 point 5 CCP). Thus, the forfeiture of assets simply cannot be ordered if they are to be returned to the victim or another entitled entity.

As a result, the rules on forfeiture and freezing in the Polish criminal legal system create duality of the legal situation of victims of crime in domestic cases and in cross-border cases subject to the direct effect of Regulation 1805/2018.[91] If the EU legal instrument is to be used directly, it creates a different set of rights and instruments available to victims of crimes in cross-border set up than the one that is provided to them through the Polish domestic criminal legal system. Thus, to remain in compliance with Regulation 1805/2018 and to serve the compensatory purpose provided in that legal instrument, Polish law should undergo a major overhaul.[92]

---

89 See Recital 13 of Regulation (EU) 2018/1805 of the European Parliament and of the Council of 14 November 2018 on the mutual recognition of freezing orders and confiscation orders [2018].

90 Ariadna H. Ochnio, 'Addressing Barriers to Victim's Rights to Recovered Assets in the Mechanism for Mutual Recognition of Freezing and Confiscation Orders' in Ariadna H. Ochnio and Hanna Kuczyńska (eds), *Current Issues of EU Criminal Law* (ILS PAS 2022) 149.

91 Ariadna Ochnio, 'O funkcji kompensacyjnej przepadku i zabezpieczeniu wykonania środków kompensacyjnych (rozważania w perspektywie prawa UE i prawa międzynarodowego)' (2023) 3 Państwo i Prawo 97–98.

92 Some suggestions how to overcome these situations were already presented by Ariadna Ochnio, 'O funkcji kompensacyjnej przepadku i zabezpieczeniu wykonania środków kompensacyjnych (rozważania w perspektywie prawa UE i prawa międzynarodowego)' (2023) 3 Państwo i Prawo 100–101.

The complicated and blurred normative regime of freezing and confiscation orders discussed above, unfortunately, cannot be explained and analyzed based on current Polish praxis as there is not enough data available and access to what is available has been made almost impossible. Although Regulation 1805/2018 has been applicable since 19 December 2020, the availability of any official data concerning the practical use of the Regulation by Polish authorities is surprisingly limited. According to the Polish Ministry of Justice, the statistics on cases involving courts concerning confiscation orders have been collected only since the beginning of 2023 and for the past year were still underreported,[93] making joint statistics unavailable at the time this contribution was written. However, independent research shows that, during the first half of 2023, numerous provincial courts reported zero cases in which confiscation was either issued or executed.[94] There is a very small chance that the results for the second half of 2023 will be slightly better, but for that data we must wait.

At the same time, the empirical research concerning the issuing and executing of freezing orders failed to provide more guidance.[95] Based on the data presented for the purpose of another project.[96] it can however be confirmed that between 19 December 2020 and 31 October 2023, the Polish public prosecution offices registered just 133 cases involving Regulation 1805/2018, of which in 45 cases Poland was acting as the issuing authority and in 88 cases as the

93 Ministry of Justice, Department of Strategy and European Funds, 9 November 2023, DSF-II.082.202.2023.

94 Statistical reports for the first half of 2023 from: Regional Court in Radom <https://radom.so.gov.pl/sor/dzialalnosc-sadu/podstawa-dzialania/sprawozdania-statystycz/2023/10147,Sprawozdania-statystyczne-z-dzialalnosci-Sadu-Okregowego-w-Radomiu-w-I-polroczu-.html> accessed 28 June 2024; Regional Court in Ostrołęka <https://ostroleka.so.gov.pl/sprawozdania-statystyczne-za-rok-2023-r,new,mg,289.html,404> accessed 28 June 2024; Regional Court in Wrocław <https://www.wroclaw.so.gov.pl/sprawozdania-statystyczne-z-dzialalnosci-sadu-za-i-kwartal-2023-roku,new,mg,85,302,.html,218> accessed 28 June 2024; and Regional Court in Warsaw <https://bip.warszawa.so.gov.pl/artykul/488/374> accessed 28 June 2024.

95 While gathering data for this project we approached the Provincial Public Prosecution Office in Wrocław requesting access to review the only case related to Regulation (EU) 1805/2018 of the European Parliament and of the Council of 14 November 2018 on the mutual recognition of freezing orders and confiscation orders handled in that office in 2022 (request from other state to execute the freezing order in Poland) – access was denied (decision of the Provincial Prosecutor of 9.10.2023, 3047-5.Ip.36.2023).

96 See project 'RECOVER (JUST-2022-JCOO)' (2022) <https://recover.lex.unict.it> accessed 29 June 2024. Note that according to the project's website the Polish report was prepared by three lawyers working in the Polish Ministry of Justice and therefore this enabled their access to data which was unavailable for us.

executing authority.[97] That means that Poland received twice as many requests to execute freezing orders as were issued by Polish prosecutors. Of all the countries that requested from Poland the execution of a freezing order, Germany is leading (37 orders), followed by France (10) and Austria (7). Poland issued the most orders to Lithuania (8), the Netherlands (6), and Germany (5).[98] This altogether shows the low level of popularity of these instruments in the country and may be considered disappointing after five years from the enactment of Regulation 1805/2018.

The lack of accessibility to statistical data is troublesome also in light of Art 35 of Regulation 1805/2018. It requires that each year Member States send to the EU Commission (preferably at a central level) data concerning the number of cases in which a victim was compensated, as well as the average time required for the execution of freezing orders and confiscation orders under Regulation 1805/2018. It has been argued that the statistics should not only be collected and reported to the European Commission according to the binding obligation but also be "comprehensible and publicly available".[99] This certainly would allow for the expanding of social control over this area of criminal proceedings, strengthening the rights of victims.

## 5 Concluding Remarks

The analysis conducted in the chapter indicates that the implementation process of the EAW FD, EIO D, and Regulation 1805/2018 is not flawless.

Generally, the transposition of the EAW FD can be assumed as proper, with two notable systemic exceptions. The first one concerns the discrepancy in the situation of Polish citizens and nationals of other Member States providing greater protection against the surrender of the former. Polish citizens may benefit from a rule that the EAW is applicable only if an offense of which they are accused of was committed outside of the territory of Poland and a double

97 Project RECOVER (JUST-2022-JCOO), 'Poland. Questionnaire on the practical obstacles and legal issues arising in the implementation of REG' (2022) <https://recover.lex.unict.it/wp-content/uploads/2023/11/Poland.pdf> accessed 28 June 2024.

98 It is however striking that in the cited report altogether 11 orders (5 when Poland acted as an issuing State and 6 as an executing State) are shown as "no data," which means that the reporting entity did not provide sufficient information as to identify the issuing or executing authority.

99 Ariadna H. Ochnio, 'Addressing Barriers to Victim's Rights to Recovered Assets in the Mechanism for Mutual Recognition of Freezing and Confiscation Orders' in Ariadna H. Ochnio and Hanna Kuczyńska (eds), *Current Issues of EU Criminal Law* (ILS PAS 2022) 144.

criminality requirement has been met. This raises doubts as to the equal treatment of all EU citizens. The second exception concerns the grounds for refusal to execute an EAW. Although all of them have been implemented in the Polish legal order, some of the grounds were implemented in a rather discretionary manner. Poland introduced five additional mandatory grounds for the refusal of an EAW not provided for in the EAW FD, among which some apply only to Polish citizens. Moreover, in some cases, the nature of the grounds for refusal was changed, making them mandatory instead of optional. These deficiencies, together with other minor flaws, resulted in infringement proceedings against Poland commenced by the European Commission in 2020 and still ongoing.

The implementation of the EIO seems to raise fewer concerns. Generally, there are no systemic or structural deficiencies which put into question the overall effectiveness of the use of EIOs in Poland. Most divergences between the provisions of EIO D and the Polish CCP are of rather minor character and they do not prevent the effective application of EIOs. The most significant problem is the transposition of Art 24–25 of EIO D, providing for hearings by videoconference or other audiovisual transmission as well as by telephone conference. The national provisions regulating these measures do not offer a sufficient legal framework to carry out hearings in such a form. This is crucial since the Polish legal provisions are to be applied in the course of the EIO's execution. If they are deficient, then the conduct of such conferences is left hanging in the air. Certainly, the executing authorities may be creative while using the existing legal provisions applicable in domestic cases, but it would be much better if the respective CCP provisions were elaborated and adjusted to the changing environment and expectations. Therefore, a reconsideration of Polish rules on interrogation by video and teleconference and their adjustment to the requirements of cooperation in criminal matters with EU Member States is indispensable.

Another important lacuna concerns the rules of admissibility of evidence obtained through the EIO. Polish CCP does not refer to this issue explicitly, which must be perceived as a deficiency. This flaw is systemic as evidence gathered abroad requires specific rules of admissibility. Therefore, at least for the sake of clarity, the lawmaker's intervention is required.

It is difficult, if not impossible, to properly assess the functioning of Regulation 1805/2018 within the Polish criminal legal system. The creation of the new legal framework relating to freezing and confiscation orders on the EU level has received virtually no response from the Polish side. It is not an exaggeration to say that it has been almost entirely overlooked, with no reaction from the Polish parliament or the Ministry of Justice. It has also received very little attention among scholars in Polish academia. This cannot be explained by the obvious fact that the discussed Regulation 1805/2018 has a direct effect on the Polish legal order and, therefore, does not require any direct form of implementation or transposition. It might stem from the low level of understanding of the emerging EU legislation concerning criminal justice matters, or from the generally poor climate for Polish cooperation with the EU between 2015 and 2023. This has serious consequences. The lack of transposition or adjustments made in the Polish CCP to meet the new perspective on freezing and confiscation as provided in Regulation 1805/2018 makes the new rules almost unseen. The untouched normative environment renders that the application of provisions concerning freezing and confiscation is no longer intuitive. While the CCP regulates the procedure for mutual cooperation concerning freezing and confiscation orders, these provisions currently apply only to Ireland and Denmark, which is at least misleading. This is confirmed by statistics that show little (in the case of freezing orders) or no (in the case of confiscation orders) use of the instruments provided for in Regulation 1805/2018 since December 2020. However, the most important issue relates to the non-compliance of the Polish legal framework with the rights of victims and the compensatory nature of the instruments provided for by Regulation 1805/2018. This is a consequence of the existence of the current unchanged normative framework on ordering a forfeiture. Polish law makes it a concurrent mechanism to restitution and compensation and not a way to enable them. As a result, the forfeiture of assets under Polish law simply cannot be ordered if these assets are to be returned to the victim or another entitled entity. This makes the main goal of Resolution 2018/1805 unmet and calls for an immediate legislative response.

Summing up, the level of implementation of the three mutual recognition instruments in Poland varies. While the implementation of the EIO is generally correct and is almost unaffected by structural deficiencies, the same cannot be said about the EAW. In this case, the problems are fundamental and sovereignty-related (differentiation between Polish and non-Polish citizens). Serious doubts can also be raised in relation to freezing and confiscation orders. While the provisions of Regulation 1805/2018 can be applied directly, their effective execution depends on the national legal framework. When the latter is deficient it does not allow the confiscation order under Regulation 1805/2018 to achieve all the aims it should serve. The crucial deficits of the national legal framework, as they cannot be neutralized by creative interpretation of the legal provisions in practice, call for immediate legislative changes.

CHAPTER 10

# Portugal: Recognition of European Warrants and Cooperation Orders in Law and Practice

*Miguel João Costa, Raquel Cardoso, António Vaz de Castro and Pedro Caeiro*

## 1 Introduction

In the Portuguese legal system there is no visible resistance on the part of either the legislator, the courts or other public authorities to mutual recognition legal instruments. The situation is somewhat contrasting in the case of EU legislation that seeks to harmonise deeply-rooted national legal instruments such as the Code of Criminal Procedure (CCP): in this case, some inertia may be said to exist on the part of the legislator in implementing them, and little eagerness on the part of the courts to give them practical application drawing on their direct effect. This attitude, however, arguably stems more from a certain perception – which is not entirely ill-founded, but is overstated and, above all, limiting of further improvement – that national law is already widely respectful of individual rights, as well as from sheer force of habit, than from any sort of enmity at the meddling of EU law with the national legal order.[1]

It is therefore not extraordinary either that, even in the field of harmonisation of procedural rights, meaningful developments have more recently taken place. Some of them are a consequence of European case law, namely of the ruling of the CJEU in *TL*, of 1 August 2022, on the rights to information and translation in criminal proceedings,[2] issued pursuant to a request for a preliminary ruling lodged by a Portuguese court, which then, on its decision of 2 August 2022, readily reflected the conclusions of the CJEU in that case.[3] Others are more clearly 'internal', such as the decision of the Constitutional Court no. 540/2022 of 16 August, which for the first time ruled on the merits of

1 In further detail, see Miguel João Costa and Pedro Caeiro, 'Portugal – The Implementation of the Directives on Procedural Rights in Law and Practice' in Giuseppe Contissa, Giulia Lasagni, Michele Caianiello and Giovanni Sartor (eds.), *Effective Protection of the Rights of the Accused in the EU Directives: A Computable Approach to Criminal Procedure Law* (Leiden: Brill | Nijhoff, 2022) 170 f.

2 Case C-242/22 PPU *TL* [2022] EU:C:2022:611; on this case, see further *infra*, § 2.2.

3 High Court of Évora, ruling of 2 August 2022 (53/19.8GACUB-B.E1).

© MIGUEL JOÃO COSTA ET AL., 2025 | DOI:10.1163/9789004705791_012 an EAW case and, drawing in part on the teleology of the EU agenda on procedural rights, held unconstitutional a certain norm of the Portuguese implementation statute which limited the right to appeal. In the same vein, after a rather apathetic first reaction by the legislator to the Directives on procedural rights, the latest amendment of the CCP, carried out through Law no. 52/2023, of 28 August, explicitly undertook to "complete the implementation" of the Directive 2010/64/EU on the right to interpretation and translation, and of the Directive 2013/48/EU on the right of access to a lawyer.

As for EU legislation on mutual recognition – or, at any rate, on judicial cooperation in criminal matters[4] –, levels of compliance in Portugal are elevated. Indeed, few implementation issues can be identified concerning the Framework Decision 2002/584/JHA on the European arrest warrant (EAW FD) or the Directive 2014/41/EU on the European Investigation Order (EIO D), the same being true of the articulation of Regulation 2018/1805 with pre-existing national legislation. Implementation of the EAW FD, which has now been in operation for over 20 years, may actually be said to be exhaustive, as the large majority of the issues that at one point did exist were gradually eradicated through successive amendments of the national statute (Law no. 65/2003, of 23 August – hereinafter "PT-EAW"). Including – after the amendment carried out through Law no. 52/2023, of 28 August – issues concerning the right to appoint a lawyer in the issuing Member State, the rights to translation and information, and the time limits for surrender.[5] Similarly, the statute implementing the EIO D (Law no. 88/2017, of 21 August – hereinafter "PT-EIO") follows the Directive "nearly verbatim",[6] leaving scant room for divergence. Finally, Regulation

4 The *caveat* concerns the EIO D, which stays further away from the mutual recognition paradigm than most EU law instruments of judicial cooperation in criminal matters, seeking instead to strike a balance between such a paradigm and the classic approach to mutual legal assistance that still presided over the 2000 Convention: see *e.g.* Lorena Bachmaier Winter, 'Transnational Evidence – Towards the Transposition of Directive 2014/41 Regarding the European Investigation Order in Criminal Matters' (2015) 2 *eucrim* 47.

5 There are some discrepancies between the EAW FD and PT-EAW, but they can be considered minor, or expressing a choice of the national legislator admitted by the EAW FD – *e.g.*: Arts 5(10)(1) EAW FD), which does not mention the obligation to make enquiries in order to determine which is the competent executing authority; Art 26, which, contrary to Art 17(7) EAW FD, does not mention the duty to inform the Council in case of repeated delays by another Member State in the execution of EAWs; and Art 18(5) (19(2) EAW FD), which provides for the rules regarding the hearing of the detainee but does not mention the "conditions determined by mutual agreement between the issuing and executing judicial authorities". The Portuguese legislator has also decided not to transpose Arts 19(3), 27(1) and 28(1) of the EAW FD, which is in line with their optional nature.

6 General Secretariat of the Council, *Evaluation Report on the Tenth Round of Mutual Evaluations on the Implementation of the European Investigation Order – Report on Portugal* (10135/1/23

2018/1805 brings about very few novelties to the national legal system, notably in view of the regime already set out in Law no. 25/2009 of 5 July, and in Law no. 88/2009, of 31 August, implementing, respectively, the Framework Decision 2003/577/JHA and the Framework Decision 2006/783/JHA.

Nevertheless, in all those cases some implementation issues can still be discerned, and the actual application of these legal instruments by the courts is also worthy of critical reflection, as will be expounded in this Chapter[7] – after providing a brief overview of the Portuguese criminal system.

### 1.1 *Overview of the Criminal Procedural System*

In the first place, it is important to bear in mind that in this legal system the suspect as such has few specific procedural rights or duties: they emerge with his or her formal designation as a subject of the procedure (*i.e.*, as an '*arguido*'), such a designation therefore being a procedural act of great relevance.[8] Regarding transnational (international judicial cooperation) mechanisms,[9] the core constitutional provision is Art 33, on extradition/EAW and expulsion, but the rights envisaged for criminal proceedings proper (mainly in Art 32 Const.)[10] expand somewhat to such mechanisms, as they are considered to some extent as special types of criminal proceedings.[11]

REV1, Brussels, 28 June 2023) 10 <https://www.parlament.gv.at/dokument/XXVII/EU/147049/imfname_11266202.pdf> accessed 14 July 2024.

7 And in further detail in Miguel João Costa, Raquel Cardoso, António Vaz de Castro and Pedro Caeiro, 'Portuguese Report' (*Facilex Project*) <https://site.unibo.it/facilex/en>.

8 Arts 57 f. CPP establish the (wide) set of procedural acts and moments in which such a designation must or can take place: see Costa and Caeiro (n 1) 174 f.

9 See Miguel João Costa and Pedro Caeiro, 'Country Report Portugal' in Martin Böse, Maria Bröcker and Anne Schneider (eds.), *Judicial Protection in Transnational Criminal Proceedings* (Cham: Springer, 2021) 271 f.

10 Art 32 is the general constitutional provision on defence rights, including the presumption of innocence; but see also, *e.g.*, Art 20, on the right to access the law and the courts, Art 27, on deprivation of liberty, Art 28, on the conditions of pre-trial custody, Art 31, on *habeas corpus*. In the CPP, the core provision is Art 61(1) to (5).

11 The Constitutional Court tends for instance to equate extradition and criminal proceedings, save insofar as concerns the rights and principles that are specific to the ascertainment of criminal liability, such as the presumption of innocence: see *e.g.* the rulings nos. 54/87, of 10 February, and 540/2022, already mentioned. That is also the view implicit in the fact that the CCP applies in a subsidiary manner to cooperation proceedings: See notably Art 3(2) of Law no. 144/99, of 31 August, and Arts 16(6), 17(4) and 34 PT-EAW.

As for their form,[12] criminal procedures in their standard modality encompass two pre-trial phases: the inquiry (*inquérito*)[13] and the instruction (*instrução*).[14] The former is the investigation phase *par excellence*. It concludes with a decision whether or not to prosecute. The instruction phase consists of a judicial evaluation by a judge of the decision taken at the end of the inquiry. It is an optional phase which takes place only upon request. If the procedure is to continue, then the phase of trial (*julgamento*) will in principle ensue,[15] after which a phase of appeal (*recurso*)[16] may yet take place – and, in some cases, the decision then taken on appeal is yet open to a further appeal before the Supreme Court.

The public authorities involved in criminal proceedings are mainly the criminal police (*órgãos de polícia criminal*), the Public Prosecution's Office (*Ministério Público*) and judges / courts (*juízes / tribunais*). The Public Prosecution's Office (PPO) enjoys institutional and functional autonomy *vis-à-vis* the Executive, namely the Minister of Justice, meaning that they cannot be instructed to act or not to act in a given manner in specific cases, which places them closer to the judicial function *stricto sensu* than to the administrative function, and warrants their classification as 'judicial authorities'.[17] The inquiry is led by the PPO, assisted by the criminal police, who act under the direct supervision and functional (but not hierarchical) dependence of the former. The judge of instruction directs the phase of instruction – also with the assistance of the criminal police, in similar terms –, but also plays a key role during the preceding phase of inquiry, where he or she is competent for executing or at least ordering or authorising the investigative measures which are more intrusive to fundamental rights,[18] thus acting as a '*juge des libertés*'. Where a different authority (notably the PPO, during the inquiry) is entitled to order or authorise investigative measures, the measure is not liable to *direct* judicial review, since the PPO has autonomy to direct the inquiry, but its validity can be challenged before a judge during the phase of instruction or later at the trial.

12 See further in Pedro Caeiro and Miguel João Costa, 'The Portuguese System' in Katalin Ligeti (ed.), *Toward a Prosecutor for the European Union – Vol. 1: A Comparative Analysis* (Oxford: Hart Publishing, 2012) 540 f.

13 Arts 262 f. CCP.

14 Arts 286 f. CCP.

15 Arts 311 f. CCP; but see Art 311 CCP (*saneamento do processo*).

16 Arts 399 ff. CCP.

17 See Jorge de Figueiredo Dias, 'Nótulas sobre temas de direito judiciário (penal)' (1995) 127 *Revista de Legislação e Jurisprudência* 354 f. and (1995) 128 *Revista de Legislação e Jurisprudência* 8 f.

18 Arts 268 and 269 CCP.

The trial runs its course before a trial court (which may be a single-judge court, a three-judge court or a court of jury), and appeals before a court of appeal (in principle a High Court), the decision then taken being in some cases liable to further appeal to the Supreme Court, as noted before. If the constitutionality of norms relevant to the case is to be challenged, appeal to the Constitutional Court is yet possible.

The institutions involved in cooperation proceedings are the same as in criminal proceedings, their competences differing only slightly from one context to the other. The criminal police may, for instance, be called upon to arrest an individual for surrender purposes. The PPO abides here too by a principle of objectivity ('*à charge et à décharge*'), such that it is not bound to plead in favour of granting cooperation. All cooperation proceedings (mutual recognition-based and classic) are streamlined, with the Attorney-General's Office operating as a central authority.[19] Courts are – here too – the main holders of the duty to secure judicial protection. That certain cooperation measures be ordered by a court is in fact imposed by the Constitution. The courts that function as courts of first instance in extradition and EAW proceedings are those that in criminal proceedings function as courts of appeal (High Courts),[20] while the Supreme Court, which in criminal proceedings intervenes in only a limited number of cases, in such proceedings is the first instance of appeal.[21] In the context of the EAW, common courts can issue warrants.[22]

### 1.2 *Overview of the Implementation Roadmap*

PT-EAW came into force on 1 January 2004. It required a constitutional amendment (in 2001), which inserted in Art 33(5) Const. an exception to the common extradition regime, so as to allow for the surrender of Portuguese citizens and for the surrender in situations where the issuing Member State may impose a life sentence or a sentence of indeterminate duration.[23] The implementation

19 See *e.g.* Arts 9 PT-EAW and 10(1) and (2) PT-EIO.

20 See Arts 12(3)(c) CCP, 46(3) and 49(1) of Law no. 144/99, of 31 August, and 15 PT-EAW (6 (2) EAW FD).

21 See Arts 49(3) of Law no. 144/99, of 31 August, and 24(5) PT-EAW.

22 See Art 36 PT-EAW.

23 See further in Pedro Caeiro and Sónia Fidalgo, 'The Portuguese experience of mutual recognition in criminal matters: five years of European Arrest Warrant' in Gisele Vernimmen-van Tiggelen, Laura Surano and Anne Weyembergh (eds.), *The future of mutual recognition in criminal matters in the European Union* (Brussels: Éditions de l'Université de Bruxelles, 2009) 446 f.; Luís Silva Pereira, 'Alguns aspectos da implementação do regime relativo ao mandado de detenção europeu' (2003) 96 *Revista do Ministério Público* 39 f.; Nuno Piçarra, 'A proibição constitucional de extraditar nacionais em face da União Europeia' (2007) 7 *Revista do Centro de Estudos Judiciários* 131 f.

statute has been subject to three modifications over its life span (in 2015, 2019, and 2023),[24] all of which were primarily aimed at addressing issues of conformity with the EAW FD[25] (and, more recently, with the overall EU legal order, notably the Directives on procedural rights). As for PT-EIO, it entered into force on 22 August 2017 and thus far was amended only once, through Law no. 42/2023, of 10 August, which implemented Directives (EU) 2022/211 and (EU) 2022/228, both of 16 February 2022. Regarding Regulation (EU) 2018/1805, no legislation has been enacted in adjustment thereto, as it was unnecessary (Art 288 TFEU). Until the Regulation came into force, mutual recognition of freezing orders was governed by Law no. 25/2009, and mutual recognition of decisions to confiscate instruments and proceeds by Law no. 88/2009, both mentioned before and which still apply to situations where the Regulation does not.[26]

## 2 European Arrest Warrant: Critical Profiles in Legislation and Case Law

### 2.1 *Scope and Issuing of an* EAW

While an EAW may be issued either for prosecuting or for enforcing a custodial sentence, changing its purpose during the procedure is disallowed, as it is seen to breach defence rights.[27]

As a fully judicialized surrender procedure, the EAW must be issued by a judicial authority. In Portugal, both prosecutors and judges are competent to issue EAWs, depending on the phase of the proceedings. During the phase of *inquiry*, competence belongs to the prosecutor (Art 257(1) CCP), if the purpose is to bring the person before the judge for the first hearing and interrogation; however, if the purpose is to subject the person to pre-trial custody, then competence falls with the judge of instruction (Art 268(1) CCP), as the application

24 Respectively through Law no. 35/2015 of 4 May, the Law no. 115/2019 of 12 September, and the already mentioned Law no. 52/2023 of 28 August.

25 For an analysis prior to the amendments, see Caeiro and Fidalgo (n 23) 447 f. For a recent analysis, see Pedro Caeiro and Raquel Cardoso, 'First Periodic Country Report [on the application of the FD EAW by Portuguese courts]: Portugal' (2022) <https://stream-eaw.eu/country-reports/> 2 f.

26 For instance, *vis-à-vis* Denmark and Ireland, which did not bind themselves to the Regulation.

27 See the ruling of the Supreme Court of Justice of 17-06-2020 (39/20.0YREVR.S1), in a case where the EAW had been issued for executing a sentence, and the issuing Member State, by means of an informal communication, sought to change its purpose to conduct criminal prosecution.

of that coercive measure is an exclusive competence of a judge. During the phase of *instruction*, competence always belongs to the judge of instruction (Art 293 CCP) and, in all subsequent phases, to the court. Both Portuguese prosecutors and judges meet the criteria required by the CJEU for determining whether the issuing authority is a judicial authority within the meaning of the EAW FD (Arts 215 to 220 Const.).[28]

No relevant implementation problems can be discerned in Portugal concerning the issuing of EAWs. However, a conclusive assessment in this respect is hardly possible, since there are very few (at least publicly available) decisions with Portugal acting as issuing Member State. At any rate, the main critical aspect appears to be proportionality in the *issuing* of the EAW.[29] For instance, it has been held that it would be disproportional to issue an EAW with the sole purpose (and without further reasoning) of putting an end to a situation of procedural default (*contumácia*), especially where it would be impossible to subject the person to pre-trial custody in Portugal.[30]

### 2.2 *Execution Procedure and Cooperation Issues between Judicial Authorities*

Upon receiving an EAW, the PPO promotes its execution within 48 hours (Art 16(1) PT-EAW). The procedure is then assigned to a judge, who must carry out a preliminary evaluation as to whether the provided information is sufficient to take a decision; if it is not, the necessary information shall be requested from the issuing Member State. Once all the information is received and the EAW translated, it is transmitted to the PPO, so that they can arrange for the detention of the individual. Within 48 hours of detention the individual must be heard by a judge, who will then decide on the validity of the detention and on whether it should continue or be replaced by another (less restrictive) coercive measure provided for in the CCP[31] (Arts 18(3) PT-EAW and 12 EAW FD). If

28 See, *inter alia*, Case C-509/18 *PF* EU:C:2019:457; Case C-508/18 and Case C-82/19 PPU *OG and PI* EU:C:2019:456; Case C-489/19 PPU *NJ* EU:C:2019:849; and Case C-556/198 PPU and Case C-626/19 PPU *JR and YC* EU:C:2019:1077.

29 For an analysis of proportionality in Portugal (not only as issuing but also as executing Member State), see Caeiro and Cardoso (n 25) 4 and 7; and *idem*, 'Country Research Brief [on the application of the EAW FD by Portuguese courts]: Portugal' (2023) 7.

30 See *e.g.* High Court of Porto, ruling of 18-03-2015 (ECLI:PT:TRP:2015:612.08.4GBOBR.A.P1.C6).

31 This includes the possibility of determining that detention is not necessary in the case. If the time limits for detention are reached (Art 30 PT-EAW: 60, 90, or 150 days), detention may be replaced by one of the coercive measures provided for in the CCP (Art 30(1) PT-EAW), in order to secure the material conditions for surrender. Such coercive measures include: statement of identity and residence; bail; obligation of periodic presentation;

the individual consents to being surrendered, this consent is irrevocable and entails a waiver of the remainder of the EAW procedure.[32]

During this procedure, the person holds all the general rights granted to an accused person,[33] as well as those specifically contained in Art 17 PT-EAW (11 EAW FD), namely the possibility to refuse or consent to being surrendered, the right to be represented by a lawyer, and (since the 2023 amendment of PT-EAW), the right to be informed of the rights to appoint a lawyer also in the issuing Member State and to be assisted by an interpreter.[34] Under Portuguese law, lack of translation of the warrant constitutes a mere irregularity (which can be remedied and therefore does not lead to the refusal of the EAW).[35] However, the 2022 judgment of the CJEU in *TL*, mentioned above, has rendered the national rules on procedural irregularities inapplicable where they carry an obligation for the holder of the rights to translation and information to invoke these rights within a prescribed period of time, under the consequence of the irregularity becoming cured.[36] When applied to the EAW, this means that if a translation is not provided, the procedural acts carried out subsequently are null and void, and must be repeated once the translation has been provided.

If there are multiple EAWs or an EAW and an extradition request for the same person, the conflict is solved based on the criteria set in Art 23 PT-EAW (Art 16 EAW FD). Arguably, these provisions are no longer fully accurate, as in

---

suspension of the exercise of profession, function, activity or rights; prohibition or imposition of conduct; house arrest (Art 196 to 201 CCP).

32 However, the right to appeal on certain grounds subsists, namely when the person disagrees with the Court regarding the sufficiency of the guarantees provided by the issuing Member State after consent has been given: see the ruling of the Constitutional Court no. 540/2022, of 16 August, and the explanation of the case in Caeiro and Cardoso (n 29) 17 f.; for an analysis of this ruling see also Margarida Santos, 'As Garantias do Detido na Execução de um Mandado de Detenção Europeu – Comentário ao Acórdão do Tribunal Constitucional n.º 540/2022' (2022) 2 *Portuguese Review of Constitutional Law* 153–168.

33 See Art 61 CCP (already addressed *supra*, § 1.1), applicable *ex vi* Art 17(4) PT-EAW.

34 See, respectively: Art 17(2) PT-EAW; Arts 17(3) and 32 PT-EAW, and Arts 61(1)(j) and 92 f. CCP.

35 For further detail, see Caeiro and Cardoso (n 25) 12.

36 This judgement clarified that the computation of the term within which the lack of translation of an essential document can be invoked shall only begin after the person "has been informed, in a language which he or she speaks or understands, first, of the existence and scope of his or her right to interpretation and translation and, secondly, of the existence and content of the essential document in question and the effects thereof" (§ 89). The judgment of the CJEU was then immediately reflected in Court of Évora, ruling of 02-08-2022 (ECLI:PT:TRE:2022:53.19.8GACUB.B.E1.EE). On this case see Caeiro and Cardoso (n 29) 9.

the light of the 2016 decision *Petruhhin* by the Court of Justice,[37] preference must be given to the EAW over extradition when it is issued by the Member State of nationality.[38]

Art 30(4) PT-EAW (transposing Art 23(5) EAW FD) now establishes that, once the time limits for detention set in Art 26 PT-EAW (Art 17(2) to (5) and (7) EAW FD) are reached, detention must cease. The implementation of this provision is quite recent: only in August 2023 was it clearly established that the consequence of the failure to execute an EAW within that timeframe is the release of the person. It is a much welcome amendment, which follows criticism that for long had been submitted in legal literature.[39] However, even before this amendment, the understanding of Portuguese courts – based on the jurisprudence of the CJEU and on the duty to interpret national law in conformity with EU law, as well as on the explicit mention in Art 1(2) PT-EAW of the execution of the EAW in accordance with the provisions of the EAW FD – was that those time limits did apply.[40]

Publicly available case law denotes no cooperation issues between Portugal and other Member States in the framework of the EAW, except for some delay in receiving requested information (usually, in relation to the 'guarantees' of Art 13 PT-EAW, that is, guarantees that the issuing Member State has provisions in its legal system for a review of the penalty imposed, or for the application of measures of clemency).[41]

---

37 Case C-182/15 *Petruhhin* [2016] EU:C:2016:630.

38 Indeed, that ruling entails a partial derogation of Art 16(3) EAW FD: see Miguel João Costa, 'The Emerging EU Extradition Law: *Petruhhin* and Beyond' (2017) 8 *New Journal of European Criminal Law* 203. The first expression of the *Petruhhin* doctrine in Portuguese case law is the ruling of the Supreme Court of 12-05-2022 (ECLI:PT:STJ:2022:8.22.5YRCBR.6E), where extradition, however, was ultimately granted. Arguably, even where *Petruhhin* case law does not technically apply, the solution to the concurrence of EAW and extradition requests under Art 16(3) EAW FD should bring into consideration the set of norms that gave rise to that case law, notably free movement and equal treatment, with the consequence that some prevalence should in general be given to the EAW over extradition.

39 See Caeiro and Fidalgo (n 23) 449.

40 Most recently, see Supreme Court, ruling of 26-07-2023 (ECLI:PT:STJ:2023:257.23.9YRLSB.A.S1.3B).

41 In one case, the Supreme Court, ruling of 03-05-2018 (879/17.7YRLSB.S1), only summary available – annulled the High Court's decision to terminate the EAW procedure due to the failure of the issuing authority to provide the requested information within the specified deadlines. It found that the High Court should persist with the requests for information until it could conclude that the issuing authority was no longer interested in the execution of the issued EAW. Regarding the content of the aforementioned information and its impact on the EAW procedure, see Caeiro and Cardoso (n 25) 10–11 and 18–19.

### 2.3 *Grounds for Non-recognition and Non-execution*

PT-EAW includes all the grounds for non-execution established in the EAW FD: the mandatory ones as mandatory, the optional ones as discretionary. This suggests that no assessment was carried out at all by the national legislator as to whether all optional grounds for non-execution were indeed necessary and/or desirable in light of the Portuguese legal tradition. Refusals to execute EAWs are also rare.[42] However, there are still some aspects where the national statute and the EAW FD differ.

One is the complete omission of reference to fundamental rights in PT-EAW, which does not include a 'fundamental rights' clause corresponding to that found in Art 1(3) EAW FD. However, it may be argued that transposing this provision is unnecessary, since it does not contain any actual obligation, but only evinces obligations already impending on Member States on the strength of other legal instruments and standards.[43] In any case, it is quite meaningful that, while potential violations of fundamental rights in the issuing Member State have been raised in some cases in Portugal, no decision can be found after *Aranyosi and Căldăraru* applying the tests set out by the CJEU in this ruling.[44]

Another ground for non-recognition that should be considered, even though it is not explicitly stated as such in either the EAW FD or the PT-EAW,[45] is the fact that the issuing authority is not considered a judicial authority under the case law of the CJEU. In order to qualify as such, an authority must be independent in the sense that it does not receive orders or instructions from the executive with regard to the discharge of their duties in specific cases. When

---

42 For some statistics, see ibid 20.

43 Namely, the ECHR, the CFREU, the Constitutions of the Member States, the common constitutional traditions, and the case law of the CJEU, inasmuch as it is directed at interpreting limitations to fundamental rights by European rules.

44 There is only an erstwhile case where the Supreme Court deployed a similar reasoning (Supreme Court, ruling of 25-03-2010 (ECLI:PT:STJ:2010:76.10.2YRLSB.S1.B3): the requested individual was suspected of being a member of ETA and one of the arguments against surrender was the potential violation of her fundamental rights in Spain, based on reports indicating that such violation often occurred in the Spanish region where the EAW was issued; the Supreme Court, however, found these allegations unsupported in terms of the actual risk of a violation in the *specific* case. In another case, concerning the applicability of a measure that had already been found to be in breach of the ECHR by the ECtHR, the Supreme Court concluded that this was not a question to be evaluated by the executing authority, but should instead be addressed within the criminal procedure in the issuing Member State: Supreme Court, ruling of 16-12-2010 (ECLI:PT:STJ:2010:176.10.9YREVR.S1.F3).

45 However, it does stem from Art 1(1) PT-EAW (corresponding to Art 1(1) EAW FD) that the EAW is a "judicial decision", and as such it must be issued by a judicial authority: see *e.g.* Case C-477/16 PPU *Kovalkovas* [2016] EU:C:2016:861.

this is not the case, the EAW cannot be executed, as it does not qualify as a "judicial decision". While, to the best of our knowledge, no EAW has been denied by Portugal on this ground, there have been cases where the defence sought to oppose surrender by arguing that the EAW was not issued by a judicial authority (namely when it was issued by a prosecutor instead of a judge). In some cases, the initial EAW was subsequently signed by a judge, thereby rendering the question moot;[46] in another case, the Court found that the prosecutor should be considered an independent judicial authority and that, therefore, the issued EAW should be regarded as valid.[47] The stance of the courts on these issues is fully in line with the CJEU's jurisprudence on the matter and it merits no reproach.[48]

An issue which is still relevant concerns Art 2(2) PT-EAW (corresponding to Art 2(2) EAW FD), on the exclusion of double criminality control. This provision requires the executing Member State to first determine if the acts fall within the listed categories and secondly if they are punishable by a custodial sentence or detention order of at least a maximum period of 3 years. If either of those requirements fails, an assessment of double criminality is permitted. Art 2(2) and (3) PT-EAW provides that, where the acts do not fall within the listed categories of (2), surrender is admissible only if the acts are also criminalised in Portuguese law, irrespective of their constituent elements or qualification. Thus, at present, the lack of double criminality constitutes exclusively a mandatory ground for refusal, whereas in the past this ground was enshrined as both a mandatory and an optional ground for refusal.[49] However, this choice should be deemed to fall within the margin of discretion left to the Member States, namely from the wording of Art 2(4) EAW FD.[50] The lack of double

46 High Court of Évora, ruling of 30-10-12 (ECLI:PT:TRE:2012:142.11.7YREVR.E1.FD) (EAW issued by Spain) and Supreme Court, ruling of 19-07-19 (ECLI:PT:STJ:2019:1728.19.7YRLSB.A.A6) (EAW issued by Germany).

47 Supreme Court, ruling of 16-12-2020 (ECLI:PT:STJ:2020:47.20.0YREVR.S1.23).

48 See the case law of the CJEU indicated *supra*, § 2.1. See also Caeiro and Cardoso (n 25) 7.

49 The mandatory ground for refusal stemmed from this legal provision, as explained, but former Art 12(1) (a) PT-EAW established as an optional ground for refusal the fact that the act that motivated the issuing of the EAW was not criminalised under Portuguese law, as long as it did not fall within the list in Art 2(2). For an analysis of the relevant provisions and case law on this matter, see, respectively, Caeiro and Fidalgo (n 23) 452 f.; Caeiro and Cardoso (n 25) 16 f.

50 Although some case law of the CJEU seems to suggest otherwise, implying that, in case of an optional ground of refusal, the executing authority must always enjoy some discretion in determining the appropriateness of the surrender (Case C-579/15 *Popławski* [2017] EU:C:2017:503 § 21), such a conclusion arguably does not apply to each and every ground of refusal: Pedro Caeiro and Miguel João Costa, 'Extradition and Surrender: From

criminality, in turn, may also have an impact on the 'relevance thresholds' of Art 2(1) PT-EAW (corresponding to Art 2(1) EAW FD): for instance, in a case where an EAW had been issued for executing a 4-month sentence for several offences, the fact that one of these offences did not exist in Portugal led to the conclusion that, although it was impossible to know the effect of such acts upon the joint sentence, by removing them from consideration the sentence would probably have been lower than 4 months, such that the EAW was refused on this ground.[51]

The most common grounds for non-execution are found in Arts 11 to 13 PT-EAW (Arts 3 to 5 EAW FD). At present, these are for the most part in line with the FD, but two aspects are still worthy of mention. The first concerns Art 12-A(4) PT-EAW (corresponding to Art 4a(3) FD): it provides that, if the individual requests a retrial or lodges an appeal, his or her detention must be reviewed according to the law of the issuing Member State. Nonetheless, the provision fails to provide that "such a review shall in particular include the possibility of suspension or interruption of the detention", and that "the retrial or appeal shall begin within due time after the surrender" (Art 4a(3) EAW FD).[52] This, however, is not problematic, as all legal systems likely admit the suspension or interruption of detention and the application of other coercive measures. Moreover, the EAW FD does not generate a right to have detention suspended or interrupted, but only to have the situation *reviewed* in the issuing Member State in accordance with its own law. Regarding the beginning of the retrial or appeal "within due time", this expression simply requires it to take place at a convenient time: it does not entail specific legal consequences, as it does not establish a fixed deadline or specify the outcome of non-compliance. Thus, and in sum, no implementation issues exist in this regard.

The second issue concerns the wording of Art 13 PT-EAW (implementing Art 5 EAW FD). While this national provision mentions "guarantees", it actually refers to certain *conditions* that the issuing Member State must fulfil in order to facilitate the execution of the EAW.[53] Thus, despite the difference in the terms

---

a Bilateral Political Arrangement to a Triangular Legal Procedure' in Kai Ambos and Peter Rackow (eds.), *The Cambridge Companion to European Criminal Law* (Cambridge: Cambridge University Press, 2023) 268.

51 See High Court of Porto, ruling of 07-03-2012 (32/12.6YRPRT).

52 Such omission is probably due to the fact that the provision already states that the standards for the review are those stemming from the law of the issuing Member State. For an analysis of national case law on this provision, see Caeiro and Cardoso (n 25) 10.

53 Indeed, no actual guarantees are requested from the issuing Member State: Portuguese courts ask only for *information*, using the envisioned mechanisms of the EAW FD to the effect. For a complete explanation, see ibid 3.

used, in substance there is no discrepancy. Art 13 envisages two situations (after the 2009 amendment of the FD). The first (a) is that in which the offence is punishable by a life sentence in the issuing Member State. In this event, execution of the warrant depends on the legal system of the issuing Member State enabling a review of the imposed penalty or the application of clemency measures, such that this constitutes a mandatory ground for refusal.[54] The second (b) constitutes a discretionary ground for refusal. It is an equivalent to Art 12(1)(g) PT-EAW (Art 4(6) EAW FD) when applied to EAWs issued for conducting a criminal procedure: in this case, surrender *may* be subject to the condition that the requested person, after being heard, be returned to Portugal to serve the custodial sentence or detention order.

Finally, in Portugal, proportionality is not regarded as a ground for refusal. This reading is consistent with the EAW FD, as proportionality is supposed to be observed by the issuing Member State but not controlled by the executing one. Thus, Portugal does not question the proportionality of the issuing of EAWs by other Member States, even though this issue is repeatedly raised by the defence.[55] Nevertheless, this principle did already serve as a deciding factor when discretionary grounds for non-execution are met in the case.[56]

### 2.4 *Remedies*

As the EAW FD lacks specific provisions on remedies, these are governed by the CCP, and they differ depending on whether national authorities are acting as issuing or as executing authorities.

When Portugal is the issuing Member State, remedies also differ according to the entity that issues the EAW in a specific case: if this entity is a public prosecutor, there is no right to appeal, right to judicial review or even (according to widely dominant understanding) to hierarchical complaint within the structure of the PPO.[57] Should a prosecutor issue an EAW in breach of the set

54 In any case, such possibilities do exist in virtually all Member State, at least formally: see ibid 18 f.

55 It is sometimes questioned by the PPO as well, especially during the issuing phase: see ibid 4.

56 See Supreme Court, ruling of 14-02-2019 (ECLI:PT:STJ:2019:120.17.2YREVR.S1.6E); see further in Caeiro and Cardoso (n 29) 7.

57 See Costa and Caeiro (n 12) 295.

legal conditions,[58] the only means of reaction would be *habeas corpus*[59] (Art 220 CCP);[60] however, since in such cases the physical act of detention takes place in another Member State, the Supreme Court has held itself prevented from intervening, on the argument that this would be tantamount to ordering another jurisdiction to execute a Portuguese procedural act in its territory.[61] In such cases, the individual – or executing authorities themselves, *ex officio* – will only be able to question the validity of the EAW on the ground that it was not issued by a judicial authority in the meaning required by the CJEU. However, this can only occur within the procedure in the executing Member State, and therefore does not constitute a true remedy to the very issuing of the EAW.

If the EAW is issued by a judge, it can be appealed by the prosecutor on the grounds that it is illegal or disproportionate. This appeal may be lodged in the High Court[62] or directly to the Supreme Court, where this is permitted.[63] Arguably, the requested person also has the right to lodge appeals against the issuing of an EAW, but it may be difficult to do so due to practical reasons, *i.e.* because the person might not even be aware that an EAW has been issued.[64] If the appeal is successful, the warrant is recalled.[65] Any other challenges to the

58 See Art 257 CCP: "Outside of *flagrante delito*, detention can only be carried out with a warrant from the judge or, in cases where pre-trial custody is admissible, from the Public Prosecution's Office: a) When there are reasonable grounds to believe that the person in question would not voluntarily appear before the judicial authority within the time frame set for them; b) When one of the specific situations provided for in Art 204 occurs, which can only be addressed by detention; or c) If it is essential for the protection of the victim". In turn, Art 202 CCP establishes the offences which allow for pre-trial custody.

59 When Portugal is the issuing authority, a *habeas corpus* appeal will not be admitted after the surrender has taken place; the claim that detention conditions are degrading or inhumane should be raised before the courts of the executing Member State in order to prevent the execution of the EAW in the first place: see Supreme Court, ruling of 23-09-2021 (ECLI:PT:STJ:2021:5553.19.7T8LSB.Q.S1.EA).

60 According to this provision, those detained at the order of any authority may request to be immediately brought before a judge on any of the following grounds: (i) expiry of the term to present the detained before the judge; (ii) keeping of the detention out of the required places; (iii) execution or order of the detention by an authority without competence for that purpose; or (iv) execution of the detention by virtue of a fact for which the law does not allow it.

61 See Supreme Court, ruling of 01-07-2020 (ECLI:PT:STJ:2020:19.20.5JBLSB.A.S1.C6).

62 See Arts 399 and 427 CCP.

63 See Art 432 CCP.

64 In any event, this appeal will not suspend the issuing of the EAW – on the suspensive effect of appeals in Portugal, see Miguel João Costa and Pedro Caeiro (n 12) 308 and 312.

65 See Supreme Court, ruling of 02-12-2013 (ECLI:PT:STJ:2013:962.09.2TBABF.E1.S2.0D), where the challenge to the EAW seems to have been made directly in the Portuguese

execution of an EAW must be made within the EAW procedure in the executing Member State.

When Portugal is the executing Member State, since competence belongs to the High Courts, appeal against the decision to execute (or refuse) the EAW is only possible to the Supreme Court, or to the Constitutional Court on constitutionality issues.[66]

## 3 European Investigation Order: Critical Profiles in Legislation and Case Law

### 3.1 *Scope and Issuing of an EIO*

No issues arise concerning the scope of PT-EIO, as Arts 1 to 5 of the national statute reflect (essentially) Arts 1 to 4 EIO D. Some details are in any case worth mentioning. Art 1(3) EIO D is implemented by 12 (4) PT-EIO, which establishes that an EIO is issued at the initiative of the judicial authority or at the request of procedural subjects, in the same conditions in which they may request the gathering or production of evidence under national criminal procedural law. In turn, Art 6(1) and (2) EIO D is implemented by Art 11(1) and (2) PT-EIO, according to which an EIO may only be issued or validated where it is necessary, adequate and proportional, and the requested measure could have been ordered in the same conditions in a similar domestic case – both of these requirements being assessed by the issuing authority in each case. Art 11(3) – pursuant to the *forum regit actum* type of approach admitted under Art 9(2) EIO D –,[67] further establishes that, should that be the case, the EIO shall indicate the formalities and proceedings to be observed by the executing authority in order to secure the validity and efficacy of the evidence.

(criminal) procedure, rather than within the EAW procedure in the executing Member State (although the person was already detained there).

66 Recall *supra*, § 1.1. It is worth adding that appeals to the Constitutional Court face very stringent conditions – see notably Arts 70 and 72(2) of Law no. 28/82, of 15 November (Law on the Organisation, Functioning and Procedure of the Constitutional Court). This goes a long way to explaining why the mentioned ruling no. 540/2022 is the first (and, thus far, the *only* one) in which this court has ruled on the merits in an EAW case.

67 To be accurate, it is a hybrid approach that seeks to combine different legal systems, with a view to appeasing the concerns of all involved parties, but which ultimately may be deemed to produce practical problems and hamper upon legal certainty: see Vânia Costa Ramos, 'Meios processuais de impugnação da Decisão Europeia de Investigação – subsídios para a interpretação do artigo 14.º da Directiva com uma perspectiva portuguesa' (2018) 7 *Anatomia do Crime* 124–125.

### 3.2 *Execution Procedure and Cooperation Issues between Judicial Authorities*

As for the provisions on time limits for recognition or execution set out in Art 12 EIO D, PT-EIO (Art 26) seems to equate the term 'recognition' to what the EIO D refers to as 'recognition *or execution*' of the EIO,[68] and the term 'execution' to what the EIO D refers to as 'carrying out the investigative measure'. Construed in these terms, the mismatch is only terminological.[69]

Regarding Chapter 4 of the EIO D, on specific provisions for certain investigative measures, there is an implementation problem with Art 22 EIO D, on the temporary transfer to the issuing State of persons held in custody for the purpose of carrying out an investigative measure: Art 22 (4) of that provision in the EIO D establishes that the transit of the person in custody through the territory of a third Member State shall be granted on application, whereas Art 32 (10) PT-EIO admits the transit through national territory or aerial space under authorisation by the Minister of Justice and provided that it does not conflict with reasons of public order or State security; moreover, it prescribes that Art 43 of Law no. 144/99 of 31 August – which is the national statute on international (non-EU) cooperation – applies *mutatis mutandis*. It is highly doubtful that this provides adequate implementation, as the conditions set in the national statute are quite restrictive of the transit. If any conditions are to apply, they should be drawn not from the legal regime of classic cooperation but from norms on EU cooperation, namely from PT-EAW (more specifically from Art 38, implementing Art 25 EAW FD).[70]

Implementation of Art 22(7) EIO D requires some reflection as well. According to this norm, the period of custody in the territory of the issuing State shall be deducted from the period of detention which the person concerned is or will be obliged to undergo in the territory of the executing State; and Art 23(2) establishes that this provision applies, *mutatis mutandis*, to temporary transfers. In turn, Art 32(5) PT-EIO has a broader reach, in more than one sense: on the one hand, because it establishes that the period of custody in the territory of the issuing State and of the State of transit does not suspend the maximum terms of pre-trial custody; on the other hand, concerning deduction of time spent on remand, because it includes the period of deprivation of

---

68 In fact, Art 18 PT-EIO, mentioned in Art 26(1) PT-EIO, refers to 'recognition and execution'.

69 Apart from that, the sole issue to be noted concerns the 'expediency requirements' of Arts 12(4) and 13 EIO D, which are not duly reflected in PT-EIO, as explained in further detail *infra*, § 3.3.

70 Obviously, for geographical reasons, Portugal will seldom be a Member State of transit in the context of EU cooperation.

liberty in the State of transit.[71] Nevertheless, this does not, in our view, conflict with the individual-oriented rationale of the matching provisions of the EIO D. To the contrary, it takes such a protection somewhat further without thereby generating any impunity concerns or meaningful risks to the punitive interests of another Member State.

Other (yet minor) issues concern *e.g.* Art 7(5) EIO D (13(5) PT-EIO), on the transmission of the EIO,[72] Art 16(1) EIO D (25 PT-EIO), on the obligation to inform,[73] and Art 19(3) EIO D (16 PT-EIO),[74] on the protection of confidentiality. The breach of confidentiality is precisely among the most interesting cooperation issues that have surfaced in national case law, namely in the ruling of the High Court of Lisbon of 7 February 2019,[75] on the offences of swindle and/or computer swindle and involving Portugal and Poland. The latter issued an EIO with a view to obtaining certain information on the activity of the Portuguese affiliate of a Polish brokerage company. The Portuguese Market and Securities Commission (CMVM) refused to provide such information to Portuguese authorities, invoking professional confidentiality. The PPO requested the judge of instruction to order the breach of confidentiality. The judge held the confidentiality claim of the CMVM valid, but submitted the case to the High Court of Lisbon so that it would evaluate whether, in the light of the principle of

71 Concerning sanctions applied by Portugal, this would already follow from Arts 80 f. Penal Code (PC) – on which see Maria João Antunes, *Penas e Medidas de Segurança* (2nd ed., Coimbra: Almedina, 2022) 80 f.

72 Namely concerning the event where the identity of the executing authority is unknown: while Art 7(5) EIO D states that, in such an event, the issuing authority "shall make all necessary inquiries (...)", Art 13(5) PT-EIO simply establishes that "[a]ssistance may be requested to the central authority, the national member of EUROJUST or the contact points of the European Judicial Network (...)".

73 Art 25 PT-EIO effects only a partial implementation of Art 16(1) EIO D, as it does not comprise the prescription of its second sentence: "Where a central authority has been designated in accordance with Art 7(3), this obligation is applicable both to the central authority and to the executing authority which receives the EIO from the central authority."

74 According to Art 16 PT-EIO: "The issuing authority shall not disclose any evidence or information provided by the executing authority which are subject to the obligation of secrecy of confidentiality, except to the extent that its disclosure is authorised by its national law and does not contravene the indication by the executing authority." This provision does not state 'except to the extent that its disclosure is necessary for the investigations or proceedings described in the EIO'. It is unclear whether this poses an actual implementation problem, but it appears to be at least a case of deficient implementation, the national provision being less protective of confidentiality than the corresponding provision in the Directive.

75 High Court of Lisbon, ruling of 7 February 2019 (ECLI:PT:TRL:2019:7078.18.9T9LSB.A.L1.9.00).

prevalence of the preponderant interest, confidentiality should be broken – to which the court replied affirmatively, thus enabling the execution of the EIO.[76]

### 3.3 *Grounds for Non-recognition and Non-execution*

The general duty enshrined in Art 9(1) EIO D to recognise and execute EIOs issued by fellow Member States is reflected in Art 18(1) PT-EIO.

However, there seems to be an implementation issue concerning Art 9(2) EIO D: the latter requires executing Member States to comply with the formalities and procedures expressly indicated by issuing Member States unless they are contrary to the "fundamental principles of law of the executing State", whereas the corresponding national provision (Art 18(2)) allows for non-compliance with such formalities and procedures if they would contravene (any) "requirements and conditions of national law on evidence". PT-EIO thus appears to be stricter than the EIO D, with the latter intending for non-compliance to be more exceptional. And the wording of the national statute can hardly be seen as inadvertent, as (4), *in fine*, of this very same provision of the EIO D (Art 9) was implemented into Art 27(1) PT-EIO with mention to "fundamental principles" rather than to "requirements and conditions". In practice, Art 18(2) PT-EIO is deemed to be usually applied narrowly, so as to cover fundamental principles only,[77] but the fact is that its wording does leave room for a broader application, which in our view justifies that it be deemed as only partially implemented.

Art 9(3) EIO D – according to which the executing authority that receives an EIO that has not been issued by an issuing authority, as specified in Art 2(c), shall return it to the issuing Member State – also raises an implementation issue, which, however, seems possible to overcome. While there is no provision in PT-EIO explicitly implementing Art 9(3), Art 18(1) PT-EIO, mentioned above, presupposes that the EIO was issued by "the competent issuing

76 The Court held that such a weighing should consider whether the information at issue is indispensable for uncovering the truth of the facts, the gravity of the offence and the necessity to protect legal interests (i.e. positive general prevention). In the case, it held the information indispensable and the offence serious, in view of the considerably high damages that it caused. It further noted that the disclosure of the information would not, in the case, carry any damage (commercial or otherwise) to the company at issue. From this decision it is not possible to grasp that the case involved an EIO; this becomes apparent only from the ruling later proffered by the Supreme Court in the same case.

77 See Vânia Costa Ramos, 'Problemas da Obtenção de Prova em Contexto Transnacional – Introdução' (2013) 4 *Revista Portuguesa de Ciência Criminal* 555 f.; *id.*, 'Admissibility of Evidence, Transnational E-Evidence and Fair Trial Rights in Portugal' in Lorena Bachmaier and Farsam Salimi (eds.), *Admissibility of Evidence in EU Cross-Border Criminal Proceedings: Electronic Evidence, Efficiency and Fair Trial Rights* (Oxford: Hart, 2024) 127 f.

authority" of another Member State, which under Art 3(c) PT-EIO must be an authority as specified in Art 2(c) EIO D. The fact remains that the return of the EIO to the issuing Member State on these grounds is not explicitly provided for, but it can arguably be carried out through an application by analogy of Art 20(3) PT-EIO. The latter, indeed, enables for such a return where the EIO has not been translated or fails to comply with other formalities set out in Art 6 PT-EIO (corresponding to Art 5 EIO D).

The grounds for non-recognition of Art 11(1) EIO D are implemented into Art 22(1) PT-EIO. This national provision does not begin by recalling the obligation to respect fundamental rights as provided for in Art 1(4)[78] (a provision which as such has not been perfectly implemented into the PT-EIO),[79] but this does not seem indispensable, as Art 22(1)(g) PT-EIO (implementing Art 11(1)(f) EIO D) gives fundamental rights the standing of an actual ground for non-execution, as opposed to a mere proclamation of principle as that of Recital 12 EAW FD, in what seems to constitute a natural post-*Aranyosi and Căldăraru* development.

In our view, the only *actual* implementation issue concerning Art 11 EIO D relates to the first sentence of (5) – according to which, in the case referred to in (1)(a), and where the power to waive the privilege or immunity lies with an authority of the executing State, the executing authority shall request it to exercise that power "forthwith". Such an expediency requirement is not to be found in Art 22(5) PT-EIO. Something similar occurs with other provisions in the Directive *vis-à-vis* the corresponding provisions in national law.[80] Trivial though these issues might be, in our view they prevent perfect implementation, conflicting with the mindset of swiftness that the EIO D seeks to introduce.

Apart from that, the only aspect worthy of reflection is that all the grounds for non-execution provided for in EIO D Art 11 were implemented into the

78 According to which the EIO D "shall not have the effect of modifying the obligation to respect the fundamental rights and legal principles (…)".

79 Criticising the lack of implementation of Art 1(4) and apparently construing it as an actual implementation problem, see Costa Ramos (n 67) 138 f.; *Id.*, 'Decisão Europeia de Investigação' (2019) II *Revista do Centro de Estudos Judiciários* 99.

80 Notably in: Art 12 (on time limits for recognition or execution) (4) EIO D ("without delay") vis-à-vis Art 26(2) PT-EIO, and Art 13 (on transfer of evidence) (1)(§ 1) EIO D ("without undue delay") *vis-à-vis* Art 23(1) and (2) PT-EIO. Again, it seems implausible that this was unintended, as other provisions in the EIO D containing requirements of the same kind – *e.g.*, Arts 11(4) ("without delay"), 12(6) (*idem*), 15(2) ("forthwith"), 16(1) ("without delay"), 16(2) ("immediately", "without delay"), 16(3) ("without delay"), 19(2) (*idem*) and 31(3) (*idem*) – are duly reflected in the national statute: see, respectively, Arts 22(4), 26(6), 24(2), 25(1), 25(3) and (4), 25(5), 30(2) and 43(3).

national statute Art 22 as optional (in the sense of discretionary).[81] However, some of them are hardly compatible with a decision of an optional character, an example of which is the ground contained in (b) – *i.e.*, the case where the execution of the EIO would harm (*inter alia*) "essential national security interests". Where this risk does exist, it is difficult to envisage on the basis of which other criteria an authority might decide whether to cooperate (due to that risk) or to refuse to cooperate (in spite of that risk).

A recurring issue in the (still rather scarce) case law on the EIO in the Portuguese legal system concerns the interplay between the issuing of an EAW and the use of the EIO system.[82] The question is well illustrated by a ruling of the Supreme Court of 3 June 2020,[83] in a case of participation in a criminal organisation and drug trafficking where France had issued an EAW. Invoking mutual trust and mutual recognition, the Supreme Court held that, although a claim might be reasonable in a given case that an EAW is disproportional or inadequate in view of existing alternatives, such as the EIO – *e.g.*, in order to hear the concerned person by videoconference[84] –, the choice to make use of an arrest warrant rather than of other mechanisms that are less detrimental to individual rights falls within the exclusive remit of issuing authorities. Thus, it cannot be disputed by the executing ones, as it does not integrate any ground for non-execution of the EAW. Such is the consistent understanding of national case law on this issue.[85]

81 In the same vein as in the context of the EAW FD: see *supra*, § 2.3. At first sight, the option to implement all grounds for non-execution as merely discretionary could suggest an attitude of adherence to the principle of mutual recognition on the part of the Portuguese legislator. However, since those grounds were merely optional under the EIO D, then Portugal could also have chosen not to implement some of them *at all* (*i.e.* either as discretionary or as mandatory), which would have been even more 'adherent'. This is arguably another example of acritical implementation on the part of the Portuguese legislator.

82 Draft Law no. 193/XIII/4 – which led to an amendment of PT-EAW (through Law no. 115/2019, of 12 September) – already mentioned 'some entropy' in the articulation between these two legal instruments: see <https://www.parlamento.pt/ActividadeParlamentar/Paginas/DetalheIniciativa.aspx?BID=43589>.

83 Supreme Court, ruling of 3 June 2020 (ECLI:PT:STJ:2020:793.20.9YRLSB.S1).

84 See Recital 26 EIO D.

85 See *e.g.* High Court of Lisbon, rulings of 05-05-2021, on extradition but referring *obiter dictum* to the EIO (ECLI:PT:TRL:2021:243.21.3YRLSB.3.7B), and of 09-03-2023 (ECLI:PT:TRL:2023:3519.22.9YRLSB.9.1D), as well as High Court of Évora, rulings of 18-02-2020 (ECLI:PT:TRE:2020:103.19.8YREVR.87) and of 23-03-2021 (ECLI:PT:TRE:2021:34.21.1YREVR.79).

### 3.4 *Issues for the Rights of the Suspect or Accused Person*

A relevant issue surfacing in the case law concerns the use in national criminal proceedings of evidence obtained through an EIO in national criminal proceedings. An example is the ruling of the High Court of Lisbon of 11 April 2023,[86] in a case of aggravated drug trafficking and criminal association. The question of interest for these purposes was the applicability of pre-trial custody, which requires 'strong evidence' that the defendant committed a given crime. In the case, most such evidentiary basis had been obtained from France pursuant to an EIO. The defendant argued that in order for it to be admissible, he should have been given access to the court orders issued by French authorities for obtaining evidence, as well as the opportunity to contest them. The evidence concerned personal (digital) data stored in a server. The court noted that decisions to *issue* an EIO can only be challenged in the issuing Member State, and that in the case the evidence had not been obtained in the context of a criminal procedure running course in Portugal but in that of a Joint Investigation Team (JIT) set up between France and the Netherlands. Portugal issued an EIO only because in that context evidence had emerged, suggesting that a criminal organisation was operating in Portuguese territory (using the encrypted communication equipment *Encrochat*). In fact – the Court held –, what was at issue was a mere transfer of data that had already been collected and preserved by foreign authorities. Since Art 125 CCP, which enshrines the principle of legality of the evidence, allows for the use of any evidence that is not prohibited by law, and since there is no legal prohibition on the use of evidence already obtained in another Member State, it followed that such information transmitted by France could also be used. As for the validity of the gathering of that evidence, the Court held that it could not be challenged, considering the principle of mutual trust.[87] Arguably, even if the national exclusionary rules contained (*inter alia*) in Art 126 CPP[88] were not applicable in such cases, Art 125 CCP is itself less permissive than the High Court seemed to suggest, as it does not simply exclude evidence which is *explicitly* prohibited by law, but it also excludes, *e.g.*, atypical evidence (that is, evidence obtained through means that are neither explicitly prohibited nor permitted) which in

86 High Court of Lisbon, ruling of 11 April 2023 (ECLI:PT:TRL:2023:267.21.0JELSB.Q.L1.5.FF).

87 In the same vein, concerning the encrypted communication system *SKY ECC*, see also High Court of Lisbon, ruling of 26-04-2023 (ECLI:PT:TRL:2023:267.21.0JELSB.W.L1.5.3E).

88 Notably, those contained in Art 126(3) CCP, which establishes that, apart from evidence obtained through the means provided for in the law (*e.g.*, the interception of telecommunications), evidence obtained through an intrusion into the private life, domicile, correspondence or telecommunications of a person without his or her (prior) consent is null and cannot be used as evidence.

essence contravenes the protection that exclusionary rules seek to provide.[89] The very recent decision of the CJEU in *M.N.* (*EncroChat*)[90] could command a different outcome for this type of cases than the one reached by the High Court, although more on the strength of the focus it placed upon the principle *audi alteram partem* than upon exclusionary rules as such.

Also relevant is the ruling of the High Court of Coimbra of 7 June 2023, in a case of aggravated rape.[91] The defendant had been acquitted in first Instance based on *in dubio pro reo*. One argument substantiating the existence of reasonable doubt was that, during the pre-trial stage, the statements of the victim were taken by videoconference (pursuant to an EIO) with her father standing next to her: this could have affected her spontaneity and truthfulness. On appeal, the High Court of Coimbra found no plausible reason for doubting that the presence of the father (who had made the complaint in the case) could have affected the statements. Otherwise – the Court noted – the judge of instruction would presumably have suspended the questioning and called the victim to make the statements in presence.[92] Moreover, and very meaningfully, the report of the psychologist attached to the case file indicated that no influence had been detected in the statements of the victim.

Another relevant issue is that as to whether the issuing of a EIO suspends the maximum terms of the phase of inquiry set out in Art 276 CCP. This issue was discussed in the ruling of the High Court of Porto of 10 March 2021,[93] concerning money laundering and involving Portugal and Spain, the former being the issuing and the latter the executing Member State. In the same criminal proceedings, a rogatory letter was also issued by Portugal to Switzerland. In Portugal, the maximum terms of the inquiry are generally seen to be merely indicative,[94] but they have an indirect impact on the subsistence of certain measures affecting fundamental individual rights (in that these may not be maintained beyond those terms): in the case, the temporary suspension of the

89 See Pedro Soares de Albergaria, 'Artigo 125.º Legalidade da Prova' in António Gama and others, *Comentário Judiciário do Código de Processo Penal – Tomo II: Artigos 124.º a 190.º* (3.ª ed., Coimbra: Almedina, 2021)36 f.

90 Case C-670/22 *M.N.* (*EncroChat*) [2024] EU:C:2024:372.

91 Case no. 793/21.1JALRA.C1, available at <http://www.dgsi.pt/jtrc.nsf/c3fb530030ea1c61802568d9005cd5bb/99f55eca540d33fc802589d3004e8cf6?OpenDocument> accessed 14 July 2024.

92 Pursuant to Arts 271(8) and 340(1) CCP.

93 High Court of Porto, ruling of 10 March 2021 (ECLI:PT:TRP:2021:109.19.7TELSB.C.P1.D8).

94 But see Cláudia Cruz Santos, 'O Controlo Judicial da Violação dos Prazos de Duração Máxima do Inquérito' (2017) 32 *Julgar* 233 f.

execution of bank operations from a given bank account.[95] Art 276(5) CCP provides that such maximum terms are suspended (albeit only for up to half of the applicable maximum term) when a rogatory letter is issued, but it does not mention the issuing of an EIO specifically. The pertinent question is whether the reference to 'rogatory letter' should at present be construed in such a way as to encompass the EIO, which did not yet exist when that norm of the CPP was enacted and last amended. Departing from the decision taken by a lower court earlier in the case, the High Court ruled that it should *not*, based on the following arguments: (i) despite their functional similarity, an EIO and a rogatory letter have different scopes, characteristics and procedures, the former being much swifter; (ii) the CCP was amended several times after the entry into force of PT-EIO, and yet the legislator did not add any reference to it in this provision; (iii) this provision has an exceptional character and it carries not only procedural but also substantive effects of impact to fundamental rights. The Court thus agreed – and, in our view, rightly so – with the argumentation of the appeal lodged by the defendants. Ultimately, however, the decision was not entirely favourable to them, as the Court also found that the maximum terms of the inquiry had been rightfully suspended on *other* grounds, namely on the strength of exceptional Covid-19 legislation.[96]

### 3.5 *Remedies*

The implementation of Art 14 EIO D, on legal remedies, raises some issues. In the first place, it is doubtful that Art 14(2) has been fully implemented, since PT-EIO contains no explicit reference to fundamental rights. In national legal literature it has been advocated that in certain situations it is possible to question before a Portuguese court the lawfulness and proportionality – the two core components of the concept of "substantive reasons" – of an EIO issued by another Member State, as well as to contest that it is based on a sufficient degree of suspicion.[97] Specifically, this might be possible where the investigative measure at issue is intrusive to fundamental rights and it is not possible to dissociate the analysis of legality from that of proportionality, including insofar as concerns special requisites on the intensity of the suspicion; and where

---

95 Arts 48 f. (esp. Art 49(2)) of Law no. 83/2017, of 18 August, which, inter alia, transposes in part the Directive (EU) 2015/849 of 20 May 2015 and the Directive (EU) 2016/2258 of 6 December 2016.

96 This ruling trails the line of (and on this topic is more detailed than) High Court of Porto, ruling of 27-01-2021 (ECLI:PT:TRP:2021:109.19.7TELSB.B.P1.44); and this case law was further reiterated in High Court of Porto, ruling of 03-05-2023 (ECLI:PT:TRP:2023:4941.21.3T9PRT.D.P1.42).

97 See Costa Ramos (n 67) 129 f., with further references.

there is no remedy available in the issuing State.[98] This stance – which finds some support in the ruling of the CJEU in *Gavanozov II*[99] – relies on the national provisions implementing Art 14(2) *in fine* EIO D (*i.e.*, Art 45(2) PT-EIO) and Art 11(1)(f) EIO D (*i.e.*, Art 22(1)(g) PT-EIO), the latter of which permits non-execution of an EIO where there are substantial grounds to believe that its execution would be incompatible with the obligations of the executing Member State under Art 6 TEU and the Charter of Fundamental Rights of the EU (CFREU). At the very least, the legislator should clarify this issue. In the second place, Art 45(5) PT-EIO does not establish that information on legal remedies should be provided "when these become applicable and in due time to ensure that they can be exercised effectively", as required by Art 14(3) EIO D.[100]

Apart from that, implementation has been accomplished, although some clarifications should be provided, the most relevant of which concerns Art 14(4) EIO D. Art 45(3) and (4) PT-EIO state that: "When Portugal is the issuing State, the decision ordering the investigation measure and, thus, the issuing of the EIO, are governed, in their admissibility and regime, by the rules of the CCP"; "When Portugal is the executing State, judicial decisions on the formalities and proceedings concerning the carrying out of the investigation measure can be appealed before Portuguese courts, in the terms provided for in the CCP on their admissibility and their regime."

This leads to the following regime, in the case where Portugal is the executing Member State:[101] (i) If the procedure is in the trial phase in the issuing Member State, competence for executing the EIO falls with a court of first instance,[102] whose decisions may be challenged before that very court or a High Court.[103] A decision of a High Court can only be appealed to the Supreme Court with a view to settling a jurisprudential conflict or if it contravenes settled jurisprudence.[104] (ii) The same applies if the EIO is issued before the trial

98 See ibid., further submitting that the same result can be achieved through Art 21 PT-EIO (10 EIO D), as it presupposes a proportionality assessment, whether made *ex ante* and in the abstract by the legislator, or in the case at hand by the competent executing authority.

99 Case C-852/19 *Ivan Gavanozov* [2021] EU:C:2021:902, although this ruling is focused on the issuing State as such. On this ruling see *idem*, '*Gavanozov II* and the need to go further beyond in establishing effective remedies for violations of EU fundamental rights' (*EU Law Live Op-Ed*, 22 November 2021) <https://eulawlive.com/op-ed-gavanozov-ii-and-the-need-to-go-further-beyond-in-establishing-effective-remedies-for-violations-of-eu-fundamental-rights-by-vania-costa-ramos/> accessed 14 July 2024.

100 See also Costa Ramos (n 67) 150 f.

101 See Costa and Caeiro (n 9) 295 f.; Costa Ramos (n 67) 145 f.

102 Art 19(3) and (6) PT-EIO.

103 See Arts 118 f., 399 f., 427 and 432 CCP.

104 See Arts 437(2) and 446 CCP.

phase in the issuing Member State and the competent executing authority is an investigative judge.[105] In contrast, if the competent executing authority is the PPO, then it is less clear that judicial review of the measure can be requested.[106] However, it has been argued – convincingly, in our view – that such a possibility is necessary to ensure respect for the constitutional principle *audi alteram partem*, in which case the ensuing judicial decision could yet be appealed.[107] Such a view underscores the particularities of criminal proceedings with transnational elements *vis-à-vis* 'ordinary' criminal proceedings, notably the fact that, in the case of the former, if Portugal is the executing Member State, there is no possibility later in the proceedings to obtain a judicial assessment of the prosecutorial decision by an investigative or a trial judge.

Last, if the execution of the EIO involves the police – which are not executing or issuing authorities under PT-EIO, but which may provide collaboration to the judicial authorities –, their intervention may be challenged before the PPO or a judge, depending on which of them is the 'executing authority' based on the above regime. In turn, the decision taken thereon by these authorities follows the conditions indicated above under (i) and (ii), respectively. The same applies to the case where Portugal is the issuing Member State, with the particularity that the acts of the PPO during the inquiry can be reviewed during the instruction by a judge, whose decisions are then yet open to complaint based on Art 291(2) CCP.[108]

## 4 Regulation 1805/2018: Critical Profiles in Legislation and Case Law

### 4.1 *Legal Basis in the National System and Scope*

The Portuguese legal system contains three types of confiscation of instruments and proceeds of (criminally) unlawful acts: (i) classic confiscation of instruments (Arts 109(1) PC and 12-B(1) of Law 5/2002, of 11 January, on the Fight against Organised and Economic and Financial Crime); (ii) classic

105 As it must per force be the case when the requested investigative measure is offensive to fundamental rights: see Art 19(1) PT-EIO and Arts 268 and 269 CCP.

106 See *supra*, § 1.1.

107 See Costa Ramos (n 67) 146–149, noting that there is diverging case law on this issue and that a dominant interpretation is yet to emerge.

108 Ibid 148. One of the few relevant rulings on remedies is High Court of Lisbon, ruling of 27-01-2023 (ECLI:PT:TRL:2023:298.22.3YUSTR.L1.PICRS.39), concerning an administrative offence, where the involved Member States were Portugal and Germany, and where the concerned entity was a legal person.

confiscation of proceeds (Art 110(1) PC);[109] and (iii) extended confiscation (Art 7(1) of Law 5/2002).

The first is subject to two core requirements: the commission of a criminally unlawful act and the dangerousness of the instruments. The second requires the commission of a criminally unlawful act as well, and the existence of proceeds generated by such act. According to a classification based on the "proximity of the confiscation scheme to the predicate offence", where "each generation of confiscation regimes moves one step further away from that offence", they both constitute *"first generation"* confiscation modalities.[110] Their common requirement (a criminally unlawful act) does not presuppose criminal liability nor, *a fortiori*, a conviction (*actus reus* and *mens rea*).[111] Rather, it will be met if the fact exists (*"perché il fatto sussiste"*), regardless of whether it constitutes a crime (*i.e.*, not *"perché il fatto costituisce reato"*).[112] These types of confiscation can therefore be applied even if the defendant is acquitted, becomes deceased in the course of the proceedings or is declared to be in procedural default (*contumácia*)[113] – provided, of course, that the fact is shown to exist[114] – and in this sense they can be non-conviction-based. If confiscation in kind is not possible, it shall be replaced by the payment of the amount matching the value of the proceeds. Confiscation of instruments and proceeds belonging to third parties is admissible and is regulated in Art 111 PC.

109 Although Portuguese law subjects 'products' and 'proceeds' (Art 110(1)(a) and (b) PC) to an identical regime, it confers some autonomy on these concepts: critically, see António Vaz de Castro, *A identificação da natureza penal de uma consequência jurídica no direito português – Os critérios Engel na jurisprudência do TEDH e o confisco das vantagens do facto ilícito-típico como ponto de partida e ponto de chegada* (Coimbra: UCILeR (forthcoming 2024)).

110 See Johan Boucht, 'Confiscation' in Pedro Caeiro, Sabine Gless, Valsamis Mitsilegas, Miguel João Costa, Janneke De Snaijer, Georgia Theodorakakou (eds.), *Elgar Encyclopedia of Crime and Criminal Justice* (Cheltenham: Elgar, 2024) § 11.3 <https://doi.org/10.4337/9781789902990.confiscation>. On the ever-increasing distance between the predicate offence and confiscation, see António Vaz de Castro, 'O Confisco Moderno na Sociedade da Transparência: a sua Natureza, o seu Fundamento, um Descafeinado e a Conta' in Norberto Martins and João Conde Correia (coord.) *O confisco não baseado numa condenação: 40 anos depois do código penal e 20 anos depois da Lei n.º 5/2002, o crime continua a compensar?* (Coimbra: Almedina, 2023) 48–50.

111 *I.e.*, it does not require a "verdict as to [the] guilt" of the person: *Varvara v. Italy* App no. 17475/09 (ECHR, 29 October 2013), § 72.

112 *Sud Fondi s.r.l. and Others v. Italy* App no. 75909/01 (ECHR, 20 January 2009), para. 65.

113 Arts 109(2) and 110(5) PC.

114 Acquittal is not limited to specific and exhaustive grounds determined by the law, contrary to what seems to have been the option of the European legislator in the Art 15 ("Non-conviction-based confiscation") of the recent Directive (EU) 2024/1260 of 24 April 2024 on asset recovery and confiscation.

Extended confiscation – the "*second generation*" of confiscation modalities[115] – is provided for in Law no. 5/2002. Its conditions are set out in Art 7 therein, and their cumulative verification gives rise to a legal presumption that, if not rebutted, allows the State to confiscate the value of the convict's unexplained property. The conditions are: conviction for an offence listed in the catalogue of Art 1(1) of that statute (that is, in this case the person must actually be held criminally liable); and disproportionate wealth (*i.e.*, a "difference between the value of the actual property of the defendant and that which is consistent with his/her lawful income"). The view has been submitted in national legal literature that extended confiscation requires a third condition: that the court be persuaded of the convict's previous *criminal activity* (not necessarily crimes or even offences, in all their elements), of the kind included in the catalogue of Art 1(1) of Law no. 5/2002.[116] The presumption will be established unless the assets at issue were held by the individual for at least 5 years prior to being designated as a defendant or were acquired with income obtained in that period, and it will only be possible to rebut by proving that the assets "result from income of lawful activity" (Art 9(3)(a)).

In Portuguese law, a 'freezing order' can be a procedural guarantee of the confiscation of assets (Art 178 CCP – *apreensão*), and also a procedural guarantee of the payment of the value of the instruments and proceeds (Arts 228 CCP – *arresto preventivo* – and Art 10 of Law no. 5/2002 – *arresto*). Each of those has a specific regime.

A central issue raised by the Regulation concerns its scope of application, which according to Art 1(1) thereto consists of "freezing orders and confiscation orders issued by another Member State within the framework of proceedings in criminal matters" ("*processos em matéria penal*"). Recital 13 assists in determining what "proceedings in criminal matters" should be taken to be. Through a positive and negative delimitation of this expression, the criterion seems to be the *object* that is confiscated or frozen: proceeds or instruments

115 See Boucht (n 110), § II.4.

116 See José Damião da Cunha, *Perda de bens a favor do Estado. Arts 7.º–12.º da Lei 5/2002, de 11 de Janeiro (Medidas de combate à Criminalidade Organizada e Económico-Financeira)* (Coimbra: Coimbra Editora, 2004) 11–17; Pedro Caeiro, 'Sentido e função do instituto da perda de vantagens relacionadas com o crime no confronto com outros meios de prevenção da criminalidade reditícia (em especial os procedimentos *in rem* e a criminalização do enriquecimento «ilícito»)' (2011) 21 *Revista Portuguesa de Ciência Criminal* 314–316. Upholding the opposite view, João Conde Correia, *Da Proibição do Confisco à Perda Alargada* (Lisboa: Imprensa Nacional – Casa da Moeda, 2012) 110; António Vaz de Castro (n 109). The latter is also the view followed by the courts: see *e.g.* Supreme Court, ruling of 24-10-2006 (06P3163).

of a criminal offence. This is corroborated by the provisions of Arts 2(1) of the Regulation ("with a view to the confiscation thereof") and 2(2) ("in relation to a criminal offence"). In this light, the manner in which confiscation is carried out or the specific terms of the freezing order are immaterial, the key point lying instead on whether they have the function of limiting ownership or possession over proceeds or instruments of a criminal offence (Art 2(4) and (5)). The scope of the Regulation therefore encompasses all modalities of confiscation of proceeds and instruments of criminally unlawful acts.[117] As for freezing orders, naturally, the Regulation only applies to the freezing of proceeds or instruments of *criminally* unlawful acts, which arguably excludes the confiscation of proceeds and instruments originating directly or indirectly from an *administrative* offence.[118]

According to this understanding, all Portuguese methods of confiscation of the proceeds and instruments of criminally unlawful acts, including extended confiscation, fall within the scope of the Regulation. So does the freezing of instruments or proceeds (*apreensão*), as well as the *arresto*, since Art 2(3)(a) and (b) of the Regulation allows for the confiscation or freezing of the value of proceeds and instruments.[119] Even if the expression "proceedings in criminal matters" were to be interpreted in a different sense, Portuguese confiscation orders and all the mentioned freezing orders would arguably still fall within that scope, because these orders are applied following criminal proceedings and they can be issued without a final conviction – and as noted Recital 13 explicitly indicates that these cases fall within the concept of "proceedings in criminal matters".

117 With this view, see Anna Maria Maugeri, "Regulation (EU) 2018/1805: Mutual recognition of freezing and confiscation orders between efficiency and safeguards. Athina Sachoulidou, '«Proceedings in criminal matters» and non-conviction based confiscation"' (2024) *New Journal of European Criminal Law* 43 <https://doi.org/10.1177/20322844241239781>; Hélio Rodrigues, 'Cooperação judiciária em casos de confisco não baseado numa condenação' in Maria Raquel Desterro Ferreira, Elina Lopes Cardoso and João Conde Correia (coord.), *Cooperação Internacional para Efeitos de Recuperação de Activos* (Coimbra: Almedina, 2021) 186–187. But see Anabela Miranda Rodrigues, 'O Regulamento (UE) 2018/1805, de 14 de Novembro de 2018, relativo ao reconhecimento mútuo das decisões de apreensão e perda como pedra angular da cooperação judiciária na União Europeia – eficácia *versus* direitos fundamentais?', in ibid 45.

118 The opposite view is upheld by João Conde Correia, 'Reconhecimento mútuo de decisões de apreensão e de confisco: o Regulamento (EU) 2018/1805 do Parlamento Europeu e do Conselho de 14 de Novembro de 2018' (2019) 39 *Julgar* 197 f.

119 See João Conde Correia (n 118) 198 f.; on these different modalities and respective legal instruments, see in further detail the Portuguese report in https://site.unibo.it/facilex/en.

### 4.2 *Grounds for Non-recognition and Non-execution*

According to Art 8(1) of Law no. 25/2009, implementing the Framework Decision 2003/577/JHA, recognition and execution of freezing orders *shall* be refused when one of the circumstances described therein is met. The matching provision of the Regulation (Art 8(1)) uses instead the expression "may" refuse. The same occurs with Art 13(1) of Law no. 88/2009, implementing the Framework Decision 2006/783/JHA when compared to Art 19(1) of the Regulation, on confiscation orders. By establishing a mere option not to recognise or execute, the Regulation narrows the room for refusal and correlatively increases the room for cooperation. However, some grounds for refusal, by their very nature, are incompatible with judicial discretion (in the same vein as in the context of the EAW FD,[120] but with the particularity that, in the context of the Regulation, the responsibility to determine criteria on the basis of which to refuse or grant cooperation is transferred *directly* to the courts, and not to the legislator, which by definition does not *implement* a Regulation). In that sense, the fact that the Regulation conceives of all grounds for refusal as optional is, in our view, a problem in and of itself. As for how the courts are actually interpreting such an option to refuse (more narrowly or broadly, in a more or a less cooperation-friendly way), it has been impossible to ascertain, given the absence of publicly available case law on confiscation and freezing orders in Portugal. One can only speculate, for instance, whether those grounds for refusal are being interpreted in line with the previous legislation whereby some of them were mandatory and others discretionary. Such unavailability of case law (as well as of statistical data on these cooperation instruments) is highly problematic. It prevents an assessment as to whether in the Portuguese legal system the norms of the Regulation are being applied properly – or applied *tout court*.

Arts 8(1)(b) and 19(1)(b) of the Regulation also entail a modification of the regime established in Art 8(1)(b) Law no. 25/2009 and in Art 13(1)(e) Law no. 88/2009, as in addition to a privilege or immunity under the law of the executing State, they include as a ground for refusal the existence of rules on the determination or limitation of criminal liability relating to the freedom of press or the freedom of expression in other media that prevent the execution of the freezing order. The Regulation therefore here seems to broaden the scope of this ground for refusal – or, at the very least, it clarifies its breadth.

120 Recall *supra*, § 2.3, § 3.3, and again Caeiro and Costa (n 50) 267 f., drawing attention to the conflation – which is visible also in official documents (*e.g.* in COM(2020) 270 final, 2.07.2020, 15, 17 f. *et passim*) – between the optional character of a ground for refusal and the type of the assessment that it requires from the courts.

There is also a novelty with the creation of a new ground for refusal in Arts 8(1)(d) and 19(1)(d) of the Regulation, namely where freezing and confiscation orders (respectively) relate to conduct committed in whole or in part in the territory of the executing Member State and not criminalised there: double criminality applies here even in relation to the offences listed in the catalogue, and its association with territoriality arguably constitutes as a manifestation of the principle of non-interference.[121] However, the Regulation does not contain grounds for refusal on territoriality and extraterritorial jurisdiction in identical circumstances – either for freezing or for confiscation orders. As a result, under Portuguese law, these remain provided for in Art 13(2)(b) Law no. 88/2009 for confiscation orders (in the terms permitted by Art 8(2)(f) of Framework Decision 2006/783/JHA).

Last, refusal of freezing and confiscation orders on fundamental rights grounds is also a novelty. Arts 8(1)(f) and 19(1)(h) of the Regulation may be seen as a natural normative development in view of *Aranyosi and Căldăraru* case law, in that they give formal expression to fundamental rights as grounds for refusal. In fact, they go so far as to encompass (any) "relevant fundamental right as set out in the Charter, in particular the right to an effective remedy, the right to a fair trial or the right of defence", which finds no parallel in preexisting legislation.

### 4.3 *Issues for the Rights of the Defendant*

Arguably, one effect of the Regulation covering all Portuguese modalities of confiscation and freezing is that Portugal is obliged to apply the essential safeguards set out in the Charter to proceedings in criminal matters that are not criminal proceedings but which are covered by the Regulation. Such is the conclusion suggested by Recital 18 of the Regulation.[122]

Admittedly, the concept of "essential safeguards" is unclear, but Recital 18 does display the potential to impact the domestic laws of the Member States regarding cases covered by the Regulation that are not criminal cases.[123] The history of the (non-)application of criminal procedural rights to confiscation

---

121 See Pedro Caeiro, *Fundamento, Conteúdo e Limites da Jurisdição Penal do Estado – O Caso Português* (Coimbra: Wolters Kluwer | Coimbra Editora 2010) 355 f.

122 Note that the Directives mentioned in this Recital "invariably concern the rights of persons suspected or accused of having committed criminal offences, and, therefore, *leave outside their scope of protection property owners and other third parties who are not themselves targets of criminal suspicion in such proceedings*": Nuno Brandão, 'The Right of Defence under Regulation (EU) 2018/1805, on the mutual recognition of freezing orders and confiscation orders' (2022) 13 *New Journal of European Criminal Law* 40.

123 See also Maugeri (n 117) 22–24.

procedures is intertwined with that of the recognition of the ECtHR's *Engel* criteria to the various confiscation procedures. Over the last few decades, the States under the jurisdiction of the ECtHR have argued before the Court that their confiscation methods – not so much those that are preconditioned by a criminally unlawful act ("offence-based confiscation"),[124] but mainly those that are not – are not criminal in nature, such that the rights arising from Arts 6(2) and (3) and 7 ECHR should not apply to them. As a result, national legislators are endowed with greater leeway to attain the desired effectiveness in this field. This was *e.g.* the case in: (classic confiscation of third parties) *Agosi, Air Canada, Yildirim, Dassa*; (extended confiscation) *Welch, Phillips, Van Offeren, Geerings*; (civil forfeiture) *Butler, Webb, Walsh, Gogitidze*; ("*confisca preventiva*") *Marandino, Raimondo, Arcuri, Riela*; ("*confisca urbanística*") *Sud Fondi, Varvara, G.I.E.M.*[125]

Of all those cases, only in *Welch, Geerings, Sud Fondi, Varvara* and *G.I.E.M.* did the ECtHR conclude that the types of confiscation at issue were criminal in nature and required application of the safeguards for criminal proceedings contained in the ECHR. Indeed, the dominant view of the Court has been that those safeguards do not necessarily apply to confiscation, because this legal consequence is not criminal in nature. Recital 18, however, by commanding the application of such safeguards in all cases covered by the Regulation, even if they are not criminal cases,[126] conflicts with that seemingly consolidated case

124 Pedro Caeiro, 'Offence-based confiscation: replacing criminal law with something better?' in Serena Quattrocolo, Sandra Oliveira e Silva and Ernestina Sacchetto (eds.), *Assets Confiscation and Prevention of Crime in Europe. An Overview upon the EU and Domestic Legislations* (CEDAM: Milan, 2022) 1–22.

125 *Agosi v. The United Kingdom (UK)* App no. 9118/80 (ECHR, 24 October 1980); *Air Canada v. UK* App no. 18465/91 (ECHR, 05 May 1995); *Yildrim v. Italy* App no. 38602/02 (ECHR, 10 April 2003); *Dassa Foundation and Others v. Liechtenstein* App no. 696/05 (ECHR, 10 September 2007); *Welch v. UK* App no. 17440/90 (ECHR, 09 February 1995); *Phillips v. UK* App no. 41087/98 (ECHR, 05 February 2001); *Van Offeren v. The Netherlands* App no. 19581/04 (ECHR, 05 July 2005); *Geerings v. The Netherlands* App no. 30810/03 (ECHR, 01 June 2007); *Butler v. UK* App no. 41661/98 (ECHR, 27 June 2002); *Webb v. UK* App no. 56054/00 (ECHR, 10 February 2004); *Walsh v. UK* App no. 43384/05 (ECHR, 21 November 2006); *Gogitidze and Others v. Georgia* App no. 36862 (ECHR, 12 May 2005); Comission, *Marandino v. Italy* App no. 12386/86 (ECHR, 15 April 1991); *Raimondo v. Italy* App no. 12954/87 (ECHR, 22 February 1994); *Arcuri v. Italy* App no. 52024/99 (ECHR, 05 July 2001); *Riela and Others v. Italy* App no. 52439/99 (ECHR, 04 September 2001); *Sud Fondi s.r.l. and Others, cit.*; *Varvara, cit.*; *G.I.E.M. s.r.l. and Others v Italy* Apps nos. 1828/06, 34163/07, 19029/11 (ECHR, 28 June 2018).

126 It may be worth emphasising that the Recital 18 question is a sort of 'implication question' which is only relevant precisely when the Regulation is applicable, *i.e.* when the requirements of Art 1 are met.

law. Regardless of which safeguards are precisely envisaged in the Recital – and even taking into due consideration that the Recital is not an actual norm –, the Regulation does seem to open a door that the ECtHR has almost always kept closed.

There is a lack of definition in the Portuguese legal system as to the principles and rights to be observed in confiscation proceedings. The national legislator has not devised a specific procedure for the classic confiscation of proceeds and instruments, nor has it clarified which safeguards apply to extended confiscation. In national literature numerous different views have been propounded on the (non-)criminal nature of the several modalities of confiscation.[127] The Constitutional Court has held that classic confiscation of proceeds is criminal in nature,[128] but little can be drawn from this case law as to precisely how the principles of criminal procedure apply in that setting. Regarding extended confiscation, in contrast, the Constitutional Court does *not* construe it as a measure of a criminal nature.[129] This case law is thus highly aligned with the dominant case law of the ECtHR, and therefore it is also

127 On the criminal nature of the classic confiscation of proceeds, see Jorge de Figueiredo Dias, *Direito Penal Português. Parte Geral, Tomo II. As Consequências Jurídicas do Crime* (Coimbra: Coimbra Editora, 1993) 638; Damião da Cunha (n 116) 7; Caeiro (n 116) 97. In the opposite sense, see Hélio Rodrigues, 'O Confisco das Vantagens do Crime: Entre os Direitos dos Homens e os Deveres dos Estados – A Jurisprudência do Tribunal Europeu dos Direitos do Homem em Matéria de Confisco' in Maria Raquel Desterro Ferreira, Elina Lopes Cardoso and João Conde Correia, *O Novo Regime de recuperação de Ativos à Luz da Diretiva 2014/42/EU e da Lei que a Transpôs* (Lisboa: Imprensa Nacional – Casa da Moeda, 2018) 46–47 and 53; Vaz de Castro (n 109).

Upholding the criminal nature of extended confiscation, see Augusto Silva Dias, 'Criminalidade organizada e combate ao lucro ilícito' in Maria Fernanda Palma, Augusto Silva Dias and Paulo Sousa Mendes (coords.), *2.º Congresso de Investigação Criminal* (Coimbra: Almedina, 2010) 39; Jorge Godinho, 'Brandos costumes? O confisco penal com base na inversão do ónus da prova (Lei n.º 5/2002, de 11 de Janeiro, artigos 1.º e 7.º a 12.º)' in *Liber Discipulorum para Jorge de Figueiredo Dias* (Coimbra: Coimbra Editora, 2003) 1348. In the opposite sense, see José Damião da Cunha, (n 116) 20; Caeiro (n 116) 311; Conde Correia (n 116) 116; Francisco Borges, 'Perda Alargada de Bens: Alguns Problemas de Constitucionalidade' in José de Faria Costa and others (org.), *Estudos de Homenagem ao Prof. Doutor Manuel da Costa Andrade* (vol. I, Coimbra: Instituto Jurídico da Faculdade de Direito da Universidade de Coimbra, 2018) 222; Vaz de Castro (n 109).

128 See Constitutional Court, ruling no. 336/2006, of 18 May.

129 Rulings no. 101/2015, of 11 January; no. 392/2015, of 12 August; and no. 476/2015, of 30 September – on which see João Conde Correia, 'Presunção de proveniência ilícita de bens para perda alargada: anotação aos acórdãos do Tribunal Constitucional n.ºs 101, 392 e 476/2015' (2016) 145 *Revista do Ministério Público* 207–221, as well as the ruling no. 498/2019, of 26 September.

challenged by the view inherent in Recital 18 of the Regulation. It is crucial that the CJEU take a stance on this issue, clarifying whether or not – and if so to what extent – there is indeed a conflict between the Regulation and the ECHR regarding applicable procedural safeguards.

### 4.4 *Execution Procedure*

The rules set out by the Regulation relating to the execution procedure are generally in line with Laws no. 25/2009 and no. 88/2009. The time limits set out for in Arts 9 and 20 of the Regulation, respectively, for executing freezing orders and confiscation orders do, however, constitute a novelty, as they find no correspondence in those national legal instruments.

Regarding the execution of confiscation orders, there is yet another noteworthy aspect. The English version of Art 18(5) provides that the 'executing authority' may decide to freeze the property concerned of its own motion. In contrast, the Portuguese version reads 'the issuing authority', which is arguably a clear mistake[130] and should rather be read as 'executing authority'.

### 4.5 *Remedies*

Art 33 of the Regulation, on legal remedies in the executing State against the recognition and execution of a freezing order or confiscation order, is in essence reflected in Laws no. 25/2009 (Art 15) and no. 88/2009 (Art 17(3) and (4)).

According to Arts 399 f. and 427 CCP, the decision to recognise and enforce freezing and confiscation orders can be appealed to the High Court. However, the decision then taken by this Court is not open to appeal. Portuguese criminal procedure provides no further possibility of reaction aimed at obtaining a re-examination of a decision by a higher court to recognise and execute a confiscation or freezing decision handed down by a foreign court. This limitation on the right to appeal follows from Art 400(1)(c) CCP, which precludes further remedies against decisions already handed down on appeal and which do not definitely settle the object of the procedure. Such is the stance of the Supreme Court of Justice,[131] and the Portuguese Constitutional Court has held this interpretation of Art 400(1)(c) CCP not to be unconstitutional.[132]

130 Compared also with, *e.g.*, the French ("*autorité d'exécution*"), the Spanish ("*autoridad de ejecución*") and the German ("*Vollstreckungsbehörde*") versions.

131 *E.g.* in Supreme Court, ruling of 02-02-2022 (3519/16.8T8LLE.E1.S1).

132 Ruling no. 76/2023, of 14 March.

## 5 Concluding Remarks

The assessment carried out above allows for the conclusion that, insofar as concerns the legal instruments of EU law covered in this study, the levels of compliance of Portuguese law are elevated.

The implementation or coordination issues that could be identified are minor both in substance and in number. In the case of the EAW FD, at present the main issue concerns Art 4a(3) EAW FD, on trials *in absentia*, but as noted even this issue is of narrow significance.[133] The remaining issues are quite immaterial.[134]

As for the EIO D, the main causes for reflection lie: with Art 9(1), as Art 18(2) PT-EIO apparently enables Portugal as executing Member State not to comply with the formalities and procedures indicated by the issuing Member State if it would contravene (any) requirements and conditions of national law on evidence, rather than only its fundamental principles;[135] and with the provisions on remedies, as PT-EIO does not (inter alia) explicitly address fundamental rights.[136] Other minor issues aside,[137] PT-EIO is highly aligned with the EIO D, and on occasion arguably even strikes a finer balance of conflicting interests.[138]

Finally, the only meaningful challenge raised by Regulation 1805/2018 is that which stems from the suggestion in Recital 18 thereto that the essential safeguards of criminal proceedings apply to all freezing and confiscation proceedings covered by the Regulation which are not criminal proceedings.[139] This collides with stable case law of the ECtHR on the issue, adding yet a further layer of complexity to the already convoluted debate about the legal nature of different types of confiscation, which may produce uncertainty as to which rights and guarantees must be observed in the proceedings where they are applied. However, this is less a problem of articulation with national law than a problem of EU law as such – on which the CJEU may have to take a clarifying stance.

---

133 See in further detail *supra*, § 2.3.

134 They concern Arts 10(1), 17(7) and 19(2) EAW FD (see *supra*, § 1).

135 See *supra*, § 3.3; yet practice suggests that the national norm is being applied consistently with the EIO D.

136 See ibid.

137 Namely, on the 'expediency requirements' found in certain provisions of the EIO D (see *supra*, § 3.2 and § 3.3), on temporary transfer (see *supra*, § 3.2), and regarding protection of confidentiality (ibid.).

138 As with the issue of the deduction of the period of custody from the period of detention: see *supra*, § 3.2.

139 See *supra*, § 4.3.

The foregoing assessment concerns essentially the conformity of Portuguese law *as it stands in the books* with EU law. And it is only natural that its actual application should also translate into high levels of conformity. Nevertheless, it is a fitting moment for engaging in a deeper reflection on the judicial application of EU legal instruments. EU law is itself an evolving system of norms, and this commands constant attention at the national level. Such an evolution takes place through the action not only of the EU's legislature but also of its judiciary, both of whom have over recent years openly shifted away from a heavy focus on security and onto a more balanced approach where upholding individual rights becomes a primary objective – no longer just something of a necessary nuisance to an effective cooperation.[140] The shift has many different facets,[141] but it should be uncontentious that *Aranyosi and Căldăraru* blazed the trail, setting 2016 as the turning point.

Meanwhile, Portuguese courts appear to have remained somewhat stuck in the criminal policy ambience of the earlier days of the Area of Freedom, Security and Justice. While it might not offer conclusive evidence of this, it should be illustrative that a decision applying the *Aranyosi and Căldăraru* tests is yet to be seen.[142] In fact, it is a relatively rare event to see an EAW refused on whichever grounds. Rather, EAWs are generally executed readily in the name of mutual trust, the importance of a swift surrender system being taken as self-explanatory in a shared area. By the same token, in the intersection between the EAW and the EIO, courts tend to dismiss promptly any claims to the effect that Portugal as an executing Member State should assess whether the goals envisaged by the EAW could be attained through other, less detrimental EU law measures. This is so even where seemingly the primary goal of the warrant is to just hear the suspect, which – as the EIO D itself recalls in Recital 26 – can be achieved through videoconference or other audiovisual transmission.[143]

Such a readiness to complying with the warrants and orders issued by fellow Member States is, of course, consistent with (a given understanding of) the principles of mutual trust and mutual recognition that underpin this cooperation system. Nevertheless, as noted, EU criminal law has evolved and has renounced the creed which "equated mutual recognition with maximal

140 See Pedro Caeiro, 'The 'licence to distrust' and the protection of individual rights in the execution of a European Arrest Warrant: a comment' (2022) 28 *European Law Journal* 238: "the protection of the targeted individual should not be seen as a hurdle, but rather as the purpose of *judicial* proceedings".

141 See Miguel João Costa, 'The External Effects of *Ne Bis in Idem* in EU Law' in Araceli Turmo (ed.), *Le Droit Européen et l'Autorité des Jugements* (Brussels: Bruylant, 2024), 165–167.

142 See *supra*, § 2.3.

143 See *supra*, § 3.3.

execution".[144] It seems critical that national courts too embrace the notion that scrutinising compliance with fundamental rights by other Member States is still a service to the Area of Freedom, Security and Justice, and a responsibility that EU law itself presently expects them to exert.

144 Pedro Caeiro, '«Scenes From a Marriage»: Trust, Distrust and (Re)Assurances in the Execution of a EAW' in Sergio Carrera, Deirdre Curtin and Andrew Geddes (eds.), *20 Years Anniversary of the Tampere Programme: Europeanisation Dynamics of the EU Area of Freedom, Security and Justice* (Florence: European University Institute, 2020) 240.

CHAPTER 11

# Spain: Critical Profiles in the Transposition of European Orders in Criminal Matters

*Ana Maria Neira-Pena*

## 1 Introduction

In Spain, all the instruments of mutual recognition in criminal matters are regulated in a single legal Act – Law 23/2014, of November 20, on the mutual recognition of criminal decisions in the European Union (hereinafter, LRM)[1] which is regularly modified as new European instruments come into force.

As stated in the LRM's Explanatory Memorandum, due to prolific EU regulatory activity, in 2014 the legislative approach for integrating European mutual recognition rules into the Spanish legal system was revised. This aimed to improve transposition and reduce the fragmentation and complexity of the legal framework, thereby facilitating legal operators' actions in a complex area.

Thus, with the approval of the LRM, the technique of incorporating each EU framework decision or directive individually in an ordinary law and its corresponding complementary organic law is considered to be overcome. A joint text where all the instruments approved in the field of mutual recognition of criminal decisions are gathered has been presented. This Act is articulated through a scheme whereby the incorporation of future directives adopted in this area may be easily accommodated.

The LRM begins with a concise Preliminary Title followed by a series of substantive titles. The Preliminary Title (Arts 1–6 LRM) establishes the foundational provisions for the general regime of mutual recognition of criminal decisions within the EU. These provisions include a list of available instruments (Art 2 LRM); Respect for fundamental rights and freedoms as the primary operational criterion (Art 3 LRM); The supplementary application of the LECrim (Art 4 LRM); Definitions of "issuing State" and "executing State" (Art 5 LRM).

Title I (Arts 7–33 LRM) outlines the general rules on the transmission, recognition and execution of all instruments of mutual recognition in the EU

1 This law was published in the Official State Gazette no. 282 of 21/11/2014. Reference: BOE-A-2014-12029. Permalink ELI: <https://www.boe.es/eli/es/l/2014/11/20/23/con> accessed 19 July 2024.

DOI:10.1163/9789004705791_013

(Arts 7–33 LRM). This section aims to consolidate common elements across the various mutual recognition frameworks. It emphasizes core characteristics of the new judicial cooperation system, such as direct judicial authority interaction between Member States. Legal practitioners are therefore required to adhere to both these overarching principles, ensuring system coherence, and the specific provisions applicable to each individual instrument.

The provisions of Title I regulate, among other aspects, the common rules governing both the transmission of European orders and judicial decisions to other Member States and their enforcement in Spain, the general grounds for refusal of recognition and execution, the rules on appeals and the general rules on costs, compensation and reimbursement.

The competence for both the transmission and the execution of the different instruments of mutual recognition is distributed among the Judges and Courts and the Public Prosecutor's Office. The law generalizes the prior hearing of the Public Prosecutor when a Judge or Court is deciding on any of the referred instruments.

A key aspect of Title I is the list of crime categories for which EU Member States have waived the double criminality requirement. The list of 'eurocrimes' contained in Art 20 LRM aligns with that provided for in EU legislation. However, the broad nature of these categories, combined with their differing nomenclature from national Criminal Codes, raises questions about whether certain offenses are covered.[2]

The different sections dedicated to mutual recognition instruments are organized according to a common pattern. Each begins with common rules defining the instrument and identifying competent issuing and executing authorities. They then detail the transmission procedure when Spain is the

2 For example, the category corruption clearly includes those corruption offenses in the public sector, such as active and passive bribery (Arts 419 to 427 bis Criminal Code), influence peddling (Arts 428 to 431 Criminal Code), embezzlement (Arts 432 to 435 bis Criminal Code), fraud and illegal exactions (Arts 436 to 438 bis Criminal Code) and negotiations and activities prohibited to public officials and abuses in the exercise of their functions (Arts 439 to 444 Criminal Code). All these crimes are included, together with some others, in Title XIX on Crimes against the Public Administration. However, the inclusion of corruption offenses in the private sector – known as business corruption offenses (Arts 286 bis, 286 ter, 286 quater and 288 bis Criminal Code) – in this category may be questionable. The latter group of offenses is included in Chapter XI (Crimes relating to intellectual and industrial property, the market and consumers), which in turn is part of Title XIII relating to Crimes against property and against the socioeconomic order.

issuing state, and conclude with rules governing the recognition and execution in Spain of instruments from other Member States.

For the purposes of this analysis, the following Titles of the LRM must be examined:

- Title II (Arts 34–62 LRM) contains the regulation of the European Arrest Warrant (EAW), incorporating the contents of the Law 3/2003, of March 14, on the European Arrest Warrant (now repealed),[3] updated in light of the experience accumulated in this matter.
- Title VII (Arts 143–156 LRM) regulates the transmission, recognition and execution of the freezing of assets and securing of evidence resolutions. This Title incorporates the content of the Council Framework Decision 2003/577/JHA, of 22 July 2003, on the execution in the European Union of orders freezing property or evidence, subsequently replaced by the Regulation (EU) 1805/2018 of the European Parliament and of the Council of 14 November 2018 on the mutual recognition of freezing orders and confiscation orders (hereinafter Regulation 1805/2018).
- Title VIII (Arts 157–172 LRM) regulates the transmission, recognition and execution of confiscation orders. With respect to confiscation, the regulations contained in the Spanish Criminal Code on the different types of confiscation (Arts 127–129 bis Criminal Code) are also relevant. As is the case with the freezing regulation, the LRM continues to reflect the contents of the Council Framework Decision 2006/783/JHA of 6 October 2006 on the application of the principle of mutual recognition to confiscation orders, subsequently replaced by the Regulation 1805/2018, which applies in the relations with all Member States except for Denmark and Ireland.
- Title X (Arts 186–223 LRM) contains the regulation of the European investigation order (EIO), adapting domestic legislation to the Directive 2014/41/EU of the European Parliament and of the Council of 3 April 2014 regarding the EIO in criminal matters (hereinafter EIO D). This title was introduced in the LRM by Law 3/2018, of June 11, amending Law 23/2014, of November 20, on the mutual recognition of criminal decisions in the European Union, to regulate the European Investigation Order.[4]

3 This law was published in the Official State Gazette no. 65 of 17/03/2003. Reference: BOE-A-2003 5451. Permalink ELI: <https://www.boe.es/eli/es/l/2003/03/14/3/con> accessed 19 July 2024.

4 This law was published in the Official State Gazette no. 142 of 12/06/2018. Reference: BOE-A-2018-7831. Permalink ELI: <https://www.boe.es/eli/es/l/2018/06/11/3> accessed 19 July 2024.

## 2 European Arrest Warrant: Critical Profiles in Legislation and Case Law

### 2.1 *General Issues*

Spain was the first country to incorporate the EAW FD into the domestic legal system, through Law 2/2003, of 14 March, on the European arrest warrant (now repealed) and the Organic Law 2/2003, complementary to the previous one. However, as already indicated above, since 2014 the legislative technique has changed and now incorporates the regime of all instruments of mutual recognition of resolutions to the LRM.

Specifically, the EAW is regulated in Title II LRM (Arts 34–62). The definitions of the instrument (Art 34 LRM) and the determination of its objective scope of application, both in cases where Spain is the issuing State (Art 37 LRM) and in cases where it is the executing State (Art 47 LRM) faithfully reflects the contents of the EAW FD.

### 2.2 *Grounds for Refusal*

Prior to Organic Law 1/2025, of January 2, on measures regarding the efficiency of the Public Justice Service, there were significant discrepancies regarding the optional or mandatory nature of grounds for refusal. The existing regulation was criticized for eliminating judicial discretion to assess the appropriateness of executing the EAWs in several instances where European regulations deemed refusal optional. These included cases of prescription under Spanish law when Spanish courts had jurisdiction, judgments rendered in absentia, final judgments for the same facts issued by non-EU third states, and dismissals or shelving of cases in Spain. These grounds, formerly mandatory in Spanish legislation, are now optional, in line with the EAW FD.

The provision of these grounds for refusal as mandatory in national legislation was contrary to the EAW FD. In these cases, Spanish legislation generally excluded the executing authority's ability to recognize an EAW, denying any discretion to consider the specific circumstances.[5] In this regard, the CJEU, in a recent ruling (Case C-396/22), addressed a German court's preliminary question regarding EAW execution following a conviction *in absentia*. The Court found that the German legislation in question generally mandates refusal

5 As indicated by the Attorney General's Office in its annual report of 2022, the conversion of the optional grounds for refusal into mandatory ones clashes with the will of the European legislator to leave a margin of discretion to the competent judicial authorities to assess the relevance of certain circumstances as grounds for refusal. Attorney General's Office, 'Annual report 2022' (2023) 1219–1221. <https://www.fiscal.es/memorias/memoria2023/FISCALIA_SITE/recursos/pdf/MEMFIS23.pdf> accessed 19 July 2024>.

of execution in such cases, precluding any judicial assessment of whether the defendant's rights were respected and thus whether the EAW should be executed (para. 44).[6] The CJEU concludes that, in those circumstances, it is obliged to declare that such national legislation is contrary to Art 4a(1) EAW FD (para. 45).

Despite the 2025 reform, other minor discrepancies between national legislation and the EAW FD remain.

Thus, for example, the fact that the Spanish legislation refers to the pardon of the requested person (Art 48(1)(a) LRM) instead of referring to the amnesty of the crime on which the EAW is based (Art 3(1) EAW FD) stands out.

Likewise, Spanish legislation seems to be more restrictive than EU law with regard to the ground for refusal consisting of the crime having been committed, in whole or in part, in Spain, by requiring that the part committed in Spain must be "important or fundamental" (Art 32(3)(a) LRM).[7]

Concerning the optional ground for refusal where the requested person is a national or resident of the executing State (Art 4(6) EAW FD), Spanish law initially referred only to nationals (prior to a 2018 reform).[8] Subsequent amendments brought domestic law into line with the EAW FD by including residents (Art 48(2)(b) LRM). A further amendment in 2025 broadened this provision to encompass individuals "habiting" in Spain. Even before 2018, case law supported an interpretation favouring social rehabilitation, reasoning that reintegration is more likely in the individual's original or acquired place of residence.[9] Spanish case law already interpreted "residence" broadly, applying this ground for refusal to those with social, labour, family, and/or linguistic roots in Spain, even without formal proof of residence. This makes it a frequently used ground for refusal in practice.[10]

6 Case C-396/22 *Generalstaatsanwaltschaft Berlin* [2023] ECLI:EU:C:2023:1029.

7 According to case law, this reference must be understood as linked to where the crime is committed, where the evidence is located and where the effects of the crime are produced. In short, the procedural criterion must prevail over the material one, based on the assumption that the crime has been committed in both jurisdictions: it is a matter of seeing whether the authorities of the claimant country are in a better position than the Spanish authorities to prosecute the facts (National High Court (Criminal Chamber, 4th Section). Order No. 89/2022 of June 27. Appeal No. 351/2022).

8 The reform was introduced by the Art 15 of Law 3/2018, of 11 June, amending Law 23/2014, of November 20, on the mutual recognition of criminal decisions in the European Union, to regulate the European Investigation Order. Ref. BOE-A-2018-7831.

9 National High Court. Order No. 33/2008, of 10 March.

10 See, among others, the following judicial decisions: National High Court. Orders No. 105/2023, of 25 July; 88/2023 of 1 July; 73/2023 of 21 May; 61/2023 of 19 April; 47/2023 of 6 March.

Finally, attention should be drawn to the fact that Spanish law provides as grounds for non-recognition or non-execution some reasons not expressly provided for in EU law. This is the case with some of the general grounds for refusal, applicable to all instruments of mutual recognition. Specifically, this situation is observed in relation to the following grounds, provided for in Art 32(1) LRM, which, in addition, are considered mandatory.

- Art 32(1)(a) of the LRM mandates refusal of any mutual recognition instrument if a final judgment (conviction or acquittal) exists in Spain or a third state for the same person and facts, and its execution would violate the *ne bis in idem* principle under Spanish law and applicable international treaties, even if the convicted person was subsequently pardoned. In the event of conviction, this will apply when the sentence has been executed, is in the process of being executed or can no longer be executed under the law of the sentencing State. This provision initially suggested a mandatory refusal even when the prior judgment came from a non-EU third state. However, a 2025 reform, consistent with Art 4(5) of the EAW Framework Decision, introduced an exception specific to EAWs. Now, a final judgment from a non-EU third state for the same facts is an optional ground for refusal in the context of an EAW (Art 48(2)(d) LRM), and in these cases, this optional ground overrides the general mandatory ground of Art 32(1)(a) LRM.
- The EAW will be rejected when the form or certificate is incomplete, manifestly incorrect, or does not respond to the measure requested, or when the certificate is missing, without prejudice to the possibilities of rectification provided for in Art 19 LRM (Art 32(1)(b) LRM). This article states that if the issuing judicial authority fails to provide a new, complete, modified, or supplemented certificate despite requests from Spanish executing authorities, the EAW will be rejected after exhausting all amendment possibilities.[11] This additional ground for refusal does not seem to be contrary to the letter and purpose of the EAW FD, which, although it does not include these defects in the form as a ground for refusal, it does establish the need for the certificate to comply with certain requirements of form and content (Art 8 EAW FD).

11 In this regard, it should be noted that the LRM allows the Spanish judicial authority competent for the execution of an EAW to request the issuing authority to remedy the deficiency of the form or certificate, when it is missing or when it manifestly does not correspond to the judicial decision whose execution is transmitted, in which case, the Spanish judicial authority will set a deadline for the certificate to be resubmitted, completed or modified (Art 19(1) LRM). If, after the deadline, no additional information is submitted and the defects are not remedied, the mandatory ground for refusal provided for in Art 32(1)(c) LRM will come into play.

- The EAW will also be rejected when there is a procedural immunity or privilege that prevents the execution of the decision, or rules on the determination and limitation of criminal liability in relation to freedom of the press and freedom of expression in other media that make it impossible for the competent Spanish authority to execute it (Art 32(1)(c) LRM). Recital (12) of EAW FD states that its application shall not prevent any Member State from applying its constitutional rules relating to the respect for the right to a fair trial, freedom of association, freedom of the press and freedom of expression in other media. However, it does not expressly include among its grounds for refusal the rules on freedom of the press or expression, unlike Spanish legislation, which has included these aspects since the 2025 reform (Art 32(1)(c)). In cases of immunity, it will be necessary to request the lifting of immunity from the competent authority (Art 31 LRM, in line with the provisions of Art 20 EAW FD). However, if the request or the necessary authorization to arrest the person enjoying such immunity is not granted, the EAW will necessarily be denied, given the impossibility of being executed. Although the EAW FD does not foresee immunity as a ground for refusal, it seems evident that if its withdrawal is not achieved, the EAW will have to be denied, so that no relevant discrepancy is observed on this point.

### 2.3 *Fundamental Rights*

Among the grounds for refusal provided for in the LRM for the EAW, there is no express provision for the possible infringement of fundamental rights that could result from the surrender. This omission is consistent with the provisions of EAW FD, which also does not expressly include the risk of violation of fundamental rights as a ground for non-recognition.

However, the Spanish legislation, in coherence with the provisions contained in Recitals (10), (12) and (13) of EAW FD, as well as in its Art 1(3), does include a general provision on fundamental rights – applicable to all instruments of mutual recognition of criminal decisions –. Specifically, Art 3 of the LRM states: "This Law shall be applied with respect for the fundamental rights and freedoms and the principles enshrined in the Spanish Constitution, in Art 6 of the Treaty on European Union and the Charter of Fundamental Rights of the European Union, and in the European Convention on Fundamental Rights and Freedoms of the Council of Europe of 4 November 1950".

In line with the CJEU's *Puig Gordi* decision (C-158/21),[12] which addressed a preliminary question from Spanish courts, an executing judicial authority is

12 Case C-158/21 *Puig Gordi and Others* [2023] ECLI:EU:C:2023:57.

permitted to refuse the execution of an EAW when it would lead to a breach of a fundamental right protected by EU law. This power, however, is constrained by Art 1(3) of the EAW FD, as interpreted by the CJEU.[13] Notably, the CJEU's jurisprudence establishes that if the executing authority possesses evidence indicating a genuine risk of violating the surrendered individual's fundamental right to a fair trial, as guaranteed by Art 47(2) of the CFR, due to systemic or widespread deficiencies within the issuing Member State's judicial system, it must conduct a detailed and precise evaluation. This evaluation must consider the individual's personal circumstances, the nature of the alleged offence, and the specific context in which the EAW was issued, to determine whether there are substantial grounds to believe that such a risk would materialize upon surrender.[14]

Consistent with CJEU case law, Spanish jurisprudence requires more than generic statements about potential fundamental rights violations in the issuing State to deny an EAW. A concrete and real risk to the requested person's rights must be reliably proven. For instance, in a case involving alleged security deficiencies in Romanian prisons, and despite ECtHR condemnations of those prison standards, the Spanish judicial authority concluded that applying Art 1(3) EAW FD necessitates demonstrating a real and patent risk of violating the defendant's fundamental rights. In this case, the Court found that the appellant's allegations about the systematic shortcomings of the Romanian prison system, without providing *prima facie* evidence of concrete risks to the appellant himself, were insufficient, especially considering Romania's membership of the EU and its attachment to the ECHR.[15]

13 In the case at hand, the Belgian State had refused the execution of an EAW issued by the Spanish State in application of a national rule according to which the execution of an EAW must be refused when there are serious reasons to consider that such execution would have the effect of violating the fundamental rights of the person concerned enshrined in Union law. According to the CJEU, such a provision, although not expressly provided for among the grounds for refusal of the EAW FD, could legitimately be applied by the national authorities provided that its scope does not exceed that of Art 1(3) EAW FD, as interpreted by the Court of Justice (para. 79).

14 See the aforementioned Case C-158/21 *Puig Gordi and Others* [2023] ECLI:EU:C:2023:57, para 97 citing the following decisions: Case C-354/20 PPU and Case C-412/20 PPU *Openbaar Ministerie* [2020] ECLI:EU:C:2020:1033, para 52 (Independence of the issuing judicial authority), and Case C-562/21 PPU and Case C-563/21 PPU *Openbaar Ministerie* [2020] ECLI:EU:C:2022:100, para 50 (Tribunal established by law in the issuing Member State).

15 National High Court. Order No. 80/2024, of 8 February.

### 2.4 *Competent Authorities and Procedure*

The Judge or Court handling the case requiring an EAW is the competent issuing authority (Art 35(1) LRM). Consequently, the issuing authority is generally the examining Court[16] at the time detention becomes necessary, although the competent court or tribunal may also issue it later. This reflects a significant level of decentralization. Conversely, however, the competent authority to recognize and execute an EAW in Spain is the Central Examining Court of the National High Court, in the event that the requested person is an adult, and the Central Juvenile Court of the National High Court, when the requested person is a minor (Art 35(2) LRM).[17] In this way, all the executions of this instrument were centralized in a single specialized body with experience in the matter, since the National High Court is the same entity that has been hearing the extradition proceedings.[18]

An EAW is transmitted to the executing authority in one of two ways. First, if the issuing judicial authority knows the requested person's location, it sends the EAW directly. Second, if the requested person's whereabouts are unknown, the Spanish issuing judicial authority may decide to enter a description of the requested person into the Schengen Information System (SIS).[19]

Upon receipt of the European Arrest Warrant (EAW), the executing competent authority will verify its compliance with Art 36 of the LRM, ensure it is

16 Organic Law 1/2025, of January 2, concerning measures for the efficiency of the Public Service of Justice (Official State Gazette no. 3 of 03/01/2025. Reference: BOE-A-2025-76. Permalink ELI: <https://www.boe.es/eli/es/lo/2025/01/02/1/con> accessed 19 July 2024), mandates the creation of the new Tribunals of First Instance. Specifically, this law stipulates that as of October 1, 2025, the existing examining Courts ("*Juzgados de Instrucción*") and Criminal Courts ("*Juzgados de lo Penal*"), like other single-person bodies, will be transformed into Sections within the respective Tribunals of First Instance. Consequently, examining Courts will transition into examining sections within the corresponding collegiate Tribunals of First Instance.

17 Organic Law 1/2025, of January 2, concerning measures for the efficiency of the Public Service of Justice, mandates the creation of the Central Tribunal of Instance within the National High Court from December 31, 2025. This constitution will involve the transformation of the current Central Courts into corresponding Sections of the new Tribunal. Consequently, the Central Examining Court will be transformed into the Examining Section of the Central Tribunal of Instance, and the Central Juvenile Court will be transformed into the Juvenile Section.

18 Ángela Gómez-Rodulfo de Solís, 'La ejecución de la Orden Europea de Detención y Entrega. OEDE pasiva' (Paper presented at the Conference on the European Arrest Warrant and Surrender 2017) <https://www.congreso.es/docu/docum/ddocum/dosieres/sleg/legislatura_12/spl_14/pdfs/36.pdf> accessed 19 July 2024.

19 These two possibilities of communication appear regulated in Art 40 LRM for the case that Spain is the issuing State in line with the provisions of Art 9 EAW FD.

translated into Spanish, and determine if any supplementary information is needed from the issuing authority (Art 19(1) and 30 LRM).

Once the aforementioned conditions have been carried out, unless it is necessary to demand a correction or additional information from the issuing authority or the EAW should be denied, the requested person will be detained in the manner and with the requirements and guarantees provided for in the LECrim (Art 50(1) LRM). This implies that the detained person will be immediately informed in writing, in simple and accessible language that s/he understands, of the facts attributed to him/her and the reasons for his/her deprivation of liberty, as well as the rights s/he has, including the right to remain silent, to appoint a lawyer, to communicate with certain persons, including the consular authorities of his/her country, to be assisted free of charge by an interpreter, to be examined by the forensic doctor, and to request free legal assistance, the procedure and the conditions for obtaining it (Art 520(2) LECrim).

In compliance with Art 50(2) LRM, the detained person is brought before a court within 72 hours of their arrest, and the issuing authority is promptly notified. During this court appearance, the detained person must be informed about the existence and content of the EAW, the possibility of consenting to their surrender to the issuing state, and their full legal rights. This includes the right to appoint a lawyer in the issuing state to advise and support their lawyer in Spain, as stipulated in Art 50(3) LRM.[20]

Within 72 hours of being brought before the court, another hearing must be held with the detainee, with the presence of the Public Prosecutor, the detainee's lawyer – retained or public – and, where appropriate, the interpreter (Art 51(1) LRM). The purpose of this preliminary hearing is multiple. The defendant will be asked whether s/he consents to surrender and whether s/he waives the principle of specialty. The parties will be heard regarding any potential grounds for refusal or conditions of surrender. Furthermore, the court will determine appropriate precautionary measures for the defendant, deciding on provisional detention or release and implementing necessary and proportionate measures to ensure the defendant's full availability (Art 53(1) LRM).

---

20 With respect to the latter right, it is established that "the detained person shall be informed in writing in a clear and sufficient manner, and in simple and understandable language, of his right to waive his right to counsel in the issuing State, of the content of said right and its consequences, as well as of the possibility of its subsequent revocation. Such waiver must be voluntary and unequivocal, in writing, and must state the circumstances of the waiver" (Art 50(4) LRM).

The arrested person's consent significantly influences the procedural path. Should the arrested person consent to surrender, and the judge, either *ex officio* or following the prosecutor's request, identifies no grounds for refusal, the surrender will be ordered by an unappealable decision (Art 51(4) LRM). However, if the arrested person withholds consent, the parties will be convened for a second hearing within a maximum of three days. This hearing will allow the judge to assess evidence proposed by the parties and accepted by the court concerning grounds for refusal or conditions to the surrender (Art 51(5) LRM).[21] If evidence cannot be presented during the hearing, the judge will set a new deadline for its production, respecting the EAW's statutory time limits (Art 51(6) LRM). This hearing may proceed without the requested person if s/he was duly summoned at the previous appearance (Art 51(7) LRM). Following the hearing, the judicial authority must issue a decision on surrender, which is subject to a direct and preferential appeal, ensuring expedited processing by the Criminal Chamber of the National High Court (Art 51(8) LRM).

During the initial hearing, the arrested person must be questioned regarding a potential waiver of the principle of specialty. If the requested person does not waive this principle, as is common, s/he cannot be prosecuted, convicted, or detained for any offense committed before surrender, other than the one for which s/he was surrendered, without the executing state's authorization (Art 60(2) LRM). Consequently, to prosecute, convict, or detain the surrendered person for a prior, different offense, the issuing state must request authorization from Spain by issuing a new EAW. After hearing the Public Prosecutor's Office, the Central Examining Judge will decide on the authorization within ten days, not exceeding thirty days from the request's receipt, through a reasoned order. Authorization is granted if the EAW execution conditions are met and no grounds for refusal apply (Art 60(3) LRM).[22]

---

21 Although the LRM foresees the celebration of two successive hearings, in the cases in which the defendant does not consent to be surrendered, in practice, it is usual to concentrate both appearances in a single act. See Gómez-Rodulfo de Solís (n 16) 7.

22 This procedure was followed by Germany in a case in which the person surrendered by Spain to the German authorities was subsequently requested by Switzerland. In this case, since the defendant had not waived the principle of specialty and did not consent to his/her surrender to the Swiss authorities, the only possibility for the surrender to the Swiss authorities of the defendant who was serving a sentence in Germany was to request authorization from Spain to carry out the surrender, since Spain was the State that had previously agreed to the surrender, through the mechanism of the EAW (National High Court. Order No. 2/2021, of January 22). The decision states that the principle of speciality does not prevent subsequent extradition, if authorization is sought from the Spanish authorities, which are ultimately obliged to grant such authorization in accordance with bilateral or multilateral conventions to which Spain is a party (Art 62(2) LRM).

The personal situation of the requested person is another critical issue in Spanish case law and legislation. As previously noted, the Central Examining Judge must determine the precautionary measures during the period from arrest to surrender. After considering the Public Prosecutor's Office opinion (Art 51 LRM), the judge will adopt necessary and proportionate measures to ensure the requested person's availability (Art 53(1) LRM). This decision, made by order, is subject to direct and preferential appeal before the Criminal Chamber of the National High Court (Art 53(4) LRM).

Decisions regarding the requested person's personal situation must consider the case's circumstances and the need to ensure EAW execution (Art 53(2) LRM). Case law clarifies that the LRM establishes the constitutionally legitimate purpose of pre-trial detention in EAW cases: to ensure successful surrender within the framework of EU judicial cooperation.[23] Consequently, pre-trial detention in EAW proceedings, focused solely on international judicial assistance, is based on compliance with extradition guarantees, not criminal liability. Therefore, the detainee's involvement in the alleged facts, the establishment of reasonable suspicion, or the blanket application of LECrim pre-trial detention rules are not assessed.[24]

Furthermore, pre-trial detention related to EAW execution has generated jurisprudential debate. The issue arises when surrender is suspended due to pending criminal proceedings or imprisonment in Spain (Art 56 LRM). In such cases, the question is whether to maintain pre-trial detention to ensure the requested person's future availability for surrender. Releasing a person whose surrender is accepted but suspended – for example, granting a temporary release permit – risks evasion of both domestic and foreign criminal responsibilities.[25]

---

Specifically, the resolution clarifies the following: "What the German authorities cannot do, and have not done, is to agree to the extraditional surrender to Switzerland, without seeking the corresponding authorization from Spain, which has been verified through the present procedure, thus complying with international commitments and safeguarding the guarantees of the requested party. This authorization comes to supplant the consent of the former, in order to avoid the impunity of serious conducts such as the ones we are dealing with".

23 National High Court (Criminal Chamber, 2nd Section) No. 397/2022, of 4 August.

24 See, among others: Constitutional Court. Judgment 5/1998, of 12 January; National High Court (Criminal Chamber, 3rd Section) Order No. 377/2022, of 28 July; National High Court (Criminal Chamber, 2nd Section) Order No. 397/2022, of 4 August; National High Court (Criminal Chamber, 1st Section). Order No. 120/2024, of 21 February.

25 On this problem, see the reflections of Juan Carlos Hernández Oliveros, 'Prisión provisional y orden europea de detención' (2023) 1 *Revista de estudios europeos* 145, 158 and ff.

This was primarily a practical issue concerning communication between authorities regarding the requested person's pre-trial status. For example, if a Spanish investigating judge orders the defendant's release in a domestic case, the question arises whether that release can be delayed to allow the Central Examining Judge, handling the EAW, to determine appropriate precautionary measures, potentially including continued detention to ensure future surrender. The National High Court's Criminal Chamber addressed this with a 'provisional detention with deferred execution' approach, issuing a detention order effective upon the defendant's release.[26] This ensured the requested person remained detained to facilitate EAW execution.

However, the Spanish Constitutional Court deemed this practice a violation of the fundamental right to liberty (Art 17 Spanish Constitution), articulating several grounds. Initially, the Court found no legal foundation, as neither the LRM nor the LECrim provided for such a measure.[27] Subsequently, the Court determined that 'deferred pre-trial detention' contradicted the principle of exceptionality, which necessitates a strict interpretation favouring liberty. Furthermore, the Court argued that 'deferred pre-trial detention' failed to meet the requirement of foreseeability, as it indefinitely suspended the execution of detention, contingent on factors beyond judicial control. Additionally, the Court concluded that deferred pre-trial detention was disproportionate due to its unpredictable nature and the objective indeterminacy of its temporal validity, which precluded a current assessment of the defendant's circumstances.[28] This temporal gap between the issuance and execution of the detention order was considered incompatible with the right to liberty. This issue was ultimately addressed through legislative intervention, which requires relevant authorities – the penitentiary center or the Court hearing a case involving a pre-trial detainee – to notify the EAW judge of impending releases, enabling

26 National High Court (Criminal Chamber) of 11 January, and National High Court (Criminal Chamber) of 12 March, both subsequently declared null and void by Constitutional Court. Judgment 210/2013, of 16 December (Amparo remedy 2501–2012).

27 In this regard, it must be taken into account that, although Art 56 LRM allows for the suspension of the surrender of the person sought by the EAW when there are pending liabilities in Spain, no provision is made regarding the impact that such suspension may have on the provisional imprisonment period. Therefore, the maximum period of precautionary deprivation of liberty provided for in Art 58 LRM must be considered, which, in line with Art 23(5) EAW FD, is linked to the maximum period foreseen for the surrender of the requested person, from the moment the surrender is agreed upon by the competent judicial authority. In this regard, the Spanish law provides that "once the maximum time limits for surrender have elapsed without the requested person having been received by the issuing State; the requested person shall be released" (Art 58(5) LRM).

28 Constitutional Court. Judgment 95/2007, of 7 May, Legal Ground 7.

the judge to make timely decisions regarding the requested person's status to ensure surrender.[29]

Furthermore, a minor legislative discrepancy exists regarding temporary surrender in cases where surrender is suspended due to pending domestic proceedings or sentences. While the EAW FD allows temporary surrender as an option (Art 24(2) EAW FD), the Spanish LRM appears to mandate it, using 'shall order' instead of 'may surrender' (Art 56(II) LRM).[30] This mandatory nature could pose issues when a domestic trial is imminent.[31]

## 3 European Investigation Order: Critical Profiles in Legislation and Case Law

### 3.1 *General Issues*

The transposition of EIO D into Spanish law occurred through Law 3/2018, of June 11, which amends the LRM, to regulate the EIO.[32] Through this regulation, a new Title X is introduced in the LRM (Arts 186–223),[33] which regulates the

29 Specifically, Art 58(4) LRM provides the following: "*In the event that the surrender of the requested person has to be suspended or postponed because he or she has criminal proceedings pending in Spain and is deprived of liberty, it must be ensured that the Spanish Judicial authority hearing the European arrest warrant proceedings receives information on the future release of the requested person so that it can immediately adopt the corresponding decision on his or her personal situation for the purpose of surrendering him or her to the executing authority. If the requested person is serving a sentence, the penitentiary center must inform the Spanish judicial authority in charge of the European arrest warrant procedure of the effective date of completion of the sentence at least fifteen days in advance, so that it can take the corresponding decision on his personal situation. In the event that the requested person is in provisional detention in a case opened in Spain, the Court hearing that procedure must immediately place the requested person at the disposal of the Spanish judicial authority hearing the European arrest warrant and surrender procedure, communicating sufficiently in advance its decision to agree to release in its procedure, so that the decision on his personal situation may be adopted within seventy-two hours to ensure the execution of the surrender*".

30 This precept provides that, in the case of surrender suspended due to criminal proceedings pending before the Spanish jurisdiction, "*the Spanish judicial authority shall order, if so requested by the issuing judicial authority, the temporary surrender of the requested person under the conditions to be formalized in writing with the said judicial authority and which shall be binding on all the authorities of the issuing Member State*".

31 Hernández Oliveros (n 23) 167.

32 This regulation is published in the Official State Gazette no. 142, of June 12, 2018. The full text of the regulation is available at <https://www.boe.es/eli/es/l/2018/06/11/3> accessed 19 July 2024.

33 As usual, the aforementioned Title X LRM is structured, in turn, into three chapters. The first is dedicated to "General Provisions". The second chapter deals with the "Issuance

EIO, replacing the European evidence warrant for the purpose of obtaining objects, documents and data for use in proceedings in criminal matters ("*exhorto*"), repealed by the European regulation.

The definition of the instrument and the determination of its scope of application, as contemplated in Art 187 LRM, faithfully reflect the content of EIO D (Arts 1, 3 and 4). No discrepancies are observed in the determination of the investigative measures nor in the type of procedure in which an EIO may be issued.

Although the Spanish legislation does not explicitly mirror Art 4(d) EIO D, which addresses proceedings against legal persons, this lack of express mention does not create a practical barrier. Given that Spanish law recognizes both administrative and criminal liability for legal entities, the subject of the issuing state's proceedings being a legal person will not preclude the execution of an EIO.

The Spanish regulation lacks an explicit provision for a defendant to request an EIO as a defense right (Art 1(3) EIO D). However, this right is effectively recognized. Art 189(1) LRM stipulates that an EIO can be issued *ex officio* or at the request of a party, provided it meets the criteria of legality, necessity, and proportionality. Consequently, the right to request an EIO extends to all parties in the proceedings, encompassing both the defense and other accusing.

In adherence to Art 3 and Recital (8) of the EIO D, Spanish legislation permits EIOs for the full range of investigative measures, excluding the establishment and evidence gathering within joint investigation teams. Nonetheless, Spanish law expressly provides that an EIO is permissible when a joint investigation team necessitates investigative actions in a Member State not part of the team, enabling requests to the relevant authorities of that state (Art 186(3)(II) LRM).

The Spanish regulation also expressly excludes from the scope of application of the EIO the regime of transmission of criminal records, which will be governed by its specific regulations (Art 186(4) LRM). In this regard, it is worth noting that the Organic Law 7/2014 of November 12, on the exchange of criminal record information and consideration of criminal court decisions in the European Union, applies.[34]

---

and transmission of a European Investigation Order". The third chapter deals with the "Recognition and execution of a European Investigation Order".

34 Published in the Official State Gazette no. 275, of 13 November 2014. Reference: BOE-A-2014-11713. Permalink ELI: <https://www.boe.es/eli/es/lo/2014/11/12/7/con> accessed 19 July 2024.

### 3.2 *Grounds for Refusal*

The Spanish regulation includes the specific grounds for non-recognition and non-execution of the EIO in Art 207 LRM. Additionally, Art 32(1) LRM includes other general grounds for refusal, applicable to all instruments of mutual recognition of criminal judgments, including the EIO.

While the grounds for non-recognition and non-execution of an EIO in Spanish law align textually with those in Art 11 EIO D, a critical discrepancy arises regarding their mandatory versus optional nature.[35] The EIO D grants enforcement authorities the discretion to "may refuse" recognition or execution, whereas Art 207 LRM mandates that Spanish authorities "shall refuse." This mandatory approach in Spanish law could potentially infringe EU law by eliminating the executing authority's discretionary assessment of refusal.[36]

However, it should be recalled that directives, unlike framework decisions, would have direct effect if their provisions were unconditional and sufficiently clear and precise.[37] Consequently, the mandatory nature of the refusal grounds in Spanish law could be subject to direct effect claims. In any case, the different nature of the grounds for refusal could give rise to infringement proceedings against Spain, which, to date, have not taken place.

Spanish law, beyond the specific grounds for non-execution of an EIO in Arts 206(5) and 207 LRM – which largely correspond to those in Arts 10(5) and 11 EIO D – introduces a supplementary general ground for refusal. This additional ground, not explicitly stated in the EIO D, is found in Art 32(1)(b) LRM. This provision mandates refusal when the EIO request form or certificate is incomplete, manifestly incorrect, does not correspond to the requested measure, or is missing.

While the EIO D does not expressly list formal defects of the certificate as ground for refusal, Art 16(2)(a) of the EIO D can be interpreted as addressing this issue. It requires the executing authority to promptly notify the issuing authority if a decision on recognition or execution is impossible due to an incomplete or manifestly incorrect form.

### 3.3 *Fundamental Rights*

With respect to the EIO, Spanish legislation, in accordance with Art 11(1)(f) EIO D, provides for the violation of fundamental rights as a specific cause for

---

35 Elena Laro González, 'Motivos de denegación del reconocimiento y la ejecución de la orden europea de investigación. ¿Reconocimiento mutuo mitigado o crisis de la confianza recíproca?' (2020) 75 *Revista de Estudios Europeos* 206.

36 Case C-396/22 *Generalstaatsanwaltschaft Berlin* [2023] ECLI:EU:C:2023:1029.

37 Case C-41/74 *Van Duyn v. Home Office* [1974] ECLI:EU:C:1974:133.

non-execution. In this sense, the EIO will be denied when there are reasonable grounds to believe that the execution of the investigative measure requested is incompatible with the obligations of the Spanish State in accordance with Art 6 of the Treaty on European Union and the Charter of Fundamental Rights of the European Union (Art 207(1) (d) LRM). This specific ground for refusal reinforces the general principle according to which the LRM "shall be applied with respect for the fundamental rights and freedoms and the principles contained in the Spanish Constitution, in Art 6 of the Treaty on European Union and the Charter of Fundamental Rights of the European Union, and in the European Convention on Fundamental Rights and Freedoms of the Council of Europe of November 4, 1950" (Art 3 LRM).[38]

The aforementioned ground for refusal must be interpreted restrictively, consistent with the CJEU's application of the principle of mutual trust. As the CJEU has established, Member States implementing EU law are required to presume that fundamental rights are upheld by other Member States. Consequently, they cannot impose a higher national standard of fundamental rights protection than that provided by EU law, nor, except in exceptional circumstances, verify the actual observance of EU-guaranteed fundamental rights in specific.[39]

Notwithstanding the principle of non-inquiry, which typically precludes challenges to the legality of foreign evidence gathering,[40] the LRM imposes a restriction on the admissibility of foreign evidence. Investigative measures conducted abroad are recognized in Spain only if they do not conflict with the fundamental principles and procedural guarantees of Spanish law (Art 186(1) (II) LRM).

While the validity of foreign investigative measures in Spain is contingent on adherence to Spanish procedural safeguards, this does not mandate strict compliance with all domestic procedural formalities. Rather, the standard is

38 Since the EIO D does not refer to national constitutions, one could question whether such a provision could give rise to incompatibility with European law. However, it should be noted that this particular provision of the Spanish regulation is not foreseen as a ground for refusal, but as a general principle of application so it does not seem inappropriate to refer to the national constitutional rules as a general framework for the application of the rules of mutual recognition.

39 Case C-562/21 PPU and Case C-563/21 PPU *Openbaar Ministerie* [2022] ECLI:EU:C:2022:100, para. 41 and referred case-law.

40 The principle of non-inquiry (*"principio de no indagación"*) is a direct consequence of the principle of mutual trust and implies that, as a general rule, the national authorities of the issuing State will not inquire into the lawfulness of the gathering of evidence by foreign authorities in the executing State.

one of fundamental fairness. Investigative acts conducted abroad are generally valid, unless a violation of the right to a fair trial is established.

Spanish courts typically uphold this principle, relying on the doctrine of non-inquiry and mutual trust between Member States when faced with challenges to the regularity or legality of investigations conducted abroad.

Furthermore, Spanish authorities consistently invoke Art 24(3) LRM when parties challenge the substantive grounds of an EIO, which are based on investigations in the issuing state. Art 24(3) LRM explicitly limits such challenges to appeals filed within the issuing Member State, reinforcing the principle that the executing state does not re-examine the substantive basis of the issuing state's decision.

Analysis of Spanish case law reveals that courts rarely refuse EIO execution based on fundamental rights infringements. Spanish courts generally prioritize the principles of mutual recognition and non-inquiry, limiting their oversight of proceedings conducted in other Member States. This approach, rooted in mutual trust, presumes that issuing states uphold fundamental rights, absent clear and specific allegations suggesting otherwise. Due to mutual trust, Spanish courts have limited supervisory authority over proceedings in other Member States, meaning they cannot require adherence to Spanish law or verify compliance with foreign legal frameworks.[41]

41 Relevant Spanish Supreme Court judgments on non-inquiry include 456/2013, of 9 June; 312/2012, of 9 April; 1281/2006, of 12 December; 19/2003, of 19 January. In short, there are many judicial decisions of the Supreme Court that indicate, "*it is not up to the Spanish judicial authority to verify the chain of legality by officials of other Member States, and specifically the compliance by foreign authorities with the legality of that country, much less to subject their actions to contrast with Spanish law* (…)". (Judgment 947/2001, of 18 May). For a detailed analysis of this jurisprudence, see Fernando Gascón Inchausti, 'La eficacia de las pruebas penales obtenidas en el extranjero al amparo del régimen convencional: apogeo y declive del principio de no indagación' in María Isabel González Cano (Ed.), *Orden Europea de Investigación y Prueba Transfronteriza en la Unión Europea* (Tirant Lo Blanch 2019) 49–52. This work identifies key arguments, including the primacy of *lex loci*, the inadmissibility of Spanish courts controlling foreign law application, the irrelevance of foreign courts knowing Spanish law, and the preeminence of mutual trust. However, the continued relevance of *locus regit actum* is questioned in light of recent EU rules allowing for the application of issuing state procedural rules. See also José Manuel Pérez Romero, 'Obtención eficaz de la prueba transfronteriza en la Unión Europea' (DPhil thesis, Universidad Nacional de Educación a Distancia 2020) 107 <http://e-spacio.uned.es/fez/eserv/tesisuned:ED-Pg-UniEuro-Jmperez/PEREZ_ROMERO_Jose_Manuel_Tesis.pdf> accessed 19 July 2024.

Spanish jurisprudence consistently affirms the existence of a European judicial space, recognizing that despite procedural differences arising from diverse legal traditions, national systems share core values and guarantees.[42]

However, the Spanish Supreme Court has established limits to the principle of non-inquiry. It has cautioned that this principle cannot resolve all doubts regarding the legality of evidence acquisition, serving primarily to ensure procedural flexibility, not to override fundamental procedural rights such as the right to defense and a fair trial.[43]

### 3.4 *Competent Authorities and Procedure*

While examining judges typically direct criminal investigations in Spain, prosecutors are also authorized to issue EIOs within pre-procedural inquiries under Art 773 LECrim. This prosecutorial competence, however, is restricted to EIOs that do not involve the limitation of fundamental rights. As Art 187(1)(II) LRM states, "prosecutors are also issuing authorities in the proceedings they direct, provided that the measure contained in the EIO is not restrictive of fundamental rights".

Furthermore, the Prosecutor's Office serves as the sole recipient of all EIOs issued by other Member State authorities, responsible for registration and acknowledgment of receipt (Art 187(2) LRM). However, the Prosecutor's Office's competence to recognize and execute EIOs is limited to those without measures restricting fundamental rights, or those where such measures can be substituted with non-restrictive alternatives. Otherwise, the Prosecutor's Office must forward the EIO, accompanied by a mandatory, non-binding report on potential grounds for refusal and the legality of the requested investigative measures, to the competent judicial authority as defined in Art 187(3) LRM.[44]

42 See, in this line, the following judgments of the Spanish Supreme Court: 1450/99 of 18 November in relation to the rogatory commission sent by the French authorities; 947/2001, of 18 May, on the Dutch authorities; 733/2013, of 8 October, Legal Ground 19.

43 Supreme Court (Criminal Chamber). Judgment No. 116/2017, of 23 February, Legal Ground 4. On the jurisprudential evolution of this principle, see Gascón Inchausti (n 39) 49–52.

44 When the execution of the EIO corresponds to the judicial authority – because either it contains measures limiting fundamental rights, or because the issuing authority has expressly indicated that a judicial body must execute the investigative measure – the following Courts shall have jurisdiction. a) The Examining or Juvenile Judges of the place where the investigative measures are to be carried out or, alternatively, where there is some other territorial connection with the crime, the investigated person or the victim. If there is no element of territorial connection to be able to specify the competence, the Central Examining Judges will be competent. b) The Central Examining Judges, if the EIO was issued for the crime of terrorism or another of the crimes whose prosecution falls

This allocation of powers leads to the Prosecutor's Office handling the enforcement of most EIOs received in Spain. Consequently, given that prosecutorial decisions are not appealable, they seldom generate judicial review, resulting in a scarcity of court rulings on EIO recognition or denial.[45]

The division of competence between judges and prosecutors has led to interpretative discrepancies, particularly when EIOs involve both rights-restricting and non-restrictive measures. Initially, some investigating judges interpreted their role as limited to executing rights-restricting measures, deferring the remaining non-restrictive measures to the Prosecutor's Office.[46]

However, Courts of Appeal clarified that judicial authority, a term that in Spain does not include prosecutors, extends to the recognition and execution of the entire EIO when any measure infringes fundamental rights. This interpretation aligns with Art 187(2) LRM, which mandates that the entire EIO, not just parts of it, be referred to the judicial body when fundamental rights are affected.[47]

The Plenary of the Criminal Chamber of the National High Court further solidified this position, rejecting the fragmentation of competence based on the nature of requested measures.[48] Consequently, a single jurisdictional body, as per Art 187(2) LRM, must execute the entire EIO when any measure restricts

---

under the jurisdiction of the National High Court, or if it is the notification provided for in Art 222 – Notification to Spain of the interception of telecommunications with interception of the address of communications of a person under investigation or prosecution who is in Spain and whose technical assistance is not necessary –. c) The Central Criminal or Juvenile Court Judges, in the case of transfer to the issuing State of persons deprived of their liberty in Spain. If the EIO has been issued in relation to several investigative measures that have to be carried out in different places, the judge or court to which the Public Prosecutor's Office refers the order will be competent for the recognition and execution of the order, from among those competent according to the rules provided in this section and, in what is not provided for in them, according to the rules of preference of the LECrim.

45 The reduced volume of judicial decisions on the matter contrasts with the number of EIO s received by the Prosecutor's Office, which in 2021 amounted to 4,606, a figure very similar to that of 2020, when 4,552 were received. Data available in Attorney General's Office, 'Annual report 2022' (2023) 1219–1221 <https://www.fiscal.es/memorias/memoria2023/FISCALIA_SITE/recursos/pdf/MEMFIS23.pdf> accessed 19 July 2024.

46 See, for example, Provincial High Court of Segovia, Order No. 91/2021, April 14, challenging the investigating judge's decision to limit their competence to the rights-restricting measure (entry and search) of an EIO, and to defer surveillance and witness statements to the Prosecutor's Office.

47 Provincial High Court of Segovia. Order No. 91/2021, of 14 April.

48 National High Court. Non-jurisdictional Agreement of December 17, 2021.

fundamental rights. This agreement rectifies the prior, fragmented approach adopted by some courts and sections of the National High Court.

It is important to recognize that, irrespective of the national investigative model, Spanish prosecutors possess broad authority in matters of international cooperation. The execution of international requests for assistance, including EIOs, is considered a separate function from domestic investigations and, therefore, is not constrained by the time limits and principles established in Art 773 LECrim. The prosecutor's assigned role in recognizing and enforcing EIOs stems from their *designation as a judicial authority solely for the purpose of international cooperation*.[49]

Concerning the confidentiality requirements of Art 19 EIO D, despite the impossibility for the Prosecutor to decree the secrecy of proceedings, their adherence to a general duty of confidentiality is considered adequate to meet the discretion mandated by European standards.[50]

More problematic is the question of remedies, as Spanish regulations appear to conflict with EU law, particularly the jurisprudence of the CJEU, regarding the non-appealability of EIO issuance and recognition decisions by prosecutors (Arts 13(4) and 24(4) LRM).

Arts 13 and 24 LRM explicitly exclude prosecutorial decisions from the general appeals regime. Specifically, Art 24(4) LRM states, "no appeal shall lie against the decisions of the Public Prosecutor's Office in the execution of the instruments of mutual recognition, without prejudice to possible challenges on the merits before the issuing authority and their subsequent assessment in the criminal proceedings in the issuing State." Similarly, Art 13(4) LRM provides, "No appeal shall lie against the decision to transfer a mutual recognition instrument made by the public prosecutor in his/her investigative proceedings, without prejudice to its subsequent assessment in the corresponding criminal proceedings, in accordance with the provisions of the Criminal Procedure Act."

The aforementioned provisions potentially clash with Art 14 EIO D, especially as interpreted by the CJEU in *Gavanozov II* (C-852/19).[51] According to this decision, Art 14 EIO D, read in conjunction with Art 24(7) EIO D and Art 47 CFR, precludes national legislation that denies legal remedies against EIOs for searches, seizures, and witness hearings via videoconference. Consequently,

---

49 Attorney General's Office, 'Circular 2/2022, of 20 December, of the Attorney General's Office, on the extra procedural activity of the Public Prosecutor's Office in the area of criminal investigation' (December 2022) 348 <https://www.boe.es/diario_boe/txt.php?id=BOE-A-2023-54> accessed 19 July 2024.

50 Elena Laro González, 'Luces y sombras de la Orden Europea de Investigación' (2023) 1 *Revista de Estudios Europeos* 129, 134.

51 Case C-852/19 *Gavanozov II* [2021] ECLI:EU:C:2021:902.

the availability of an appeal is deemed essential for EU law compliance. However, Art 13(4) LRM denies appeals against prosecutorial EIO issuance decisions.[52]

Nevertheless, the State Attorney General's Office argues that Art 13(4) LRM aligns with EU case law due to the pre-procedural nature of prosecutorial investigations. They contend that subsequent appeals before the investigating judge in criminal proceedings sufficiently ensure effective judicial protection against EU rights infringements.[53]

The non-appealability of prosecutorial decisions in criminal investigations aligns with the national appeals system and the limited prosecutorial role in investigations.[54] This is justified by the limited temporal and material scope of prosecutorial preliminary proceedings, which are merely preparatory and assess prosecution suitability. They do not replace judicial investigation or possess evidentiary value, hence the non-appealability. Additionally, the lack of remedies against prosecutorial EIO decisions is consistent with the national regulation for domestic cases, suggesting alignment with Art 14 EIO D.

However, *Gavanozov II* (C-852/19)[55] raises doubts about compatibility, potentially leading to refusals of prosecutor-issued EIOs. A CJEU preliminary ruling is the most appropriate method to clarify the compatibility of Spanish legislation with the EIO D as interpreted by the CJEU.

Moreover, it is necessary to underline a discrepancy regarding the concept of "parties concerned" as used in Art 14(4) EIO D. According to the Advocate General's conclusions in the case *Gavanozov I*, this term encompasses witnesses subject to EIO investigative measures and individuals facing criminal charges but not directly subject to those measures.[56] However, Spanish law requires procedural party status for individuals to appeal judicial decisions,

52 Several authors have expressed their opinion on this possible incompatibility: Antonio Martínez Santos, '¿Emisión de órdenes europeas de investigación por el Ministerio Fiscal español? Consideraciones sobre la compatibilidad del Art 13(4) de la Ley de Reconocimiento Mutuo con el derecho de la Unión a la luz de las sentencias del TJUE en los asuntos *Gavanozov I y II*' (2022) 57 *Revista General de Derecho Europeo* 272–317; Laro González (n 49) 138–141.

53 Attorney General's Office, 'Circular 2/2022, of 20 December, of the Attorney General's Office, on the extra procedural activity of the Public Prosecutor's Office in the area of criminal investigation' (December 2022) 348 <https://www.boe.es/diario_boe/txt.php?id=BOE-A-2023-54> accessed 19 July 2024.

54 Laro González (n 49) 140.

55 Opinion of Advocate General delivered on 11.04.2019 in Case C-324/17 *Gavanozov* [2019] ECLI:EU:C:2019:312.

56 Opinion of Advocate General delivered on 11.04.2019 in Case C-324/17 *Gavanozov* [2019] ECLI:EU:C:2019:312.

a condition not met by witnesses or persons subject to investigative measures like searches without being suspects.[57]

Further discrepancies arise regarding the enforcement authority's control over issuing authority decisions. Specifically, the lack of transposition of Art 6(3) EIO D is striking. This article allows enforcement authorities to review the legality, proportionality, and necessity of issuing authority decisions and to consult on the EIO's importance when suspicions arise. However, Spanish legislation limits checks to grounds for refusal (Art 207(3) LRM), omitting such consultative review.

A minor discrepancy is also observed in the regulation of civil servant liability. Contrary to Art 18(4) EIO D, which generally prohibits Member States from claiming damages from each other except for third-party payments, Art 26 LRM states, "The Ministry of Justice shall claim from the issuing State the reimbursement of the amounts which, in accordance with Spanish law, it has had to pay as compensation for damages caused to third parties, provided that these are not the exclusive responsibility of Spain due to the abnormal functioning of the Administration of Justice or due to a miscarriage of justice," without explicitly excluding claims for other damages.

Regarding specific investigative measures, beyond minor inconsistencies,[58] the most significant issue is the absence of legal provisions for witness or expert testimony via telephone conference (Art 25 EIO D). Recognizing this gap, Spanish law includes a transitional regime outlining rules for such procedures if they are incorporated into future criminal procedural legislation (Additional Provision 6th LRM).[59] Currently, the absence of a legal basis prevents the practice of these proceedings in Spain.

57 Laro González (n 50) 138.

58 For example, with regard to the execution of an EIO for an appearance by videoconference or other means of audiovisual communication, while the EIO D states that the executing authority must ensure respect for the "*fundamental principles*" of the law of the executing State (Art 24(5) EIO D), the Spanish law seems to grant it broader powers of control, indicating that, during the statement, the competent Spanish judicial authority must ensure respect for the "*Spanish legal system*" (Art 216(3)(a) LRM). Although in its wording it may appear to be a relevant contradiction, a judicial interpretation in accordance with the EIO D would serve to bridge the discrepancy.

59 According to this provision, entitled *Testimony of witnesses or experts by telephone conference*, "[i]n the event that the hearing of witnesses or experts by telephone conference is introduced in the Spanish criminal procedural legislation, the following rules shall apply for the issuance and execution of a European Investigation Order providing for such measure: (a) When the competent Spanish authority hearing criminal proceedings in Spain considers it necessary to hear, as a witness or expert witness, a person who is in the territory of another Member State, it shall issue a European investigation order for

## 4 Regulation 1805/2018: Critical Profiles in Legislation and Case Law

### 4.1 *General Issues*

Regulation 1805/2018, directly applicable to freezing and confiscation certificates from December 19, 2020, replaced FFDD 2003/577/JHA and 2006/783/JHA among Member States bound by the Regulation. However, Titles VI and VII of the LRM still contain provisions based on the superseded FFDD, and Spanish legislation has not been amended to reflect Regulation 1805/2018.

Given the aforementioned context, the central question is the ongoing validity of the LRM regarding freezing and confiscation orders following the implementation of Regulation 1805/2018. It is understood that the LRM's provisions remain applicable insofar as they do not conflict with Regulation 1805/2018 and address matters not covered by it.[60] Additionally, the LRM continues to apply to Denmark and Ireland, which are not bound by Regulation 1805/2018.

Regarding the LRM's role in the recognition and enforcement of freezing and confiscation orders, while Regulation 1805/2018 is directly applicable, certain procedural aspects necessitate supplementary national rules. In fact, the State Attorney General's Office, in its 2022 annual report,[61] highlights the need to amend the LRM to develop rules complementing Regulation 1805/2018, which, despite its direct applicability, requires appropriate legal adaptation. The coexistence of Titles VI and VII of the LRM with Regulation 1805/2018 significantly complicates the practical tasks of judicial authorities in issuing and enforcing freezing and confiscation decisions.

In addition, the need to adapt the domestic rules to the Regulation 1805/2018 was noted following the public consultation carried out by the Spanish Government on November 29, 2019.[62] At that time, it was considered

---

the testimony of the witness or expert witness to be given by telephone conference, provided that it does not consider it more convenient for the person to appear in person in its territory and it would not have been possible to use another more appropriate means. b) Unless otherwise agreed, the procedure for the hearing of witnesses or experts by telephone conference, both for the issuance and for the execution of a EIO including such a hearing, shall be governed by the provisions of Art 216(2)(3)(4) and (5) LRM. For the purposes of this additional provision, the competent Spanish authority shall be understood as that defined in Art 187 LRM".

60 Jesús Conde Fuentes, 'El Reglamento (UE) 2018/1805 y la ejecución de resoluciones de embargo y decomiso' (2021) 151 *La Ley Penal*.

61 Attorney General's Office, 'Annual report 2022' (2023) 1219–1221. <https://www.fiscal.es/memorias/memoria2023/FISCALIA_SITE/recursos/pdf/MEMFIS23.pdf> accessed 19 July 2024.

62 Ministerio de Justicia, 'Consulta pública sobre la adaptación al reglamento (ue) 2018/1805 del parlamento europeo y del consejo, de 14 de noviembre de 2018, sobre el

that legislative intervention at the internal level was necessary, both to clean up national legal system, as well as to implement the Regulation 1805/2018, determining the "non-existence of a non-regulatory alternative" for the adjustment of the national regulations to the Regulation 1805/2018. This statement, perhaps somewhat convoluted in its wording, proclaimed the need for intervention at the legislative level to adapt our legal system to the Regulation 1805/2018, given the insufficiency of non-legal instruments, such as circulars from the public prosecutor's office or case law. However, to date, this legislative intervention has not yet taken place, which has been criticized by the doctrine for jeopardizing legal certainty and hindering the effectiveness of the European regulations on freezing and confiscation.[63]

Although Regulation 1805/2018 does not represent a drastic overhaul of the prior framework, there are specific aspects that, notwithstanding its direct applicability, necessitate explicit national legislative articulation to ease the recognition of freezing and confiscation orders issued in Member State criminal proceedings. However, even without explicit legislative action, the LRM incorporates numerous provisions of Regulation 1805/2018, exhibiting no substantial inconsistencies.

Alongside the rules governing mutual recognition between Member States, national regulations on freezing and confiscation must likewise be taken into account. With respect to confiscation, the regulation contained in the Spanish Criminal Code on the different types of confiscation (Arts 127 to 128 Criminal Code) is extremely relevant. In alignment with Directive 2014/42/EU on the freezing and confiscation of instrumentalities and the proceeds of crime in the European Union, the Spanish Criminal Code provides for several forms of confiscation, including direct confiscation, confiscation by substitution or equivalent value, extended confiscation, non-conviction-based confiscation, and confiscation of third-party assets. Additionally, the Spanish Criminal Code regulates the possibility of freezing property for subsequent confiscation (Art 127 octies (1) Criminal Code) and the destination to be given to the confiscated property (Art 127 octies (2) and (3) Criminal Code).

---

reconocimiento mutuo de las resoluciones de embargo y decomiso' (November 2019) <https://www.mjusticia.gob.es/es/AreaTematica/ActividadLegislativa/Documents/1292430895810-ConsultapublicaEMBARGODECOMISO.PDF> accessed 19 July 2024.

63 Teresa Aguado Correa, 'Reconocimiento mutuo de las resoluciones de embargo y decomiso: de la Ley 23/2014 al Reglamento (UE) 2018/1805: ¿Y la ley de adaptación al Reglamento (UE) 2018/1805, para cuándo?' in José Antonio Posada Pérez and Borja Mapelli Caffarena (eds.), *Análisis empírico y doctrinal de la Ley 23/2014 de reconocimiento mutuo de resoluciones penales* (Aranzadi, 2022) 352, 351.

It is important to emphasize that Art 127 Criminal Code legally characterizes confiscation as an "accessory consequence," thereby avoiding its classification as a penalty or criminal sanction. Conversely, Art 157 LRM aligns with the definition in Regulation 1805/2018 by treating confiscation as a sanction.

At the domestic level, the criminal procedural legislation's regulation of third-party intervention in confiscation and the autonomous confiscation procedure (Title III ter, Arts 803 ter (a) – 803 ter (u) LECrim) is noteworthy. These provisions address the summoning and intervention rights of individuals who, though not parties to the criminal proceedings, may be affected by a confiscation order. It also establishes a special procedure dedicated solely to the confiscation of assets, proceeds, or their equivalent value, independent of criminal prosecution. This constitutes an autonomous or non-conviction-based confiscation. As this autonomous confiscation procedure occurs within "proceedings in criminal matters," as defined by EU law (Art 1(1) and Recital (13) Regulation 1805/2018), Regulation 1805/2018 applies.[64] Consequently, within the context of this procedure, the issuance of a seizure or confiscation order may be required for transnational enforcement. Similarly, this procedure may be utilized for the domestic execution of a confiscation order originating from another Member State.

Finally, a conceptual discrepancy exists regarding the term freezing. The LECrim employs a broad definition, encompassing not only assets subject to future confiscation but also assets secured for civil liabilities, effectively a real precautionary measure (Art 589 LECrim). Conversely, the LRM defined freezing orders as those aimed at provisionally preventing the destruction, transformation, displacement, transfer, or alienation of both confiscation-liable assets and evidentiary items (Art 143(1) LRM).

Given the varied definitions of "freezing" at domestic level, clarification regarding the applicability of Regulation 1805/2018 is essential. The Regulation's application to the execution of freezing orders hinges on the purpose of the freezing. Specifically, if a freezing order aims to secure civil liabilities or evidence, even within criminal proceedings, Regulation 1805/2018

---

64 Regarding the scope of application of the Regulation 1805/2018, it should be noted that it applies to all confiscation orders issued by a court in the context *"proceedings in criminal matters"*, the latter being an autonomous concept of European Union law (Recital (13) Regulation 1805/2018). Moreover, it should be borne in mind that the classification of proceedings as criminal in the issuing State implies the acceptance of that nature in a different State. See Conde Fuentes (n 60) 3.

does not apply.[65] However, the Regulation does apply when a freezing order is issued to secure a future confiscation decision.

### 4.2 *Grounds for Refusal*

A comparison of the grounds for refusal in the LRM and Regulation 1805/2018 reveals three categories of discrepancies. First, as in the case of the other mutual recognition instruments previously analysed, the LRM mandates certain grounds for refusal that are discretionary under Regulation 1805/2018.[66] Second, Regulation 1805/2018 includes grounds for refusal absent from the LRM.[67] Finally, the LRM contains grounds for refusal not found in Regulation 1805/2018.

This last discrepancy is particularly significant, as it expands the grounds for refusal beyond those in Regulation 1805/2018. Notably, the following national grounds for refusal are present in the LRM but not in Regulation 1805/2018.

Firstly, Spanish authorities may refuse the recognition and execution of confiscation orders when they pertain to acts that Spanish law considers to have been committed wholly, substantially, or fundamentally within Spanish territory (Art 32(3)(a) LRM). Secondly, the Spanish authority may also refuse the recognition of freezing and confiscation orders when they relate to acts for which Spanish authorities have jurisdiction to prosecute, and if a conviction had been issued by a Spanish court, the offense or the imposed sanction would have been prescribed according to Spanish law (Art 32(3)(b) LRM). Finally, Spanish law mandates refusal of confiscation orders in the following circumstances: violation of interested parties' rights, including bona fide third parties as defined by Spanish law (Art 170(1)(a) LRM); contravention of fundamental rights and freedoms guaranteed by the Spanish Constitution through the

65 Regulation 1805/2018, as clarified by Recital (13) and Art 1(4), expressly excludes freezing orders issued in civil proceedings. Therefore, civil actions are not subject to the Regulation. The concurrent exercise of civil and criminal actions within criminal proceedings does not alter the fundamental civil nature of the former, which remains separate and distinct from the latter.

66 Discrepancies include *ne bis in idem* (Art 32(1)(a) LRM), incomplete or incorrect certificates not corrected after consultation (Art 32(1)(b) LRM) and privilege or immunity preventing enforcement (Art 32(1)(c) LRM).

67 In this sense, discrepancies are observed in the ground for refusal provided for in Arts 8(1)(d) and 19(1)(d) of the Regulation 1805/2018 for freezing and confiscation respectively. This ground relates to an offense committed, in whole or in part, outside the territory of the issuing State and, in whole or in part, in the territory of the executing State, when the facts in relation to which the order has been issued do not constitute an offense in the executing State. This ground, which implies an extension of the double criminality control in the case of concurrence of jurisdictions, is not provided for in Spanish law.

application of extended confiscation provisions from the issuing State's legislation (Art 170(1)(b) LRM); and confiscation orders relating to offenses committed outside the issuing State that Spanish law does not permit to be prosecuted extraterritorially (Art 170(1)(c) LRM). These refusal grounds are absent from Regulation 1805/2018.

However, the aforementioned discrepancies are mitigated by the fact that Regulation 1805/2018's entry into force effectively repeals prior conflicting provisions regarding the recognition and execution of freezing and confiscation orders among participating Member States. Nevertheless, due to the absence of rulings regarding these instruments, it remains uncertain whether Spanish courts are applying the superseded national law or the Regulation 1805/2018.

### 4.3 *Fundamental Rights*

Prior to 2025, the LRM lacked an explicit provision for refusing freezing and confiscation orders based on well-founded reasons, supported by concrete and objective evidence, that execution would manifestly violate a fundamental right enshrined in the Charter, particularly the rights to effective judicial protection, a fair trial, and defense (Arts 8(1)(f) and 19(1)(h) Regulation 1805/2018). However, Art 32(1)(d) of the LRM now expressly includes this ground.

Furthermore, in the context of confiscation orders, Spanish law mandates refusal when there is a violation of the rights of interested parties, including bona fide third parties as defined by Spanish law (Art 170(1)(a) LRM). Refusal is also required if the Judge finds that the application of extended confiscation provisions from the issuing State's legislation contravenes fundamental rights and freedoms guaranteed by the Spanish Constitution (Art 170(1)(b) LRM). Again, it must be emphasized that these grounds for refusal should not be applied. Given that they are not included in the Regulation 1805/2018, which provides an exhaustive list of grounds for refusal, they should be considered tacitly repealed.

### 4.4 *Competent Authorities and Procedure*

Art 23 of Regulation 1805/2018 delegates the determination of competent authorities to national law. In Spain, issuing competence for freezing orders lies with the judges or courts presiding over the proceedings where the measure is to be implemented (Art 144(1) LRM). Similarly, judges or courts responsible for executing sentences that include confiscation as an accessory consequence hold competence to issue corresponding confiscation orders (Art 158(1) LRM).

For recognition and execution, Spanish legislation, exercising its discretion, assigns distinct authorities for freezing and confiscation orders, despite their frequent sequential execution. Investigating judges in the location of the assets subject to freezing are competent to execute freezing orders (Art 144(2) LRM). Conversely, criminal courts[68] in the location of any assets subject to confiscation enforce confiscation orders. If the asset location is unknown to the issuing authority, the criminal court of the person's residence or registered office against the order had been issued shall be competent to execute the confiscation order (Art 158(2) LRM).

Moreover, in accordance with the declaration submitted by Spain to the European Commission on December 18, 2020, pursuant to Art 2(9) of Regulation 1805/2018, the International Cooperation Unit of the Attorney General's Office (UCIF) is designated as the receiving authority for freezing and confiscation certificates solely to determine the location of assets to be seized or confiscated when the issuing authority lacks such information.

Simultaneously, the Public Prosecutor's Office holds competence in asset investigations through the EIO, provided it does not involve measures infringing fundamental rights (Art 187(2)(a) LRM).

The existing system for enforcing freezing and confiscation orders has been criticized for inefficiency, leading to delays and, in some cases, asset dissipation.[69] To address these issues, the Specialized Unit for International Criminal Cooperation of the Attorney General's Office proposes amending the LRM to designate the Public Prosecutor's Office as the sole receiving authority for freezing and confiscation certificates. This reform aims to resolve the current dysfunctions stemming from the division of competence among the prosecutor for EIOs, investigating judges for freezing orders, and criminal judges for confiscation orders, which creates confusion for European issuing authorities. Centralizing the receipt of all confiscation certificates within the Public Prosecutor's Office would ensure necessary national-level coordination for executing these instruments.[70]

---

68 Remember, as previously indicated, that from October 1, 2025, the Investigating Courts (*"Juzgados de Instrucción"*) and Criminal Courts (*"Juzgados de lo Penal"*) will be transformed into Investigating Sections and Criminal Sections, respectively, within the new Tribunals of First Instance.

69 This criticism is supported by various sources, including Conde Fuentes (n 60) 5; Rosa Morán Martínez, 'España como país ejecutor de decisiones de embargo y decomiso en el Reglamento (UE) 2018/1805' in Ignacio Berdugo Gómez De La Torre and Nicolás Rodríguez García (eds.), *Decomiso y recuperación de activos. Crime doesn't pay* (Tirant lo Blanch, 2020) 461; Carmen Rodríguez-Medel Nieto, 'España como país emisor de decisiones de embargo y decomiso en el reglamento (UE) 2018/1805' in Ignacio Berdugo Gómez De La Torre and Nicolás Rodríguez García (eds.), *Decomiso y recuperación de activos. Crime doesn't pay* (Tirant lo Blanch, 2020) 440; Aguado Correa (n. 63) 358–359.

70 The Attorney General's Office, in its 'Annual report 2022' (2023) 1219–1221, available at <https://www.fiscal.es/memorias/memoria2023/FISCALIA_SITE/recursos/pdf

The procedure for the enforcement of freezing orders is regulated in Arts 150 to 156 LRM, while the enforcement of confiscation orders is regulated in Arts 166 to 169 LRM. This regime, in general terms, is in accordance with the provisions of the Regulation 1805/2018, despite being prior to the adoption of the new EU instrument.

Concerning the execution of freezing orders, the enforcement decision must be adopted immediately and communicated without delay to the issuing judicial authority and the Public Prosecutor's Office, by any means ensuring a written record, within 24 hours of receiving the order (Art 151(1) LRM). Additionally, the competent authority receiving the freezing order must take necessary steps to ascertain the location of the assets to be frozen within five days of receipt (Art 151(2) LRM).

It is important to note that Art 9(3) of Regulation 1805/2018 extends the time limits specified in the LRM. Specifically, the deadline for deciding on a freezing order is extended from 24 to 48 hours when the issuing authority requests immediate freezing. Furthermore, the Regulation allows, though not expressly stated in the LRM, the issuing authority to specify a date for freezing execution (Art 9(2) Regulation 1805/2018).

The resolution granting recognition and execution of asset freezing will specify the precautionary measure to be implemented. This measure may include asset deposit, preventive freezing, bank account blocking, or restrictions on financial instruments, as well as disposal prohibitions or other precautionary measures consistent with Spanish law (Art 152(1) LRM). Regarding confiscation execution, Spanish law mandates that the competent Criminal Court ascertain the location of assets to be confiscated, with the discretion to liaise with the issuing judicial authority for supplementary execution information (Art 167(1) LRM). Subsequently, following reports from the Public Prosecutor's Office and other involved parties within five days, the Criminal Court will order the execution of the transmitted confiscation decision within

/MEMFIS23.pdf, and the Spanish National Member of Eurojust, in 'Memoria de actividades del miembro nacional de España en Eurojust 2019' (April 2020) 103, available at https://www.fiscal.es/documents/20142/377345/Memoria+de+actividades+del+miembro+nacional+de+Espa%C3%B1a+en+Eurojust+_2019.pdf/a53039fb-01ca-54e2-f916-6ffd6b896125?t=1587375387854> accessed 19 July 2024, advocate for this reform. The national member of Eurojust highlights persistent delays and errors in distributing and executing EU freezing orders, often treated as national freezing orders by court services. It proposes extending the EIO's competence criteria from Art 187(2) LRM to freezing and confiscation orders, with the Public Prosecutor's Office as the central receiving authority, forwarding certificates with recognition reports to examining courts. This model has proven effective for EIO s (Art 187(2)).

ten days of receipt (Art 167(2) LRM). It is noteworthy that the concise time-frames prescribed in the LRM are superseded by the extended deadlines provided in Regulation 1805/2018 (Art 20).

The execution of a confiscation order depends on whether it pertains to a specific asset or a monetary sum (Art 168 LRM),[71] and Spanish law establishes specific rules for the execution of multiple confiscation orders (Art 169 LRM) and expressly regulates various possibilities for suspending enforcement (Art 171 LRM).

While there are no significant discrepancies regarding the enforcement procedure, a gap exists in national regulation concerning the allocation of confiscated assets for victim compensation. In relation to the restitution of frozen or confiscated property to victims (Arts 29 and 30 Regulation 1805/2018), the LRM's Explanatory Memorandum (para. XII) explicitly excludes property restitution to rightful owners from its scope.[72] This gap can be addressed by direct application of Regulation 1805/2018, though legislative adaptation of the LRM would be advisable.

Finally, legal scholars have identified a potential conflict between Art 374(2) of the Spanish Criminal Code and Regulation 1805/2018. This arises because the former excludes victims as beneficiaries of confiscation in drug trafficking offenses. Specifically, Spanish law stipulates that assets confiscated in certain public health crimes cannot be used to satisfy civil liabilities or procedural costs, and must be fully awarded to the State. This prohibition on victim compensation from crime proceeds raises concerns about its consistency with Regulation 1805/2018's principle that confiscation measures should not prejudice legitimate victim expectations.[73]

---

71 Generally, confiscation orders are recognized and enforced as if issued by a national judge. If specific assets cannot be confiscated, confiscation for equivalent value is employed (Art 168(1) LRM and 127(3) Criminal Code).

72 For domestic cases, Art 334(IV) LECrim on property confiscated at crime scenes is relevant. It mandates immediate return of victim-owned effects unless needed as evidence. This precept provides as follows: "*The effects that belonged to the victim of the crime will be immediately returned to the victim, unless exceptionally they should be kept as evidence or for the practice of other proceedings, and without prejudice to their restitution as soon as possible. The effects shall also be returned immediately when they must be preserved as a means of evidence or for the practice of other proceedings, but their preservation may be guaranteed by imposing on the owner the duty to keep them at the disposal of the Judge or Court. The victim may, in any case, appeal this decision in accordance with the provisions of the preceding paragraph*".

73 Cristina Martínez Arrieta Márquez De Prado, *El decomiso y la recuperación y gestión de activos procedentes de actividades ilícitas* (Tirant Lo Blanch. 2018) 138. For his part, José Antonio Díaz Cabiale, 'El decomiso tras las reformas del CP y de la LECrim de 2015' (2016)

## 5 Concluding Remarks

The transposition of all mutual recognition instruments through a single legislative instrument – the LRM – avoids regulatory dispersion and enhances systemic coherence. However, the existence of general provisions, applicable to all mutual recognition instruments, sometimes leads to discrepancies between Spanish and European legislations.

Concerning the EAW, the 2025 reform has achieved alignment of the grounds for refusal with the EAW FD, thus resolving prior discrepancies related to mandatory versus optional application. Although certain minor discrepancies remain, this general alignment addresses previous criticisms, particularly those from the Attorney General's Office, and upholds the European legislator's intent to confer judicial discretion in the assessment of refusal grounds.

Jurisprudentially, provided EAW requirements are met, certificates are valid, and no refusal grounds exist, execution is swift. However, surrender is frequently denied when individuals with Spanish residency or ties refuse extradition, often resulting in sentence execution in Spain.

Overall, the EAW FD's implementation remains positive, with accumulated experience fostering a balanced national framework that respects both extradited individuals' rights and mutual recognition principles.

Regarding the EIO, discrepancies persist concerning refusal grounds and their mandatory nature. However, the most significant inconsistency is the lack of appeals against prosecutorial EIO issuance and execution decisions. While this aligns with national appeal systems, its compatibility with Art 14 EIO D is questionable, particularly following *Gavanozov II*.

Notwithstanding the legal transposition inconsistencies identified, it is essential to highlight the robust jurisprudential application by Spanish courts of the principle of mutual trust, which, in the context of transnational evidence, manifests as the "principle of non-inquiry." This principle effectively prevents Spanish courts from scrutinizing the methods by which evidence was obtained abroad, resulting in an extremely low incidence of recognized fundamental rights violations in such evidence acquisition.

Finally, regarding Regulation 1805/2018, Spanish law remains unadapted, despite acknowledgments from various institutions, including the Government and the Attorney General's Office, concerning the advisability of domestic legislative alignment with this EU cooperation mechanism.

18 *Revista electrónica de ciencia penal y criminología* 34–35, justifies this provision by referencing the 1988 UN Convention, which emphasizes funding for anti-drug trafficking bodies.

The absence of express legislative adaptation is mitigated by the Regulation's direct applicability. Additionally, existing legislation transposing Framework Decisions 2003/577/JHA and 2006/783/JHA remains applicable to competent authorities and national procedures, provided it does not conflict with Regulation 1805/2018. However, unresolved ambiguities necessitate domestic legislative adjustments to address the new legal landscape created by Regulation 1805/2018.

For instance, Spanish legislation lacks specific regulations on freezing for confiscation purposes. While Spanish freezing regulations are unified across various purposes – securing evidence, civil liabilities, or subsequent confiscation – Regulation 1805/2018's rules apply exclusively to freezing orders securing future confiscation, including non-conviction-based confiscation in criminal or autonomous proceedings. The legislative landscape is, in any case, complex and confusing.

Similarly, Spanish legislation lacks consistent regulations on victim restitution or compensation from frozen or confiscated assets. Therefore, a review of domestic legislation is advisable to rectify this legal gap and prevent interpretative uncertainties concerning Regulation 1805/2018's interaction with existing national provisions regarding the disposition of confiscated assets.

By way of conclusion, it is affirmed that the Spanish legislator's decision to unify all regulations pertaining to the mutual recognition of criminal decisions within a singular legislative instrument is a positive development. This legislative approach fosters systemic coherence and facilitates the application of legal norms by competent judicial authorities. Nevertheless, further refinements are required to achieve complete alignment of domestic legislation with European law. In the interim, it is imperative that judicial authorities interpret and apply national rules in a manner consistent with the letter and the spirit of EU Law.

CHAPTER 12

# The Netherlands: Implementation and Application of the EAW, EIO, and Freezing and Confiscation Orders

*Camila Ugaz Heudebert, Teddy Zwackhalen, Gijs van Dijck and Menno Dolman**

## 1 Introduction

This chapter provides a comprehensive overview of the transposition and application of the EAW FD, the EIO D, and the Regulation 1805/2018 in The Netherlands. Below, the EAW FD (*section 2*), the EIO D (*section 3*), and the Regulation 1805/2018 (*section 4*) will be discussed. The analysis brings together and builds on previous work on the EAW FD,[1] the EIO D,[2] and the Regulation

* The first two authors contributed equally to this chapter.

1 R. Da Silva Athayde Barbosa, V. Glerum and others, *European Arrest Warrant: Practice in Greece, The Netherlands and Poland* (Boom Juridisch 2022); E.G. Kurtovic, P.M. Langbroek, 'The EAW in The Netherlands' in B. de Santos Sousa (eds), *The European Arrestwarrant in law and in practice: A comparative study for the consolidation of the European Law-enforcement Area* (Coimbra 2010); S. Buisman, 'First Periodic Country Report: The Netherlands' <https://stream-eaw.eu/wp-content/uploads/2022/01/STREAM-Country-Report_The-Netherlands.pdf> accessed 17 July 2024; V.H. Glerum and N. Rozemond, 'Overlevering', in R. van Elst, E. van Sliedregt (eds.), *Handboek Internationaal strafrecht. Internationaal en Europees strafrecht vanuit Nederlands perspectief* (3rd edn, Wolters Kluwer 2022); W.R. Jonk and R. Malewicz, 'Het Europees arrestatiebevel' [2020] 6 TvBS&H 324; A.M. Timorason and R. Malewicz, 'De evolutie van het begrip, rechterlijke autoriteit'' in *de overleveringsprocedure* [2019] 102 TPWS 262; V. Glerum and K. Rozemond, 'Overlevering van Nederlanders: copernicaanse revolutie of uitlevering in overgang?' (2008) 58 DD; J.W. van der Hulst, 'De uitleg van het begrip rechterlijke autoriteit bij de uitvaardiging van een Europees arrestatiebevel' [2019] 5–6 NtEr 158; H. Sanders, 'Overlevering' [2012] 3 DD 247; V. Glerum and K. Rozemond, 'Een evaluatie van de Nederlandse Overleveringswet' [2006] 9 DD 187.

2 W. Geelhoed and J.W. Ouwerkerk, 'Wederzijdse rechtshulp in strafzaken 2.0' [2017] NtEr 16; T.M. de Groot and P. van Glabbeek, 'Het Europees onderzoeksbevel: vergaande Europese samenwerking op basis van het beginsel van wederzijdse erkenning' [2022] 3 NTS 140; J. van Eekelen and A. Schild, 'Rechtsbescherming na beslag gelegd ter uitvoering van een Europees Onderzoeksbevel' [2018] NJB 2153; M. van Noorloos and J. Ouwerkerk, P. Verrest, 'Kroniek van het Europees strafrecht' [2023] 33 NJB 2917; P. Geelhoed and J. Ouwerkerk, 'The role and position of public prosecutors in the application of the European Investigation Order: A view from The Netherlands', in M. Luchtman, F. de Jong, F. Kristen and others *Of swords*

1805/2018[3] as well as insights from case law. For each of the three instruments, the implementation, scope and issuance, execution and cooperation between judicial authorities, fundamental rights, grounds for non-recognition and non-execution, and remedies are discussed. The analysis is followed by concluding remarks (*section 5*). This chapter will reveal that compliance with the three instruments has incrementally increased.

## 2 European Arrest Warrant: Critical Profiles in Legislation and Case Law

### 2.1 *Implementation*

The EAW FD was first transposed in The Netherlands in 2004 through the *Surrender of Persons Act* (SPA) (*Overleveringswet*).[4,5]

Since its entry into force in 2004, the SPA has been substantively amended several times due to EU legislation strengthening the rights of suspects. The most relevant amendments occurred in response to rulings by the CJEU: the first through emergency legislation in 2019, and the second with more comprehensive amendments (re-implementation) in 2021.

---

*and shields: due process and crime control in times of globalization* (Eleven International Publishing 2023); B. de Jonge, 'Grensoverschrijdende misdaad. Wanneer moeten opsporing en vervolging de grens over' [2022] 3 Boom Strafblad 78.

3 S. Bollens and D. van Daele, 'De wederzijdse erkenning van confiscatiebevelen: de innovatieve aspecten van Verordening (EU) 2018/1805' [2022] 3 Boom Strafblad 98; M. van Noorloos and J. Ouwerkerk, P. Verrest, 'Kroniek van het Europees strafrecht' [2023] 33 NJB 2917.

4 Overleveringswet 2004. A full-text version can be accessed at <https://wetten.overheid.nl/BWBR0016664/> accesed 17 july 2024.

5 The SPA is divided into five chapters: Chapter 1 (Arts 1–4) covers general provisions, key terms, principles, and the law's applicability concerning the EAW. Chapter 2 (Arts 5–43a) outlines procedures for handling EAWs received by The Netherlands, judicial review processes, and the rights of individuals, including legal representation and appeals. Chapter 3 (Arts 44–48a) details the issuance of EAWs by Dutch authorities to other Member States of the European Union, securing surrenders, and cooperation mechanisms. Chapter 4 (Arts 49–58) addresses broader legal cooperation in criminal matters beyond the scope of the EAW, such as the rules for transferring criminal proceedings between The Netherlands and other jurisdictions, and the conditions for executing foreign judicial decisions in The Netherlands. Chapter 5 (Arts 59–76) includes provisions for pending cases, amendments, repeals, and implementation details. Additionally, there are two appendices which provide standardized forms and supplementary guidelines to apply the law.

The Act of 10 July 2019 amended the SPA in response to the CJEU's judgment in the joined cases *C-508/18 OG* and *C-82/19 PPU PI*.[6] Prior to this amendment, the Amsterdam public prosecutor was authorized to both issue and execute an EAW under Arts 1(f)[7] and Chapter 3[8] of the SPA. The amendment modified these provisions to comply with the CJEU ruling, which emphasized that a prosecutor must be able to exercise their responsibilities objectively and free from external influence, particularly from the executive branch. In the Dutch case, following the CJEU ruling in *Case C-510/19*,[9] it was determined that the Amsterdam public prosecutors do not meet these requirements, as they may receive instructions from the Minister of Justice and Security in exercising their decision-making powers.

The April 1, 2021, amendments to the SPA encompassed several significant changes, with particular emphasis on those made to Art 6, which regulates the procedures and conditions under which persons may be surrendered from one jurisdiction to another for the purposes of a criminal investigation against them or the enforcement of sentences. Notably, the requirement for a Dutch residence permit of unlimited duration to qualify as a national for the purposes of the SPA was replaced with a mandate for five-year continuous residence. Furthermore, Art 6a was introduced, granting judicial authorities the discretion in assessing refusal grounds, considering factors like reintegration. Moreover, these amendments introduced provisions allowing for the postponement of surrender in cases of fundamental rights violations, with surrender being refused if risks are not mitigated, as outlined in Art 11 of the SPA. Further elaboration on these modifications and others will be provided *infra*, § 2.5.

Nevertheless, in June 2021 the European Commission issued a letter of formal notice to The Netherlands, stating that it "incorrectly transposed the provisions related to, amongst others, the obligation to execute an EAW, the grounds for non-execution, the competent executing judicial authority, and

6 Cases C-508/18 and C-82/19 PPU *Public Prosecutor's Office in Lübeck v OG*, *Public Prosecutor's Office in Zwickau v PI* [2019] ECLI:EU:C:2019:456.

7 Art 1(f) before 2019 amendment: "In this Act the following terms shall have the following meanings: (…) f. Examining magistrate: the examining magistrate, responsible for the handling of criminal cases, at the District Court of Amsterdam."

8 Before the 2019 amendment, Chapter 2 of the Surrender of Persons Act, encompassing Arts 44 to 48b, governed the process of surrender to The Netherlands and designated the public prosecutor as the issuing judicial authority for a European Arrest Warrant (EAW). For instance, Art 44 stated: "Any public prosecutor in The Netherlands can act as an issuing judicial authority."

9 See Case C-510/19 *Belgium v AZ* [2020] ECLI:EU:C:2020:953.

the time-limits for surrender of the person".[10] This notice has led to draft legislation in June 2024, which addresses the issues pointed out by the European Commission.[11] At the time of the writing of this chapter, the draft is under consideration at the senate and therefore in the final stages of the legislative process. The proposed modifications will be detailed in their respective sections.

### 2.2 *Scope and Issuance*

In The Netherlands, an EAW may be issued either for the purpose of prosecuting an individual or enforcing a custodial sentence, as provided by Article 2(1)[12] in accordance with Article 7(1) of the Surrender of Persons Act (SPA). This framework is aligned with the FD 2002/584/JHA following amendments by the District Court of Amsterdam, which corrected the initial incorrect transposition.[13] The EAW is intended to address serious crimes, and therefore specific criteria apply to its issuance: i) for prosecution, the acts in question must be punishable by the law of the issuing Member State with a custodial sentence of at least twelve months; ii) for enforcement, the sentence to be enforced must be at least four months.

The principle of proportionality is critical in the issuance of an EAW. Dutch authorities must ensure that the gravity of the offense justifies the recognition and the ensuing obligation to comply with the EAW, avoiding its use for minor offenses. In line with previous judicial decisions of the District Court of Amsterdam,[14] the assessment of (dis)proportionality under the EAW requires distinguishing between general proportionality under the EAW and proportionality in specific cases. The EAW system, based on the underlying Framework Decision, is based on the principle that enforcement powers should not exceed what is necessary to achieve its objectives. However, the issuing of an EAW may be disproportionately burdensome for the individual in certain situations.

---

10 INFR (2021) 2004, 9 June 2021.

11 Kamerstukken I 2023–2024, 36491, A.

12 Art 2(1): "A European arrest warrant may be issued only for acts punishable by the law of the issuing Member State and punishable by a custodial sentence of a maximum term of at least 12 months or where a sentence or detention order has been imposed, the duration of which is at least four months."

13 This was incorrectly transposed in Art 7 of the Surrender of Persons Act but was later amended by the District Court of Amsterdam, which aligned its interpretation with the FD 2002/584/JHA, as will be further addressed *infra*, § 2.5.3.

14 See as examples District Court of Amsterdam, judgement of 23 August 2011, ECLI:NL:RBAMS:2011:BR5804; and District Court of Amsterdam, judgement of 1 March 2013, ECLI:NL:RBAMS:2013:BZ3203.

Claims of disproportionality can only succeed in exeptional circumstances, as illustrated by the case analysed in section 2.4.

Since 2019, in The Netherlands an EAW may only be issued by an investigating judge of each of the eleven District Courts, pursuant to Art 44[15] of the SPA.[16] Originally, all Dutch prosecutors on the District Court level were considered to have competence to issue an EAW. After the CJEU ruling 'Public Prosecutor's Offices in Lübeck and Zwickau' of May 27, 2019[17], however this article was amended. The current decentralized approach ensures that local judicial authorities can promptly issue warrants as needed. The amendment to restrict the issuing of EAWs to investigating judges rather than prosecutors represents a significant change to ensure increased judicial oversight and impartiality in the issuing process. This change aligns Dutch practice with the principles outlined by the CJEU, strengthening the protection of fundamental rights and the rule of law. By requiring a judicial authority to issue the EAW, the process potentially reduces the risk of misuse and ensuring that decisions are made on the basis of a thorough legal assessment rather than prosecutorial discretion.

The competent public prosecutor initiates the issuance process by submitting a request to the appropriate District Court.[18] In many prosecution instances, a national arrest warrant for the requested person issued by the public prosecutor typically precedes the issuance of the EAW.[19] Under Dutch law, although the prosecutor's formal authority to issue an EAW has been withdrawn, s/he still has the power to issue a national arrest warrant. Such a warrant can demonstrate the seriousness of the offence and the need to pursue surrender by means of an EAW. As a result, the judicial authority of the competent District Court may determine that the issuance of an EAW is justified.

### 2.3 *Execution and Cooperation between Judicial Authorities*

For the execution of an EAW by the Dutch authorities, the District Court of Amsterdam (*Rechtbank Amsterdam*) is the central authority, exclusively

15 Art 44: "Any examining magistrate may act as an issuing judicial authority."

16 Originally, pursuant to Art 44 of the Surrender of Persons Act, all Dutch prosecutors in District Court level were considered to have competence to issue an EAW, this until the CJEU ruling Cases C-508/18 and C-82/19 PPU *Public Prosecutor's Office in Lübeck v OG, Public Prosecutor's Office in Zwickau v PI* [2019] ECLI:EU:C:2019:456, after which this article was amended.

17 Ibid.

18 For further information as to which information is provided by the Prosecution to the competent District Court, go to V. Glerum, H. Kijlstra, A. Klip, C. Peristeridou, M. Wąsek-Wiaderek, A. Zbiciak (n 1) 124.

19 V. Glerum, H. Kijlstra, A. Klip, C. Peristeridou, M. Wąsek-Wiaderek, A. Zbiciak (n 1) 126.

empowered as the court of first instance to handle applications for issuance of an EAW executions. Consequently, once an EAW is issued and the individual is apprehended, all execution proceedings fall under the jurisdiction of this court. While uncommon, the Dutch Prosecutor may invoke Art 23(1)[20] of the SPA and thereby petition the court to decline the surrendering of the requested individual in particular cases. Such instances typically revolve around concerns that surrendering the individual to the issuing Member State could lead to violations of fundamental rights, including issues related to detention conditions and fair trial guarantees. Through the case sampling for this work, a case was found in which the prosecutor raised Article 23 SPA.[21] In this instance, the requested person, terminally ill with a life expectancy of only twelve months, faced surrender for prosecution on drug offenses. The court agreed with the prosecutor's argument, determining that the surrender would impose an excessive burden on the requested person, and decided to refuse surrender under such exceptional circumstances.

An EAW is sent to the public prosecutor in Amsterdam (Art 20 of the SPA),[22] who assesses if the EAW meets the basic requirements. If the prosecutor determines that the EAW *prima facie* fails to meet these requirements, they must inform the issuing authority immediately (Art 23[1] SPA). However, the power to refuse surrender based on the presence of a ground for refusal rests with the executing judicial authority, as stipulated by Art 6(1) of the EAW FD and further elaborated in Art 15(1) of the EAW FD, which mandates that the judicial authority decides on the execution of the EAW.[23] The recent legislative draft provides for a role for the Amsterdam court in these determinations.[24] The proposed

20 Art 23(1): "If the public prosecutor immediately takes the view that surrender cannot be authorised on the basis of the European arrest warrant at issue, he shall immediately inform the issuing judicial authority thereof."

21 See District Court of Amsterdam, judgement of 1 March 2013, ECLI:NL:RBAMS:2013:BZ3203.

22 Art 20(1): "A European arrest warrant, if not sent to the public prosecutor, shall be forwarded to him without delay". (2): "A European Arrest Warrant may only be processed if it meets the requirements set out in Art 2." (3): "If, in the opinion of the Public Prosecutor, a European Arrest Warrant does not meet the requirements set out in Art 2, he shall offer the issuing judicial authority the opportunity to complete or correct it." (4): "If, in the opinion of the Public Prosecutor, additional information in addition to the European Arrest Warrant is necessary, in particular in connection with Arts 7 to 9 and 11 to 13, he shall give the issuing judicial authority the opportunity to complete or correct it, taking into account the time limits referred to in Art 22."

23 V.H. Glerum and N. Rozemond, 'Overlevering' in R. van Elst and E. van Sliedregt (eds.), (n 1) 5.1.6.

24 The proposed Art 23(1) reads: "If the Public Prosecutor already at an early stage considers that the surrender cannot be authorised on the basis of the European Arrest Warrant before it, he shall bring this opinion to the attention of the court no later than on the

Article 23(1) SPA perfects this process by requiring the prosecutor to notify the court within three days if he considers that surrender cannot be authorised. The court then has ten days to decide on the refusal of surrender. This change strengthens the role of the court in ensuring that all legal and human rights considerations are thoroughly assessed, thus reinforcing the integrity of the surrender process. If the court refuses surrender, the prosecutor must immediately inform the issuing judicial authority. Regarding the postponed surrender of the requested individual, the SPA designates the Amsterdam Public Prosecutor as the responsible authority. This is specified in Art 36(1), applicable when the requested person is the subject of criminal proceedings in The Netherlands or if a criminal judgment rendered against him by a Dutch court is still subject to execution in whole or in part. Similarly, Art 36(2) of the SPA assigns the authority for conditional surrender of the requested individual to the Minister of Justice and Security for the same situations as stated in Art 36(1). In collaboration with the Public Prosecution Service, the Minister determines whether and under what conditions the individual may be temporarily handed over to the issuing judicial authority.[25] The rationale for assigning this authority to the Minister likely stems from their ability to impose conditions ensuring the individual's return to The Netherlands after completing the foreign legal process. Regardless, the proposed legislation transfers this power from the Minister to the District Court of Amsterdam.[26]

If the requested individual does not agree to surrender, a panel of three judges will determine the execution of the EAW following a public hearing. If the requested individual consents to surrender, a single judge (*unus judex*) will decide in what are known as summary proceedings (*verkorte procedure*), having heard the individual in camera, in accordance with Art 39 of the SPA.[27]

Under Art 29 of the SPA, decisions rendered by the District Court of Amsterdam are immediately enforceable. Typically, these decisions are not subject to appeal, except when the interest of justice justifies it. In such

third day after receipt of the European Arrest Warrant, submitting the European Arrest Warrant and its translation. In that case, the court may disapply the provisions of Art 23(2) of the Code of Criminal Procedure. The court shall decide within a period of 10 days on the immediate refusal of the surrender. If the court decides that the European arrest warrant shall be refused, the public prosecutor shall immediately notify the issuing judicial authority of this decision."

25 For further information as to the rationale to allow non-judicial authorities to make these decisions, see V. Glerum, H. Kijlstra, A. Klip, C. Peristeridou, M. Wąsek-Wiaderek, A. Zbiciak, (n 1) 134.

26 Art 36 is amended as follows: "In the second and third paragraphs, "Our Minister" is replaced by "the court" each time and "his trial" is replaced by "his prosecution"."

27 For further information, see V. Glerum, H. Kijlstra, A. Klip, C. Peristeridou, (n 1) 131–133.

cases, cassation appeals can be initiated solely by the Procurator General at the Supreme Court, as stipulated in Art 456(1) of the Dutch Code of Criminal Procedure ('*Wetboek van Strafvordering*', hereafter to be referred to as CCP). A cassation refers to the process of appealing a legal decision to the highest court, the Supreme Court of the Netherlands (*Hoge Raad*). The primary function of cassation is to review whether the lower courts have correctly applied the law, rather than to re-examine the factual aspects of the case.

The term "interest of justice" refers to an extraordinary remedy used to obtain a Supreme Court decision on a legal question that needs to be answered in the interests of legal unity or legal development.[28] Importantly, cassation in the interest of justice has no legal effect on the parties involved in the original proceedings. Regardless of the Supreme Court's ruling, the earlier judgment will continue to apply to those parties, pursuant to Art 456(3) CCP. The Supreme Court's decision in such cases is intended to provide clarity for future ones, guiding judges on how to decide in similar situations. Thus, the significance of cassation extends beyond the correct application of the law in a specific case. It plays a crucial role in shaping legal judgments for future cases and fostering legal development, potentially leading to the formation of new law. Therefore, while cassation in the interest of justice is a valuable tool for fostering legal development and ensuring uniformity in the EAW procedure, its limitation lies in the fact that it does not provide a remedy for the parties involved in the original case. Whether this is a positive or negative aspect depends on the perspective: it is beneficial for the legal system as a whole, but it might not be satisfactory for individuals seeking redress in their specific situations.

Cooperation between the Dutch judicial authorities and their foreign counterparts plays a key role in ensuring the effective execution of EAWs. Interviews with judges and prosecutors suggest that the collaboration with their foreign counterparts is generally considered effective.[29] When there is a case in which the details provided in the EAW are insufficient for the Dutch authorities to make a decision regarding the surrender request for surrender, they may seek additional information from the issuing Member State, such as the description of the offence (e.g., the role of the requested person), and the applicable maximum sentence for each separate offence.[30]

---

28 *Cassatie in het belang der wet*, 'Jaarverslag Hoge Raad' (n.d.) <https://www.hogeraad.nl/jaarverslag/parket-hoge-raad/cassatie-belang-wet/> accessed 17 July 2024.

29 E.G. Kurtovic, P.M. Langbroek, 'The EAW in The Netherlands' in B. de Santos Sousa (eds), (n 1) 285.

30 For the complete list of supplementary information requested by the Dutch authorities, go to V. Glerum, H. Kijlstra, A. Klip, C. Peristeridou, M. Wąsek-Wiaderek, A. Zbiciak, (n 1) 176.

Furthermore, the Dutch authorities commonly request additional information on the detention conditions in the requesting Member States, especially when cooperating with certain Member States such as Poland and Belgium.[31] Indeed, ensuring humane treatment and appropriate detention conditions for persons to be surrendered is a requirement to recognise an EAW, under the Framework Decision. The case law of the Amsterdam District Court shows that Dutch authorities are inclined to postpone the execution of an EAW if they lack sufficient information to decide.[32] Nevertheless, this does not imply a violation of the limits imposed by Art 17 of the EAW FD on the maximum duration of the enforcement procedure.

### 2.4 *Fundamental Rights*

Recital 13 of the EAW FD, along with Article 1(3), prohibits the surrender of individuals to the issuing Member State if there is a risk of violating their fundamental rights as guaranteed by the European Convention for the Protection of Human Rights and Fundamental Freedoms (ECHR). This principle is integrated in Dutch law under Article 11 of the SPA, which mandates refusal of surrender on these grounds to align with the EAW FD.

#### 2.4.1 Proportionality and Detention Conditions

The examination of potential human rights infringements is closely tied to the proportionality considerations that must be addressed by the executing Member State. However, the SPA lacks a provision for evaluating the proportionality of executing an EAW.[33] Although the EAW FD does not explicitly mention proportionality, it has been contended that it is addressed implicitly.[34] Glerum and Kijlstra suggest that the conditions for issuing an EAW, as outlined in Art 2(1) of the EAW FD, inherently require consideration of proportionality. We agree with their position, particularly because Art 2(1) ensures that an EAW can only be issued for offenses punishable by a custodial sentence or detention order of at least twelve months, or for sentences of at least four months if already passed. This requirement inherently links the issuance of an EAW to the severity of the offense, ensuring that the request is proportional to the

---

31 *Infra*, § 2.4.

32 *Infra*, § 2.4.

33 Glerum & Kijlstra are of the opinion that the EAW FD should contain a provision on verifying the proportionality of issuing an EAW, detailing the relevant criterion and alternatives to issuing an EAW, as well as stating to what extent the judicial authority should check the proportionality of it. For more information on this topic, see V. Glerum, H. Kijlstra, A. Klip, C. Peristeridou, M. Wąsek-Wiaderek, A. Zbiciak, (n 1) 230.

34 V. Glerum, H. Kijlstra, A. Klip, C. Peristeridou, M. Wąsek-Wiaderek, A. Zbiciak (n 1) 134.

seriousness of the crime. Notwithstanding, exceptional cases may arise where executing an EAW under these provisions would not be proportional.

The case law analysis conducted by Glerum and Kijlstra highlights that there has been only one case in which the District Court of Amsterdam declined to execute an EAW due to lack of proportionality.[35] In this instance, as mentioned supra § 2.3., the requested person, terminally ill with a life expectancy of only twelve months, faced surrender for prosecution on drug offenses. This case underscores concerns that the act of surrender itself could potentially violate Art 4 of the Charter of Fundamental Rights of the European Union, regardless of the quality of medical care or prison conditions in the issuing Member State.[36]

#### 2.4.2 Examination of Human Rights Violations

In the first version of the SPA, Art 11 only allowed refusal of surrender when there were strong suspicions of a flagrant violation of fundamental rights. However, a 2021 amendment, prompted by the CJEU ruling in *Aranyosi and Căldăraru*,[37] introduced new provisions. Now, courts can delay surrender if there is a chance that fundamental rights violations may be prevented by any changing circumstances (Art 11, paragraph 2). If conditions do not improve within a reasonable time, surrender can be refused (Art 11, paragraph 4). This change is significant as it acknowledges that mutual trust between Member States is not unconditional. It also allows the issuing Member State to modify conditions to respect the fundamental rights of the requested person and prevent his impunity.

For example, in a case in August 2019, the District Court of Amsterdam dealt with a Hungarian surrender request.[38] Defence counsel argued against surrender due to lack of assurance regarding humane detention conditions. The court, referencing past violations and a negative report from the European Committee for the Prevention of Torture and Inhuman or Degrading Treatment or Punishment (CPT), postponed the hearing indefinitely to allow for further investigation into detention conditions in Hungary.

---

35 See District Court of Amsterdam, judgement of 1 March 2013, ECLI:NL:RBAMS:2013:BZ3203.

36 V. Glerum, H. Kijlstra, A. Klip, C. Peristeridou, M. Wąsek-Wiaderek, A. Zbiciak, (n 1) 135.

37 The CJEU ruled that if, after a two-stage assessment, the executing judicial authority finds that there is a real risk of an Art 4 violation for the requested person once surrendered, the execution of the arrest warrant must initially be deferred and, where such a risk cannot be discounted, the executing judicial authority must decide whether or not to terminate the surrender procedure. Case C-486/14 *Piotr Kossowski v Generalstaatsanwaltschaft Hamburg* [2016] EU:C:2016:483.

38 See District Court of Amsterdam, Judgement of 06 August 2019, ECLI:NL:RBAMS:2019:5853.

### 2.4.3 Court's Approach to Detention Conditions

In most cases regarding potential violations of Art 11 of the SPA due to prison conditions, the District Court of Amsterdam relies on general communications from the issuing Member State. These communications typically assure compliance with CPT standards, without detailed case-by-case analysis. For instance, in a ruling of December 2021, the court accepted a non-specific guarantee from Belgian authorities regarding detention conditions, considering it valid for all cases.[39] This trend was also evident in a ruling of March 23, 2022, where the court concluded there was no risk of inhumane treatment in a Belgian prison based on the same non-specific guarantee from October 7, 2021.[40] This approach was reiterated in a judgment of September 6, 2022, regarding a Belgian request for the surrender of a Dutch citizen involved in criminal activities.[41] Overall, the District Court of Amsterdam tends to prioritize mutual trust between Member States, despite some exceptions. This approach, however, may conflict with the CJEU ruling in *Aranyosi and Căldăraru*, which emphasizes that Member States must assess case-by-case the specific prison conditions before executing an EAW when concerns arise about compliance with fundamental rights such as the prohibition of inhuman or degrading treatment.[42]

### 2.4.4 Recommendations for Improvement

To enhance the protection of human rights in EAW cases, the District Court of Amsterdam could conduct individualized assessments in each case rather than solely relying on general assurances from issuing Member States. This entails carefully examining the specific circumstances surrounding the requested person's potential surrender, particularly regarding detention conditions, although it could also create an additional burden for the court, as it can be difficult to obtain the relevant information to properly assess the protection of human rights in issuing Member States.

The recent 2021 amendment to Art 11 of the SPA allows for a more flexible approach. It grants the court the authority to postpone surrender if there is a risk of rights violations, pending changes in circumstances. If fully utilized,

39 See District Court of Amsterdam, Judgement of 9 December 2021, ECLI:NL:RBAMS:2021:7414.

40 See District Court of Amsterdam, Judgement of 23 March 2022, ECLI:NL:RBAMS:2022:2273.

41 See District Court of Amsterdam, Judgement of 6 September 2022, ECLI:NL:RBAMS:2022:5363.

42 Case C-486/14 *Piotr Kossowski v Generalstaatsanwaltschaft Hamburg* [2016] ECLI:EU:C:2016:483 paras 88 and 92.

it can be ensured no one is surrendered if their fundamental rights are endangered.

When concerns arise about detention conditions, the court should proactively investigate. This may involve seeking additional information, such as reports from independent bodies like the CPT, to make well-informed decisions.

In terms of compliance with the EAW FD, the 2021 amendment guarantees that the SPA aligns with EU legal standards and CJEU rulings. It upholds the principle that fundamental rights must be protected, even within the framework of mutual recognition. By allowing the possibility to delay or refuse surrender based on concerns over fundamental rights, the amendment demonstrates a commitment to balancing effective judicial cooperation with the protection of individual rights.

### 2.5 *Grounds for Non-recognition and Non-execution*

#### 2.5.1 Transposition

In The Netherlands, the implementation of the EWA FD included all refusal grounds and guarantees, with one notable exception: Amnesty (Art 3, paragraph 1 EAW FD), which conflicts with Dutch law.[43]

Art 122(1) of the Dutch Constitution (*'Grondwet'*) explicitly mentions that pardon is granted by royal decree after advice from a court designated by law and in compliance with established regulations. On the other hand, Art 122(2) recognizes that amnesty is granted by or pursuant to law, but there is no provision or established procedure within Dutch law that allows for the declaration of amnesty. Consequently, the absence of such legal mechanisms or regulations means amnesty cannot be declared under Dutch law. Therefore, this ground for refusal does not apply to The Netherlands as a requested State. Additionally, it was decided not to include the guarantee related to life sentences (Art 5, paragraph 2 of the EAW FD).

In assessing these differences, it appears that the Netherlands gives priority to maintaining the integrity and specificity of its legal system while adhering to the EAW FD. The lack of an amnesty provision could be seen as a limitation in providing full legal safeguards. However, it also underlines the importance of adhering to national constitutional principles. Similarly, the exclusion of the guarantee of life imprisonment reflects the commitment of the Netherlands to its established legal procedures, which already include robust safeguards and procedures in place concerning the imposition and review of life sentences in compliance with international human rights obligations under the ECHR.

43 V. Glerum, H. Kijlstra, A. Klip, C. Peristeridou, M. Wąsek-Wiaderek, A. Zbiciak (n 1) 97.

Originally, all grounds for refusal and guarantees were transposed in the SPA as mandatory.[44] However, the 2021 reform made most of the grounds for non-recognition provided for in Arts 4 and 4a of the Decision as optional under Dutch law.[45] It should be noted that optional grounds should not be applied when mandatory grounds are applicable. This ensures no overlap or conflict between the grounds under Dutch law. This approach is compliant with the EAW FD, as it respects the hierarchy and application of mandatory grounds while allowing flexibility for the optional ones.

As to the transposition of Art 4a EAW FD, the Dutch Government explained that the proposal to partially amend it was made because they were previously of the belief that, except in the specific situations described in Art 4a(1)(a-d), there could be no circumstances in which surrender could be permitted if the requested person did not appear in person at the trial which gave rise to the decision (the latter was transposed in Art 12 of the SPA).[46] This position was erroneous.[47] The Dutch Government's approach seemed to overlook other possible scenarios in which the requested person might not have been present at his or her trial and yet his or her rights might still be sufficiently protected. For example, there may be valid reasons for a person's absence that do not prevent a fair trial, such as being properly informed of the proceedings or having legal representation. Accordingly, we are of the opinion that the change of this ground of refusal from mandatory to optional was correct.

The mandatory grounds for non-execution of the EAW, set out in Art 3 of the Framework Decision, have been integrated into the SPA. Art 9(2)(b)(1) of the SPA, which mirrors Art 3(1) of the EAW FD, provides that surrender shall not be granted if the requested person has been convicted by a final judgment of a Dutch court or a court of another Member State of the European Union provided the sentence or measure imposed has been executed in its entirety. This provision maintains the *Erledigungsprinzip* (*ne bis in idem*), which ensures that persons are not punished several times for the same offence within the EU, underlining the importance of the finality and integrity of judicial decisions in all Member States. This raises the question of the standing of cases where a person has been convicted but has not yet served their sentence or are simply being prosecuted in The Netherlands. In such cases, optional grounds for refusal come into play, allowing Dutch authorities to consider whether

44 V. Glerum, H. Kijlstra, A. Klip, C. Peristeridou, M. Wąsek-Wiaderek, A. Zbiciak (n 1) 98.
45 Ibid.
46 V. Glerum, H. Kijlstra, A. Klip, C. Peristeridou, M. Wąsek-Wiaderek, A. Zbiciak (n 1) 134.
47 Ibid.

surrender should be postponed or refused depending on the specific circumstances, ensuring a balance between the rights of the person and the interests of justice.

Furthermore, Art 9(2)(b)(1–4) of the SPA, transposing Art 3(2) of the EAW FD, outlines additional circumstances under which surrender is prohibited. Specifically, surrender is not allowed if the punishment or measure imposed has been fully served, is no longer subject to execution, involves a judicial pardon, or if the punishment is being served in The Netherlands. These clauses ensure that once a person has been dealt with legally in one Member State, they are not subjected to repetitive legal actions elsewhere within the EU.

Moreover, Art 9(1)(d) of the SPA, which transposes Art 3(2) of the EAW FD, allows for refusal of surrender if a court in a third country has given a final decision. This provision recognizes the judicial authority of non-EU countries in specific cases, such as when the person has been acquitted, convicted, or has served their sentence or been pardoned in that third country. This ensures respect for the *ne bis in idem* principle and prevents people from being tried or punished several times for the same offence, including outside the EU. Finally, Art 10 of the SPA, in line with Art 3(3) of the EAW FD, provides that surrender shall not be granted if the person was under twelve years of age at the time of the commission of the offence.[48] It is worth mentioning that this is in line with Art 486 CCP, which stipulates that no one may be criminally prosecuted for an offence committed under the age of twelve. This provision reflects the commitment to the principles of juvenile justice and the protection of children during court proceedings.

The SPA explicitly transposes the optional grounds for non-execution provided for in Art 4 of the EAW FD. Art 4(1) of the EAW FD has been transposed into Art 7(1)(a)(2) of the SPA, which allows surrender to be authorized in cases where the issuing Member State or the European Public Prosecutor's Office (EPPO) has initiated a criminal investigation. This provision is significant as it allows the executing judicial authority to consider requests for surrender in situations where the requested person is suspected of having committed another offence punishable under both the law of the issuing Member State and the law of The Netherlands with a minimum custodial sentence of twelve months.

48 Through case sampling, we have not found any court rulings where an EAW was denied because the requested person was under the age of twelve at the time of the offense. However, we have encountered several rulings where Art 10 was invoked by the defence counsel, but without success, as the court determined that the requested person had already reached the legal age at the time of the crime. See as an example District Court of Amsterdam, Judgement of 23 September 2021, ECLI:NL:RBAMS:2021:5377; District Court of Amsterdam, Judgement of 11 June 2020, ECLI:NL:RBAMS:2020:2969.

In such cases, surrender may also be refused, which gives the executing authority the discretion to refuse surrender depending on the specific circumstances of the case.

Likewise, Art 4(2) of the EAW FD is mirrored in Art 9(1)(a) of the SPA, which refers to the refusal of surrender for a requested person if criminal proceedings are ongoing against them in The Netherlands for the same offense as specified in the EAW. This prevents double jeopardy or simultaneous legal actions across jurisdictions. Art 4(3) of the EAW FD has been transposed into two provisions under the SPA. Firstly, Art 9(1)(b) allows for refusal if the person has been prosecuted in The Netherlands for the same offence and it is not possible to prosecute him anew. This includes cases where renewal of prosecution is excluded under Art 255 (1–2),[49] or Art 255a (1–2)[50] CCP. It also includes situations where the right to prosecute has lapsed because the individual has fulfilled the conditions set by the prosecutor prior to trial to avoid prosecution. Similarly, Art 9(1)(c) allows for refusal if the individual cannot be prosecuted in another Member State due to a final decision having been rendered. These provisions ensure legal certainty and respect for judicial decisions across borders. These provisions are in line with the EAW FD, as they uphold the principles of avoiding double criminality, respecting ongoing national proceedings, and recognising final judicial decisions, thereby aligning with the objectives of the framework.

Art 4(4) of the EAW FD manifests in Art 9(1)(f) of the SPA, which allows for the refusal of surrender if jurisdiction could be exercised under Dutch law for the offense, but a statute of limitations prevents prosecution. Additionally, if surrender is requested for the purpose of executing a punishment or measure, and punishment can no longer take place due to a statute of limitations, surrender may also be refused. This ensures individuals are not surrendered for time-barred offenses, maintaining legal certainty and fairness.

These provisions are in compliance with the EAW FD, as they uphold the principles of legal certainty and fairness by ensuring that individuals are not surrendered for offenses that are time-barred under Dutch law, thereby aligning with the framework's objectives.

---

49 Art 255 (1) states that: "The accused may not be charged again in respect of the same offence after his acquittal, after the order served on him declaring that the case has ended, or after the notification of no further prosecution, in the latter case subject to Art 12i or Art 246, unless new objections have become known". Art 255 (2) refers to: "New objections can only include statements by witnesses or the accused and documents, records and minutes that have come to light later or have not been examined."

50 Art 255a (1) declares that: "If an order of punishment has been issued against the accused, which has been fully enforced, he cannot, subject to the provisions of Art 12i, be charged again in respect of the same offence." Meanwhile Art 255a (2) indicates that: "The first paragraph applies mutatis mutandis if the public prosecutor withdraws a penal order."

Art 4(5) of the EAW FD is integrated into Art 9(1)(d) and Art 9(2)(b)(1–4) of the SPA, aligning with the transposed mandatory ground provided in Art 3(2) of the EAW FD. Art 4(6) of the EAW FD has been transposed into three provisions in the SPA. First, Art 6(1) of the SPA permits the refusal of surrender of Dutch citizens if the court is satisfied that the enforcement of the custodial sentence imposed will be taken over by The Netherlands. In such cases, if surrender is refused, the court simultaneously orders the enforcement of the custodial sentence. This provision ensures that Dutch citizens are not surrendered for enforcement of sentences if alternative arrangements for serving the sentence can be made, promoting the efficient administration of justice, and safeguarding the rights of citizens. Additionally, Art 6(2)(a–c) mandates the court to assess whether grounds as referred to in Art 2 exist when evaluating a surrender request for surrender. Art 6(3) stipulates that if the duration of the custodial sentence imposed exceeds the maximum sentence applicable for the offense under Dutch law, the duration of the sentence is reduced to match the maximum sentence. These provisions ensure that requests for surrender are evaluated comprehensively, and that the duration of the sentence aligns with Dutch legal standards. These measures are in line with the EAW FD, ensuring respect for the principles of fairness, protection of citizens and legal consistency.

Finally, aligning with the EAW FD, Art 4(7)(a) of the EAW FD is mirrored in Art 13(1)(a) of the SPA, allowing for refusal of surrender for offenses committed wholly or partly within Dutch territory or on Dutch vessels or aircraft. This upholds Dutch jurisdiction and sovereignty over such offenses. Correspondingly, Art 4(7)(b) of the EAW FD is reflected in Art 13(1)(b) of the SPA, allowing for refusal of surrender for offenses committed outside the issuing State's territory if not prosecutable under Dutch law. This safeguards individuals from surrender for offenses falling outside Dutch jurisdiction.

### 2.5.2 Surrender of Nationals and Equivalent to Nationals

#### 2.5.2.1 *Requirements for Equivalence to Nationals*

Art 6 of the SPA is a pivotal piece of legislation as it establishes the conditions under which nationals or individuals deemed equivalent to nationals can be surrendered to the issuing Member State.

Initially, Art 6, paragraph 5 (currently paragraph 3) of the SPA stated the conditions for being considered equivalent to a national, being one of them being a residence permit of indefinite duration in The Netherlands.[51] However,

51 The three conditions stated by Art 6(5) were: 1) that the requested person held a residence permit of an indefinite period in The Netherlands; 2) that they could be prosecuted in The Netherlands for the same offenses as requested in the EAW; and 3) that there was no

prompted by CJEU judgments like *Wolzenburg*,[52] this requirement was removed through the 2021 amendment of the SPA. Instead, the requested person must only prove a continuous residence of at least five years in accordance with Art 8, under a) to e) and l), of the Aliens Act 2000, ensuring sufficient integration in the executing Member State.[53]

In current national case law,[54] the Amsterdam District Court considers sufficient information provided by the defence counsel proving a continuous residence of five years, as well as information provided by the Immigration and Naturalization Service (hereinafter: IND) corroborating the above and issuing an opinion as to whether the person's residency status would be affected by an eventual sentence. This change reflects the EU's non-discrimination principle and highlights the responsiveness of Dutch law to the evolving jurisprudence of the CJEU.

#### 2.5.2.2 *Judicial Discretion in Cases Final Judgments' Enforcement*

The legislative amendments, particularly between the SPA 2004 and its updated version in 2021, mark a notable shift in approach. The surrender of Dutch nationals for the execution of a custodial sentence previously was strictly prohibited unless the executing state expressed a willingness to undertake

---

risk of the requested person losing their residence status as a result of a punishment or measure imposed after the surrender.

52 A question was raised by the District Court of Amsterdam to the CJEU in 2008 in the *Wolzenburg* case. The CJEU, Case C-123/08 Wolzenburg [2009] EU:C:2009:616ECR I-09621, concluded that, to ensure that the person from another Member State in respect of whom the EAW was issued is sufficiently integrated in the executing Member State, it is required that they have resided for an uninterrupted period of five years. To this effect, the CJEU underlined that the EU rules on the right of residence have expressly established this time limit as a condition for Union citizens to acquire a permanent right of residence in the host Member State. It emphasized that this aligns with Art 12 of the EC Treaty (principle of non-discrimination).

53 Through the amendment of the law of 2021, Art 6(5) was removed, and 6(3) was introduced, which maintained requirements two and three (prosecution possible in The Netherlands and no risk of losing the right of residence because of the potential punishment), but modified the first requirement, establishing that the requested person must only prove a continuous residence of at least five years in accordance with Art 8, under a) to e) and l), of the Aliens Act 2000 "and because that provision also encompasses third country nationals with a Dutch residence permit of limited duration, they are no longer obliged to be in possession of a Dutch residence permit of unlimited duration". V. Glerum, H. Kijlstra, A. Klip, C. Peristeridou, M. Wąsek-Wiaderek, A. Zbiciak, (n 1) 116–117.

54 As an example, see District Court of Amsterdam, Judgement of 30 March 2023, ECLI:NL:RBAMS:2023:3713.

the sentence's enforcement, without providing a concrete guarantee.[55] This provision conflicted with Art 4(6) of the EAW FD, which requires an undertaking as an exception to refusal. Therefore, through its 2021 amendment, Art 6a was introduced, outlining the factors that Dutch magistrates must consider for taking over the enforcement of judgements. These factors include whether there are grounds for refusal as specified in relevant articles of the Mutual Recognition and Enforcement of Custodial and Conditional Sanctions Act (para. 2a), whether the offense is also punishable under Dutch law (para. 2b), and whether the sentence needs adjustment to align with Dutch legal standards (para. 2c).

#### 2.5.2.3 *Dual Criminality in Cases of Final Judgments' Enforcement*

The principle of dual criminality, established in Art 2(2) of the EAW FD, is another significant consideration in cases of surrender of nationals or equivalent to nationals. While the EAW FD allows for the execution of sentences for offenses punishable in the issuing Member State without verifying double criminality, it also allows for execution for offenses not listed, provided they are punishable in both issuing and executing Member States. In instances where the offense is not punishable under Dutch law, the District Court of Amsterdam has the discretion to refuse surrender of a national to the issuing Member State and undertake enforcement.[56] The execution of this discretion is crucial for protecting the claimed person's social reintegration interest.

However, the new draft amendment to Art 6(3) of the SPA proposes the deletion of the clause "insofar as he or she may be prosecuted in The Netherlands for the facts on which the European Arrest Warrant is based".[57] The justification for this change is to simplify and speed up the surrender process. The deletion of this clause is intended to avoid unnecessary legal complications and delays related to determining whether the person can be prosecuted in The Netherlands for the same facts. This change is intended to facilitate more efficient execution of EAWs, thereby improving judicial cooperation, and ensuring a smoother surrender process within the EU.

---

55 V. Glerum, H. Kijlstra, A. Klip, C. Peristeridou, M. Wąsek-Wiaderek, A. Zbiciak, (n 1) 103–104.

56 As an example, see District Court of Amsterdam, Judgement of 18 November 2021, ECLI:NL:RBAMS:2021:6776.

57 Art 6 is amended as follows: "(...) 2. In the third paragraph, the words 'insofar as he can be prosecuted in The Netherlands for the facts on which the European arrest warrant is based and' are deleted."

#### 2.5.2.4 *Guarantee for Return in Cases of Surrender for Criminal Prosecution*

Another critical aspect addressed by the SPA is the condition for the issuing Member State to provide a guarantee of return in cases where surrender for criminal prosecution is requested. This guarantee ensures that nationals, if sentenced, will return to serve their sentence in the executing Member State. The objective behind this provision is, again, to protect the requested person's interest in reintegrating into their own Member State while serving a custodial sentence. This guarantee can be found in the District Court of Amsterdam rulings, which consistently show that a written submission of the guarantee by the issuing Member State is considered sufficient for the Dutch magistrates.[58]

#### 2.5.2.5 *Recommendations for Improvement*

While the recent amendments to the SPA have brought it closer in line with European law, there may be room for improvement by focusing on protecting the reintegration interests of claimed persons in surrender decisions, including their social ties and rehabilitation prospects. To achieve this, the SPA could explicitly require the consideration of these factors rather than leaving it to judicial discretion. This applies equally to both cases of requests for criminal prosecution and enforcement of sentences. Assessment of factors such as family connections, employment history, community involvement, and participation in rehabilitation programs would then be integral to surrender decisions.

The current draft to modify the SPA has adopted this position, specifically adding to Art 6(1) that "the court shall assess in particular whether serving the sentence in The Netherlands will contribute to the social reintegration of the Dutch national."[59] Furthermore, the draft proposes adding a new subparagraph b) to Art 6a(2), which requires the court to assess, when considering a request for the surrender of a Dutch national, "whether the transfer of the execution of

---

58 As an example, see District Court of Amsterdam, Judgement of 27 December 2022, ECLI:NL:RBAMS:2022:8453.

59 Art 6 is amended as follows: "(…)1. The first paragraph shall read: 1. Surrender of a Dutch national may be permitted insofar as it has been requested for the purposes of a criminal investigation against him. In the event that the Dutch national is sentenced to an unconditional custodial sentence in the issuing Member State for the acts for which surrender may be permitted, the court may impose the condition that the requested person may serve his sentence in The Netherlands. In doing so, the court shall assess in particular whether serving the sentence in The Netherlands will contribute to the social reintegration of the Dutch national."

the custodial sentence will contribute to the social reintegration of the Dutch citizen."[60] These modifications align with the previous recommendations.

### 2.5.3 Double Criminality

Originally, Art 7, paragraph 1 of the Dutch SPA aimed to transpose Art 2, paragraphs 1 and 4, in conjunction with Art 4, paragraph 1 of the EAW FD. However, this transposition was flawed. The most significant omission was the treatment of double criminality. The Dutch law mistakenly established the lack of double criminality of non-listed offenses as a mandatory ground for refusal, contrary to the intention of the EAW FD.

The issue was addressed in *Case C-665/20 PPU*, in which the CJEU emphasized that Member States cannot require judicial authorities to categorically refuse to execute EAWs based on optional grounds for non-execution without allowing them to consider the specific circumstances of each case.[61] This ruling clarified the discretionary nature of grounds for non-execution under the EAW FD. To rectify the transposition errors, the Dutch legislator made amendments. The language of Art 7(1) of the SPA was changed from mandatory ("may only be permitted for") to optional ("may be authorized for"). This change clarified that the lack of punishability under Dutch law for non-listed offenses is an optional ground for refusal. Additionally, the Amsterdam District Court interpreted the amended Art 7(1) as an optional ground for refusal.[62] The court stated that even if the double criminality requirement is not met, surrender may not be refused if the circumstances warrant it.[63]

#### 2.5.3.1 *Resolving Cumulative Conditions for Non-listed Offenses*

Another issue with the transposition was found in Art 7(1) of the SPA, which outlined two cumulative conditions for refusing surrender in EAW cases for non-listed offenses: i) the sentence must be at least four months in the issuing

---

60 Art 6a is amended as follows: "1. In the second paragraph, a subparagraph is inserted, renumbering parts b and c to parts c and d, worded as follows: b. whether the transfer of the execution of the custodial sentence will contribute to the social reintegration of the Dutch citizen."

61 Case C-665/20 PPU *Local Court Tiergarten v X* [2021] ECLI:EU:C:2021:339.

62 As an example, see District Court of Amsterdam, Judgement of 15 April 2021, ECLI:NL:RBAMS:2021:1803.

63 In this specific case, despite the conclusion that non-payment of maintenance without intent to endanger or abandon the child did not constitute an offence under Dutch law, the court still considered the surrender admissible. This was based on the need to enforce other custodial sentences imposed in Poland and to facilitate the consolidated resolution of all pending custodial cases, which was considered beneficial to the person concerned.

Member State, and ii) the offense must carry a maximum sentence of at least twelve months. However, this conflicts with Art 2(1) of the EAW FD, which sets these conditions as alternatives for both criminal prosecution and execution of a custodial sentence.

Furthermore, Art 7 of the SPA incorrectly required that for an EAW involving a non-listed offense – either for the prosecution of a criminal offense or the enforcement of a custodial sentence – it must be: i) an offense under Dutch law and ii) have a maximum sentence of at least twelve months, contrary to Art 2(4) in conjunction with Art 4(1) of the EAW FD. The CJEU ruled in *Case C-463/15 PPU* against refusal of the execution of an EAW solely because the offense is not punishable by a custodial sentence of at least twelve months in the executing Member State.[64]

These transposition errors were addressed by the District Court of Amsterdam, which aligned its interpretation with the EAW FD.[65] Currently, for surrender for the purpose of prosecution, the offense must be punishable by a custodial sentence of at least twelve months in the issuing Member State, while for surrender for the purpose of execution, only a minimum sentence of four months is required.

#### 2.5.3.2 *Amendments Proposed by Legislation Draft*

The draft amendments to Art 7 of the SPA aim to enhance clarity and flexibility in the surrender process between Member States of the European Union.

Firstly, the proposed modification of paragraph 1 expands the grounds for surrender by allowing individuals to be surrendered for acts punishable under both the issuing Member State's law and Dutch law, beyond specific listed offenses.[66] This ensures that individuals cannot evade surrender simply because their alleged offense is not explicitly mentioned in the surrender request.

Secondly, the draft amendment specify conditions under which surrender may be refused. For instance, surrender can now be denied if the act in question is not considered a crime under Dutch law, regardless of how it is classified

64 Case C-463/15 PPU *Public Prosecutor at the Court of First Instance Brussels v A* [2015] ECLI:EU:C:2015:634.

65 See District Court of Amsterdam, Judgement of 30 October 2015, ECLI:NL:RBAMS:2015:7470.

66 Art 7 is amended as follows: "1. In the first paragraph, part b, the words 'or 2°' are deleted and the words 'or for another act punishable under both the law of the issuing Member State and the law of The Netherlands' are inserted after the words "intended"."

or defined in the issuing Member State.[67] This prevents individuals from being surrendered for acts that do not meet Dutch legal standards.

Moreover, the draft clarifies that surrender requests cannot be rejected solely based on differences in financial or regulatory laws between Member States, pursuant to the new paragraph 3.[68] This means that variations in taxes, customs, or other regulations do not hinder the surrender process if the underlying criminal offense meets the surrender criteria.

Lastly, the draft amendment regarding paragraph 7, introduces flexibility when handling surrender requests involving multiple offenses.[69] Even if some specific acts within a request do not individually meet the severity conditions initially required for surrender, individuals can still be surrendered if other related acts fulfil these conditions. This adjustment aims to expedite surrender proceedings while ensuring that serious criminal activities are appropriately addressed across borders. This result is compliant with the EAW FD, as it aligns with the framework's objectives of facilitating efficient and effective judicial cooperation while maintaining the necessary legal standards for serious offenses.

### 2.5.4 *Ne bis in idem*

#### 2.5.4.1 *Transposition Challenges*

In the first version of the SPA, the Dutch legislature clearly aligned with the *Erledigungsprinzip* applied in Dutch law by transposing number 2 of Art 3(1)

---

67 Art 7 is amended as follows: "(…) 2. Two paragraphs are inserted, renumbering the second to fifth paragraphs as the fourth to seventh paragraphs, worded as follows: 2. Except as provided in the third paragraph, surrender may be refused if: a. Another act as referred to in the first paragraph, part a, under 2°, but which is not punishable under Dutch law, regardless of its elements or qualification; or b. The execution of a custodial sentence of four months or a longer period to be served by the requested person in the territory of the issuing Member State for another act referred to in the first paragraph, point (b), but which is not punishable under Dutch law, regardless of its constituent elements or description. (…)"

68 Art 7 is amended as follows: "(…) 3. In respect of charges and taxes, customs and exchange, extradition may not be refused on the grounds that The Netherlands does not levy the same type of charges or taxes, or does not have the same type of regulations on charges, taxes, customs and exchange, as the issuing Member State."

69 Art 7 is amended as follows: "(…) 3. The sixth paragraph (new) shall read: 6. Where the European arrest warrant relates to several separate acts which are punishable either under the law of both the issuing and executing Member States or under the law of the issuing Member State alone, but one or more of which do not fulfil the condition as to the severity of the penalty referred to in point (a)(2) of the first paragraph or in point (b), surrender may also be authorised for those acts, at the same time as surrender for the act or acts which do fulfil that condition."

of the EAW FD, which concerns the *ne bis in idem* principle, into Art 9(1) of the SPA as a mandatory ground for refusal. However, the April 2021 amendment inadvertently changed this to an optional ground for refusal, which is in contravention of both Art 54 of the Convention Implementing the Schengen Agreement (CISA) and Art 50 of the Charter of Fundamental Rights of the European Union. In this regard, the CJEU clarified in *Case C-665/20 PPU* that the executing judicial authority has no discretion under Art 3 of the EAW FD and must adhere to the *ne bis in idem* principle as enshrined in Art 50 of the Charter.[70]

#### 2.5.4.2 *Prosecutor's Penal Orders*

Another issue identified in the transposition of Art 3(1)(2) of the EAW FD concerns Art 9(2) of the SPA. This Art explicitly outlines the conditions under which surrender can be refused. It requires either: i) an acquittal or discharge from legal proceedings by a Dutch court, or a final EAW FD by a court of another EU Member State "which materially corresponds to a Dutch judgment to that effect"; or ii) a *res judicata* conviction by a Dutch court or by a court in another EU Member State.

The way the provision has been transposed poses a problem, since it fails to address situations where the prosecutor issues a penal order (*strafbeschikking*) against a defendant after fulfilling certain obligations, such as the payment of economic reparations, or when the prosecutor decides to discontinue proceedings based on the merits of the case.[71] These decisions, not being court judgments, are not covered by the current transposition. However, the CJEU, in interpreting Art 54 of the CISA, has concluded that such prosecutorial decisions should be equated to final court judgments, even though they are made without court involvement and do not have the form of judicial decisions.[72]

According to Glerum & Kijlstra, Art 9(2) of the SPA should be invoked in such cases, instead of relying on Art 9(1)(b) or (c), which currently provide for optional grounds for refusal. We agree with this position, since it aligns with the principle that mandatory grounds should take precedence over optional ones when determining the refusal of requests for surrender. This position was partly endorsed by the Amsterdam District Court in a case concerning the issuing by the Dutch public prosecutor's office of a penal order for the same facts on which the surrender request was based. The District Court considered

70 Case C-665/20 PPU *Local Court Tiergarten v X* [2021] ECLI:EU:C:2021:339.

71 V. Glerum, H. Kijlstra, A. Klip, C. Peristeridou, M. Wąsek-Wiaderek, A. Zbiciak, (n 1) 107.

72 Case C-486/14 *Piotr Kossowski v Generalstaatsanwaltschaft Hamburg* [2016] ECLI:EU:C:2016:483.

that the prosecutor's penal order sentencing the requested person to community service constituted a final judgment within the meaning of Art 3(2) of the EAW FD. Accordingly, the refusal to surrender should be mandatory and not discretionary.

#### 2.5.4.3 *Exception Clause*

Art 9 of the SPA has included an exception since its inception, allowing the refusal of surrender if the requested person is being prosecuted in The Netherlands for the same offenses. For this exception to apply, the Dutch Minister of Justice, based on advice from the Public Prosecutor, must order the discontinuance of the judicial proceedings to allow the prosecution to take place in the issuing Member State. During the case law analysis conducted for this work, we encountered a ruling that exemplified the application of this exception. The court deliberated on whether a prosecution, as defined in Art 9, paragraph 1(a) of the SPA, had commenced.[73] If the grounds for refusal under Section 9(1)(a) existed, the Minister's decision under Section 9(3) effectively resolves this issue.

#### 2.5.4.4 *Proposed Modification to Art 9(1) by Amendment Draft*

The amendment to the first paragraph, subsection b, specifies that surrender may be refused if in The Netherlands a decision has been made not to prosecute for the criminal offense for which the EAW has been issued, or to discontinue such prosecution.[74] This amendment clarifies that a decision not to prosecute in the requested state can serve as a ground for refusal of surrender, ensuring that individuals are not surrendered for offenses where prosecution has been abandoned or where there is no intent to prosecute.

#### 2.5.4.5 *Recommendations for Improvement*

To address the challenges posed by the transposition of Art 3(1)(2) of the EAW FD into the SPA, several steps can be taken. Firstly, the Dutch legislature may align Art 9 of the SPA with the mandatory nature of number 2 of Art 3(1) of the EAW FD to ensure consistency with EU law and fundamental rights.

Secondly, Art 9(2) of the SPA requires clarifications to explicitly include situations where prosecutors issue penal orders or discontinue proceedings,

---

73 See District Court of Amsterdam, Judgement of 23 September 2021, ECLI:NL:RBAMS:2021:5372.

74 Art 9 is amended as follows: "1. The first paragraph, part b, shall read: b. in The Netherlands, a decision has been taken to abandon prosecution for the offence for which the European arrest warrant was issued or not to pursue prosecution for that offence."

ensuring legal clarity. Based on CJEU interpretations, amendments might need to be made to the SPA to provide clear procedures for situations involving prosecutorial decisions, treating penal orders as equivalent to final judgments in the surrender refusal process. This would enhance legal consistency and predictability. These proposals have been incorporated into the draft legislation, which suggests supplementing the second paragraph of Art 9 with a new subsection (c).[75] This addition ensures that individuals cannot be surrendered if prosecution rights have lapsed in The Netherlands due to compliance with conditions imposed by the public prosecutor before the start of proceedings aimed at preventing criminal prosecution.

Finally, the exception clause in Art 9 of the SPA should be clarified to establish specific criteria for refusal, reducing ambiguity. This should include clear guidelines on when it should be considered that prosecution for the same offenses in The Netherlands has commenced. By establishing clear criteria for invoking this exception, the consistency and effectiveness of surrender procedures can be ensured.

### 2.5.5 Trials in Absentia

#### 2.5.5.1 *2011 Amendment*

The Dutch system complies with the EAW FD by transposing Art 4a into Art 12 of the SPA in 2004, making the refusal of surrender mandatory if the requested person did not attend their trial, unless proper notification can be proven.

On February 26, 2009, Council Framework Decision 2009/299/JHA amended the EAW FD, introducing grounds for refusing surrender of persons tried and convicted in absentia. One such ground involves cases where the person was not aware of the proceedings. However, it is important to note that this amendment did not establish a mandatory ground for refusal, instead leaving it to the requesting authorities to demonstrate the person's awareness of the proceedings for the purpose of surrender. This amendment did not seek to harmonize national legislation across Member States.

75 Art 9 is amended as follows: "(…) 2. The following subparagraph is added to the second paragraph, replacing the full stop at the end of subparagraph (b) with a semicolon: c. he has been prosecuted in The Netherlands, but renewed prosecution is excluded on the basis of Art 255 or Art 255a of the Code of Criminal Procedure, or the right to prosecute has lapsed in The Netherlands because he has complied with conditions imposed by the public prosecutor prior to the commencement of the hearing to prevent criminal prosecution, or a corresponding decision has been taken in his respect in another Member State involving a final judgment for the same facts."

This amendment was incorporated into the SPA on August 1, 2011, through Art 12(a), yet this ground for refusal remained mandatory, which led to a high incidence of refusals to execute EAWs.[76]

Specifically, when applying Art 12(d), which outlines the requirements for surrender when the person has not been served with the decision in person, the District Court of Amsterdam employs a two-fold test:[77] i) the person must be served in person promptly after surrender and informed of their right to an objection or appeal procedure. This procedure allows for the re-examination of the case with the possibility of presenting new evidence and reviewing the original decision; and ii) the individual must be informed of the timeframe within which they must lodge an objection or appeal, as specified in the EAW.

To this point in time, it could be said that the SPA did not fully comply with the EAW FD, since Article 4a was transposed as mandatory, which reversed the intended logic of the provision.

#### 2.5.5.2 *2021 Amendment*

On 26 May 2016, in the *Dworzecki* case the CJEU clarified that Art 4a of the EAW FD allows for optional refusal of surrender.[78] It underlined that the situations described in Art 4a constituted exceptions where non-recognition was not mandatory, allowing the executing judicial authorities to weigh other factors to avoid any violation of the individual's right to a fair trial. This was reaffirmed in the *Zdziaszek* case, where the CJEU stressed the discretionary nature of Art 4a.[79] This practice strikes a crucial balance between promoting judicial cooperation between Member States and safeguarding individual rights. It allows for a tailored approach that ensures adequate protection of rights, especially the right to a fair trial, while maintaining flexibility to address the diverse circumstances of each case.

In line with these rulings, the SPA was amended in April 2021, making Art 12 an optional ground for refusal. This remedies the defective compliance and will reduce the number of refusals.[80] However, while this amendment does not explicitly allow the court to consider other circumstances, such as the lack of diligence of the requested person, the District Court of Amsterdam has taken

76 K.H. Brodersen, V. Glerum and A. Klip, 'The European arrest warrant and in absentia judgments: The cause of much trouble', (2022) 13 New Journal of European Criminal Law.

77 See as example District Court of Amsterdam, Judgement of 30 October 2015, ECLI:NL:RBAMS:2015:7460.

78 See Judgement of 26 May 2016, Case C-108/16 *Dworzecki* [2016] ECLI:EU:C:2016:346.

79 See Judgement of 10 August 2017, Case C-271/17 *Zdziaszek* [2017] ECLI:EU:C:2017:629.

80 V.H. Glerum, 'De Overleveringswet op de helling: de herimplementatie van Kaderbesluit 2002/584/JBZ', Nederlands Tijdschrift voor Strafrecht [2021] 5, 5.2.

this into account when deciding under this provision. In an April 2021 ruling,[81] the court stated that, to comply with CJEU standards, it must first determine if the requested person appeared at the process leading to the decision. If not, it assesses if any of the circumstances mentioned in the law occurred. If none apply, it may take other circumstances into account to ensure no violation of the person's defence rights. For instance, in cases where the person was properly notified, the court may request assurances from the issuing authority that the person was in fact properly notified.

#### 2.5.5.3 *Compliance Assessment*

The Dutch system's compliance with the EAW FD has improved through significant amendments in 2011 and 2021. Initially, the transposition of Article 4a into the SPA as a mandatory ground for refusal led to frequent rejections of EAWs, contrary to the optional nature intended by the EAW FD. Following the CJEU rulings in the *Dworzecki* and *Zdziaszek* cases, which emphasized the discretionary aspect of Article 4a, the SPA was amended in 2021 to make Article 12 an optional ground for refusal. This change, allowing the District Court of Amsterdam to consider additional circumstances to protect defence rights, has brought the Dutch system into better alignment with the EAW FD, balancing judicial cooperation and individual rights more effectively.

### 2.5.6 Territoriality

#### 2.5.6.1 *Transposition Problems*

Initially, both refusal grounds were transposed as mandatory in Art 13, paragraph 1(a) and (b) of the SPA, respectively. An additional paragraph 2 was introduced, stating: "At the request of the public prosecutor, a refusal of surrender shall be waived solely pursuant to subsections 1(a) and 1(b), unless, in the opinion of the court, the public prosecutor could not reasonably have arrived at his request."

Due to the vagueness of this second paragraph, the District Court of Amsterdam had to establish through case law the requirements for its application through case law. In their study, Kurtovic & Langbroek[82] referred to a judgment of July 2, 2004, in which the court refused the surrender of the requested person to French authorities, finding that the prosecutor could not reasonably

81 As an example, see District Court of Amsterdam, Judgement of 15 April 2021, ECLI:NL:RBAMS:2021:1818.

82 E.G. Kurtovic and P.M. Langbroek, 'The EAW in The Netherlands' in B. de Santos Sousa (eds), (n 1) 262.

waive the refusal to surrender since she did not consider the requested person's interests in being tried as a Dutch national in his own country and not being subjected to indefinite pre-trial detention abroad.[83] The court further concluded that, in assessing whether to waive the refusal under Art 13 of the SPA, the public prosecutor must balance the interests of the issuing authority and the requested person.

However, in its ruling of November 28, 2006, the Supreme Court of The Netherlands held that humanitarian reasons cannot be considered as grounds to refuse surrender under Art 13 of the SPA.[84] It clarified that the legislative intent behind Art 13 is to prevent Dutch judicial authorities from cooperating in surrendering individuals for acts committed in The Netherlands that are either not punishable under Dutch law or do not warrant prosecution in the country. The Supreme Court further noted that the provision allowing waiver of refusal grounds at the request of the public prosecutor was created to ensure the proper administration of justice, particularly in cases where Member States have cooperated in investigations, and concentrating prosecution in one of the Member States is deemed appropriate.

In conclusion, the initial transposition of the grounds for refusal as mandatory in Article 13 of the SAP was not in conformity with the EAW FD, as the latter provides for these grounds to be optional. The vague wording of the additional paragraph 2 further complicated compliance, making judicial clarification necessary. However, the 2006 Supreme Court ruling, which excluded humanitarian reasons as valid grounds for refusal and clarified the legislative intention, brought the SAP closer to meeting the objectives of the EAW FD by ensuring a more uniform and cooperative approach to the surrender process in the EU.

#### 2.5.6.2 *2021 Amendment*

Following an amendment on April 1, 2021, the second paragraph of Art 13 was removed, leaving the first paragraph as an optional ground for refusal of surrender. When analysing national case law, it was observed that since this amendment, the Amsterdam District Court has focused on determining in which country it would be most appropriate to conduct the investigation, considering factors such as where the proceedings have already been initiated, where the most evidence is located, and in which jurisdiction the co-accused

---

83 See District Court of Amsterdam, Judgement of 02 July 2004, ECLI:NL:RBAMS:2004:AQ6068.

84 See Supreme Court of The Netherlands, Judgement of 28 November, 2006, ECLI:NL:HR:2006:AY6631.

are being prosecuted.[85] For the court, the mere fact that offenses are considered to have been committed wholly or partly in The Netherlands is insufficient reason to apply the ground for refusal.[86]

In conclusion, the amendment of 1 April 2021, which removed the second paragraph of Article 13 and left the first paragraph as an optional ground for refusal of surrender, brought the SPA in line with the EAW FD. The Amsterdam District Court's shift of focus towards practical considerations, such as the location of proceedings, evidence and jurisdiction of co-defendants, is in line with the intention of the EAW FD to facilitate effective judicial cooperation. This approach ensures that the grounds for refusal are applied in a manner consistent with the EAW FD, avoiding automatic refusals based solely on the connection of the offence to the Netherlands.

### 2.6 *Remedies*

According to Art 29(2) of the SPA, the District Court of Amsterdam's judgments on the (non-)execution of an EAW are immediately enforceable, with no legal remedies available except for an appeal in cassation in the interest of justice as specified in Art 456 of the CCP, as explained in section 2.3. It should be reiterated that if the Supreme Court overturns the District Court's judgment, this does not alter the disposition of the case at hand. Before 2022, the Prosecutor-General had lodged an extraordinary appeal on points of law in only five EAW cases.[87] This state of affairs restricts broader appellate review, which, while common in legal frameworks, may limit avenues for challenging decisions and potentially impact procedural fairness.

In cases where the requested person has been detained while awaiting the decision of the Dutch judicial authority on the request for surrender pursuant to an EAW, the public prosecutor can appeal a decision to release the requested person provisionally pursuant to Art 64(2) of the SPA in conjunction with Art 87(1) CCP. According to the same provisions, the requested person can appeal a decision to deny conditional release from detention, but only once. If the decision is issued by the investigating judge, the Amsterdam District Court has jurisdiction to hear the appeal; if it is given by the Amsterdam District Court, the Amsterdam Court of Appeal has jurisdiction. These proceedings are governed by Art 64(2) of the SPA in conjunction with Art 87(1) CCP. The

85 See District Court of Amsterdam, Judgement of 06 April, 2021, ECLI:NL:RBAMS:2021:1628.

86 See District Court of Amsterdam, Judgement of 09 August, 2022, ECLI:NL:RBAMS:2022:5185.

87 V. Glerum, H. Kijlstra, A. Klip, C. Peristeridou, M. Wąsek-Wiaderek, A. Zbiciak, (n 1) 133. The publication does not include the references to the cases.

restriction to a single appeal for denied conditional releases may be viewed as limiting, especially given its implications for the requested person's detention status.

Additionally, both the public prosecutor and the requested person can appeal a decision of the District Court of Amsterdam regarding the awarding of damages for wrongful detention, pursuant to Art 67(1) of the SPA in conjunction with Art 535(1) CCP. These appeals are heard by the Court of Appeal of Amsterdam, as stipulated in Art 67(2) of the SPA. This remedy ensures that both parties have an opportunity to challenge rulings on an equitable basis.

The current framework of the SPA provides specific appeal mechanisms related to EAWs, which align with the EAW FD's requirements to an extent. While the provisions for immediate enforceability and appeals regarding detention and damages ensure compliance with the need for judicial protection and fairness, the limitations on broader appellate review and the restriction to a single appeal for denied conditional releases indicate partial compliance. Enhancing these mechanisms could improve alignment with the EAW FD, ensuring comprehensive procedural fairness and judicial protection.

## 3 European Investigation Order: Critical Profiles in Legislation and Case Law

### 3.1 *Implementation*

The Directive has been transposed through the Act of 31 May 2017 amending the Dutch CCP. As of then, Title 4 of Book 5 of the CCP applies to the recognition and execution of EIOs.[88] More precisely, implementation has taken place through the amendment of Arts 5.4.1 to 5.4.31 of the CCP. In some of the amended provisions, reference is made to pre-existing Dutch legislation that was already applicable in The Netherlands prior to the implementation of the Directive and relates to domestic criminal matters, but by virtue of the adopted provisions 5.4.1 to 5.4.31 of the CCP, are also applicable in EIO cases. To date no amendments have been made to the implementing legislation.

In the past, refusal to recognize and execute a foreign criminal order was possible based on the grounds of Art 7 of Framework Decision 2003/577/JHA,[89] which were implemented through Art 552II (2)(3) of the CCP.[90] Now,

88 Staatsblad van het Koninkrijk der Nederlanden 2017, 231.

89 Council Framework Decision 2003/577/JHA of 22 July 2003 on the execution in the European Union of orders freezing property or evidence.

90 Staatsblad van het Koninkrijk der Nederlanden 2005, 310.

Art 5.4.4 of the CCP lists the grounds for refusal for non-recognition or non-execution of an EIO. Apart from the exact wording, some of the EIO grounds for refusal, which are currently included in the CCP, bear similarities to the Framework Decision's 2003/577/JHA grounds for refusal at the time. For instance, the second ground for refusal (section b) of FD 2003/577 was related to the situation where a privilege or immunity applicable under Dutch legislation precludes seizure; the third ground for refusal (section c) to the situation where the seizure would ultimately lead to cooperation in a prosecution or trial that under Dutch legislation is deemed to violate the principle of ne bis in idem; the fourth ground for refusal (section d) concerned the situation where double criminality is absent.[91] Art 13 of Framework Decision 2008/978/JHA[92] included the grounds for refusal of an evidence order. Art 13 of Framework Decision 2008/978/JHA was implemented in Dutch legislation through Art 552yy of the CCP.[93] Thus, the grounds for refusal applicable in The Netherlands under Art 5.4.4 of the CCP are not entirely novel and Dutch legal practitioners already had some practical experience with certain grounds for refusal.

### 3.2 *Scope and Issuance*

In The Netherlands, an EIO may be issued to obtain evidence in criminal matters or to obtain evidence already in the possession of the competent authorities of the executing State (Art 5.4.1(1) CCP). An EIO may also be issued in proceedings initiated by an administrative or judicial authority in respect of acts which are punishable under the national legislation of The Netherlands provided that the decision may be appealed against before a court having jurisdiction in criminal matters (Art 5.4.1(2) CCP). However, an EIO cannot be used to establish a joint investigation team (Art 5.4.1(3) CCP), which refers to the possibility of the public prosecutor, in some cases provided for in Art 5.2.1 of the CCP, to set up an investigation team together with competent authorities of other countries.

The authorities that, in principle, have the competence to issue an EIO in The Netherlands are the public prosecutor, examining magistrate, or court (Art 5.4.21(1) CCP).[94] These are also designated as possible competent issuing

---

91 Kamerstukken II 2004–2005, 29845, 3.

92 *Council Framework Decision* 2008/978/JHA of 18 December 2008 on the European evidence warrant for the purpose of obtaining objects, documents and data for use in proceedings in criminal matters.

93 Staatsblad van het Koninkrijk der Nederlanden 2013, 10.

94 Art 5.4.21(1) of the CCP: "The prosecutor, examining magistrate or a court, as the issuing authority, may issue a European Investigation Order applying investigative powers in another Member State, with the exception of Denmark and Ireland."

authorities in Art 2(c)(i) of the Directive. In addition, the CJEU has ruled that an EIO may be issued by a public prosecutor even if they are not completely independent of the executive authority.[95] Based on the Dutch implementing legislation upon first examination there do not appear to be any cases where the magistrate judge should be mandatorily involved in the issuance of an EIO, contrary to the execution of an EIO.[96] However, Art 5.4.25(2) of the CCP states that the practical arrangements for the application of videoconferencing shall be agreed upon by the magistrate judge or the court issuing the EIO. In this, it appears, there is therefore no role for the public prosecutor. Furthermore, where the decision to issue the EIO is concerned, the court before which the criminal case is pending is competent to assess whether that decision was taken in accordance with Art 5.4.21(2) of the CCP. This includes an assessment of the substantive grounds for issuing the EIO. To the extent that the issue of the EIO has already been decided on by the examining magistrate, the judge in the criminal case may assess whether the examining magistrate could reasonably have reached his decision on the issuance of the EIO.[97]

Art 5.4.21(2) of the CCP clarifies the prerequisites that should be met before an order can be issued: (1) the issuance of the order must be necessary for the investigation and proportionate to the purpose of the investigation, taking into account the rights of the suspect or accused person; (2) the EIO could have been ordered under the same conditions in a similar domestic case.[98] These prerequisites are in conformity with Art 6(1) of the Directive and the means of transmitting the EIO to the executing Member State stipulated in Art 7(1) of the Directive and transposed to Art 5.4.23(1)[99] of the CCP. The Dutch legislature has chosen to adopt the wording of the general provisions of the

---

95 Judgement of 8 December 2020, Case C-584/19 *A and others v Staatsanwaltschaft Wien*, [2020] ECLI:EU:C:2020:1002; J.H. Crijns, S.M.A. Lestrade and others 'Het OM uit de positie? De institutionele positionering van het Openbaar Ministerie ter discussie' [2022] 2 Boom Strafblad 45, 50–54.

96 For more clarification on the mandatory involvement of the examining magistrate, in some matters, in the execution of an EIO see 3.3.

97 See Supreme Court, Judgement of 13 June 2023, ECLI:NL:HR:2023:913.

98 See Art 5.4.22 in conjunction with Art 5.4.3(1) of the CCP, which establish additional requirements regarding the content of the issued EIO.

99 Art 5.4.23(1) of the CCP: "The issuing authority shall transmit the European Investigation Order completed in accordance with Arts 5.4.21 and 5.4.22 directly to the authority of the executing State competent to recognize and execute it in such a way that it may be recorded in writing and the executing State may establish its authenticity."

Directive almost entirely verbatim, with occasional nuances more appropriate to the Dutch language.[100]

### 3.3 *Execution Procedure and Cooperation between Judicial Authorities*

In The Netherlands, the public prosecutor is the authority authorised to execute an EIO (Art 5.4.2(1) CCP). If a Dutch authority other than the public prosecutor receives an EIO, it shall immediately forward the order to the public prosecutor and inform the issuing authority thereof (Art 5.4.2(3) CCP).

Although in most cases, the public prosecutor is authorized to conduct investigative acts independently within EIO proceedings, there are cases in which involvement of the examining magistrate is made either optional or mandatory. Pursuant to Art 5.4.8 of the CCP, an optional ground for involvement of the examining magistrate, the public prosecutor, if necessary or desirable for the execution of the EIO, shall submit the EIO to the examining magistrate. The public prosecutor specifies in a written requisition the operations required of the examining magistrate and may withdraw the requisition at any time.

There are also investigative acts that require the involvement of the examining magistrate. This is the case regarding an EIO that seeks to have a witness or expert who is in the territory of the executing state, to be heard by videoconference or other audio-visual transmission. The public prosecutor shall, to this effect, submit the order to the examining magistrate (Art 5.4.13(1) CCP).[101] Another case of mandatory involvement of the examining magistrate is that of interception of telecommunications carried out in the Netherlands, by another Member State, without the technical assistance of The Netherlands. If the public prosecutor, using the form provided by Annex C to the Directive receives a telecommunication recording notification, they shall immediately put the notification in the hands of the examining magistrate (Art 5.4.18(1) CCP).[102]

---

100 Separate provisions have been provided for the issuance of interrogation by videoconference (Art 5.4.25 CCP), the temporary transfer of a foreign detainee to the Netherlands (Art 5.4.26 CCP), the temporary transfer of a detainee to a foreign country for the execution an EIO issued by the Netherlands (Art 5.4.27 CCP) and the recording of telecommunications (Arts 5.4.28 and 5.4.29 CCP).

101 Art 5.4.13(1) of the CCP: "The examining magistrate is authorized to execute an EIO that aims to hear a witness or expert who is located on the territory of the executing State (...) via videoconference or other audiovisual transmission. The public prosecutor (...) shall place the order to this effect in the hands of the examining magistrate. The order may also relate to the interrogation of a suspect by videoconference or other audiovisual means of transmission."

102 Art 5.4.18(1) of the CCP: "(...) The notification shall be provided in either Dutch or English."

The magistrate judge shall decide within 48 hours of receiving notification whether to agree to the recording (Art 5.4.18(2) CCP).[103]

Art 5.4.3(1) of the CCP[104] contains minimum requirements regarding the content of an EIO, which are transposed from Art 5(1) (a–e) of the Directive. This provision further includes rules on the language in which the EIO should be drawn up, what the public prosecutor should do when a request has been transmitted by an unauthorized foreign authority, information is missing in the form provided by Annex A to the Directive, and/or an EIO is deemed disproportionate to the investigation in the issuing Member State.

The Directive states that the gathering of evidence should take place in the same manner as in a domestic case and that, in principle, there is an obligation to execute the EIO.[105] In The Netherlands the public prosecutor, as the executing authority, shall decide on the recognition and execution of the order as soon as possible and at the latest within 30 days of receiving it in conformity with Art 12(3) of the Directive.[106] An EIO capable of recognition and execution should be addressed with the same speed and priority as a similar domestic case. If necessary, the Netherlands shall consult with the issuing authority about the execution of the order and the expected duration of execution (Art 5.4.5(1) CCP). In executing an EIO, investigative powers may be applied under the same conditions as they would be in a domestic Dutch investigation concerning the same facts. However, this does not include requirements of proportionality or an assessment of the investigation interest (Art 5.4.7(1) CCP). In addition, the formal requirements and procedures indicated by the issuing authority shall be complied with in the execution of the request unless this

103 Art 5.4.18(2) of the CCP: "The examining magistrate shall decide within 48 hours of receiving the notification, in accordance with Arts 126m and 126t, whether consent for the recording may be granted. Consent may be denied, if in a similar Dutch criminal case, the recording of telecommunications would not be permitted."

104 Art 5.4.3(1) of the CCP: "Susceptible to recognition is an EIO containing at least the following information: (a) details of the issuing authority and, where applicable, the validating authority; (b) the subject matter and grounds for the order; (c) the available necessary information on the person(s) concerned; (d) a description of the offence that is the subject of the investigation or criminal case, as well as the legal qualification of the offence under the law of the issuing State; (e) a description of the jurisdiction requested and the evidence to be obtained."

105 Art 1 of EIO D; Case C-584/19 *A and others v Staatsanwaltschaft Wien* [2020] ECLI:EU:C:2020:1002.

106 Art 5.4.2(4) of the CCP; Art 5.4.5 of the CCP: "If this is deemed impossible, the public prosecutor shall inform the competent authority of the issuing State without delay, stating the reasons for the delay and the time deemed necessary to take the decision. The period may then be extended by a maximum of 30 days."

violates fundamental principles of Dutch legislation (Art 5.4.5(2) CCP). A fundamental principle of Dutch criminal procedural law is, for example, the prohibition of *détournement de pouvoir*.[107] The latter means that a power shall not be exercised for a purpose other than that for which it was given.[108] Furthermore, Art 5.4.5(5) of the CCP[109] reflects that unless there are grounds for delay under Art 5.4.6 of the CCP,[110] or if what is required in the EIO is already available, the EIO must be executed within 90 days of the decision to do so.

Geelhoed and Ouwerkerk argued that for the procedure to be swift and efficient, the short procedural deadlines and the prosecutor's information and consultation obligations require action at regular intervals and within prescribed, relatively short, timeframes, or at the very least, consideration of whether action is necessary.[111] Concerns can be voiced regarding the uncertainty that remains with respect to whether a response to a request for legal assistance will be received in a timely manner and whether that response will be usable.[112] The Netherlands is a logistical hub, which causes it to receive more requests than it issues and this can negatively affect the Dutch investigative capacity.[113] Moreover, swift and efficient judicial cooperation may create tension with the legal safeguards that The Netherlands can grant to the person affected by the EIO.[114] This criticism is further discussed in paragraph 3.6, which elaborates on Dutch remedies against an EIO.

---

107 See District Court of Overijssel, Judgement of 04 March 2019, ECLI:NL:RBOVE:2019:1013, for an example of the application of this principle.

108 P.H.P.H.M.C. van Kempen, 'Subsidiariteit, proportionaliteit en doelbinding als algemene beginselen: codificatie graag, maar meer volledig' [2018] 8 DD 85, 85.

109 Art 5.4.5(5) of the CCP: "Unless there are grounds for delay under Art 5.4.6 or if what is required in the order is already available, the authority shall execute the power without delay and, notwithstanding paragraph three, within ninety days of the decision referred to in Art 5.4.2(4)".

110 Art 5.4.6(1) of the CCP: "The public prosecutor may suspend recognition and execution of the EIO if: (a) the interests of an ongoing criminal investigation in The Netherlands oppose the execution of the order; (b) the documents, objects or data to which the order relates are already being used in another judicial proceeding."

111 W. Geelhoed and J.W. Ouwerkerk, 'Wederzijdse rechtshulp in strafzaken 2.0' [2017] NtEr 16, 21–23.

112 B. de Jonge, 'Grensoverschrijdende misdaad. Wanneer moeten opsporing en vervolging de grens over' [2022] 3 Boom Strafblad, 83.

113 T.M. de Groot and P. van Glabbeek, 'Het Europees onderzoeksbevel: vergaande Europese samenwerking op basis van het beginsel van wederzijdse erkenning' [2022] 3 NTS 140.

114 Ibid.

### 3.4 *Fundamental Rights*

Recital 18 of the Directive, alongside Art 1(4) of the Directive, stipulate that the Directive does not have the effect of modifying the obligation to respect the fundamental rights and fundamental legal principles of the Treaty on European Union (hereafter: TEU) and the Charter of Fundamental Rights of the European Union (hereafter: CFREU). In addition, Art 11(1)(f) of the Directive states that where investigative measures in the execution of the EIO conflict with fundamental rights, execution may be refused. This ground for refusal is explicitly transposed in Dutch legislation, under Art 5.4.4(1)(f) of the CCP.

Questions have been referred both to Eurojust,[115] by Member States (in respect of the Directive) and to national courts by individuals on whose behalf an EIO was (about to be) executed (in respect of the CCP), regarding the (possible) incompatibility of an EIO with fundamental rights enshrined in the TEU and/or the European Convention of Human Rights (hereafter: ECHR). The primary issue which emerged before the national Dutch courts up to now is whether there has been a violation of Art 8 ECHR in conjunction with Art 7 CFREU. Counsel requested the return of data carriers that contained, among other things, photographs of the deceased partner and (grand)children of the complainant. The counsel considered the seizure and inspection to be in violation of Art 8 ECHR. The seizure was deemed not in accordance with Dutch law, as it was effected without prior judicial review in which the interests of the complainant were considered. The District Court of Amsterdam assessed this complaint under Art 5.4.4(1)(f) of the CCP, since the violation of private life is a fundamental right included under Art 7 CFREU. The restriction on the right to respect for private life was deemed permissible, as the infringement was based on the CCP and sought to implement an EIO deemed necessary in the issuing State, established for the protection of the rule of law and the prevention of crime.[116]

Eurojust highlighted that the national legislation of the Member States differs, sparking debates about what constitutes fundamental rights. Questions mostly arise, due to difference in the interpretation of fundamental rights, specifically Art 6 TEU and/or the CFREU. As a result, concerns arise about whether the procedural law of the executing Member State is in conformity with Article 6

115 Eurojust, 'Report on Eurojust's casework in the field of the European Investigation Order' (Revisited version 24 November 2020) <https://www.eurojust.europa.eu/sites/default/files/assets/2020_11_eio_casework_report_corr.pdf> accessed 20 May 2024.

116 See District Court of Amsterdam, Judgement of 04 November 2021, ECLI:NL:RBAMS:2021:6315.

TEU and/or the CFREU.[117] However, in most cases it is just a matter of interpretation differences instead of noncompliance.

The concept of fundamental rights seems, at first glance, to have different scopes within Dutch legislation as well. The legislator chose to word the ground for refusal of Art 5.4.4(1)(f) of the CCP differently than in Art 11 of the SPA, which was already in force before the new Arts of the CCP were drafted. This was done to align the newly written text of the ground of refusal in the CCP with the ground of refusal in the Directive. However, the fundamental protections enshrined in Art 11 SPA, as established through ECtHR and Dutch Supreme Court case law, are clearly preserved within the scope of the current wording of the CCP provision.[118]

In conclusion, based on the legislation and a relatively small quantity of case law, especially regarding this ground for refusal, the Netherlands currently seems to conform to the Directive. Art 5.4.4(1)(f) of the CCP explicitly stipulates what is also provided for in Art 11(1)(f) of the Directive, and national courts assess possible violations of fundamental rights protected by the CRFEU under Article 5.4.4(1)(f) of the CCP, when counsel for example invokes Article 8 ECHR, which, like Article 7 of the CRFEU, protects the right to privacy.

### 3.5 *Grounds for Non-recognition and Non-execution*

The Dutch legislator has transposed the grounds for refusal mentioned in Article 11(1) of the EIO D through Art 5.4.4 of the CCP. The decision was made to designate all the grounds for refusal as imperative. In this regard, Dutch legislation is at odds with the Directive.[119] Until now, however, this has not resulted in debates or discussions in practice. Perhaps this can be explained from the fact that the EIO D and the Dutch implementing legislation require consultation with the issuing authority in all cases before invoking a ground for refusal. A ground for refusal is thus only at issue if consultation has not led to a solution.[120]

In assessing whether a ground for refusal referred to in Art 5.4.4 of the CCP arises, the court shall consider the contents of the complaint and what has

117 Eurojust, 'Report on Eurojust's casework in the field of the European Investigation Order' (Revisited version 24 November 2020) <https://www.eurojust.europa.eu/sites/default/files/assets/2020_11_eio_casework_report_corr.pdf> accessed 20 May 2024.

118 Kamerstukken II 2016–2017, 34611, 3.

119 As also noted in Brussels, 20.7.2021, Report from the Commission to the European Parliament and the Council on the implementation of Directive 2014/41/EU of the European Parliament and of the Council of 3 April 2014 regarding the European Investigation Order in criminal matters, COM (2021) 409.

120 Kamerstukken II 2016–2017, 34611, 3.

been put forward in that regard by the public prosecutor and by or on behalf of the person concerned at the hearing of the complaint. However, there is no obligation for the court to show *ex officio* that it has examined whether the public prosecutor, after receiving the EIO, complied with all the requirements of Arts 5.4.2 to 5.4.5 of the CCP before recognizing and executing the EIO.[121]

With the grounds having been adopted almost *verbatim* in the same order for nearly all grounds, it suffices to examine here only the few exceptions and grounds that require clarification. Art 5.4.4(1)(a) of the CCP, transposing Art 11(1)(a) of the Directive, is a pivotal piece of legislation as it encompasses several elements for refusal, including incompatibility of execution with a privilege or immunity applicable under Dutch legislation, as well as incompatibility with rules establishing and limiting criminal liability concerning freedom of the press and freedom of expression in other media.[122] Unlike Framework Decision 2003/577/JHA and Framework Decision 2008/978/JHA the last part – "as well as incompatibility with rules establishing and limiting criminal liability concerning freedom of the press and freedom of expression in other media" – is explicitly included as part of a ground for refusal. In the Framework decisions, this was only listed in the preamble. The Dutch legislator has chosen to adhere to the manner in which this ground for refusal is incorporated into the Directive, as a result public prosecutors can now explicitly invoke 'incompatibility with rules establishing and limiting criminal liability concerning freedom of the press and freedom of expression in other media' as a ground for refusal.

In Dutch legislation privilege and immunity relate to cases in which Arts 218 and 218a of the CCP apply. These Arts are applicable, for example, when a lawyer or medical professional successfully appeals to their right to decline to testify. The categories of professionals who can invoke the right to privilege are limited in number. Generally recognized as persons entitled to privilege are doctors, clergymen, notaries, and lawyers. The Dutch Supreme Court ruled that probation officers and legal assistants working for legal aid offices can also qualify.[123] If a Dutch authority has the power to waive an immunity or privilege, that authority shall be requested to waive it by the public prosecutor as soon as possible (Art 5.4.4(5) CCP). Despite the clear designation of persons deemed to be privileged in Arts 218 and 218a of the CCP, there was a case before

121 See Supreme Court, Judgement of 28 June 2022, ECLI:NL:HR:2022:965.

122 To gain perspective on how Dutch courts apply this ground for refusal see: Supreme Court, Judgement of 15 December 2020, ECLI:NL:HR:2020:1970.

123 P.P.J. van der Meij, 'Verschoningsrecht op grond van geheimhoudingsplicht' (in: T&C Strafvordering 2024, art. 218 Sv) accessed 20 May 2024.

the Supreme Court, which concerned a lack of clarity as to whether the person concerned could claim the privilege. This pertained not so much to the position of the person concerned, but to a discrepancy in wording between the Directive – *person concerned* – and the CCP – *interested party*. The Supreme Court has ruled that the right to complain for individuals entitled to privilege is not limited by the fact that the Directive refers to – *person concerned* – rather than – *interested party*.[124]

Art 11(1)(e) of the Directive has been transposed to Art 5.4.4(1)(e) of the CCP and allows for non-recognition and execution of an EIO where the latter relates to an offence committed outside the territory of the issuing State and committed at least partially on Dutch territory, which is not punishable under Dutch law. This is the only ground for refusal for which it was considered making it optional. Notwithstanding this consideration, the legislator made this ground for refusal mandatory in line with the other grounds for refusal.[125]

In conclusion, legislation and case law have not given rise to significant debates or discussions about the application of or compliance with EIO D. The Netherlands quite explicitly adheres to the wording of the grounds for refusal in the Directive. However, all grounds for refusal are imperative instead of optional as is the case for the grounds for Refusal in Art 11(1) of the Directive. In this respect, the Netherlands seems to be in noncompliance with the Directive, but consultation with the issuing authority is obligatory in all cases before invoking a ground for refusal. A ground for refusal is thus only raised if consultation has not led to a solution, which makes it unlikely for a ground for refusal to be formally invoked. For this reason, there seems to be little issue in practice.

### 3.6 *Remedies*

The CJEU ruled in the *Gavanozov II* case that the right to an effective remedy requires that in the Member State issuing an EIO, an appeal against that issuing decision must be available.[126] This ruling can be interpreted with different levels of strictness. Dutch commentators favour a less strict reading, as the CJEU does not comment on when that remedy should be available.[127]

Art 14(1) of the Directive stipulates that Member States should provide a remedy against the investigative measures defined in an EIO equivalent to the remedies in a domestic case. In The Netherlands, persons whose properties

124 See Supreme Court, Judgement of 15 December 2020, ECLI:NL:HR:2020:1970.

125 Kamerstukken II 2016–2017, 34611, 3.

126 Case C-852/19 *Ivan Gavanozov* [2021] ECLI:EU:C:2021:902.

127 M. van Noorloos, J. Ouwerkerk and P. Verrest, 'Kroniek van het Europees strafrecht' [2023] 33 NJB 2928; Annotation to Case C-852/19 *Ivan Gavanozov* [2021] ECLI:EU:C:2021:902.

have been seized within the course of the execution of an EIO have the right to file a written complaint about the seizure, about the use of the objects seized, or for the purpose of having their properties returned (Art 5.4.10(1) in conjunction with 552a CCP).

The Dutch Supreme Court clarified the role and responsibilities of executing authorities in proceedings in which a complaint against the seizure is filed, which should be active in safeguarding the rights of the person concerned. However, the role of the court in complaint proceedings should be limited to assessing whether there are grounds to refuse or delay the recognition or execution of the EIO.[128] The substantive grounds (Art 5.4.10(3) CCP),[129] proportionality and transfer of evidence (Art 5.4.7(1) CCP), may not be assessed by the Netherlands as executing Member State. This contributes to the concern that Dutch judges, as executing authorities, are sometimes unsure of what they may or may not assess. In response, the Supreme Court has developed a framework for review if the interested party files a notice of complaint under Art 5.4.10(1) in conjunction with Art 552a of the CCP for the purpose of executing the EIO.[130] The court may assess whether: (1) there are grounds for suspension or refusal (Arts 5.4.3, 5.4.4, 5.4.6 CCP); (2) whether the authority by which the EIO was executed was lawfully applied. In doing so, the court must limit itself to an examination of the formalities with which the seizure must comply. Any defences touching on the lawfulness of the prolongation of the seizure must, in view of the principle of mutual recognition, be disregarded; and (3) the seized objects concern the evidence to which the EIO relates and which the issuing authority seeks to obtain by that order. The presence of an interest in the issuing Member State in issuing an EIO is central and is automatically assumed after establishing that the seized objects are evidence to which the EIO relates.[131]

Questions were also raised about the scope of legal protection to which interested parties are entitled, both in the context of the issuance and execution

---

128 P. Geelhoed and J. Ouwerkerk, 'The role and position of public prosecutors in the application of the European Investigation Order: A view from The Netherlands', in M. Luchtman, F. de Jong and others (n 2).

129 Art 5.4.10(3) of the CCP: "Arts 552a(1) to (6), 552d(1) and (2), and 552e(1) shall apply mutatis mutandis, except that the court shall not examine the grounds for issuing the order, the execution of which led to the filing of the complaint."

130 See Supreme Court, Judgement of 21 December 2021, ECLI:NL:HR:2021:1940.

131 T.M. de Groot and P. van Glabbeek, 'Het Europees onderzoeksbevel: vergaande Europese samenwerking op basis van het beginsel van wederzijdse erkenning' [2022] 3 NTS 140; See for example, District Court of Rotterdam, Judgement of 22 February 2024, ECLI:NL:RBROT:2024:2261.

of EIOs and the role of the authorities involved.[132] These questions revolve around the exception that there are merely fourteen days to file a complaint against the seizure (Art 5.4.10(1) CCP). Indeed, contrary to the regular complaint procedure in a domestic case (Art 552a(3)(4) CCP), a short complaint period of fourteen days applies to the EIO (Art 5.4.10(1) CCP), which seems to be in contradiction with of Art 14(4) of the Directive. This provision stipulates that Member States shall ensure that the time-limits for seeking a legal remedy shall be the same as those that are provided for in similar domestic cases. It is therefore questionable whether The Netherlands has implemented this provision in conformity with the Directive. If no complaint is made within the short complaint period of fourteen days, the seized objects can be transferred to the judicial authorities of the issuing Member State. According to Van Eekelen and Schild there are two main issues. Next to the exceptionally short timeframe for submitting the complaint, the notification of the seized person of his right to complain in practice (Art 5.4.10(1) CCP) occasionally fails, because in the case of a regular criminal domestic seizure (Art 94 CCP), there is no obligation to give notice of the complaint period.[133]

Art 19(2) of the Directive stipulates that confidentiality of the EIO is a basic principle.[134] The legislative history does not disclose if the legislator considered how to ensure effective legal safeguards in view of the EIO's confidentiality obligation. It has been left to the executing Member State to navigate through how to ensure effective legal safeguards.[135] The challenge in EIO proceedings is that given the obligation of confidentiality, an EIO cannot be contested in the complaint procedure, and in addition, the public prosecutor will, in some cases, not be obliged to notify interested parties of their right to lodge a complaint. However, the confidentiality of EIO proceedings does not mean that the public prosecutor need not carry out any activity regarding protecting the

132 M. van Noorloos and J. Ouwerkerk, P. Verrest, 'Kroniek van het Europees strafrecht' [2023] 33 NJB 2917.

133 J. van Eekelen and A. Schild, 'Rechtsbescherming na beslag gelegd ter uitvoering van een Europees Onderzoeksbevel' [2018] NJB 2153; P. Geelhoed, J. Ouwerkerk, 'The role and position of public prosecutors in the application of the European Investigation Order: A view from The Netherlands' in M. Luchtman, F. de Jong and others (n 2) 438–439.

134 Art 19(2) of Directive 2014/41/EU: "The executing authority shall, in accordance with its national law, guarantee the confidentiality of the facts and substance of the EIO, except in so far as such information must be disclosed for the purpose of implementing investigative measures. If the executing authority is unable to comply with the obligation of confidentiality, it shall inform the issuing authority without delay."

135 J. van Eekelen and A. Schild, 'Rechtsbescherming na beslag gelegd ter uitvoering van een Europees Onderzoeksbevel' [2018] NJB 2153, 2153–2154.

rights of the interested party.[136] To provide effective legal protection, the public prosecutor could ask the authorities of the issuing Member State whether there are any objections to the disclosure of the EIO in the complaint's procedure. In addition, if the issuing Member State does not give its consent, the possibility remains for the chamber to apply Art 23(5) of the CCP,[137] which allows only the chamber and not the complainant to examine the EIO. This enables for the assessment of the criminal procedural interest in the enforcement of the seizure. However, this will not change the fact that the complainant is impeded in their ability to substantiate his complaint, for which there is no solution within Dutch legislation in EIO proceedings.[138]

Art 14(7) of the Directive stipulates that issuing Member States shall take into account a successful challenge against the recognition or execution of an EIO in accordance with their own national law. In 2023, the Dutch Supreme Court provided a preliminary ruling at the request of the District Courts of Overijssel and Noord-Nederland in the EncroChat/Sky cases. It was ruled that concerning evidence obtained by means of an EIO, the judge in the criminal case must ensure that the use of that evidence complies with the right to a fair trial and the rights of the defence, as stipulated in Art 14(7) of the Directive. This means that the court must ensure the 'overall fairness' of the proceedings in question when using that evidence.[139] In 2024, the Supreme Court delivered another judgement after answering the preliminary questions. It ruled that where the reliability of investigation results used for evidence is concerned, a court would only use evidence that it considers reliable. Exclusion of evidence is possible if irregularities have occurred that have substantially affected the reliability and accuracy of investigation results. It makes no difference whether those investigation results were obtained under the responsibility of other Member States or in a Dutch criminal investigation. Ordinarily, courts will take as a starting point that investigations conducted under the responsibility of other Member States were conducted in such a way that the results obtained

136 J. van Eekelen and A. Schild, 'Rechtsbescherming na beslag gelegd ter uitvoering van een Europees Onderzoeksbevel' [2018] NJB 2153, 2153–2154; P. Geelhoed and J. Ouwerkerk, 'The role and position of public prosecutors in the application of the European Investigation Order: A view from The Netherlands', in M. Luchtman, F. de Jong and others (n 2) 439.

137 Art 23(5) of the CCP: "The prosecution shall submit to the chambers the documents relating to the case. The accused and other participants in the proceedings, as well as their counsel or attorney, shall be authorized to peruse the contents of these documents."

138 J. van Eekelen and A. Schild, 'Rechtsbescherming na beslag gelegd ter uitvoering van een Europees Onderzoeksbevel' [2018] NJB 2153, 2153–2154.

139 Supreme Court, Judgement of 13 June 2023, ECLI:NL:HR:2023:913.

by those investigations are reliable. However, if there are concrete indications to the contrary, the court is obliged to examine the reliability of those results.[140]

In conclusion, there is no clear-cut answer to the question whether the possibilities under Dutch law to argue against the use of evidence obtained through an EIO can be considered adequate. For the time being, however, there is no pressing need to adjust legislation or practice. The Netherlands seems to conform to the rules laid down in the Directive regarding remedies. The review framework developed by the Supreme Court regarding what Dutch courts may or must assess in the context of a complaint's procedure against an EIO is in conformity with the Directive. Also, the Dutch Supreme Court's rulings in the EncroChat cases, although prior to the CJEU ruling, seem to correspond to what was stipulated herein regarding exclusion of evidence without an effective remedy. The main shortcoming of the Dutch implementation legislation concerns the short complaint period, which differs from the national procedure, while the Directive expressly states that Member States should ensure time limits for appeal that are the same as those in comparable domestic cases. This seems to be at odds with the Directive.

## 4 Regulation 2018/1805: Critical Profiles in Legislation and Case Law

### 4.1 *Implementation*

Dutch legislation provided rules on the recognition and execution of freezing and confiscation orders before the Regulation 1805/2018 (hereafter: Regulation) was adopted. The Regulation simplified and accelerated the procedures for taking away criminal assets concealed in another European Member State. The so-called prohibition on overwriting European regulations meant that the existing national rules could not apply to freezing and confiscation orders covered by the Regulation and had to be removed. The deletion of these existing Dutch provisions was deemed undesirable as Denmark and Ireland were (and are) not bound by the Regulation. Therefore, the already existing rules in Title 5 of Book 5 of CCP and the Mutual Recognition and Enforcement of Monetary Penalties and Confiscation Act (hereafter: MREMPCA)[141] were retained in respect of those Member States. With respect to a freezing order from another Member State not bound by the Regulation, including Denmark

140 Supreme Court, Judgement of 13 February 2024, ECLI:NL:HR:2024:192.

141 Wet wederzijdse erkenning en tenuitvoerlegging geldelijke sancties en beslissingen tot confiscatie, overheid.nl, https://wetten.overheid.nl/BWBR0022604/2023-04-19 accessed 17 july 2024.

and Ireland, Arts 5.5.1 to 5.5.13 of the CCP apply. For a confiscation order from another Member State not bound by the Regulation, including Denmark and Ireland, Arts 22 to 33 of the MREMCPA apply. With respect to the other Member States, which are bound by the Regulation, the directly applicable provisions of the Regulation entered into force as of December 19, 2020.[142] In addition, with regard to Member States bound by the Regulation a new Third Section has been added to Title 5 of the Fifth Book of the CCP (Arts 5.5.14 to 5.5.19) and also a new Third section was added to Chapter 3 of the MREMPCA. As a result, Chapter 3 of the MREMCPA came to consist of three sections. The first two sections apply to confiscation orders against Member States not bound by the Regulation, the third section deals with confiscation orders from Member States that are bound by the Regulation.[143] This approach, in which new articles were added to the existing Dutch legislation in addition to the Regulation having direct effect, was adopted with the intention of effective practical application of the Regulation in the Netherlands.[144] As of then no amendments have been made.

The Regulation has innovative aspects compared to previous legislation. Firstly, the Regulation has a broad scope of application, which allows to take into consideration the differences between Member States on confiscation procedures. The Regulation applies to all confiscation orders issued in the context of criminal proceedings and is thus not limited to the confiscation measures harmonised by the European Union legislator. It may involve classic confiscation, but also confiscation that goes beyond the confiscation of property directly related to the offence for which the person was convicted. In this context, the standard of proof is often lower, or the burden of proof is reversed or shifted. Also, the Regulation applies to all national legislation that creates a confiscation power, including confiscation without a final conviction: so-called non-conviction-based confiscation (hereinafter: NCBC).[145]

A draft bill on confiscation of criminal assets was published by the Dutch Minister of Justice and Security on 16 November 2021, proposing the possibility of taking away criminal assets without prior criminal conviction. A parliamentary letter dated 15 March 2024 revealed that this bill will not be submitted to the House of Representatives in its current form.[146] It was planned to amend

---

142 Kamerstukken II 2019–2020, 35402, 3.

143 Ibid 167.

144 Kamerstukken II 2019–2020, 35402, 3.

145 S. Bollens and D. van Daele, 'De wederzijdse erkenning van confiscatiebevelen: de innovatieve aspecten van Verordening (EU) 2018/1805' [2022] 3 Boom Strafblad 98.

146 Kamerstukken II 2023–2024, 29911, 435.

the bill in response to the European Union Confiscation Directive when agreed on by the European Council and the European Parliament.[147] A draft bill is currently being prepared to implement Directive 2024/1260 on asset recovery and confiscation, which has now been published. The Non-Conviction-Based Confiscation (NCBC) procedure will be included as part of this legislative initiative. The aim is to present a draft bill for consultation around the end of 2024.[148]

When examining the Dutch legislation and case law it is apparent that the provisions in the Regulation have direct effect in The Netherlands. In addition, some articles of the CCP and MREMCPA should be consulted, for example to ascertain who is the issuing authority in the Netherlands, in cases governed by the Regulation. This implies that in some cases three instruments (Regulation, CCP, MREMCPA) need to be considered in conjunction.

### 4.2 *Scope and Issuing*

The Third Section to Title 5 of the Fifth Book (Arts 5.5.14 to 5.5.19), named "freezing orders under Regulation 2018/1805", was added. In addition, Arts 34 and onwards of the MREMCPA were added to the Third section of Chapter 3, named "confiscation order under Regulation 2018/1805".[149]

Art 5.5.14(b) of the CCP[150] refers to the authorities mentioned in Art 2(8)(a) of the Regulation as issuing authorities. The Regulation states that "issuing authority" means any judge, court, or public prosecutor in charge of the case, or another competent authority which is designated as such by the issuing State, and which is competent in criminal matters to order the freezing of property or to execute a freezing order in accordance with national legislation. Art 5.5.19 of the CCP designates the public prosecutor as the issuing authority. Besides, this provision there are no other provisions in the CCP that explicitly deal with the issuance of an order. Also, regarding the issuance of confiscation orders, no provisions can be found in the MREMCPA. Reference is made to the direct effect of the provisions in the Regulation only.[151]

147 Ibid; M. van Noorloos, J. Ouwerkerk and P. Verrest, 'Kroniek van het Europees strafrecht' [2023] 33 NJB 2917, 2923.

148 Kamerstukken II 2023–2024, 32317, 880.

149 Kamerstukken II 2019–2020 35402, 3.

150 Art 5.5.14(b) of the CCP: "Issuing authority means the authority referred to in Art 2, section 8, subsection a, of External link: Regulation 2018/1805."

151 Kamerstukken II 2019–2020, 35402, 3.

### 4.3 *Execution Procedure and Cooperation between Judicial Authorities*

Art 3(1) of the Regulation specifies for which offences freezing orders and confiscation orders should be executed without verification of the double criminality requirement. Art 3(2) complements that, for all other offences, Member States may assess whether the conduct also constitutes an offence under domestic legislation. Both paragraphs have direct effect in The Netherlands. Regarding the second paragraph, it is noted that the Dutch Criminal Code and particular legislation provide for the penalization of offences other than those mentioned in Art 3(1) of the Regulation.[152]

Art 5.5.14(c) of the CCP[153] refers to the authorities mentioned in Art 2(9) of the Regulation as executing authorities. The Regulation states that "executive authority" means an authority that is competent to recognize a freezing order and to ensure its execution. Art 5.5.15(1) of the CCP designates the public prosecutor as executive authority. In addition, Art 5.5.15(2) specifies the way the freezing order is executed, namely by seizure of property, with the application, *mutatis mutandis*, of the third section of Title IV of the First Book, unless otherwise provided for in this title. Title 4 of the First Book provides special coercive measures, more specifically, the third section provides rules about seizure in domestic matters. Furthermore, Arts 8 to 13 of the Regulation provide rules on the execution of a freezing order which are applicable in The Netherlands by virtue of direct effect.

Art 35(1) of the MREMCPA distinguishes between execution of an order referring to a sum of money and an order referring to an object, with respect to manner of execution in The Netherlands. Provisions are cited that apply only to the execution of an order that pertains to a sum of money or an object, respectively.

In the case of an order relating to a sum of money, enforcement must be carried out in accordance with Arts 6:1:1 to 6:1:5, 6:1:9 and 6:6:25 of the CCP, the second title of the Fourth Chapter of the Sixth Book of the CCP and the rules established by or pursuant to a general administrative order based on Art 6:4:19 of the CCP. The claim for the application of the coercive measure of committal and the opposition to the execution of a coercive order shall be filed with the District Court of North Netherlands. Art 6:1:1 of the CCP designates the Minister of Justice and Security as the authority to enforce court decisions and criminal orders. The public prosecutor shall provide the Minister of Justice and Safety with the decision to that effect at the latest fourteen days after it has become

152 Ibid.

153 Art 5.5.14(c) of the CCP: "Executive authority means the authority referred to in Art 2(9) of External link: Regulation 2018/1805."

enforceable, attaching, if applicable, the judge's opinion on enforcement. In addition, Art 6:1:5(1) of the CCP grants the Minister of Justice and Safety the authority to issue general or special orders to officials or officers designated by the Minister for that purpose. By virtue of Art 6:1:9 of the CCP, Art 96a(3) of the CCP is also applicable, which ensures that, among others, the persons referred to in the aforementioned Arts 218 and 218a of the CCP, as this would contravene their duty of confidentiality, are not obliged to provide information to the Minister of Justice and Security, if requested for the execution of a judgement.

In the case of an order relating to an object, the same provisions apply as those in respect of an order that relates to a sum of money, except for Arts 6.1.1 and 6.6.25. Based on Art 6.6.25 of the CCP, the public prosecutor may make an application to be authorised to apply the coercive measure of hostage-taking against the convicted person, if full recovery in accordance with Arts 6.4.4, 6.4.5 and 6.4.6 of the CCP is not possible in the case of (1) a fine imposed in a penal order; (2) an obligation to pay a sum of money to the state for deprivation of illegally obtained benefit. In addition to the Second Title of the Fourth Chapter of the Sixth Book of the CCP is not applicable. This Chapter provides a wide variety of provisions on national procedures relating to monetary penalties and sanctions, more specifically provisions on the collection of fines and compensatory measures, deprivation of illegally obtained profits and investigation into the offender's assets. However, the Fifth Chapter of the Sixth Book of the CCP is applicable. Chapter five of the Sixth book concerns provisions regarding confiscation. One article provides the basis for the Decree on Enforcement of Criminal Decisions,[154] which contains provisions about, among other things, the payment of monetary fines and other monetary sanctions.

Art 35(2)(3) of the MREMCPA refer to provisions in the Regulation to be complied with in the execution of a confiscation order where the issuing authority has decided to return an object, or a corresponding sum of money, to the victim, or if the confiscation order is for the transfer of an object or sum of money to the issuing Member State.

Art 23(1) of the Regulation provides that an order shall be executed according to the law of the executing Member State. The aforementioned Dutch provisions make this practically possible. The provisions of the Regulation have direct effect, but in some cases specific provisions dealing with the practical execution of the Regulation in the Netherlands define the way an incoming

154 Besluit tenuitvoerlegging strafrechtelijke beslissingen, overheid.nl, <https://wetten.overheid.nl/BWBR0042962/2024-07-01https://wetten.overheid.nl/BWBR0022604/2023-04-19> accessed 17 july 2024.

confiscation order is executed, in particular which provisions of Dutch legislation apply to the execution.

### 4.4 *Fundamental Rights*

Recital 16 and 17 of the Regulation stipulate that the Regulation does not modify the obligation to respect fundamental rights and legal principles of the Charter and ECHR. As indicated in Recital 34 of the Regulation, this ground is an exception to the mutual trust that exists within the Union and to the assumption that all Member States comply with Union law, in particular fundamental rights.[155] Further, the grounds for refusal in Art 8(1)(f) and Art 19(1)(h) are premised on this.

Art 5.5.16 of the CCP and Art 36 of the MREMPCA make explicit reference to the grounds for refusal pertaining to freezing and confiscation orders outlined in the Regulation. Many of these grounds for refusal align with the previous mandatory grounds for refusal in Arts 24 and 24a of the MREMPCA that applied prior to the enactment of the Regulation. In addition, the Regulation has introduced a new ground for refusal for the situation where the execution of the confiscation order would lead to a manifest violation of fundamental rights contained in the Charter, which had not previously been enacted into legislation.[156]

### 4.5 *Grounds for Non-recognition and Non-execution*

Art 5.5.16 of the CCP refers to Art 8(1) of the Regulation, and Art 36 of the MREMCPA refers to Art 19(1) of the Regulation, with the only difference that the public prosecutor is designated as the competent authority for refusing recognition or enforcement on the grounds mentioned in Art 8(1) of the Regulation, and with respect to refusal of recognition or enforcement on the grounds mentioned in Art 19(1) of the Regulation also the Minister of Justice and Security.[157]

Especially during the legislative process, there was debate about the nature of the grounds for refusal. The Dutch legislator initially intended to implement the Regulation so that all grounds are mandatory grounds, but eventually opted for optional grounds for refusal, following the opinion of the Council of State's Advisory Division (hereinafter: council). The council pointed out that the Regulation states the executing authority may decide not to recognize or execute a confiscation order if one of the grounds for refusal applies, whereas the proposed national legislation stated that the public prosecutor

155 Court of Noord-Nederland, Judgement of 14 December 2022, ECLI:NL:RBNNE:2022:4959.
156 Kamerstukken II 2019–2020, 35402, 3.
157 Ibid.

or the Minister should refuse the recognition or execution of a confiscation order.[158] The latter was deemed inconsistent with the *Poplawski I* judgment.[159] The approach differs from the system of partly mandatory and partly optional grounds for refusal adopted in the domestic system implementing Framework Decision 2006/783/JHA.[160]

In the existing case law, a framework is developed for assessing complaints based on Art 5.4.10 in conjunction with Art 552a of the CCP, which also applies to assessing a complaint against the execution of a freezing order based on the Regulation.[161] The court should, in that instance, also consider *ex officio* whether any of the grounds for refusal under Art 5.5.16 of the CCP in conjunction with Art 8(1) of the Regulation are present.

To date, there is relatively little case law on Art 5.5.16 of the CCP in conjunction with Art 8 of the Regulation, and Art 36 of the MREMCPA in conjunction with Art 19(1) of the Regulation. The adoption of a ground for refusal by the courts hardly ever occurs and, in addition, the reasoning is usually meagre. Two of the most extensively addressed grounds for refusal in domestic case law concern Art 19(1)(d) (on double criminality) and Art 19(1)(h) (on fundamental rights) of the Regulation. Important in this regard is that the District Court of Noord-Nederland proceeded to assess a complaint that was not based on Art 36 in relation with Art 19(1)(d), of the Regulation, when it was noticed that the lawyer cited the wrong ground from the MREMCPA.[162] Thus, the incorrect citation of national legislative provisions by lawyers, following the entry into force of the Regulation, seems to be rectified by the judiciary. Art 19(1)(h) of the Regulation has the most "extensive" elaboration in case law. The courts ruled in all cases that there had been no violation of fundamental rights.[163] As indicated in Recital 34 of the Regulation, this ground is an exception to the mutual trust that exists within the Union and to the assumption that all Member States comply with Union law, in particular fundamental rights.[164] This may be one of the reasons for not setting aside this ground lightly.

---

158 Kamerstukken II 2019–2020, 35402, 4.
159 Judgement of 29 June 2017, Case C-579/15 *Poplawski* [2017] ECLI:EU:C:2017:503.
160 Kamerstukken II 2019–2020, 35402, 3.
161 Court of Amsterdam, Judgement of 17 August 2023, ECLI:NL:RBAMS:2023:5995.
162 Court of Noord-Nederland, Judgement of 13 December 2023, ECLI:NL:RBNNE:2023:5252.
163 Court of Noord Nederland, Judgement of 14 December 2022, ECLI:NL:RBNNE:2022:4959; Court of Noord-Nederland, Judgement of 14 December 2022, ECLI:NL:RBNNE:2022:4960; Court of Noord-Nederland, Judgement of 12 October 2022, ECLI:NL:RBNNE:2022:4188; Court of Noord Nederland, Judgement of 12 October 2022, ECLI:NL:RBNNE:2022:4190.
164 Court of Noord-Nederland, Judgement of 14 December 2022, ECLI:NL:RBNNE:2022:4959.

### 4.6 *Remedies*

Due to the direct effect of the Regulation persons affected by a freezing order have the right to seek effective remedies in the executing Member State against the decision to recognize and execute the order (Art 33(1) Regulation). Art 5.5.18 of the CCP makes this appeal practically possible in The Netherlands.[165] To this end, reference is made to several articles that also apply in domestic proceedings, including Art 552a of the CCP, that also applies in the EIO complaint procedure. In addition to the possibility of complaint under Art 552a of the CCP, the civil judge has jurisdiction to hear disputes regarding the application of Art 94d of the CCP, which concerns the retention of the right to recourse, by the public prosecution authority. If one of these remedies is raised by an interested party, the issuing authority must be notified (Art 33(3) Regulation). The court may not intervene in the examination of the basis of the freezing order and the complaint also has no suspensory effect.[166]

Art 32 of the Regulation, which has direct effect, states that after the execution of a freezing order or the decision to recognise and execute a confiscation order, the executing authority shall without delay inform the persons known to it to be affected by the procedures in accordance with domestic law. That notice must indicate the remedies available to the affected persons.[167] Art 39 of the MREMCPA provides the practical possibility for convicted persons as well as interested parties to appeal the decision of the public prosecutor to recognize and enforce the confiscation order. The appeal must be filed with the District Court of Noord-Nederland. Arts 21 to 25 of the CCP, which deal with the examination by the chambers, are declared applicable. Appeals shall be lodged within seven days from the day on which the convicted person or interested party became aware of the decision recognizing and executing the confiscation order and, as in the case of appeals concerning freezing orders, shall not have a suspensive effect. Art 39 of the MREMCPA also indicates the provisions to which third parties who believe they are entitled to objects from which recourse is taken may rely. These provisions are laid down in the Code of Civil Procedure, which has differing regimes for the settlement of seizure under foreclosure, distinguishing between movable property that is not registered property (Art 439 onwards) and immovable property (Art 502 onwards).

---

165 Art 5.5.18 of the CCP: "(…) Arts 552a, 552c to 552d, subsection 1, and 552e, subsection 1, shall apply mutatis mutandis, on the understanding that the court shall not enter into an examination of the basis of the freezing order. The complaint shall have no suspensive effect."

166 Kamerstukken II 2019–2020, 35402, 3.

167 Ibid.

For example, a third party may oppose the foreclosure sale of confiscated objects (Arts 456(1) and 538(1) Code of Civil Procedure). A third party may also claim a portion of the proceeds after the foreclosure sale.[168]

There are certain principles that govern the assessment of an appeal pursuant to Art 39 of the MREMCPA: (1) the court must assess whether the public prosecutor could reasonably come to his decision to recognize the order; (2) the public prosecutor, in making his assessment, must not interfere with the proceedings and decisions made in another Member State.[169]

## 5 Concluding Remarks

The analysis has shown compliance with the three instruments that has gradually increased over time. The journey from the inception of the EAW FD to its integration into Dutch law has been characterized by a continual evolution shaped by judicial rulings and legislative adjustments. Initially, the SPA mirrored all grounds for refusal and safeguards outlined in the EAW FD. However, the landscape gradually shifted due to the interventions of the Supreme Court of The Netherlands and, notably, the Court of Justice of the European Union. These interventions prompted revisions in the SPA and established interpretative guidelines for the EAW FD, leading to a more nuanced understanding of its provisions. Significant changes can be observed, such as the transformation of grounds and guarantees for refusal from mandatory to optional, except for those explicitly mentioned in Art 3 of the FD. A legislative proposal is expected to result compliance with the EAW FD for the most part, although there remains room for improvement, for instance with respect to the exception clause in Art 9 of the SPA, which could be clarified to establish specific criteria for refusal.

The Dutch system has generally implemented the provisions of the EIO D into national law, specifically through the amendments to the Dutch CCP. The Dutch legislation incorporates the grounds for refusal, the procedures for issuing and executing an EIO, and the necessary safeguards for fundamental rights as stipulated by the EIO D. While the Dutch system demonstrates substantial compliance with the EIO D, certain aspects, such as the imperative nature of grounds for refusal and the short complaint period, may require further alignment to fully meet the EIO D's standards. Nonetheless, these discrepancies do not significantly hinder the overall functionality and compliance of the Dutch EIO D implementation.

168 Kamerstukken II 2019–2020, 35402, 3.

169 See Court of Noord-Nederland, Judgement of 3 April 2024, ECLI:NL:RBNNE:2024:1448.

The Dutch legal framework demonstrates substantial compliance with Regulation 1805/2018. Dutch legislation, specifically the Criminal Code of Procedure (CCP) and the Mutual Recognition and Enforcement of Monetary Penalties and Confiscation Act (MREMCPA), has been appropriately amended to accommodate the Regulation. While minor legislative updates are ongoing to further align with evolving EU directives, the amendments ensure the direct applicability of the Regulation while retaining necessary provisions for Member States not bound by the Regulation, such as Denmark and Ireland.

# PART 3

CHAPTER 13

# Comparative Remarks on Mutual Recognition Instruments of Judicial Cooperation in Criminal Matters

*Giulia Lasagni, Michele Caianiello and Isadora Neroni Rezende*

## 1 Introduction*

The objective of this Chapter is to give a concise report on some of the most relevant trends emerging from a comparative analysis of national legal frameworks concerning the three cooperation tools studied in this research: the European Arrest Warrant (*infra*, §13.3), the European Investigation Order (*infra*, §13.4) and the Regulation 2018/1805 on freezing and confiscation orders (*infra*, §13.5).[1]

Such mechanisms have been examined from a twofold perspective.

The first approach is a transversal legal comparative methodology. Due to the limited remit of this contribution, the analysis does not aim at listing all incongruencies in the cooperation framework and practices in the selected Member States (Bulgaria, Croatia, France, Germany, Italy, Poland, Portugal, Spain, and the Netherlands). On the contrary, it focuses on identifying different normative or jurisprudential approaches that seem to generate or incentivize divergent solutions in the functioning of the examined cooperation mechanisms.

In this perspective, the comparison seems to point out how it is more difficult than it appears at first glance not only to ensure a smooth and fair cooperation but also to deeply understand the causes that impede this outcome,

* Although the Chapter is a joint reflection of the authors, its drafting is broken down as follows: Giulia Lasagni §§ 1; 2; 5; 6 (Regulation conclusion and general part); Michele Caianiello, §§ 4–6 (EIO conclusion); Isadora Neroni Rezende §§ 3–6 (EAW conclusion). A special thanks for his precious suggestions to Antonio Pugliese.

1 Council Framework Decision of 13 June 2002 on the European arrest warrant and the surrender procedures between Member States; Directive 2014/41/EU of the European Parliament and of the Council of 3 April 2014 regarding the European Investigation Order in criminal matters; Regulation (EU) 2018/1805 of the European Parliament and of the Council of 14 November 2018 on the mutual recognition of freezing orders and confiscation orders.

 | DOI:10.1163/9789004705791_015

especially when looking not just at every single mechanism, but to the whole implementation of mutual recognition tools in the criminal matter.

The second perspective adopted in the research originates from a multi-disciplinary approach, that combines legal and computer science expertise (*infra*, § 13.2). Thanks to a semantic and textual examination of legal texts, in a previous research project,[2] the elaboration of "harmonization indexes" and "heat maps" based on Artificial Intelligence (AI) technology, facilitated the identification of similarities and lacunas in the design of implementation measures across domestic systems.

This method, now reproposed in the field of judicial cooperation, allowed for cross-checking the results of traditional legal analysis, trying to bypass, by way of automated assessments, some problematic features typical of comparative studies, such as linguistic discrepancies and ontological divergencies.

The results of this combined effort, as it will emerge, highlight several critical profiles that, on one side, show the difficulties in reaching effective cooperation in the criminal law field and, on the other, may help trace a potential way forward toward a higher level of fairness in these proceedings throughout the EU.

## 2 An Innovative Comparative Methodology: Combining Legal and Automated Analysis

The Facilex project adopted an integrated perspective to examine the state of play of judicial cooperation in criminal matters in the EU.

This innovative point of view grows upon a semantic analysis and annotation of the legal provisions contained in the three studied mechanisms.

The methodology, developed by computer scientists in cooperation with legal experts, takes its cues from the "translation" of legal text into a numerical text representation, following a computational approach that exploits Natural Language Processing (NLP) techniques, which is an application of AI technologies. According to it, text excerpts, such as legal provisions, have been transformed into a vector by which words are represented by numbers.

The main aim of such semantic analysis was the tracking of a significant frequency of occurrences from mere counts or redundancies. In other words, the output of the methodology does not substitute human analysis, but it supports it in the identification of gaps and misalignments. A common problem

2 CrossJustice, Grant Agreement no. 847346, Giuseppe Contissa, Giulia Lasagni, Michele Caianiello, Giovanni Sartor (eds) *Effective Protection of the Rights of the Accused in the EU Directives. A Computable Approach to Criminal Procedure Law* (Brill, Leiden, 2022).

in the use of AI for law is the 'black box' of the models, which makes it difficult to justify the results. The methodology developed in Facilex, based on an analysis that uses explicit and implicit concepts, provides more interpretable tools. This means that legal experts can not only see if two regulatory texts are similar, but why they are (or are not) so, based on concrete and verifiable concepts. This, in turn, represents a possible advantage for legal experts, who can reduce the time spent on comparative analysis and focus on the interpretative and strategic aspects of the regulations.

The impact of the developed approach can be appreciated on several levels, from the simplification of the work of comparative analysis to the possibility of improving the quality and consistency of national implementations of European legislation.

Indeed, one of the main problems in legal practice is the comparison between European legislation and the national regulations that implement it. Traditionally, this is a manual and challenging activity, especially if applied on a multi-level system, such as the EU.

In this regard, the creation of an "Harmonised Glossary", enriched with implicit notions and relationships between concepts through Large Language Models (LLM), allows for automatic alignment between legislative sources, highlighting discrepancies and simplifying the identification of key concepts in national implementations.[3]

For the cooperation tools that require implementation (EAW and EIO) the methodology also brought to the development of a "Harmonization Index", that is of the possibility to compare the level of harmonization among Member States with an automated approach. More specifically, the Index, which works on asymmetric and symmetric metrics to assess the similarity between European legislation and national implementations, is a useful indicator to spot harmonization gaps or a distortion in implementation. This can facilitate the identification of compliance issues with EU law; improve the uniformity of regulatory interpretations between different Member States; and support policy makers and supervisory bodies in monitoring the effectiveness of harmonisation.

In addition to retrospective analysis of national implementations (*ex-post*), the methodology can also be used to assess the degree of harmonisation *ex-ante*, i.e. before a piece of legislation is implemented. This could help European and national policy makers to anticipate transposition difficulties; national legislators to write regulations more in line with European law; and scholars and jurists to develop predictive models on future implementation.[4]

3 See, for more details, infra, Chapter 17.

4 Practical applications are also foreseeable for law firms, companies and institutions. For law firms, to obtain support in the comparative analysis of regulations between Member States,

## 3 Comparative Remarks on the Implementation of the EAW

The comparative analysis conducted reveals a contradictory picture of the state of implementation of the principle of mutual recognition in the EU, as both positive and negative trends can be discerned in the holding of the EAW system.

On the one hand, national legislators seem to show greater adherence to the spirit of the framework decision and have enacted subsequent reforms to adjust the national transposition to the European text. The transposition of some grounds for refusal, however, remains refractory to this phenomenon, for instance, when specific State interests come into play (such as for the grounds for refusal based on the *ne bis in idem* principle and the surrender of nationals).

On the other hand, the emergence of fundamental rights concerns in the EAW mechanism prompts other issues for EU criminal cooperation. Despite the clear position of the CJEU on the matter after *Aranyosi and Căldăraru*, the appreciation of this newly established "ground for refusal" is quite scattered across the Member States. In particular, the range of fundamental rights triggering the non-execution, as well as the threshold to refuse the surrender, are often interpreted quite flexibly in the national case law. These positions, together with the protective attitude expressed by some Member States in the transposition of certain grounds for refusal, continue to represent pitfalls for the integrity of the EU mutual recognition system in criminal matters, as argued below.

### 3.1 *Grounds for Refusal: towards Greater Adherence to EU Provisions?*

The transposition of the grounds for refusal has been a delicate issue in the implementation of the EAW FD across Member States. Concerned about losing their competencies in criminal matters, national legislators had often introduced additional grounds for refusal in the national law or transposed them as mandatory even where these were formulated as only optional in the European text. This trend raised – and still raises, as shown below – compliance issues with EU law. In fact, the CJEU considers that the primacy of EU law precludes a national legislation that translates as mandatory a ground for refusal that is only considered optional in the framework decision, thus excluding any margin of appreciation of judicial authorities on the decision to execute the EAW.[5]

useful for example for companies with transnational activities; for companies, to achieve greater certainty in assessing regulatory compliance in the various European markets.

5 Case C-396/22 *Generalstaatsanwaltschaft Berlin* [2023] ECLI:EU:C:2023:1029, paras 19–20; Case C-665/20 PPU *Local Court Tiergarten v X* [2021] EU:C:2021:339.

Over the years, however, a positive evolution has occurred, which displays a greater adherence by several Member States to the principle of mutual recognition. Some national legislators (as in Italy, France, Croatia, and the Netherlands, to some extent) have aligned their domestic laws to the framework decision, by converting some mandatory grounds for refusal into optional ones.[6] Moreover, in the cases of most blatant mismatches between the European and the national text (for example, in Italy), subsequent reforms have expunged from the domestic system the grounds for refusal that do not appear in the EAW FD.[7]

In particular, an interesting example of this phenomenon regards the transposition of the double criminality requirement that, more than others in the past, has symbolized the preeminence of national sovereignty interests over the needs for cross-border cooperation. The first EAW FD transposition in some Member States provided the lack of double criminality as a mandatory ground for refusal but this has now been converted into a merely optional one in some domestic legislations (France, the Netherlands).[8] Other States have kept the requirement as a basis for mandatory rejection of the EAW (Portugal, Italy), although this choice may – for the particular wording of Art 2(4) EAW FD – fall within the margin of appreciation of Member States without raising compliance issues.[9]

Some notable exceptions, however, still cast doubts on this progressive approach of national legislations to the text of the EAW FD. Specifically, Spain and Poland have signaled significant compliance issues in the implementation of the grounds for refusal, specifically, for the provision of additional bases not foreseen in the framework decision and the transposition of optional grounds as mandatory in the national law.[10]

---

6 See, for Croatia, Zlata Đurđević and others, Chapter 5, §2.1.3. (although, in this case, the amendment was prompted by an infringement procedure activated by the European Commission); for France, Eleonora Cervellera, Chapter 6, §1.2.1; for Italy, Isadora Neroni Rezende and others, Chapter 8, §2.2; for the Netherlands, see Camila Ugaz Heudebert and others, Chapter 12, §2.5.1.

7 Isadora Neroni Rezende and others (n 6) §1.

8 See, for France Eleonora Cervellera (n 6) §1.2.1.; for the Netherlands, see Camila Ugaz Heudebert and others (n 6) §2.5.3.

9 See FACILEX Italian national report, §7.2.2.2, available at <https://site.unibo.it/facilex/en> accessed 14 August 2024; for Portugal, Miguel João Costa and others, Chapter 10, §1.2.3. In fact, while Arts 3 and 4 EAW FD are directly addressed to the executing judicial authorities, Art 2(4) of the same decision appears to be addressed to the Member States, leaving it up to them to decide on the transposition of the principle of dual criminality into national law.

10 See, for Poland, Wojciech Jasiński and others, Chapter 9, §1.2.4; for Spain, Ana Maria Neira Pena, Chapter 11, §1.2.2.

Furthermore, the comparative analysis has unveiled some more specific issues that transversally affect national legislation on the grounds for refusal, often as a result of Member States' historical backgrounds. On the one hand, the transposition of the grounds inspired by the *ne bis in idem* principle still appears to be one of the most problematic across Member States. On the other hand, the refusal of the surrender of nationals and residents by the executing country is regulated in a very fragmented fashion in EU countries, raising problems for the principle of equal treatment. Both profiles are examined more in detail below.

#### 3.1.1 A Strong Commitment to the *ne bis in idem* Principle

The implementation of the grounds for refusal – both mandatory and optional – inspired by the *ne bis in idem* suggests that the principle still bears great importance in Member States' legal cultures. Except for the Netherlands, which inadvertently transformed the relevant ground for refusal from mandatory into optional in 2021,[11] many Member States (for example, Germany, Poland, and Spain) have transposed the optional grounds of refusal based on the *ne bis in idem* (Arts 4(3) and 4(5) EAW FD) as mandatory, thus betraying the spirit of the EU text.[12]

Following a similar trend, other Member States have extended the scope of the mandatory ground for refusal in the framework decision (Art 3(2) EAW FD) in the national transposition, sometimes including situations that would have entailed judicial discretion by the executing authorities, rather than an automatic rejection of the warrant.

This is the case, for instance, of Italy, which has included judgements of no grounds to proceed (*sentenze di non luogo a procedere*) into the list of decisions that satisfy the requirement of "finally judged" under Art 3(2) EAW FD.[13] Despite some ambiguities on the right framing of such decisions between national and EU law,[14] it should be borne in mind that judgements of no grounds to proceed never become "final" under Italian procedural law, even when they are no

11 Camila Ugaz Heudebert and others (n 6) §2.5.4.1.

12 See, for Germany, Anna Albrecht and Anne Schneider, Chapter 7, §1.2.2.3 (where, however, the transposition of Art 4(3) EAW FD as a mandatory ground for refusal is not seen as problematic by the Authors); for Spain, Ana Maria Neira Pena (n 10) §1.2.2. (referring to both Arts 4(3) and (5) EAW FD); for Poland, Wojciech Jasiński and others (n 10) §1.2.4. (referring to Art 4(5) EAW FD only).

13 Isadora Neroni Rezende and others (n 6) §2.2.

14 In fact, the CJEU has considered Italian judgements of no ground to proceed as "final judgements" barring further prosecution in the EU under Art 54 of the Schengen Convention, see Case C-398/12 *M* [2014] ECLI:EU:C:2014:1057.

longer subject to appeal, meaning that the case can always be reopened when new evidence comes to light. In this sense, the judgements of no grounds to proceed appear more in line with the concept of a "final" judgement that has been passed upon the requested person in a Member State and that prevents further proceedings. Under Art 4(3) EAW FD, such decisions can only serve as a basis for an optional refusal; therefore, the transposition of this ground for refusal cannot be considered satisfying in this respect. Likewise, in Poland and Spain, the scope of the *ne bis in idem* exception has been broadened in the national transposition. Specifically, final decisions of third countries have been included – alongside those of EU Member States – among those that trigger a mandatory refusal of the warrant, although these can serve only as optional grounds according to the framework decision (Art 4(5) EAW FD).[15]

Against this background, the tendency to extend the outreach of the *ne bis in idem* as a ground for refusal appears to be a critical issue across Member States and represents an interesting exception to the phenomenon of progressive alignment of national transposition laws to the EAW FD.

### 3.1.2 Historical Resistance and Discrimination Issues in the Surrender of Nationals and Residents

Another common (and problematic) trend in the implementation of the grounds for refusal concerns the surrender of nationals and residents in the executing State, as provided by Art 4(6) EAW FD.

Originally, the adoption of the framework decision raised issues regarding the constitutional provisions of some Member States (Croatia, Poland, Germany) that, for historical reasons, forbade the extradition of their nationals. In Croatia, for example, the removal of the complete ban on the extradition of Croatian citizens foreseen in the Constitution was a benchmark in the country's negotiations to accede to the EU.[16] In Poland as well, constitutional amendments were necessary to allow the surrender of Polish nationals to other EU States, although some obstacles to the execution of EAWs were kept for these situations.[17] Similarly, Germany has introduced narrow exceptions to the constitutional ban on the extradition of its citizens, which are to be strictly interpreted by the judiciary.[18]

15 See, for Poland, Wojciech Jasiński and others (n 10) §1.2.4.; for Spain, Ana Maria Neira Pena (n 10) §1.2.2.

16 Zlata Đurđević and others (n 6) §2.1.1.

17 Wojciech Jasiński and others (n 10) §1.2.1.

18 Anna Albrecht and Anne Schneider (n 12) §1.2.2.4.

Still to this day, citizens in some of these countries are afforded preferential treatment in the EAW mechanism. In Poland, for example, the national law requires that the double criminality requirement is always respected when the surrender of a Polish national is at stake, even if the warrant concerned one of the 32 categories of offences of Art 2(2) EAW FD.[19] Moreover, Art 4(6) EAW is transposed as a mandatory ground for refusal for Polish citizens and refugees, and as an optional one for other residents, despite this distinction not being made in the European text.[20] In Germany, the regulation of the surrender of nationals and other EU or third-country citizens appears equally scattered. For instance, the surrender of nationals is forbidden unless the issuing State can claim a substantial (mainly territorial) link with the commission of the offence and promises to transfer the person back for the enforcement of the sentence. While the appreciation of the issuing State's substantial link with the crime allows for some judicial discretion, the refusal of surrender is considered mandatory if the abovementioned requirements are not met.[21] The same ground for refusal is provided as thoroughly optional for EU citizens, whose surrender is thus subject to a wider margin of appreciation. While this judicial discretion is per se compatible with Art 4(6) EAW FD, the unfavorable treatment of EU citizens in comparison with German nationals raises issues for the principle of non-discrimination.[22] Likewise, the surrender of third-country nationals, habitually resident in Germany, is permitted even without a substantial link of the crime to the issuing State but can be refused if their interests to remain in the country prevail. In this case, the decision on surrender is partly delegated to the executive authorities, a circumstance that further underlines the discretionary nature of the assessment. Unsurprisingly, the criteria according to which the interests of the foreign citizen not to be surrendered prevail remain

19 Wojciech Jasiński and others (n 10) §1.2.3.

20 Ibid §1.2.4.

21 To be true, section 80 IRG is very complex and allows the judge, in certain cases, to perform a balancing of the interests of the German national not to be surrendered and the interests of the issuing State to prosecute him or her. Although this leaves the judge some room for manoeuvre, from the theoretical point of view the balancing is still a condition for a pre-determined consequence: if the judge finds that the interests of the German citizen do not prevail and the other requirements of the paragraph are met, the judge is obliged to allow the surrender. See Anna Albrecht and Anne Schneider (n 12) §1.2.2.4.

22 Nonetheless, EU citizens are treated the same as German nationals only after five consecutive years of being legally resident in Germany, in accordance with the indications of the CJEU in *Wolzenburg* (see Case C-123/08 *Wolzenburg* [2009] ECLI:EU:C:2009:616; see also OLG Frankfurt a.M., decision of 08.12.2016, BeckRS 2016, 13556).

unclear, although they often refer to external factors such as the person's language skills, his or her work, and family ties.[23]

It is unclear whether these differences in treatment raise compliance issues with Art 4(6) EAW FD per se, but they surely undermine the respect of the EU principle of non-discrimination. Under this principle, some Member States have progressively amended provisions allowing for the surrender of nationals and other citizens legally resident in their territory, following the positive trend described above. In Italy, for example, the scope of the domestic provision transposing Art 4(6) EAW FD has been extended multiple times under the influence of the Constitutional Court and the CJEU, and now covers both Italian citizens and other persons legally residing in Italy for five consecutive years (although this requirement is assessed differently in case law).[24] In both instances, the refusal is only optional, in accordance with the text of the framework decision. In the Netherlands, the surrender of nationals was strictly prohibited unless specific guarantees were given by the issuing State but is now subject to judicial discretion after a 2021 reform. According to Art 4(6) EAW FD and the interpretation of the CJEU in *Wolzenburg*, the surrender of other nationals legally resident in the country for at least five years follows the same regime.[25] Spanish legislation was also amended in 2018 to include residents – beyond nationals – among the categories of people protected under the optional ground of refusal foreseen in Art 4(6) EAW FD. Even before that, however, the domestic case law interpreted the criterion of residence quite broadly, also including situations where the person concerned could not prove legal residence but only the existence of social, linguistic, family, and work-related links with Spain.[26]

Under a slightly different profile, Croatian judges also express a high commitment to the principle of mutual recognition when it comes to the surrender of Croatian nationals. It is the settled case law of the Supreme Court that national executing authorities are obliged to order the surrender of Croatian citizens to other Member States even where the prosecution or the execution of the sentence for the criminal offence is statute-barred in Croatia, contrary to the approach followed in other EU countries.[27]

23 Anna Albrecht and Anne Schneider (n 12) §1.2.2.4.
24 Isadora Neroni Rezende and others (n 6) §2.2.
25 Camila Ugaz Heudebert and others (n 6) §2.5.2.1.
26 Ana Maria Neira Pena (n 10) §1.2.2.
27 Zlata Đurđević and others (n 6) §2.2.1.

### 3.2 *A Fragmented Approach to Fundamental Rights as Grounds for Refusal*

As widely known, the protection of fundamental rights considerations has made inroads in the EAW cooperation mechanism only at a later stage, imposing itself as a counterbalance to the principle of mutual recognition.[28] After some early CJEU decisions,[29] it was with *Aranyosi and Căldăraru* that the risk of fundamental rights violations emerged as a ground for refusal of a EAW. In the comparative perspective, the later development of fundamental rights considerations in the EAW system emerges in the fragmentary way in which national laws still incorporate this newly established ground for refusal, as well as in the way domestic courts approach it. These issues are examined in more detail below.

#### 3.2.1 Fundamental Rights Clauses in National Legislation

Concerning the first aspect, most Member States involved in the analysis (Germany, Spain, Italy, Croatia, Poland, the Netherlands) include in their national legislation on the EAW a general clause about the protection of fundamental rights, although this is not always explicitly formulated as a ground for refusal.[30] The genesis of such provisions may, however, differ across EU countries. In Germany, for instance, a generic clause on the "EU public order" already existed in the national legislation but was only later interpreted as a basis to introduce fundamental rights risks as grounds for refusal.[31] Other Member States (Croatia, the Netherlands),[32] instead, incorporated a specific provision on this matter only as a follow-up to *Aranyosi and Căldăraru*.

Conversely, only a few countries (Bulgaria, Portugal, and France) do not include any specific grounds for refusal based on fundamental rights in their

---

28 On this topic, see *inter alia* Valsamis Mitsilegas, 'The Symbiotic Relationship Between Mutual Trust and Fundamental Rights in Europe's Area of Criminal Justice' (2015) 6 NJECL 4; Petra Bárd, Sergio Carrera and Marco Stefan, 'The Judicialisation of the European Arrest Warrant: Rule of Law and Fundamental Rights as Preconditions for Merited Mutual Trust' (*CEPS*, 11 August 2023), <https://cdn.ceps.eu/wp-content/uploads/2023/08/Judicialisation-of-the-European-Arrest-Warrant-STREAM-Report.pdf.> accessed 14 August 2024.

29 cf, for instance, Case C-399/11 *Melloni* [2013] ECLI:EU:C:2013:107; Case C-396/11 *Radu* [2013] ECLI:EU:C:2013:39.

30 See, for Croatia, Zlata Đurđević and others (n 6) §1.2.2.1.; for Poland, Wojciech Jasiński and others (n 10) §1.2.5. (where, however, the provision about fundamental rights is explicitly formulated as a ground for refusal); for Spain, see Ana Maria Neira Pena (n 10) §1.2.3.

31 Anna Albrecht and Anne Schneider (n 12) §1.2.2.1.

32 See, for Croatia, Zlata Đurđević and others (n 6) §2.2.3.1.; for the Netherlands, see Camila Ugaz Heudebert and others (n 6) §2.4.2.

national law. This "lacuna" does not seem to raise issues in Bulgaria and France, where the case law directly considers fundamental rights in surrender decisions, referring to other international obligations (e.g., the ECHR in Bulgaria)[33] or the very text of the framework decision (i.e., Art 1(3) EAW FD in France).[34] The commitment to fundamental rights considerations in France also emerges in the provision of a peculiar ground for refusal based on the principle of non-discrimination, which forbids surrender when this may expose the person to discriminatory treatment in the issuing country (e.g., political persecution), but which finds no correspondent in the text of the framework decision.[35] Differently, in Portugal, the absence of any specific provision on fundamental rights may be symptomatic of the lack of such considerations in EAW proceedings, since no decisions applying the *Aranyosi and Căldăraru* test have been identified in jurisprudence.[36]

#### 3.2.2 Fundamental Rights Considerations in National Case Law

Concerning the second aspect, despite the established approach of the CJEU, domestic courts across the examined Member States seem to interpret the risk of fundamental rights violations quite differently. Only in Italy, Spain, Poland, and Croatia, national judges refer explicitly to the *Aranyosi and Căldăraru* test.[37] Conversely, in France and the Netherlands, domestic courts interpret this ground of refusal in a rather flexible fashion, considering that generic statements on the deficiencies of the issuing State can be enough to reject the execution of the EAW.[38] This approach – which eludes the second part of the *Aranyosi and Căldăraru* test – arguably sets a lower threshold to refuse surrender and disproportionally prioritizes fundamental rights over the needs of mutual recognition, possibly raising compliance issues with EU law.

A similar trend is also developing in relation to the range of fundamental rights that may trigger the application of this ground for refusal. For instance, several Member States appear ready to refuse the execution of a EAW to prevent the violation of *any* fundamental right enshrined in the national constitution. This is the case of Germany, where the Constitutional Court has developed a

33 Miroslava Manolova and Ekaterina Salkova, Chapter 4, §1.2.3.

34 Eleonora Cervellera (n 6) §1.2.2.1 (citing, for example, Cass. Crim., 28 February 2012, no. 12-80.744).

35 Eleonora Cervellera (n 6) §1.2.1.

36 Miguel João Costa and others (n 9) §1.2.3.

37 See, for Poland, Wojciech Jasiński and others (n 10) §1.2.5.; for Spain, Ana Maria Neira Pena (n 10) §1.2.3.

38 See, for France, Eleonora Cervellera (n 6) §1.2.2.1.; for the Netherlands, see Camila Ugaz Heudebert and others (n 6) §2.4.3.

right to reject the surrender, if this would infringe the constitutional rights and thus threaten the identity of the Constitution (so-called "*Identitätskontrolle*", i.e., identity control).[39] In this light, German courts have refused to execute a EAW where this would have entailed a serious violation of fair trial guarantees, namely the right of access to a lawyer or of access to the file.[40] Likewise, Croatian courts have also included fair trial rights into the list of rights allowing for refusing a EAW, even if surrender is denied only if this would result in a flagrant denial of justice in the issuing State.[41]

While the CJEU has broadened the categories of rights allowing for rejecting a EAW,[42] similar practices conceal risks for the holding of the mutual recognition system. Refusals in these circumstances should indeed be limited to the most serious violations of fundamental rights, for example, where the surrender may expose the person to a real risk of inhumane and degrading treatment according to the *Aranyosi and Căldăraru* test.

However, not all Member States seem to apply this high threshold in the application of fundamental rights-based grounds for refusal. An interesting example of this interpretative drift is the extensive use of private life considerations to refuse surrender in the French case law and, more recently, in Croatia. In fact, the settled case law of the French Court of Cassation requires investigating chambers to check *in concreto* that the surrender of the person does not disproportionately affect the respect for the right to private and family life under Art 8 ECHR.[43] Likewise, Croatian judges have been recently manifesting

39 BVerfGE 140, 317; see Anna Albrecht and Anne Schneider (n 12) §1.2.2.1.

40 OLG Karlsruhe BeckRS 2020, 27088; see Anna Albrecht and Anne Schneider (n 12) §1.2.2.1.

41 Zlata Đurđević and others (n 6) §2.2.3.4.

42 If in the early case *Radu* the CJEU denied that the violation of a procedural safeguard (such as the right to be heard) could ground the refusal of a EAW, since *Aranyosi and Căldăraru* the Court has progressively widened the range of fundamental rights that can prevent the execution of the warrant. In *LM* (Case C-216/18 PPU *LM* [2018] ECLI:EU:C:2018:586), for instance, the CJEU admitted that the right to a fair trial (specifically, to an independent and impartial tribunal) could lead to the rejection of a EAW if the *Aranyosi and Căldăraru* two-fold test was satisfied. After the Covid-19 pandemic, this possibility was also extended to the right to health (see Case C-804/21 PPU *C and CD v Syyttäjä* [2022] ECLI:EU:C:2022:307 and Case C-699/21 *E.D.L.* [2023] ECLI:EU:C:2023:295).

43 Eleonora Cervellera (n 6) §1.2.2.1. In particular, the Author refers to a 2010, where the Court of Cassation overturned the decision of an investigating chamber that had agreed on the surrender of a person who had been living in France for several years, with her five school-going children, for the theft of a wallet worth 40 euros (Cass. crim., 12 May 2010, no. 10-82.746). In another ruling, the Court of Cassation confirmed an investigating chamber's refusal to surrender a wanted person to Germany for the offence of driving without a license, since the execution of the warrant would have caused a disproportionate breach of the person's right to respect for private and family life under Art 8 ECHR. In fact, the

greater attention to the right to private life when deciding whether to execute a EAW, requiring national executing authorities to acquire data on the specific circumstances of the case (e.g., time of residence in Croatia of the surrendee, the seriousness of the offence, best interests of the children involved) and assess whether the surrender would be proportionate to said right.[44] While this approach shows more sensitivity to fundamental rights, a systemic oversight on the impact on private life of the surrender, such as that applied in France and Croatia, does not seem to realize an adequate balance of such needs with the principle of mutual recognition. In these cases, the judicial assessment seems to circumvent the two-fold test of *Aranyosi and Căldăraru* – recently reaffirmed by the CJEU in *GN* also in relation to the right to private and family file[45] – so the threshold to refuse surrender is *de facto* much lower than that required by the CJEU.

## 4 Comparative Remarks on the Implementation of the EIO

### 4.1 *Introductory Overview*

The national reports show that, so far, the transposition and implementation of the EIO D have not given rise to any major problems. Member States have transposed the EIO D on time, given that, by 2018, all had adopted the necessary amendments in their national legislation as required by the directive. Moreover, no passage has given rise to particularly critical debates, with the exception perhaps of Germany, where the transposition law seems to leave show little concern for the mutual trust and mutual recognition that should characterise the actions of States (scholars have not failed to criticise the legislator in this respect).

Overall, the implementation of the EIO D does not appear problematic. This may be due to a few reasons. First, the EIO D was conceived with the main problems originating in the EAW FD already in mind. This allowed the EU legislator to take them into account and introduce some clauses that were missing in the EAW FD. Secondly, the concrete use of this instrument is perhaps still limited (although the numbers give hope for a progressive success also in quantitative terms: in this regard, the data provided by the Croatian

person concerned had worked regularly on French territory for several years, shared his life with a French woman, and was the father of two children living in France (Cass. crim., 5 May 2015, no. 15-82.108).

44 Zlata Đurđević and others (n 6) §2.2.3.2.

45 Case C-261/22 *GN* [2023] ECLI:EU:C:2023:1017.

report are interesting). Thirdly, it should not be forgotten that the EIO D avoids adopting common rules on the mutual admissibility of evidence, which is the most delicate aspect of evidentiary matters, leaving its decisions to national laws. This has led to a postponement in dealing *ex professo* with the exclusion of evidence, whenever a party (usually the defence) opposes admissibility. The simplification and the postponement of the issue have been largely achieved by invoking mutual recognition (in the name of which, national courts tend to admit evidence from a jurisdiction other than their own unless errors markedly conflict with their fundamental principles).

The impression, however, is that there is still too little data on the admissibility of evidence and remedies because the full operation of the EIO D is still too recent. Indeed, the EIO D, albeit implicitly, aims to create the general framework for jurisprudence to develop some common rules on the admissibility of evidence (the *Encrochat* judgment itself is an example).[46] In time, when these common rules start to emerge more clearly, it is realistic to think that we will have new sensitive legal issues brought to the attention of the Court of Justice.

### 4.2 *Respect for Fundamental Rights and Proportionality*

Having said, therefore, that the transposition of the directive does not seem to have given rise to too many problems so far, it must be emphasised that all States have implemented the general rejection clause, in the name of which an EIO cannot be adopted (or executed) if it is contrary to fundamental rights and inconsistent with the principle of proportionality. From this point of view, it is evident that the lesson drawn from the case law of the MFA-DF has indeed been considered by all States. Actually, the lesson had been taken on board by the European legislator in drawing up the EIO D, in which hypotheses of non-enforcement (or postponement) for violation of fundamental principles or failure to comply with proportionality were already introduced. Rather, in this respect, it should be noted that many States (Italy, Germany, Poland, Spain) have also included in the clause the due respect for national constitutional principles. This is certainly a legitimate and opportune choice, although perhaps superfluous, given that both the Charter of Fundamental Rights and the Treaty recognise respect for national traditions (albeit common ones). In addition, the Netherlands has also chosen to invoke the principle of subsidiarity, for which the same considerations apply as to constitutional principles:

46 On this point, please refer to what is discussed below in paragraph 4.5, on the admissibility of evidence.

this is undoubtedly correct, but it is already covered by the Treaties and the case law of the Court of Justice.

On the other hand, Poland's choice to subordinate the issuance and execution of the EIO to the respect of national interests raises some doubts. This step could eventually give rise to friction with the jurisprudence of the Court of Justice. Certain national interests must take precedence, such as national security, which, already in the provisions of the directive, legitimises the non-execution of the EIO. However, such a generic and neither punctual nor selective reference to national interests, always superordinate – according to the textual wording of the Polish transposition text – over the EIO, could give rise to conflicts, which will have to be resolved by the Court of Justice (or by an appropriate dialogue between the apex courts). It is, however, desirable that an interpretation inspired by the general principles of the EU legal system be able to resolve the risks of conflict a priori by interpreting the clause in harmony with supranational jurisprudence (and the legal sources on mutual recognition in EU judicial cooperation).

Finally, it should be noted that most of the jurisdictions examined have chosen to transpose all refusal clauses, both mandatory and optional. This choice does not give cause for concern. Indeed, the effectiveness of the implementation of the directive does not seem to be linked so much to the number of refusal clauses introduced on paper as to their application in practice. So far, from this last point of view (which is the one that counts), it must be acknowledged that the EIO seems to be implemented with prevailing consistency regarding the principle of mutual recognition and a mutual trust approach.

### 4.3 *Competent Authorities*

Most States include the prosecutor among the authorities legitimated to issue an EIO (see, for example, Italy, France, Netherlands, Poland). Likewise, the prosecutor is the referring figure when it comes to the execution of the EIO in the passive procedure. Some include also other authorities, such as the police (in Poland, where the police are competent for the so-called Petty Offences).

This choice does not entail too many problems, as it is generally provided that when the national law provides for judicial review of the requested act, the EIO must be issued by a judge in the strict sense of the word, or any case after a judge has authorised the police or public prosecutor to issue it. It must also be recognised that in several countries (e.g., France, but also Spain), the prosecutor is responsible for the phase preceding the investigation (the so-called preliminary inquiry). It was therefore inevitable that the choice fell on this figure, given that, in any case, when a sensitive act is to be performed (such as wiretapping) the intervention of a judge is required.

Rather, some problems may arise concerning the independence of the body, since in some systems the prosecutor acts under the direction (or at least the supervision) of the executive. So far, the problem has not arisen, but the possibility is not remote that it might arise, should the EIO be issued during a court case with significant political implications, and the acting prosecutor not offer adequate guarantees of independence from the executive. In such hypothetical eventualities, it is realistic to think that the jurisprudence of the Court of Justice on the matter would become relevant again and would have to dispel the uncertainties linked – we imagine – to a risk of conditioning by the executive.

From another perspective, it is worrying that most States have neglected the position of the defence. According to the research conducted only Italy (via an explicit provision) and Spain (which interprets ad hoc an already existing legal provision) offers the possibility for the defence counsel to take action, requiring the judge to issue an EIO. This is a gap that gives rise to some concern in perspective. Indeed, increasingly, the success of mutual recognition of court decisions will highlight the disproportion of resources between the prosecution and the defence. The former is now able to move within a network of effective connections, developed over decades (starting with the liaison magistrates in the late 1980s). The latter, on the other hand, still operates in isolation, because connections between defence offices are occasional and episodic, left to the resources and sagacity of individual professionals (or individual law firms). This disproportion must be mitigated by encouraging and incentivising the growth of effective channels of connection between professionals and law firms across the EU. An indirect way to foster such growth is to empower defences when involved in a transnational case, for example by giving them the power to request the court to issue an EIO. Acting to solicit an EIO, in fact, preliminarily requires that a defence lawyer develop adequate transnational contacts with colleagues in other EU countries, to be able to gather the necessary information to substantiate one's claims (and to be able to rely on a law firm to serve as a logistical base when one has to operate abroad).

It is true that, in most EU countries, the prosecutor should also investigate by looking for exculpatory evidence. However, such a legal choice alone, as we well know, is not sufficient to safeguard the needs of an effective defence, for which a proactive defence counsel who is aware of the transnational dimension of the modern criminal trial is also necessary. The fact that the role of the lawyer has been forgotten and that in most national laws transposing the EIO D this figure does not appear among those authorised to act, is not a good sign and denotes a cultural delay on the part of national legislators in conceiving the role of the defence counsel.

### 4.4 *Remedies*

In relation to remedies, no particular legal issues arise at first sight. An EIO may be issued when the law, for the evidence sought, is provided for in a similar domestic case by existing domestic law. The same then applies to the enforcement of an EIO in passive proceedings.

Of course, as became clear in the *Gavazonov* case,[47] the problem becomes relevant when the domestic legal system (this was the case in Bulgaria) does not provide any remedy against the possible violation of legal provisions concerning an investigative measure or evidence to be gathered. However, beyond that (Bulgaria itself adapted its system to the requests of the CJEU), no specific issues seem to arise.

Rather, it is worrying how most countries (France, The Netherlands) extensively use the secrecy clause to delay the communication to the defence of the possibility of challenging before a court the investigative measure or evidentiary operation performed. In most cases, investigative secrecy predominates, resulting in the defence not being notified of the possibility of challenging the EIO when it is executed. This also implies that often notification is made when it is very late, and it is difficult for the defence to effectively avail itself of effective legal remedies. Once again, the weakness of the defender emerges here, in the transposition of the EIO D. A weakness, in turn, which, in this case, was also made possible by the legal provisions of the directive, which are very sensitive to safeguarding national investigative secrecy. The opposite should apply. Once executed, the EIO is no longer secret. Thus, there should no longer be any problem alerting the defence of the legal remedies to which it has access. On the face of it, indeed, this is the minimum condition – officially alerting the defence of its prerogatives – that should be respected. One might perhaps think here that the directive should be amended to allow for timely and effective notice to the defence once the EIO has been executed. Of course, the possibility of appeal will have to coexist with the persistence of secrecy (secrecy, however, which may remain on acts other than the EIO, of which the defence has now come, or at least must be made, aware).

### 4.5 *Admissibility*

The admissibility of evidence, in a framework still in its infancy of EIO D, does not seem to give rise to problems. An open attitude generally prevails regarding the admissibility of evidence gathered through the EIO. An example, from this point of view, is Poland, which allows readings of all or almost all records of

47 Case C-852/19 *Gavazonov II* [2021] EU:C:2021:902, ECR I-7879.

evidence and information taken abroad. But similar solutions are also found in other systems, such as Spain or Italy, where the principle of mutual recognition ends up prevailing. Yet, both systems would have a general clause on the exclusion of evidence. However, in practice, openness to evidence gathered abroad (an attitude that goes back a long way, related to the need to accept deviations from the legal national model when cooperation from other States is required) still predominates. A similar solution applies, for example in Croatia, where it was decided not to penalise the failure to video-record the interrogation of the defendant (which is nevertheless required under the domestic rules under threat of exclusion of evidence).

Finally, the rule that, in the logic of mutual recognition, the justification and legitimacy of the EIO must only be appealed before the jurisdiction of the issuing State is certainly not conducive to the flourishing of exclusion cases. Usually, the defence is at a disadvantage, since it is difficult for it to prepare an effective strategy of attack if it is located, as is predominantly the case, in the State of execution of the EIO.

The *Encrochat* case itself, which has been touched upon sporadically in current research, does not seem to have changed the picture we have described so far. After all, the judgment of the Court of Justice of 30 April 2024[48] recalled that the admissibility of the evidence, understood as its legality and the justification of the measure, must only be appealed in the jurisdiction of the State where the data were originally collected, and cannot be dealt with in the jurisdiction of the State where the data are transferred thanks to an EIO. It is true, however, that the judgment recognises an exclusionary rule for cases where the defence could not effectively challenge the results of the data collected through EIO. This observation, in perspective, could open the way to relevant questions of admissibility for cases in which the defence receives too late official notice of the power to challenge the evidentiary measures carried out with EIO, or for cases in which it is not allowed effective disclosure of exculpatory evidence (an issue that, in theory, could be relevant in investigations carried out with the Encrochat and SkyEcc operations and has so far received little consideration from the courts before it was raised).

Furthermore, the thesis that a State issuing an EIO to obtain the transfer of evidence or information already in the possession of the executing State cannot question the legality and proportionality, with regard to how the evidence was originally obtained in the executing State, should perhaps be questioned, at least in part. Indeed, it is true that Art 11 EIO D provides that "information

48 Case C-670/22 *M.N.* (*EncroChat*) [2024] EU:C:2024:372.

or evidence which is already in the possession of the executing authority [...] always have to be available under the law of the executing State". However, this does not preclude the issuing State, when issuing an EIO, from verifying whether the measure is necessary and proportionate, taking into account the rights of the defence and whether it could have been issued in a similar domestic case, as stipulated in Art 6.

At any rate, the *Encrochat* court case presents numerous complexities that deserve careful examination, particularly regarding issues that have not been adequately assessed so far. Central to this discussion is the right of the defence to request access to potentially relevant and exculpatory communications. In this sense, a good practice seems to be the Dutch one, developed in the course of the investigations stemming from the SkyEcc case. The defence was granted access to data on its clients through the same forensic platform used by the police authorities, which deserves the attention of other States. This, as has been pointed out by the scholars who studied the case,[49] indeed seems to be a good practice to facilitate access to data for the defence as part of the right to a fair trial. This right is fundamental to ensuring a fair trial, as it allows defendants to effectively challenge the prosecution's evidence. Furthermore, understanding the methods by which communications were originally collected and decrypted is equally crucial, as transparency in this area is necessary to assess the legality of operations, balancing national interests with individual rights. Information concerning the modalities with which data were gathered originally is also essential to determine if the EIO can be issued respecting the requirements of the admissibility in a similar domestic case, as these cannot be derogated even when the EIO regards evidence already in the possession of the executing authority according to Art 11.

## 5 Comparative Remarks on the Implementation of Regulation 1805/2018

Last, in this comparative analysis, the application of Regulation 1805/2018 plays a somewhat special role. Being a regulation, this cooperation tool does not require any form of transposition or implementation and shall apply directly at the domestic level. The choice of such a legal basis, still rather uncommon in the criminal justice area, seems to produce ambivalent outcomes in the examined Member States.

49 Jan-Jaap Oerlemans ,Sofie Royer, 'The future of data-driven investigations in light of the Sky ECC operation' [2023] 14 *New Journal of European Criminal Law* , 434.

On the one hand, as in the European legislator's intention, the use of a regulation has reduced the margin of discretion for national policymakers, decreasing the rate of error and discrepancies across domestic systems. On the other hand, however, what emerges from the comparative study is a certain degree of uneasiness in the direct handling of a European instrument by national legal practitioners, courts, and parties alike.

In this regard, a first contradiction arises between the general data, which hints at a broad application of the Regulation,[50] and the analysis of domestic case law, which appears extremely scarce in all the examined legal orders.[51] Against a majority of States where no jurisprudence before the highest court can be reported yet (Bulgaria, France, Spain, Poland, and Portugal), a few others provide for a limited array of decisions focused on thematic issues depending on the country at stake. While in Germany, cases are referred almost exclusively to the territoriality clause of the Regulation;[52] in the Netherlands, they are concentrated on two specific grounds for refusal (double criminality and fundamental rights violation);[53] and in Italy, attention has mainly focused on compliance with the principle of proportionality, on specific issues in the execution of measures (when Italy is an executing State), or on the completeness of certificates.[54] Peculiar in this context is the Croatian case, where a preliminary reference has already been issued to the Court of Justice to inquire on a series of interpretative questions (from the possibility of enforcing confiscation in case of acquittal, to the rights of the third parties involved in the procedure).[55]

Four years after its entry into force, the reasons for such an underrepresentation of Regulation-related issues in the jurisprudence and (perhaps consequently) the limited attention given to it by legal doctrine is not straightforward, although some hypotheses can be formulated in light of the elements presented below.

---

50 As confirmed by Eurojust, interviewed on May 13, 2024, within the FACILEX project; the data supporting the claim are being elaborated by Eurojust, and will be published in an upcoming report on Regulation 1805/2018.

51 In this regard, a major difficulty of this study on the Regulation has been represented by the lack of substantial statistical information, regardless the provision of Art 35 Regulation that requires Member States to collect and submit relevant data.

52 See Anna Albrecht and Anne Schneider (n 12) § 1.4.2.2.

53 See Camila Ugaz Heudebert and others (n 6) § 4.5.

54 See Cass. Pen. sec. II, n. 34212 of 27/05/2022, reported on the FACILEX Italian report, available on: https://site.unibo.it/facilex/en/the-project/results.

55 See Zlata Đurđević and others (n 6) § 4.2.

### 5.1 *An Overlayered Field of Law*

The first aspect that seems to heavily impact the general enforcement of the Regulation is the extreme complexity of the whole legal regime concerning seizure, freezing, and confiscation in the European Union.

Legal systems that have been significantly impacted by the transposition of Framework Decisions 2003/577 and 2006/783,[56] and perhaps to a lower extent, by Directive 2014/42,[57] appear to be currently struggling in reconstructing a coherent operative framework that includes also the Regulation.

On the one hand, the Regulation has a limited scope of application as far as territoriality is concerned since it does not cover the cooperation with Denmark and Ireland (where, therefore, the previous legislation continues to apply). On the other hand, even within its scope, the succession of legislative sources in a short period[58] has likely contributed to a certain amount of confusion, which seems to have somewhat delayed the awareness by legal practitioners of the potential offered by the new legislation.

In this sense, the very discipline of the Regulation, which does not provide for clear coordination with the previous legislation, certainly plays a role. An example in this sense is shown by the grounds for refusal, which are provided for as both mandatory and optional in the Framework Decisions, whereas they are only optional in the Regulation. This discrepancy is reported as a major factor of uncertainty in all the States examined, to the point that in some instances national courts directly opt for the application of the older, and better-experimented regimes (e.g. in Bulgaria).[59] Another example is given by execution deadlines, established in the Regulation, but only seldom backed up at the national level by adequate provisions, that make the enforcement of the orders effective in practice.[60]

---

56 Council Framework Decision 2003/577/JHA of 22 July 2003 on the execution in the European Union of orders freezing property or evidence, and Council Framework Decision 2006/783/JHA of 6 October 2006 on the application of the principle of mutual recognition to confiscation orders.

57 Directive 2014/42/EU of the European Parliament and of the Council of 3 April 2014 on the freezing and confiscation of instrumentalities and proceeds of crime in the European Union.

58 A trend that is not giving any sign of discontinuity even after the entry into force of the Regulation, as clearly shown by the approval of Directive (EU) 2024/1260 of the European Parliament and of the Council of 24 April 2024 on asset recovery and confiscation.

59 Miroslava Manolova and Ekaterina Salkova (n 33) §1.4.2. In this uncertainty finds its origin also the request for a preliminary reference by the Croatian authorities, mentioned above and in Zlata Đurđević and others (n 6) § 4.2.

60 In this sense, especially France (Eleonora Cervellera (n 6) §1.4.2) and Portugal (Miguel João Costa and others (n 9) § 1.4.4).

In this regard, it is not surprising that, although a regulation does not require any form of transposition into national law, most of the analyzed systems felt the need to introduce some sort of coordinating provision or at least to partially amend the previous legislation in an attempt to restore unity to the overall discipline, or to cover some fundamental issues related to the designation of the competent authority, the certificate procedure, and, to a lesser extent, remedies. Poland and Spain still represent an exception to this trend, although numerous calls are made for the implementation of similar instruments in those countries as well. Even where coordination has been implemented, however, the effort seems insufficient to ensure enough clarity in the regime of seizure, freezing, and confiscation.

A first conclusion thus strongly emerges from this comparative analysis: rather than a series of subsequent interventions that never fully overlap with each, the situation urgently calls for a rationalization of the whole sector at the European level, possibly with a single instrument that provides for a clear, all-encompassing regulation.

### 5.2 *A Still-Too-Vague Ontological Dimension*

A further element of complexity, strictly related to the first one, is the high level of fragmentation that can be reported regarding the ontological dimension of concepts and notions in this domain. In other words, despite the numerous interventions for harmonization, this cooperation field appears still extremely diverse when it comes to defining the single legal tools.

The extension of the scope of freezing, seizure, and confiscation orders, indeed, has a considerable impact on the effectiveness of the whole cooperation mechanism, as it increases or decreases the number of cases in which a Member State can request the execution of such measures on assets located in another Member State.[61]

An exemplification, in this sense, is the definition of "freezing order", which is interpreted in very different ways across the European jurisdictions (for instance, for what concerns the purpose it can be used for).[62] A great deal of fragmentation can also be observed about the forms of confiscation, which vary from State to State both as far as the typologies are concerned (conviction-based/non-conviction-based[63]/civil forfeiture) and in relation to the requirements that define each of such measures.

---

61 In this sense, also Eleonora Cervellera (n 6) § 1.4.

62 E.g. in Spain it cannot be used for confiscation purposes, while this is possible in other legal orders, see Ana Maria Neira Pena (n 10) § 1.4.1.

63 In particular, non-conviction-based confiscations are reported in all the examined Member States, with the exception of the Netherlands, where a proposal to introduce

It is true that, in general, the influence of European legislation extended the scope of freezing and confiscation tools in domestic systems, therefore marking an advance in the efficiency of the fight against cross-border crime. Nonetheless, at times, this same extension also represented a factor for further complications. For instance, the fact that the Regulation also applies to proceedings that are not strictly speaking of a criminal nature in accordance with Recital 18, without a clear definition of the substantial nature of the single confiscation measures, has been identified as an obstacle to a smooth cooperation.[64]

### 5.3 *Divergent Operational Rules*

Against these more transversal divergence issues, the comparative analysis brought to light a series of punctual discrepancies that are also reportedly diminishing the impact of the Regulation in its practical implementation.

The first aspect concerns the competent authorities, which each Member State must identify according to the new regime, and which have been chosen with a lot of variety across the countries. In some, the decision fell upon courts, however of different status, at the district level for instance in Bulgaria; depending on the state of procedure in Spain and Italy; in Croatia and Poland, courts are flanked by prosecution offices; in Germany and the Netherlands, prosecutors have a prominent role, while in France a significant position is held by an administrative authority (the Agency for the Management and Recovery of Seized and Confiscated Assets). Such a divergence may also be found within national systems, for example, in Poland and Italy, where the authority in charge varies also depending on the single tool at stake (freezing or confiscation).

A second aspect of discrepancy emerges, rather unsurprisingly in truth, about remedies. The need to establish effective remedies, vague as ever in the European legislation, has been variously interpreted by the national legislature regarding the Regulation.

In a few cases, that brought to the establishment of new forms of appeal (for instance in Germany, or Bulgaria, in the latter however only where the State acts as executing authority);[65] in others, the chosen solution was to extend

---

them is ongoing (see Camila Ugaz Heudebert and others (n 6)). On this matter, in any case, Directive 2024/1260 is likely to have a significant impact, once implemented at the national level.

64 This aspect is reported as especially problematic in some jurisdictions, e.g. Portugal, see Miguel João Costa and others (n 9) § 1.4.3, and Italy, see Isadora Neroni Rezende and others (n 6) § 4.2.

65 See Anna Albrecht and Anne Schneider (n 12) § 1.4.4 and Miroslava Manolova and Ekaterina Salkova (n 33) § 1.4.6.

remedies already available in the domestic framework also to the cases covered by the Regulation.

Finally, a third major factor of divergence can be observed with the status of third parties, especially where they can be identified with the crime victims. In this regard, differences among Member States are quite striking. In some, for instance, victims cannot be at all the beneficiary of confiscation measures (in any case, as in Poland, or in some circumstances, as in Spain),[66] while in others, victims may indirectly benefit from such measures, although without directly activating the single tools provided in the Regulation (as in France and in Italy).

## 6 Concluding Remarks

The picture that emerges from the analysis carried out shows that the path toward smooth and fair cooperation in the criminal justice field is a complex proceeding. In light of the above considerations, each of the examined cooperation mechanisms can be observed singularly, and for each, a specific conclusion could be drawn. The comparative analysis conducted indeed reveals a contradictory picture of the state of implementation of the principle of mutual recognition in the EU.

The EAW is the oldest of the EU mutual recognition instruments in criminal matters, and its use is generally well-established in the national practice. Over the years, Member States seem to have become more willing to adapt their transposition laws to the spirit of the framework decision, thus showing a greater commitment to the principle of mutual trust. Despite this widespread trend, however, some problems still seem to affect the integrity of the EAW mechanism. Even if some transposition issues are quite common for specific grounds for refusal – in particular, those related to the *ne bis in idem* and the surrender of nationals and other residents – the more complex legal issues for the holding of mutual recognition will likely stem from the incorporation of human rights considerations in the EAW system. The recent nature of the relevant grounds for refusal, which was not initially provided in the EU surrender mechanism, is evident in the fragmented approach that is developing across Member States. Domestic case law differs on the interpretation of the range of fundamental rights that may trigger the non-execution of a EAW and the threshold to refuse surrender. These divergences undermine the consistent

66 See Wojciech Jasiński and others (n 10) § 1.4.3 and Ana Maria Neira Pena (n 10) § 1.4.4.

application of the principle of mutual recognition in the EAW system, despite the efforts made by the CJEU in this regard since *Aranyosi and Căldăraru*. Against this scattered background, a more harmonized approach may likely be achieved with a reform of the EAW FD, clearly stating the conditions for refusing a EAW due to the real risk of fundamental rights violations.

The analysis carried out on the transposition of the EIO D shows a rather unproblematic picture so far. However, the EIO D is still in its beginning and has already shown considerable success. It is therefore conceivable that certain critical aspects, in particular, the marginal role left to the defence of the accused, may in the future give rise to complex legal issues, on which it may be necessary to intervene, either by amending the text of the directive (as in the case of the need to respect, at all costs and without exception, the secrecy of the investigation) or by changing certain interpretative solutions adopted so far. This last remark applies in particular to the so-called data-driven investigations,[67] which represent a new way of operating, very different from what is regulated by the EIO (which treats each investigative and evidentiary measure as a *unicum* and does not address the issue of massive data acquisition).

It is still too early to draw firm conclusions in this regard, but it is easy to imagine that the issue of admissibility of evidence will, therefore come up again. After all, while avoiding explicitly regulating the topic, the EIO D indirectly intervenes on admissibility, inviting national States to simplify their systems to focus on protecting the essential principles of their respective legal systems. The more transnational investigations proliferate, the more the indirect push to simplify national systems on evidentiary admissibility will be felt. It is, therefore to be expected that new problems will emerge, given that the admission of evidence is an area in which States have always appeared very jealous of their sovereignty.

Last, the Regulation, which, as a tool, could have seemed the best legislative option to prevent many of the implementation problems highlighted with regard to the EAW FD and the EIO D, seems to suffer from similar problems with opposite origins. The direct applicability of the instrument, in fact, perhaps still due to the peculiarity of similar solutions in criminal matters, seems – in

67 See Giulia Lasagni, 'Admissibility of Evidence in Criminal Proceedings: Lessons (and Problems) from the "Data Retention Saga"' in Lorena Bachmaier Winter and Farsam Salimi (eds), *Admissibility of Evidence in EU in Cross-Border Criminal Proceedings: Electronic Evidence, Efficiency and Fair Trial Rights*, (Bloomsbury Publishing, 2024), 29–48; Jan-Jaap Oerlemans,Dave van Toor, 'Legal Aspects of the EncroChat Operation: A Human Rights Perspective', [2022] 30 Eur.J.Crime Cr.L.Cr.J. 309; Jan-Jaap Oerlemans, Sofie Royer, 'The future of data-driven investigations in light of the Sky ECC operation', [2023] 14 NJECL 434.

these early years – to have perplexed numerous legal practitioners, first and foremost the courts, with the result that they often fail to exploit the full potential of the system. In this difficulty, as in the case of EAW FD and EIO D, the role of the national legislator also seems to have a prominent position. In the absence of a duty to transpose, in fact, the absence of rules or guidelines coordinating with the new discipline often seems to have left interpreters in doubt as to how and when to apply the Regulation. Without prejudice to these more general considerations, however, the certainly more problematic issue appears to be the fragmentary nature of the legislative basis for the confiscation and freezing of assets. In fact, the centrality of the issue, in the European and international context, would require today a complete systematisation of all legal acts still in force in the sector, starting from a clear definition of which legal institution (e.g., seizure, freezing, confiscation) can be used under which conditions and for which purposes.

In light of these considerations, it would seem natural to conclude that, in the end, the legal tool used to establish a cooperation mechanism is certainly a crucial factor, but maybe it is not the resolutive one. Clarity in the legal bases and knowledge of the legal operators of what could be achieved thanks to a certain tool remain pivotal in making cooperation effective in practice, not only on a theoretical level. This consideration is particularly important, especially for the position of defence lawyers, who, as private individuals, appears today as the party of the proceeding that struggles more in transposing their action on transnational grounds. In this regard, defensive exceptions, raised till the level of preliminary references to the CJEU, have significantly contributed to strengthening the degree of protection of fundamental rights in all the three cooperation mechanisms analysed here. Still, especially the EIO D and the Regulation, insisting on subject matters where a transnational approach is less developed than with the surrender of suspects, show the limits of an approach that continues to portray the figure of the defence lawyer only seldomly on the European dimension. Thus, a change in the approach seems increasingly necessary.

Pointing the finger against gaps and lacunas, however, should not let us forget how much has actually been accomplished in the last few years. This is even more so, considering that procedures regulating investigation and trials, so far, have not been harmonized at the EU level and, therefore, present a significantly high level of divergence among Member States.

Just to mention one of the major achievements, reference could go to the effective functioning of all mechanisms in a context in which judicial authorities, police, and lawyers still widely disregard the legal systems of others and their languages and legal traditions.

Indirectly, the practice related to the three mechanisms also provided a push forward towards some approximation, if not harmonization, of investigative measures (for instance, as far as the requirement of judicial authorization is concerned).

Although at times frustrating in terms of foreseeability of the applicable procedural norm and effectiveness of cooperation, this complex but continuous accumulation of practice steadily contributes to the creation of a common culture on criminal proceedings in the EU that is starting to go well beyond the harmonization of single procedural safeguards. The reflection of this study tried to support this trend by increasing the level of mutual knowledge and understanding for legal operators, for a path that – in the current European and international context – appears today as fragile and fascinating as ever.

CHAPTER 14

# Piercing the Veil of Ignorance of Fundamental Rights Protection. What Is Transnational in EU Judicial Cooperation?

*Mariavittoria Catanzariti*

## 1 Introduction

The area of judicial cooperation is very broad both from the perspective of the legal institutions involved and from the perspective of its purposes. This implies, on the one hand, that there is a difficult cooperation between the police and judicial institutions and, on the other hand, that increasingly broader areas related to criminal matters are addressed by different competencies. This contribution poses the question to what extent the protection of fundamental rights can be considered the common core that informs the rationale of three mechanisms in the field of judicial cooperation. The main tasks addressed by the judicial cooperation instruments at glance – Regulation 1805/2018, the EAW FD, and the EIO D – are information sharing between Member States, the fight against corruption, cybercrime, fraud and money laundering and the effectiveness of the fight against crime.

In these contexts, the use of such cooperation mechanisms that are different in scope,[1] shed light on the possible systemic framework on fundamental rights' protection as precondition of judicial cooperation.

The EAW is a simplified cross-border judicial surrender procedure for the purpose of prosecution or executing a custodial sentence or detention order, replaces extradition procedures and operates via direct contact between judicial authorities.[2] It is a very expedited procedure, because the country where the person is arrested must take a final decision on the execution of the EAW within 10 days, if the requested person consents to surrender. Otherwise, the final decision on the execution of the EAW should be taken within a period of

1 These instruments represent the core research of Facilex Project (G.A. 101089634).

2 Regarding the scope, the EAW can be issued for acts punishable by the law of the issuing Member State by a custodial sentence or a detention order for a maximum period of at least 12 months or, where a sentence has been passed or a detention order has been made, for sentences of at least four months.

60 days after the arrest of the requested person. Moreover, for 32 categories of offences, there is not any verification obligation on whether the act constitutes a criminal offence in both countries.

Regulation 1805/2018 replaces the framework decisions on the mutual recognition of freezing orders as regards the freezing of property and on the mutual recognition of confiscation orders of 2003 and 2006. While freezing temporarily aims at retaining property while a decision is pending, confiscation aims at preventing criminals from the use of property obtained by breaking the law.

The European Investigation Order (EIO) is an instrument of mutual recognition, which in principle obliges the executing state to recognise and ensure execution of the request of the other country, in the same way and under the same modalities as if the investigative measure concerned had been ordered by an authority of the executing country. The execution of the Order can be refused only in specific cases. It may also include electronic evidence gathering. In fact, the Council Regulation (EC) 1206/2001 on cooperation between the Courts of the Member States on civil and commercial evidence has been recently adopted on 25 November 2020 to adapt the judicial cooperation to technical development.[3]

## 2 Transversal Issues of Judicial Cooperation

The judicial activism in the field, as well as the uniformizing role of Eurojust in facilitating consultation between authorities, shows how judicial cooperation may also produce or restrict individual safeguards' cascades. If this connection between the use of instruments of judicial cooperation and individual rights is normal in a context of rule of law, it becomes an objective to be achieved in the daily practice of national and European institutions.

The transnational dimension of crimes requires judicial cooperation instruments that can cope with the territorial fragmentation of states and national criminal law. The exchange of information and recognition of judicial measures thus becomes crucial to provide a global response to crimes that increasingly exploit cross-border characteristics. Moreover, the choice of the instrument to be used is relevant not only in terms of the most effective response to fighting crimes, but also to limit as much as possible the impact of the instruments on fundamental rights, both in terms of procedural and substantive rights.

3 Regulation (EU) 2020/1783 of the European Parliament and of the Council of 25 November 2020 on cooperation between the courts of the Member States in the taking of evidence in civil or commercial matters [2020] OJ L 405.

Conversely, fundamental rights' protection may act as a legitimate limit for the execution of judicial cooperation's instruments.[4]

As well known, the legal basis of judicial cooperation in criminal matters includes Arts 82, 83, 84, 85 and 86 Treaty in the Functioning of the European Union (TFEU). Judicial cooperation in criminal matters in the Union is based on the principle of mutual recognition of judgments and judicial decisions. Parliament and Council shall act in accordance with the ordinary procedure on: (a) the mutual admissibility of evidence between Member States; (b) the rights of individuals in criminal procedure; (c) the rights of victims of crime; (d) other specific elements of criminal procedure, identified by the Council in advance by means of a decision; to adopt such a decision, the Council shall act unanimously after obtaining the consent of the European Parliament. The related measures are subject to control by the Court of Justice of the European Union (CJEU).

This means that the Commission shares the right of initiative with the Member States provided that they represent a quarter of the members of the Council (Art 76 TFEU), whereas the Parliament has a purely advisory function with regard to measures on judicial cooperation in criminal matters, which are adopted unanimously by the Council. In the absence of unanimity in the Council, nine or more Member States seek consensus requesting that the draft measures be referred to the Council.

A crucial role in strengthening judicial cooperation is played by Eurojust, which is the European Union Agency for Judicial Cooperation in Criminal Matters. It supports and enhances coordination and cooperation between national authorities responsible for investigating and prosecuting serious crime affecting two or more Member States or requiring prosecution on a common basis, on the ground of operations carried out and information provided by Member States' authorities and Europol. In this context, Council and Parliament may, by means of regulations in accordance with the ordinary legislative procedure, determine Eurojust's structure, operation, field of action and tasks.[5] For example in the case of European Arrest Warrant the sensitiveness

4 European Union Agency for Fundamental Rights *European Arrest Warrant Proceedings. Room for improvement to guarantee rights in practice*, Report March 2024 (Luxembourg: Publications Office of the European Union 2024).

5 Those tasks may include: (a) the initiation of criminal investigations and the proposal for the initiation of prosecutions by the competent national authorities, in particular those relating to offences affecting the financial interests of the Union; (b) the coordination of investigations and prosecutions; (c) the strengthening of judicial cooperation, including through the settlement of conflicts of jurisdiction and through close cooperation with the European Judicial Network.

of issues at stake, including the lack of a legal basis for adopting a regulation,[6] did not permit the adoption of an uniformizing instrument that would help a common inspiration to standards and fundamental rights protection.[7] However, the adoption of specific rules building on the right to a fair trial and the right of defence – including the right to interpretation and translation, the right to information, the right of access to a lawyer and the right to have a third party informed upon deprivation of liberty and to communicate with third persons and with consular authorities while deprived of liberty, the right to legal aid, procedural safeguards for children – guarantee the procedural rights of persons suspected and accused.[8] While individual rights shall inform the rationale of judicial cooperation mechanisms, sometimes they may contrast with their execution.

In the EIO D, for instance, Art 11(1)(f) introduces a specific rule stating that the executing authority may refuse to recognize or execute the order if there are serious grounds for considering that the execution of the requested investigative measure would be incompatible with the obligations of the executing State under Art 6 of the Treaty on European Union (TEU) and the Charter of Fundamental Rights (CFREU). This ground for non-execution is also included in Regulation 1805/2018 at Art 8(1)(f), but it is not mentioned in the EAW FD.

In light of the above, the choice of the instrument may have an impact on the individual safeguards on a different scale.

The case of confiscation and freezing orders is significant as far as the choice of the Regulation 1805/2018 has represented an innovative modality to ensure the uniformized recognition of judgements pursuant to Art 82 of the Treaty on the Functioning of the European Union. Generally, in fact, the European Parliament and the Council, acting in accordance with the ordinary legislative procedure, shall adopt measures – thus, without specifying which pieces of secondary legislation are involved – to lay down rules and procedures to

6 Thomas Wishmeyer, 'Generating Trust Through Law? Judicial Cooperation in the European Union and the "Principle of Mutual Trust"' (2016) 17 German Law Journal 354.

7 Stefano Montaldo, *I limiti della cooperazione in materia penale nell'Unione Europea* (Napoli 2015); Evelien Brouwer, 'Mutual Trust and Human Rights in the AFSJ. In Search of Guidelines for National Courts' (2016) European Papers 893.

8 The six directives on procedural rights are the following: Directive on the Right to Legal Aid in Criminal and EAW Proceedings (2016/1919/EU); Directive on Procedural Safeguards for Children (2016/800/EU); Directive on the Presumption of Innocence and the Right to be Present at Trial (2016/343/EU); Directive on the Right of Access to a Lawyer in Criminal Proceedings and in European Arrest Warrant Proceedings (2013/48/EU); Directive on the Right to Information (2012/13/EU); Directive on Interpretation and Translation in Criminal Proceedings (2010/64/EU).

ensure recognition throughout the Union of all types of judgments and judicial decisions.

In the last decade, the CJEU has compensated the lack of legal framework by means of judicial activism. To highlight such a potential, this chapter focuses on the role of fundamental rights protection as a limit to the mutual trust between Member States. It transversally examines the three mechanisms of mutual trust identifying the areas of law in which fundamental rights protection emerged in this respect and focusing on specific aspects that are related to individual safeguards and rule of law standards. It finally explores to what extent fundamental rights protection may represent a 'veil of ignorance' that justifies the grounds for non-execution.

## 3 The European Arrest Warrant

As is well-known, the European arrest warrant is a judicial decision issued by a judicial authority of an EU Member State for the arrest and surrender by another Member State of a person wanted for a criminal prosecution or the execution of a custodial sentence. It has been established by the Framework Decision on the European Arrest Warrant (EAW FD),[9] which has replaced the system of extradition to speed up the surrender of accused or convicted persons from one Member State to another. It is in fact a tool that strengthens cooperation between Member States' judicial authorities based on the principle of mutual recognition of decisions in criminal matters.

This instrument is grounded upon the institutionalization of the principle of mutual trust by which it is presumed that the law enforcement authorities of the executing Member States comply with the right to a fair trial and other (related) fundamental rights recognized in the issuing State.

Several EU directives on procedural rights adopted between 2010 and 2016 ensure that persons who are subject of a European arrest warrant have the right of access to a lawyer and to legal aid; are entitled to interpretation

9 Council Framework Decision 2002/584/JHA of 13 June 2002 on the European arrest warrant and the surrender procedures between Member States [2002] OJ L 190/1, as amended by Council Framework Decision 2009/299/JHA of 26 February 2009 amending Framework Decisions 2002/584/JHA, 2005/214/JHA, 2006/783/JHA, 2008/909/JHA and 2008/947/JHA, thereby enhancing the procedural rights of persons and fostering the application of the principle of mutual recognition to decisions rendered in the absence of the person concerned at the trial [2009] OJ L 81/24 (FDEAW).

and translation of the European arrest warrant; shall receive information on their rights.[10]

The main aspects of the legal framework that are relevant for the fundamental rights' protection and that will be addressed throughout the analysis of the CJEU's caselaw are the following: the validity of the instrument, its compatibility with fundamental rights, the domestic guarantees related to the competence of the issuing authority. Regarding the definition, the EAW is defined as a judicial decision (Art.1(1)). This leads to a first interpretative problem regarding the competent authority issuing an EAW that will be examined in this paragraph.

The requested person should be granted fundamental rights (Arts 11, 13 and 14): the right to be informed about the content, the right to be assisted by a legal counsel and by an interpreter, the right to consent or renunciation, and the right to be heard.[11]

We will deal with this instrument, focusing on specific legal issues arising from the emerging case law.[12] The methodology followed aims at testing the weight of fundamental rights protection as a parameter of legitimacy even beyond the cases related to specific rights to be granted to the requested persons.[13]

### 3.1 *Validity of the Instrument*

With regard to the validity of the EAW instruments, some leading cases shall be mentioned.

---

10 On the most relevant issues related to the implementation of the six directives on procedural rights, see Giuseppe Contissa and others (eds) *Effective Protection on the Rights of the Accused in the EU Directives: a Computable Approach to Criminal Procedure Law* (Brill Nijoff, 2022).

11 For a complete analysis, see Petra Bárd,Sergio Carrera and Marco Stefan, *The Judicialisation of the European Arrest Warrant: Rule of Law and Fundamental Rights as Preconditions for Merited Mutual Trust* (Centre for European Policy Studies, 2023) https://cdn.ceps.eu/wp-content/uploads/2023/08/Judicialisation-of-the-European-Arrest-Warrant-STREAM-Report.pdf (accessed: 19/04/2025).

12 The selected case-law has been collected based on the Eurojust Report on the Case-law by the Court of Justice of the EU on the European Arrest Warrant of 2023, (European Union Agency for Criminal Justice Cooperation, 2023) <https://www.eurojust.europa.eu/sites/default/files/assets/eurojust-eaw-cjeu-case-law-report-10-2023.pdf> (accessed: 19/04/2025). See also Anne Pieter van der Mei, 'The European Arrest Warrant System: Recent Developments in the Case Law of the Court of Justice' (2017) 24(6) Maastricht Journal of European and Comparative Law 882, https://doi.org/10.1177/1023263X17745804.

13 Thomas Wahl, 'CJEU Rules on Compliance of FD EAW with Charter of Fundamental Rights'(2021) Eucrim https://eucrim.eu/news/cjeu-rules-on-compliance-of-fd-eaw-with-charter-of-fundamental-rights/ (accessed: 19/04/2025).

On the one hand, In *Advocaten voor de Wereld* (2007),[14] the issue at stake concerned the legal basis for the EAW FD and its compliance with the principles of legality in criminal matters and equality and non-discrimination. The main question regarded the validity of the EAW FD with respect to the Belgian Law on the EAW, whether the choice of the legal instrument (a Framework Decision) was compatible with the Treaties, that would have required to regulate the matter with a convention, rather than with a framework decision. Moreover, the CJEU was asked whether the exclusion of the double criminality requirement for the list of 32 offences in Art 2(2) EAW FD determined (i) a violation of the principle of legality, given the rule that dispenses with the verification of the double criminality requirement in relation to the categories of offences (ii) an infringement of the principle of non-discrimination, since individuals could be treated differently depending on whether they were accused of having committed one of such offences or others excluded from the list. The Court concluded that these questions do not undermine the validity of the EAW FD, because this is not aimed at ensuring the harmonization of substantive criminal laws across Member States. Also, the exemption from the double check criminality for the 32 categories of crimes involved[15] does not violate the principle of legality of criminal offences and the principle of equality and of non-discrimination, as the distinction between the offences included in the list and those excluded is founded on the criterion of the seriousness of the offenses.

---

14 Case C-303/05 *Advocaten voor de Wereld VZW v Leden van de Ministerraad* [2007] ECR I-3633.

15 The list of the offences eligible to surrender pursuant to Art 2(2) of the EAW Framework Decision are the following: participation in a criminal organization, terrorism, trafficking in human beings, sexual exploitation of children and child pornography, illicit trafficking in narcotic drugs and psychotropic substances, illicit trafficking in weapons, munitions and explosives, corruption, fraud, including that affecting the financial interests of the European Communities within the meaning of the Convention of 26 July 1995 on the protection of the European Communities' financial interests, laundering of the proceeds of crime, counterfeiting currency, including of the euro, computer-related crime, environmental crime, including illicit trafficking in endangered animal species and in endangered plant species and varieties, facilitation of unauthorized entry and residence, murder, grievous bodily injury, illicit trade in human organs and tissue, kidnapping, illegal restraint and hostage-taking, racism and xenophobia, organized or armed robbery, illicit trafficking in cultural goods, including antiques and works of art, swindling, racketeering and extortion, counterfeiting and piracy of products, forgery of administrative documents and trafficking therein, forgery of means of payment, illicit trafficking in hormonal substances and other growth promoters, illicit trafficking in nuclear or radioactive materials, trafficking in stolen vehicles, rape, arson, crimes within the jurisdiction of the International Criminal Court, unlawful seizure of aircraft/ships, sabotage.

On the other hand, in *Spetsializirana prokuratura* (2021),[16] the challenge was focused on the right of information of the accused persons, based on the main question of whether the safeguards provided by Directive 2012/13 apply to a person who has been arrested based on an EAW. Persons who are arrested for the purposes of the execution of an EAW are in fact to be provided promptly with an appropriate Letter of Rights containing information on their rights according to the law implementing the EAW FD in the executing Member State. In this respect, they are already granted a specific safeguard with the Letter of Rights that reconciles individual safeguards with the need of an expedite procedure such as the EAW. The Court then answered that the additional rights provided by Directive 2012/13 (besides the Letter of Rights) exclusively apply after the moment of surrender because only after this moment the arrested person assumes the status of accused person. Similarly, in another case related to Bulgaria, the *IR* case (2021),[17] the CJEU has been called upon to pronounce on a preliminary ruling regarding the applicability of the information rights provided by the Directive 2012/13 – e.g. the right to be provided with a written Letter of rights upon arrest that informs about the possibility of challenging the lawfulness of the arrest, obtaining a review of the detention, and making a request for provisional release – to an absconding suspect of a tax crime (trafficking cigarettes), against whom an EAW had been issued. Once again, the Court denied the application of these rights in the context of EAW proceedings. By excluding the application of additional information rights in these cases, the CJEU considered the EAW valid and rightly issued and dismissed the preliminary questions.

### 3.2 *Obligation of the Executing Judicial Authorities*

Another interesting topic is of the admissibility of a request for preliminary ruling by an issuing judicial authority concerning obligations of the executing judicial authority in the context of EAW proceedings. This issue has been handled in different cases by the CJEU, which held that an issuing judicial authority can request a preliminary ruling concerning obligations of the executing judicial authority (for example, *AY Mandat d'arrêt Témoin*, 2018).[18] In this case, the admissibility of the request for preliminary ruling by the issuing authority was justified by the Court based on the fact that the assessment of the requirements for issuing an EAW lies with a national court. It does not depend on the obligations of the executing authority because, in any event, the responsibility

16 Case C-649/19 *IR Spetsializirana prokuratura* ECLI:EU:C:2021:75.

17 *Ibid.*

18 Case C-268/17 *AY* [2018] ECLI:EU:C: 2018: 602.

for fundamental rights' protection primarily falls under the responsibility of the issuing authority. Under this capacity, this authority retains the possibility to refer questions for preliminary rulings. The CJEU dealt with such a topic in the case of an EAW that had already been annulled to maintain, withdraw or adopt a new EAW (*Spetsializirana prokuratura*; *Puig Gordi and Others*),[19] or when a question on the compatibility of the EAW with Art 50 CFR had been arisen (*AB and Others Révocation d'une amnistie*).[20]

### 3.3 *Competence of the Issuing Authorities*

In another group of cases the CJEU set up the remit of the issuing authorities' competencies in relation to EU law. In the case *Özçelik* (2016), the CJEU clarified that the confirmation by public prosecutor's office of a national arrest warrant issued by a national police department is considered a judicial decision within the meaning of Art 8(1) EAW FD.[21] In another case, *Bob-Dogi* (2016), the term 'arrest warrant' has been clarified as referring to a national arrest warrant that is distinct from the EAW. If the executing judicial authority concludes that the EAW is not valid because it was issued in the absence of any national warrant separate from the EAW, the executing judicial authority must refuse to give effect to it.[22]

On the same topic, in the *MM* case (2021), the CJEU held that in the lack of a "[national] arrest warrant or any other enforceable judicial decision having the same effect", it is up to the referring court to decide, in conformity with its national law, what are the consequences that the absence of a national arrest warrant as legal basis for the issuing of an EAW may have on the decision to keep a person who is subject to criminal prosecution in provisional detention.[23]

However, in the *Spetsializirana prokuratura* case (*Informations sur la décision nationale d'arrestation*),[24] the CJEU further clarified that the issuing authority is not obliged to forward to the person who is the subject of the EAW, upon arrest, the national judicial decision and information on the possibilities

19 See Thomas Wahl, 'CJEU Upholds Restrictive Fundamental Rights Jurisprudence on the EAW in Catalan Surrender Cases' (2023) 1 Eucrim; Case C-105/21 *Spetsializirana prokuratura* (*Informations sur la décision nationale d'arrestation*) [2022] ECLI:EU:C:2022:511.

20 Case C-203/20 *AB and Others* (*Révocation d'une amnistie*) [2021] ECLI:EU:C:2021:993.

21 Case C-453/16 *Openbaar Ministerie v Halil Ibrahim Özçelik* [2016] ECLI:EU:C:2016:860.

22 Case C-241/15 *Niculaie Aurel Bob-Dogi* [2016] ECLI:EU:C:2016:385.

23 Case C-414/20 PPU *MM* [2021] ECLI:EU:C:2021:4.

24 Case C-105/21 *Spetsializirana prokuratura* (*Informations sur la décision nationale d'arrestation*), [2022] ECLI:EU:C:2022:503; Case C-158/21 *Puig Gordi and Others* [2023] ECLI:EU:C:2023:56.

of challenging that decision, because this might hinder the executing judicial authority's implementation of the simplified system of surrender. This would entail a third level of protection that is in any event not required. As soon as the person is surrendered, she has the right to receive all the information regarding the EAW as well as the information on the remedies in the issuing Member State and is given access to the materials of the case.

Concerning the discretional powers of the executing authorities, instead, it is worth noting that in the case *Openbaar Ministerie* (*Décision de remise différée en raison de poursuites pénales*, 2022),[25] it was pointed out that it is instead exclusive competence of the executing judicial authority the decision to postpone the surrender. If the postponement has not been decided by the executing judicial authority, the competent authority of the executing Member State must release the requested person.

Moreover, the CJEU ruled that executing authorities cannot refuse to execute an EAW on the sole basis that another State has already refused to execute a previous EAW issued against the same person and for the same acts. Executing authorities are obliged to examine the request and take a decision in any event, except for cases of non-execution provided for by the framework decision.[26]

### 3.4 *Judicial Independence of the Issuing Authorities*

On a different level, the concept of judicial independence as a specific requirement of the issuing authority gained traction in the last decade due to the rule of law crisis.[27] In particular, in the *LM* case (2018) the CJEU linked this concept to the correspondence between fundamental rights and rule of law standards: "it must be pointed out that the requirement of judicial independence forms part of the essence of the fundamental right to a fair trial, a right which is of cardinal importance as a guarantee that all the rights which individuals derive from EU law will be protected and that the values common to the Member States set out in Article 2 TEU, in particular the value of the rule of law, will be safeguarded" (*LM* case, para 48). This means that the lack of judicial independence might symptomize substantial deficiencies of rule of law and legitimize the refusal of the execution only in exceptional circumstances where, after carrying out a specific and precise assessment of the particular case, the executing

25 C-492/22 PPU, *CJ* (*Décision de remise différée en raison de poursuites pénales*) [2022] ECLI:EU:C:2022:964.

26 Case C-268/17 *AY* (*Mandat d'arrêt – Témoin*) [2018] ECLI:EU:C:2018:593.

27 Leandro Mancano, 'European Arrest Warrant and Independence of the Judiciary. Evolution or revolution?' (2019) Diritticomparati.

authority finds that there are substantial grounds for believing that the related person after her surrender runs a real risk of breach of her fundamental right to an independent tribunal and, therefore, of the essence of his fundamental right to a fair trial (*LM* case, para 73).[28]

However, the Court mitigated the concept of judicial independence of the issuing authority as a requirement to issue an EAW in the Joined Cases C-354/20 PPU and C-412/20 PPU, *Openbaar Ministerie* (*Indépendance de l'autorité judiciaire d'émission*, 2020),[29] stating that denying the status of 'issuing judicial authority' to all judges or courts of a Member State where there is a suspicion of generalized lack of independence, would extend disproportionately the limitations that may be placed on the principles of mutual recognition and mutual trust. It would also mean that courts of that Member State could no longer submit references to the CJEU for preliminary rulings. This implies that the systematic or generalised deficiencies concerning the independence of the judiciary in the issuing Member State should be verified case by case.

### 3.5 *Effective Judicial Protection and the Remit of Judicial Decisions*

The validity of the EAW was instead addressed in a few cases highlighting the requirement of the effective judicial protection. For instance, the Cases *Svishtov Regional Prosecutor's Office* and *Prosecutor of the regional prosecutor's office in Ruse, Bulgaria* (2021)[30] clarified the meaning of an 'arrest warrant or any other enforceable judicial decision having the same effect' pursuant to Art 8 EAWFD. Read in accordance with Art 47 ECFR, the Court stated that the requirements inherent in the effective judicial protection that must be afforded to a person who is the subject of an EAW for the purpose of criminal prosecution are not satisfied where both the EAW and the judicial decision on which that warrant is based are issued by a public prosecutor[31] – who may be classified as an

28 Case C-216/18 PPU, *LM* [2018] ECLI:EU:C:2018:589.

29 Joined Cases C-354/20 PPU and C-412/20 PPU *Openbaar Ministerie* [2020] ECLI:EU:C:2020:1033.

30 Case C-648/20 *PPU Svishtov Regional Prosecutor's Office* [2021] ECLI:EU:C:2021:187; Case C-206/20 *VA Prosecutor of the Regional Prosecutor's Office in Ruse* [2021] ECLI:EU:C:2021:509.

31 The content of the EAW is strictly provided by Article 8, which shall include: (a) the identity and nationality of the requested person; (b) the name, address, telephone and fax numbers and e-mail address of the issuing judicial authority; (c) evidence of an enforceable judgment, an arrest warrant or any other enforceable judicial decision having the same effect, coming within the scope of Articles 1 and 2; (d) the nature and legal classification of the offence, particularly in respect of Article 2; (e) a description of the circumstances in which the offence was committed, including the time, place and degree of participation in the offence by the requested person; (f) the penalty imposed, if there is

'issuing judicial authority' within the meaning of Art 6(1) EAW FD – but whose decision cannot be reviewed by a court in the issuing Member State prior to the surrender of the requested person. The emerging legal principle is that an effective judicial protection presupposes that the judicial review of either the EAW or the judicial decision on which it is based is possible before that warrant is executed. Consequently, the judicial review of a prosecutor's decision to issue an EAW, which takes place only after the requested person is surrendered, does not satisfy the obligation of the issuing Member State to implement procedural rules allowing a court to review, prior to that surrender, the lawfulness of the national arrest warrant, also adopted by a prosecutor, or of the EAW.

The CJEU deal with this issue also in the case *Minister for Justice and Equality (Mandat d'arrêt – Condamnation dans un État tiers, membre de l'EEE* (2021)),[32] where it was asked whether the EAW may be issued on the basis of a judicial decision of the issuing Member State ordering the execution, in that Member State, of a sentence imposed by a court of a third State pursuant to a bilateral agreement between those States. The CJEU stated that in such circumstances an EAW may be issued when the judgment in question has been recognised by a decision of a court of the issuing Member State. However, the issuing of the EAW is subject to the condition, first, that a custodial sentence of at least four months has been imposed on the requested person and, second, that the procedure leading to the adoption in the third State of the judgment recognised subsequently in the issuing Member State has complied with fundamental rights and, in particular, the obligations arising under Arts 47 and 48 CFREU.

In relation to the meaning of 'judicial decision', in another group of cases the CJEU clarified the concept of judicial authority pursuant to Art 6 EAW FD. In the case PPU, *Poltorak* (2016),[33] the CJEU stated that the police (even executing a custodial sentence) and Ministries of Justice cannot considered issuing judicial authorities under EU law because police services fall within the province of the executive, while Ministries of Justice are not eligible for being considered judicial authorities because of lack of independence.[34] Surrender

a final judgment, or the prescribed scale of penalties for the offence under the law of the issuing Member State; (g) if possible, other consequences of the offence.

32 Case C-488/19 *JR Minister for Justice and Equality* (*Mandat d'arrêt – Condamnation dans un État tiers, membre de l'EEE*) [2021] ECLI:EU:C:2021:206.

33 Case C-452/16 PPU, *Poltorak* [2016] ECLI:EU:C:2016:858.

34 Petra Bárd,Sergio Carrera and Marco Stefan, *The Judicialisation of the European Arrest Warrant: Rule of Law and Fundamental Rights as Preconditions for Merited Mutual Trust* (2023) https://cdn.ceps.eu/wp-content/uploads/2023/08/Judicialisation-of-the-European-Arrest-Warrant-STREAM-Report.pdf (accessed: 19/04/2025).

should take place through *direct cross-border judicial cooperation* and be issued and executed exclusively by authorities identified as 'judicial'.

Two years after, the CJEU held that the concept of 'judicial decision' does not exclusively encompass decisions of judges or courts of a Member State, but must include, more broadly, the decisions adopted by the authorities participating in the administration of criminal justice in that Member State if, according to the law of the issuing Member State, the conditions for issuing such a EAW – and in particular its proportionality[35] – are subject to judicial review, as stated in Case *C-625/19 PPU, Openbaar Ministerie*.[36]

In the Joined Cases *OG and PPU* (2019),[37] the Court has been called to clarify whether public prosecutors' offices of a Member State that are subordinate to a body of the executive and may thus be subject – directly or indirectly – to directions or instructions from that body on the adoption of a decision to issue an EAW, fall within the concept of 'issuing judicial authority'. The Court hold that Art 6(1) EAW FD does not include prosecutors in such cases.

In the case *Puig Gordi and Others* (2023), the Court also clarified that it is the competence of issuing authorities to issue several successive EAWs against a person, if the decision meets two requirements: the change of circumstances and the proportionality – taking into account the nature and gravity of the offence for which the requested person is being prosecuted, and the consequences for that person of the EAWs previously issued against him or her, or the prospects of execution of any new EAW.[38] This case also ruled out the possibility for the executing authority to autonomously assess whether the issuing authority is a judicial authority and refuse to execute the EAW when it retains that the relevant conditions are not met. By virtue of the principle of

35 The issuing judicial authorities should carry out a 'proportionality check' before deciding whether to issue an EAW. Even where the circumstances of the case fall within the scope of Art 2(1) of the Framework Decision on EAW, the issuing judicial authorities are advised to consider whether issuing an EAW is justified in that specific case. Considering the significant impact that the execution of an EAW has on the requested person's liberty and the restrictions of free movement, the issuing judicial authorities should consider all relevant factors in order to determine whether issuing an EAW is justified. In particular, the following factors should be considered: (a) the seriousness of the offence; (b) the likely penalty imposed if the person is found guilty of the alleged offence; (c) the likelihood of detention of the person in the issuing Member State after surrender; (d) the interests of the victims of the offence.

36 Case C-625/19 PPU, *Openbaar Ministerie (Swedish Public Prosecutor's Office)* [2019] ECLI:EU:C:2019:1078.

37 Joined Cases C-508/18 *OG* (*Parquet de Lübeck*) and C-82/19 PPU, *PI* (*Parquet de Zwickau*) [2019] ECLI:EU:C:2019:456.

38 Case C-158/21 *Puig Gordi and Others* [2023] ECLI:EU:C:2023:56.

procedural autonomy, in fact, it is for each Member State to designate competent judicial authorities to issue the EAW.

In addition, in another case *PPU, MN* (2020) the Court specified that when the EAW is issued for the purposes of executing a custodial sentence (rather than for criminal prosecution on the basis of a detention order, as in *Svishtov*) by an authority that, although participating to the administration of justice, is not a court, the existence of a separate judicial remedy against the decision to issue such an EAW is not necessary. In fact, the judicial review of proportionality, which is necessary to meet the requirements of effective judicial protection, is carried out by means of the enforceable judgment on which that arrest warrant is based. The Court clarified that a separate judicial remedy is not necessary also in the case where the judicial authority was a prosecutor managed and controlled by superiors and under the authority of the Ministry of Justice, provided that the conditions for issuing that warrant andthe proportionality thereof, are subject to judicial review in that Member State.[39]

In the *Parquet de Vienne* (2019)[40] case, another important principle has been set up. In order to ensure that public prosecutors' offices issuing a warrant do not undergo any influence, EAWs must be subject to endorsement by a court that reviews them independently and objectively. Having access to the entire criminal file, to which any specific directions or instructions from the executive authority are added, the court may assess the conditions to issue the EAW, including proportionality, and adopt an autonomous decision that gives them their final form.

In another case, *Parquet général du Grand-Duché de Luxembourg and de Tours* (2019),[41] the CJEU stressed that the public prosecutors of a Member State, who act under the direction and supervision of their hierarchical superiors, are covered by the term 'issuing judicial authority' provided that statutory rules and the institutional framework exclude any influence by the executive power in issuing the EAW. However, the requirement of effective judicial protection is not a condition for classification of the authority as an issuing judicial authority (para 48).[42] In fact, the EAW system entails a dual level of protection of fundamental rights and procedural rights: the national level of protection related to the national arrest warrant and the European level of protection

39 Case C-813/19 PPU, *MN* [2020] ECLI:EU:C:2020:18 (Order).

40 Case C-489/19 PPU, *NJ* (*Parquet de Vienne*) [2019] ECLI:EU:C:2019:849.

41 Joined Cases C-566/19 PPU and C-626/19 PPU, *Parquet général du Grand-Duché de Luxembourg and de Tours* [2019] ECLI:EU:C:2019:1077.

42 The same conclusion has been reached also in Case C-414/20 PPU, *MM* [2021] ECLI:EU:C:2021:4, para 44.

related to the EAW. Regarding the first level of protection, this means that a decision meeting the requirements inherent in the effective judicial protection should be adopted, at least, meeting one of the two levels of that protection, the fundamental rights' protection or the procedural rights' level. The second level of protection of the rights of the person concerned means that the judicial authority competent to issue an EAW must review whether the conditions necessary for the issuing of the EAW have been observed and whether the issuing of the EAW was proportionate.[43] Effective judicial protection is ensured if, according to the law of the issuing Member State, the conditions for issuing such a warrant, and in particular its proportionality, are subject to judicial review in that Member State.

In the *MM* case,[44] mentioned above, the CJEU took a further step stating that the jurisdiction of a court that is called upon to decide on the lawfulness of the provisional detention of a person surrendered in execution of a EAW extends to the review of the lawfulness of a EAW issued by public prosecutor, in the absence of any remedy under national law.

### 3.6 *Fundamental Rights Protection as a Ground for Non-recognition and Non-execution*

After the overview on the main CJEU case law concerning the remit of effective judicial protection and rule of law standards – such as the independence of the issuing authority – as the key of fundamental rights' protection, it is time to move more precisely to the topic that is most relevant for our research question, that is the human rights protection as ground for refusal.

Over the years, as renown, the CJEU engaged in the elaboration of a two-step assessment that the executing judicial authority is obliged to undertake before deciding on the execution of the EAW, as exemplified in the leading case *Aranyosi and Caldararu* that sets a general rule: "where the judicial authority of the executing Member State is in possession of information showing there to be a real risk of inhuman or degrading treatment of individuals detained in the issuing Member State, in the light of the standard of protection of fundamental rights guaranteed by EU law and, in particular, by Article 4 of the CFREU, that judicial authority is bound to assess the existence of that risk when it is called upon to decide on the surrender to the authorities of the issuing Member State of the individual concerned by a European arrest warrant. The consequence of the execution of such a warrant must not be that that individual suffers

43 Similar conclusions have been reached in Case C-813/19 PPU, *MN* [2020] ECLI:EU:C:2020:31 (Order).

44 See ft n 8.

inhuman or degrading treatment".[45] More precisely, the first-step assessment revolves around the presence of factors demonstrating generalized and systemic deficiencies regarding prison conditions or tribunals established by law, based on reliable reports and materials showing that there is a real risk of breach of fundamental rights. The second-step assessment consists in the evaluation of impact of the deficiencies considered under the first-step assessment, whether they can determine a real risk of inhuman treatment for detention's conditions (e.g. sanitary conditions and free movement in prison).

Regarding the second step, it should be distinguished between EAWs issued for prosecution and EAWs issued for custodial sentence. In the first case, the assessment relies on the information provided by the requested person about the personal situation, the nature of the offense and the factual context or any other circumstance related to the independence of judges called to hear the case. In the second case, the executing authority must consider the information provided by the requested person about the composition of the panel of judges who heard her criminal case.

The refusal based on fundamental rights grounds can then be issued only in exceptional circumstances.[46] Hereinafter some of the pivotal principles enshrined in the case law of the CJEU will be presented that highlight the most relevant grounds for refusal based on fundamental rights' protection.

---

45 Joined Cases C-404/15 and C-659/15 PPU, *Aranyosi and Căldăraru* [2016] ECLI:EU:C:2016:198.

46 The mandatory grounds for non-execution are expressly provided by Art 3: 1) if the offence is based is covered by amnesty in the executing Member State; 2) if the executing judicial authority is informed that the requested person has been finally judged by a Member State in respect of the same acts; 3) if the person who is the subject of the European arrest warrant may not, owing to his age, be held criminally responsible for the acts under the law of the executing state. The optional grounds for non-execution (Art 4), instead, include the following cases: 1) the act is not an offence in the executing state; 2) the person is being prosecuted in the executing Member State for the same act; the judicial authorities of the executing Member State have decided either not to prosecute for the offence or where there has been a final judgement not to prosecute; 3) the criminal prosecution or punishment of the requested person is statute-barred according to the law of the executing Member State; 4) the executing judicial authority is informed that the requested person has been finally judged by a third State in respect of the same acts provided; 5) the European arrest warrant has been issued for the purposes of execution of a custodial sentence or detention order, where the requested person is staying in, or is a national or a resident of the executing Member State and that State undertakes to execute the sentence or detention order in accordance with its domestic law; 6) the EAW relates to offences occurred in the executing State or outside the jurisdiction of the issuing state.

In the *Radu* case (2013),[47] the main question was whether the EAW FD, read in the light of Arts 47 and 48 CFR, must be interpreted as meaning that the executing authority can refuse to execute an EAW for the purpose of prosecution on the ground that the issuing judicial authority did not hear the requested person before the EAW was issued. The Court replied that is it is not sufficient for the refusal of the executing authority that the requested person was not heard in the issuing Member State before that arrest warrant was adopted, otherwise the effectiveness of the EAW system could be compromised.

In the case *Melloni* (2013),[48] the CJEU ruled out that a surrender of a person convicted *in absentia* was unlawful because Art 4(a)(1) as amended in 2009 precludes the executing judicial authorities from making the execution of a EAW issued for the purposes of executing a sentence conditional upon the conviction rendered *in absentia* being open to review in the issuing Member State.[49] For the same reasons, also Art 53 CFR must be interpreted as precluding a Member State to make a surrender of a person convicted *in absentia* conditional upon the conviction being open to review in the issuing Member State, in order to avoid an adverse effect on the right to a fair trial and the rights of the defence guaranteed by its constitution. Allowing a Member State to avail itself of Art 53 of the CFREU to make the surrender of a person convicted *in absentia* conditional upon the trial being open to review in the issuing Member State, by casting doubts on the uniformity of the standard of fundamental rights' protection in the EU, would undermine the principles of mutual trust and recognition which the EAW FD decision purports, compromising its efficacy. The CJEU motivated this decision on the ground that assessing the lawfulness of the surrender based on the presence of a requirement in the national law that is missing in the EAW FD casts doubts on the legitimacy of this instrument as well as on the meaning of mutual trust. In practice, this implies that the right to be present at trial, being a potential specific safeguard required by national

47 Case C-396/11 *Radu* [2013] ECLI:EU:C:2013:40.

48 Case C-399/11 *Melloni* [2013] ECLI:EU:C:2013:107.

49 However, the executing state may require specific guarantees (Art 5), such as: 1) for *in absentia* decisions: the issuing judicial authority must ensure that the person subject to EAW can apply for a retrial of the case in the issuing Member State and to be present at the judgment; 2) for offences punishable by custodial life sentence or life-time detention order: the issuing Member State must ensure in its legal system the conditions for a review of the penalty or measure imposed or a measure of clemency; 3) where a national or resident of the executing Member State, surrender may be subject to the condition that the person, after being heard, is returned to the executing Member State in order to serve there the custodial sentence or detention order passed against him in the issuing Member State.

law or legitimizing at national level the possibility of judicial review for surrenders of convicted persons *in absentia*, cannot be waived with the principle of mutual trust as well as with the consensus reached by Member States on the procedural rights in criminal matters.

In *Aranyosi and Căldăraru* case (2016),[50] abovementioned, the executing authority believed that the detention conditions to which both men might be subject in the prisons of the issuing authority, respectively, were contrary to fundamental rights' protection. Therefore, it referred to the CJEU a request for preliminary ruling asking whether a refusal can be motivated by serious indications that the detention conditions are not compatible with fundamental rights. The CJEU replied that the executing authority must determine specifically the real risk by requesting supplementary information from the issuing authority. The general principles are mutual recognition and mutual trust, according to which an EAW should be executed unconditionally, unless one of the grounds for non–recognition (Arts 3, 4 and 4a EAW FD) or one of the guarantees (Art 5 EAW FD) is identified or raised. However, "where the judicial authority of the executing Member State is in possession of information showing there to be a real risk of inhuman or degrading treatment of individuals detained in the issuing Member State, in the light of the standard of protection of fundamental rights guaranteed by EU law and, in particular, by Article 4 of the CFREU, that judicial authority is bound to assess the existence of that risk when it is called upon to decide on the surrender to the authorities of the issuing Member State of the individual concerned by a EAW. The consequence of the execution of such a warrant must not be that that individual suffers inhuman or degrading treatment" (para 88).

The specific consideration of the real risk implies the double step assessment mentioned above. The first is the assessment of a general risk based on precise information. This information may be obtained, for example, from judgments of international courts, such as the ECtHR, judgments of courts of the issuing Member State as well as decisions, reports and other documents produced by bodies of the Council of Europe or under the aegis of the United Nations. The deficiencies may be systemic or generalized or may affect certain groups of people or certain places of detention. Once the general risk has been verified, the executing authority must determine whether, in the circumstances of the case, there are substantial grounds to believe that the requested person, if surrendered, will run a real risk of being subject to inhuman or degrading treatment.

50 See supra at 48.

In particular, the Court has recently fine-tuned the remit of the concept of real risk. In the case *ML*,[51] the CJEU has excluded that an executing judicial authority may rule out the existence of a 'real risk' merely because the requested person has, in the issuing Member State, a legal remedy to challenge the detention conditions. The executing judicial authority must solely assess the actual and precise detention conditions that are relevant for determining whether that person will be exposed to a 'real risk' of inhuman or degrading treatment.

In the famous case *LM* (2018),[52] besides the two-steps assessment, the CJEU further redefined the scope of the notion of real risk. Mr. LM objected to his surrender from Ireland to Poland based on his suspicion of being exposed to a real risk of a flagrant denial of justice. The CJEU ruled that the two-step assessment is always required. The assessment of a systemic the suspension of the EAW mechanism in one Member State is always subject to a decision of the European Council. If the executing authority believes that there is a real risk of violation of the right to fair trial, it should assess *in concreto* having regard the personal situation, the context and the nature of the offence if such a risk is real.

The case *Dorobantu* (2019), deals with the extent of the judicial review of the decision to execute an EAW. In particular, the German Constitutional Court suspended the decision to surrender a Romanian citizen to lodge a preliminary ruling to the CJEU in relation to certain factors that could be considered relevant to the assessment of the detention conditions in the issuing Member State.[53] The CJEU replied that the executing authority should take into account not only obvious deficiencies but also minimum standards under Art 3 ECHR, such as for instance minimum personal space in a multi-occupancy cell (cf. *Muršić* v *Croatia*).[54]

In another case, *LP* (2020), the CJEU clarified that the executing judicial authority cannot presume that there are substantial grounds to believe that that person will run a real risk of breach of her fundamental right to a fair trial, without carrying out a specific and precise verification through the two-step examination set out in *Minister for Justice and Equality* (*Deficiencies in the system of justice*), mentioned above. The existence of systemic and generalized deficiencies does not necessarily affect every decision that the courts of that

51 Case C-220/18 PPU, *ML* (*Conditions of detention in Hungary*) [2018] ECLI:EU:C:2018:589.

52 Case C-216/18 PPU, *Minister for Justice and Equality* (*Deficiencies in the System of Justice*) [2018] ECLI:EU:C:2018:586.

53 Case C-128/18, *Dumitru-Tudor Dorobantu* [2019] ECLI:EU:C:2019:857.

54 App. 7334/13, Judgement 20 October 2016.

Member State may adopt in each case, nor the status of issuing judicial authorities for all judges or all courts of that Member State acting by their nature entirely independently from the executive.[55]

Most recently, in the *EDL* case (2023) the concept of systemic and generalized deficiencies in the issuing State has been deepened in relation to the situation of a serious threat to the health of the person concerned which would result from surrender due to chronic illnesses of a potentially indefinite duration. The referring court, the Italian Constitutional Court, wondered whether the concept of generalized and systemic deficiencies as a ground for refusal can be extended to the above-mentioned case. The CJEU concluded for the possibility of non-execution only after the assessment of a real risk and a temporary delay of the surrender aimed at asking the executing authority information about the compatibility between the detention conditions and the personal situation of the convicted person.[56]

The analysis of the case law shows that the EAW FD should be interpreted in light of compliance with fundamental rights' standards that legitimize the issuing and the execution of EAW. In fact, the validity of the EAW can be considered with respect of its compliance with the CFR but also in light of its contents and the competencies of the issuing and executing authorities. In this case, fundamental rights' protection acts as a limit to judicial cooperation not only internally within the EAW system but also externally against its misuse.

## 4 European Investigation Order

The EIO D (Directive 2014/41/EU)[57] sets up a new comprehensive system that simplifies and speeds up cross-border criminal investigations in the EU, enabling judicial authorities in one EU country ('the issuing State') to request that evidence be gathered in and transferred from another EU country ('the executing State'). It was adopted on 3 April 2014.

As well known, the EIO has become the primary legal tool to collect trans-border evidence, substituting the traditional mutual legal assistance agreements.

This directive applies to all EU countries except Denmark and Ireland, which opted out. It replaces existing EU mutual legal assistance schemes,

55 Joined Cases C-354/20 PPU and C-412/20 PPU, *LP* [2020] ECLI:EU:C:2020:1033.
56 Case C-699/21 *EDL* [2023] ECLI:EU:C:2023:295.
57 Directive 2014/41/EU of the European Parliament and of the Council of 3 April 2014 regarding the European Investigation Order in criminal matters [2014] OJ L 130.

namely the 2000 EU Mutual Legal Assistance Convention and Framework Decision 2008/978/JHA on the European Evidence Warrant.

In this regard, the Eurojust report states: "The EIO Directive is generally seen as an improvement on the legal framework of mutual legal assistance (MLA). In many cases, the existence of standard forms (available in all languages), the increased role of judicial authorities (as issuing or validating authorities), the limited grounds for refusal and the time limits have proved successful and had a positive impact on judicial cooperation. Yet, to be fully successful, it is crucial that the templates be duly filled in, the grounds for non-recognition be applied correctly and time limits be fully respected. This has not always been the case. In fact, time limits (Art 12 EIO DIR) – at the time seen as one of the major improvements compared with the MLA regime – are not always met. Often those countries that had long execution terms under the MLA regime still have long execution terms despite the new EIO regime".[58]

The EIO must be issued or validated by the judicial authority of the issuing state to ask the executing State to carry out specific investigative measures to obtain evidence or to obtain evidence that are already in the possession of the competent authorities of the executing State. It covers all phases of criminal proceeding except for setting up a joint investigation team. An 'issuing authority' could be a judge, a court, an investigating judge, a public prosecutor competent in the case concerned, or any other competent authority as defined by the respective issuing State, which, in a specific case, is acting in its capacity as an investigating authority in criminal proceedings with competence to order the gathering of evidence in accordance with national law. The issuing of an EIO may also be requested by a suspected or accused persons within the framework of applicable defence rights in conformity with the respective national criminal procedures. The recognition or execution of EIO may be refused in the executing State in limited cases, such as essential national security interests or respect for fundamental rights.[59] As well as the EAW, the EIO also foresees a bilateral setting between the issuing authority and the executing authority, where Eurojust can play a bridge-building role. As the EIO is based on the mutual recognition principle, each EU country is obliged in principle to recognise and carry out such a request. The EIO improves on previous

58 Eurojust, *Case-law by the Court of Justice of the European Union on the European Arrest Warrant* (European Union Agency for Crimnal Justice Cooperation, October 2023) 51 <https://www.eurojust.europa.eu/sites/default/files/assets/eurojust-eaw-cjeu-case-law-report-10-2023.pdf> (accessed: 19/04/2025)

59 Alexandra Tsvetkova, 'EU Legislation on EIO and Its Implementation in the Member States', in Maria Angela Biasiotti and Fabrizio Turchi (eds.) *European Investigation Order. Where the Law Meets the Technology* (Springer 2023).

EU laws covering this field by setting strict deadlines for gathering the evidence requested and by limiting the grounds for refusing such requests. It also reduces paperwork by introducing a single standard form for authorities to ask for help when seeking evidence.

The key aspects of the EIO are related to the fact that: a judicial decision can be issued or validated by a EU country's judicial authority to carry out one or several investigative measures in another EU country in order to obtain evidence in line with this directive; it can also be issued to get evidence that is already held by the responsible authorities of the executing country; it can be requested by a suspected or accused person, or by their lawyer, in line with the applicable defence rights in a EU country; it must not unlawfully affect human rights or legal principles, e.g. the right of defence in criminal cases; it covers any investigative measure, apart from setting up a joint investigative team; it can be issued for prosecuting offences considered criminal or acts/infringements of law that are punishable under an issuing state's national law. After receiving a EIO, the executing state must quickly act on the request within 90 days. It can only refuse to do so under certain circumstances, e.g. if the request is against the country's fundamental principles of law or harms national security interests.

In the field of legal remedies, we can also test this instrument considering fundamental rights' protection.[60] However, differently from the analysis of the case law on EAW – where we saw how the legal framework can be expanded throughout fundamental rights'-oriented interpretation – the case law on EIO shows how sensitive is the issue of margin of appreciation in criminal matters. For this, the individual safeguards related to judicial protection offered by EU law represent the shutoff valve of a complex architecture that aims at reconciling effective evidence gathering and fight against crime with access to legal remedies.

### 4.1 *Effective Judicial Protection*

The first cases dealing with this issue are *Gavanazov I and Gavanazov II*[61] and they involve the issuing of a EIO in the context of a large-scale VAT fraud. Based on a EIO the Bulgarian authorities requested searches and seizures as well as a

60 Anne Weyenberg, 'About the Gavanazov II and HP judgments of the CJEU on the European Investigation Order Directive: strengthening the judicial protection in the issuing Member State' EJ20 Anniversary essays <https://www.eurojust.europa.eu/20-years-of-eurojust/gavanazov-ii-and-hp-judgments-cjeu-european-investigation-order> (accessed: 19/04/2025).

61 Case C 324/17 *Gavazanov I* [2019] ECLI:EU:C:2019:876 and Case C-852/19 *Gavazanov II* [2021] ECLI:EU:C:2021:894.

witness hearing by videoconference in the Czech Republic. Since the Bulgarian law does not provide any legal remedy against the issuance of a EIO dealing with these measures, the Specialized Court referred a request for preliminary ruling asking whether national laws must provide for the possibility of an appeal against the issuance of an EIO.

Pursuant to Art 14 EIO D, in fact, Member States shall ensure equivalent remedies to those available in a similar domestic case. In particular, in the first case on the interpretation of the EIO (*Gavanazov I*, 2019),[62] the Court reformulated the questions of the Bulgarian Court and solved them procedurally by looking at the annex to be filled in: in this form, the issuing authority shall not include the list of legal remedies available at national level but only indicate whether a legal remedy has been provided. After CJEU's reply, the referring Court presented a second referral asking whether a national law that does not provide a legal remedy is compatible with the EIO D and with Art 47 CFR and whether a EIO is legitimately issued under these circumstances. The CJEU, in *Gavanazov II*,[63] answered to the first question highlighting the lack of harmonization in the evidentiary field in different Member States and holding that Art 14 EIO D does not require Member States to provide additional legal remedies to those existing in similar domestic cases but only equivalent ones. Since Bulgarian law does not provide remedies for national measures either, Art 14 is not violated. However, implementing EU law also means being compliant with the right to an effective remedy enshrined in Art 47 CFR. The second question instead gives the CJEU the possibility to reply in the sense that a EIO issued in such circumstances is not legitimate as it does not provide any remedy against the search and seizure as well as to the organization of the witness hearing by videoconference. The reasoning is interesting as it is based on the concept of mutual trust, which includes the presumption that Member States comply with European Law. The lack of legal remedies is considered problematic by the CJEU, this should impede the issuing of an EIO, due to a violation of Art 47 CFREU. Although the Court does not explicitly qualify it as a ground for refusal, in practice this effect may arguably derive from the *Gavanazov II* decision. In any case, in the words of the Directive this represents an optional ground for refusal and not an automatic one. The extent of judicial control on the issuance of an order under certain conditions also encompasses the control of individual rights' protection. We are visibly far from the recognition of procedural rights, as in the case of EAW, however on a compatible trend with basic

62 *Gavazanov I* (n 64).

63 Gavazanov *II*, (n 64).

requirements of effective judicial protection that links the concept of mutual trust to the trust in the judiciary.[64]

### 4.2 *Competence of the Issuing Authorities*

In another case, the *HP* case (2021),[65] the CJEU had the chance to answer two important questions. The first was related to the possibility for a public prosecutor to issue a EIO asking for the collection of traffic and location data whereas at national level the adoption of such an investigative measure usually is competence of the judge. The CJEU provided a logical answer, by reading Art 6(1)(b) in the sense that the issuing authority, i.e. the authority competent to issue an EIO, is the same authority having the power to adopt the investigative measure under national law. The second question was related to the possibility for the executing authority to replace the act required by the judicial authority of the issuing State. In this respect, the Court responded negatively in the sense that national law cannot allow a public prosecutor to issue an EIO, where instead the judge has exclusive competence to adopt an investigative measure seeking to obtain the data. In this case, the executing authority would be obliged to return the EIO to the issuing State where it receives an EIO which has not been issued by a competent issuing authority and should not attempt to remedy the non-compliance. This was the case, for example, in the opinion of the AG, of "an EIO seeking to obtain traffic and location data associated with telecommunications [which] cannot be issued by a public prosecutor where that public prosecutor not only directs the criminal pre-trial procedure, but also brings the public prosecution in subsequent criminal proceedings" (para 43).

On the other side, in the very recent *Encrochat* case,[66] the CJEU dealt with the concept of the legitimate issuing authority, recalling in a certain way the requirements sought in the caselaw on the EAW. The case concerned illegal drug trafficking involving the use of the encrypted telecommunications service EncroChat. A German public prosecutor issued a EIO to obtain from France the transmission of data obtained through the interception of EncroChat users in Germany, authorized by a French judge. The Court of Justice clarified that,

---

64 Andrew H. Weiss, 'Effective Protection of Rights as a Precondition to Mutual Recognition: Some Thoughts on the CJEU's Gavanozov II Decision' (2022) 13(2) New Journal of European Criminal Law 180; Jan Stajnko, Mário Simões Barata and István Szijártó, 'Comments re Gavanozov I and Gavanozov II' in Kai Ambos, Alexander Heinze, Peter Rackow and Miha Šepec (eds), *The European Investigation Order: Legal Analysis and Practical Dilemmas of International Cooperation* (Duncker & Humblot2022) 265.

65 Case C-724/19 *HP Spetsializirana prokuratura* [2021] ECLI:EU:C:2021:1020.

66 Case C-670/22 *M.N.* [2024] ECLI:EU:C:2024:372.

for the sake of the evidence preservation principle, a EIO for the transmission of evidence already in possession and gathered by the competent authorities of the executing State may, under certain conditions, be issued by a public prosecutor instead of a judge. However, it does not need to satisfy the conditions applicable to the gathering of evidence in the issuing State but only those applicable to the transmission of the evidence in the same State.[67] However, the Court concludes by stating that fundamental rights' protection always needs to be subject to judicial review. Moreover, an interception measure carried out by one Member State on the territory of another Member State must be notified in due time to that Member State. In addition, the Court also stated that national courts cannot utilize evidence that cannot be contested by the persons concerned.

In the examined cases fundamental rights' protection plays a granular role that aims at compensating the lack of some safeguard or some exceptions admitted by the Court – as for the case of the EIO issued by public prosecutors under certain circumstances.

## 5 Regulation (EU) 2018/1805 on the Mutual Recognition of Freezing Orders and Confiscation Order

Regulation (EU) 1805/2018 aims to facilitate the cross-border recovery of criminal assets and to lead to more efficient freezing and confiscation of funds of illicit origin in the EU. It sets out the rules under which an EU country recognizes and executes in its territory freezing and confiscation orders issued by another Member State in the context of proceedings in criminal matters. Like the EAW FD and the EIO D, Regulation 1805/2018 excludes the double criminality check in the execution of freezing and confiscation orders for a series of serious crimes (Art 3).[68] This instrument has to be differentiated from Directive 2014/42/EU[69] on the freezing and confiscation of instrumentalities (any property used or intended to be used, in any manner, wholly or in part, to commit a criminal offence, Art 2(1)) and proceeds (any economic advantage

67 On mutual admissibility of evidence see Lorena Bachmaier, 'Mutual Admissibility of Evidence and Electronic Evidence in the EU: A New Try for European Minimum Rules in Criminal Proceedings?' (2023) 2 Eucrim 223.

68 For crimes that are not listed in Art 3 Regulation 1805/2018 the lack of the double criminality requirement may constitute a ground for refusal.

69 Directive 2014/42/EU of the European Parliament and of the Council of 3 April 2014 on the freezing and confiscation of instrumentalities and proceeds of crime in the European Union [2014] OJ L 127.

derived directly or indirectly from a criminal offence; it may consist of any form of property and includes any subsequent reinvestment or transformation of direct proceeds and any valuable benefits, Art 2 (3)).[70] Both instruments have been recently complemented by Directive EU/2024/1260[71] (entered into force on 22 May 2024) on assets' recovery and confiscation, which applies to freezing and confiscation measures within the framework of criminal proceedings (Art 1(1)) as well as in proceedings in civil or administrative matters (Art.1(2)) While Regulation 1805/2018 applies to certain crimes that are not only serious crimes (Art 3) without the requirement of the double criminality check for the execution of freezing orders and confiscations, the Directive EU/2024/1260 generally applies to all proceedings in criminal matters regardless of civil or administrative instruments. It addresses instrumentalities, proceeds of crime and assets that could potentially be object of confiscation or freezing orders (Art 1).

The Regulation 1805/2018 has replaced the Framework Decisions 2003/577/JHA[72] on freezing property and evidence 2006/783/JHA on confiscation orders has the following key features: a) it covers issues linked to the implementation of existing legal instruments by establishing a single regulation – including both freezing and confiscation orders – that is directly applicable in the EU; b) it is inspired from the general principle of mutual recognition, entailing that there is only a limited number of reasons for non-recognition and non-execution; c) it provides for standard certificates and procedures to allow for quicker and more efficient freezing and confiscation actions; d) it sets a deadline of 45 days for the recognition of a confiscation order and, in urgent cases, a deadline of 48 hours for the recognition and 48 hours for the execution of freezing orders, with the possibility of postponement under strict conditions; e) it foresees provisions to ensure that victims' rights to compensation and restitution are respected in cross-border cases.

Art 2 of the Regulation defines freezing order as a "decision issued or validated by an issuing authority in order to prevent the destruction, transformation, removal, transfer or disposal of property with a view to the confiscation thereof" and a confiscation order as a "final penalty or measure, imposed by a

---

70 For a deep analysis see Sandra Oliveira e Silva, Serena Quattrocolo and Ernestina Sacchetto, *Assets Confiscation and Prevention of Crimes in Europe: An Overview upon the EU and Domestic Legislation* (Cedam 2022).

71 Directive EU/2024/1260 of the European Parliament and of the Council of 24 April 2024 on asset recovery and confiscation [2024] OJ L.

72 Council Framework Decision 2003/577/JHA of 22 July 2003 on the execution in the European Union of orders freezing property or evidence [2003] OJ L 196.

court following proceedings in relation to a criminal offence, resulting in the final deprivation of property of a natural or legal person".

What is important to notice is that, as it is provided in Rec. 13, the Regulation 1805/2018 has a very broad scope as it applies "to all freezing orders and to all confiscation orders issued within the framework of proceedings in criminal matters". The concept of proceedings in criminal matters covers all types of freezing orders and confiscation orders issued following proceedings in relation to a criminal offence, not only those addressed by Directive 2014/42/EU, as well as types of orders issued without a final conviction. The news is that even though such orders might not exist in the legal system of a Member State, the latter should be able to recognize and execute such an order issued by another Member State. Proceedings in criminal matters are not only limited to judicial proceedings but could also encompass criminal investigations by the police and other law enforcement authorities. On the contrary, freezing orders and confiscation orders that are issued within the framework of civil or administrative proceedings should be excluded from the scope of this Regulation 1805/2018 (Art 1(4)).

Within this picture, fundamental rights' protection comes to the front with respect to the victims' right to compensation or restitution of frozen property. Victims are prioritized to issuing and executing's State interests. Property rights can be claimed in the issuing state provided that (1) the victim's title to the property is not contested; (2) the property is not required as evidence in criminal proceedings in the executing State; and (3) the rights of affected persons are not prejudiced.

Among the grounds for non-recognition and non-execution, three different cases are particularly relevant for our purposes. The executing authority may decide not to recognise or execute a freezing order where: such recognition or execution would prevent as a privilege or immunity the executing State from applying its constitutional rules related to freedom of the press or freedom of expression in other media (Rec. 33 and Art 19 (b)); there are substantial grounds to believe, on the basis of specific and objective evidence, that the execution of the confiscation order would, in the particular circumstances of the case, entail a manifest breach of a relevant fundamental right as set out in the CFREU in particular the right to an effective remedy, the right to a fair trial or the right of defence (Art 19 (h)); the rights of affected persons can be compromised (Art 19 (e)). Affected persons have of course the right to be informed by the executing authority with the indication of the name of the competent authority as well as of the name of the legal remedies available (Art 32). Legal remedies can be exercised before the courts of the executing State against the decision of issuing a freezing or a confiscation order but cannot involve the substantive reasons leading to that decision (Art 33).

### 5.1 *Fundamental Rights Protection*

In this area, the selected case law of the CJEU sheds light on possible conflicts between freezing or confiscation and fundamental rights. However, the reference to fundamental rights' protection is again considered as a limit to the judicial cooperation because it is often raised as a ground for refusing the confiscation. Also in the Regulation 1805/2018, in fact, the suspect of a manifest infringement of a relevant fundamental right as set out in the EU Charter of Fundamental Rights (CFREU), such as the right to an effective remedy, the right to a fair trial and the right of defence - constitutes a ground for not recognizing or executing a freezing and confiscation order (Art 8). Interestingly, the lack of a precise reference to the rights included in the procedural rights Directives shows the difference in considering the transnational character of each judicial cooperation instrument as elaborated by EU law.[73]

It is also important to point out that the case law outlined below is related to the compatibility of Directive 2014/42/EU of the European Parliament and of the Council of 3 April 2014 on the freezing and confiscation of instrumentalities with the CFREU and does not refer to Regulation 1805/2018.

For instance, the *OM* case[74] concerned the interpretation of Art 17(1) of Directive 2014/42/EU and Art 47 CFR. The request for preliminary ruling was submitted in the context of criminal proceedings brought against OM concerning the confiscation, following his conviction for aggravated smuggling, of property used to commit that infringement which belongs to a third-party acting in good faith. The Court of Justice has been questioned regarding the compatibility of curtailing property rights of third parties on grounds of confiscation of property used to commit crimes and fundamental rights protection. The Court held that the good faith of third parties and the possibility of third parties to be granted legal remedies must prevail on the execution of the confiscation. In fact, Art 2(1) of Council Framework Decision 2005/212/JHA,[75] read in the light of Art 17(1) CFREU, must be interpreted as precluding a national law allowing

73 Nuno Brandão, 'The Right of Defence under Regulation (EU) 2018/1805 on the Mutual Recognition of Freezing Orders and Confiscation Orders' (2022) 13(1) New Journal of European Criminal Law 28.

74 Case C-393/19 *Okrazhna prokuratura* [2021] ECLI:EU:C:2021:8.

75 Council Framework Decision 2005/212/JHA of 24 February 2005 on Confiscation of Crime-Related Proceeds, Instrumentalities and Property [2005] OJ L 68.

the confiscation of an instrumentality used to commit an aggravated smuggling offence where that property belongs to a third party acting in good faith, whereas Art 4 of Framework Decision 2005/212/JHA, read in the light of Art 47 CFREU, must be interpreted as precluding a national law which permits the confiscation, in the context of criminal proceedings, of property belonging to a person other than the person who committed the criminal offence, without the former being afforded an effective remedy.

The aforementioned case expanded the rights of third parties with respect to the *Meroni* case,[76] where the applicant was not heard before the issuance of the order. The case referred to the freezing of a certain number of assets, as a precautionary measure aimed at preventing one of the parties depriving the other party of subsequent access to those assets. Accordingly, the order was also directed to third persons, including the applicant in the main proceedings, who hold rights over those assets. In that case, the Court of Justice held that the recognition and enforcement of an order issued by a court of a Member State, without a prior hearing of a third person whose rights may be affected by that order, cannot be regarded as manifestly contrary to public policy in the Member State in which enforcement is sought, or manifestly contrary to the right to a fair trial, in so far as that third person is entitled to assert her rights before that court.

In another more recent case, *DR and TS case* (2021) the Court assessed the incompatibility of a national law with the CFREU where third parties are not allowed to appear as a party in the confiscation proceedings and to be heard in those proceedings, when the property which is claimed to belong to a person other than the perpetrator of the criminal offence.[77] It also clarified that Directive 2014/42 on freezing of instrumentalities and proceeds also applies to proceeds of a criminal offence of which the person has been convicted that, directly or indirectly, gave rise to economic benefit.

Lastly, another case, *JP EOOD*,[78] is very interesting because it shows how broad is the remit of confiscation measures also in relation to administrative proceedings. The case regarded the possibility for customs authorities to issue confiscation measures under EU law (in particular pursuant to the Union Customs Code, Regulation (EU) 952/2013) as well as to apply the Framework Decision 2005/212/JHA of 24 February 2005 on Confiscation of Crime-Related Proceeds in the absence of a crime. The Court clarified that the

76 Case C-559/14 *Meroni* [2016] ECLI:EU:C:2016:349.

77 CJEU Joined Cases C-845/19 and C-863/19 *Okrazhna prokuratura* [2021] ECLI:EU:C:2021:864.

78 Case C-752/21 *JP EOOD* [2023] ECLI:EU:C:2023:179.

Bulgarian customs authorities that are competent for issuing forms of confiscation, but not in connection with a crime, do not fall within the notion of "court, as required by Art 2(4) of Directive 2014/42", as the confiscation ex art 4 of Directive 2014/42 presupposes a crime. Moreover, they also stated that national legislation not providing for a right to appeal against an administrative penalty notice against a person whose property has been seized, based on such a decision, but who is not the person committing the administrative offence connected with the penalty imposed, is not legitimate under EU law. It also held that the Framework Decision 2005/212/JHA of 24 February 2005 on Confiscation of Crime-Related Proceeds does not apply to decisions concerning an act that does not constitute a criminal offence.

This decision may be understood as requiring a necessary link between the assets to be confiscated and the commission of a crime, without which the confiscation measure is not legitimate.[79]

## 6 Relationships across the Instruments of Judicial Cooperation

Besides for the specific issues, related to the three judicial cooperation instruments illustrated above, in the field of judicial cooperation there might be a general problem of choosing one instrument of judicial cooperation instead of another. Such a complex decision may also have a relevant impact on individual rights. On the contrary, instead, the legitimate means for fighting crimes should be neutral as much as possible in terms of individual safeguards.

The Court of Justice for example stated that the European Investigation Order, unlike an EAW, is not capable of affecting the right to liberty of the person concerned. This means that the notion of 'issuing judicial authority', which under the EAW FD does not include prosecutors' offices of a Member State exposed to the risk of being subject to individual orders or instructions from the executive power, is not applicable in the context of the EIO, which does not require the same level of guarantee.[80]

The same reasoning could be applied in the context of the Regulation which expressly provides that the public prosecutor is included among the authorities considered to be "issuing authorities" (Art 2, 8(a)(i) Regulation 1805/2018)

---

79 This case draws from another recent ECtHR case, *Torodov and Others v. Bulgaria*, Apps nos. 50705/11 and others (ECHR, 13 July 2021), ruling that in the absence of a link between proceeds and criminal activity, the confiscation violates the right to property.

80 Joined Cases OG C-508/18, PI C-82/19 PPU and PF C-509/18 *OG* (*Parquet de Lübeck*) [2021] ECLI:EU:C:2019:456.

or which has the power to validate a seizure order before it is transmitted to the executing authority, if such an order has been issued by "another competent authority" (Art 2, 8(a)(ii) Regulation 1805/2018). In fact, a seizure order does not concern the right to liberty, but the right to property and freedom of economic initiative of the person concerned. Additionally, it is a temporary measure.[81]

Sometimes it is not sufficiently clear whether the EIO can be always used, or other instruments can be used instead to gather transborder evidence. Generally, not all provisions of the traditional MLA conventions and protocols can be replaced by the EIO but only the "corresponding provisions".[82] For example, the definition of a EIO provided by Art 2 clarifies the conditions under which it is possible to issue a EIO pursuant to Art 1 of the Directive: a) a decision issued (or validated) by a judicial authority; b) in the context of criminal proceedings (in the sense defined in Art 4 of the Directive); c) consisting in investigative measures of trans-border nature; d) aimed at gathering evidence; e) among the Member States bound by the EIO Directive.

In the presence of all these conditions, the EIO can be issued, within in the absence of even one of these conditions the EIO cannot. Art 34 of the Directive also states that the EIO replaces and prevails over pre-existing MLA conventions, namely the European Convention on Mutual Assistance in Criminal Matters of the Council of Europe of 20 April 1959, as well as its two additional protocols, and the bilateral agreements concluded pursuant to Article 26 thereof; the Convention implementing the Schengen Agreement; the Convention on Mutual Assistance in Criminal Matters between the Member States of the European Union and its protocol. Evidence gathering provisions from the MLA agreements and freezing orders are replaced by the EIO. However, Ireland and Denmark are not subject to the EIO D, and thus remain parties to MLA treaties. Moreover, the EIO Directive only applies to corresponding provisions. Among the examples of non-replaced provisions, we can include traditional rogatory letters, mutual legal assistance requests such as service of documents and summons, spontaneous exchange of information, returning objects to the injured party and transfer of proceedings or information with a view to proceedings being opened by another country.

81 See on this Anna M. Maugeri, 'The Proposal of a New Directive on Asset Confiscation' (2024) 1 Diritto Penale Contemporaneo 1, 17.

82 Jorge A.E. Ramos, 'The European Investigation Order and Its Relationship with Other Judicial Cooperation Instruments: Establishing Rules on the Scope and Possibilities of Application' (2019) 1 Eucrim 53.

Art 34 saves the possibility, however, to apply other bilateral and multilateral MLA agreements instead of EIO when three conditions are met: the alternative instrument a) further strengthens the aims of the EIO Directive; b) simplifies or further facilitates the procedures for gathering evidence, and c) respects the level of safeguards set out in the Directive. However, between the compatibility rule and the replacement rule, the latter applies. This has also been stated in the matter of EAW by the CJEU in the case *Goicoechea*[83] where the Spanish Government requested the extradition of Mr. Goicoechea, rejected by France, and afterwards issued an EAW although this was not temporarily applicable to facts committed before the entry into force of the EAW FD. The Court held that the extradition request based on a Convention that became applicable only after the entry into force of the EAW FD could be accepted by the executing Member State. Arts 31 and 32 of the EAW FD do not preclude the application of extradition arrangements related to these specific circumstances. The issue of the replacement among judicial cooperation's instruments is relevant as far as it implies different protection for involved individuals as well as different impact on individual rights. It in fact requires striking delicate balance between the principle of mutual trust, the principle of legality mostly exemplified by national competence in criminal matters, and fundamental rights' protection. However, when equal treatment is ensured, other grounds related to the effectiveness of international relations – as regards for instance extradition's conventions – need to be taken into consideration.

## 7 Concluding Remarks

From the analysis conducted so far, a diverse landscape of instruments aiming at protecting different interests emerges. Although the three instruments considered serve different logics, we saw how fundamental rights' protection represents in fact a limit of mutual trust. This may be paradoxical, because often mutual trust is justified by the adhesion to common European values. At the same time, the protection of fundamental rights and the compatibility of mutual recognition instruments with the CFREU plays an important unifying function aimed at fostering the judicial dialogue between courts around an unbreakable core of guarantees. The areas of law examined are different, of course, but it is precisely this diversity that pierces the veil of the lack of harmonization, which often hinders judicial cooperation. What clearly emerges is

83 Case C-296/08 PPU, *Gioicoechea* [2009] ECR I-06307.

the fact that EAW seems to gauge higher relevance as regards individual safeguards with respect to EIO and Regulation 1805/2018, however case-by-case analysis shows that fundamental rights' protection is a granular concept that may be tailored upon specific circumstances. Conversely, the safeguards provided similarly for different instruments always need to be interpreted according to their different context.

The indivisible character of the protection offered by the fundamental rights paradigm thus overcomes the sectoral character of mutual trust. In such a light we can read the Opinion of the European Union Agency for Fundamental Rights on the development of an integrated tool of objective fundamental rights indicators able to measure compliance with the shared values listed in Art 2 TEU, based on existing sources of information,[84] which could go beyond the peculiarity of specific instruments and stabilize the aims of the fight against crimes within the remit of inviolable rules and principles. What emerges from the CJEU case law is that judicial cooperation is increasingly becoming a playground where the basic requirements of effective fundamental rights' protection are recurringly oscillating between the extent of the notion of judicial authorities and the one of judicial review. This tension, although being subject to sophisticated differentiation elaborated by the jurisprudence of the CJEU, highlights a common trajectory for judicial cooperation inspired to basic requirements of the rule of law that cannot be waived, although they are constantly balanced with the margin of appreciation of States.

---

84 FRA-Opinion 2/2016, 'Opinion of the European Union Agency for Fundamental Rights on the development of an integrated tool of objective fundamental rights indicators able to measure compliance with the shared values listed in Article 2 TEU based on existing sources of information' (European Union Agency for Fundamental Rights, 2016) <https://fra.europa.eu/sites/default/files/fra_uploads/fra-2016-opinion-rule-of-law-art-2-02-2016_en.pdf>_(accessed: 19/04/2025).

CHAPTER 15

# Mutual Recognition and Double Criminality in EAW: Comparative Challenges and Future Prospects

*Alessandra Santangelo*

## 1 Introduction

The primary shortcomings of the European framework for double criminality are so well known that they now appear almost self-evident. The European Union has failed in its attempt to accomplish a political process of harmonisation: a single code covering all the Member States is far from being achieved, even more so in the punitive dimension. Instead, each legal system detains largely divergent criminal provisions, fuelling continuous challenges for judicial cooperation in criminal matters. In this perspective, double criminality encapsulates a relevant stress test for the enforcement of mutual recognition,[1] in contrast with the rationale of Arts 67 and 82 TFEU even though not always on grounds of protecting fundamental rights.[2]

Double criminality is a key mechanism which stems from the notion of national sovereignty, and particularly encompasses the principle of legality, legal certainty and proportionality in international criminal law.[3] Yet, it gains different nuances when framed in the European perspective,[4] being – inevitably – influenced by the ongoing (and never accomplished) path towards

---

1 A "cornerstone" of EU judicial cooperation according to Recitals 6 and 12 of EAW FD 2002/584: Cases C-562/21 PPU and C-563/21 PPU *Openbaar Ministerie* [2022] ECLI:EU:C:2022:100, para 44.

2 See Lorena Bachmaier, 'European Arrest Warrant, Double Criminality and Mutual Recognition: A Much Debated Case' (2018) European Criminal Law Review 152.

3 ibid 155 where the author lists as double criminality's rationale also political comity, the reciprocity principle and the protection of the *ordre public*. On this issue, see also Pedro Caeiro, 'The Contribution of Advocaten voor de Wereld for the Protection of Human Rights in the Context of Supra-State Law and for the Doctrine of Double Criminality', in Valsamis Mitsilegas, Alberto di Martino and Leandro Mancano (eds) *The Court of Justice and European Criminal Law* (Hart 2019) 357.

4 Adam Nieto Martín, 'The Foundations of Mutual Recognition and the Meaning of Dual Criminality' (2018) European Criminal Law Review 161, observing that '[s]ince this cession of sovereignty, judicial cooperation in criminal matters should be read and understood in the context of judgements such as *Melloni, Akerberg Fransson* or *Taricco*'.

integration in the criminal field and revealing penumbras and struggles still to be solved.

Against this background, the paper focuses on EAW revolving around a thesis that has already been widely argued more than a decade ago: even though it embodies a general principle,[5] it is not clear yet whether judicial cooperation is merely allowed, mandatory or prohibited in the absence of double criminality.[6] Here, some of the renowned issues that dwell on the reasonableness of the list of offences intertwine with the most recent caselaw on legality, proportionality and the protection of fundamental rights to the detriment of mutual recognition and mutual trust.[7]

More in detail, the Chapter first examines the European double criminality legislative framework (*infra*, §2), together with the most relevant case law of the Court of Justice (*infra*, §3). The European tribunals, in fact, have not achieved a final stance yet, prompting uncertainties on the side of national judicial interpretation. Some of the most relevant domestic outlines will be examined in a comparative perspective (*infra*, §4), so as to draw few conclusive considerations about the challenges judicial cooperation is currently facing on the ground of mutual trust or – sometime – 'distrust' among Member States (*infra*, §5).

## 2 The Inner Rationality of the Regulatory List

The principle of double criminality stands among the general principles of international cooperation, to the extent that it is considered implicitly enshrined even when not expressly provided for in a Convention.[8]

---

5 For a deep analysis of the five – and then seven – cooperation domains affected by double criminality, see Wendy De Bondt, 'Double criminality in international cooperation in criminal matters' in Gert Vermeulen, Wendy De Bondt and Charlotte Ryckman (eds) *Rethinking international cooperation in criminal matters in the EU* (Maklu 2012) 109.

6 As it is well-known, the notion itself of double criminality is uncertain, as some scholars have preferred referring to – just to mention few examples – double penalisation, double punishability, dual liability, dual incrimination: recalling the most debated arguments, Michal Plachta, 'The role of double criminality in international cooperation in penal matters' in Nils Jareborg (eds), *Double Criminality* (Uppsala Iustus Forlag 1989); Sharon A. Williams, 'The Double Criminality Rule and Extradition: A Comparative Analysis' (1991) Nora Law Review 581.

7 As for the interaction between mutual trust and mutual recognition, André Klip, *European Criminal Law. An Integrative Approach* (Intersentia 2021) 110.

8 Regarding extradition, see Ivan Shearer, *Extradition in international Law* (Manchester University Press 1971) 138. For a different perspective, see again Sharon A. Williams, 'The

This standard has never seriously been disputed, resting as it does on the balance between national sovereignty and the protection of fundamental guarantees, on the one hand, and reciprocity as a functional tool for opposing the most odious crimes, on the other. More in detail, the principle at stake embodies national prerogatives in criminal policies, a cornerstone of extradition to begin with.[9] Furthermore, double criminality entangles the respect of *nullum crimen sine lege*: personal freedom shall not be restricted due to provisions not recognised as criminal by the requested State. Following a familiar pattern for jurisdictions built upon the rule of law, a person shall not be punished for a behaviour which was not clearly defined as criminal by the legislator in advance.[10] In a nutshell, the need for calculability of the legal consequences of personal behaviours and the prohibition of 'catch-all' criminal sanctions evokes the constitutional guarantee of predictability referring to the principle of legality as well as, indirectly, to responsibility and culpability.[11]

It is therefore not surprising that the principle of double criminality is expressly included in the Framework Decision regulating EAW. In a brief review of the relevant provisions, the European legislator provides a two tracks approach: it departs from a precise statement that selects the offences involved according to the seriousness of the illicit conduct or, more precisely, the gravity of penalties. In fact, Art 2(1) states that a European arrest warrant may be issued for acts punishable by the law of the issuing Member State by a custodial sentence or a detention order for a maximum period of at least 12 months or, where a sentence has been passed or a detention order has been made, for sentences of at least four months. To speed up judicial cooperation, the second paragraph continues by enumerating a list of offenses where the test needs not be passed, provided that the custodial sentence or the detention order entail a maximum period of at least three years. This legislative solution has been

Double Criminality Rule and Extradition: A Comparative Analysis' (1991) Nora Law Review, 582.

9 In this light, as early as the 1970s see Paolo Pisa, *Previsione bilaterale del fatto nell'estradizione* (Giuffrè 1973) 156, focusing on extradition.

10 Also considering the risks of erosion of the legality principle, Douglas Husak, 'Wilful Ignorance, Knowledge, and the Equal Culpability Thesis', in Id., *The Philosophy of Criminal Law. Selected Essays* (Oxford University Press 2010) 202.

11 In this perspective, it is interesting to observe the development of criminal responsibility gaining a central role even in common law legal orders: Andrew Ashworth, 'Ignorance of Criminal Law, and Duties to Avoid it', in Id., Positive Obligations in Criminal Law (OUP 2013) 81; Nicola Lacey, *In Search of Criminal Responsibility: Ideas, Interests and Institutions* (OUP 2016) 135 and, also, Id. 'In Search of the Responsible Subject: History, Philosophy and Social Sciences in Criminal Law Theory' (2001) Modern Law Review 357.

described as revolutionary, as it enables smooth cooperation and hampers the grounds for refusal by preventing the use of double criminality.[12]

As for the crimes not covered by paragraph 2, the check emerges from Art 2(4) where the legislator states it is necessary the behaviour constitutes an offence in the executing Member State 'whatever the constituent elements or however it is described'. This condition represents, in accordance with EAW FD Art 4(1), a ground for optional non-execution.[13]

Thus, the European Union opts for a rather clear solution. Leaving aside the *in abstracto* doctrine (as for the case law, see *infra*, §3), according to which it is necessary to identify corresponding criminal offences in the concerned jurisdictions, the 2002 legislator seems to emphasise the *in concreto* double criminality, i.e. the actus reus shall be punished at the national level, regardless of the legislative labelling and also of the punitive treatment envisaged.[14] Yet, it is anything but easy to state a position on this quarrel, inasmuch as considerable diversity exists on the exact understanding of *in abstracto* and *in concreto* double criminality at the national level.[15]

This normative option raises considerable concerns, especially in view of subsequent developments in the Court of Justice case law. Therefore, it seems useful to further investigate these aspects, testing the resilience of the European regulatory framework in relation to the fundamental guarantees which underpin the punitive field. Undoubtedly, the EAW FD's underlying goal is to facilitate the execution of pre-trial measures and judgements restricting personal freedom within the Union's territory.[16] And it is also true that the approximated crimes, i.e. frauds affecting the financial interests of the Union, place rather fewer concerns. Nonetheless, the listed offences present several inconsistencies which imply the risk of breaching fundamental guarantees at

12 Considering the problems arising from different judicial applications of the 32 offences at national level, Bedanna Bapuly, 'The European arrest warrant under constitutional attack' (2009) Journal on International Constitutional Law 4.

13 A 'yardstick for dual criminality as a condition of recognition', as stated in Case C-718-18 *X* [2020] ECLI:EU:C:2020:142, opinion of A.G. Bobek, para 38.

14 Wouter van Ballegooij, *The Nature of Mutual Recognition in European Law: Re-examining the Notion from an Individual Rights Perspective with a View to Its Further Development in the Criminal Justice Area* (Intersentia 2015) 127.

15 In this way, Case C-289/15 *Grundza* [2017] ECLI:EU:C:2017:4, opinion of A.G. Bobek, para 21.

16 For an all-encompassing analysis, Valsamis Mitsilegas, *EU Criminal Law* (2nd edn, Hart 2022) 196.

the national level[17] as well as infringing the more general rules on conferral in the EU dimension.[18]

Focusing on the legality principle, a first problem revolves around the very wording of the listed offences: the normative indication is extremely vague and refers to a significant array of crimes, which cannot exactly be predetermined in advance. An example is the inclusion of 'computer-related crime' or 'racism and xenophobia'. In the absence of a clear legislative indication, it is inevitable that the selection will be left – afterwards – to the discretion of national judicial authorities, in breach of separation of power as a cornerstone of the rule of law. Thus, the risk would be weakening the EAW mechanism by increasing judicial discretion, recalling the hesitancy of the opponents of further integration into the criminal matters. In this regard, it is worth mentioning the claim that this tool would work perfectly if all listed offences were fully harmonised, making the EAW serve as a sort of incentive to strengthen the 'unification' of Europe.[19] Besides, this issue has significant importance since it triggers the sophisticated counter-limits strategy,[20] as the 'Taricco saga' has made undisputedly clear.[21]

Moreover, one of the 'classic' pitfalls of closed lists is to be encountered: the passage of time. Leaving aside the problems of interpretation (*infra*, §3 and §4), the legislator's decision to enumerate the offences – or, rather, the range of offences – excluded from double criminality test is in danger of aging badly.

17 Analysing the possible infringements of Italian Constitutional guarantees, with particular attention to *nullum crimen* and fair trial, see Stefano Manacorda, 'La deroga alla doppia punibilità nel mandato di arresto europeo e il principio di legalità (note a margine di Corte di giustizia, *Advocaten voor de Wereld*, 3 maggio 2007)' (2007) Cassazione penale 4346, as well as Vincenzo Caianiello and Giuliano Vassalli, 'Parere sulla proposta di decisione quadro sul mandato di arresto europeo' (2002) Cassazione penale, 462.

18 On the proper legal basis to adopt criminal legislation, see Case C-303/05 *Advocaten voor de Wereld VZW v Leden van de Ministerraad* [2007] ECR I-03633, para 18. See the notes relating to the decision, *inter alia*, of Daniel Sarmiento 'European Union: The European Arrest Warrant and the quest for constitutional coherence' (2008) International Journal of Constitutional Law 171.

19 In this perspective, see again Vincenzo Caianiello and Giuliano Vassalli (n 17) 462.

20 For a broader analysis on the interplay between legality and the EU primacy, Emanuela Fronza, 'Primacy, Duty of Loyalty and Interpretation' in Kai Ambos and Peter Rackow (eds) *The Cambridge Companion to European Criminal Law* (Cambridge University Press 2023) 65.

21 On the judicial saga, *inter alia*, see Silvia Allegrezza, 'On Legality in Criminal Matters between Primacy of EU Law and National Constitutional Traditions. A Study of the Taricco Saga' and Vittorio Manes, 'Taricco, Endgame' both in Valsamis Mitsilegas, Alberto di Martino and Leandro Mancano (eds) *The Court of Justice and European Criminal Law* (Hart 2019) 165, 188.

What will happen in the presence of further legislative approximation with respect to new offences? Would it not have been better to conceive in the EAW FD a general provision which qualified cooperation as automatic in case of EU obligations of criminalisation?

Considering all those aspects, the debate on overcoming double criminality as a 'two-party talk' appears interesting: the idea would be fostering judicial cooperation even though single behaviours are not regarded as criminal in nature at the national level.[22] In this light, the highest favour for efficient rendering of justice would be achieved, striving for consistency in EU policy making (more broadly *infra*, §5).[23]

## 3 Judicial Assessments at the EU Level

As already mentioned in the introduction, the concerns surrounding the double criminality test could represent an incentive towards maximum harmonisation between national criminal provisions.[24] The issue appears even more serious if the inconsistencies in judicial application that arise both in the national and European dimension are taken into consideration.

More in details, the Court of Justice had immediately to clarify whether the FD provisions could – to borrow a paradox – violate the legality principle.[25] The Court took *nullum crimen* seriously, as the standard against which EU secondary provisions should be measured.[26] However, it did not specifically rule on *nullum crimen* and, instead, considerably relied on the European Court of Human Rights' case law.[27] In this light, it is well established that penal

22 As for the possibility that a political union allows for the interest in cooperation to weight more, see the mentioned paper by Pedro Caeiro (n 3) 357, where the author claims that '[i]n a sense, the recognition of values acquires a formalistic nature: judicial cooperation no longer refers to the protection of the common legal interest harmed or endangered by, e.g., murder, or trafficking in human beings, but to the effectiveness of the penal justice system of the requesting (issuing) state'.

23 See again Wendy De Bondt (n 5) 109, 111, reflecting on a four-party talk which includes both European institutions and the interested persons.

24 On the issue, it has also been observed that 'harmonisation efforts may raise the level of scrutiny necessary to ensure the double criminality requirement is met': Gianmarco Bondi, 'Double criminality and the European Arrest Warrant: current trends and future developments in light of the KL case' (2024) New Journal of European Criminal Law 12.

25 On the subject, see the already mentioned Pedro Caeiro (n 3) 349.

26 Case C-399/11, *Melloni v Ministerio Fiscal* [2013] ECLI:EU:C:2013:107.

27 To this effect, see Christina Peristeridou, *The Principle of Legality in European Criminal Law* (Intersentia 2015) 178 ff.

provisions shall be accessible and foreseeable, i.e. meet minimum qualitative requirements for enabling an effective compliance with the rule of law.[28] As the clear wording of criminal laws is an essential requirement (*lex certa*), the ECtHR has long clarified that drawing up of exhaustive lists complies with Art 7(1) since it allows citizens to identify in advance unlawful behaviours.[29] The issue becomes ensuring the legislative enumeration to be exhaustive.

The problem – it is quite evident – concerns interpretation of Article 2(2):[30] the risk for Member States is to violate the legality principle not because they fail to transpose or incorrectly transpose a European provision. Rather, the contrast with *nullum crimen* stems from the vagueness of the European provision itself. In *Advocaten voor de Wereld*, the Court of Justice dealt with the issue with questionable arguments. First, the Court considered the applicant's claims according to which the offences set out in that list were not accompanied by legal definition and, rather, drew unpredictable series of unlawful conducts.[31] Hence, the judges convincingly maintained that legality requirements were met whenever the individual concerned was in a position, on the basis of the wording of the relevant provision and with the help of the interpretative assistance given by the courts, to acknowledge which acts or omissions will make him criminally liable.[32]

Here, the most critical reasoning. Art 2(2) exclusively stated in clear terms the penalties thresholds, while referring to the categories of offences in rather vague terms. As a result,

28 For an effective overview on qualitative requirements as interpreted by the Strasbourg Court, see the case of *Del Rio Prada v Spain* App no. 42750/09 (ECtHR, 21 October 2013), para 91, and the case of *Vasiliauskas v Lithuania* App no. 35343/05 (ECtHR, 20 October 2015), para 153.

29 Expressly, *Cantoni v France* App no. 17862/91 (ECtHR, 11 November 1996), para 28. Considering the consistency on undetailed references (i.e. 'in any way'), case of *Georgouleas and Nestoras v Greece* App no 44612/13 (ECtHR, 20 May 2020), para 62.

30 As it is well-known, according to the Court of Justice, in order to establish the scope of the condition of double criminality of the act, it is necessary to consider not only the wording of Articles 2(4) and 4(1), but also the context in which they occur and the objectives pursued by the rules of which those provisions form part: see Case C-649/19 *Spetsializirana prokuratura* [2021] ECLI:EU:C:2021:75, para 42. Consistently, the judgements C-533/08 *TNT Express Nederland* [2010] ECR I-04107 and C-181/19 *Jobcenter Krefeld* [2020] ECLI:EU:C:2020:794, para 61.

31 See the already mentioned Case C-303/05 *Advocaten voor de Wereld VZW v Leden van de Ministerraad* [2007] ECR I-03633, para 48.

32 ibid 50, expressly referring the Court of Justice to the case of *Coëme and Others v Belgium* (ECtHR, 22 June 2000), para 145.

> even if the Member States reproduce word-for-word the list of the categories of offences set out in Article 2(2) of the Framework Decision for the purposes of its implementation, the actual definition of those offences and the penalties applicable are those which follow from the law of 'the issuing Member State'.[33]

Accordingly, compliance with the principle of legality is entrusted to national authorities, called upon to regulate in detail each offence falling within the category referred to in Art 2(2). Thus, EAW FD is not invalid on the ground that it infringes the principle of legality (§54).[34] Well, it is doubtful that such an approach would strengthen European cooperation, instead of defending the 'nationalisms' that by tradition characterise the penal sphere.

Yet, not least to break the impasse, the European Court sets out the minimum requirements of double criminality in the context of the interpretation of Council FD 2008/909/JHA.[35] More in details, assessing the condition of double criminality of an act requires the executing judicial authority to verify whether the factual elements underlying the offence, as reflected in the issuing State's judgement, would also, per se, be criminal in nature in the executing State. It is not necessary – as the Court later recalls in *KL* – to assess 'an exact match between the constituent elements of the offence, as defined in the law of the issuing State and the executing State, respectively, or between the name given to or the classification of the offence under the national law of the respective States'.

Consistently in *KL*,[36] the Court of Luxembourg confirms this approach.[37] In particular, surrender is only possible on condition that the defendant

33 ibid 52.

34 For deep reflections on the judgement, see Pedro Caeiro (n 3) 359.

35 See *Grundza* (n 15) paras 34–38, adding the Court that 'in assessing double criminality, the competent authority of the executing State must ascertain, not whether an interest protected by the issuing State has been infringed, but whether, in the event that the offence at issue were committed in the territory of the executing State, it would be found that a similar interest, protected under the national law of that State, had been infringed' (49).

36 Gianmarco Bondi (n 24) 6.

37 Case C-168/21 *Procureur général près la cour d'appel d'Angers* [2022] ECLI:EU:C:2022:558, concerning a request made in the context of the execution in France of a European arrest warrant issued by the Italian judicial authorities against KL for the purpose of enforcing a custodial sentence of 12 years and 6 months for acts classified as theft committed in conjunction with others and while carrying a weapon, devastation and looting, carrying a weapon and detonation of explosive devices, committed in Genoa (Italy) in 2001. The case concerned the refusal to surrender the defendant to the Italian authorities by way of execution of the European arrest warrant in so far as two of the acts underlying

for identical acts could also have been punished in the executing State. The European Tribunal reiterates the 'autonomous notion' approach,[38] awarding a concept of relevant offences for the execution of the EAW which focuses on punishability and it is independent from the crimes' legal interests.[39] But not every scholar is convinced that this outline strengthens mutual trust, as wide margins of discretion remain with the national authorities (*infra*, §4).[40]

Another very remarkable aspect: the referring court challenges proportionality under Art 49(3) CFREU as a valid ground for the executing State to refuse to execute a EAW.[41] In *KL*, the issuing Member State has referred to the commission, by the requested person, of a single offence consisting of multiple acts, only some of which constitute a criminal offence in the executing Member State. The argument is not new. Apart from *Grundza*, the Court had already ruled on the interplay between proportionality and double criminality, albeit with reference merely to offences punishable by a custodial sentence of a maximum of at least twelve months.[42] However, the *KL* case addresses the issue in broader terms.

According to the Court, the aim to facilitate and accelerate surrenders between the judicial authorities of the Member States in the light of the mutual confidence prevails and requires a strict interpretation of the refusal grounds.

---

in Italy the offence of 'devastation and looting' – namely, first, the destruction of premises belonging to Credito Italiano and, secondly, the destruction by fire of a Fiat Brava vehicle – did not constitute an offence in France. While in Italy destruction and damage shall be punished as they cause a breach of the public peace by threatening the normal course of life in civil society, the French law exclusively evaluates the loss to the owners of the property in question.

38 L. Mancano, 'Mutual Recognition in Criminal Matters, Deprivation of Liberty and the Principle of Proportionality' (2018) Maastricht Journal of European and Comparative Law 718–732.

39 However, scholars are not unanimous commenting on this landmark decision. According to some views, the Court prefers a technical approach to the problem through an objective comparison of legal systems: Marta Ramat, 'The Court of Justice and the Assessment of Double Criminality Under the European Arrest Warrant Framework Decision: KL' (2023) European Papers, 1000. Following others, it would be rather a preference for the *in abstracto* approach, moreover of an 'extreme' nature (Florentino Ruiz Yamuza, 'CJEU case law on double criminality. The Grundza-Piotrowski paradox? Some notes regarding the Puigdemont case' (2019) ERA Forum, 473).

40 Lorena Bachmaier (n 2) 153.

41 On proportionality in the EU criminal sphere, see Valsamis Mitsilegas and Emmanouil Billis, 'Article 49 – Principles of Legality and Proportionality of Criminal Offences and Penalties' in Steve Peers, Tamara Hervey, Jeff Kenner, and Angela Ward (eds), *The EU Charter of Fundamental Rights. A Commentary* (Hart 2021) 1473.

42 Case C-463/15 *A* [2015] ECLI:EU:C:2015:634, paras 21–31.

The EAW's effectiveness is essential for European criminal policy, entangling to 'water down' double criminality.[43]

As repeatedly held by the EU case law, the execution of EAW is subject only to one of the conditions exhaustively laid down in Art 5.[44] Thus, in *KL* the principle of proportionality is not infringed:[45] accordingly, on the one hand, the observance of the rights of the person whose surrender is sought falls primarily within the responsibility of the issuing Member State.[46] On the other, possible disproportionality of the sentence handed down in the issuing Member State is not among the grounds for mandatory and optional non-execution of a European arrest warrant set out in Articles 3, 4 and 4a of EAW FD.[47] Finally, double criminality does not allow the executing judicial authority to assess the sentence handed down in the issuing Member State in the light of Article 49(3) CFREU.[48]

The solution envisaged by the Court is not fully convincing. The EU case law reiterates that EAW seeks, by the establishment of a simplified and effective system for the surrender of persons convicted or suspected of having infringed criminal law, to facilitate and accelerate judicial cooperation with a view to contributing to the attainment of the objective set for the European Union of becoming an area of freedom, security and justice, and has as its basis the high level of trust which must exist between the Member States.[49] The question is whether this may occur even at the expenses of the fundamental rights of the individual.

After all, mutual trust is built primarily on respect for the fundamental guarantees of the individual. The option of narrowing the proportionality's scope of application, which instead is increasingly relevant at European level and to the constitutional traditions of the Member States,[50] is not convincing.[51]

---

43 Adam Nieto Martín (n 4) 164.

44 Case C-717/18 *X* [2020] ECLI:EU:C:2020:142, para 41.

45 Case C-168/21 *Procureur général près la cour d'appel d'Angers* (n 37), para 64.

46 Case C-367/16 *Piotrowski* [2018] ECLI:EU:C:2018:27, para 50.

47 In this light, see point 63 of the opinion of Advocate General Rantos delivered on 31 March 2022 in the case at stake.

48 Case C-168/21 *Procureur général près la cour d'appel d'Angers* (n 37), para 67. See also *Grundza* (n 15), para 46.

49 See the above mentioned *Openbaar Ministerie* (n 1) judgement para 42.

50 Besides, the two levels seem to be strictly connected since recent *NE* case law directly engages the national judges: C-205/20 *NE* (CJEU, GC 8 March 2022). On the national perspective, see as far as the Italian Constitutional Court, Francesco Viganò, *La proporzionalità della pena. Profili di diritto penale e costituzionale* (Giappichelli 2021) passim.

51 For a broader analysis on proportionality and mutual recognition, L. Mancano, 'Mutual Recognition in Criminal Matters, Deprivation of Liberty and the Principle of Proportionality' (2018) Maastricht Journal of European and Comparative Law 723.

Rather, it seems useful to insist on the front of harmonisation or, even before that, of a serious discussion on the cultural *milieu* of European criminal law enhancing the rule of law principles. Besides, considering the actual limited harmonisation in the criminal field, it is likely not to find exact matches among national provisions with the threat to further jeopardise mutual recognition as it will be considered in the next paragraphs.[52]

## 4 A Glimpse into Comparison between Member States

As examined before, according to the most recent EU case law, double criminality cannot require the executing judicial authority to verify the impairment of the legal interest protected by the offence.[53] Otherwise, the teleological goal of combating the impunity of a requested person and, at the same time, fostering judicial cooperation would not be met. Hence, it could be argued that the application of EAW rules by national authorities should proceed in the direction of minimising obstacles to cooperation by enhancing, case-by-case, scenarios where the relevant conduct is punished at the domestic level.

The effectiveness-oriented approach is quite clear in theory but presents several challenges in practice.

Hence, comparative research is indispensable not only to appreciate the application of judicial cooperation tools but also to test the endurance of European remedies in the dialogue with national authorities. It is, of course, not possible here to recall all the relevant insights that emerge from the previous chapters focusing on domestic legal systems, which is made full reference to. Nonetheless, it seems useful to dwell on few aspects appraising the impact of the EU cooperation concerns analysed so far (*supra*, §2 and 3) in a comparative perspective.

A first problematic issue concerns the options available for national legislators. The Spanish authorities, for instance, decided in 2014 to rationalise the rules on judicial cooperation in a single legal text – Law 23/2014, of November 20. Indeed, to ensure maximum alignment with European provisions, the legislator replicated the list of offences excluded from the double criminality test, adopting similar vague terms. This option, however, makes it more complex to determine in advance which offences will be exempted: considering

52 On the 'disharmony' among Member States' legislations, Massimo Fichera, *The Implementation of European Arrest Warrant in the European Union Law: Law, Policy and Practice* (Intersentia 2011) 120.

53 Case C-168/21 *Procureur général près la cour d'appel d'Angers* (n 30), para 49.

'corruption' as an example, scholars question whether this category could also be extended to bribery between private individuals.[54]

No wonder that this legislative option has not been unanimously embraced. In the case of France, in fact, the principle of double criminality was initially construed in a strong sense, so as to strengthen national defences against European integration.[55] National legislator only allowed the execution of the EAW if the relevant conduct had also domestic criminal relevance. Indeed, a mitigating factor came firstly from national case law, which adopted a more lenient approach not requiring an exact match between the offences involved but, rather, settling for a common substantive criminal nature in spite of different legal definitions.[56] Following this direction, the legislator itself opted for a '*revirement*': starting with the reform of 2021, the legislative provision was changed and the word 'must' replaced by 'may', to the effect of removing the double criminality test from mandatory requirements.[57]

A comparable reform has not yet found its way into the Polish system, which has introduced an even further legal dodge. The national provisions transposed the EAW FD with regard both to double criminality and to the 32 excluded offences, except not applying the smoother way to Polish citizens for whom domestic judges must always assess whether the relevant facts are criminal in nature according to domestic legislation.[58] In order to temper the risk of discrimination, also in Poland national courts tend to avoid 'to examine the issue of guilt, social harmfulness or illegality of the alleged prohibited act'.[59] Rather, criminal judges just assess that the offence at stake has a counterpart in national legislation. While the purpose of the national authority is clear, the alignment with the Court of Justice's approach seems not perfect, especially after *KL*. This is a rather complex issue which will be analysed in broader terms, at the end to the comparative analysis.

Following a different approach, Dutch legislation had initially envisioned the double criminality test as a mandatory refusal ground, with the consequence of circumventing the national courts' discretion on the peculiar circumstances of the case. On the topic, the Court of Justice itself stepped in,

---

54 For a deep analysis, Ana Maria Neira Pena, Chapter 11, *supra* §1.1.

55 Discussing a 'nationalist' approach by the 2004 legislation, see Eleonora Cervellera, Chapter 6, *supra* §1.2.

56 ibidem, referring to Cass. Crim. 5 April 2018, n 18-81.528.

57 Law n 2021-1729 of 22 Dec. 2021 pour la confiance dans l'institution judiciaire, JORF n 0298, 23 Dec. 2021.

58 See Wojciech Jasiński, Karolina Kremens and Agnieszka Frąckowiak-Adamska, Chapter 9, *supra* §1.2.3.

59 ibid.

stating how 'executing judicial authorities may, in principle, refuse to execute such a warrant only on the grounds for non-execution exhaustively listed by the Framework Decision. Accordingly, while execution of the European arrest warrant constitutes the rule, refusal to execute is intended to be an exception, which must be interpreted strictly'.[60] Afterwards, as for Spain and France, the national position had to be reconsidered, granting more discretion to the judicial authorities.[61]

Considering their essential role, it is now worth turning to judicial authorities. It is interesting to observe that domestic tribunals do not always succeed in furthering the aim of cooperation but, instead, may offer a certain resistance, not always when the protection of fundamental rights is at stake.

Starting from Germany, the *Puigdemont* case occupied a prominent role as demonstrated by the newspaper's front pages.[62] The Spanish authorities, it is well-known, ordered an EAW against the leader of the Catalan separatist movement for the crime of 'rebellion' and 'corruption'. Considering that the EAW FD rules on double criminality have been transposed (Art 81 IRG), the German judge agreed that the act at stake, i.e. wasting public money, could represent a form of corruption on the ground of Art 2(2) EAW FD. On the contrary, the national judge observed that the crime of 'rebellion' did not meet the double criminality test as in Germany it included violence as an essential element, preventing cooperation in this particular concern.[63] The approach outlined by the Court of Justice finds acknowledgement at the national level, stressing the possibility to punish the behaviour involved. As convincingly maintained, the question did not concern the violation of fundamental rights – the defendant could clearly foresee in Spain his acts were criminal in nature – but, rather, the defence of national political interests.[64] The guard level must be kept high on the danger of the EAW being manipulated for political purposes (*infra*, §5).[65]

60 Case C-665/20 PPU *X* [2021] ECLI:EU:C:2021:339, para 39, focusing the case mainly on *ne bis in idem* and non-mandatory grounds for refusal. For a deeper analysis, see Camila Ugaz Heudebert, Teddy Zwackhalen, Gijs van Dijck and Menno Dolman, Chapter 12, *supra* §2.5.3.

61 ibid.

62 For a deeper analysis of the case, Lorena Bachmaier (n 2) 152.

63 On the judgement OLG Schleswig BeckRS 2018, 19152, see Anna Albrecht and Anne Schneider, 'EU mutual legal assistance instruments and German law – a clash of systems', *supra* §1.2.1.

64 Lorena Bachmaier (n 2) 157.

65 Actually, Recital n 12 of the EAW FD states in clear terms that '[n]othing in this Framework Decision may be interpreted as prohibiting refusal to surrender a person for whom a European arrest warrant has been issued when there are reasons to believe, on the basis of objective elements, that the said arrest warrant has been issued for the purpose of

Another interesting case can be traced in the Bulgarian system. Again, national legislator has correctly followed European provisions on the ground of EAW FD Arts 2(2) and 2(4); nonetheless, in a relevant judgement the application of the test fails to enhance cooperation.[66] More in detail, the Bulgarian judges as executing authorities observed that the relevant behaviour – assessed in Hungary and triggering the EAW – was committed with negligence. However, the correspondent Bulgarian offence required intent as *mens rea* (Art 340 CC), the negligent conducts could be criminal in nature only if causing considerable property damages, medium or grave bodily injury or death to one or more persons (Art 341 CC). In this frame, national judges could not surrender the defendant. Considering the essential elements of the offence, there was no exact matching, thereby barring recognition of the foreign judicial measure.

Applying double criminality does not seem above reproaches. Facing chaotic legislation, one much-debated issue, for example, relates to the possibility of surrendering the defendant if the crime is time-barred.[67] Likewise, it is not easy to determine how double criminality may influence the relevant penalty thresholds. Exemplary, in this respect, the case of Portugal. Having transposed the European provisions (Arts 2(2) and 2(3) PT-EAW), the Portuguese authorities had to unravel the knot concerning the likelihood – not even certainty – of not meeting legislative thresholds.[68] The problem raised in a case of several concurrent offences. The overall penalty was at the lower threshold necessary to execute the EAW. However, by applying the double criminality test, one of the offences was to be excluded since the behaviour was not unlawful in Portugal. Consequently, a different penalty treatment had to be assumed, likely below the legislative limit. The solution was not straightforward. National courts considered legal certainty and predictability to prevail on mutual trust and rejected the EAW even though 'it was impossible to know the effect of such acts upon the joint sentence'.[69]

---

prosecuting or punishing a person on the grounds of his or her sex, race, religion, ethnic origin, nationality, language, political opinions or sexual orientation, or that that person's position may be prejudiced for any of these reasons'.

66 See, in particular, a judgement by the Haskovo District Court, 3 July 2019, as analysed by Miroslava Manolova and Ekaterina Salkova, Chapter 4, *supra* §1.2.1.

67 It is quite emblematic the complex 'affair' involving the Croatian legislature and courts – including the highest courts – on statute of limitations and double criminality, in the attempt to provide citizens with equal protection compared to other Member States: Zlata Đurđević, Elizabeta Ivičević Karas, Marin Bonačić, Zoran Burić, Chapter 5, *supra* §2.2.1.

68 On the issue, see Miguel João Costa, Raquel Cardoso, António Vaz de Castro and Pedro Caeiro, Chapter 10, *supra* §1.2.3.

69 ibid.

Turning, in conclusion, to Italy, the challenge between double criminality and proportionality has already emerged (*supra*, §3). The referring court observed that in certain circumstances, the proportionality of the measure can only be determined by the executing authority. In the *KL* case, the defendant claimed that the EAW became disproportionate not at the time of its issuance but later. The enforcement of the EAW was to be considered disproportionate to the time of execution, considering the legal interests protected by the specific wording of the national offence ruled by the executing Member State.[70] Nonetheless, the Court of Justice preferred an unyielding outline by hampering the application of proportionality in surrender proceedings.[71]

The application of the EAW reveals several concerns, which are all the more relevant insofar as they intertwine – at least implicitly – with proportionality of penal prosecution.[72] Hence, it is useful to recall the role played by EU policy makers' goals. In fact, the tools for judicial cooperation emphasise the importance of strengthening the approximation *acquis*. Once a certain offence meets a reasonable degree of approximation among Member States, the scenario appears smoother.[73] On the one hand, national authorities which complied with the criminalisation obligation have not to bother with the double criminality test and domestic legislators which did not comply, on the other, cannot use inaction as an argument against cooperation.[74] In this way, it seems arduous to cast double criminality as a refusal ground to undermine cooperation.[75]

## 5 An Effectiveness-Oriented Approach towards Mutual Recognition?

Attempting to draw some conclusions, the EAW double criminality test provides an interesting specimen to essay the challenges that shape the arduous

70 In Italy, the crime of 'destruction and damage' implied the endangerment of the public peace by threatening the normal course of life in civil society; on the contrary, the French legislator exclusively considered property interests, greatly diminishing the seriousness of the crime. For a critical analysis, see Gianmarco Bondi (n 24) 6, arguing that the notion of legal interest 'may still play a pivotal role in other domains, such as the harmonisation of criminal offences and penalties'.

71 As for some further considerations on the *KL* case (n 37), see *supra* §3.3.

72 Wouter van Ballegooij (n 14) 350.

73 Massimo Fichera (n 52) 120.

74 In this perspective, see Gert Vermeulen and Laurens van Puyenbroeck, *Appreciating Approximation. Using common offence concepts to facilitate police and judicial cooperation in the EU* (Maklu 2010) 43.

75 As for the possibility of still using capacity as a refusal ground even when double criminality is met, see the already mentioned Wendy De Bondt (n 5) 115.

balance between teleological interpretation of mutual trust[76] and the protection of fundamental rights. On the one hand, the principle of legality, legal certainty and harmfulness is not always favoured, as the European authorities try not to discourage judicial cooperation (*supra*, §3). Indeed, it is undisputed that the EAW was introduced with the aim of smoothing relations between States as regards the execution of criminal measures, with the ultimate goal of encouraging integration in the criminal sphere.[77] Nevertheless, the decrease in mutual trust through the double criminality test does not always entail the violation of fundamental guarantees. Rather, it is possible to envisage other less noble reasons.

The effectiveness-oriented approach cannot go so far as to undermine those inviolable principles that the Union itself recognises in the Charter, in line with the ECHR. In *E.D.L.*,[78] in fact, national authority wondered whether, if the surrender of a person suffering from a serious chronic and potentially irreversible disease might expose that person to the risk of suffering serious harm to her health, the executing judicial authority should refuse to surrender her.[79] Against this background, the Court of Justice 'creates' a new mandatory ground for refusal where the real risk of a significant reduction in the defendant's life expectancy or of a rapid, significant and irreversible deterioration in her state of health cannot be excluded within a reasonable period of time.[80] Hence, the Union continues encompassing a prominent evaluation of individual guarantees:[81] even at the cost of curtailing judicial cooperation, as general interests can never sacrifice individual fundamental prerogatives.

Notwithstanding, in cases where fundamental rights are not at risk, how can the step backwards on mutual trust be justified?

76 With specific regard to confiscation of properties, Ciro Grandi, *Mutuo riconoscimento in materia penale e diritti fondamentali. Il nodo delle confische* (Giappichelli 2023) 29.

77 Adam Nieto Martín (4) 162, where the author affirms the automatic nature of mutual recognition is essential 'to shorten the time taken for judicial cooperation and ensure its effectiveness.'

78 Case C-699/21 *E.D.L.* [2023] ECLI:EU:C:2023:295, where the Italian Constitutional Court referred a preliminary ruling on the interpretation of EAW FD Art 1(3).

79 ibid 20, specifying that the first step should be that the issuing judicial authority provide information allowing the existence of such a risk to be ruled out; so that the refusal is justified whether the national authority does not obtain assurances to that effect within a reasonable period of time. For further details on the issue with regard to the protection of the right to health, see the decision of the Italian Constitutional Court no 177 of 2023 available in English at <https://www.cortecostituzionale.it/documenti/download/doc/recent_judgments/sentenza-n177-del-2023-en.pdf> last accessed 13 August 2024.

80 ibid 55.

81 On the issue, see again Adam Nieto Martín (4) 162.

In the above mentioned *Puigdemont* case (*supra*, §4), no *nullum crimen* issue arises in the sense that the defendant committed an unlawful offense under the Spanish penal law. This case rather entangles the risk that Member States could jeopardise judicial cooperation not so much guided by the protection of fundamental rights as by the protection of national sovereignty and political interests,[82] i.e. at odds with the European scope of fostering cooperation.[83] Thus, it is even more important for the Court of Justice to shed light on the boundaries of double criminality; as shown by the previous comparative analysis, national authorities fail to always apply EAW FD correctly and, sometimes, they are groping in the dark, not acknowledging the right balance between mutual recognition and the safeguarding of fundamental rights in the criminal field.

Indeed – just a few months before *E.D.L.* – the case *Puig Gordi* has been decided in an opposite direction in favour of the effectiveness-oriented approach.[84] In brief, the Court seems to bypass the two-step examination to refuse surrender in case of an alleged violation of fundamental rights: it is possible to stop examining general or systematic shortcomings, without carrying out the individual assessment.[85] Limited to the issue of jurisdiction, the European court appears to weaken the standard required by previous case law[86] and pave the way for an enhancement of the effective application of EAW.[87] This approach is not necessarily in contrast to safeguarding individual guarantees: is not mutual trust among Member States based primarily

82 It is important to recall that EAW is certainly based on the respect of Member States' national identity: see Adam Nieto Martín (4) 164.

83 Considering the rationale of double criminality in extradition, see Antonio Vallini, 'Il superamento della clausola della "previsione bilaterale del fatto" nell'estradizione per i reati di criminalità organizzata: obsolescenza o regresso antigarantistico?', in Giovannangelo De Francesco (ed) *La criminalità organizzata tra esperienze normative e prospettive di collaborazione internazionale* (Giappichelli 2001) 123, where the author denies a sort of "judicial nationalism" could legitimise the international tool which foster judicial cooperation in line with Art 13 Italian Constitution.

84 Case C-158/21, *Puig Gordi* [2023] ECLI:EU:C:2023:57, ruling on the refusal to execute a EAW issued by the Spanish authorities against several Catalan separatists. See, also, the *Puigdemont* case: *supra*, §3.4.

85 ibid 111.

86 See *Openbaar Ministerie* (n 1) [53–56] as well as the judgement *Bivolaru and Moldovan v. France* (ECtHR, 25 Mars 2021).

87 Para 116, where the Grand Chamber states that the EAW 'framework decision, read in the light of the provisions of the Charter, cannot be interpreted in such a way as to call into question the effectiveness of the system of judicial cooperation between the Member States'.

on the common respect for freedom, equality, and fundamental rights of the individuals?

Even though the two judgements do not clearly refer to double criminality, the Court of Justice seems to have better delineated its viewpoint towards mutual recognition, requiring strict oversights only if fundamental rights are at stake.[88] More and more clarity on this point can indeed be expected, to facilitate national authorities to interpret EAW FD in an effective way[89] and, at the same time, to prevent the overflow of mutual 'distrust' between Member States.[90]

88 On the CJEU case law and the possibility to state new judicial grounds for refusal when violations of fundamental rights are envisaged, Nicola Canestrini 'La cooperazione giudiziaria penale europea esige il rispetto della tutela dei diritti fondamentali, fondamento della fiducia reciproca fra gli stati membri. la vicenda degli indipendentisti catalani' (2023) Cassazione penale 2124.

89 Enhancing the division of work as a EAW fourth foundation, see Adam Nieto Martín (4) 162, stating that 'mutual recognition is fast and secure because it is grounded on a trust-based division of tasks: judges assume that their counterparts are competent and develop their activity in accordance with the rule of law'.

90 Lorena Bachmaier (n 2) 153.

# PART 4

CHAPTER 16

# Access to Justice through AI

*Marco Billi and Alessandro Parenti*

## 1 Information Technologies in Legal Practice[1]

In the European Union (EU) legal system, characterized by its multilevel structure, legal professionals are required to have a deep understanding of both national and EU regulations to navigate this complex web. This intricate system is further complicated by numerous international conventions, bilateral agreements, and national instruments with overlapping rules.

In our increasingly interconnected world, legal professionals must account for the interplay of multiple normative systems, especially in international or European matters, and social interactions involving different countries. These intersecting normative systems can introduce conflicts or differing consequences, making it challenging for legal experts to determine which sources of law to consider when preparing a case. Due to the EU's multilevel legal framework, identifying the applicable legal provisions for a specific case can be extremely demanding.

In this context, Artificial Intelligence (AI) can assist users in retrieving legal information, identifying and applying relevant EU and national regulations, and assessing the degree of harmonization of national laws with the EU acquis. To support legal experts in these tasks, we will use a range of technologies, from expert systems designed to model legislation to large language models for user interaction.

The focus of this chapter is the Facilex Advisory Module, a system built on a computable version of the law, on which an expert system can be based on. By translating legal norms into rules written in a programming language, the system can apply legal reasoning to the rule base. The objective of the modelling is therefore the creation of a reasoning platform that can assist any user in finding and applying the relevant rules, by understanding which conditions have been met and which factual elements have influenced the decision.

The tool has been designed to assist legal experts and professionals in resolving practical cases involving the application of EU procedural directives

1 The article is a joint reflection of the authors, but its drafting is broken down as follows: Billi §§ 1; 1.1; 2.1; 2.2; 2.5; 3.3; 4 Parenti §§ 1.2; 1.3; 2.3; 2.4; 3.1; 3.2; 5.

and mutual recognition instruments, as it enables legal practitioners to define a cross-border case by answering a series of questions and receiving a customized legal assessment on available legal remedies and potential cooperation issues within the specific legal system.

Below we introduce what are the main approaches taken to develop Artificial Intelligence technologies in the legal domain and provide an overview of the strengths and challenges of each one of them.

### 1.1 *Symbolic AI*

AI has traditionally been developed using a symbolic approach to represent the entirety of knowledge at its core. Such systems (expert systems) consist of two main parts. The first one is a knowledge base developed using methods such as logic or ontologies (i.e., symbolic methods). This represents, in a computable form, large amounts of information about the specific field the system is developed for. Most importantly, the knowledge features large sets of predefined rules that the system applies to carry out its reasoning (*rule-based systems*).[2]

The second part is an inference mechanism. This component represents the system's engine that enables the application of the rules contained in the knowledge base to the factual scenario provided by external users. Using both components, the system can carry out automated reasoning.

Symbolic systems experienced widespread employment in the legal domain and specifically those based on logic because of its suitability to represent legal rules.[3] Legal rules, in fact, often take the form of conditional statements: "*If* certain conditions are met, *then* a specific legal consequence follows." This if-then structure aligns perfectly with logical implication, making it straightforward to represent legal rules using logical constructs.

An illustrative example of such symbolic systems in the legal domain is the CROSSJUSTICE (CJ) project. [4] This project employs rule-based systems to represent and provide automated reasoning about the European laws related to the rights of suspects and accused in criminal proceedings. Both the European directives as well as several national laws applying them were transposed using logic programming. In the final platform, the system can be interrogated to know which European and national rules apply to specific scenarios provided.

---

2 Jurgen Karpf, 'Quality assurance of legal expert systems' (1989) Artificial Intelligence and Law.

3 Marek J. Sergot and others, 'The British Nationality Act as a Logic Program' (1986) 29 Communications of the ACM 370.

4 CrossJustice project (2022) <https://site.unibo.it/cross-justice/en> accessed 18/04/2024.

One of the main strengths of symbolic AI systems is the transparency and justifiability of the reasoning, thus making their overall functioning explainable.[5] Being based on precise rules defined by humans, the process leading to the final output can be easily audited. This means that, in case of a wrong output, the process can be traced back to identify where the system made a mistake.

However, despite their strengths, rule-based systems present notable challenges, particularly in communicating their outputs to non-experts.[6] The high-level programming languages used to express these logical conclusions often result in outputs that are difficult for laypeople to understand. This complexity can hinder the broader accessibility and usability of these systems, making it hard for non-specialists to appreciate the reasoning behind the decisions. From this perspective, the newer ML techniques and LLM can provide many advantages.

### 1.2 *Data Driven AI*

A different approach to the development of AI systems is represented by Machine Learning (ML). Rather than on sets of specific rules, systems are based on learning algorithms that extract patterns, i.e. learn, from large amounts of data. Several learning models were developed and implemented to obtain the best results in terms of learning outcomes.[7] Among these, we can mention the Neural Networks (NN) model. NN s consist of large number of nodes (neurons) interconnected with each other, whose functioning is inspired to those of the neurons found in human brains. It can process the data received as in input into meaningful information and propagate it to the entire network for it to learn. Deep learning, a subset of machine learning involving NN s with multiple hidden layers, has significantly advanced the capabilities of neural networks. Deep neural networks (DNN s) are particularly adept at handling high-dimensional data and extracting hierarchical representations, making them suitable for complex tasks that require multiple levels of abstraction.[8]

5 Katie Atkinson, T.J.M. Bench-Capon and Danushka Bollegala, 'Explanation in AI and law: Past, present and future.' (2020) Artificial Intelligence 289.

6 Harry Surden, 'Artifcial intelligence and law: An overview' (2019) Georgia State University Law Review 35.

7 Tala Talaei Khoei, Hadjar Ould Slimane and Naima Kaabouch, 'Deep Learning: Systematic Review, Models, Challenges, and Research Directions' (2023) 35 Neural Computing and Applications 23103.

8 OA Montesinos López, Abelardo Montesinos López and José Crossa, 'Fundamentals of Artificial Neural Networks and Deep Learning' (2022) Multivariate Statistical Machine Learning Methods for Genomic Prediction 379.

In the most recent years, this approach showed a great development specifically in the field of Natural Language Processing (NLP). These techniques, when applied to the legal domain, enable the extraction and interpretation of legal concepts from vast amounts of textual data. Furthermore, they enhance the accessibility of legal information for non-experts by translating complex legal and technical jargon into more user-friendly language.

AI technologies trained to process and generate natural language, developed at a faster-ever increasing scale and have recently exploded in popularity with the creation of Large Language Models (LLM s). These powerful systems of generative AI trained on huge amounts of natural language datasets can understand and answer questions in a human-like form. Similar capabilities allow for a wide range of applications. In legal applications, LLM s have proven useful for tasks ranging from retrieving legal information[9] to drafting contracts and legal documents, to predict judgement predictions.[10] Being designed to understand and generate human language, their output is, by nature, accessible and intelligible for humans, and non-IT experts. This feature results particularly crucial in the legal domain, where connection with laypeople is a necessary requirement.

All these advantages, however, do not come without drawbacks. The other side of LLM s, just like most other data driven models, is that they are intrinsically probabilistic. This means that results can never be verified and trusted at one hundred percent, but they always entail a certain degree of mistake or, in general, non-determinism.[11] A direct consequence is the phenomenon of hallucinations,[12] i.e., when the model provides information that is false, non-real, or otherwise incorrect.

---

9 Aniket Deroy, Kripabandhu Ghosh and Saptarshi Ghosh, 'Ensemble Methods for Improving Extractive Summarization of Legal Case Judgements' (2023) Artificial Intelligence and Law. Andrew Blair-Stanek, Nils Holzenberger and Benjamin Van Durme, 'Can GPT-3 Perform Statutory Reasoning?' (2023) Proceedings of the Nineteenth International Conference on Artificial Intelligence and Law.

10 Dietrich Trautmann, Alina Petrova, and Frank Schilder, 'Legal prompt engineering for multilingual legal judgement prediction.' (2022). Zhongxiang Sun, 'A short survey of viewing large language models in legal aspect' (2023) <https://arxiv.org/pdf/2303.09136> accessed 14 July 2024.

11 Bartosz Brożek, Michał Furman, Marek Jakubiec and Bartłomiej Kucharzy, 'The Black Box Problem Revisited. Real and Imaginary Challenges for Automated Legal Decision Making' (2023) Artificial Intelligence and Law.

12 Matthew Dahl and others, 'Large Legal Fictions: Profiling Legal Hallucinations in Large Language Models' (2024) Journal of Legal Analysis 64.

Moreover, in contrast to rule-based approaches, these systems are opaque by design and don't allow a verification of the process that led to the final output. The unreliability and nonexplainable nature of LLMs undermines the trust in their outputs, especially in critical legal applications where the motivations behind decisions are crucial.

### 1.3 *A Hybrid Approach*

Conscious of the strengths and constraints just described, we decided to take a hybrid approach and leverage the advantages of both AI paradigms.[13]

By integrating LLMs into legal expert platform we can address the communicability issues inherent in rule-based systems. While the latter excels in formalizing law with justifiable precision, LLMs enhance the usability of these systems by ensuring that their outputs are understandable to a broader audience. This symbiotic relationship between rule-based logic and LLMs creates a comprehensive tool that not only maintains the rigor of legal formalization but also makes it accessible and practical for all users, expert and layperson alike.

LLMs, with their advanced generative AI capabilities, can facilitate the incorporation of extensive domain knowledge into the system while maintaining the advantages of reliable legal reasoning and explanation inherent to logic-based methods.

The following paragraphs will first introduce the technologies applied to this project and explain how they were utilized for different tasks. In the second paragraph, we will outline the general legal principles behind the formalization of the law and their application to the current domain. The third paragraph will describe the integration of LLMs in the architecture and the conclusive paragraph will explain how everything was linked together in the available platform.

## 2 The Modelling of Norms

### 2.1 *General Principles of Modelling*

In this section, we will showcase the development of the rule-base layer of the Facilex advisory module, which provides the automation of reasoning within the entire system.

13 Marco Billi, Alessandro Parenti, Marco Sanchi and Giuseppe Pisano, 'A hybrid approach for accessible rule-based reasoning through large language models' (2024) Proceedings of JURISIN.

Among the legislation under study in the project, we concentrated on the provisions concerning the grounds for refusal of EAW, EIO, and EU freezing and confiscation orders. We chose these specific provisions due to their suitability for automation and their practical utility compared to other provisions. These rules consist of well-defined conditions for applying a norm, making them ideal for direct user queries.

We started the development of the rule-based system by building a computable representation of the targeted provisions following the methodology established for the CrossJustice project.[14] For this reason, we have used the same programming language, Prolog.

During this discussion, we will focus on the relevant legal requirements to be considered while modelling different legal sources, which have first been introduces as far back as 1992:[15]

– *Isomorphism*, defined as one-to-one correspondence between norms in the formal model and natural language. This is achieved by representing each paragraph from each article individually and visually separated from the others, so that all grounds of refusal are kept distinct. For example, let's look at the formalization of Art 3(3) of Decision 2002/584, which states that Member States shall refuse to execute the EAW "*if* (1) *the person who is the subject of the European arrest warrant* (2) *may not, owing to his age, be held criminally responsible for the acts on which the arrest warrant is based under the law of the executing State.*" This specific paragraph is represented in Fig. 1 by a specific and corresponding prolog rule that is identified with the label of the article number [article3_3].

– In lines 1–3 of Fig. 1, we can see that there are two conditions for applying the article. First, that the matter concerns the EAW, second that the person is not considered criminally responsible. There are two sub rules connected, although only one is shown.

The first sub-rule (*eaw_matter*) is verified when certain conditions are fulfilled, such as declaring that the offence is covered by arts 2(2) or 2(4), that there exists an issuing authority, and an executing authority, and that the proceedings fall under the scope of Art 1. This is not shown in Fig. 1.

14 Giuseppe Contissa, Giulia Lasagni, Michele Caianiello and Giovanni Sartor (eds), *Effective protection of the rights of the accused in the EU directives: a computable approach to criminal procedure law* (Brill, 2022).

15 T.J.M. Bench-Capon and Frans P. Coenen, 'Isomorphism and legal knowledge based systems' (1992) 3 Artificial Intelligence and Law.

```
mandatory_refusal(article3_3, ExecutingMemberState,
europeanArrestWarrant):

       eaw_matter(PersonId, IssuingMemberState, ExecutingMemberState,
Offence),

       person_status(PersonId, under_age, ExecutingMemberState).

person_status(PersonId, under_age, ExecutingMemberState):-

       person_age(PersonId, Age),

       Age < 14,

       executing_member_state(ExecutingMemberState).
```

FIGURE 1 Formalization of art.3(3) Decision 2002/584

The second condition (*person_status*) is shown from lines 4–7, and states that a person is considered criminally responsible when the age is above the threshold chosen by the executing member as the age of criminal responsibility.

Therefore, although multiple sub-rules are considered, all are referred to a single paragraph of Art 3 to preserve isomorphism.

- *Reification*: rules representing legal norms need to be treated as objects that feature different properties regulated by other rules. This allows different aspects of legal systems such as jurisdiction, authority or temporal properties. In the Facilex representation, such properties are formalized only when specifically required by the norm.

  Let's consider the provision of Art 4(4) of Decision 2002/584. This provides that executing authorities may refuse to apply an EAW *"where the criminal prosecution or punishment of the requested person is statute-barred according to the law of the executing Member State and the acts fall within the jurisdiction of that Member State under its own criminal law";*

  Although, generally, the jurisdiction of each state is not part of our representation, it's been explicitly stated in this article as a condition for the application of this rule. This is the only article where jurisdiction is an explicit part of the representation.

Let us now consider temporal properties of rules. We can distinguish between the external time of a rule (when a rule is in force), and its internal time (temporal issues involved in the application of a norm). The former is never explicitly formalized because there's the assumption that a rule which has been transposed is valid. The latter, instead, is captured in the modelling. For example, consider Art 18-*bis* (2-2*bis*) of the Italian Provisions to adapt national legislation to the Council Framework Decision 2002/584/JHA of 13 June 2002 on the European arrest warrant and the surrender procedures between Member States, which transposes Art 4(6) of Decision 2002/584. The article states that

```
optional_refusal(article18bis_2, MemberState, europeanArrestWarrant):-
        [...]
        person_continuous_residence(PersonId, ExecutingMemberState, Time),
        Time >= 5,
```

FIGURE 2 Partial formalization of art. 18bis(2) of Italian legislation

```
exception(optional_refusal(article4a_1_a, ExecutingMemberState,
europeanArrestWarrant), _)
```

FIGURE 3 The formalization of exceptions

*When the European arrest warrant has been issued* [...], *the Court of Appeal may refuse to surrender of the Italian citizen or of a person who lawfully and effectively resides continuously for at least five years on the Italian territory,* [...]. In this case, the period of five years must be specifically considered, and the result is the following:

In Fig. 2 you can see a partial formalization of the article. The internal time is formalized as a variable, "Time", and must possess a value greater than 5, showing that at least 5 years of continuous residence must have passed.

- Finally, we will consider *defeasibility*. Briefly, this means providing the means to solve conflicts between rules. Rules, in fact, may have incompatible legal effects, that can be resolved through rule priorities, such as: lex specialis (which gives priority to the most specific rule), lex superior (which gives priority to the rule from the higher authority), lex posterior (which gives priority to the rule enacted later). The same logic applies to exclusionary rules, which are rules that provide a way to explicitly undercut other rules, making them inapplicable. We represent it by employing the Prolog based syntax for defining negation as failure. In our formalization (Fig. 3), this is achieved by having a specific predicate, called "exception" which is aimed at defining all those cases where a rule may not be applied.

For example, the conditions in Arts 4(a)(1)(a) and following in Decision 2002/584 are exceptions to the application of Art 4(a)(1). From the technical perspective, exceptions are represented as meta rules containing other rules. When an exception is valid, it prevents the contained rule from succeeding.

- The final legal requirement, which has been introduced by us due to the scope of this project, is "*harmonization.*" In the following section, we will explore in detail how European and national legal sources have been formalized and combined for a better outcome, to provide the user with an overview of the applicable grounds for refusal.

### 2.2 *Framework Decision 2002/584*

For this section, we refer to the EU provision in Fig. 1 above and showcase how that is transposed under Italian and French law.

As shown in Fig. 4 below, the transpositions feature a general rule reflecting the general EU decision provision, as well as an additional rule where the age of criminal responsibility is introduced. As we can see from the computable representation, the age of criminal responsibility is different in between France and Italy (14 in Italy, 13 in France).

It is interesting to note that, whenever the conditions allow it, 2 articles related to the same ground of refusal may simultaneously apply. Take for example a citizen of age 13, who is the subject of a European arrest warrant from France to Italy. In that case, our system will apply the Art 3(3), as well as the Italian transposition, thus showing that Italy has perfectly implemented the European article. If the issuing and executing state were reversed, as the age of criminal responsibility is respected in France, no grounds of refusal apply.

The process of harmonization, when this legal framework is considered, is grounded on the fact that the European Union leaves areas where national states are free to legislate, such as setting the age of criminal responsibility. This can be achieved by either (a) having an additional rule formalizing the conditions each state applies (as seen in the example above); or (b) by having

```
mandatory_refusal(article18_1_c, italy, europeanArrestWarrant):-
        eaw_matter(PersonId, IssuingMemberState, italy, Offence),
        person_status(PersonId, under_age, italy).
person_status(PersonId, under_age, italy):-
        person_age(PersonId, Age),
        Age < 14,
        executing_member_state(Italy).
_____________
mandatory_refusal(article695_22_3, france, europeanArrestWarrant):-
        eaw_matter(PersonId, IssuingMemberState, france, Offence),
        person_status(PersonId, under_age, france).
person_status(PersonId, under_age, france):-
        person_age(PersonId, Age),
        Age < 13,
        executing_member_state(france).
```

FIGURE 4 French and Italian transposition of art.3(3) Decision 2002/584

a predicate that the user must select to identify an event in the executing member state, when the formalization results too complex to be captured. For example, Art 4(4) of Decision 2002/584 states that an optional ground of refusal applies "*where the criminal prosecution or punishment of the requested person is statute-barred according to the law of the executing Member State and the acts fall within the jurisdiction of that Member State under its own criminal law*".

In this case the highlighted information is formalized as a single predicate, which the user must select ["executing_proceeding_status(Offence, ExecutingMemberState, statute_barred)"]. Another way to achieve the same result would have been to have additional rules which calculate the time passed for the crime committed, and then compare it to the legal requirement for each offence, in each of the Member States. We thought that such formalization would have been too time consuming and falls outside the scope of the formalization.

### 2.3 *Directive 2014/41*

To showcase the formalization of Directive 2014/41, let us take a look at Art 11(1)(c), which states that Member States may refuse to execute the European Investigation Order when "*the EIO has been issued in proceedings referred to in Article 4(b) and (c) and the investigative measure would not be authorized under the law of the executing State in a similar domestic case*".

The first difference we can highlight, between the Decision and the Directive, is that we have changed one of the main variables needed to apply the EIO. When verifying whether the matter concerns the application of the Directive, we ask the user to insert the "Measure" needed by the issuing Member State, instead of the offence committed by the person as we do for EAWs. As the focus of the legal source is different, we decided to reflect the same change in our formalization, as the alleged offence is accessory, and the requested measure is the main objective of the EIO.

Let us now showcase the way the connection between European sources and national sources has been formalized in our representation. As we can see from Fig. 5, the directive often leaves room for Member States to decide on their own when a measure is authorized [national_law_does_not_authorize].

Let us consider, for example, the case of Portugal. According to Arts 188 and 189 of the code of criminal procedure, in case of interception of telecommunications, the judge is the only authority that may authorize the measure.

This is transposed in our formalization as shown below.

It is important to note that the goal of this rule is not the ground of refusal itself, but one of the conditions for the application of the ground of refusal

```
optional_refusal(article11_1_c, ExecutingMemberState, europeanInvestigationOrder):-
    eio_matter(IssuingMemberState, ExecutingMemberState, Measure),
    (
        art4_b_applies
    ;   art4_c_applies
    ),
    national_law_does_not_authorize(ExecutingMemberState, Measure),
    \+ exception(optional_refusal(article11_1_c, ExecutingMemberState,
europeanInvestigationOrder), _).
```

FIGURE 5 Formalization of Art 11(1)(c) Directive 2014/41

```
national_law_does_not_authorize(portugal, interception_of_telecommunications):-
        eio_matter(IssuingMemberState, portugal, Measure),
        issuing_authority(interception_of_telecommunications, IssuingAut),
        validating_authority(interception_of_telecommunications, ValidatingAut),
        ValidatingAut \= judge_or_court.
```

FIGURE 6 Conditions ex. Arts 188–189 Portuguese code of Criminal Proc.

contained in the European Directive. In particular, the last three conditions showed in Fig. 6 implement the prohibition of executing interception of telecommunications under Portuguese law when the authority validating the measure is different from a judge or a court. This Portuguese provision is integrated within the system so that when that is satisfied, it automatically triggers the application of Art 11(1)(c) of the EIO D.

Such a system enables a direct connection between national and European rules, favoring a harmonized view of the entire framework. By aligning the execution of the EIO with the specific legal conditions of each Member State, the formalization ensures that national legal standards are respected while promoting a single procedural framework across the EU. This allows each state's sovereignty and legal traditions to be preserved. Additionally, it mitigates potential conflicts by preemptively addressing discrepancies, thus showing a single outcome, instead of multiple, when the national rule is explicitly called by the European directive.

### 2.4 *Regulation 1805/2018*

As far as Regulation 1805/2018 is concerned, the discussion is brief. As the legal source is directly applicable in the Member States, there should theoretically be no issues in the harmonization of the Regulation.

Nonetheless, the same topics presented in the earlier chapters still apply. The regulation often sets as a condition a matter to be evaluated by the judicial authority of the executing member state, such as the principle of ne bis in idem. The formalization follows the same techniques presented above, by either adding rules contained in the member states, when requested by the regulation, or expanding the meaning/definition of certain matters, when national laws differ.

Something that should be clarified is that there's one condition, set by all European legal sources, which we found to be particularly troublesome. The ground for refusal applying when "*the conduct in connection* [to the instrument] *does not constitute a criminal offence under the law of the executing State*" is present in all three sources (EAW FD, EIO D, Regulation 1805/2018) and has been transposed as a simple "national_law_not_offence(Offence, ExecutingMemberState)". This is mainly because an automatic recognition of whether a conduct constitutes an offence is a member state falls outside the scope of this formalization, as it would require a completely different set of rules to be studied and collected.

The only exception to this consists in the offences contained in Art 2(2) EAW FD, Annex D EIO D and Art 3(1) Regulation 1805/2018. When an offence falls under one of these cases it is excluded from the verification of double criminality, and therefore, there is no need to verify whether the conduct constitutes a crime.

### 2.5 *Modelling of Case-Law (and Struggles)*

When dealing with the harmonization of the legal framework, it's essential to consider more than just European and national laws. Case law can play an important role in identifying how rules are to be applied. In particular, it is extremely useful when it specifies further requirements for the implementation in practice of EU provisions, rather than when it mechanically applies them.

Transposing case law into a harmonized legal framework, however, presents significant challenges, primarily due to the inherent complexity of extracting pertinent information from judicial decisions. Case law is context-specific and often contains varied interpretations contingent on each case's unique circumstances.

The extraction of universally applicable principles from case law is a difficult task due to the specificity and complexity of individual cases. We tasked legal experts with analyzing each case to generalize essential legal principles across different jurisdictions, especially when it relates to a ground of refusal, following the template below:

> The case concerns the crime of [name of the offence] provided by [e.g. art x, criminal code] and is referred to the [EIO/EAW/REG 1805]. The countries involved in the cooperation procedure are [x] and [x]. In the case, the relevant ground for refusal(s) is/are [use the same wording of the EU legislation]. The main facts relevant to the case, that triggered the application (or potential application) of the ground for refusal are: [e.g. the person to be surrendered is a citizen/there is a proceeding on the same facts that has concluded with a final decision/etc ...]. Against all these factors, the court concluded that ... [summary of the conclusion of the court].

Following this methodology, we could find some rules that increased our understanding of the conditions necessary for the application of certain grounds of refusal. For example, Bulgarian sentence n. 21/2023 provided that: "*serving the sentence in the country of origin, namely Bulgaria, is related to the principle of humanity and humane treatment as far as the requested person will be placed in a prison near her permanent residence in order to maintain social contact between her and her family.*". We can transpose the information above as stating that, whenever the person requires to stay near his family, this will be considered as humane treatment of the person, therefore fulfilling one of the conditions for applying Art 4(6) of EAW FD. The formalization of this rule can be seen in Fig. 7.

Although this specific task yielded some interesting results, overall, it presented several limiting challenges. For instance, the variability of judicial reasoning and the intricate fact patterns that always feature a court case greatly complicate this process. The summaries, in fact, were always influenced by the expert's interpretation of the legal issues and often struggled to provide homogenous information. Moreover, the result often concerned the application of general national principles or procedural rules, which falls outside the purpose of our formalization. Another critical point is that case law on the

```
caselaw(article4_6, bulgaria, europeanArrestWarrant):-
      human_treatment(PersonId, MemberState).
human_treatment(PersonId, MemberState):-
      close_to_family(PersonId, MemberState).
```

FIGURE 7 Example of case law formalization

topic is quite limited, and extracting provisions that go beyond the mere application of national law has stymied our efforts in this task.

In the end, such manual summarization has proven to be time-consuming and potentially exacerbating the challenge of creating a harmonized legal framework, as this process demands significant human resources and expertise, limiting the efficient integration of case law into a cohesive legal system.

## 3 LLM Integration

### 3.1 *Architecture*

As outlined above, we implemented a hybrid architecture that leverages the strengths of both symbolic and sub-symbolic artificial intelligence to obtain a result that is at the same time verifiable and accessible. In particular, we employed Large Language Models to process the output produced by the rule-based system and gave it a form that is understandable to laypeople.

We use the GPT-4 model developed by Open-AI, in that it has proved to be the most effective and provides the highest percentage of positive performance.[16] We used an API to enable the setting of various parameters. We set the system's temperature to the lowest possible, i.e., 0. This minimizes the system's tendency to be creative and generate words or sentences that do not strictly derive from the knowledge provided by the user.

At the center of the methodology is the creation of a prompt carrying all the necessary information and instruction needed by the LLM to carry out its task. This includes two main elements.

First, the output of the rule-based system. This consists of a prolog tree indicating the rules that were applied to solve the specific scenario. As described in section 2, the Facilex automated reasoning system focuses on the regulation of the grounds of refusal of EAW, EIO, Freezing Order (FO) and Confiscation Order (CO), as defined by EU legislation. Therefore, the output of the system describes if and which ground of refusal applies together with all the satisfied conditions that led to the application. This is presented in a prolog tree indicating the rules applied, written in the prolog programming language.

The second part of the prompt features the command given to the LLM. The task is described, giving exact instructions on the content and form requested, and on the procedure to be followed to carry it out. As anticipated, our goal is

16 See <https://huggingface.co/spaces/lmsys/chatbot-arena-leaderboard> accessed 18 June 2024.

to obtain a transposition (or explanation) in natural language of the of the outcome provided by the rule-based system, thus allowing understanding for end users regardless of their IT expertise. This means providing the main result, i.e., whether and which ground of refusal apply. Moreover, in order for this explanation to be exhaustive and effective in giving a full understanding of the legal situation to the users, it should also include the reasoning behind the application of the ground of refusal in connection with the specific scenario provided.

### 3.2 *Prompt Engineering and Challenges*

We encountered several issues. An initial challenge was to obtain a fixed structure in the output, which was often presented in different formatting (e.g., bullet lists, numbered lists, free-form text). We found that it was necessary to give a fixed structure for the LLM to follow, in order to decrease the degree of variance between answers and maximise repeatability and reliability.

Second, we noticed a propensity to miss and not mention key facts part of the specific scenario. To address this, we included in the prompt the requirement for the LLM to take into consideration all legal terms and facts from the scenario, and to refer to those when building the explanation.

Finally, the most challenging aspect was to overcome the tendency of the model to ascribe meaning to legal text where not explicitly mentioned nor provided. Often, meaning was guessed based on the most general significance, disregarding the specificity of juridical norms and legal lexicon.

Trying to address all these challenges we engineered the prompt shown in Fig. 8. The LLM is provided with a clear structure to follow (Summary, What, Why). Moreover, the prompt stresses the importance of referencing all the Prolog terms found in the tree, which also include the part of the factual scenario.

```
You have been provided a Prolog inference tree using a legal norm in a specific
case (Prolog Tree). Provide the following info according to the given structure:

  -  Summary : simplified text of the legal norm . Use everyday language with a
     serious register . Add any information you have on the source of law;
  -  What grounds of refusal apply : what kind of grounds of refusal apply
     (mandatory or optional), if any, according to the Prolog explanation;
  -  Why do they apply : inference steps and reasoning that led to the grounds of
     refusal. Use all the Prolog terms in the explanation explicitly referencing
     the original Prolog when needed. Ignore empty Prolog variables (_number).

Use enumerations in the ' What grounds of refusal apply ' and ' Why do they apply'
sections if needed.
```

FIGURE 8 Natural language explanation prompt

### 3.3 Implementation

For exemplification purposes, we will now demonstrate the functioning of the LLM integration using a real-world scenario. Consider the following legal case inspired by a real court case: Seydou is a boy born in France on January 1, 2010, to Ivorian parents and residing in Bobigny. On the evening of December 31, 2023, together with a group of friends, he committed the crime of theft of spirits. After being caught and temporarily released by the French police under the custody of his parents, Seydou was taken to Italy by his parents to distance him from bad company. The French authorities, having identified Seydou through security cameras, issued a European arrest warrant.

Such a case can be submitted to the Facilex platform to identify which, if any, grounds of refusal may apply to the EAW issued for Seydou. After issuing all the necessary information related to the case, the system will return an outcome as shown in Fig. 9. This indicates the grounds for mandatory refusal according to Art 3(3) of EAW FD. It also includes a Prolog tree that outlines all the inference steps taken by the system to reach this conclusion.

Clearly, however, the output is not intelligible to the average user. While it mainly features natural language terms, these follow a form and syntax specific to the Prolog programming language, which is opaque to non-IT experts.

To improve the readability of this output and make it accessible to laypeople, we feed it to an LLM along with the prompt described above.

The resulting output is notable and shown in Fig. 10. The LLM organizes its output according to the given structure: first, it provides a summary of the applicable norm; second, it indicates the type of refusal ground; third, it details all the inference steps that led to the application of this refusal ground. In doing so, the LLM explicitly references the Prolog terms present in the original output, as requested, enabling the verification of the answer. This last part is particularly significant as it allows the user not only to understand the applied provision but also how the specific elements of the scenario influenced the outcome. Lastly, the answer included a summary of the legal case and its solution at the end.

In this specific case, Art 3(3) of EAW FD finds application. This provides that a European arrest warrant must be refused when the person who committed the crime cannot be considered criminally responsible under the law of the executing state. In our scenario, Seydou was 13 when he committed the crime, while the threshold for criminal responsibility according to Italian law is 14.

To conclude, the LLM respected the guidelines given as to the form of the output, regarding both the structure and the lexicon of the answer. Moreover, the answer is also juridically correct. On the one hand, it reports all the information present in the Prolog output and, most importantly, it does not include

```
[mandatory_refusal(article3_3,italy,europeanArrestWarrant),[eaw_matter(seydou,franc
e,italy,theft),[issuing_proceeding(france,_7966,seydou),[issuing_member_state(franc
e),[system_predicate],person_role(seydou,subject_eaw),[system_predicate]],offence_t
ype(theft),[system_predicate],art2_2applies(theft),[system_predicate],executing_pro
ceeding(italy,seydou,criminal_prosecution),[executing_member_state(italy),[system_p
redicate],executing_proceeding_purpose(seydou,criminal_prosecution),[system_predica
te],system_predicate,person_role(seydou,subject_eaw),[system_predicate]]],person_st
atus(seydou,under_age,italy),[person_age(seydou,13),[system_predicate],system_predi
cate,executing_member_state(italy),[system_predicate]]]]
```

FIGURE 9 Facilex platform's output

```
Summary
The legal norm concerns Article 3(3) of the European Arrest Warrant (EAW) Framework Decision
2002/584/JHA, which allows for mandatory refusal of an EAW if the person sought is under the age of
criminal responsibility according to the law of the executing member state. In this case, the executing
member state is Italy, and the individual involved is Seydou, who is 13 years old. The EAW was issued by
France for the crime of theft.

What grounds of refusal apply
The ground of refusal that applies in this case is **mandatory refusal** according to Article 3(3) of
the European Arrest Warrant Framework Decision.

Why do they apply
1. **Issuing Proceeding (issuing_proceeding(france,_7966,seydou))**: France has issued an EAW for Seydou
in relation to the crime of theft.
   - **Issuing Member State (issuing_member_state(france))**: The EAW is issued by France.
   - **Person Role (person_role(seydou,subject_eaw))**: Seydou is the subject of the EAW.
   - **Offence Type (offence_type(theft))**: The EAW concerns the offence of theft.
   - **Art2_2 Applies (art2_2applies(theft))**: Theft falls under the offences listed in Article 2(2) of
the EAW Framework Decision.

2. **Executing Proceeding (executing_proceeding(italy,seydou,criminal_prosecution))**: Italy is the
executing member state where the EAW is being considered for execution.
   - **Executing Member State (executing_member_state(italy))**: Italy is responsible for executing the
EAW.
   - **Executing Proceeding Purpose (executing_proceeding_purpose(seydou,criminal_prosecution))**: The
purpose of the proceeding is criminal prosecution.

3. **Person Status (person_status(seydou,under_age,italy))**: Seydou is classified as under age
according to Italian law.
   - **Person Age (person_age(seydou,13))**: Seydou is 13 years old.
   - **Executing Member State (executing_member_state(italy))**: Italy's laws apply in determining the
age of criminal responsibility.

The mandatory ground for refusal applies because Seydou, at 13 years old, is below the age of criminal
responsibility in Italy. Under Article 3(3) of the EAW Framework Decision, Italy must refuse to execute
the EAW issued by France for the criminal prosecution of Seydou for theft, as he is not considered
legally responsible for criminal actions under Italian law.
```

FIGURE 10 LLM's transposition to natural language

any self-generated facts or information. This methodology proved successful in improving accessibility to the Facilex system, while preserving the soundness and trustworthiness of the underlying rule-based reasoning.

## 4 Platform Integration

### 4.1 *User Interface*

To conclude, we will demonstrate the practical application of this system. As previously discussed, we have formalized several rules in a programming language to represent European and national legal sources. However, executing these rules successfully requires specific conditions to be met, which is where the user interface becomes essential. By accessing the Facilex Advisory Module through this link[17] users can input all relevant facts related to their scenario by answering the platform's questions. Based on this information, the tool can analyze all relevant European and national legal norms and present inferred solutions with a detailed assessment. Each question is linked to a single Prolog fact, and, through the answer, the fact is adjusted to be tailored to the user.

The questions have been (mostly) taken from the annexes provided by the European Union, at the foot of the legislative document. These represent the official form that authorities must fill in when issuing the request for the instrument. To these questions, we have added others which are essential for applying the specific grounds of refusal.

The first questions are general, and are used to determine which further questions should be displayed to the user:

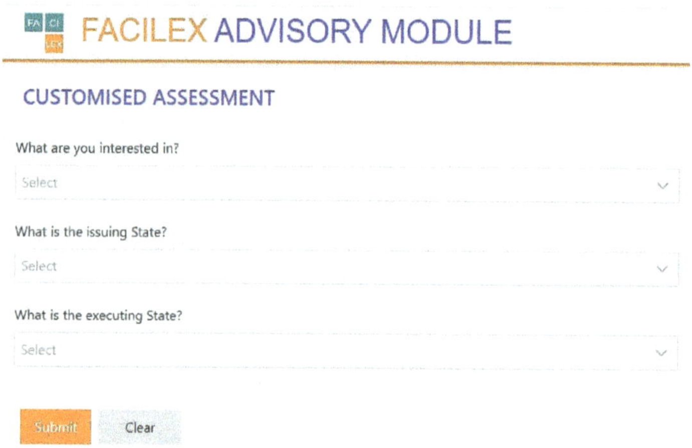


FIGURE 11 User interface: general questions

The user shall select which legal instrument he's interested in, and then select the issuing and executing state. As these questions should be answered every time the platform is called upon, they are mandatory. All other questions are optional, although failure to provide answers may result in the platform being unable to generate a positive outcome.

17 See Facilex Advisory Module <https://facilex-tool.eu/Advisory/customised-assessment> (2024) accessed 18 June 2024.

If we were to select "European Arrest Warrant" as the instrument, the following questions would be asked, which represent points (a) and (e) of the Annex on EAW.

In some cases, the information is inserted as free text (e.g, the person's name). Other times, instead, the user is restricted to a multiple-choice answer, such as in the representation of point (e) of the Annex. This is because, while the person's name can have a random value, the list of offences must be confined to those analyzed by legal experts.

To elaborate, a variable can be substituted with any value and remain valid. However, there are rules that apply only to specific offences and are included in our formalization's logic. This makes the precise naming of the offense crucial for our purpose.

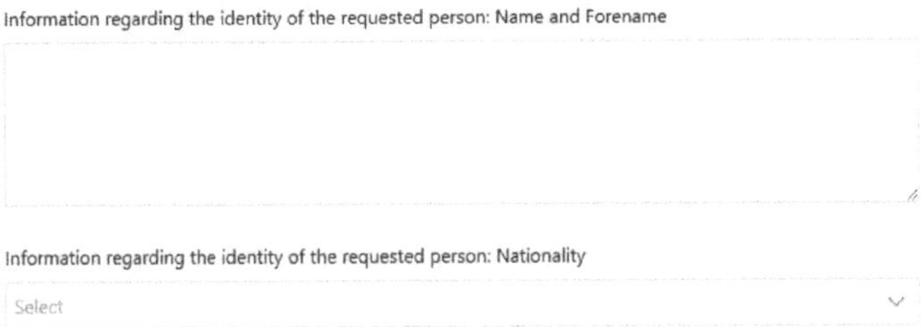


FIGURE 12 User interface: annex point (a)

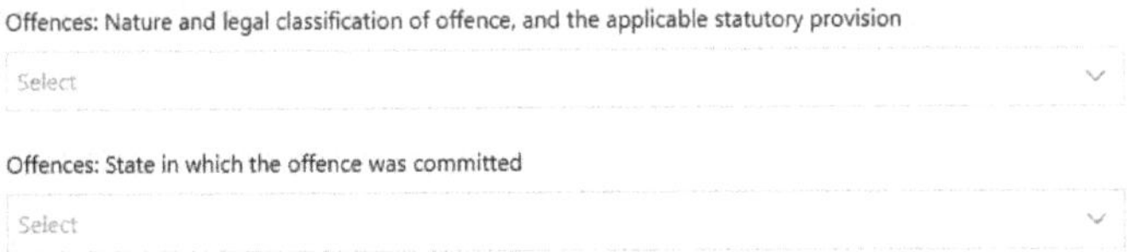


FIGURE 13 User interface: annex point (b)

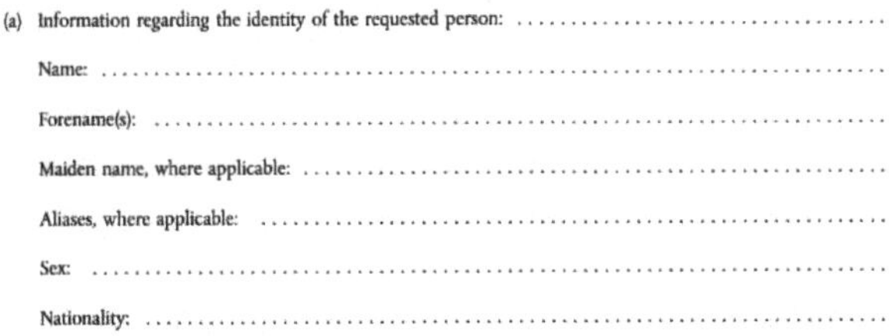
(a) Information regarding the identity of the requested person: ....................

Name: ....................

Forename(s): ....................

Maiden name, where applicable: ....................

Aliases, where applicable: ....................

Sex: ....................

Nationality: ....................

FIGURE 14 Annex point (a)

(e) Offences:

This warrant relates to in total: ............................ offences.

Description of the circumstances in which the offence(s) was (were) committed, including the time, place and degree of participation in the offence(s) by the requested person:

...............................................................................

...............................................................................

...............................................................................

Nature and legal classification of the offence(s) and the applicable statutory provision/code:

...............................................................................

...............................................................................

...............................................................................

...............................................................................

...............................................................................

FIGURE 15 Annex point (e)

Is the offence covered by amnesty in the executing Member State?

Yes

No

FIGURE 16 User interface: amnesty question

Additionally, we include questions beyond those provided in the annex, which are necessary for the executing member state to determine whether any grounds for refusal exist. For example, the user may be asked to consider if the offense in question is covered by amnesty.

The intended user of this platform is the authority in the executing member state who receives the EAW (or another instrument) and is deliberating on its execution. There are certain grounds that apply only based on questions connected to the annex, while others need additional information to be provided, such as amnesty.

One limitation of this approach is that the system heavily relies on the legal knowledge of the user to answer certain questions. While a few conditions are straightforward, most require at least some familiarity with legal terminology and concepts. This restricts the user base to those with relevant expertise, such as authorities involved in drafting the instrument or lawyers seeking support for their clients.

Finally, once the system evaluates the outcome, the solution presented in §3.3 is displayed.

## 5 Concluding Remarks

In this chapter we have shown the results obtained by combining two approaches in the domain of legal informatics. The Facilex project integrates these approaches to address the formalization of grounds of refusal in the three mutual recognition instruments, effectively applying legal rules and explaining them in natural language. This project harnesses old and new technologies to perform various tasks that are essential to legal informatics.

Firstly, we introduced the technologies applied in this project, explaining their use for different tasks. Subsequently, we outlined the general legal principles behind the formalization of the law and demonstrated their application in the current domain. Furthermore, we described the integration of LLMs within the architecture, highlighting their role in enhancing the project's capabilities.

The Facilex project exemplifies reliability and trustworthiness, standing out as an innovation in the field. This integrated approach not only ensures accuracy and precision but also enhances accessibility and comprehension for users. Additionally, this effort is essential in harmonizing the cooperation of states in mutual recognition instruments, facilitating smoother cross-border legal interactions. In conclusion, the Facilex platform represents a significant advancement in legal informatics, offering a robust and innovative solution for the formalization and application of legal principles.

CHAPTER 17

# Harmonizing Legal Terminology and Case Law Retrieval in European and National Legislation

*Davide Audrito, Ivan Spada, Rachele Mignone, Emilio Sulis, Luigi Di Caro, Eduard-Raul Kontos and Rohan Nanda*

## 1 Introduction

In legal informatics,[1] the effort to analyse the phenomenon of legal harmonization in the European Union (EU) has been the subject of research in recent years.[2] The EU has gained experience in harmonizing domestic legislation with the legal acts of its own legal order.[3] In this context, a relevant issue concerns the theoretical development and partial implementation of both a Harmonized Glossary and a Harmonization Index. The current Chapter explores the topic based on the efforts developed in the European project "Facilex", hereafter referred to as FX, which can be considered an extension of a previous project "CrossJustice" (CJ).[4]

Harmonization is a complex process at both vertical and horizontal levels, based on the EU's decision-making processes and the implementation process within national systems. From a formal perspective, pursuant to Art 288 of the Treaty on the Functioning of the European Union (TFEU), a directive binds the Member State to which it is addressed regarding the result to be achieved while leaving the choice of form and methods to national authorities. Consequently, directives serve as the primary legislative instrument driving the process of legal harmonization in Europe, although framework decisions and regulations also play a role. It is not uncommon for such instruments to also require implementing measures that transpose their content into the legal systems of the

1 Daniel M. Katz, Ron Dolin, and Michael J. Bommarito, Legal Informatics (2021).

2 Luigi Di Caro and others, 'EU Directives Implementation: Automated Analysis of Complexity and Harmonization' in Effective Protection of the Rights of the Accused in the EU Directives (2022) 309–328".

3 Gerda Falkner, 'Complying with Europe: EU Harmonisation and Soft Law in the Member States' (2005).

4 CrossJustice Project: <https://www.crossjustice.eu/en/index.html> accessed 28 april 2024.

 | DOI:10.1163/9789004705791_019

Member States.[5] Therefore, the nature of EU legislative sources demonstrates the interdependence between European and national laws and the EU motto "United in diversity".[6]

On this topic, some recent efforts in the field of legal informatics have proposed work in several areas, including semantic search[7,8] similarity computation[9,10] and ontologies.[11]

This work contributes to research in this area and proposes a practical application in a real case study. This Chapter is divided into two main parts, focusing on creating a Harmonized Glossary and Harmonization Index and on the identification of relevant case law in relation to the EU mutual recognition instruments in criminal matters. The last section, together with the conclusions, presents some possible future work.

## 2 Harmonized Glossary and Harmonization Index

This portion of the Chapter delves into the creation of a Harmonized Glossary and the calculation of a Harmonization Index. In particular, the first section explores the initial dataset used for our research, which consists of Transposition Tables (TT) manually created by legal experts within the FX project. These tables contain relevant European legislation and the aligned Member States' transposing legislation, adopted to comply with the requirements established at the European level.

5 Paul Voigt, Axel Von Dem Bussche, 'Practical Implementation of the Requirements under the GDPR' in The EU General Data Protection Regulation (GDPR): A Practical Guide (2017) 245–249.

6 Jurgita Malinauskaite, 'EU Conceptual Framework of Harmonisation: Setting the Scene' in Harmonisation of EU Competition Law Enforcement (2020) 39–79.

7 Ivan Spada and others, 'Adopting Video-Recordings to Extract Embedded Domain Knowledge and Automate Legal Case Reading' in *Proceedings of Workshop on Annotation of Legal Data* (in press, 2023).

8 Roger Ferrod and others, 'Pairing EU Directives and Their National Implementing Measures: A Dataset for Semantic Search' (2023) 51 Computer Law & Security Review 105862.

9 Emilio Sulis and others, 'Exploiting textual similarity techniques in harmonization of laws.' In International Conference of the Italian Association for Artificial Intelligence (2021) 185–197.

10 Rachele Mignone and others, 'Augmented Reading and Similar Case Matching: from Legal Domain Experts' Modus Operandi to a Computational Pipeline' in Joint Ontology Workshops (2023).

11 Davide Audrito and others, 'Analogical Lightweight Ontology of EU Criminal Procedural Rights in Judicial Cooperation' (2023) 31 Artificial Intelligence and Law 629–652.

The second section describes the methodology, beginning with the creation of a manually crafted dataset suitable for modeling the glossary and the index. This dataset consists of concepts extracted from the EU Council Framework Decision on the European arrest warrant, hereinafter referred to as "EAW FD". These concepts are interrelated and modeled in a graph structure, employing a robust methodology. This initial effort lays the foundation for integrating the same or similar concepts enshrined in the national transposing legislation to provide a data representation suitable for assessing the degree of legislative harmonization throughout the European Union.

As a further step, the section outlines the methodology used to automate the analysis of legislative harmonization, based on the similarity comparison between EU legislation and corresponding national legislation, as well as between EU and national concepts therein codified. The deployed Natural Language Processing (NLP) techniques culminate in calculating an asymmetric similarity between legal texts. Based on this, a composite index approximates the level of harmonization achieved within our legislative corpus.

Finally, the third section outlines the initial results of the research work, pointing to future research opportunities and integrations.

## 2.1 *Dataset*

This study employs a comprehensive dataset designed for both manual and computational analysis, encompassing tables of European legislation and corresponding national transpositions, which have been accurately divided into articles and paragraphs. Since the tables include national legislation that is inherently multilingual, the entire dataset has been manually translated into English to facilitate uniform analysis. This data was also made available in JSON format making it machine-readable.

Figure 17 presents an excerpt of the Transposition Table and shows, on the left side, Art 1 EAW FD split into cells and, on the right side, the corresponding French transposing legal sources.

Despite the exhaustiveness of the TTs, some processing steps are required to enable effective computational analysis, such as applying textual similarity metrics to verify the semantic correspondence between European and domestic legislation, which represents a preliminary layer of legislative harmonization that excludes judicial interpretation, legal doctrine, and linguistic misalignments.

The purpose of our research is to delve into a deeper analytical level that is grounded on the extraction of concepts and their definitions from the

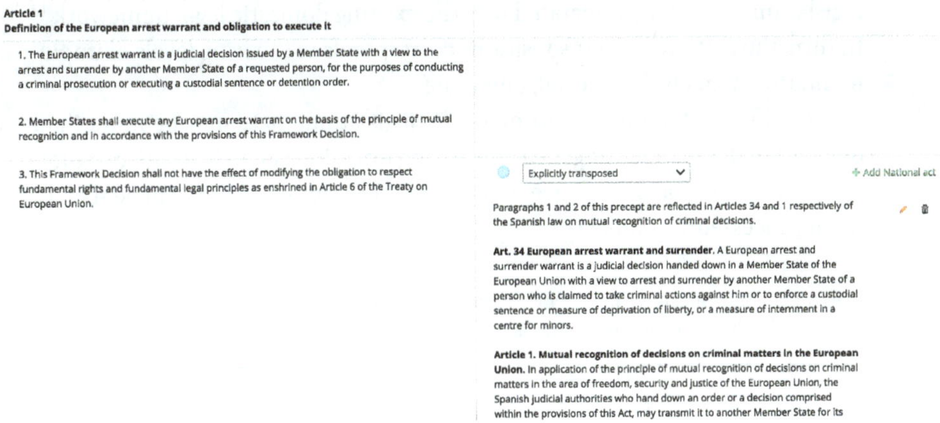

**Article 1**
**Definition of the European arrest warrant and obligation to execute it**

1. The European arrest warrant is a judicial decision issued by a Member State with a view to the arrest and surrender by another Member State of a requested person, for the purposes of conducting a criminal prosecution or executing a custodial sentence or detention order.

2. Member States shall execute any European arrest warrant on the basis of the principle of mutual recognition and in accordance with the provisions of this Framework Decision.

3. This Framework Decision shall not have the effect of modifying the obligation to respect fundamental rights and fundamental legal principles as enshrined in Article 6 of the Treaty on European Union.

Explicitly transposed

+ Add National act

Paragraphs 1 and 2 of this precept are reflected in Articles 34 and 1 respectively of the Spanish law on mutual recognition of criminal decisions.

**Art. 34 European arrest warrant and surrender.** A European arrest and surrender warrant is a judicial decision handed down in a Member State of the European Union with a view to arrest and surrender by another Member State of a person who is claimed to take criminal actions against him or to enforce a custodial sentence or measure of deprivation of liberty, or a measure of internment in a centre for minors.

**Article 1. Mutual recognition of decisions on criminal matters in the European Union.** In application of the principle of mutual recognition of decisions on criminal matters in the area of freedom, security and justice of the European Union, the Spanish judicial authorities who hand down an order or a decision comprised within the provisions of this Act, may transmit it to another Member State for its

FIGURE 17 Excerpt of Transposition Table (TT)
Transposition Table example

Transposition Tables in view to facilitate computational analysis. This alignment allows for precise comparative legal analysis, crucial for understanding the implementation patterns and discrepancies across different legal systems.

## 2.2 *Methodology*

This section will elaborate on the data structures used to facilitate the exploration of the dataset provided. Subsequently, the Harmonized Glossary will be formally defined and its implementation delved into. Concerning the latter, greater emphasis will be placed on the methodology employed for the extraction of concepts used to evaluate each national transposition measurement. The visualization of the Harmonized Glossary will be presented as a result of the above-mentioned extraction.

Finally, this section will present the definition and implementation of a Harmonization Index regarded as a metric for evaluating the similarity between transpositions.

### 2.2.1 Data Structures

The dataset has been processed into data structures to support its consultation. According to legal experts, there are two types of transpositions: explicit and implicit. Explicit transposition involves the adoption of *ad hoc* legislative measures aimed at incorporating EU legislation into the domestic legal system. In contrast, implicit transposition occurs when the provisions of EU legislation are already integrated into the existing domestic legal framework.[12] In turn, the category of transpositions corresponds to differing levels of implementation, namely full, partial, and none.

More in detail, for each portion of EU legislation, there may be more than one national implementing measure arising from diversified legislative or judicial sources. Such an imbalance in the number of transpositions can be seen in the reprocessed TT (Table 1).

TABLE 1 Transposition Tables (TT) reprocessed (an example where A, B, and C represent the national transpositions of Art1_par1)

| EU | ITA | ES | FR |
|---|---|---|---|
| Art1_par1 | A, B | A, B, C | C |

In order to make the work of legal professionals more efficient, we propose a structure of rapid detection of the effective implementation, even partial, of segments of European directives. The following Mapping Table (MT) identifies the presence or absence of national transpositions of the corresponding segment of the European directive:

TABLE 2 Mapping Table (MT) (example)

| EU | ITA | ES | FR | ... |
|---|---|---|---|---|
| Art1_par1 | 2 | 3 | 0 | ... |
| ... | ... | ... | ... | ... |

### 2.2.2 Harmonized Glossary

The Harmonized Glossary graph is a useful tool for quick and user-friendly identification of EU legal concepts, their national implementations, and their respective definitions. It consists of a network of EU concepts, Arts, and Council Frameworks manually extracted by legal domain experts from the Decision 2002/584.

12 Emilio Sulis and others, 'Exploiting textual similarity techniques in harmonization of laws' in International Conference of the Italian Association for Artificial Intelligence (2021) 185–197.

#### 2.2.2.1 *Theoretical Data Analysis and Manual Extraction*

The extraction of concepts from legal texts adheres to a meticulous process, according to the following three steps.

i. Legal experts, following a careful reading and examination of the text, systematically annotate terms indicating semantically significant concepts within the document, starting from the first normative provision. A concept is deemed relevant to the extent that its absence would significantly alter the meaning of the entire law or even just one of its paragraphs and is sufficiently specific to be determinative for the comprehension of the essential components of the law under scrutiny.

By way of illustration, Figure 18 portrays the annotation of concepts in the text of Art 1 of the EAW FD. The concept of "*European Arrest Warrant*" is fundamental because the term represents the final goal of the Framework Decision. Likewise, the *principle of mutual recognition* of judgments and judicial decisions, which lays the foundation of the European judicial cooperation in criminal matters under Art 82 of the Treaty on the Functioning of the European Union, is essential for the functioning of the mechanism of the EAW.

Further examples are provided to clarify the task. For instance, the concept of "entry into force" is not considered semantically relevant. This is indeed a permanent legislative arrangement indicating the scope of application *ratione temporis* of all legislative acts and lacking a meaning able to alter the semantic content of the text, despite its importance for the terms of validity of the norm. In contrast, concepts such as "terrorism," "human trafficking," or "corruption" are relevant to the EAW FD. These criminal offenses may result, in the absence of any other grounds for refusal, in the surrender of a sought-after person by the competent authorities of one Member State to another even if the offence is not provided in the same terms in the law of the executing Member State. The absence of any of these offenses would significantly alter the meaning of Art 2 of the Framework Decision.

Likewise, the concept of "fundamental rights" under Art 1(3) (Figure 18) will not be included in the extracted terminology, considering the broad scope of its meaning. The provision intends to underline that legislative requirements codified into the Framework Decision cannot have the effect of restricting obligations to comply with European fundamental rights. This can be considered a standard legal obligation of European laws aimed to reiterate the subordination of legislative sources to European founding Treaties and does not essentially contribute to defining the fabric of the EAW FD.

It is not essential for identified terms to be explicitly defined in the text because their collection occurs at a granularity level that reduces the risk of omitting useful concepts, albeit resulting in a significant increase of the

CHAPTER 1

**GENERAL PRINCIPLES**

*Article 1*

**Definition of the European arrest warrant and obligation to execute it**

1. The European arrest warrant is a judicial decision issued by a Member State with a view to the arrest and surrender by another Member State of a requested person, for the purposes of conducting a criminal prosecution or executing a custodial sentence or detention order.

2. Member States shall execute any European arrest warrant on the basis of the principle of mutual recognition and in accordance with the provisions of this Framework Decision.

3. This Framework Decision shall not have the effect of modifying the obligation to respect fundamental rights and fundamental legal principles as enshrined in Article 6 of the Treaty on European Union.

FIGURE 18 Concept annotation example

annotated corpus. However, mapping these undefined concepts enriches the semantic modeling of the textual content, yields a more comprehensive and accurate glossary of interconnected concepts, and potentially facilitates resource consultation.

ii. The second step of textual analysis involves the possible taxonomization of identified terms. In doing so, concepts of lesser scope are included in broader categories that facilitate their use for easier exploration and NLP purposes, specifically for automatic classification activities. This step allows an increase in the number of defined concepts and reduces those concepts without definitions, as shown in Figure 19 below.

This portion of text from Art 1(2) of the EAW FD lists the categories of offenses that, without verification of the double criminality of the act, give rise to the surrender of the requested person according to the EAW FD. The list of concepts is fundamental in the fabric of the judicial cooperation mechanism because Member States' competent authorities will have the obligation to surrender the requested person if charged with one of the listed offenses, notwithstanding the absence of double criminality (unless other grounds for refusal apply). However, the terms are not defined in the Framework Decision. Accordingly, instead of providing *ad hoc* definitions, the relevant concepts will be part of the broader definition of the concept "offense giving rise to surrender

2. The following offences, if they are punishable in the issuing Member State by a custodial sentence or a detention order for a maximum period of at least three years and as they are defined by the law of the issuing Member State, shall, under the terms of this Framework Decision and without verification of the double criminality of the act, give rise to surrender pursuant to a European arrest warrant:

— participation in a criminal organisation,

— terrorism,

— trafficking in human beings,

— sexual exploitation of children and child pornography,

— illicit trafficking in narcotic drugs and psychotropic substances,

— illicit trafficking in weapons, munitions and explosives,

— corruption,

— fraud, including that affecting the financial interests of the European Communities within the meaning of the Convention of 26 July 1995 on the protection of the European Communities' financial interests,

FIGURE 19 Specific concept annotation example

pursuant to the European Arrest Warrant". In so doing, the text of the definition will be suitable for NLP Tasks, including text similarity techniques. In the meantime, undefined concepts will be extracted for semantic web modeling efforts, including knowledge graphs and legal ontologies.

iii. In conclusion, the corpus of concepts must be validated. Two legal experts are involved in this task. A first annotator validates the concepts by repeating the procedure at least once on the same corpus. This task starts with the reading and examination of the clean, unmarked legislative text. A second annotator is engaged with assessing the results of the first annotator, according to the same procedure. A third annotator is involved in case of disagreement.

This approach achieves a positive and effective balance between the number of identified terms and the computational operability of the corpus of concepts and definitions. The result is a synergistic harmony conducive to robust legal scholarship and scholarly discourse within the legal domain. Indeed, within the Facilex project, this corpus of concepts and definitions proves suitable for concept classification tasks using similarity metrics. The ultimate

TABLE 3 Concept Table (CT) (example)

| EU | Concepts |
|---|---|
| Art1_par1_letA | concept1, concept2 |
| Art1_par1_letB | concept3 |
| Art1_par2 | concept4 |
| Art3 | concept5 |
| … | … |

TABLE 4 Concept Relation Table (CRT) (example)

| Concepts (from) | Relations | Concepts (to) |
|---|---|---|
| concept1 | relation1 | concept2 |
| concept1 | relation2 | concept3 |
| … | … | |

goal is to create a Harmonization Index capable of approximately measuring the semantic correspondence between EU legislative norms and national implementing measures. This tool is valuable for providing an overview of the applicable law in the Member States and assessing the conformity of national laws with the European legislative framework defined as Harmonization Mass Testing function.

The above-described process resulted in the creation of two tabular artifacts. The Concept Table (CT) containing the identified concepts and their location within the EAW FD (Table 3) is created as a support. Together with the Concept Relation Table (CRT), which contains binary relations between the concepts identified by legal-domain experts (Table 4), the CT is also used to create the graph described in the following sections. Employing this data structure, it is possible to interconnect concepts on both a topological and semantic basis.

#### 2.2.2.2 *Confidence Index*

Once the manual extraction of EU concepts is accomplished (see Table 3), the Mapping Table shows in which national legal systems the concepts have been possibly transposed. Following this step, it is possible to locate the national definitions within the transposed text and to evaluate the system's confidence in their identification.

This process results in the definition of the Confidence Index Table (CIT) concept:

TABLE 5 Confidence Index Table (CIT) (example)

| EU | Concepts | ITA | ES | FR | … |
|---|---|---|---|---|---|
| Art1_par1_letA | concept1 | 100% | 100% | 40% | … |
| Art1_par1_letA | concept2 | 70% | 30% | 20% | … |
| Art1_par1_letB | concept3 | 40% | 84% | 58% | … |
| Art1_par2 | concept4 | 55% | 70% | 70% | … |
| Art3 | concept5 | 20% | 100% | 100% | … |
| … | … | … | … | … | … |

#### 2.2.2.3 *Data Modeling*

Building upon the Concept Table (CT), and Concept Relation Table (CRT), the data is modeled using a Neo4j[13] graph as follows.

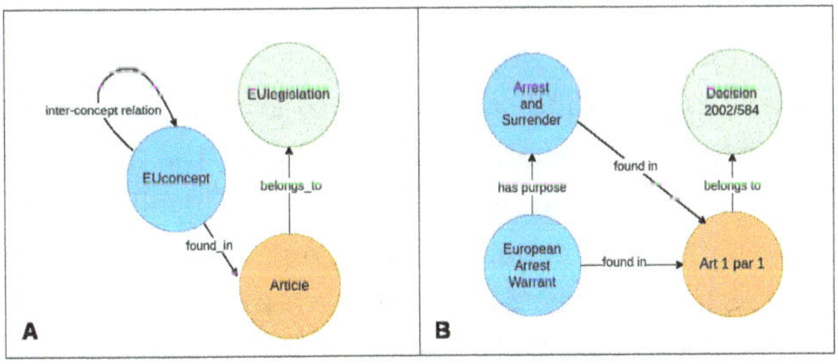


FIGURE 20 A) Neo4J schema B) Graph sample showcasing the Neo4J schema

Entities and relations in Figure 20 are described below.

Entities:

- EUCONCEPT represents the extracted concepts, interconnected through relations manually defined by legal domain experts. For every EUconcept node, the following attributes are defined:
  - ID: item identifier
  - NAME: full name of the concept as manually extracted by domain experts
  - SHORT_NAME: shortened name to be displayed on the node for readability reasons

13 Neo4j, Neo4j Graph Database (Neo4j, Inc 2024) <https://neo4j.com/> accessed 25 May 2024.

  - EU_DEFINITION: segment of the European directive defining the concept (if present)
  - [NATION]_CONFIDENCE_INDEX: for each nation, it indicates how confident the system is of the presence of the concept in national legislation. If absent, the attribute is not present
- ARTICLE specifies the location in which each EUconcept was found, expressed as an article, paragraph, and sub-paragraph (if present). For every Article node, the following attributes are defined:
  - ID: item identifier
  - NAME: full name of the concept as manually extracted by domain experts
- EULEGISLATION specifies the document to which the Article belongs. For every EUlegislation node, the following attributes are defined:
  - ID: item identifier
  - NAME: full name of the concept as manually extracted by domain experts

Relations:

- INTER-CONCEPT RELATION(S) are custom relations between concepts obtained after manual annotation
- FOUND_IN links the concept to the related segment of the EU Directive
- BELONGS_TO links the segment of the EU Directive to the EU Directive

#### 2.2.3 Harmonization Index

The Harmonization Index (HI) is an indicator aimed to evaluate the extent to which two legislative text portions overlap. In other words, the HI can be defined as a similarity measure between texts to capture and highlight their shared meanings. Accordingly, in the context of this project, the HI aims to evaluate the extent to which a European legal act, such as the EAW FD, is implemented into domestic legal systems. The objective is to obtain an index that quantifies the extent to which an EU Member State has transposed a certain segment of European legislation into its legislation.

A comparative analysis was conducted between two iterations of the Harmonization Index (HI): a symmetrical and an asymmetrical versions. The computational pipeline for the indicator is structured in the following steps: (1) data modeling, (2) generation of embeddings at two distinct levels of granularity, and (3) computation of the HI.

Given a piece of European legislation *EUtext* containing a set of components {A, B} and the national legislation *Ntext* transposing *EUtext*, HI(EUtext, Ntext) reaches its maximum value if the set of components expressed in *Ntext* contains both A and B. Nevertheless, due to the nature of the texts under scrutiny, *Ntext* can express a greater number of components than those defined in the *EUtext* (e.g. {A, B, C}); this does not impact the value of the HI as long as each EU concept is correctly transposed at the national level. For this reason, the HI could be considered an asymmetric similarity measure at two levels of granularity (*segment* and *eu-art*) compared to a symmetric version considered as baseline on both levels. The article level granularity aggregates every $HI_{segment}$ values related to a specific article *EUart* by computing the average. Components may be words, paragraphs, text partitions, concepts, quotations, etc. In this case study, the *EUtext* and *Ntext* components are paragraphs and words.

The data modeling process commenced with an analysis of the transposition tables provided within the Facilex project framework. Relevant fields for the comparative analysis of European legislation and corresponding national transpositions were extracted. This yielded a structured JSON file organized across three hierarchical levels: "document_name," "eu_segment_id," and "nation." The "nation" field contains the national transposition, derived by merging all national legislative segments associated with a specific "eu_segment_id" within the legislative framework denoted by "document_name." Subsequently, the textual data underwent preprocessing, which encompassed HTML tag removal, elimination of non-alphanumeric characters, and conversion to lowercase. This document will henceforth be referred to as "tt_merge".

The embedding generation and indicator computation methodologies diverge for the symmetrical and asymmetrical versions of the Harmonization Index.

In the symmetrical HI implementation, the "nlpaueb/bert-base-uncased-eurlex"[14] model was employed to generate paragraph embeddings using a window of 512 tokens. This window size was determined based on the average token count observed for the "nation" field within the tt_merge document. Subsequently, the [CLS] token embedding was extracted for each paragraph. Conversely, the asymmetrical version also utilized the "nlpaueb/bert-base-uncased-eurlex" model, but for the extraction of word embeddings. Specifically, input embeddings corresponding to tokens present in a predefined vocabulary were extracted.

The symmetrical Harmonization Index is computed by calculating the cosine similarity between the European and national paragraph embeddings. Subsequently, a min-max scaling function is applied to constrain the indicator values to a range of 0 to 1. Conversely, the asymmetrical version is computed

14 Nlpaueb, 'bert-base-uncased-eurlex' (HuggingFace 🤗, November 2020) <https://huggingface.co/nlpaueb/bert-base-uncased-eurlex> accessed 28 June 2024.

using the following formula was inspired by these two works,[15] leveraging the word embeddings generated in the preceding step:

$$HI_{segment}(EUtext) = (\Sigma_{w_q \in EUtext} \; W(w_q, EUtext) \; max_{w_c \in Ntext_{EUtext}} \sigma(w_q^T w_c)) \, / \, |EUtext|$$

$$W(w, EUtext) = min\_max\,norm(\textsc{itf\_df}(w, EUtext)) =$$

$$= min\_max\,norm(log_2(\frac{\#tokens\ in\ EUtext}{count(w)\ in\ EUtext}) * \frac{\#EU\ segments\ with\ w}{\#EU\ segments})$$

$$\sigma(x) = \frac{x+1}{2}$$

Where *EUtext* is the European legislative segment, $Ntext_{EUtext}$ is the national transposition related to *EUtext*, $w_q$ is the *query-word*, $w_c$ the *candidate-word*, $W(w)$ the weight function performed as Inverse Term Frequency – Document Frequency (ITF-DF) with a min-max normalization and $\sigma(x)$ the scale function. In the computation of ITF-DF, stop words were excluded, and the Porter Stemmer algorithm was employed to aggregate tokens sharing a common stem. This asymmetrical version, similarly, yields scores within the unit interval [0, 1]. The newly defined HI function reaches its maximum value when each component contained in *EUtext* appears at least once within the transposition set *Ntext*.

The ITF-DF weighting function was selected due to the non-recursive nature of legal definitions. Consequently, it is anticipated that defined terms will exhibit low frequency within individual legislative segments but higher frequency across the entire corpus. This assumption stems from the observation that legal documents typically establish a framework with a specialized lexical context. Therefore, terms such as "European," "arrest," and "warrant," which hold significant relevance for legislative comparison, are expected to appear infrequently within individual segments but frequently within the broader legislative framework.

15 The formula drew inspiration from Kathryn Ricci and others, 'Unsupervised Partial Sentence Matching for Cited Text Identification' (2022) and Luigi Di Caro and others, 'EU Directives Implementation: Automated Analysis of Complexity and Harmonization' in Effective Protection of the Rights of the Accused in the EU Directives (2022) 309–328.

The subsequent formula presents the aggregation function employed on both versions to derive the Harmonization Index from the segment-level scores of a given legislative article:

$$HI_{art}(EUart) = \frac{\sum_{EUtext \in EUart} HI_{segment}(EUtext)}{|EUart|}$$

### 2.3 *HG Results and HI Evaluation*

The Neo4J graph obtained as a result of the manual extraction of concepts performed on the EU EAW FD No. 2002/584 (EUlegislation entity taken into account) contains 124 articles (and consequently '*belongs_to*' relations), 198 EUconcepts, 212 'found_in' relations, and 225 inter_concept relations (see Figure 21 and 22).

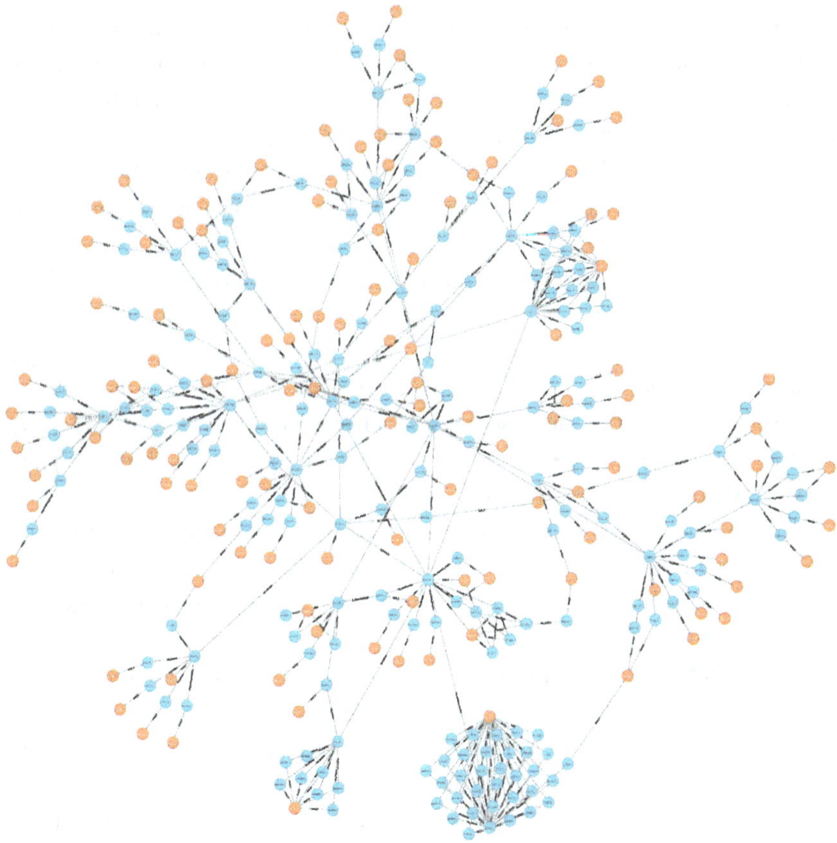

FIGURE 21 Neo4J graph overview

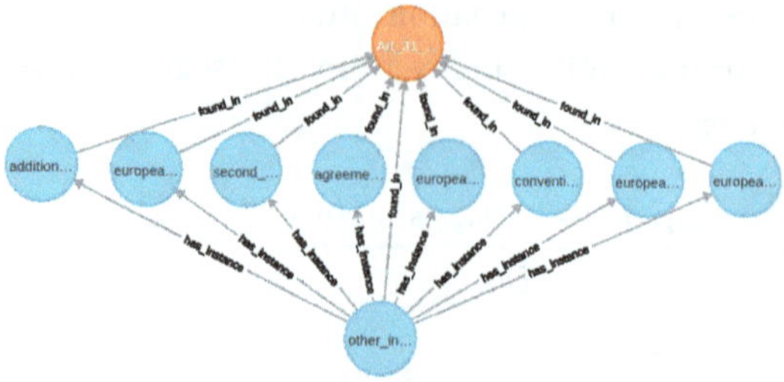


FIGURE 22 Cluster example

The high presence of hubs in the graph occurs for several reasons. Firstly, the granularity level in concept identification is high, leading to numerous subclasses of broader concepts, such as crimes listed automatically triggering the issuance of a European Arrest Warrant. Secondly, concepts and relations are organized to support information retrieval. Legal experts have prioritized focusing on the competencies and functions of the main institutions involved in the EAW procedure, namely the issuing and executing national authorities, while depicting the obligations incumbent upon the Member States. Consequently, these nodes exhibit significantly greater interconnection compared to others. Thirdly, some articles contain many concepts, whereas other provisions are less represented; therefore, their nodes present a lower degree of content.

Regarding the Harmonization Index (HI), the distribution of segment-level scores was analyzed for both symmetrical and asymmetrical versions. The symmetrical version exhibited a mean score of 0.93 and a median of 0.95, while the asymmetrical version yielded a mean of 0.73 and a median of 0.69. A threshold, set at the mean score for each version, was used to categorize segments into two sets: UP (scores greater than or equal to the threshold) and DOWN (scores below the threshold).

Excluding instances with a score of 0, which signify the absence of transposition, the symmetrical version yielded 1150 UP elements and 755 DOWN elements. Conversely, the asymmetrical version resulted in 778 UP elements and 1127 DOWN elements.

Concordance between the two indicators was observed for 683 UP elements and 660 DOWN elements, leaving 562 instances of disagreement. From this discordant subset, a random sample of 30 instances was selected and manually annotated by a legal expert. Annotations were assigned as either UP or DOWN based on the perceived degree of transposition of European legislation (high or low, respectively). The asymmetric version achieved a higher level of total agreement with the manual annotations, as detailed in Table 6:

TABLE 6 Agreement scores for symmetric and asymmetric versions

| | UP agreement | DOWN agreement | Total |
|---|---|---|---|
| Symmetric version | 21 | 1 | 22 |
| Asymmetric version | 5 | 3 | 8 |

The manual annotation suggests a higher degree of congruence between the symmetrical version of the Harmonization Index and the human assessment of legislative transposition levels compared to the asymmetrical version. Therefore, the symmetrical version is deemed more suitable for this task. This finding raises questions regarding the comparative performance of the indicator against alternative versions that operate on different levels of textual granularity. For instance, a potential avenue for exploration involves developing metrics based on the overlap of legal concepts identified within legislative segments. Such concepts could potentially be extracted automatically using resources like the Harmonized Glossary as a gold standard.

## 3 Identification of Relevant Case-Law

The major goal of this task is to find the most relevant case law for a particular input (query) court case to facilitate legal research. We developed a NLP pipeline for the identification of relevant case-law from different Member States. The pipeline is presented in Figure 23.

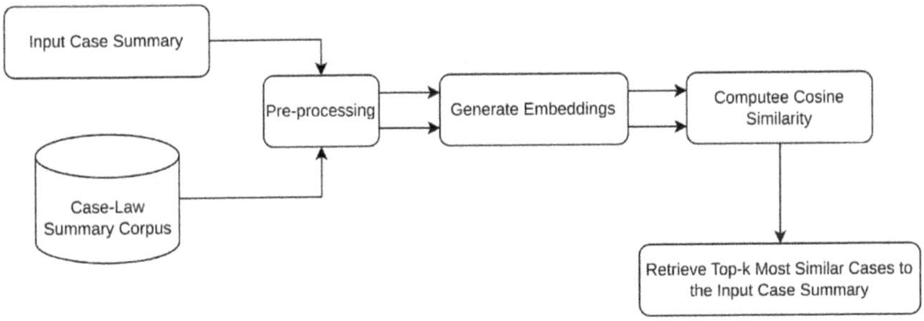


FIGURE 23 NLP pipeline for identification of relevant case-law

### 3.1 *Dataset*

The dataset consists of 433 case summaries obtained from the FACILEX platform. The cases consist of the following jurisdictions: Bulgaria, Italy, Netherlands, Portugal, Germany, Poland, Spain, Croatia and the EU, with the exact composition being shown in Table 7.

TABLE 7 The number of cases for each jurisdiction present on the FACILEX platform

| Bulgaria | Italy | Netherlands | Portugal | Germany | Poland | Spain | Croatia | EU | Total |
|---|---|---|---|---|---|---|---|---|---|
| 81 | 77 | 72 | 60 | 54 | 50 | 29 | 8 | 2 | 433 |

The relevant case law for each of the three EU mutual recognition instruments has been populated on the FACILEX platform with annotations made by the national legal experts of each Member State. In order to evaluate our methodology (i.e. the case-law retrieval system as discussed in section 3.2), we need a standard ground truth against which the performance of the system can be measured. Ground truth is normally defined as a label (i.e. relevant or non-relevant) made by human experts. In our context, this would refer to a legal expert identifying relevant cases manually for a particular query case and assigning labels to them.

Due to the lack of ground truth labels on the FACILEX platform, we derived two types of proxy ground truth labels. To derive these ground truths, we used the annotations made by legal experts with references to EU instruments when populating the FACILEX platform. A common citation refers to a scenario where two cases share at least one reference to the same EU mutual recognition instrument. The first ground truth refers to the common citations at the document level of the EU instrument. The second ground truth refers to the common citations, only at article level (citations at paragraph or subparagraph levels were excluded) of the EU instrument. Some cases did not contain any citations and were thus excluded from our analysis.

### 3.2 *Methodology*

The NLP pipeline is modeled as a legal information retrieval system for case-law retrieval. The FACILEX platform consists of case summaries written by legal experts in the English language for each jurisdiction. The main objective of the system is to retrieve the most similar case summaries for an input case summary. Initially, the input case summary and the entire case-law corpus (consisting of all the case summaries) are pre-processed by removing the

HTML tags. This is followed by the removal of non-word characters and punctuation. The text was then converted to lowercase.

The next step consisted of generating the semantic vector embeddings[16] (numerical representations that capture the meaning of text) for the input case and the entire case-law summary corpus. Three different embedding models were utilized to generate the vector embeddings: Term Frequency-Inverse Document Frequency (TF-IDF),[17] a pre-trained BERT[18] model, and an MPNET[19] sentence transformer model. BERT only provides word-level embeddings. In order to understand the whole summary of a case and not just individual words, we averaged the word-level embeddings to obtain a representation for the entire case summary. The MPNET model readily generates embeddings for the entire summary that can be used for the task at hand with no additional overhead.

The final step consists of measuring the semantic similarity[20] between the embeddings of the input case summary and all other case summaries present in the FACILEX dataset. Thus the input case summary is compared against all the other cases in the dataset. After obtaining the semantic similarity scores, the top five most similar (with the highest semantic similarity scores) cases are retrieved.

### 3.3 *Evaluation Metrics*

The system was evaluated on four metrics: Precision, Recall, Mean Reciprocal Rank (MRR), and Normalised Discounted Cumulative Gain (NDCG). The choice of metrics was dictated by several factors. First, it would not be optimal to present a user with all of the 433 available cases sorted by the similarity score, therefore, the amount of presented documents was limited to at most 5 documents contained within a retrieval window. Thus, the evaluation was similarly performed on the top 5 retrieved cases, henceforth referred to with the notation of "@5". Furthermore, with the use of the first ground truth, there were many more cases labelled as relevant outside the retrieval window. One drawback of

16 Jurafsky Dan and Martin James, Speech and Language Processing (3rd edn, Prentice Hall 2024) 105–132.

17 Binarized count vectors, using uni- and bi-grams, with an NLTK word tokenizer.

18 Google, 'Bert-base-uncased' (HuggingFace🤗, November 2018) <https://huggingface.co/google-bert/bert-base-uncased> accessed 28 June 2024.

19 Sentence transformers, 'Multi-qa-mpnet-base-dot-v1' (HuggingFace🤗, August 2021) <https://huggingface.co/sentence-transformers/multi-qa-mpnet-base-dot-v1> accessed 28 June 2024.

20 Computation was done using cosine similarity; Jurafsky Dan and Martin James, Speech and Language Processing (3rd edn, Prentice Hall 2024) 114–115.

this evaluation is that with such a short retrieval window, recall will be significantly lower for an input case summary that shares the same citation with a high number of cases, especially exceeding the size of the retrieval window.

### 3.4 *Results and Analysis*

Figure 24 presents the evaluation metrics for various vector embedding models for the identification of relevant case law. The plot on the left represents the evaluation when using the first ground truth (common citations to EU instruments). The plot on the right represents the evaluation when using the second ground truth (common citations to the EU instrument articles as the ground truth).

There is a stark contrast in performance between the two ground truth types (first and ground truth as mentioned in the dataset subsection). The number of labels in the first ground truth is comparatively lower than the number of labels in the second ground truth because the latter is at a finer level of granularity (article level). Therefore, the performance of the case-law retrieval system which is based on semantic similarity is better in the case of the first ground truth. Recall@5 values are lower in the first ground truth as compared to the second ground truth because in the former there were more documents outside the retrieval window.

Across all metrics, as seen in *Figure 24 (left side)*, the MPNET-based model performed best when using the first ground truth, while TF-IDF was the best

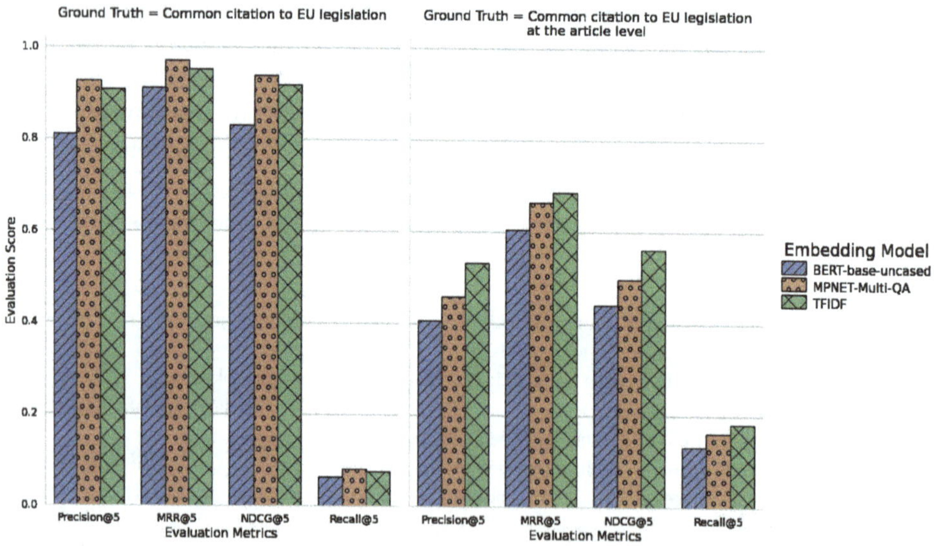


FIGURE 24 Comparison of vector embedding models (BERT, MPNET, and TF-IDF) for identification of relevant case-law

when considering the second ground truth (*Figure 24; right side*). A further important distinction is between MRR@5, NDCG@5, and precision@5. The former two are rank-aware and precision@5 is rank-agnostic. Precision@5 is significantly higher than recall@5 because it ignores all relevant cases outside the retrieval window. MRR@5 is higher than NDCG@5 across all models and ground truths because it is less strict in its calculation as it only considers the rank of one item. On the other hand, NDCG@5 looks at all ranks within the retrieval window, thus yielding a lower score.

## 4 Concluding Remarks

This research explores the adoption of automated methods to address the EU harmonization process. A method for assessing legislative harmonization using transposition tables and concepts extracted from the EAW FD is presented. The methodology employs NLP techniques toward the computation of asymmetric and asymmetric similarity indicator to measure the level of harmonization achieved across the EU and the identification of relevant case-law. Initial results and future research opportunities in this field are discussed.

As a future work, we plan to explore the use of Large Language Models (LLM s) for the extraction of both implicit and explicit definitions of national legal concepts. This will allow for a more comprehensive understanding of how these concepts are implemented within different national contexts. One further development would be that of evaluating the LLM s' ability to extract EU concept definitions against the ones manually extracted by domain experts, which can be used as a gold standard.

Secondly, we aim to explore and evaluate a wider range of asymmetric similarity metrics. These asymmetric similarity measures will be compared against concept-based metrics, utilizing the extracted concepts as components of the computation of the HI. Finally, we intend to enrich the existing historical graph by incorporating the full corpus of documents. This will provide a richer and more comprehensive knowledge base for future analysis, facilitating deeper insights into the evolution and interplay of national concepts over time.

# Conclusion

This research paved the way to a methodology on how to rigorously and usefully integrate automated technology with the practice of criminal proceedings.

These results, however, are far from representing an ending point, but rather move forward the starting line for the studies about to come.

In this regard, there are several profiles that already appear interesting to further investigations.

First, the integrated analysis and reasoning methodology experienced in the projects could find application to other areas of judicial cooperation, both where legal bases have been recently amended (as in the case of seizure and confiscation, with Directive 2024/1260/EU) and where new cooperation mechanisms have been created (as in the case of the European Production Order).

Second, the approach developed in these studies may be useful for the objective of evidence-based policy making, as it provides ways to analyse the impact of the law, supporting the legislator in understanding gaps, inconsistencies and interpretative issues that may impede smooth cooperation practices. Such approach is even more necessary in a time where policy makers have to face the challenges posed by the digitalization of criminal conducts and investigative potential, struggling to update the efficiency of criminal justice systems without hampering procedural safeguards and fundamental rights.

Third, a hybrid approach to the development and functioning of AI legal technologies, which combines symbolic and data-driven paradigms, provides a decisive advantage over simpler data-driven only approaches: thanks to the symbolic paradigm, the system grounds its reasoning into an explicit model of the law, and this ensures transparency and explainability of the outcomes, enabling the human user to integrate such outcomes in its decision-making activity. Then, the integration of a Large Language Model enhances the usability of the systems by ensuring that its outputs are understandable to a broader audience, making the use of the system accessible and practical for experts and laypeople alike.

Other relevant research lines have then been only partially examined in the present studies but are acquiring a growing weight in shaping the effectiveness of procedural safeguards on a national and supranational dimension.

For instance, the increasing deployment of digital technology does require a much deeper reflection on the integration between criminal procedure rules, remedies, and potential violation of the rights to privacy and data protection.

All these developments, however, represent only a part of what needs to be done to ensure a swifter cooperation across the EU and more substantial

 | DOI:10.1163/9789004705791_020

implementation of fundamental rights. The other side lays in practical, but essential aspects, that no digitalisation can (at least for the time being) substitute: basic linguistic and technological skills for lawyers, judges, prosecutors and law enforcement; and awareness of all legal operators on how to position themselves in a transnational dimension. That naturally also requires adequate financial support to qualified training programs, as well as the willingness and mental flexibility of all legal operators to get involved over and over again.

We hope that this research, regardless all its limit, can provide an example in this direction, contributing to lay the basis for a new integrated methodological approach that should probably become increasingly common in our complex, transnational, technological society.

The task is certainly difficult and tiring, as the protection of fundamental rights always is, but exciting at the same time. And we are proud to have taken up the challenge.

*Giulia Lasagni*
*Giuseppe Contissa*

# Index

www.ingramcontent.com/pod-product-compliance
Lightning Source LLC
LaVergne TN
LVHW020653300926
849161LV00004B/921